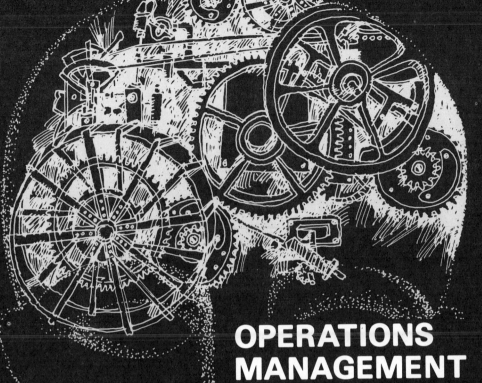

OPERATIONS MANAGEMENT

A SYSTEMS MODEL-BUILDING APPROACH

THOMAS E. VOLLMANN University of Rhode Island

ADDISON-WESLEY PUBLISHING COMPANY
Reading, Massachusetts
Menlo Park, California
London • Don Mills, Ontario

To Tani

PREFACE

This book is intended to serve two groups of readers—instructors and students. Since students rarely read prefatorial comments, these introductory remarks are primarily intended for the first audience; however, if you happen to be a student, you still may find something of interest here. Introductory remarks that are primarily student-oriented are embodied in Chapter 1.

This book is intended for a first or introductory course in operations management, typically taught during the junior or senior year in an undergraduate business curriculum, or in the first year of an MBA program. It provides a survey of operations management techniques that will be useful for those not planning further study in the area, as well as a base for those desiring to go into the field in more depth.

THE OPERATIONS MANAGEMENT COURSE

Although providing a survey of operations management techniques is one goal of this book, it is not the most important, or even a basic one. I see three closely related major goals for a first course in operations management: to understand the basic operations function, to gain a viable knowledge of the systems approach to the design of operations procedures, and to provide an applications forum where the skills gained in other areas of the curriculum can be utilized and applied. These three major goals are discussed in Chapter 1.

Present student disenchantment with the academic process is professedly based upon a quest for relevance; business administration students manifest this quest in pragmatism and a related disinterest in detached theoretical pedagogy. A properly designed operations management course can channel this pragmatic interest into an enriched educational experience.

The basic operations management course should build upon an applications forum of problems, case studies, computer simulations, games, and real-world situations that students find plausible or representative of the kinds of problems with which they will have to cope in their careers. The pursuit of answers to these credible problems involves what I see as the central theme for integration of the course material: problem delineation and solution from a systems point of view.

A systems orientation stresses the uniqueness of problem delineation, the essential role of criteria or goals in that delineation, the never-ending evolutionary nature of problem delineation and solution, the need for modeling mechanisms that both accommodate and foster evolution, and the necessary interaction between expert model-builders and users or consumers of that expertise.

Particular techniques or models that have been developed in the operations management area (e.g., inventory models, time study, or computerized layout models) can be examined as current but not ultimate approaches to certain problems; and the weaknesses of the tools can be assessed when the system boundaries or problem delineations are expanded. A historical perspective of the field can be seen as the progression of ever better models.

Of at least equal importance is the tie to other model-building courses. The operations management course should be able to clearly demonstrate the worth (in terms of credible problem-solution quality) of quantitative techniques and computer power. In short, the operations-management course can contribute credibility to quantitative-analysis and computer courses which all too often are regarded by students merely as something to be survived.

If by now I appear to be talking about the kind of *gestalt* normally reserved to a business policy course, my message has been well received. The notion of holding out business policy as the integrative capstone of the curriculum is analogous to asking the student to build a tree where he is given a few leaves in each course (perhaps a twig from a very good instructor), and not given the trunk until the end. I believe that we should *start* with an integrative viewpoint and that the systems concept provides the right vehicle. We should be able to provide a basic structure which, although not in the beginning fully understood by the student, is rich enough to build upon; understanding of the structure involves a spiral learning process where the understanding is being reinforced continually.

A serious gap exists in business curricula between the present emphasis on quantitative material at the core or basic level and the almost complete reliance on intuitive approaches to business policy. I see no reason why a properly designed operations management course should not start the student on the way to increasingly interdependent policy-oriented problems that can be attacked with rigorous models, particularly those utilizing digital computers. Just as more rigorous models can be shown to produce results superior to rule of thumb for inventory or layout problems, industrial-dynamics type models can yield profound insights into complex policy problems.

This text has been designed for use in a well integrated operations-management course, where emphasis is placed on relevant applications in a systems context, with particular models taking an ancillary role. This relationship means that the book is not a guided tour of the operations research/management science literature. Although topics such as the assignment of facilities to locations are very interesting to a few of us, I do not feel that a detailed history of theoretical approaches belongs in the introductory operations management course.

The emphasis on applications and a systems context in the operations management course potentially permits a useful division of labor in the curriculum. Far too many courses in the functional areas do only a superficial job of teaching quantitative techniques, which are better relegated to a course specifically designed to develop quantitative model-building expertise for later use in functional courses. Although some of us who teach operations management courses enjoy teaching quantitative materials, I find even greater enjoyment in meeting the challenge of integration.

I have tried to write this book for students, avoiding mathematical elegance wherever possible, and using repetition of important concepts as an integral part of the presentation. I have been sparing in the use of footnotes to make for easier reading, and I hereby apologize to all slighted sources. The references cited at the end of each chapter indicate places where a student might go to find alternative or more comprehensive coverage; they are not intended as an exhaustive list of classical sources.

An attempt has been made to continually tell the student where he is going and what he can expect to gain from his efforts. Chapter 1 briefly lays out the overall goals; introductions to each of the six major parts of the text give more detailed overviews and expected results. Reviews are provided for each chapter which assist in reinforcing the major ideas; these are particularly useful for the first few chapters where the students will probably be "in over their heads." The integrative approach of the book means that successive building takes place; the use of reviews does, however, permit some chapter skipping.

APPROACH

Like many other authors, I would like to believe that my approach is new and better than existing approaches. The primary feature that sets this book apart is its integration built upon the systems context and an evolving case study which is carried throughout the book. By seeing the ways in which problems evolve and interact in a particular real-world company, students develop a working understanding of problem identification and solution from a systems point of view.

Because I believe in curricular division of labor, this book will not provide detailed descriptions of many operations research methodologies, such as linear programming. Although the contents page might lead a prospective reader to think otherwise, only modeling procedures with wide conceptual applicability (such as queues and digital simulation) are treated in depth. Chapters 9 and 10 provide an overview of the benefits obtained from quantitative techniques; both chapters can be covered in one assignment devoted to curricular bridge-building.

Instructors often wonder about the level of mathematical ability required for using a particular text; the mathematical background necessary for using this text is minimal. At the same time, I expect that students with considerable mathematical exposure will also be challenged by the material. This seeming inconsistency is resolved by the systems/model-building approach, which emphasizes that there is no such thing as *the* ultimate analysis of a problem. Other considerations can always be added to any analysis; making such additions requires more comprehensive modeling procedures, and students with strong facility in numerical representation will be able to capitalize on that ability.

On the other hand, students coming to the operations management course with social science strengths have different kinds of contributions to make; often the value of these contributions lies in questioning the goals or assumptions used in quantitative models. A lively interaction allows for a considerable degree of synergy; and for this reason, diversity in student backgrounds represents a strong potential asset to a course in operations management. The chapter-end assignments are designed to appeal to that diversity, since each student learns a great deal from seeing how his fellow students approach similar problems. The assignments tend to build in difficulty; those which are particularly well suited to computer implementation will be marked by an asterisk.

ORGANIZATION

The arrangement of chapters proceeds toward increasingly quantitative materials. This arrangement allows for the operations management course to be taught concurrently with courses in operations research, quantitative methods, or computers. When assignments for these courses can be integrated, considerable benefits are achieved.

The text is divided into six major parts. Part I has the ambitious goal of providing each student with an initial working understanding of the systems approach. Included in this understanding are the notions of systems, models, and roles of expert system designers and those who use such systems in an evolutionary approach to problem-solving. A working understanding of the systems approach is a major goal of the course, and the initial exposure provided in Part I will be reinforced spirally in subsequent parts. It is only through application that the concepts become a part of the student's problem-solving approach.

Part II is concerned with models of cost and value. Almost all operations management problems involve costs which are expended in an attempt to create some kind of value; it is essential for students to understand how to isolate the costs that are relevant to particular problems and goals. Also, since these decision problems often involve costs and benefits which accrue over time, it is necessary to develop a facility with capital budgeting models which account for differences in the timing of cash flows. The inclusion of PERT and PERT/COST models at this point in the operations management course illustrates tradeoffs in relevant costs and time, as well as providing another useful way to structure problems.

Part III is entitled "Quantitative Models" because the basic groundwork is usually taught in quantitative analysis courses. An overview of deterministic and stochastic models illustrates real-world problems and the insights provided from rigorous models. A chapter on queues provides the flow orientation which pervades so many operations management problems; the next chapter describes the application of digital-simulation models in the investigation of complex flow-oriented problems.

Part IV treats many of the traditional operations management problems and models. There is growing sentiment among those who teach operations management courses for decreasing the emphasis given to these materials. While sharing that sentiment, I nevertheless feel that exposure to a minimum core is a necessary part of the operations-management course. Work measurement is a good case in point: accounting standard cost data are derived from this system. Organizational-behavior courses often consider problems which arise from work-measurement systems; and relating performance to wages will continue to be of real-world interest. The strengths and weaknesses of one of the few concrete measurement systems used in industry is a useful part of the business student's education. The basic ideas of quality control similarly are useful; quite aside from other applications in operations management, my experience is that students can understand hypothesis testing much more readily through quality control than by means of the usual treatment given in statistics courses.

Part V is devoted to materials-flow systems. It is the most difficult portion of the text, requiring both a working understanding of the systems concept and some facility with probabilistic models; the latter is partially developed as a natural outgrowth of Part IV. The approach in Part V is decidedly pragmatic. There are many forecasting methods, but exponential smoothing for routine control of many items will usually produce excellent results. Emphasis is placed upon the design of a set of decision rules to routinely monitor inventory control, production-planning/inventory control, and logistic system problems.

Part VI attempts once again to drive home the integrative theme of the book—problem identification and solution from a systems point of view. Just as the text began with an open-ended case study, it ends with another open-ended case study; the change in student ability to deal with such a situation is one good measure of the benefits obtained from the operations management course.

ACKNOWLEDGMENTS

A complete list of all those who have helped me in one way or another in the preparation of this text would be overly lengthy. The genesis goes back to graduate-school days and notable discussions with Professors Robert Andrews, Elwood Buffa, and Alfred Nicols, as well as with fellow students Joseph Biro, Richard Chase, and John Miller. The continuing interaction with my friend and mentor Elwood Buffa has provided encouragement that goes beyond what can be expressed in a brief acknowledgment.

A similar large debt is owed to my very good friend and former colleague Professor Christopher Nugent, now at the Harvard Business School. The systems approach—which is the integrative thread of the book—grew from a joint venture involving many hours of discussion and many pages of written materials. Above and beyond that particular piece of work are professional and personal interactions which have profoundly influenced my life.

The few references to the works of Professor Jay Forrester at Massachusetts Institute of Technology do not do justice to his influence on my thinking. His summer course at MIT in 1965 put a great many things into perspective; subsequent interactions with him and rereadings of his ideas have played an important role in my approach to operations management.

Colleagues at Dartmouth who have helped me in quite different ways include former Dean Karl A. Hill, Dean John W. Hennessey, and Professors Richard Bower, Wayne Broehl, Brian Quinn, Leroy Schwarz, Barnard Smith and Donald Stone. I have profited by my association with many students, particularly Harold Howell, Joseph Rokus, John Ruml, Robert Schuldenfrei, James Westfall, Thomas Warren, and Robert Zartler. Resources were provided by The Amos Tuck School Associates Fund, Dartmouth Computation Center, General Electric Company, Hearst Foundation, Sloan Foundation, and Project Themis.

Several individuals at the University of Rhode Island have continued to support this effort, particularly Dean Richard Weeks.

The case study presented as Chapter 2, and expanded upon in subsequent chapters, is based upon a five-year research project with the Baumritter Corporation, manufacturers of Ethan Allen furniture. I am deeply indebted to many individuals in this company, most particularly to Nathan Ancell, president, and William Morrissey, vice president of manufacturing. All aspects of the company operations were open to me, on a no-holds-barred basis.

I have also benefited from reviews by Professors Sumer Aggawal at Pennsylvania State University, Geoffrey Churchill at Georgia State University, Gary Dickson at the University of Minnesota, Lewis Goslin at Portland State University, Warren Hausman at Massachusetts Institute of Technology, Thomas Hendrick at the University of Colorado, and Fredrik Williams at North Texas State University. The continuing interaction with Professor Goslin has been of special value to me.

Thomas Warren and Keith Finck have been immensely helpful in problem writing and editing. I have also been aided editorially by Mrs. Jean Lawe. The encouragement given me by the staff of Addison-Wesley had an important influence on the decision to undertake and complete this work. Miss Jane Overman cheerfully typed more pages than she would like to remember.

To Villa San Francesco di Paola where the first draft was largely completed, I dedicate the promise of a return trip. To my long-suffering family, I dedicate the promise of spending more time with them on that return trip.

T.E.V.

Kingston, Rhode Island
November, 1972

CONTENTS

PART II COST/VALUE MODELS

Chapter 5   Relevant Costs 102

Chapter 6   Capital Budgeting 129

Chapter 7   Analysis of Value and Function 163

Chapter 8   Project Management 188

PART III QUANTITATIVE MODELS

Ave Cost of inventory

INTRODUCTION TO PART I

Part I has a very ambitious goal: to provide each of you with a working understanding of the systems approach. This goal can be only partially achieved in this part, however, and the ideas presented will be applied to specific problems throughout the balance of the book. The systems approach is a conceptual framework for integrating the materials in your operations management course, for integrating other materials in the curriculum and for identifying and solving problems throughout your career.

The fairly abstract ideas put forward in Part I may be difficult to grasp with a single reading, and it is recommended that some of the materials be reviewed as your knowledge becomes more sophisticated. Indeed, the initial exposure to this conceptual base will be strengthened and built upon spirally throughout your course in operations management.

Part I is composed of four chapters. The first brief chapter is devoted to laying out the goals of the text, what you can expect to get out of your operations management course, and the pedagogical strategy that will be used.

Chapter 2 involves doing, rather than talking about, the process of problem identification and solution. One large problem situation or case study will be presented. At the end of the chapter, you will be asked to prepare a written set of suggestions without benefit of the systems structure or the particular problem solving procedures or models which will be considered subsequently. This first large problem situation is based upon a real company, the Baumritter Corporation, and will be revisited in later chapters as an example of the systems-model building approach in action and to illustrate and assess the worth of particular analytical tools. Although you will be least able to answer the question posed in Chapter 2 at the beginning of your course, the continuing search for improved answers provides an important focus for subsequent materials.

Chapter 3 attempts to provide a tight description of the systems approach and the essential role of model building in achieving the benefits of a systems approach to problem solving. A key feature of this chapter is the way in which goals, objectives, or criteria direct both the design of a particular problem solution and the evolution to a more encompassing problem definition.

Chapter 4 expands the conceptual base to include the roles of particular individuals in an evolving systems approach to problem solving. A major goal is to increase the evolutionary speed toward improved understanding of increasingly encompassing problem delineations. The user-designer concept is presented as a way of recognizing and capitalizing on the strengths of expert outside or staff system designers and inside or line system users.

CHAPTER 1

INTRODUCTION

Before we get started, let us briefly discuss where we are going. This book is intended for a first or introductory course in operations management. Such a course is typically required as a junior or senior course in undergraduate schools of business administration or in the first year of an MBA program. There has been a steady evolution in the design of such courses, with a major trend being toward a more inclusive definition of the term "operations." Other important trends have been toward the use of more quantitative techniques and toward a more integrative approach to the models of problem-solving tools used.

This book continues these trends and hopefully encourages you as a student to become more excited about your course in operations management; the intent of the course is to define and solve problems that you personally find relevant, because the problems are similar to ones you face or will face in your career. It is the hope of the author and your instructor that you will feel a definitive improvement in your ability to cope with these realistic problems as a result of your efforts in this course.

GOALS

A typical goal of a first course in operations management is to provide a survey of techniques or models that have been used for operations man-. agement problems. Although this goal will be partially achieved in this book, it is by no means the only goal; neither is it the most important one. It will be partially achieved as a by-product of three major related goals for the course: to develop an understanding of the basic operations function in any enterprise, to gain a viable knowledge of the systems approach for solving problems, and to provide an applications forum where skills you have gained in other areas of the curriculum can be utilized and reinforced. Let us examine these goals in more detail.

The Operations Function

The term *operations management* encompasses the design, implementation, operation, and control of systems made up of men, materials, capital equipment, information, and money to accomplish some set of objectives. The production function in a business is concerned with the goods producing activity. The term "production" brings to mind machine shop technology and the manufacture of goods such as automobiles or steel. A broader term, "operations," has been coined for the goods or service producing activity in any business undertaking, private or public, profit or nonprofit.

As the title of this book indicates, our interest is in operations management rather than production management; connoted is the application of existing and evolving tools or models of production management to a wider class of problems and to problems whose underlying technologies may be quite different from those of typical manufacturing. We will see that important similarities exist between flows of material in furniture manufacturing, customers checking out at a supermarket, processing claims in an insurance company, and satisfying patient needs in a hospital. We will also see that it is possible to readily grasp an understanding of diverse technologies sufficient to perform meaningful analyses and to interact with those who have specialized technical knowledge.

The broader scope implied in the term operations management also attempts to recognize the important benefits obtained through delineation and solution of problems which cross the functional boundaries of production, marketing, and finance. Thus, we will see how decisions affecting the creation of a product and its storage or inventory can be usefully integrated with those affecting distribution and sales of that product. Indeed, the needs established by marketing should partially establish goals for production, and production capabilities should in turn establish goals for marketing. The cost of maintaining inventories of a product is directly related to a firm's financial capacity; a forecast of expected inventories and concomitant cash requirements are useful inputs to the finance function, and a financial input of seasonally varying capital or interest charges can call for changes in production plans.

A special insight into an enterprise (public or private, profit or nonprofit) can be gained by identifying the basic operations function of the enterprise or portion of the enterprise. An analysis of what fundamental product or service is desired in the marketplace and what kinds of systems, methods, or procedures are being used to create that product or service can lead to important improvements in both the end product or service offered and the means used to achieve the desired ends.

The benefits attendant to sophisticated design of an operations function are well illustrated by proper understanding of franchise potentials. To many, a franchise is largely the right to use a name which is known in the marketplace, but such a viewpoint is shortsighted. A franchise agreement potentially allows for the franchiser to economically invest in the design of a superior operations system that when transplanted will lead to highly efficient product or service creation by many franchisees.

Thus a Colonel Sanders Kentucky Fried Chicken franchise includes an efficient method for buying, preparing, packaging, and pricing a product. It also includes detailed marketing procedures such as newspaper advertising copy (note how the "production" and "marketing" functions are inextricably related).

In the furniture industry, the Baumritter Corporation has Ethan Allen Showcase Store franchises in which a large investment has been made in interior decorating, architectural, and other talents to provide efficient ways for showing home furnishings in highly appealing room plans. Customers can examine their needs for "mood" or "environment" and determine the kinds of furnishings (including lamps, accessories, wallpaper, etc.) that best satisfy their highly individualistic needs. The franchisee does not dilute his energy on designing systems or methods for doing business that can be better or more efficiently designed by the franchiser, whether those systems be furniture arrangement or financial accounting. Rather, the franchisee spends his time in personal contact with customers; the result is the mass marketing of interior decorating services (note here how we have identified the more basic customer needs or goals of mood or environment, rather than more narrowly focusing attention on what we will call "proximate" or "surrogate" criteria such as selling pieces of furniture—the more basic goal identification can lead to profound changes in the design of operations systems).

The Systems Approach

The second major goal of this book is for each of you to develop a viable understanding of problem identification and solution from a systems point of view. The term "system" is perhaps the most overused word in business education today, but systems concepts can provide an improved orientation to problem identification and solution.

Simply stated, the *systems approach* is a conscious orientation toward more encompassing problem definitions which when solved yield benefits that are increasingly in line with the highest order or most basic goals of a firm. A model is a representation, and all problem solving techniques or tools are models. In order to implement the systems approach we need models capable of representing continually larger systems or situations, which can be evaluated in terms of an evolving set of interactive multiple goals or objectives.

Problem statements or delineations determine the applicability of particular models, and change or evolution in problem delineation affects model appropriateness. We will want to assess the "richness" of models, in terms of the extent to which they can accommodate (and encourage) evolution in problem delineation.

You students can usefully regard yourselves as model builders; a good part of your professional education process is the development of a familiarity with existing problem-solving techniques or models. However, I don't believe that your course in operations management should consist of a potpourri of techniques without integration or a structure. Although the important operations management models will be treated in this book, the systems approach will provide an integrative thread for understanding the strengths and weaknesses of particular models. The organization of the text has been guided by the systems approach; the ordering of topics is toward increasingly more encompassing problem definitions, with each chapter broadening the scope of investigation.

A viable understanding of the systems approach has value beyond integration of operations management ideas. I strongly believe that the approach allows you to obtain a better understanding of other functional courses, and for the integration implied in your business policy course to be understood on a more concrete operational basis.

An Applications Forum

The third major goal of this book is to provide an applications forum where skills gained throughout the curriculum can be utilized and reinforced. A properly designed operations management course can add increased perspective and credibility to the technique oriented courses you are taking. The most notable of these courses are those in quantitative analysis and computers, which all too often are regarded as "something to survive." A large part of your operations management course will be based upon real life, case, or plausible problem situations, and it will become abundantly clear that more rigorous approaches to these problems pay off in terms of solution quality.

A unique approach embodied in this book is the use of one case study throughout the text. This case study is based upon a real world company, the Baumritter Corporation, manufacturers of Ethan Allen furniture. Although we may have no particular interest in the furniture industry, per se, students find it encouraging to see that the technology of a particular industry can be mastered sufficiently to make meaningful recommendations.

By continually returning to a particular company and its problems, you will gain an improved appreciation of the ways in which problems interact and the systems approach which copes with these interactions. You will also find that your knowledge is not at all limited to a particular company or industry. The problems faced by Baumritter are similar in very important ways to problems faced by many other firms. Even more importantly, you will find that the *approach* used to problem identification and solution for this particular firm will be of continuing value.

STRATEGY OF THE TEXT

The arrangement of chapters proceeds toward increasingly quantitative materials. This arrangement permits you to achieve cross-course benefits when taking your operations management course concurrently with courses in operations research, quantitative methods, or computers. To whatever extent work in these courses can be integrated, your understanding of the business enterprise should be enriched.

Students often wonder about the mathematical background expected in a particular course. I hope that the background necessary for using this text is minimal. At the same time, I expect that if you have had considerable mathematical exposure you should still be challenged by the material. This seeming inconsistency is resolved by the systems-model-building approach where we will see that there is no such thing as *the* ultimate analysis of a problem. Other considerations can always be added to any analysis; making such additions requires more comprehensive modeling procedures, and if you have strong facility in numerical representation you will be able to capitalize on that ability.

On the other hand, students coming to the operations management course with social science strengths have different kinds of contributions to make; often these contributions lie in questioning the goals or assumptions used in quantitative models. A lively interaction allows for a considerable degree of synergy, and I believe that diversity in student backgrounds represents a strong potential asset to a course in operations management. The chapter-end assignments are designed to appeal to that diversity, since each of you can learn a great deal from seeing how your fellow students approach similar problems. The assignments tend to build in difficulty and those which are particularly well suited to computer implementation will be asterisked.

In the Introduction to Part I, I attempted to tell you what is in this chapter as well as what to expect in Chapters 2, 3, and 4. There are introductions to each of the other five major parts of the book as well; in each of these I have tried to tell you where we are going, what you can expect to gain, and how your understanding of prior materials can be built upon. Each chapter (except Chapters 1 and 2) will have a review which attempts to reinforce the major ideas. Although you will not find these reviews to be an alternative to careful reading of the chapters, you will find them useful as a study guide. The course is for you, and I believe that a diligent effort on your part will result in a personal payoff well worth the effort.

AN OPERATIONS PROBLEM

Chapter 2 presents an open-ended case study and an introduction to the Baumritter Corporation and one of its manufacturing divisions—Westfall Furniture Company. The problems contained in this case will serve us well in subsequent chapters to illustrate the application of both abstract ideas and particular model building procedures. The case will also provide an opportunity to see how various technological, behavioral, and environmental factors influence the ways in which problems may be identified and attacked.

WESTFALL FURNITURE COMPANY

"Now's the time to put in for the 24-inch belt conveyor. Man, once we get that baby humming, we'll be able to knock out about 900 chairs per day." The speaker was Jim Howell, industrial engineer at the Westfall Furniture Company. He had recently become a member of a three-man study team to investigate the chair assembly line. The other members of the team were Harry Ruml, plant manager, and John Hughes, assistant plant manager.

The Company

The Baumritter Corporation manufactured two lines of colonial furniture, the most important being an integrated line sold under the Ethan Allen brand name. Sales in fiscal year 1971 were approximately $65 million, and the goods were manufactured in 18 factories which specialized on the basis of woods and particular furniture.

The Westfall Furniture Company was located in Westfall, Vermont, and was largely a manufacturer of yellow birch dining room furniture. Sales of furniture produced at Westfall were approximately $7 million in 1971. A four-year monthly breakdown of sales is shown in Fig. 2.1. Westfall also served as a shipping orbit for seven other Baumritter plants

	1971	1970	1969	1968
January	497	558	490	458
February	483	495	462	427
March	610	558	524	498
April	650	610	574	549
May	583	604	568	560
June	631	627	587	557
July	438	410	298	310
August	690	680	601	590
September	597	543	512	502
October	698	674	562	532
November	632	620	570	541
December	570	562	497	468
Total	7,079	6,941	6,245	5,992

Fig. 2.1 Monthly sales data (thousands of $).

located nearby; these plants would ship their entire production output to Westfall where railroad pool cars and truck shipments were coordinated in order to achieve low freight costs.

MANUFACTURING PROCESS

The Westfall Company had a fairly versatile production capability including chair production and the usual dining room pieces, but with an ability to produce other wood or "case good" furniture. While Westfall could produce bedroom furniture, a nearby plant which specialized in bedroom furniture would have had difficulty in manufacturing dining room furniture since the parts tend to be more complex.

Raw Materials

The major raw material in furniture is wood. Furniture manufactured by Westfall was almost completely solid wood, as opposed to veneer construction. Although the company produced some cherry pieces, the majority of production was in yellow birch. Westfall purchased yellow birch lumber and also yellow birch logs which were sawed into lumber. Logs were purchased locally (from within about 50 miles) and lumber was purchased from a wider growing area (a considerable proportion came from Canada). Lumber was graded according to its coloring, knots, and other defects. Because furniture manufacturing called for wood that was largely defect free, Westfall was continually trying to purchase lumber of a high quality. On the other hand, the lumber sellers traditionally tried to pass off lumber of one grade as a higher grade and to overestimate percentages of higher lumber within individual shipments. Since the cost of lumber was estimated to represent approximately 20% of the finished furniture cost, Westfall placed considerable importance upon efficient use of wood.

Westfall used about 200,000 board feet of lumber per week. (A board foot of lumber is equal to 12" x 12" x 1".) All lumber was stockpiled on carefully arranged skids to permit efficient air drying. The quantity of lumber in the stockpiles varied, but was generally between a two and five month supply.

Dry Kilns

The Westfall Furniture Company had four dry kilns which were used to reduce moisture content in the lumber. The natural moisture content in lumber can be as high as 80 percent. It was necessary to reduce this moisture level to prevent warpage or shrinkage in the final items (Westfall usually attempted to maintain a moisture content of approximately 6%). Westfall's four kilns had a total capacity of approximately 275,000 board feet. The time required for a load of lumber to be dried or cured depended upon several factors, including the initial moisture content and the thickness of the lumber; typical cure times were between three and ten days.

After drying, lumber could be placed in what was called a "tempering shed." The tempering shed had a capacity of about 50,000 board feet and allowed for dried lumber to be maintained at a reasonably constant moisture level.

Rough Mill

Dried lumber began its conversion into furniture at cutoff saws. The stacks of dried lumber were automatically raised to a convenient height so that cutoff saw operators could slide boards of varying lengths into positioning for sawing. The cutoff saw operators attempted to cut boards into lengths which provided for efficient use of each board. An attempt was made to have four or five different lengths cut at the same time so that waste could be minimized. These lengths were, obviously, dependent upon the length requirements for finished parts. Any time a board was found with a defect free area long enough to be made into a table top, it was so cut. All of the boards in a particular load were of uniform rough thickness, but varied in quality, width, and length.

Boards coming from the cutoff saws fell on a conveyor belt to a machine which planed both sides of the boards to a uniform clean thickness. After planing, the boards were dropped on a revolving table which allowed for separation and stacking of clean boards of a particular length.

When a skid load (or completed job) was accumulated, it was taken to the rip saws. The rip saws cut off the two rough edges, and also removed any defects in the boards. That is, if an 18" long by 4 1/2" wide board had a 1/2" knot in the center, the rip saw operation would be to clean up the two edges and thereafter saw the board into two 2"-wide boards and one 1/2"-wide board with the defect in the middle of it. Output from the rip saws represented defect-free clean boards of uniform length but varying widths. The exception to this rule was for parts which required boards of a width less than 3 1/2". Such boards were ripped to required width rather than glued up from smaller boards. About 30% of the parts fell into this category.

Loads of defect-free boards from the rip saws were moved to the panel gluing area where different width boards were glued together to make up panels of uniform length, width, and thickness. Boards were placed on a table and combined so that grain and color patterns would match well. The resultant group of boards was then ripped to a desired width (the excess ripped off was used in the next panel to be made up). In order to preserve the matching for color and grain structure, a crayoned semicircle was drawn on the boards so that the gluing operators would know the order in which the finished panel was to be glued.

Panels of wood were coated with glue on the edges and placed in a large glue wheel, which clamped the panels in place while the glue set. Completed panels were removed from the glue wheel, stacked on skids, and placed in a humidified glue drying room for 24 to 48 hours depending upon thickness. Because of the large number of parts produced by Westfall, approximately 4000 different panel sizes were made.

Finish Mill

All parts flowed through the rough mill and gluing operation in a uniform fashion; such was not the case for the finish mill operation. In the finish mill, panels of various sizes were machined into particular parts to be used in the final product. Typical machines included molders which could impart any desired shape to all four sides (but not the ends) of a board or panel simultaneously; double-end tenoners which were similar to molders except that they cut at right angles to the grain and were used to maintain exact lengths; shapers which were used to cut irregular designs in the edge of a panel such as might be required for a chair seat; and lathes for imparting circular shapes such as are required for chair spindles or legs. Some machines were used for many parts, and others were used for only one or a few parts. All the machines required operators; there was no automatic equipment.

The flow of work through the finish mill was dependent upon the particular part configuration required. Some parts required many more finish mill operations than others. Work in process was stored all over the finish mill floor area, with location usually being decided on a space-available basis. Finished parts were accumulated at an area near the end of the finish mill next to an elevator which took them upstairs to the sanding operation. Parts were usually not moved to the sanding operation until all of the required parts for a particular piece of furniture had been completed in the finish mill.

Sanding

When all the parts for a particular item had been accumulated in the hold area near the elevator, they were moved upstairs to a sanding operation. Here, semiautomatic sanding equipment could be used for flat surfaces where boards were fed from one end to the other; the majority of finished parts, however, required skilled labor using simple sanding devices such as drum and belt sanders. Round parts, such as chair legs and spindles, were sanded on a special sanding machine which brought the rotating parts into contact with sandpaper of increasingly fine grit.

After sanding, considerable care was exercised in handling the parts so that resanding of assembled parts could be minimized. Sanded parts were referred to as "white goods" and were stored in controlled humidity rooms so that warpage could be minimized.

Assembly

Sanded parts and some subassemblies were usually brought to the particular assembly line in a total group. This procedure, however, was often violated because of rush requirements and because of limited storage areas in the assembly areas. The final assembly operations were divided into five major assembly lines. The first line was for tables and was staffed in different ways depending upon the particular table being assembled. Thus, some tables were shipped in a disassembled or knocked down version, while others were shipped completely assembled; the same line was sometimes used for assembling small occasional tables. The second major assembly line was for hutches or china cabinets. This line utilized large case presses or clamps which held the sides of a hutch in proper parallel so that the parts could be joined with glue, screws, or other fasteners. Doors, drawers, and some kinds of hardware were attached during this operation. The third major assembly line was for smaller cases such as dry sinks, desks, or low serving pieces. The fourth major assembly line was for plastic-topped tables. For these the wooden legs or frames were assembled separately and finished; this operation was accomplished on the table line. A separate purchased plastic top was thereafter installed, but since plastic-topped tables required no further finishing after assembly, this assembly line was placed adjacent to finished goods storage. The fifth and largest major assembly line was for chairs. Chair assembly required more personnel and more floor space than the other assembly lines. There were

No. 10-6006/No. 10-6008 Server with Hutch Cabinet. Overall 71" H. Three drawers.

No. 10-6046 Grilled Corner Hutch. 39" x 23" x 75" H. Adjustable shelf behind cabinet and grilled glass doors. Upper shelves grooved for display of dishes.

No. 10-6063 Spoonfoot Harvest Drop Leaf Table. 22" x 45" x 66" with leaves extended. Seats 8-10.

No. 10-6063P Same item with Formica plastic top.

No. 10-6124P Round Pedestal Table. 42" diameter. Extra-heavy Formica   plastic top. Non-extension.

No. 10-6105 Four Drawer Dry Sink. 40" x 20" x 35" H. Partitioned, felt-lined silver compartments in top drawer. Adjustable shelf behind shutter doors which are fully paneled in rear to protect interior from dust. Matching woodgrained plastic top lid opens to large working surface or closes to conceal deep storage area. Removable copper tray and swivel casters.

Fig. 2.2 Westfall items

No. 10-6100A   No. 10-6100
Spindleback Formal Chairs 37½″ H.
Upholstered seat padded with Urethane Foam.

No. 10-6030A   No. 10-6030
Duncan Phyfe Chairs 34½″ H;
upholstered seat.

No. 10-6072A   No. 10-6072
Duxbury Chairs 39″ H.

No. 10-6002
Concord Chair. 34″ H.

No. 10-6031
Captain's Chair. 29″ H.

*No. 14-6072A and No. 14-6072 available in
Decorated Finishes 601, 604 or 610.

Fig. 2.2 (*cont.*)

many kinds and styles of chairs produced on the line, such as ladder-back, captain, Duncan Phyfe, Duxbury, and Queen Anne. The majority of these different chairs were placed on the same overhead conveyor line to chair finishing, where the most popular finish was applied.

Finishing

After assembly all goods (except plastic-topped tables) went to the finishing area where several coats of stains and lacquer were applied with various ovens used for drying between coats. The finishing process was semiconveyorized in a way that allowed for some flexibility in the mix of product being finished. Westfall produced furniture with two major finishes, the standard Nutmeg and a limited volume more expensive finish called Classic Manor which was somewhat darker and incorporated distressing and antique spotting. The two finishes were applied on different lines; in order to utilize finishing personnel effectively, it was necessary to impose some constraints on the mix and volume of assembly line operations. After finishing, the furniture was hand rubbed to give it a high degree of lustre and smoothness. It was then inspected, packaged, and placed in finished goods inventory for subsequent shipment.

Staffing

Westfall employed approximately 450 people who could be put in the following rough classifications:

Raw Materials	18	Assembly	85
Dry Kilns	4	Finishing	110
Rough Mill	35	Maintenance	30
Gluing	8	Shipping	10
Finish Mill	60	Office and clerical	35
Sanding	35	Supervision	20

PRODUCTION SCHEDULING

The Baumritter Corporation maintained an open stock policy which meant that additional pieces of a dining room set produced by Westfall could be purchased at any time. Westfall manufactured approximately 1,000 different items or pieces of furniture, but about 80% of their sales were in 200 fast selling items. Figure 2.2 shows a sample of the items made at Westfall. When a particular item was desired, a "cutting order" was issued for a manufacturing lot size of that particular item. Thus, if a chair was made up of seat, four legs, two leg cross braces, two stretcher braces, two back posts, back, and four spindles, and the manufacturing lot size for the chair was 250 units, then a cutting order would be issued for 250 chair seats, 1000 legs, 500 cross braces, etc. The parts requirements were translated into lumber requirements and appropriate orders were given to the cutoff saws. Once cut, the parts continued throughout the rough and finish mills as formerly described.

Order Acknowledgments

Orders for particular pieces of furniture came from retail dealers to the New York office. The New York office acknowledged orders on the basis of the current total backlog of orders (in sales dollars) at the factory which manufactured the particular item desired. Since Westfall produced sales of $7 million per year, an average week's output was $140,000. Thus, if a particular dining-room table was manufactured at the Westfall Furniture Company, and Westfall had an overall seven week backlog ($980,-000), the customer would be notified that his table would arrive in eight weeks. Figure 2.3 gives the production, inventory, and backlog position over the last year. Because of the fixed lead times for activities such as preparation of shipping papers, and minimum times for production runs, orders were never acknowledged for delivery in less than four weeks. Also, a maximum order acknowledgement interval of 15 weeks was imposed by the marketing department which felt that customers should never have to wait more than 15 weeks for delivery. This constraint was, however, somewhat artificial; although orders were never acknowledged for delivery in more than 15 weeks, 15 week delivery promises were often broken.

	Production	Beginning backlog	Beginning inventory
January	568	773	1,112
February	552	783	1,193
March	610	771	1,250
April	627	893	1,372
May	607	847	1,303
June	598	854	1,334
July*	320	822	1,269
August	635	982	1,311
September	681	1,408	1,682
October	647	1,454	1,812
November	645	1,332	1,639
December	633	1,278	1,598
January 1972		1,028	1,411
Total	7,123		

*Annual 2-week vacation shutdown.

Fig. 2.3 1971 production, inventory and backlog (thousands of $).

Shipping Schedules

Shipping schedules were prepared on the basis of orders acknowledged in order to achieve freight cost savings through pooled railroad cars. This was accomplished by the traffic department at Westfall keeping track of the accumulated acknowledged sales by particular shipping points. When the dollar total that represented an average freight car full of furniture was achieved, the car was planned for that particular location. Cars were scheduled 3 weeks in advance so that necessary adjustments in production could be implemented. As the time for a particular car shipment drew near, adjustments were made in the actual items to be shipped based upon volume considerations and on stock availabilities.

Because Westfall shipped full cars not only of furniture manufactured there, but also of furniture manufactured in other nearby Baumritter plants, a considerable amount of "juggling" was required to achieve the pool car savings. A weekly "short list" was prepared which was designed to fill up whatever needs were required for pool car shipments. Items on the short list were expedited through whatever operations were required; usually some finish mill, sanding, and assembly operations.

Lot sizes

Many of the machines in the finish mill area required extensive setup times. All furniture manufacturers attempted to manufacture in large lots so that the setup times could be amortized over many items. Thus, lot sizes at Westfall were always at least for 100 units; some nonchair items were cut in lots of 400 to 500, with the average lot size being about 175.

Lot sizes for chairs tended to be larger than those for other items since customers typically purchased a four to six piece set. The smallest lot size of chairs was 200 and the three most popular chairs were cut in lots of 2000, with the average being about 700.

Forecasting

The long lead times involved in the operation (from raw lumber to the finished product took eight to twelve weeks) necessitated some sort of forecasting methodology. Lead times were influenced by many factors including the size of lumber. Thus, most parts required 1" thick lumber, but a few parts required 1 1/2", 2", and 2 1/2" lumber. One kiln load of these less frequently used sizes might represent a two or three month supply. Westfall used a six week moving average for estimating the demand for the items they produced.

Shop Floor Control

The system used by Westfall for routing materials through the rough and finish mills was fairly simple. Cuttings were put into the rough mill and tended to flow directly into panels and boards of desired width, thickness, and length. The boards and panels would then go to the various finish mill machine centers as indicated on the shop papers.

Individual machine centers tended to run jobs on a first come-first served basis, but there were some important exceptions. Many times jobs might be completed in one operation and not immediately move on because of a lack of room at the subsequent operation. Such jobs were often placed wherever there was room on the machine room floor, and might remain there undetected until that particular item found its way onto the short list. Another exception came about because some jobs were inherently easier for the workers to earn large incentive wages on than others. A major influence on work flow was a flurry of activity near the end of monthly accounting periods to increase the amount of work completed. Still another reason for violation of the first come-first served processing of jobs on machines was a tendency of some foremen to ask their workers to process jobs with oldest initial cutting dates first. Needless to say, the short list also caused certain jobs to be placed ahead of other jobs.

A SYSTEMS STUDY

Several persistent problems that were typical in the furniture industry were becoming increasingly critical for Baumritter. This was so because the company was an innovator in furniture marketing. Baumritter followed a deliberate policy of reducing the number of retail outlets, concentrating their efforts on a small number of carefully designed franchised Ethan Allen Showcase Stores. This policy afforded much greater control over the destiny of the company, but at the same time it implied important responsibilities to the franchisees.

Finished Goods Inventories

One problem of immediate concern was finished goods inventories. The financial executives in New York seemed to be always complaining about the high level of finished goods inventories, and during low sales periods the intensity of the complaints increased; it was not unusual for the president to voice his dissatisfaction during these times.

A related charge was directed to the constitution of finished goods inventories. The vice-president in charge of marketing was a frequent critic; no explanation for the simultaneous existence of large inventories and backlogs of sold merchandise seemed to satisfy him. Figure 2.4 gives a random sample of inventory balances for 50 Westfall items.

Work in Process Inventories

Another frequent complaint from the New York office concerned what appeared to be a continually increasing work-in-process inventory level. In studying this issue, one Westfall executive felt that the factory re-

Item number	Quantity sold (1/1/71–7/1/71)	Inventory 7/1/71
1	8	0
2	14	0
3	0	14
4	4	0
5*	217	12
6	33	0
7	12	68
8	9	0
9	47	0
10	223	0
11*	51	147
12	3	12
13	12	0
14	399	0
15	17	0
16	29	4
17	47	0
18	9	2
19*	10800	147
20	176	8
21	10	0
22	4	46
23	12	0
24	27	0
25*	3,5	18
26	49	0
27	12	98
28	318	0
29	14	0
30	250	8
31	8	0
32	15	0
33	68	0
34	19	0
35*	4112	153
36	14	0
37*	3720	80
38	18	0
39	33	0
40	219	47
41	47	14
42	9	0
43	12	0
44*	2980	48
45	14	0
46	287	0
47	291	0
48	72	12
49	3	0
50	253	0

Fig. 2.4 Random sample of sales activity and inventory for 50 items (July 1, 1971) (*=chair).

quired a high work-in-process inventory level for three major reasons. First, in order to achieve good lumber utilization, the cutoff saw operators always required at least one relatively short length (17 inches was the smallest usable size). Unfortunately, this practice led to substantial stock piles of smaller sized lumber. Second, Westfall's manufacturing people desired to keep the expensive equipment in the finish mill as busy as possible; this seemed to require considerable work-in-process inventory. The third major cause of high work-in-process inventory levels was thought by many Westfall executives to be the short list. That is, in order to achieve pool car shipments it was always necessary to expedite certain items through the finish mill, assembly, and subsequent operations. When such expediting was called for, it was usual to split the lot size going through and only expedite what was needed for the pool car shipment.

Market Specials

In April and October, Baumritter participated in the Southern Furniture Markets held in the High Point, North Carolina area. In order to stimulate sales at these markets, existing or newly designed pieces of furniture were exhibited and promoted as market specials at lower prices. It was expected that retailers would use these pieces to draw in customers during the two major annual selling peaks, August and December. The vice-president in charge of marketing exerted considerable pressure on the factories to provide good delivery service on market specials. Westfall often found it necessary to devote the plant almost exclusively to market specials during August and September; the effect on deliveries of furniture other than market special items was often severe.

The Study

In June 1969, a formal study was initiated with the goals of increasing manufacturing efficiency and improving customer service in terms of product deliveries. The study was headed up by the vice-president in charge of manufacturing, Mr. Bill Fisher, who was located in New York. The New York office took on the overall responsibility for the systems study and the design of improvements which crossed functional lines. The two most notable of these were order acknowledgment, which necessarily involved marketing and production, and field warehouse stocks, which required a coordination between marketing policy, order acknowledgments, production scheduling, and the traffic function. Another goal of the study was integration of efforts between factories and preventing duplication of efforts.

Historically, Baumritter had followed a policy of decentralization, to the extent that each factory was run as virtually an autonomous company. Since the systems study would almost certainly reduce the autonomy, the vice-president in charge of manufacturing was anxious to get factory people actively involved in the formal systems study.

Each factory was given some latitude in defining its participation in the systems study. Accordingly, after some discussion of alternatives, it was decided that Westfall managers would undertake a study to improve performance in their assembly operations. Several managers had wanted to make some changes in this activity anyway, and they felt that the systems study gave them a chance to make some necessary changes. At the same time, they felt that "getting on board" the systems study with enthusiasm was politically expedient.

Since the chair line was the largest major assembly line, they proposed to start their investigation there. However, it was hoped that a better understanding and improvement in one assembly area would lead to similar improvements in the other assembly lines, and perhaps to a general capability that could be applied in other factories.

THE CHAIR LINE

As noted above, chair building tended to be done in volumes larger than those associated with other items, since customers typically purchased four to six chairs at one time to go with a single dining room table. Westfall produced chairs in two major finishes with about 85% of the volume being in the more popular Nutmeg. A fixed speed overhead conveyor took Nutmeg chairs to the finishing room; the maximum number of chairs that could be placed on this conveyor in an eight-hour shift was 785.

By not placing chairs on each hanger of the overhead conveyor, smaller volumes would result. The maximum number of chairs produced in one shift was 715, but this rate severely taxed the Nutmeg chair finishing operation; it was necessary to carefully load the conveyor so that chairs with a large number of spindles, such as a Duxbury arm chair, were followed by chairs with less complex finishing surfaces, such as a Duncan Phyfe side chair. When the daily volume was held to less than 600 chairs, the conveyor could be loaded with much less care. Chairs in the Classic Manor finish were sent to the finish room along with other Classic Manor items.

Chair Building

Chair building typically was accomplished in four 2-man building stations, three for Nutmeg finish and one for Classic Manor. One man assembled the back, spindles, and arms into the seat; the other man assembled the legs and cross braces into the preassembled seat and back. Both operations involved the application of glue, and assembly was aided with

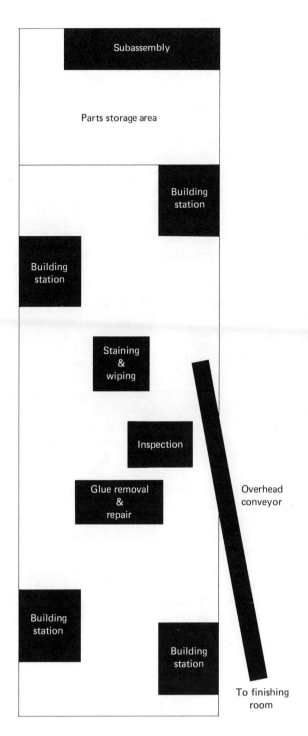

Fig. 2.5 Layout of the chair assembly area.

Fig. 2.6 Pictures of the chair assembly, other activities, and the overall plant.

Fig. 2.6 (*cont.*)

Fig. 2.6 (*cont.*)

simple alignment devices and rubber hammers. A one-man subassembly station assembled leg cross-braces and stretchers for those chairs designed with stretchers.

The procedure varied somewhat when the rear leg and back post was one integral part; the backs of these chairs were assembled in a fixture which pneumatically held the parts in proper location, and the chair was completed in another pneumatic fixture which clamped the front legs and seat supports to the back while wood screws were inserted.

In addition to the nine workers in subassembly and chair-building stations, two men were employed in the department to move stock to the work stations and help move completed chairs away, two men dipped Nutmeg chairs in a vat of stain and wiped them semi-dry, one man inspected all chairs before they went on the conveyor to the finish room, two men cleaned off any excess glue (glue does not absorb stain and finish in the same way as wood), three men made any necessary repairs, and a foreman, Mel Ryding, supervised the operation. Total employment was twenty of which four, the foreman, inspector and two stockmen, were considered as indirect labor; the others were regarded as direct labor

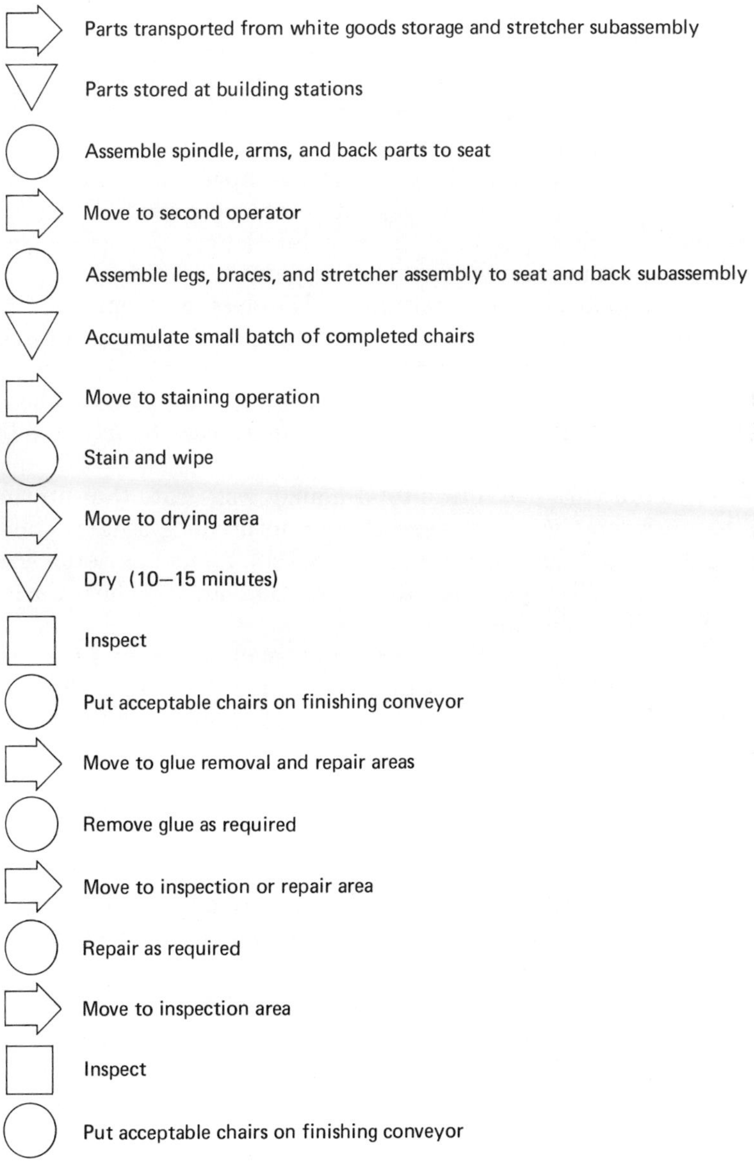

⇨ Parts transported from white goods storage and stretcher subassembly

▽ Parts stored at building stations

◯ Assemble spindle, arms, and back parts to seat

⇨ Move to second operator

◯ Assemble legs, braces, and stretcher assembly to seat and back subassembly

▽ Accumulate small batch of completed chairs

⇨ Move to staining operation

◯ Stain and wipe

⇨ Move to drying area

▽ Dry (10–15 minutes)

▢ Inspect

◯ Put acceptable chairs on finishing conveyor

⇨ Move to glue removal and repair areas

◯ Remove glue as required

⇨ Move to inspection or repair area

◯ Repair as required

⇨ Move to inspection area

▢ Inspect

◯ Put acceptable chairs on finishing conveyor

Fig. 2.7 Process flowchart for chair assembly.*

*The following symbols are commonly used for describing activities in
the flow of materials through a conversion or manufacturing process:

◯ = Operation   ⇨ = Transportation   ▽ = Storage or delay   ▢ = Inspection

workers and were on an incentive wage program geared to production output. Ten men worked in the finishing room exclusively on Nutmeg chairs. Although it was possible to increase or decrease output by changing the number of chair builders, the result was usually a bottleneck or slack operation in staining, glue removal, repair, or finishing.

Employee relations were quite good. The company was the major employer in the area and tried to treat its employees well. Thus, for example, when Baumritter acquired the Westfall factory, free paint was offered to anyone in the town who wanted to paint his house.

All Westfall employees were nonunion. The average length of employment on the chair assembly line was 9 1/2 years. The inspector and foreman were salaried, and the stockmen were paid about $2.15 per hour. Direct labor workers on the chair line had an average base wage of about $1.80 per hour, but incentive wages increased the average hourly rate to about $2.60.

There was more variance in the total hourly wage rate than in the base rate, because some workers were able to outproduce others. Thus, one chair building team made up of a father and son named Carleton was able to average about $3.50 per hour; as Mel Ryding put it, "Those Carletons really shake it all day long."

Location of the chair assembly operation was on the second floor in an area approximately 200 feet long by 40 feet wide. Figure 2.5 shows a layout of the existing operation; photographs of chair building, other activities, and the overall plant are shown in Fig. 2.6. Figure 2.7 is a process flowchart of the chair building operation.

Problems

The chair assembly process always seemed to require a flurry of activity. Keeping the four-chair building stations supplied with parts and supplies was a constant battle; moreover, since the conversion of parts into actual chairs created a manifold increase in required floor space, log jams of chairs seemed to be constantly present. Expediting and lot splitting to satisfy short list requirements confounded the operation still further.

In order to keep the building stations supplied, the stockmen sometimes had to hunt down particular parts and get them expedited. Sometimes it was not possible to get the desired parts on time; although it was against company policy, parts for other chairs were sometimes used (there were very few parts of identical design). Whole lots of parts were sometimes "lost," necessitating a rush replenishment order. Occasionally in order to keep the chair assembly area busy, the style of chairs produced would not be those desired. This condition usually occurred when parts for desired production were unavailable and when supplies of purchased parts such as special castors or rush seat materials ran out. One chair seat was specially made in Spain; one day a girl in the finishing room told Mel Ryding that a two day supply was left, and a six month stockout occurred.

About once every four months, the stain tank required servicing. When this happened, 1 1/2 days of chair production piled up to the ceiling and into the aisles while the chair finishing personnel were sent home. When they came back, the finishing line would run at virtual maximum capacity for several days to work off the semifinished chair inventory. During these periods, the work load for the three repair men was also quite high, because chairs were more easily damaged when they were piled up.

The foreman assigned particular chairs to the building teams. The more complicated chairs naturally had a higher building time, but on some chairs it was inherently easier to make large incentive wages than on others. Mel Ryding tried to spread these "gravy jobs" as evenly as possible, but there was always grumbling about favoritism.

The opposite problem also existed. There were some chairs with very "tight" time standards. A closely related problem concerned the workers' reactions to small orders, expediting, and lot splitting. It was easier to make incentive wages on long runs where a team could develop a knack for the particular chair and the particular batch of parts used to make it.

One of the most vocal complainers was the elder Carleton. Because he and his son were so fast, he felt that they got more than their share of rush jobs. He also alleged that jealousy on the part of other workers and the foreman caused him and his son to receive most of the jobs with tight standards and short runs.

Estimating when particular batches of chairs would be completed and when more parts would be needed to keep the building stations busy was quite difficult. If a particular batch went to the Carletons, it would probably be finished in three-fourths of the time required for another team.

There was some friction between the chair builders and the glue removers and repairmen. If a chair builder was sloppy in applying glue, he could get his job done faster, but the resultant work required of the men who removed excess glue was substantially increased. A similar problem arose with repairmen when chairs and parts were carelessly handled.

The 24-Inch Conveyor

Jim Howell, the industrial engineer, had been working full time for Westfall for six months since he graduated from a midwestern state university. However, he had grown up in Westfall, and had worked for the company five summers while a student. Soon after joining Westfall on a full-time

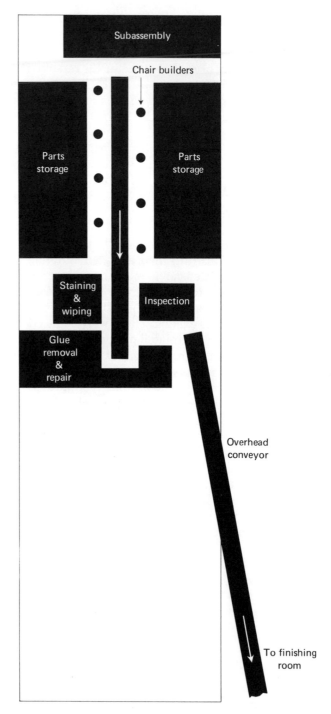

Fig. 2.8 The proposed 24-inch conveyor line.

basis, he proposed to Harry Ruml and John Hughes that a 24-inch wide floor level conveyor be used for assembling chairs.

His proposal was that all chair builders act as a single team to make one kind of chair at a time. In this way, the time required to finish an order for any one batch of chairs would be small enough so that quick adaption to the latest demand situation would be facilitated. In addition, the inventory of semifinished chairs would be substantially reduced and the delivery of components would be to one major location instead of to four separate places in the department. He also believed that the use of a conveyor might reduce damage sufficiently so that one less repair man would be needed. A rough drawing of his proposal is given as Fig. 2.8.

ASSIGNMENT

You have been hired as an assistant to Mr. Bill Fisher, Baumritter's vice-president of manufacturing, to work on the systems study. As your first task, you have been assigned to help Messrs. Ruml, Hughes, and Howell with their investigation of the chair line. In a four page (maximum length) written memorandum, tell them what you think they should do.

Why. did what I did

Outline form

CHAPTER 3

SYSTEMS AND MODELS

One of the major goals of this book is to provide each student with his own viable framework for understanding and solving problems in terms of their widest possible ramifications. To achieve this goal, we will consider many particular problems and solution methods proposed for these problems. Since "the systems approach" is concerned with solving particular problems in relation to their widest consequences, this chapter is devoted to a description of the *process* of problem formulation and solution from a systems point of view. With this exposition as a base, we will be able to better assess the worth or relevance of particular problem statements and their solutions.

Problem solving can be viewed as a process of system design, whether it is attempting to perform chair-building activities on a moving conveyor belt in the Westfall Furniture case, deciding where to locate a warehouse, or making choices about how to spend a month in Italy. Viewing such diverse problems as system design problems allows one profitably to investigate the underlying system design process and thereafter to obtain considerable insight into particular problems.

Since problem solving as system design is done for a reason or goal, we will consider the part played by a goal, set of goals, or evaluative criteria in the design process. Although differentiating between "goals," "objectives," and criteria might be of some intellectual interest, we will use the terms interchangeably.

In this chapter, we will also gain an appreciation of model building since models are representations of systems. The use of models allows us to economically test alternative system design strategies.

DEFINITION OF A SYSTEM

Many definitions of a system exist, but the following definition is particularly well suited to an understanding of the system design process:

A system is a collection of entities and the relationships among the attributes of those entities.

A somewhat less ambitious (and perhaps more comprehensible) definition might be:

A system is a collection of things and the relationships among those things.

The differences between the two definitions, however, are significant. *Entity* is here used as a more general term than *thing*. That is, things are physical entities. But systems often must include conceptual entities, e.g., the foreman's *view* of how chair builders will react to a change in job methods. An entity does not require present existence or stability over time. That is, an entity might be physical such as a conveyor; it might be conceptual such as the foreman's view of chair builder reaction (which could also be time variable); it might be organizational such as a procedure for inspecting chairs; it might be semipermanent such as the Rock of Gibraltar or a building; or it might be relatively ephemeral such as a particular chair passing through the line.

The other major extension in our definition is concerned with the notion of attributes of entities. By *attributes* we mean characteristics, descriptors, or properties. This extension is important because one's desire for entities is really a desire for attributes possessed by those entities; e.g., the industrial engineer's desire for a conveyor is for its material handling capacity, not its belt and motor. System performance is affected by relationships among the attributes of entities; e.g. the performance of the conveyor is strongly influenced by relationships such as the motor's pulling power and the friction of the bearings (it is also clear that these relationships change over time due to causes such as bearing wear).

Although every entity has more attributes than those in which one is interested at a particular time, an entity has value *only* because of its attributes. A particular entity may be valued in one system because of other attributes, and what is valuable at one time is not necessarily equally valuable at another. Thus, the Carleton chair building team has many attributes, including speed, belligerence, and perhaps English ancestry. Clearly, some of these attributes are more important than others, the importance is dependent upon the system in which the Carletons operate, and the importance can change over time (perhaps they would grow to loathe an Irish made conveyor).

Subsystems and Supersystems

From the belt, motor, conveyor, chair building personnel and other examples used above, it should be clear that every system is an entity in larger systems (so that it is a subsystem in many supersystems) and that every entity is really a system composed of smaller entities. The belt is composed of webbing and other parts; chair builders are an integral part of the assembly process, but are also part of family and social organizations;

the motor is made up of components including the armature, laminations, and main frame, Westfall is but one part of the furniture industry.

The concept of systems, subsystems and supersystems in which every system is composed of subsystems and is part of larger supersystems is one which will be used throughout this book, and virtually every business problem can usefully be viewed in this framework. A problem involving an inventory system interacts with many other systems, e.g., production scheduling, marketing, and systems involving individuals or communities. Some method of eliminating short list demands on the chair assembly line could have a profound impact on performance levels. Clearly, what is "good" for a system in isolation may or may not be good for another system or for a supersystem which includes other significant entities.

THE SYSTEM DESIGN PROCESS

In the extremely general way in which a system has been defined above, the number of existing systems is infinite since it is the sum of all the possible ways of arranging all the entities in the universe from the beginning until the end of time. Further, there is only one *total* system, that conceptual system which consists of all entities with their attributes related in all ways. A system is an artifact or construct; as such, it is artificial in that bounding is required, and the bounding process necessarily omits entities having some influence. Although the bounding process is artificial, it is virtually synonymous with analysis; that is, one identifies, bounds, or isolates some problem and then attempts to solve it —often by in turn bounding smaller parts or subsystems for analysis. Since the bounded or isolated problem is not really isolated, the analysis, no matter how useful, is somewhat artificial.

Only a very small number of all possible systems are useful, meaningful, or of interest to students of operations management. They consist of those systems made up of relevant entities, the attributes of which are related in meaningful ways for the solution of operational problems. The meaningfulness of systems can *only* be evaluated in terms of the criteria or objectives or goals of the system. This is a critical point that will be developed in the next major section of this chapter.

Man-made systems are all imperfect in that they include some irrelevant entities, exclude some relevant entities (assumed to be part of the environment), and relate the attributes of the included entities imperfectly. Thus, in the design of a conveyorized chair-building operation, relevant entities like the production rate in the finishing room may be excluded (considered to be part of the chair building system's environment), while fairly irrelevant entities like some worker's abhorrence for fat inspectors may be included (considered to be within the system boundaries). Also, the magnitudes and variabilities of included entities such as conveyor capacity, costs of a conveyor breakdown, and the costs of ordering and carrying maintenance parts are certain to be imperfectly related.

An approach to the problem of conveyorized chair building which excluded the rate of chair finishing and the extent of short-list changes would clearly be open to serious question. However, important as it may be to include these entities in the problem approach, analysis of the resultant system is very likely to be more difficult. The dilemma, therefore, is that wider system bounding usually leads to more realistic identification of problems, but the delineated problems are more difficult to solve.

Having established these ideas, the system design problem at the conceptual level can be stated quite simply: *The system design problem is to discover which system, from the infinite population of all systems, to use to satisfy a stated need.* This statement of the problem applies whether the system being designed (discovered) is a new system or an ongoing system being redesigned. It is the search for the desired system which we shall call the system design process. In this process, the system designer acts in two capacities:

1. He decides what entities are to be included in (or excluded from) the system (the *INCLUSION* process).

2. He decides how to structure the attributes of the set of chosen entities (the *STRUCTURING* process).

The system designer is guided in these decisions by a set of criteria which establishes the goals of the system being designed.

Consider some examples. Glenn Miller, Herb Alpert, and Mantovani each had a musical *criterion* or *goal* which indicated the attributes of the musical output sought. Assuming technical competence, musical output depends primarily on two factors, instrument choice and arrangements. The first is the inclusion process, the second the structuring of the attributes of the chosen entities. It can be argued that a similar set of decisions exists for the fields of musical composition, junk sculpture, poetry, painting, or operations management. Notes, pieces of junk, words, colors, and various operations management ideas are known and available. An infinite variety of systems (tunes, sculptures, poems, paintings, and operational problem solutions) exists conceptually. The composer, sculptor, poet, painter or management system designer selects (includes) entities for the value of their attributes and combines (structures) those attributes in certain ways, thereby creating a system in order to achieve a desired output. Those most skillful in the system design process in some of these areas we call artists. But *all* good system design calls for artistry

—artistry in the imaginative and insightful selection of entities and structuring of their attributes.

Artistry is called for because, although the system design problem can be stated simply, finding a solution to the problem is not a clear-cut process for the following reasons:

1.   The system designer cannot know of all systems. He cannot even know of all entities.

2.   The system designer cannot know of all the attributes of entities. He also cannot know how all of the various attributes relate, e.g., he may predict correctly one relationship but not know of a concomitant relationship which may or may not be desirable.

3.   The system designer has quite limited knowledge of how the system will perform over time.

4.   The "stated need" or criterion is often imprecise and/or inaccurate.

By coupling his artistic skill and the operational tools of system design available to him, the designer develops a "feeling" for the "key" attributes sought, the entities which might yield these attributes and how to establish the key attribute relationships among the key entities in a system. Thus the system design process is a search to find the key entities and establish the key relationships which will produce the objectives sought.

The Inclusion Process
The inclusion process is the process of determining what entities are to be part of the system. Although in practice a system designer alternates between emphasizing the inclusion and the structuring processes, the inclusion process logically precedes the structuring process, as the entities to be included must be considered before relationships among their attributes can be imagined. It is the inclusion process that you as a student have to face when preparing a written assignment such as in Chapter 2, when you decided what "facts" (entities) of the Westfall Furniture case to put into your four-page memorandum. (It is worth noting that fact entities other than those in the case being considered, e.g., information from a course in industrial relations or organizational behavior, are candidates for inclusion in your analysis.)

In the inclusion process entities are chosen for the value of their attributes, not for any inherent value. A coach values a certain member of a football team because of his kicking or throwing ability, his height, speed, weight, or agility, and because the coach can structure those attributes with those of other team members to do well in terms of his criteria. In the business world we value a prospective manager, a piece of production equipment, a new strategically located warehouse, or a management information system for their attributes and the effectiveness with which those attributes can be structured. In the Westfall case you may have valued the Carleton building team for its ability to produce, a conveyor belt for its ability to move material, or a larger work-in-process inventory area for its ability to allow more autonomous operations.

In every system design, an explicit or implicit decision is made as to the inclusion of each possible entity. Exclusion is undesirable but necessary; undesirable because some relevant entities are always excluded from the system, necessary because only a limited number of entities can be examined and managed. A major factor affecting entity choice is the ability to structure the attributes of chosen entities, i.e., a system designer may recognize the importance of an entity but not be able to deal with a system which includes it. As we shall discuss later in this chapter, models may be used to examine larger numbers of alternatives and to help the system designer to deal with systems which include larger numbers of entities.

The Structuring Process

The structuring process is concerned with the determination of key relationships among the attributes of chosen entities. In this phase a given set of entities is closely analyzed to see how their attributes shall be related in order to perform as well as possible in terms of the criteria set. This phase would correspond to the determination by an econometrician of the precise relationships (the functions and their coefficients) among chosen explanatory variables and dependent variables. The chemical engineer is structuring when he used EVOP (EVolutionary OPeration) to determine the proper settings of chosen inputs in a chemical process. The management scientist uses this process when he turns from the *identification* of key variables in a simulation to the *manipulation* of those variables to affect performance. When the business analyst shifts from the decision to integrate demand forecasts, production capabilities, fiscal resources, and customer service, and attacks the question of how to accomplish this integration, he is involved in the structuring process. When you turned from the selection of fact entities in the Westfall Furniture case to a study of how to put those facts into a sound position paper to the chair assembly study team, you were involved in the structuring process.

Although the structuring process is important and yields payoffs, often efforts are directed toward improvements in structure when inclusion changes might yield higher returns. Misplaced effort can be put into improved structure for a number of reasons. First, it is easier. Working with existing entities just takes less "brain strain" or creativity than determining the truly relevant criteria or goals, imagining appropriate and realizable attributes and imagining new entities with the attributes sought. In such a search the system designer may well have to break out of long-standing thought patterns. It is easier just to concentrate on making the existing entities work better. Second, the structuring process is more predictable and straightforward, more certain of some positive results. Third, the common management science tools usually cited as valuable in system design (queuing theory, mathematical programming, game theory, etc.), assist more in the analysis of a chosen set of entities than in the process of selection of those entities.

Finally, our educational process emphasizes structure; few, if any, disciplines formally address the inclusion question. Existing entities (theories, tools, institutions) are studied closely and occasionally their interrelationships are examined. While serving the valid educational purpose of handing down knowledge, this style of education is limited in developing the inclusion-oriented abilities of the student.

THE CRITERIA SET

The worth of a system and the system design effort can be assessed only in terms of particular criteria, goals, or objectives. The criteria dictate, direct, or drive the system design process, because changes in inclusion and structure are made for the purpose of achieving some objective or objectives. The system designer uses the set of criteria to assess the relevance of entities and the quality of relationships among the attributes of the chosen entities. Consequently, an inventory system devised with the criterion of minimizing stockouts would be different from one with a goal of minimizing a sum of stockout costs and carrying costs or of minimizing an even more global cost function including production costs. Thus good system design must start with identification of criteria: One simply cannot know how to design a system without knowing the purpose or use to which the system will be put. The highly individualistic nature of criteria is well illustrated by the story presented in Box 3.1.

An urbanite driving through Vermont came to a fork in the road with signs indicating that both roads led to White River Junction. When he asked a Vermonter whether it made any difference which road he took, the Vermonter replied, "Not to me it don't."

Box 3.1

The Criteria Set as a System

Most useful systems are driven by more than one criterion. In an inventory control situation there are many criteria, including decreasing production fluctuations, backing up salesmen with large inventories, minimizing capital investment in inventories, enhancing the personal goals of inventory clerks, and presenting a healthy-looking set of accounting statements to the shareholders. At Westfall objectives or criteria include more output, better delivery performance, improved quality, lower costs, satisfied employees, and perhaps increased political power within the organization. These criteria may be viewed as entities (some with considerably more attributes of potential input than others), and the collection of these criterion entities with the relationships among their attributes may be viewed as a *criteria system*.

Even though the design of a criteria system is a very difficult task, there is no need to treat the underlying design *process* of this more complex class of systems more explicitly than that of other systems. The system design process described in the preceding section is still appropriate; each criterion is an entity, the relationships among the attributes of these entities (structure) can be good or poor, and improvements can be made by changes in the inclusion of criterion entities and/or by changes in the structuring of entity attributes. Thus, short and long-term profit, good morale, and steadiness of work force might be included in a criteria set for a whole company or for a fairly small subsystem within a company and might be related in various states of "goodness." Also present might be unarticulated criterion entities such as perpetuation of job or company, or the growth of one's domain. It is important to note that the inclusion of particular criteria in a given system does not necessarily have to be planned or even conscious and that the ways in which such criteria entities relate to other criteria can be profound. In Westfall the criterion of increasing the amount shipped before the end of a monthly accounting period probably leads to significant costs in the early days of the succeeding month when the work-in-process "pipeline" is "dry."

Goal Congruence

In order to consider the worth or appropriateness of criterion entities for a subsystem (which entities and how they are related), the criteria sets for the supersystems in which the subsystem is embedded must be considered. The criteria set of a holding company is used in designing the criteria set for a particular diversified corporation—the corporation's for its divisions', a division's for its subsystems' and theirs for their subsystems' down to the smallest entity of interest. Each subsystem's criteria set is hopefully designed so that its measurement of subsystem performance matches (or is in keeping with) that of its higher level criteria set, i.e., there is "goal congruence." Thus goals, objectives, constraints, or criteria for Westfall's operation must be assessed in terms of the entire Baumritter Corporation. Such an assessment could be important in the consideration of questions such as whether Westfall should build a specialized chair assembly line with limited flexibility; the place of product line size in achieving marketing objectives is critical.

A significant problem in the design of criteria sets lies in achieving goal congruence and in assessing the degree of matching between subsystem criteria sets and higher level sets. What goals for chair assembly line production match best with those for car load shipments? For marketing? For suppliers of purchased materials? For the personal systems of the employees? And what goals for these systems match best with those of Westfall Furniture Company, Baumritter, the town of Westfall, Vermont, or larger societal goals? To what extent does Westfall Furniture Company *care* about employee or societal goals?

Unwise selections of lower level criterion entities and poor structuring of their attributes can result in suboptimization of higher level criteria. It should be clear that a Baumritter marketing criterion of sales maximization based upon substantial increases in the product line, interacting with a production criterion of cost minimization achieved through specialization may thwart the fulfillment of higher enterprise objectives of growth, stability, and profitability.

Such suboptimization may be reduced by redesigning the subsystem criteria sets in such a way that they are more in tune with the higher level criteria; so that when subsystem criteria are met, the results in terms of the supersystem set of criteria will be more favorable (the subsystems may or may not be combined into a larger system). In the investigation of operations management problems it is extremely important to assess goal congruence, both with criteria within the operations function, and with other subsystems. For Baumritter, the production criteria set must include flexibility to meet product line objectives; similarly, product line changes need to be constrained by production capabilities and should build upon productive strengths.

Surrogate Criteria

Another significant problem in the design of criteria systems is the vagueness, lack of definition and nonquantifiability of higher level criteria, e.g., long term growth, stability, community service, or corporate integrity.

The integration of these criterion entities with others such as profitability is extremely difficult and is usually resolved in a somewhat arbitrary fashion. Practical substitutes, stand-in, surrogate, or "proximate" criteria, are typically found for vague high level criteria which hopefully will yield desired results. Thus, various financial ratios are used as tests or criteria for financial stability, minimization of stockouts is used as a surrogate for customer service, and chairs produced per day is used as a measure of chair-line effectiveness. It is worth reiterating that each of these surrogate or proximate criteria is an entity in a system and its attributes can relate to attributes of other criteria in profound ways. Thus, the chair builders can more readily produce one chair than another, but if the less readily produced chair has a high backlog, it would seem appropriate to produce it at the expense of the surrogate criterion of chairs produced per day.

As noted above, noncongruency of goals leads to suboptimization. The omission of relevant criteria entities in the design of subsystems and the use of proximate criteria also lead to suboptimization. The concept of suboptimization refers to the penalty one pays in higher system criteria for imperfect design—imperfect in choice of entities (criteria entities or otherwise) and structure. Suboptimization comes about from imperfection in:

a) the choice of entities in the system (inclusion); e.g., a chair conveyor with no speed adjustment;

b) the relationships of entity attributes (structure); e.g., worker job satisfaction and the setting of chair conveyor speeds.

c) criteria inclusion; e.g., no wage incentive paid to workers on the conveyorized chair line; and

d) criteria structure: e.g., an incentive system that resulted in poorer quality production.

Since all systems are imperfect in entity choice and structure, every system is inevitably suboptimal. For a system to be truly optimal in the ultimate sense it would have to include all entities (since all entities are related in some way, none is totally irrelevant to any system) and relate their attributes perfectly. This is obviously impossible.

It is told that a Russian nail factory was being evaluated on the basis of output tons of production. After some time it was noticed that only very large nails were produced with a resultant high backlog for small sizes. A new surrogate criterion for measuring plant efficiency was therefore determined, namely, the number of nails. At that point, only tacks were produced.

In at least one large American city, police precincts are rated or evaluated on how well they keep the crime level down. This criterion, however, leads to a large number of crimes going unreported. In the same city, it is said that the arrest of a juvenile on a narcotics charge requires 121 forms to be filled out by the arresting officer. This constraint acts to inhibit juvenile narcotics arrests.

Box 3.2

It is suboptimal to consider operation of the chair assembly line separately from chair finishing, but it is also suboptimal not to include dry kiln charging or the executives' desire for carpeted offices. The distinction is that at this time our understanding of flow oriented systems such as the chair-building activity has progressed to a level where the inclusion of additional flow entities such as chair finishing is economically feasible and justifiable. What is good practice today will not be tomorrow. The solution of one problem often leads to a statement of a more important problem—important in terms of higher level, more inclusive criteria.

The essential role played by criteria in the system design process is well illustrated by Box 3.2.

SYSTEM EVOLUTION

Our discussion of systems and the system design process for problem solving has not yet explicitly included a time dimension. That is, it is easier to think initially of problem solving as a one-time or static activity in which we identify the criteria, imagine attributes that would help in achieving these criteria or goals, imagine entities that have the attributes, build the system, and consider the task finished.

But what happens if at some point in the process or after completion, a new entity with superior attributes is discovered, such as a more compact electronic component, a motor with greater power, a bearing with less friction, or a conveyor with less cost? What happens if the selected entities and anticipated structures do not achieve the desired results? What happens if desired results are achieved but are accompanied by undesirable unanticipated side effects, e.g., the output from chair finishing is increased, but the workmen quit? What happens if the desired results are achieved, but even more desirable results can be achieved with additional changes?

In an earlier section, it was noted that the system design process is not clear cut and requires "artistry"; and in the last section we noted the inevitability of suboptimization. Thus, in terms of a time dimension, the result is that there is no such thing as "the ultimate weapon," that improvements are always possible, and that evolution is inevitable.

In considering improvements or evolution, it is useful to differentiate between two different varieties of improvement. First, it may be possible to make improvements in the design of a system in terms of an existing or specific set of criteria (there are certain problems where this is *not* so; e.g., a mathematically exact solution for optimizing throughput in a refinery). Second, it is *always* possible to make improvements in the design of a system by changing the criteria (that is, by an evolution or redesign of the criteria system that dictates the system design process). The redesign may be in the structure or weighting of existing criterion entities or by the inclusion of additional criterion entities.

The notion of the inevitability of evolution carries with it, if not a negative connotation, at least not a positive one. It should be noted emphatically that evolution is indeed positive. In fact, a major criterion entity in the system design *process* should be for rapid evolution of the system, both within the specified set of criteria and (perhaps more importantly) for the system of criteria which drives, directs, or dictates the system design process.

Chapter 4 will deal explicitly and in some detail with the roles of expert problem solvers or system designers and system users; for now it is worth noting that the speed of system evolution is often severely hampered by an unfortunate fact of life, particularly in business organizations. In order to get systems installed or operating in a human environment, it is often necessary for an individual to put his personal prestige, power, or status "on the line." Subsequent evolution in these systems is often unfortunately viewed as an assault on this individual prestige, and the result is that many good ideas either take considerable time to be implemented or do not come to fruition at all.

Adaptability

A concept that is related to evolution (indeed it would be impossible to draw a clear dividing line) concerns the adaptability of a system. Many systems, when operating, process input entities into output entities; indeed, a widely held view of a system is as a black box (containing entities) which processes inputs into outputs. For example, the chair line processes parts of various designs into different chairs. In most input-output systems there are variations and/or changes in the inputs and outputs over time, and the ways in which particular inputs are treated affects the ways in which other inputs can be treated. The extent to which a system is able to deal with or adapt to variations, changes, and interdependencies in input entities is an important criterion for evaluating that system design effort. Thus, some chair-building systems will be much better able to cope with poor fitting parts than others.

In addition to variable behavior in the input entities, there will be variations, changes, and interdependencies in the "interior" of transformation entities. In fact some of these will occur *because* of the behavior of input entities. Perhaps a ¼" oversize chair leg requires extra effort that necessitates a redivision of effort on the conveyorized chair line.

Systems are designed with varying degrees of tolerance for variations, changes, and interdependencies in input entities and interior entities. The word *tolerance* implies that change is an evil to be guarded against; this is of course not necessarily true. A good system should in fact be highly adaptive; that is, the design should allow for the system to capitalize on behavioral changes. Perhaps strategic placement of the Carletons and redivision of chair-building activities can permit greater output.

In the design of a good conveyorized chair-building line at Westfall, it would be critical to build in the flexibility to handle different chairs, methods improvements, and different production rates. All of these capabilities imply proper balance or division of efforts between workers and the ability to rebalance to achieve improvement possibilities.

In a general sense, explicit inclusion of evolution in the framework for system design connotes that systems are designed to perform over time, that systems and conditions will change, that the system designer should assess the adaptability of his design to changes, that a system will evolve over time, and that a very appropriate objective should be to speed that evolution.

MODEL BUILDING

A model is an abstraction of a system; e.g., a pilot plant, a hydraulic model of an inventory system, a mathematical model of consumer behavior, a verbal description or model of the Westfall chair-building activity, a mental model of the Washington Monument, or *my* mental model of *your* mental model of the Washington Monument. The abstraction is made for a purpose (criterion)—the modeler has a problem to solve or a system to design, and he will use the model to obtain results from which he can draw important inferences about the system being modeled. The model will not be identical with the real world system; it will be synthetic, a construct, artifact, or "fake." But if one has modeled well, the results obtained from the model will be "valid" with respect to the particular aspects of the system that are of interest. That is, the synthetic abstraction will contain the essential qualities of the system being modeled and the inferences made about the system will be satisfactory—which does not necessarily mean that inferences can be drawn in regard to other problems, interests, or systems with this particular model.

The model-building process follows from an interest in some system. One such interest might be to design a system: for example, an airplane, a refinery, a procedure for chair building on a belt conveyor, a production control system or a system for gambling at Las Vegas. Implicit in the interest of designing a system is the notion of evolution or redesign. The first designs for an airplane, refinery, chair-building procedure, or production control system yield poor results; or we lost most of our money at Las Vegas. Since Westfall undoubtedly will make changes in the procedure for building chairs, one necessarily must be concerned with redesign.

In addition to an interest in designing a system, one might also be interested in training someone in the use of a system: e.g., a pilot to fly an airplane, an engineer to operate a refinery, a workman to fit legs to stretcher braces, a foreman to use the production control system, or a shill to make bets. One might also be interested in how to achieve improved operation of a system; how to develop superior flying patterns in order to avoid enemy groundfire, how to increase the yield from the refinery, how to get more chairs per hour, how to achieve few shortages or late orders, or how to increase expected payoff from the gambling venture.

Another interest in a system might be to predict its behavior: for example, at what diving speed is the airplane unable to pull out? What happens if the catalytic cracker temperature is increased by 10°? How many men will be required to run the chair line if the demand for ladder back chairs increases by 20%? What happens to machine utilization if jobs are run on a first come-first served basis? What happens if one only plays blackjack when the fives and sixes have been played from the deck?

Still another interest in a system might be to sell it: to convince the Defense Department to order a new fighter aircraft, to build a new refinery for an oil company, to convince a foreman that chair building on a conveyor belt is superior to the present method, to persuade a manufacturer of the design superiority of a proposed production control system, or to get financial backing for a gambling scheme.

There are undoubtedly additional interests in systems, but for any of the above interests, there are basically two ways in which the interest can be satisfied. One can either experiment with the real system (if it exists), or one can use some model or synthetic system. Thus, an airplane could be built to see if it flies, a raw trainee could be put in the cockpit and wished luck, various flying patterns through groundfire could be tried, the driving speed could be increased until the plane could not pull out, or the plane could be built before selling it to the Defense Department. The other obvious choice is to use models such as a wind tunnel replica, a Link trainer, a computer simulation of groundfire, or a mathematical representation of driving stresses.

The airplane example is one where the model-building choice seems more appropriate than using the real system, but this is not always true, even for interests involving airplanes. Some questions about aircraft performance are best answered with flying experience. Refinery operations often are tinkered with through "EVolutionary OPeration" during which the results of various micro-changes are carefully examined. There are things about conveyorized chair building that will only be learned in actual operation. Production control systems are tempered to take account of differences in worker abilities for particular jobs. And the Las Vegas gambler may shade his bets by watching the dealer's eyes.

The major reason for using a model instead of a real system is economy. Some kinds of experimentation with real systems can be relatively expensive, slow, or dangerous. Thus building, testing, or experimenting with various airplanes or refineries could be very time-consuming and expensive. And trying odd settings for a refinery or atomic reactor could be dangerous if not insane.

The Model-Building Process

Model building is one type of system design, and the model-building process is, therefore, the same as the system design process depicted earlier in this chapter. The only real difference is that models are systems of abstracted entities or concepts; the modeler utilizes both the inclusion and the structuring processes to build a system of abstracted entities in order to represent a real world system. Modeling is difficult for the same reasons that system design in general is difficult. A model may be poor because of inappropriate criteria, faulty or imperfect choice of entities, or faulty structuring of their attributes. For example, a model to aid in the design of a procedure for conveyorized chair building may fail to give valid results because personal goals of the workers have not been considered, because variability in worker speed has been ignored, or because the interactions of speed variability have not been properly treated.

A unique problem-oriented set of criteria is used to identify the aspects or qualities of the real world system to be represented. This set of criteria or needs is determined by the interest one has in building a model and dictates both the entities to be represented and the level of detail or abstraction of these entities. Once selected, the model entities (blocks of wood for a wind tunnel model, variables in a mathematical model, or subroutines in a digital simulation model) are then combined so that their attributes are related (with glue, by mathematical operators, or other subroutines) so as to produce the qualities desired for the model interest.

Although the role of criteria is addressed explicitly in the next section, it is worthwhile here to note the importance of the criteria system. If one wants to model an oil refinery, it is absolutely essential to define the use for which the model is intended. Only in this way can the necessity for representation of the crude oil smell or the catalytic cracker temperature be determined. Clearly for some purposes either or both could be important or irrelevant.

Figure 3.1 is a diagram of the model building process. On the left side of Fig. 3.1, the real world has been depicted as a large system or set. Within that set is a smaller set or system of interest such as a refinery (of course, the refinery need not physically exist—that is, the set could be

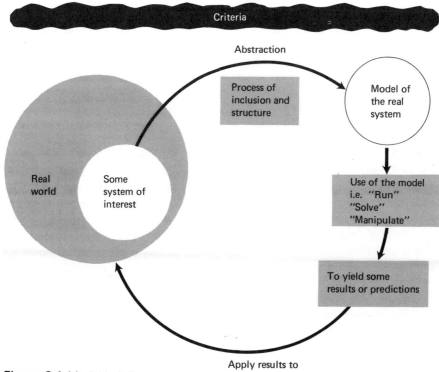

Figure 3.1 Model-building process.

a conception of a refinery). Based upon some problem, interest, goal, or criterion, certain entities in that system of interest are selected as having some properties or attributes that need study in a model. For example, one might be interested in the balance of various distillate flows in a refinery in terms of ascertaining the capacity needs for various components (e.g., a catalytic cracker, fractionating towers, and cokers), and it is necessary to examine these needs under various operating conditions such as seasonal changes in needs for gasoline and fuel oil or changes in types of crude oil input.

With this balance of flow interest in mind, *some* attributes of *some* entities of a proposed refinery system are selected for representation in the model. Also, by elimination, attributes are selected which should *not* be represented in the model. Thus, many operating characteristics of catalytic crackers are important to the particular problem under study, but the color of the cracker is probably unimportant. The use to which the model is to be put also determines the kind of model or type of abstraction chosen. Thus if we were concerned with laying out the refinery on a block of land, a physical scale model or a graphical model with two-dimensional templates might be selected. For an interest in distillate flow balance, some sort of a symbolic or mathematical representation of refinery component attributes seems appropriate.

Once the model entities are selected, they are structured or put together so that the interaction of their attributes matches or represents the interactions deemed important in the real world system. Thereafter, following the clockwise arrow flow of Fig. 3.1. the model is "run," "solved," or "manipulated" to examine hypotheses of both model behavior and indirectly, behavior of the real system. Thus the results accruing from this activity would give insight into the wisdom of a particular set of refinery components and some insight into how well these components have been represented in the model.

At this time, one typically recycles through the modeling process and examines different choices of components in the real system by making appropriate changes in the model. For example, a run of the original model might have revealed that one refinery component was much closer to capacity than others. Or one might now wish to examine other hypotheses; for example, additional component needs if different kinds of crude oil were used or if different kinds of transportation devices (e.g., water or pipeline) enabled entrance into new markets.

These kinds of hypotheses or problems are often called "what if" questions, and a thoroughgoing analysis should treat many such questions. Many of these questions can only be treated in a model; the modeling process enables reasonable examination of a much greater number of alternatives, and the choice of model can influence one's ability to examine such alternatives.

The Role of Criteria

Figure 3.1 depicts a criteria cloud hanging over the model-building process. Earlier in this chapter the notion of a system or set of criteria which drives, directs, or dictates the system design process was presented. Put very simply, systems are built for particular purposes. The same argument holds true for model building, which is system design with abstracted entities. Models are built for particular purposes.

The above paragraph may seem repetitious or intuitively obvious, but it is worth emphasizing that in this area an abstract statement and actual practice can be dramatically separated. Experience indicates that the greatest deficiency in model-building efforts well may be the lack of a clearly delineated set of criteria. It can virtually be *guaranteed* that each student will fall into this trap during his course in operations management as well as in other endeavors. Indeed, one of the most important lessons to be learned from this course is how to fall into the trap less frequently and to recognize the condition sooner when it occurs.

Suppose, for example, that you were asked to construct a diagrammatic or flowchart model of a bank teller's operation. To make the task even simpler, let us suppose that all he does is cash checks. How would you construct such a model? What would you include? How would you relate the model entities? Does the teller always count out the paper money before the silver? Is it necessary to include the counting of silver separately from that of paper money? Is it necessary to include the process of counting money separately from the process of account verification?

The only way one can adequately answer such questions is to consult the criteria system. That is, *why* is this model being built and what questions are to be examined with the model? If one were interested in knowing how to improve the teller's efficiency or speed, he might reasonably break the task down to very small detail, studying the individual hand motions involved in counting silver and paper money. If, however, he were willing to accept the present job methods, but were concerned with how many teller stations to have open at various times during the day, the selection of model entities (and the concomitant data collection process) would be quite different.

Level of Aggregation

The criteria system not only dictates the appropriate entities to be represented in a model, but also the *way* they are to be represented. The necessary degree of detail, or what is often called the appropriate "level of aggregation," can only be determined by falling back on the criteria system. The level of aggregation issue is at the heart of the modeling process. As stated above, the major reason for using a model is economy; a model is a fake that contains the essence of the real—but only the essence for a particular set of criteria. It therefore follows that the essence implies a necessary level of detail, and the necessary level will vary for different problems.

In our description of the model-building process, the notion of recycling was discussed as different entities were included in the model, as they were related in improved ways, and as different "what if" questions were asked. All of these activities suggest an evolution in the model-building process similar to that considered in the system design process. As that evolution occurs, the appropriate level of aggregation changes.

In prior considerations of evolution, we dealt with evolution or change both under a fixed set of criteria and with evolution in the system of criteria which directs the system design effort. Both kinds of evolution also apply to model building, and it is only an appeal to the set of criteria (fixed or evolved) which allows one to assess model relevance and the appropriate level of detail. Thus a flow-oriented model (such as we will discuss in Chapter 11) could be concerned with studying the effects of various chair designs on chair-building efficiency. The model could be improved or evolved by including various changes in methods or staffing that would result in decreased times for particular tasks. The model could also be improved by considering the additional criteria or goals of improved chair quality and worker satisfaction; clearly the appropriate attributes of model entities as well as the entities themselves might change to meet the more encompassing problem definition.

A very interesting impact of the evolution in model building is the evolution in the criteria system itself which is fostered by model-building efforts. One set of model-building results leads to another question and still another. As these questions arise, changes are called for in the level of aggregation, in the entities selected for inclusion in the model, and in the criteria which drive the model-building process.

Kinds of Models

Since model building is a highly individualistic process based on unique criteria, it is not surprising that there are many different kinds of models and that some kinds of models are more appropriate for particular problem situations than others. Various classification schemes have been proposed for categorizing models, the most common being iconic, analog, or symbolic. For our purposes, we will now find it useful to consider the strengths and weaknesses of physical, mathematical, mental, verbal, graphical, and digital simulation models.

Physical models are those that look like the real thing. Examples might be a pilot plant for a chemical processor, a mockup of an airplane to examine cabin decor, or a three-dimensional model of the conveyorized chair-building line. Physical models are particularly well suited to what might be broadly termed education. In general, however, they are relatively expensive and somewhat limited in their use for analysis, since the range and complexity of issues or "what if" questions that can be studied through physical models is more limited than is true for other modeling procedures.

Mathematical models use symbols to represent both entities and their interrelationships. Thus in the equation $A^2 = B^2 + C^2$, a precise model is given for predicting the length of the hypotenuse of a right triangle. Examples which are useful for operations management problems include inventory, queuing, and linear-programming models. The use of mathematical models is constantly growing, and for good reason. Mathematical models are more abstract and hence more general than others. They can be easily modified to represent differing situations. For example, how would one examine the cabin decor of a proposed SST with the interior mockup of a fighter plane? Clearly, however, the same mathematical model for estimating lift as a function of wing area could be used for both aircraft. Similarly, the three-dimensional representation of the conveyorized chair-building line would be of limited use to understanding chair production under differing production rates. Mathematical models also have the advantage of not being limited to things we can visualize, e.g., negative numbers and n-dimensional space.

Mental models are by far the most common. Each of us has millions of mental models. Indeed, whatever one thinks about something is a mental model. Thus we have mental models of the effects of gun control legislation on crime, the effect of changing chair production rates at Westfall, the relationships between angles and sides of triangles, and the worth of a course in operations management. Mental models have a great strength in that *some* mental model can be produced quickly in a situation which would be difficult if not impossible to describe physically or mathematically, such as skiing on a wintry day. This great generality of application has, however, another side to it: Different people possess different mental models for the same phenomenon. My mental model for skiing might be quite different from yours.

Verbal models are an attempt to communicate and improve on mental models. Thus as I attempt to verbalize my mental model for skiing, I will be better able both to express the model to you and to understand and articulate my feelings about skiing. Verbal models, however, lack the rigor of mathematical models. And, if one considers the written word as a model form different from verbal models, a similar increase in rigor may also be obtained. All of us have experienced this rigor in attempting to write unambiguously what we feel we can easily say.

Graphical models are a step in rigor above the written word and include such manifestations as blueprints, flow charts, organization charts, and process charts. At one time the dominant mode of analysis in production and operations management, many of the earlier graphical techniques have been superseded by more dynamic, unambiguous, flexible models.

Digital simulation models are a combination of mathematical models or relationships and the computer. They involve numerical and logical relationships and rely on mass computation power in order to make the tremendous number of necessary calculations feasible. This tool will be treated explictly in Chapter 12; but for now, in terms of model-building potential, it is worth noting that digital simulation fills a large void in the supply of readily applicable modeling procedures. It has the rigor of mathematical analysis, but can handle wide classes of problems for which mathematical models are not appropriate and can include a much larger number of model entities. In addition, use of digital simulation is not limited to the mathematically gifted. In fact, digital simulation is in many ways a logical extension in the evolution of modeling from mental to verbal to written to graphical (flow chart), and now to digital simulation. Students of operations management will find in this modeling procedure a particularly congenial atmosphere in which to extend and develop their thinking about operational problems.

An important concept is related to the notion of extensions or evolution in model building from mental to verbal to written to graphical to digital simulation to mathematical. That is, there are great benefits to be derived from making models explicit. In this way both communication between individuals, and analysis can be fostered. When discussing the systems approach, we talked of expanding system boundaries; this is the key to real improvements in the criteria set and in the systems under study. In order to achieve these benefits, the size of the system often must cross organizational and behavioral boundaries. The biggest barrier to such extensions is usually found in a communication gap or a lack of understanding of other organizational or individual needs; the benefits from explicit model formulation, therefore, become increasingly important. The "black cigar" model-building approach depicted in Fig. 3.2 simply cannot compete with more rigorous varieties.

Model Validation

In Fig. 3.1, results were achieved by running, solving, or manipulating the model. From these results, inferences were made about the real world system and actions taken upon these inferences. It should be noted explictly that the act of inferring and applying model results in the real world is an audacious one. The results that accrue from running a model are really applicable only to the model. The model is a tightly bounded abstraction of a complicated, messy, highly interactive real world system. The model is a fake and cannot possibly depict the real world system in all its detail.

Since it is impossible for the model to completely depict the real world system without being the real world system, how do we assess the worth or validity of one of these partial constructs? There are those who say that this question can be resolved in terms of model prediction for the real world, but such an activity may be somewhat analogous to building a model without explictly defined criteria. That is, the worth of a model can only be defined in terms of a set of criteria. Models are valid or not valid depending upon the use to which they are put. What is valid for one purpose is not necessarily valid for another, and what is an extremely useful prediction for one purpose can be unimportant for another (e.g., a prediction of required time for the bank teller to get pennies with his left

Figure 3.2 The black cigar model.

hand in order to balance getting nickels with the right could be useful for improving the teller's efficiency, but might not be highly relevant to long-range plans for the bank).

Model validation is therefore intimately connected with the criterion issue and the evolution in both criteria systems and models constructed under those criteria. As one thinks of the sensibility of model results or predictions for the real world system, improvements are made in model structure and entities represented. When results pass various tests (intuitive or explicit) a typical process is the examination of a new and perhaps broader question with a different model. The result is that there is no such thing as *the* model which is all things to all men. There are only particular models for particular purposes.

In assessing the usefulness or validity of a particular model, it is necessary to make the test on a comparative rather than an absolute basis. A model which describes the velocity of a ball thrown down from a roof just before it strikes the ground as $v = gt$ will give better predictions, in general, than will the model $v = $ constant, which does not include the accelerating force of gravity. The better model is not as good as the model $v = $ initial velocity $ + gt,$ however, because it ignores the fact that the ball was initially thrown down. But the Newtonian model is not the last word either, for it neglects the effect of air resistance and the changes in acceleration with altitude. A model is only a "good model" until a better one comes along.

Summary

Models are systems of abstracted entities, built for particular purposes or interests in real world systems such as design, operation, training, prediction, or sales. The primary reasons for using models instead of real world systems are economies in time and expense and for the prevention of danger. Kinds of models include mental, verbal, written, graphical, digital simulation, and mathematical. An increase in rigor, generality, and communicative ease is experienced as we substitute verbal models for mental, written for verbal, graphical for written, etc. The newer techniques or models of operations research and management science represent a continuing effort to develop better, more rigorous modeling procedures. The model-building process involves the processes of inclusion and structuring of abstracted entities to obtain a model which is run, solved, or manipulated to yield some results or predictions from which inferences are made about a particular real world system. The entire process is driven or directed by a set of criteria (i.e., the needs or questions to be answered by the model), and there is typically an evolution or cycling through both the modeling process and the criteria system as needs are more completely examined and different and more inclusive needs are stated. Model validation necessarily must appeal to the particular criteria or purposes for which a particular model is designed. There is no such thing as "the" model which will answer every question or even answer particular questions "best" for all time.

As we proceed with this book we will examine many operations management problems and models which have been suggested as appropriate for dealing with these problems. Within the context of this chapter, we should recognize each of these problems as being somewhat unique in the way it resides in an operational environment (i.e., each problem situation or business endeavor is somewhat unique) and think very carefully about the way in which we would like to abstract the real world problem into a model. In this way we can better appreciate the strengths and weaknesses of particular modeling procedures that have been used by others and not blindly accept existing or proposed models.

EXAMPLES

Numerous examples have been used as an adjunct of the description of the concepts presented in this chapter. At the risk of redundancy, this section is devoted to presenting a few more complete examples where many of the concepts can be applied within the context of a single problem.

Desk Arrangement

How should the desk of a clerk checking invoice totals be arranged? Let us start by identifying a relatively simple criterion system in which the major criterion is the processing of the invoices at a maximum rate constrained by a specified maximum probability of error. Other criteria include norms of decorum for the particular business institution (are several cardboard boxes full of messy papers tolerable?) and need satisfaction of the individual worker (are all workers entitled to two 15-minute coffee breaks and does this particular girl hate red staple machines?).

Assuming that the latter two kinds of criteria can be satisfied within rather wide limits, the system designer might now decide, based on the desirability of certain attributes, which entities to include. He obviously has the input entities (invoices) with many particular attributes (the one of concern is an unchecked dollar total). The output entities are the invoices with *checked* dollar totals. The more imaginative inclusion question is concerned with what entities are to be used to process the input entities. A list of the combinations of human and mechanical entities which could be used might be a good first step in the inclusion process. The list might include the female clerk or other employees working in conjunction with various pieces of equipment; for example, a pencil, a harder pencil, a softer pencil, a red pencil, stapler, other types of staplers, staple removers, adding machines, computers, slide rules, abacus, or a footrest to facilitate counting with toes.

Once the difficult and somewhat arbitrary choice of entities has been made (because of their attributes a #2½ pencil does not require sharpening as often as a #2), the structuring process can begin. Where should the input box be placed? Should work flow from right to left? Should the adding machine be operated with the right hand?

The result of this system design effort is an explicit specification of how the task is to be performed, including an expected output rate. In the above description of the desk arrangement design process, however, we glossed over some important considerations. How did the designer find or know of the various equipment entities? Did they all exist? Did he have mental models of them? How "valid" were his models? By what means did he decide how various entities would interact? What models exist for examining such interactions? How "valid" are those models? In terms of what criteria are they valid?

Various formal models exist for understanding the capacity of workers to do manual tasks and for analyzing work flows. These models are superior to intuitive or mental models and will be presented in Chapter 13. Such models are not, however, the "best" models that will ever be developed. There is always room for improvement, both for models under specified criteria and more importantly for models which operate under a more inclusive or well-developed set of criteria. For example, should the invoice processing model consider the *use* of checked dollar total invoices? What are the costs of incorrect dollar totals? What other checks exist in our company system? In the system that includes other companies?

It is probably also worth pointing out that the installed system as designed is not the last word. It will and should evolve over time. The operator interchanges the positions of the stapler and paper clips. A new foot-operated stapler comes on the market. The operator finds a "shortcut." Having a particular desk calendar becomes a status symbol. Someone finds a way to eliminate the task completely!

Other Examples

Many other examples could be described. Consider the problem of decorating a room or a house. What is the mood or environment wanted? What entities should be included (rugs, chairs)? What attributes should they have (colors, texture)? How should they be structured (furniture arrangement, color coordination)? What models exist to help with such problems? How "good" or "valid" are they?

Consider any file system—library, house, or office. What are the criteria? Entities? Desired attributes? One would have to be concerned not only with documents, but with files—how many should there be? How should their attributes be related? What documents should go in which files? Should documents go in more than one file? Should there be notes between files? What models are available for analyzing alternatives?

Consider the architect's problem in designing a house, or the problem of designing a piece of hardware or a data-processing system. The list of examples is unlimited. This book is itself a system design problem: There is no shortage of entities (words, ideas, concepts), and the entities have attributes, and the wish is to combine these entities in such a way that various pedagogical goals are maximized with a given student input.

Westfall Furniture Company

By now it should be obvious that a virtually infinite number of systems, subsystems, and potential systems exist for the Westfall case. In this section, the goal is to take one simple problem and examine it in an evolutionary systems context. In this process, we will identify far more questions than will be answered; the pursuit of answers to these questions leads to various modeling mechanisms to which the rest of the book will be largely devoted.

Let us address ourselves to the problem of chair building on a conveyor. What are the objectives or criteria? We might start by stating an interest in having all operators working at a high rate of productivity, since this surrogate goal should yield low cost-high volume production which in turn should be congruent with Baumritter's basic objectives as a corporation. We also need to concern ourselves with the necessity of producing chairs of acceptable quality, with the satisfaction of marketing needs for product line variations, with attaining adequate customer service levels, with keeping inventory levels within prescribed bounds with the size of the capital outlay, and with the personal goals of the employees.

It should be clear that some of these criteria are in conflict with others and can to some extent be traded off. For example, a degradation in customer service can permit lower inventory levels, and greater inventories can allow longer production runs with concomitant increases in worker productivity. It should also be clear that the ability to properly structure this system of criteria will be quite limited at the outset. Our objective will be to design a conveyorized chair-building system that initially will be "good" or "satisfactory" (not optimal) for all the criteria, a system that can adapt to permit better performance levels as tradeoffs between the criteria become better understood and that can accommodate additional criteria.

In an analysis of conveyorized chair building, what are the fact or datum entities that should be considered as candidates for inclusion in a model? What model should be used for the analysis? The following are some potentially important production oriented fact entities (obtaining some of these fact entities will necessitate additional model building efforts):

1.   What are the most fundamental building blocks that comprise the chair assembly operation? (e.g., must all four legs be assembled by one operator? Can one leg be half assembed by each of two operators?) To what extent are these fundamental work activities unique to particular chair designs? Chapters 13 and 14 present some models that will be useful in providing answers to these questions.

2.   What are the average times for these fundamental building block activities, and what is the variability of time for these operations? For any operator? For a specific operator (e.g., one of the Carletons)? Chapters 11 and 12 are closely related to these questions.

3.   What are the work methods best suited to accomplishing the fundamental work activities on a conveyorized line? What capital equipment can be purchased or designed to eliminate potential bottlenecks? Chapters 6, 13, and 15 consider aspects of these questions.

4.   Can all of the fundamental work activities be performed on a moving conveyor? Can all activities be performed without waiting time between them (e.g., glue drying)? What are the sequential constraints (e.g., can we stain parts before assembly)? Chapter 15 presents models that consider implications of these questions.

5.   What are the production rates for the chairs to be built on this line? Must all Westfall chairs be built on the conveyor line? How long will it take to change from one design to another? Will it be easier to change from certain designs to others? What are the implications of product line changes (e.g., will certain designs be more amenable to conveyorized production)? Chapters 17, 19, and 20 will provide an improved perspective for the consideration of these questions.

Other fact or data entities would be required for the other criteria, as well as for other production oriented activities affected by a change to conveyorized chair building, e.g., the implications for parts supplying, expediting, finish mill operations, and chair finishing. The net result achieved *should* represent a "solution space" or area of feasible alternatives which can be investigated with a model or models to find a "good" initial design. The word "should" has been italicized because it is entirely possible that no method for conveyorized chair building can be found that will satisfy all the criteria; such a result would indicate that the criteria need to be changed or that conveyorized chair building is not a viable proposal.

Assuming that a solution space of feasible alternatives did exist, the analysis of alternatives could be based on mental or verbal models, but it is a fundamental tenet of this book that superior results would accrue to analysis based upon more rigorous models. We will examine many of these models in later chapters, but for now, let us briefly turn our attention to the chair-building problem as it resides in the larger Westfall and Baumritter supersystems.

As a starter, let us recall that the output from chair building represents the input to chair finishing. If chair-building capacity is to be increased, it will be necessary to consider the resultant demands placed upon chair finishing. The present chair-finishing rate is a constraint on chair building. Moreover, the highest finishing rate achieved of 715 chairs per day required careful attention to the way in which the chair conveyor was loaded; chairs of complex finishing requirements could not be produced solely in high volume unless an inventory of completed chairs of several varieties is held between chair building and chair finishing.

Similarly, increased chair production implies increases in parts production. Inferred is a need to schedule more exactly the assembly of particular chairs sufficiently far ahead so that parts can be produced with dependability and some means of guiding the flow of parts through production so that schedules can be met. Also inferred are methods for monitoring inventories and for forecasting requirements.

Increased chair production also has implications in the marketing function of the corporation. Will the added volume be sold? If more chairs are sold, is there a causal influence on the demand for tables and hutches? Alternatively, do we need to promote table sales in order to sell the increased chair production? Will increased sales be accomplished with the existing product line? If not, what are the implications for a high volume somewhat inflexible chair-building facility?

The process of enlarging the subsystem under consideration can go on and on. Clearly we could consider subsystems that are not under the control of Westfall such as the field warehouses. We could also add systems that are not within Baumritter's scope of authority such as lumber supply and retail store operations. We noted in Chapter 2 that Baumritter's franchise system afforded considerable control over retail operations. Within the systems concept, that control has many potential benefits; we will see this quite clearly in Chapter 21. As we continue to add real world complexities, our statement of the problem gets increasingly less artificial and close to the most important goals of the company; unfortunately, analysis of that problem becomes increasingly difficult with fewer rigorous models to help us.

SUMMARY REMARKS

This chapter has presented some abstract concepts that will be useful for integrating the materials that follow in the text, class discussions, other facets of your course in operations management, other courses in the curriculum, and your growing awareness of the business environment. These abstract concepts are not easy to grasp with a single reading; indeed, the remainder of your course in operations management is largely designed to create a point of view based on these concepts.

There is a growing and almost universal enthusiasm for "the systems concept" or "the systems approach" in business and other curricula. Unfortunately, these terms are difficult to define and often are equated with "good," "right-way," or "motherhood and apple pie" (appropriately shortened by one creative student to "applehood"). The word *system* is perhaps the most widely used "buzzword" in business education today. However, difficult as it may be to explain, those who have a viable feeling for the concept of a system almost universally believe that the concept is both important and useful.

The systems *concept* is indeed hard to define since to this author's way of thinking it represents an open-minded problem approach that recognizes the fantastically large number of subsystems interacting with a particular problem which has been identified or bounded for analysis. The systems *approach* seems easier to define explicltly. The systems approach recognizes the importance of the systems concept and attempts continually to widen the boundaries of the system or problem being investigated. The systems approach is based upon the belief that greater returns (in terms of the highest criteria) are often obtained by enlarging the boundaries of a system (and the system of criteria that directs the system design) than by refining the approach to a tightly bounded problem.

Being able to *apply* the systems approach, however, requires more than appreciation; as noted several places in the chapter, larger system bounding leads to more realistic problems which are more difficult to solve and to some extent it seems incumbent upon one who identifies such problems to aid in their solution. The use of the system approach, therefore, requires modeling procedures for larger systems. This book will provide some of these models and hopefully indicate the direction for obtaining additional models.

In concluding our discussion of the systems approach, it is perhaps appropriate to attempt to relate the systems approach to day-in, day-out problem-solving activities for those who would say, "That all sounds good, but we have to deal with practical realities and come up with fast answers." As one sage put it: when you are up to your neck in alligators, it is hard to pursue your mission of draining the swamp. There has to be a middle ground and if on your first day of your first job you are asked to sharpen a pencil, it would not be advisable to take the systems approach and badger the president about his long-range goals for the company. What one *can* do, however, is to examine each problem at *some* level of complexity greater than that presently specified or bounded.

REFERENCES

Boulding, Kenneth, "General Systems Theory—A Skeleton of Science," *Management Science,* **2,** no. 3 (April 1956): 197–208.

Bross, Irwin D. J., *Design for Decision,* Macmillan, 1953.

Hall, Arthur D., *A Methodology for Systems Engineering,* Van Nostrand, 1962.

Hitch, Charles J., "Suboptimization in Operations Problems," *Operations Research,* **1,** no. 3 (March 1953): 87–99.

Nugent, Christopher E. and Thomas E. Vollmann, "A Framework for the Systems Design Process," *Decision Sciences,* **4,** no. 1, January 1972.

Quade, E. S., *Analysis For Military Decisions,* Rand McNally, 1964.

Simon, Herbert A., *The Sciences of the Artificial,* MIT Press, 1969.

CHAPTER REVIEW

Well, you have made it through what in some ways is the most difficult chapter in the book. If you feel a bit blear-eyed and unsure of what it all means, you probably are not alone. It is only by coming back to these ideas again and again with specific problems and techniques that you will derive a working understanding of the systems approach. Regard that working understanding as a major goal of your operations management course, and remember that our approach to achieving the goal is to build spirally upon the base provided by this chapter.

There are a lot of words in the chapter; we have tried to approach the systems concept from several directions. It will be useful for you to give detailed consideration to some of the ideas, e.g., the distinction between entity and thing and the notion of entity attributes. However, it is not my goal to create exact definitions which must be spit back on examinations. Moreover, the ideas can be pushed to extremes. A colleague and I once spent an entire day walking the woods of New Hampshire wondering if attributes were also entities. We finally decided that it really did not make much difference! The objective is a way of thinking or a framework for analysis that yields results superior to those obtained from other frameworks. Let us turn to an outline of the chapter and major ideas. Thereafter, we will briefly consider the central issues.

OUTLINE OF THE CHAPTER

Introduction	(objectives of the chapter)
Definition of a system	(entities and attributes—why important)
Subsystems and supersystems	(relationships between systems)
The system design process	(artistry in matching system to needs)
The inclusion process	(choice of entities for system)
The structuring process	(relationships among entity attributes)
The criteria set	(driving mechanism for system design)
The criteria set as a system	(multiple interactive goals)
Goal congruence	(appropriate subsystem criteria)
Surrogate criteria	(measurable objectives approximating less measurable)
System evolution	(iterative problem solving)
Adaptability	(system robustness)
Model-building	(abstraction for a purpose)
The model-building process	(system design with abstract entities)
The role of criteria	(models built for particular purposes)
Level of aggregation	(appropriate level of detail)
Kinds of models	(value of more rigorous models)
Model validation	(judged by purpose)
Summary	(models versus problems)
Examples	(concepts applied)
Desk arrangement	(particular problem and models)
Other examples	(goals and framework for analysis)
Westfall furniture company	(return to Chapter 2 issues)
Summary remarks	(systems approach defined)

CENTRAL ISSUES

This chapter presents a framework for problem analysis. By examining specific problems within a systems context, you will find yourself armed with an approach that can lead to more relevant problem delineations and solutions. Any system is by its nature related to many other systems; the bounding of a system is necessary for analysis or design, but bounding is also artificial since it ignores other systems. The systems approach recognizes this artificiality. There are times when you will achieve greater returns from expanding the system boundaries than from improved analysis of a specified problem as system.

The role of criteria in problem solving cannot be overemphasized. Criteria drive the system design process, since systems are designed for particular purposes. The fact that most systems are designed with multiple objectives complicates achievement and recognition of superior results. The need to have measurable criteria by which performance can be judged leads to use of surrogate or proximate criteria. The congruence of surrogate criteria with more fundamental objectives must be frequently assessed.

Model building is described as a process of system design with abstracted entities. More rigorous models tend to produce superior results. Wider system bounding implies a need for models which include more entities, so model building is necessary to achieve the systems approach. Goals or criteria determine model validity as well as the appropriate level of detail to be represented.

Concepts of the chapter are illustrated by several examples, including a return to the Westfall Furniture Company presented in Chapter 2.

ASSIGNMENTS

1. Consider a one-month vacation as a system design problem utilizing the framework presented in this chapter. Come to class prepared to present and defend your "design" for a personal vacation.

2. Identify a problem of personal interest and treat that problem as a system design effort utilizing the system design framework. Again, be prepared to present and defend your "design."

3. Prepare a two page (maximum length) written critique of your written memorandum to Messrs. Ruml, Hughes, and Howell prepared in Chapter 2. Base your critique upon the ideas contained in Chapter 3.

4. Recent research on traffic flow has shown that the volume of traffic that crosses a point on a highway is a function of the vehicle density. Furthermore, the volume decreases past some optimum density as in Fig. 3.3.

   Assume that you are an engineer with the Massachusetts Department of Public Works. Your department has responsibility for the South-East Expressway (Fig. 3.4 Route 3, Braintree to Boston). Morning rush-hour traffic has caused increasingly bad tie-ups on this route during recent years. Your department has installed stoplights on the north-bound entrance ramps labeled A-E. By limiting the number of cars on the highway at a given moment you hope to improve the situation. Your problem is to determine the operat-

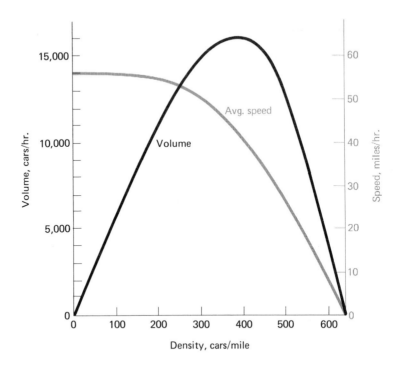

Fig. 3.3 Density-speed-flow relationship for a hypothetical 3 lane highway.

ing rules for the stoplights. You are authorized to place sensing devices on the highway and on the entrance ramp if they seem necessary.

What criteria are relevant? On which will you base your decision? Pay particular attention to the boundary problem. What implications do your operating rules have on subsystems (e.g., the motorist) and supersystems (e.g., the city)?

5.   Skiway Inc. has just hired your firm as consultants for the design of a new ski area. What criteria are important to the system? What entities will you initially include in the design? Which relationships between the attributes of included entities do you consider to be critical?

6.   The Council on Uniform Security Identification Procedures (CUSIP) has compiled a list of all the widely held securities in the United States with more than $500,000 outstanding. In addition they have assigned an alpha-numeric code to each issue. What criteria are relevant for this system, which is used primarily by brokers, bankers, and investment analysts? What particular attributes or entities might the system have if you had designed it?

7.   The experienced back packer is a master in the design of a particular type system, one that provides all the comforts of home and yet weighs considerably less. Choose a three-day route. Specify the criteria for the hike and equipment to be taken. What would you bring? What supersystem attributes are important to your decision?

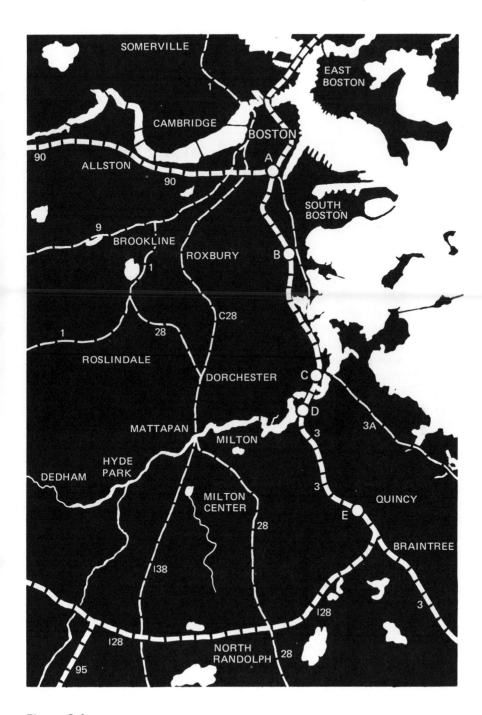

Figure 3.4

CHAPTER 4

PROBLEM SOLVERS AND PROBLEM SOLUTIONS

In the last chapter we said that any problem-solving activity can be considered as system design, that a process for system design can be articulated and made a part of each student's problem-solving approach, and that improved solutions to particular problems can be obtained by structuring those problems in the system design framework. The systems approach was presented as a continual striving toward larger system bounding; to make the systems approach operational we extended the notion of system design into model building, where abstractions of problem situations are designed and studied in order to make inferences which lead to better problem solutions. In the same chapter we also briefly discussed improvements in modeling procedures and an evolution in problem identification, model formulation, and problem solution. In this present chapter we will consider more explicitly the process of system design evolution in terms of *how* that evolution takes place and *how* evolutionary speed may be increased. To do this it will be necessary to consider the roles of particular individuals, namely, model builders and model users, in that evolution, and the kinds or types of models which best lend themselves to rapid evolution.

THE USER-DESIGNER CONCEPT

In our increasingly specialized world, a quasi-standard procedure has come about for designing complex problem solutions or systems of all kinds. The procedure typically involves two kinds of individuals or two sets of personnel. The first is the "user" of a system or potential system who has a problem and some idea of the relevant system goals or criteria; he has some idea of what he would like the problem solution to accomplish. The second is the expert system designer, model builder, or consultant (either external or internal to the organization).

The user is intimately connected with the total criteria system from which the particular problem became identified, and that total criteria system must be considered for determining appropriate changes in the evolving problem identification, model formulation, problem solution cycle. The expert system designer, however, is not intimately connected with the criteria system. He is a specialist in solving certain kinds of problems.

Another way of classifying the differences between users and designers is by the kinds of modeling procedures with which they operate. In the hierarchy of models presented in Chapter 3, the user tends to use models of a more inclusive or general but less rigorous variety; the designer uses models which are specialized to match his own specialization. Thus, an operations researcher might be intimately familiar with mathematical programming models, a child psychologist might use a particular set of behavioral models, an econometrician might have a mathematical model for predicting disposable income, an architect could make inferences about the warmth of a room from a blueprint, a physician could utilize a diagnostic model (perhaps mental) based on indicators such as temperature or blood count, a travel agent has a mental model for seeing seven countries in nine days, an auto mechanic has a diagrammatic model of a transmission assembly, or a plumber has a mental model of the consequences of various drainage pipe slopes.

A Communications Gap

Typically the user calls in the designer or consultant to solve the problem. We are all familiar with the situation of dealing with the specialists we call in to "design a system" for us, whether the specialist is a plumber, auto mechanic, travel agent, architect, physician, computer system designer, or whatever. A communications gap exists between the user who has the need (quite surely ill-defined, particularly at the initiation of system design efforts) and the designer who has the model-building abilities or system design expertise, a gap which tends to become increasingly acute as evolution in the system design effort occurs. We also all know of poor results in the system design process frequently caused by this gap.

The designer first identifies as well as is practicable the properties of the system he is to design by extracting from the prospective system user his needs as he currently perceives them. The designer then selects from his repertoire of model-building procedures a model or models, collects appropriate data, makes inferences, and thereafter designs and delivers a system to meet the perceived needs. If the design is a good one, it meets the original needs satisfactorily. However, once the system becomes operational, new problems and criteria, perhaps more basic and fundamental, are perceived by the user, necessitating further model building and system modifications by the designer. But the first modification is not the last. The user's perception of his needs or problems continues to change, improve, or sharpen in an evolutionary manner.

It should be emphasized that evolution in the user's needs (demanding new model-building efforts and appropriate changes in the system) does not mean that the user did a "poor" job in the initial formulation of the problem or criteria. Many important problems or potential opportunities can be identified only after models have been formulated or systems designed to cope with a different problem. A significant part of the problem-solving process is in fact the identification of the problem; indeed, in our discussion of criteria in Chapter 3 we noted the inherent artistry involved in the design of a criteria system. And, just as there is no such thing as *the* model or *the* system, there is no such thing as *the* problem; evolution is inevitable, should be expected and should be sought.

As evolution occurs in the problem identification, model formulation, problem solution cycle, the user of the system often becomes less familiar with both the models used by the expert to make inferences and the corresponding system modifications. To the user they become black boxes or unknown quantities.

There is also frequently an erosion of the designer's relative expertise. The designer is a specialist but problem evolution is often toward more general or inclusive problem formulation. Such problem formulations call for modeling procedures which are also more general or inclusive.

The net result of the communications gap between designers and users is that many logical extensions of the models which would be easy to implement (potentially valuable inferences) are unrecognized by the user; logical extensions of the user's thinking become increasingly difficult for the designer to capture in his specialized models and systems. Both situations are undesirable, causing a reduction in the evolutionary speed of problem identification, model formulation and problem solution. It is not at all unusual in the business world for such an evolution to reach a stage where the next step calls for a virtual scrapping of a long and expensive system design effort.

Box 4.1 illustrates the kind of evolution in system design that can occur and allows us to make some observations about the evolutionary process.

There are several interesting observations that can be made. First, evolution in the problem identification, model formulation, problem solution cycle must be accompanied by significant changes in the criteria system driving both the system design effort and the operating or organizational systems in the company. Second, the investigation that has

A company selling consumer durables responded to customer complaints by identifying the need for a pricing study. The study was initially undertaken by an "in-house" (as opposed to "out-house") marketing group. The study focused on relative prices and found that the firm's prices were consistent with its quality. Further efforts indicated that the customer complaints were not so much directed at price as at deliveries. An investigation of delivery times indicated that the actual problem seemed to involve delivery promises rather than delivery times. Customers were angry with unfulfilled promises. At this point attention shifted to the order acknowledgment process which in turn led to the need for better information on production schedules, and it was then found that planned production schedules were rarely met. Although attention now shifted from the marketing function to the production function, it did not, interestingly enough, remain solely in the production function. Investigations found that broken promises led to personal phone calls to company executives. These executives made further promises and backed up their off-the-cuff promises by issuing demands to factory managers. Factory managers responded to these personal demands by expediting the goods promised by the executives. Unfortunately, while these goods were expedited, normal work was pushed aside. Therefore, normal work was always late, the schedule was never met, and delivery promises were poor.

Box 4.1

been quickly summed up above represented more than four years of actual time and an estimated manpower expenditure of about twenty-five years. Variations in evolutionary speed are, therefore, of critical importance. Third, the skills of the original system designers (for a comparative price study) became increasingly noncongruent with the evolved problem statement. The actual users and designers involved in the study necessarily changed many times. Fourth, an observation that is related to the first three concerns the fact that the evolution described might never have come to fruition. In order for sufficient evolutionary speed and appropriate direction to be maintained, a continuing involvement of top management was required.

It is especially significant to note the way in which the evolution crossed functional or authority lines. Although the evolution was in line with overall company objectives, at many stages it definitely was not congruent with some individual and functional goals. If that individual or function had had absolute control over the system design effort, the evolution depicted in Box 4.1 well might have been different. An attitude which facilitated change was required; an attitude where individual problem solutions were regarded not as sacrosanct, but merely as stepping stones to increasingly improved solutions.

Overcoming the Communications Gap

There are two fairly appealing ways of overcoming the gap of understanding or communication between system users and system designers. First, the expert system designer can take on the job of the system user; second, the system user can take over more of the model building or analytical work performed by the outside expert or system designer. Both approaches have always been somewhat infeasible. For example, there is no particular reason why an economist who studies relative prices would make a good marketing manager. And even if a specialist did understand a particular problem, as we have seen from Box 4.1, problems can and do evolve in unforeseen ways which call for quite different kinds of specialized knowledge or model-building capabilities.

It is equally infeasible to suggest that every system user or manager acquire a detailed knowledge of specialized model-building techniques such as those used by our economist to study relative prices. However, a central thesis of this chapter is that it may be possible to address the question of evolution explicitly and thereafter establish a modeling environment that is particularly congenial to evolution. With such an environment it may be desirable and feasible, at least in certain situations, for systems users to take a much more active role in the modeling portion of the problem identification, model formulation, and problem solution cycle for problems within their domain. We also will see that because such evolution-oriented modeling environments will encourage explicit model formulation and communication between system users, problem evolutions that cross functional or authority lines will be facilitated.

The Feedback between Needs, Models and Systems

We have described an evolutionary cycle of problem identification, model formulation and problem solution, and the importance of speeding this evolutionary cycle has been noted. It also has been noted that evolutionary speed is hampered or affected by the extent to which a gap in understanding or communication exists between system users who perceive needs and system designers who have expertise. What, then, can be done to reduce this gap? to quicken evolutionary speed? What kinds of models will keep pace with a rapid evolution in perceived user needs? And, since an evolution in perceived user needs is not independent of the modeling process, what kinds of models will not only keep pace with the evolution in perceived user needs, but will, in fact, *feed* or *drive* a more rapid evolution in perceived user needs?

To illustrate the evolutionary interaction between user needs, models, and designed systems or problem solutions, let us turn to Fig. 4.1, which is a greatly simplified model of the evolutionary process.

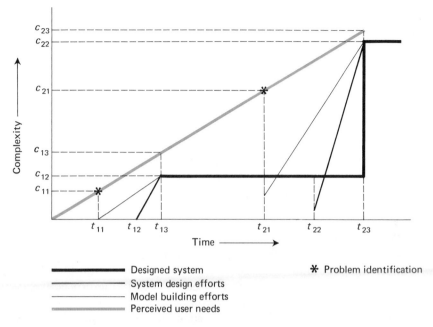

Figure 4.1 Needs and systems.

In Fig. 4.1 our axes are complexity and time, and we see perceived user needs increasing linearly over time. We assume that we start with no system available to satisfy those needs, or if there is such a system it is represented by the abscissa. At a point in time, t_{11}, a sufficient amount of perceived user needs, c_{11}, has been built up so as to call for the identification of a problem. At this point model-building efforts are initiated and grow in complexity. At time period t_{12} the problem solution or designed system is started. At time period t_{13} the "problem" is "solved;" an operational system is in existence. The degree of complexity or "goodness" of the problem solution at the time period t_{13} is indicated by c_{12}, which is greater than c_{11}, the perceived problem at time period t_{11} because the designers have made some evolution or change in the problem statement during the model-building and system design stages. The system designed or problem solution is depicted as static in complexity or "goodness" until time period t_{23}. However, at time period t_{21}, a new gap $(c_{21} - c_{12})$ exists, and someone has decided that this gap is large enough to call for the "identification of a new problem." Model-building efforts begin at time period t_{21} but are depicted as not starting from "gound 0." That is, the knowledge obtained from our prior model-building and system design efforts should be of some value for this new model-building and system design effort. Similarly, the system design effort can utilize certain pieces or aspects of the prior system in the new one. The new system is completed and operational at time period t_{23} with a degree of complexity c_{22}. The "complexity gap" ($c_{23} - c_{22}$) at time period t_{23} is depicted as being less than the complexity gap at time period t_{13} ($c_{13} - c_{12}$). This indicates that the model-building and system design effort for the second identified problem was more visionary than for the first. In particular situations this would not necessarily be true; in fact, the opposite might occur.

Let us illustrate this evolutionary process with the Westfall conveyorized chair-building example. Time t_{11} is the situation described in Chapter 2, and Jim Howell, Harry Ruml, and John Hughes perceive a problem of complexity c_{11}. You have been called in largely because of your model-building expertise, and the group engages in problem identification, model formulation, and problem solution until time t_{13}. At time t_{12}, sufficient knowledge has been obtained to start construction of a conveyorized chair line, but small changes are made up to the final installation date, t_{13}. The goodness of the conveyorized chair-building procedure, c_{12}, is shown as static until time t_{23}. At time t_{21}, a new problem is perceived, e.g., perhaps the finishing line cannot cope with the output from chair building. New model-building efforts begin at time t_{21}, actual construction changes (e.g., additional spray booths) begin at time t_{22}, and a system of goodness c_{22} is completed at time t_{23}.

Figure 4.1 is, of course, greatly simplified. Perceived user needs do not actually increase linearly; they are affected by the model-building and system design processes, and they will tend to increase rapidly after the worth of a particular system design effort is recognized. Thus, user needs, model-building efforts, and system design efforts are related in a circular causality or feedback manner. Also, Fig. 4.1 does not accede much visionary credit to the system designers. In some instances it is quite possible to see the drift of things to come and design accordingly. Thus perhaps Fig. 4.2 might be a better representation.

Figure 4.2 depicts the feedback interaction between perceived user needs, model building, and system design efforts. As was true for Fig. 4.1, Fig. 4.2 depicts a gap between system availabilities and user perceived needs at time t_{11} of the complexity c_{11} minus whatever exists at the origin. At time t_{11} model-building efforts are initiated and continued until time t_{13} when the new system is operational. The system design effort begins as before at time t_{12}. Note, however, that unlike the situation depicted in Fig. 4.1, this designed system does not remain static from time t_{13} until t_{23}. Figure 4.2 shows the system as experiencing a slow but constant evolution during that time interval (e.g., the conveyerized chair-

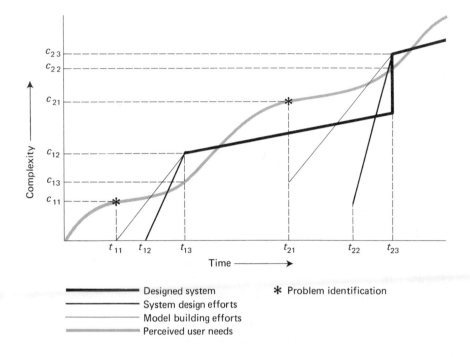

Figure 4.2 Needs and systems (dynamic).

building methods are improved). Note also that in Fig. 4.1 a gap of desired complexity or goodness exists continuously. In Fig. 4.2 this is not so. Here, the design effort is depicted as being somewhat visionary so that at time period t_{13} the system can provide goodness or complexity of the order c_{12} while the users of the system only perceive a level of need of c_{13} (e.g., a variable speed conveyer is installed). A similar visionary design effort is depicted at time t_{23}.

Although Fig. 4.2 is not a model of the way all model-building and system design effort comes about, in terms of vision, etc., it is at least a plausible model of how one particular system design effort might have evolved. Other plausible models could be drawn which might depict system design and model-building efforts affecting perceived user needs (and vice versa) in different ways. The point is, model-building and system design efforts are intimately intertwined with the perception of needs by the user(s) in an ongoing evolutionary environment. It is, therefore, terribly important to consider a model-building and system design effort in terms of its feedback effect on the evolution of perceived user needs.

Evolution Oriented Models

A significant way to stimulate evolution in the need identification, model formulation, and system design cycle is for the user (who has the criteria) to be as close as possible to the actual model-building process. This can be done by creating a modeling environment that is particularly congenial to the user's standard methods of operation. It is now possible to design many kinds of models so that the user can make changes in them and thereby test highly individualized hypotheses as they arise through the evolutionary process. Such changes require an apparently inappropriate investment by the user in understanding the model-building technology; that is, it may seem that the responsibility for model changes should not be foisted off on the system user. One might reasonably argue that a particular change could be much more easily implemented by a model-building specialist. This would be true if there were only one change, but we are thinking of a process of change or model evolution that can be virtually endless. The process of change can only be directed by the user (who has the criteria), and since a major goal is to speed the change process, intimate involvement by the user can lead to substantial benefits.

It is possible to design certain kinds of model environments so that the user's "start up cost" or investment in understanding the modeling process is minimal and closely parallels his own evolution in perceived needs. In this book we will call the way in which users can take a much more active role in system design the user-designer concept.

In the user-designer concept, the role of the designer is not primarily to solve problems, but to create the proper model-building environment for the user to solve his own problems—in fact to teach the user to become a "designer." In this situation, rather than experiencing an increasing need for expert model-building aid, the user will gradually take over a large aspect of the system design process. Figure 4.3 depicts this user-designer interaction over a period of time.

In Fig. 4.3 the original problem is initially investigated by the system designer, but in a very broad way, and he establishes a model-building environment specifically oriented toward facile implementation of user identified changes. The designer then teaches the user some elementary notions of model building, some specifics about this particular model, and the proper role of the user in a rapid ongoing evolutionary process of problem identification, model formulation, and problem solution. Then, following the dashed lines in Fig. 4.3, the designer and user solve the initial problem, the user identifies a new problem, the user is motivated to learn more modeling techniques, and the designer and the user (with the relative role of the user increased) solve the new problem. Figure 4.3 is a feedback model, where the user's skills continually increase and, therefore, the relative role of the designer decreases. It should be empha-

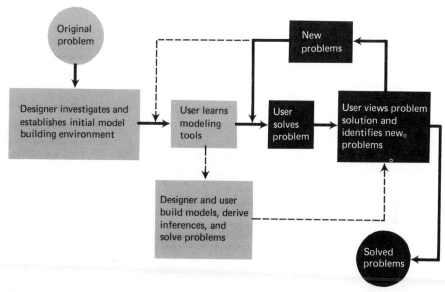

Fig. 4.3 User-designer interaction.

sized that the critical stage in this feedback model is the establishment of a proper environment in which the user can easily see the relevance of additional modeling skills to whatever *his* problem delineation is at a particular time. Thanks to improvements in certain modeling procedures, most notably computer technology, the user's modeling skill need never equal that of a professional.

Explication

A primary reason for the communications gap between users and designers is the lack of clearly stated or explicit criteria. Of perhaps equal importance is a lack of clearly stated or explicit models. We noted in Chapter 3 that explicit, more rigorous models had many advantages, including a fostering of communication.

An essential feature of the interaction between users and designers is the need for users to unambiguously state what they want. This can rarely be done perfectly; explicit statements of basic goals are improved as the users and designers interact, and explicit models encourage the process.

As anyone who has learned computer programming knows, the most difficult hurdles are to think logically and to unambiguously state the actions which follow from the various conditions. *Decision rule formulation* is the process of explicitly stating the actions to be taken when various conditions are observed.

Decision rule formulation is closely related to the management process. It is the substitution of policy for reaction, and the use of creative abilities for understanding and changing basic causes of phenomena rather than reacting solely to the phenomena. A cornerstone for the systems approach, decision rule formulation permits the necessary communication involved in analyses that cross the boundaries of individuals or functions.

One of the big evolutionary aspects of the user-designer interaction depicted in Fig. 4.3 derives from improved statements of explicit criteria and relationships among entity attributes. In the balance of this book, we will repeatedly see how users gain improved perspectives of their own problems (intracommunication) as well as problems involving other criteria (intercommunication) with explicit models which foster evolution.

The user-designer concept is not intended to be an argument for not utilizing expert consultants. Nor is it argued that in all contexts users can and should be their own designers, and it most certainly is not argued that business executives should become "do-it-yourselfers" for what are essentially clerical operations. It is believed, however, that in certain highly creative aspects of the system design process, interaction with users can lead to significant payoffs. In order to achieve these payoffs, it is usually necessary for the user to make a modest initial investment of time in learning about the modeling environment and his critical role in the ongoing evolutionary cycle of problem identification, model formulation, and problem solution. It is very important for the designer to make this investment a minimal one which is not accompanied by either disdain or fear.

Up to this point we have been discussing the user-designer concept in a rather abstract way. The balance of this chapter is largely devoted to exemplification of the user-designer concept as it has been implemented in some actual situations. Most of these examples utilize the computer, but it is not the author's intention to equate the user-designer concept with computer model building or to devote this chapter to an exposition of computer programming. Rather, it is intended that these examples be viewed here in a broad context with the emphasis on the user's increasing role in the model building-process and the subsequent effect on evolutionary speed, rather than concentrating on the intricacies of these particular models. Some of these intricacies that are particularly amenable to other situations will be discussed in later chapters; but for the present the emphasis should be on understanding the user-designer concept and seeing the general nature of modeling environments which lead to significant evolutions in perceived user needs. We will start by revisiting the Westfall example and seeing the roles of users and designers in specific analyses.

WESTFALL FURNITURE COMPANY

It may come as somewhat of a surprise, but to a large extent the user-designer concept cannot be applied to the Westfall case as it is presented in Chapter 2. The *reason* is informative.

The case study presented as Chapter 2 is a model of the "real" Westfall Furniture Company. As such, and this is true for all models, it is an abstraction and the abstraction does not include many entities that exist in the actual Westfall Furniture Company. One such entity, terribly important to implementation of the user-designer concept, is a *user*. Without a user, we simply do not have someone who can drive the evolution in perceived user needs. A closely related consideration has to do with the nondynamic nature of a case study. A case study represents a snapshot not only of a portion or model of the company, but of that portion or model at a particular point in time. But real world companies do not stand still —they are living organisms that are continually changing and, indeed, we have noted the importance of fostering this evolutionary process.

In our treatment of the Westfall Furniture Company case in Chapter 3, we noted that a virtually infinite number of problems and potential solutions existed. We selected a problem of conveyorized chair building, identified some potentially interesting fact entities, and advocated the use of rigorous models to evaluate feasible design alternatives. We then briefly took the systems approach and attempted to widen the boundaries of our analysis; we included for consideration subsystems that are affected by the flow of material into and out of the chair-building operation and suggested some other extensions that might later be made.

On what basis was the conveyorized chair-building problem selected? In Chapter 3 we just "selected it" and then considered how one might intelligently or cleverly attack such a problem. But there is a missing or assumed entity in this process. That entity is the user. In Chapter 2 Jim Howell was described as being interested in conveyorized chair production, but he is the junior man on the Westfall study team to investigate chair assembly. Are we assuming that Harry Ruml and John Hughes concur? Even if they do concur, are we assuming that the three man team will allow us to identify the problems? Are they completely passive in this process, refusing to identify fact entities for inclusion into our models? Or do we make a different kind of assumption, namely, that *we* are the user(s)—perhaps that we are the three man study team?

The Student's Analytical Role

In case studies as well as in actual operational situations, it is critical to know just who "you" are, to know just what sort of a role you have or you are playing. Virtually all of the work in your operations management course and a good part of your business education is devoted to improving your powers as an analyst. It follows, therefore, that your role is most often that of an outside expert; your role in an actual company when you take a job might be somewhat similar, a "young Turk" who wants to see some changes made.

Seeing "changes made" implies implementation, and implementation requires more than good analysis. A major problem discussed in the management science literature is the high degree of nonimplemented good solutions. It is a reasonable conjecture that one reason for this problem is improper consideration of the user-designer concept. It is important to consider who the user is, what his analytical powers are, what his particular criteria and constraints are, and what problems are of interest to him both now and potentially. With such an assessment, it becomes possible for the expert or young Turk to be more realistic about what kinds of ideas will and will not be implemented and what kind of a modeling environment will foster evolution. The assessment and the knowledge can and should be considered with a time dimension. That is, for example, there well may be important or fundamental ideas that could not initially be studied or implemented, but that could be made operational later if another problem which is of immediate interest were tackled in a particular way. In deciding upon that way, one comes face to face with the modeling-environment question.

Without a particular user, construction of a user-oriented, computer-modeling environment for the Westfall case is artificial. The result well might turn out to be a good idea in which no one is interested. If, however, we wish to consider some hypothetical user (let us say the three-man study team), perhaps a supplement to the case could be added which described some of their more important individual attributes such as analytical ability, particular criteria and constraints, to what extent they tend to be immediate action oriented, and problems of pressing concern. Supposing the team members were college graduates with average college graduate intelligence, at least an acquaintance with computers, their criteria were in line with those stated in Chapter 3, the constraints placed on their operation allowed for a reasonable time period for analysis as well as for reasonable capital expenditures, and they were personally interested in conveyorized chair building; *then* perhaps the analysis might proceed as described in Chapter 3. One kind of user-oriented modeling environment would be a computer simulation of the assembly of various chairs, where times to perform different fundamental work activities could be generated, and the output could be evaluated under differing assumptions. One such model will be described in Chapters 11, 12, and 15. Let us now turn to an *actual* user-oriented investigation that took place at the Westfall Furniture Plant.

Problem Identification

The author and several colleagues used the Baumritter systems study as a research vehicle in the formulation, evaluation, and evolution of the user-designer concept. A detailed exposition of the entire research effort is beyond our present scope but many aspects will be covered in later chapters. At this point let us see how a user-oriented modeling environment was established for a particular problem situation. Specifically, we will describe a modeling environment for scheduling production for the assembly lines at Westfall; first, however, we should summarize the user-designer interplay leading to the identification of production scheduling as an area of interest.

The academic orientation of the author and his colleagues toward the system design effort provided them with certain strengths and weaknesses. On the one hand, the group was able to tackle without prejudice whatever it deemed appropriate. On the other hand, this detachment also meant that opinions reached by the outside group required selling to the company personnel. From time to time, various factions in the company sought the stamp of "unbiased authority" from the outsiders in support of their point of view.

Initially the research group was convinced that the aggregate productive capacity planning problem was a subsystem in need of extensive design efforts. The problem was believed to be central to the entire systems study; because of relative skills, this was an area where the research team felt they could be of significant service. In the approach to this problem, several available models were considered. It was finally decided to use a rather inelegant model which the researchers felt could be understood (and thereafter evolved) by company personnel more easily than a more mathematically oriented model. A considerable amount of time was put into the initial formulation of this model, and it was presented to an assembled group of personnel responsible for factory operations. The presentation included some lively discussion, and the research team believed that the importance of both the problem and the model was understood.

Unfortunately, in spite of initial interest, the commitment required to get the aggregate planning model operational for Baumritter was not forthcoming. In retrospect the lack of commitment seems intuitively obvious. Although everyone agreed that this was a significant problem, each man found himself with no shortage of "significant problems" and most of these were much more closely allied to his day-to-day efforts and criteria. That is, no one in the company had been formally concerned with the aggregate planning problem; in addition, there was widespread feeling that if some of the day-to-day problems could be solved, long-range problems would be ameliorated and executive talent would be more readily available for their solution.

The outside research group, being confirmed user-designer advocates, saw little point in pursuing the aggregate planning problem without interested users. So they let the insiders (who after all had the criteria) themselves determine what was a significant problem and thereafter established a user-oriented modeling environment to provide aid to the solution of the problem identified.

Factory Scheduling

It was found that a significant problem facing each plant manager was the scheduling of his production. Many orders were late, and expediting orders and the short-list seemed to dominate factory operations. We have already observed how production-scheduling problems are linked to many other problems in an organization; the outside research group had to bound the initial problem so that it was meaningful to the factory manager within his own particular set of criteria, yet could be expanded to include other pertinent considerations.

In our discussion of models in Chapter 3, we considered a concept called the level of aggregation. In the present context, the issue was how detailed a schedule should be. Should each man or piece of equipment be scheduled? Should each part be scheduled? each subassembly? each major assembly? the aggregate capacity of the plant?

The Westfall factory manager and his assistants spent a great deal of time trying to schedule the production of the finished goods assembly lines for particular products. The factory people essentially were attempting to schedule each line by using a graphical bar chart type model. In order to achieve a "feasible" schedule, they manipulated pieces of paper representing assembly time requirements over about twenty feet of table space. The attempt was to produce a schedule for ten weeks into the future, and the process of using such a schedule required two-to-three man days of effort. A schedule produced by this procedure was not only not an "optimum" schedule, it wasn't necessarily a very good schedule— it was only a "feasible" schedule. Even the lack of goodness of the schedule did not bother the plant manager, if in fact the plan could be met. But the model had no provision for uncertainties, and as actual events occurred, fairly large discrepancies from the plan created a need for frequent trips to the "20-foot table."

Many of these discrepancies occurred because of poor "models" used for providing input data to the production scheduling problem. A good example was the lack of a clear model for forecasting work content and output from particular tasks; we will consider such models in Chapters 13 and 14.

Clearly here was an area where significant executive talent was being expended. Their model was not only time-consuming and incapable of producing superior results; it was virtually incapable of coping with actualities in the plant. The decision was made to construct a time-shared computer model for production scheduling. Time-sharing was used because evolution in the problem identification, model formulation, and the problem solution cycle was expected to be significant. Company personnel expressed hope that after some time a more or less standarized production scheduling format would come about which could be implemented on their regular computation facilities.

Model Development

When the research team first talked about constructing a time-shared computer model for production scheduling, factory personnel regarded the whole idea as being akin to something out of a science fiction novel. One executive said flatly that it couldn't be done; another said the outside group was wasting its time and he was damned if he would waste his. There were, however, a few people in the organization who believed the idea had merit. In addition, an investment by the researchers in golfing and beer drinking with Westfall personnel was beginning to pay dividends. One particular individual in the factory became enthusiastic at the prospects of such a modeling environment. He not only cooperated with the outside design effort, he rapidly became a part of it and fought the necessary battles within Westfall.

In about three months, an initial model was formulated and programmed, and the first schedule for ten weeks was run. The factory enthusiast was crestfallen when it didn't work, and many of his colleagues gave him the all too familiar "I told you so." He had been warned, however, that it was not expected to work the first time. He was promised, however, that the defects would be obvious since the model required an explicit statement of many considerations which were handled intuitively in the former modeling effort.* Within one additional month, the model could produce results that were superior to the "20-foot table" for a longer time period (18 weeks) and could be updated to incorporate changes in less than a half hour.

As the model was used, improvements were made not only in the model, but in many of the actual production operations themselves. Incon-

---

*Note the communicative power of explicit decision rule formulation—how it enabled this user to "communicate with himself." We will see that subsequently the evolutionary development involved communication with other people with additional ideas and criteria. Their ideas and criteria were in existence long before the model was formulated, but the explicit model allowed for new levels of understanding to be attained.

sistencies and potential improvements were more easily identified. A particular evolution in the criteria set is especially interesting: At the outset of the investigation, plants were being partially evaluated on the basis of dollars of finished goods produced per week. The effect of this criterion on the assembly lines was the assembly of goods not on the basis of customer demand, but on the basis of dollar output relative to assembly time. A noteworthy example involved the table line that produced both regular tables and tables with plastic tops. The tables with plastic tops required no further finishing and could, therefore, be assembled and finished at a rate double that of regular tables. In addition the sales price of tables with the special plastic tops was higher than for the regular tables. The net result was that assembly operations on this line were often devoted to plastic tables when in fact a backlog for regular wooden tables was significantly higher. This type of behavior had an interesting feedback effect; as plastic tables were produced in higher percentage than the demand would indicate, the proportion of nonplastic tables needed in subsequent weeks increased. But, in those subsequent weeks, that particular line found itself in even more trouble in terms of the criterion of dollar output if it tried to produce only nonplastic top tables. The formalized model showed up this type of noncongruency in criteria. The search for new criteria led to scheduling with the surrogate criterion of equalizing the inventory or backlog position of each item produced by a particular line.

Extensions

The application of an explicitly formulated model for production scheduling demonstrated that explicit models were required for other parts of the factory operation. That is, once a rational schedule for final assembly was determined, it was mandatory to provide the necessary component part inputs at the required times. Therefore, a system for controlling the timing of purchased parts was necessary. Also the need to plan for the availability of various parts dictated the need for a system to control part flow through the machine shop and a system to plan the dry kiln operations. With a production plan that could be relied upon, the problems involved in scheduling full railroad car shipments of furniture were diminished. Thereafter, the number of panic or rush orders issued to fill cars was greatly reduced.

At the outset, some of those opposing use of the model felt that it could not take account of all the factors that a good plant manager needs to consider. It is true that *no* model includes all the pertinent entities. As we stated in Chapter 3, every model is an abstraction that attempts to include the essence of the real—for a particular problem. The production scheduling model allowed for a man-machine interaction where a great degree of insight possessed by a factory manager would not be drained in day-to-day "fire fighting." Instead his wealth of knowledge could be utilized for finding inconsistencies in the model and eliminating them, and for finding new significant entities and criteria that should be represented in a new expanded model.

Users and Designers

The role of the outside research group as expert designers in this process was initially to formulate the skeleton of the model, and to involve users in its evolution. Once the model started to work, enthusiasm rapidly spread both through Westfall and throughout Baumritter. People who had been openly hostile toward the project at first rapidly became model users and advocates. The role of the research team in production scheduling was rapidly reduced. The enthusiast at Westfall (who had never done any computer programming before) became the resident expert in the model. Other factories, hearing of the success, were most anxious to obtain the model. It turned out that most of what had been done in the first factory was transferable to other factories, although a small amount of model generalization was necessary. These other factories were usually able to get a model suited to their own use operational within a month.

The designers wished to extricate themselves from the detailed operation of the production-scheduling model and to leave evolution of the model in the hands of the users. They thereafter shifted their attention to interesting linkages with production scheduling; most notably the way in which production output is maintained as inventories in various factory, regional and field warehouses. Again, a particular individual in the company was found who was quite concerned with physical distribution, and the development began in the area of his immediate concern.

In concluding this section, it is worth reemphasizing that the purpose of describing the implementation of the user-designer concept of Westfall was not to discuss computers or production scheduling per se. Instead it is to illustrate the roles that must be adopted by users and designers in order to achieve the significant benefits of rapid evolution in problem identification, model formulation, and problem solution. Let us now turn to some other examples to illustrate the broad applicability of these concepts.

A USER-ORIENTED DATA BASE LANGUAGE

The user-designer concept was not formulated as an abstract exercise, but rather evolved slowly from a series of empirical system design studies, some of which predate the Westfall scheduling project. A complete history of how the concept evolved would be lengthy and probably would not add to the goal of making the user-designer concept an internally viable aspect of each student's approach to problem solving. We will start then with a somewhat abbreviated history of the initial major use of the user-designer concept. A problem situation will be described, then a user-oriented modeling environment for attacking that problem, and then the roles of various people in the process and the results. Thereafter a generalized modeling skeleton that has evolved from this first application will be presented.

A Student Health Clinic

Many authors have talked of the generality of production and operations management concepts, stating that they should be useful for hospitals, banks, cities, etc. As an extension of the business-oriented problem environment, student projects were initiated in a college student health clinic. The problem statement was made particularly open-ended: "To do something useful for the staff at the student health clinic by applying concepts and techniques learned in the classroom to problems identified at the student health clinic." An early project involved the development of a simple computer system to provide the staff with an improved set of up-to-date inpatient information. The first concrete outputs from this project were several time-shared computer programs which produced certain reports of interest (e.g., daily statistics on facility utilization). Although this project satisfied the criterion of "doing something useful," the major effect was to stimulate additional effort.

A subsequent project was approached in what might be viewed as a classical consulting manner. A student trained in computer technology met regularly with a group of physicians and a head nurse and attempted, through discussions, to identify their criteria or objectives—to determine something really important to them that a computer system could help achieve. He then began to design a computerized information system based upon these criteria. However, the student and his faculty advisers were dissatisfied with the problems selected for solution. They simply did not seem to be in tune with the fundamental concerns of the physicians; rather the problems seemed to be connected with day-to-day operational details. When this relatively low-level approach was recognized, the research emphasis shifted in two important ways. First, a different type of problem was identified and attacked. Second, it became necessary to investigate the underlying problem formulation and solution approach itself; at an early stage it became clear that some methodology was needed which would allow for rapid evolution in individualized attacks on the more fundamental problems of the physicians.

The doctors dealt with medical problems for which computational power was potentially very useful. For example, one doctor had been collecting information on hockey injuries with the intent of possibly developing new protective equipment designs. This research was tedious and time-consuming, involving the sifting of masses of student health records. Other doctors were also involved with interesting problems amenable to computer-modeling techniques, such as predicting epidemics, correlating medical and student grade information, and testing hypotheses about drug usage in terms of various drug user attributes such as personality test scores.

Each doctor's interest was highly individual; moreover, satisfaction of his needs as he presently understood them required computer model features conflicting with the particular model features needed by other doctors. Furthermore, as depicted in Figs. 4.1 and 4.2, a doctor's "needs" are not static. They would mutate or evolve over time as hypotheses are formulated, data acquired, and analyses performed. It is quite clear that the evolutionary nature of the doctor's understanding of his needs is dependent upon the modeling environment that he uses. Having observed the painfully tedious efforts involved in the hockey injuries research, it became a major goal to provide the doctors with a modeling environment that could be highly individualized and that also would not only *accommodate* their changing needs but *encourage* that evolution. Formulation of this research goal led to the development of the user-designer concept. Implementation of the user-designer concept required the design of a particular computer modeling environment which has been called INF*ACT.

The INF*ACT Model

As previously noted, implementation of the user-designer concept requires models constructed in ways so that problem evolution can proceed rapidly in directions unforeseeable at the outset. Since the user must be quite close to the model-building efforts, the models themselves must be constructed in the user's terms with a minimal investment required for the user to achieve communication with the model.

For a user unskilled in computer technology, the effective use of a computer requires the existence of a man-machine communications system more geared to the user's communication skills than are most present day computer systems. The key to implementation of the user-designer concept is the ability of nonprofessionals to make major changes in their models. This is not possible in most computer systems.

In order to take full advantage of the computer's manipulative powers and to achieve highest efficiency, most computer systems programming is accomplished by writing in an assembly language at the level of the computer's basic machine language. For example, the translators or compilers for higher level languages such as COBOL, FORTRAN, BASIC, and ALGOL are usually written in assembly language, as are those systems utilizing the latest input-output devices. A highly skilled professional systems programmer is required to program systems at this machine level. The user of languages such as FORTRAN is, relatively, a nonprofessional computer systems man, and needs no knowledge of programming at the machine level. His communications with the computer are all in the higher level language; and the computer compiler translates his wishes into machine code which is then executed by the computer before the results are returned.

An alternative to writing the translating language or compiler in machine language is to go through an additional computation step—to use a higher level language such as FORTRAN as the "compiler" or translator for statements written in some new unique language. Then, rather than having the new language's statements translated directly at the machine level, they are translated by the FORTRAN statements, which are then further translated to the machine language level. The user of the new language need have knowledge neither of machine language nor of the FORTRAN-level language—only the new language in which he will write his commands. The new language can be highly simplified and oriented to the particular problem and would require only a small investment of effort for the user to achieve communication with the computer.

Languages written with the additional translation step, while they will generally be less efficient in terms of computer usage than those written at the machine level, will be much easier to program initially and, most important, easier to change later; and they can be programmed by a nonprofessional with relatively minimal programming skill. Since the nonprofessional can make changes in the model, users can become much closer to the model-building effort and be more directly involved in the system redesign and implementation processes. As this process takes place a more rapid evolution of the system can be achieved.

INF*ACT, which is a computer language of this variety, is a higher level computer language written in Dartmouth BASIC* for execution on time-shared computers. INF*ACT is a modularized general computer system or language for creating a user-oriented modeling environment for data retrieval and manipulation in a wide variety of problem areas. INF-*ACT consists of a collection of BASIC subroutines or modules useful in

---

*BASIC is an algebraic language with the flavor of FORTRAN and ALGOL, but easier to learn and use. Hereafter in this chapter when we refer to BASIC we mean this higher level Dartmouth BASIC rather than any basic machine language.

constructing languages oriented to particular problems. In adaptation to a new problem area, many of the subroutines can be used with no change. Some new subroutines may have to be written, but the modular construction of INF*ACT makes changes in existing modules and the addition of new modules easy. To illustrate the kind of user-oriented modeling environment made possible by INF*ACT, let us now turn to one actual implementation at the student health clinic.

Student Health INF*ACT

One major problem area identified by four staff doctors and the head nurse at the student health clinic was an interest in testing hypotheses about infectious mononucleosis, such as patient attributes which predict duration of stay in the hospital and the effects of various drugs. Let us describe this problem area by first giving an overview of the INF*ACT computer modeling environment which was established for testing hypotheses on a data base comprised of infectious mononucleosis patient attributes; thereafter, we investigate the ways in which the doctors and nurse were able to integrate this modeling power into their own highly individualized analytical styles.

For data, 26 facts for each of the 50 mononucleosis patients were stored. The facts stored included the day, month, and year of a mononucleosis patient's admittance to the hospital, his doctor, age, sex, race, and results of medical tests such as white blood count. Each fact was given an alphabetic code (e.g., WBC for white blood count, AGE for age); each patient had a numerical code. Nine commands were implemented: one for retrieval (RET), four for limited manipulation (ADD, SUB, MPY, DIV), one for output (PRT), one for editing (LIM), one for grouping (EQU), and one for terminating execution.

Details on these commands are really beyond the scope of this chapter. It is generally true that any kind of numerical analysis can be accomplished. Also, command names are easily changed and new commands easily added. Codes are easily changed. Thus if a particular doctor finds TEMP more congenial than FEVER for the highest fever the patient had while in the hospital, that change could easily be made in that doctor's own model or working version of the system.

The size of the data base in this preliminary version was dictated by limitations on the particular time-sharing system used at the time and on the resources available for data acquisition. Both these limitations have since been overcome; however, neither prevented valuable use of the system, and expansion was easy with no new conceptual problems.

Retrieval and manipulation take a conversational form between man and machine in which the man presents one command at a time for execution and the system indicates its readiness to accept the next command by printing a question mark. The conversation typically begins with a retrieval of selected pieces of data of interest to the researcher. The data are then either printed out or computation is performed on them which perhaps combines them with other retrieved data. For example, in the following exchange a user is interested in a certain group of students who had a maximum fever higher than 100 degrees.

```
? EQU S;STU (701-707;LIM;FEVER>100)
? RET FEVER;MD;DAYD;AGE;S
? PRT FCT

        FEVER   MD   DAYD   AGE

703     102.3    7     6     18
704     103.3    7    16     20
707     100.8   14     8     23

?  END
JOB TERMINATED
TIME: 1.63 SECS
```

In response to the first, "?", the user says "equate (EQU) the symbol 'S' to those students who have numbers from 701 through 707, and who had a maximum fever greater than 100 degrees." The second "?" printed by the computer indicates that the first instruction has been carried out, and that the computer is ready for another command. Now the user says, "retrieve (RET) the following four facts on each of the students that I have previously designated by the symbol 'S': the highest fever (FEVER), the code number for the doctor in charge (MD), the number of days before the patient was discharged (DAYD), and the patient's age (AGE)." When the computer signifies (by the third "?") that this command has been carried out, the user asks for a printout of the previously retrieved information. The computer prints it out, and responds with another "?". The user types "END" to signify that he is through, but he could have continued the exchange indefinitely. The "1.63 SECS." indicates the computer central processor time involved in the exchange.

The User Investment

INF*ACT can be used by researchers with a wide disparity of programming sophistication in Dartmouth BASIC. We have illustrated the level of use at one extreme—the user who does not know BASIC at all, but wants to access a particular data base with an INF*ACT program. In about one hour physicians with no prior computer experience have been taught elementary commands of an INF*ACT computer model and have accessed existing data bases.

However, the ability to use an existing version of INF*ACT does not take advantage of the model's ability to change with the user's changing perception of his needs. Since the user's needs or problems evolve, it is to be expected that the computer model to meet those needs will also have to evolve. A major effort in the design of INF*ACT has been to make that evolution as simple and as flexible as possible—in fact to speed the evolution.

Users on the next level of sophistication still do not need to know Dartmouth BASIC and yet can implement some substantial changes to their models. In particular, Student Health INF*ACT has been written so that a user may easily change the data base; this was quite important since the design of the data base itself was a significant portion of the research effort. Physicians with no computer-programming knowledge have been taught to make significant changes in the organization and composition of the data base in about two hours.

The third level of sophistication is what gives INF*ACT its real versatility. Any user with an elementary programming knowledge of BASIC can learn to redesign the INF*ACT modeling environment to fit his own particular evolving needs. This level of sophistication requires a somewhat increased investment in time, the actual time being a function of the user's programming ability and the magnitude of the changes that he desires to make. A good BASIC programmer might expect to take 5 to 10 hours to change the program, a beginning programmer 10 to 20 hours. Ease of changing the computer model is enhanced by modular construction; any module can be altered fairly easily and new modules, perhaps utilizing calls on existing modules, can be added easily.

This ability to readily make model changes in response to evolving user needs is crucial for implementation of the user-designer concept. The INF*ACT modeling environment provides the system user with this ability to redesign computer models as his needs change without having continual communication problems with an outside expert. If INF*ACT were written in machine language, no user would find it ideal for his particular needs, and it would be extremely difficult to change. Since it is written in BASIC, however, each user can have his own personal version or model and change it as he wishes. One may start using INF*ACT at its most elementary level and move up in versatility to the second and third levels. The speed of this movement is usually quite rapid, as users can see the need for developing general programming expertise and particular modeling "tricks" that are useful for their problems. Thus, model-building expertise is put into the context of particular problems of interest to the user. Let us now see how the physician users responded to the availability of the student health INF*ACT computer-modeling environment.

Model Use

Because the student health project was of a developmental nature, predictions of the success of the doctors in gaining expertise in model use were made cautiously. However, there were some general expectations about the direction the staff's development would take, First, it was expected that the doctors would be able to learn enough about the INF*ACT computer model to begin to formulate and test individual hypotheses without outside aid. Second, it was expected that the staff would grow to understand the user-designer concept and be able to evaluate its operational effectiveness. Third, it was expected that the staff would be able to design useful extensions of the model (either with or without outside help) for implementation.

There were also some expectations as to the potential accomplishments of the individual personnel involved. Since previous computer model-building experience seemed to be a strength at the outset, it was felt that those having had previous exposure to Dartmouth BASIC would progress more rapidly. However, this did not prove to be true. It is now believed that rapid evolution in an INF*ACT type computer-modeling environment is not as dependent upon programming expertise as it is upon the recognition by the user of the user-designer concept and his own very critical role in the evolutionary design process. This is illustrated by the fact that one doctor, who had no previous experience with a computer, progressed at least as rapidly as any other member of the staff. He was able to see clearly his own important role in the evolutionary process. He understood the personal benefits to be obtained by learning additional computer-modeling procedures, and therefore they were relatively easy to achieve.

In actual experience, all of the general expectations noted above were realized, and with encouraging speed in terms of user commitment and outside aid. The staff and outside consultants (two students) held weekly meetings for nine weeks. After the first meeting two of the four doctors involved asked for additional help in learning Dartmouth BASIC; this help was provided by one student on a weekly one-half hour tutorial basis for the nine weeks. Since the doctors were simultaneously maintaining their regular medical work load, the entire effort necessarily was done at odd hours and to some extent on the doctors' own time.

The exact determination of the contents of the data base for infectious mononucleosis involved considerable discussion and thought among the staff members, and was regarded as an integral part of the investigation. In the discussion of the data base above, only the final data base was described. As hypotheses were formulated data were required for testing those hypotheses. In several instances it was found that the available data were inappropriate for testing the hypotheses and appropriate data had not been collected. In addition, the analysis indicated substantial inconsistencies in the data collection process; data were often not comparable between doctors or patients.

In the course of the investigation many tests were conducted. One involved investigation of the factors affecting the length of stay in the hospital for infectious mononucleosis. Hypotheses were formulated and tested for factors such as differences in drugs, in temperature at admittance, in days from admittance until the time of highest temperature, and in time of the year admitted (perhaps, it was suggested, students stay in the hospital longer near examination periods). None of these hypotheses received significant statistical weight. Finally a hypothesis was formulated which was supported by significant statistical measures. That hypothesis was simply that the length of stay in the hospital was a function of which doctor had admitted the student. One doctor believed that infectious mononucleosis was a very serious disease and that a student afflicted with it should stay in the hospital for at least three weeks; others dismissed patients in a week to ten days.

Before one dismisses such a result as "amusing" or "obvious," it is pertinent to remember that many discoveries look obvious in retrospect. The plain fact of the matter is that a group of highly intelligent men had a "problem," and many hypotheses about its cause. After a modeling environment was established which allowed these hypotheses to be tested sequentially, a result was found by *them* that was significant in terms of *their* criteria. It is quite doubtful that outsiders could have achieved this result.

New procedures have since been adopted in the health clinic for dealing with infectious mononucleosis. Those procedures involve treatment of the disease as well as data collection procedures. In addition, one member of the staff formulated and tested some hypotheses that led to results which merited testing on a larger data base. This individual went on to collect additional data from other student health clinics in order to test his hypotheses, and believed that his additional effort would lead to the publication of a scholarly paper in a medical journal.

Other kinds of efforts with additional data and new data bases were also investigated by the health staff. These efforts proceeded with a minimal use of outside design aid. However, rather than discussing these medical extensions, let us now turn to a brief description of some other INF*ACT applications which are more closely allied to the business world.

A Generalized INF*ACT

It was clear that the computer model-building environment established for the student health clinic could be generalized and used for many kinds of problem-solving activities involving large data bases. We will not, however, describe these other INF*ACT applications in detail.* Rather, our interest will be to illustrate the generality of the INF*ACT approach to data oriented problems, and its value in regard to the user-designer concept.

The INF*ACT model is being used by marketing managers who are concerned with computing various market shares, the effects of special deals, and various statistical measures utilizing routines such as correlation, regression, projection, or forecasting. One data base consisted of wholesale weekly product movement data for many products, in several marketing areas, for many weekly periods, for dollar sales or equivalent cases. Many new commands were added for this particular application.

In terms of the user-designer concept, marketing managers represent users who normally must call on expert "systems" people in order to obtain desired computer analyses; certain computer analyses are performed on a routine basis, but the evolutionary aspects of problem identification and solution inevitably lead to the formulation of individualistic hypotheses. The successful marketing manager indeed is paid partially for his ability to formulate and test individualistic hypotheses. With a modeling environment such as INF*ACT, these hypotheses can be generated and tested in highly individualistic ways with efficient speed and cost. Without such a modeling environment, the alternative is long hours of "coolie" work at a desk calculator. The difference in results as well as the difference in challenge provided to the creative abilities of a marketing manager under these two alternative analytical modes is extraordinary. And, as was true for the medical example, only the marketing men themselves can identify the relevant directions for model and system evolution. Computer experts simply cannot decide what kinds of analyses are pertinent by themselves since they do not have the proper criteria.

A personnel type record system with a data base of 18 attributes for approximately 4,000 alumni has been developed as an offshoot from the INF*ACT model. The system was again somewhat like other systems except that, following the user-designer principle, the commands and structure of the language were user-oriented and included some unique features. In addition to providing a continuously up-to-date alumni file, the computer-modeling environment allowed various kinds of inquiries, such as which alumni work for a particular company, which alumni live in a particular city, which alumni work in a particular kind of industry at the vice-presidential level in either the Southeast or Northwest. Again, the kind of questions to ask can only be determined by particular users;

---

*The interested reader should see INF*ACT User's Manual, International Time-sharing Corporation, Minneapolis, 1970.

a placement officer or dean has his own specialized alumni interests which can vary substantially from time to time.

Two other applications concerned the banking world. An INF*ACT language was developed to facilitate analyses by top management based on a bank's daily financial statement for many days. Another banking application evolved around a data base made up of various published and financial information about the bank's major competitors. Again, analyses with these data bases could only be directed by bankers; outside system design experts who know little of banking simply could not do it.

In the realm of financial analysis, INF*ACT systems have been built for published financial data (such as Standard & Poor's) as well as for more individualistic financial analyses of a particular company (internal quarterly accounting data). A related effort involved detailed monthly cost information for a manufacturing concern. Still another application involved demographic data for developing countries for projects in comparative entrepreneurship. Again, in each of these situations, users examined highly individualistic needs by performing analyses that were significant in terms of their own particular evolving criteria.

SUMMARY REMARKS

In this chapter we have attempted to examine the interactions between system design experts and system users. An assessment of this relationship was found to be vital for implementation of significant inprovements, both initially and more importantly in subsequent evolution. Many authors have talked about the importance of communication between analysts who study a problem and people who are affected by the solution to that problem. Such approaches as "the staff must sell—not tell" and "participative management" have been addressed to this issue. However, there is an important difference between these approaches and the user-designer concept. The former have the flavor of consideration for people as individuals but do not question the superiority of outside expert analyses. The latter does not downgrade outside expertise, but the user-designer concept explicitly recognizes the importance of rapid evolution in perceived user needs and the necessary role played by users in that evolution. This means that the individuals directly concerned with the system under study, rather than playing a passive role in the analytical process and thereafter being sold on the results, take an active part in the actual problem identification, model formulation, and problem solution cycle. They do so because they alone have the criteria by which evolution can be directed. The outsiders' job is to provide the proper modeling environment rather than to obtain a solution to an initial problem which, even if it were superior to that obtained by the users in conjunction with

Fig. 4.4 Copyright 1969 Saturday Review, Inc. Reprinted by permission of the publisher and the author.

the outside designers, would not be as beneficial when seen from a long-run or evolutionary viewpoint.

In implementing the user-designer concept, we noted the benefits of explicitly stating the actions which follow from various conditions. Decision rule formulation is important for intrahuman, functional, or organizational analyses. Thus even if the production scheduling problem were entirely under the domain of one individual, we have seen how there is still great benefit to be derived from examining the interactions of various policies (existing and proposed) in a model. Once the policies have been explicitly stated, many ideas for improvement will be suggested, particularly by other individuals who come to the explicit model with a "fresh" viewpoint.

It is worth emphasizing that as the number of conditions and actions increases, the ability to intuitively understand the interactions and system performance diminishes rapidly. This is particularly so for those ubiquitous situations where feedback is involved (that is, where an observed condition initiates an action which changes the condition). Since real world problems are often very complex and have many feedback mechanisms, we shall be interested in modeling mechanisms which can depict complexity and feedback; those models will rely very heavily on the notion of explicit decision-rule formulation.

The user-designer concept is an extension of the materials discussed in Chapter 3. In that chapter we talked of the importance of the systems approach where larger problem bounding is accomplished through appropriate model formulation. In this chapter we have been concerned with making the systems approach operational; that is, with implementation of the benefits suggested through analyses utilizing the systems approach. In order to do this, we have taken the pragmatic approach that the outside expert should assess the existing organization and its personnel and build on whatever he finds. This approach recognizes the evolutionary nature of problem solving, and is not so much concerned with the initial solution to a problem as with the potential benefits to be obtained through rapid evolution based on an evolution-oriented modeling environment. Figure 4.4 sums up our intent nicely.

REFERENCES

Ackoff, Russell L., "Management Misinformation Systems," *Management Science,* **14,** no. 4 (Dec. 1967): 147–156.

Bower, R. S., C. E. Nugent, J. P. Williamson, and B. C. Myers, "A Language for the Aid of Financial Fact Finders," *Financial Analysts Journal* (Jan.–Feb. 1967), pp. 83–94.

Mayer, C. S., C. E. Nugent, and T. E. Vollmann, "On Line Data Retrieval and Analysis," *Proceedings of the International Marketing Congress,* American Marketing Association, Atlanta (June 1969), pp. 121–129.

Nugent, C. E., T. E. Vollmann, A. H. Howell, R. L. Schuldenfrei, and J. R. Westfall, "User-Oriented Computer Modeling Environments," *Management Science,* **17,** no. 7 (January 1971): 372–4.

Simon, Herbert A., *The New Science of Management Decisions,* Harper, 1960.

Withington, Frederick, *The Real Computer: Its Influence, Uses, and Effects,* Addison-Wesley, 1969.

CHAPTER REVIEW

The basic intent of Chapter 4 is to specifically consider the implementation process.

You may be able to design a good system or problem solution, but getting it implemented requires an additional set of skills. By focusing our attention on the interaction between experts in particular kinds of system design and users of that expertise, we see the need to add criteria to the model-building process.

The chapter is heavily laced with computer model examples. My objective is not to impress you with computerized razzle-dazzle, nor to equate the systems approach with computers. Other kinds of user-oriented modeling environments are possible, and the models described should only be considered as examples. On the other hand, the systems approach requires models which can accommodate many entities. Evolution intensifies the need for open-ended models which can accommodate many entities. The attributes of the computer make it particularly appealing.

OUTLINE OF THE CHAPTER

Introduction (goals and how system evolution happens)

The user-designer concept (use of specialists)

A communications gap (evolving criteria)

Overcoming the communications gap (users take more active role in modeling)

The feedback between needs, models and systems (goal-rapid evolution in perceived needs)

Evolution oriented models (recognition of proper modeling environment)

Explication (ambiguity and communication)

Westfall furniture company (requirements for user-oriented model)

The student's analytical role (problem delineation related to particular perception)

Problem identification (a good problem at the wrong time)

Factory scheduling (a clearly perceived problem by users)

Model development (user validation and evolution)

Extensions (other subsystems)

Users and designers (nothing works like success)

A user-oriented data base language (evolution oriented model)

A student health clinic (unique user needs)

The INF*ACT model (an open-ended approach)

Student health INF*ACT   (the model)

The user investment   (recognition of user time constraints)

Model use   (user payoffs)

A generalized INF*ACT   (user-oriented modeling environment)

Summary remarks   (a bottom-up approach)

CENTRAL ISSUES

The user-designer concept recognizes the evolutionary nature of problem solving, and an implied goal of speeding the evolution. The user or consumer of expertise is the primary possessor of criteria by which evolutionary direction is determined. The process of identifying new steps in the evolutionary process is iterative; solution of one problem leads to delineation of the next problem. By having the user more actively involved or closer to the actual model-building process, increased evolutionary speed in iterative problem perception can be attained.

Moving the user closer to the model-building process implies construction of models that are particularly user-oriented. A key feature of user-oriented models is the reduction of ambiguity and poor communications, achieved through criteria and model explication. Explicit decision rules and explicitly stated criteria permit a more rational examination as well as an improved assessment of surrogate criteria appropriateness.

The user-designer concept in actual use was illustrated by production scheduling and related problems at Westfall. It also was exemplified by the student health clinic and other INF*ACT models. In all of these actual problems, the initial problem scope was determined by particular users. A rapid evolution in perceived user needs occurred in each case, but the evolution was unique to particular users and their corresponding unique criteria sets.

ASSIGNMENTS

1. Returning to problem 1 in Chapter 3, a one-month vacation as a process of system design, attempt to identify and describe the way in which evolution occurred in problem identification, model formulation, and problem solution. In what ways did the kinds of models used change?
2. How would your approach to the one-month vacation problem change if you were aiding someone else in planning such a vacation as compared to the approach used for your own vacation?
3. In what ways are the system design efforts of problems 1 and 2 different?
4. Selection processes often reflect an evolution in criteria. Choose one of the following and specifically treat the evolution of criteria which you experienced when making a selection: a college, a car, a course, a wife or husband, or a house. What kinds of models can be used for these problems?
5. For problem 4 in Chapter 3 assume that the solution that is accepted is for the red light to come on whenever the density on that stretch of highway

exceeds the optimal. The criterion satisfied by this scheme is maximization of throughput. Using the ideas presented in Chapter 4, describe how this problem solution might have come about.

6.   Assume that you have been hired for the summer by a relatively small suburban bank. Because of your experience as a computer programmer you are assigned to the trust department where they are in the process of implementing a computerized accounting and information retrieval system. The system was purchased as a finished product from one of the country's largest accounting/consulting firms and consists of over 130 programs. In addition to bookkeeping there are check writing routines for all stipends and recurring payments. Standard reports range from a coded copy of the indenture or will governing each trust to comparative earnings on different types of accounts or investments. Data processing is done by a separate organization, owned by a group of banks including yours. Batch processing and the subcontracting of card punching operations lead to long turn-around times. It often takes two weeks to make any substantial programming changes.

The trust officer in charge of the project has had no computer experience but is intimately familiar with every aspect of the department's operation. His attitude toward the computerized accounting and information retrieval system is as though it were a legal document to be interpreted and enforced but *not* changed.

The implementation process is being carried out mostly by a group of four similar employees of which you are the senior member. As the summer progresses your experience gains you more and more responsibility. In fact you come to be regarded as the expert on the computerized package, and when the project director takes his vacation you are left in charge.

What would you do or try to do which would be best for the trust department when you return to school in the fall?

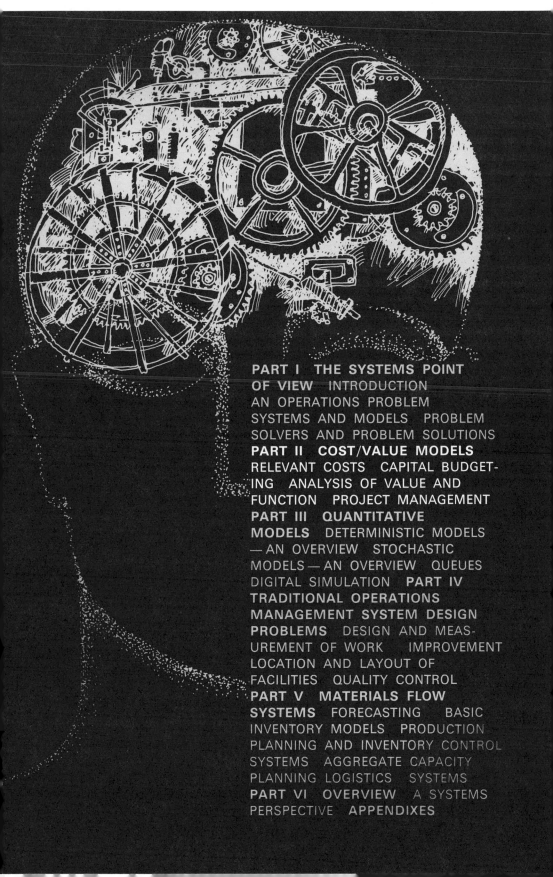

INTRODUCTION
TO PART II

Perhaps the most prominent concept presented in Part I is the essential role played by criteria in the system design or problem-solving process. We stated the need for surrogate or proximate criteria that are used to measure more encompassing goals such as corporate growth and profitability; the minimization of cost is a frequently used surrogate criterion. As is true for *any* surrogate criterion, however, you should continually test the appropriateness of the proximate relationship by assessing improvements in terms of both the surrogate criterion and more global criteria.

Cost/value data do not somehow magically exist; modeling procedures for generating these data are required. As such, our general remarks apply to the inevitability of model imperfections and to model validity or appropriateness being necessarily determined for particular purposes. In most instances, the value or worth of some good or service is determined by its use, not its cost. Simply stated, what is a "good" (not optimal) representation of an economic phenomenon has to be determined on the basis of use or criteria; what is "good" for one purpose can be quite improper for another.

Part II is devoted to attaining an understanding of surrogate criteria based upon costs and values, some specific models used for measuring costs and values, and an organizational form for achieving cost/value objectives. The goal is to make each of you a more sophisticated consumer of cost/value data and to recognize how certain criteria sets are implied from certain models which generate cost/value data; these data will be appropriate for some problems and inappropriate for others. It will be necessary to tailor cost/value data to specific problems, and we will see examples of data collection systems built specifically for particular projects.

Chapter 5 delineates the major criteria which have led to the development of existing cost-data generating models, and emphasizes the need for tempering or tailoring the outputs of such models for operations management problems. A major objective is for you to derive an improved understanding of the difference in criteria orientation between financial accounting models and specialized analyses for particular problems. Cost data are only a subset of data which might be deemed pertinent to a particular problem. Because cost data often come from cost-data generating models with a high degree of precision, there is a tendency to regard such data as accurate or pertinent. We all have a penchant for such "hard" data that many times are not nearly as pertinent as "soft" data which are the output of much less rigorous models, e.g., Baumritter *opinions* about how customers will react to a new line of cherry furniture well may be more important than the cost of the products in setting prices.

Chapter 6 takes on a related but more clear-cut problem, how to make appropriate adjustments to cost and revenue data to reflect differences in timing. Also presented are some of the most widely used models for coping with investment decisions involving cash-flow timing differences. Without this basic understanding, it will not be possible for you to properly consider many kinds of operations management problems, such as those which substitute capital for labor or those involving an investment which generates a stream of revenues.

Chapter 7 builds upon the healthy skepticism for cost data and cost-data generating models developed in Chapters 5 and 6. It is in this chapter that the notions of value are more fully developed, and a model for measuring value is presented. The functional analysis model is much less precise than the cost models examined previously, but you will find it very useful for many kinds of problems. By attempting to define the basic "function" or activity provided by a system, a standard of comparison can be created which leads to insightful system design improvements.

Chapter 8 is devoted to the control of project oriented activities on the basis of both time (PERT-CPM) and cost (PERT/COST). Key features of this chapter are the definition of a problem which crosses organizational boundaries, division of the problem or project into component tasks, establishment of sequential constraints among the tasks, and a reporting-control procedure for monitoring time and cost criteria as the project is being completed. In addition to understanding some important models for trading-off time and cost to achieve functional values, you should gain an appreciation of the benefits derived from an organizational form which facilitates achievement of concrete objectives.

CHAPTER 5

RELEVANT COSTS

The great majority of operations management problems demand the trading off of one kind of cost against another or the payment of some cost to achieve a benefit or value. Examples include the tradeoff of costs of holding larger inventories versus those of being more frequently out of stock, costs of warehouses versus high speed transportation costs, costs of more rapid delivery to achieve increased sales, costs of capital investments versus those of labor, costs of greater inspection versus those resulting from shipping poor quality merchandise, and the costs of using executive talent for routine tasks versus the costs and benefits associated with using that talent to find or design long-run solutions or decision rules for those routine tasks. In the discussion of Westfall in Chapter 3, we talked of the need for obtaining certain important fact or data entities; many of these involved costs, such as for a conveyor belt, for installation, for the development of conveyorized chair-building procedures, or for the unit production costs.

Since cost data are required for the majority of operations management problems, we should now consider their *relevance.* Cost data require tailoring or special design for the purposes to which they are put. The criteria system not only dictates problem identification or selection as well as the choice of appropriate modeling representation, it also establishes the relevancy of cost data and the benefits or values obtained from costs.

From where do cost data come? There is obviously no such thing as a giant cost "bush" with cost "berries" of all descriptions hanging on it that can be easily picked for a particular occasion, but the assumption that such data in usable form can be readily obtained from an accounting system is almost equally naive. Some of the costs we have identified in the opening paragraph as necessary for analyses (such as the costs of utilizing executive talent for routine matters or developing conveyorized chair-building procedures) clearly do not reside in an accounting system; even more unfortunately, many of the data that *do* reside in an accounting system (such as the unit cost of conveyorized chair building) may be inappropriate or not relevant for particular analyses or purposes (e.g., the "cost" of a conveyor breakdown well might be based upon lost sale considerations; the "value" of a conveyor less prone to breakdown may be quite unrelated to its purchase price).

This chapter explains how and why cost data must be tailored for specific problems, analyses, or purposes. We saw in Chapter 3 that models are built for particular purposes, but what is a good model for one purpose is not necessarily good for other purposes, and what is an important fact entity in one model may not be important in another constructed for a different purpose. To these ideas another can be added: Simply stated, fact names do not always unambiguously represent one and only one fact or datum (e.g., *which* chair-component cost—are they all produced at the same cost? Do we include amounts representing necessary internal transportation, holding, or paperwork procedures?). The key word in this idea is "represent." As in model building, we represent a set of occurrences or a system with an abstraction, and the properly abstracted cost representation must be based upon the situation-dependent interest, goal, need, or criterion for that cost datum.

We must obtain cost facts or data through model building; interests or criteria dictate the relevancy of cost data, which in turn require relevant, tailored fact or data-generating models. Serious errors in decisions can be made at least as frequently through poor attention to data relevancy as through inappropriate model selection or manipulation.

THE FINANCIAL ACCOUNTING MODEL

An income statement and balance sheet (sometimes with supporting documents) are attempts to depict the economic health of a company. As such, they are models, and the financial accounting process is one of model building. Our comments in Chapter 3 about models only being valid for particular criteria should be remembered. In using the outputs from this modeling process, it will behoove us to carefully examine the criteria by which the model building has been directed. A comparison of these criteria with those directing many individualized analyses often indicates a basic incompatibility and the need for different data-generating models. The incompatibility is largely because criteria which are appropriate for one gross level of aggregation are not appropriate for analyses requiring a different and much more detailed level of aggregation.

Criteria

The criteria for financial accounting largely originate from outside the firm, and the primary goal or criterion of financial accounting is to "fairly" reflect the financial health of the total company to various outside interests including shareholders, potential investors, security-regulating bodies, lending institutions, and taxing authorities. The financial accounting process should be looked at in a social context where the goal is economic health for a very large system, such as the United States or perhaps the world economy. If companies large enough to require capital investments (from many people) are to flourish, it is necessary that information about those companies be made available on a consistent and reasonable basis. In addition, in a society where it is believed that companies and individuals should share the tax burden fairly, it is necessary for a consistent across-the-board accounting system to be used. Governmental agencies see these goals as extremely important; they use their regulatory powers accordingly.

The distinction between costs and values is interesting in the social responsibility sense. Financial accounting makes virtually no attempt to measure values. However, there is increasing social pressure for firms to report on what kinds of progress they are making towards societal goals, such as employment of minority groups, elimination of poverty, pollution control, other environmental problems, and improvement of international relations. These kinds of values increasingly are discussed in annual reports, with financial goals increasingly not accepted as the only pertinent criterion entities.

As is true for any system design effort, the rather lofty goals associated with fairly representing the economic health of a company must be translated into subordinate, proximate, or surrogate criteria for the design of particular accounting systems and the appropriate disposition of particular transactions (see Box 5.1).

It is worth reiterating that a surrogate or proximate criterion is one used as an *attempted* measure of performance which is hopefully congruent with higher order goals or criteria of the organization. Thus, financial ratios are attempted measures of enterprise well-being, and minimization of idle time is *one* surrogate for appraising the efficacy of conveyorized chair building. One must never neglect the implications of "attempted" in the definition; it is almost always possible to take actions that better the surrogate at the expense of the fundamental goal (e.g., pay off accounts payable with cash to increase the current ratio, or run the chair line at reduced speed to decrease idle time).

Box 5.1

Many accounting theorists are continually attempting to refine the set of accounting surrogate criteria, but it is not our present goal to describe this process. Rather, our purpose is merely to note a few of these criteria and examine their effects on the accumulation of cost data.

One of the most important surrogate financial-accounting criteria is "reasonableness," which is very much like the so-called reasonable man doctrine in the interpretation of law. The criterion of reasonableness is implemented through the professionalization of accounting. Financial accounting reports are required to be attested to by unbiased professional outside accountants. Most of these accounting professionals belong to the American Institute of Certified Public Accountants which allows them to assess various accounting model-building choices in terms of what their colleagues would deem "appropriate" or "reasonable." One of the major outputs from the professionalization of accounting is a continuously evolving set of "generally accepted accounting principles."

A related accounting criterion entity is called "disclosure." The idea of disclosure is that if a particular model-building choice were made that has a hidden effect on the reporting of firm economic health, such effect or effects should be clearly stated so that proper inferences can be drawn.

A major problem with reasonableness and disclosure, however, is that both require some frame of reference; that is, just exactly what is "unreasonable?" Who is to decide? Doesn't such a decision necessarily have to be made on the basis of user criteria? Thus a difference of $100,000 in the annual income of a large corporation might be relatively insignificant to the average potential investor. On the other hand, for a particular problem or analysis the outcome of a decision well might revolve on the treatment of that $100,000. A similar but even more basic criticism is that both disclosure and reasonableness have a detached or "average" orientation rather than an orientation that recognizes and feeds the particular biases or criteria of particular needs or individuals.

A somewhat more operational accounting criterion is captured in the term "consistency." Consistency states that if an accounting treatment (model-building choice) has been used in prior years, it should be retained. The reasons for consistency are fairly obvious. It discourages company management teams from manipulating their financial statements by changing accounting methods. Many investors make choices based on analyses of accounting data over several time periods and require consistent reports.

Nonetheless, important as it may be to maintain data for outsiders on a consistent basis, an insider's evolutionary cycle of problem identification, model formulation, data selection, and problem solution brings to mind Emerson's aphorism, "Consistency is the hobgoblin of small minds." We will discuss the need to abandon consistency more thoroughly in the section dealing with situation-dependent cost models. For now it is worth noting that as problems either change or evolve, the ways in which particular cost data are generated must similarly change or evolve.

Matching is another surrogate criterion entity for the accounting model-building process. The concept of matching states that sales revenues should be matched against the costs which were incurred in order to achieve those revenues. It is the matching concept that dictates depreciation.* Matching also requires that each product or service sold carry its "fair share" of the more general, fixed, or "overhead" expenses of the enterprise, e.g., heat and power, the president's salary, supplies.

Although matching is very important in order to reflect enterprise health in gross or highly aggregated terms, the systematic application of matching to the accumulation of cost data can mask significant managerial decision-making alternatives which are almost always at a lower level of aggregation. Thus for example when considering holding costs for the design of an inventory control system, it is appropriate to assume that each individual unit held will cause the firm to incur a cost based upon dividing the stockroom clerk's salary by the average number of units held? Will the firm realize a savings of that amount if one unit less is held?

A concept related to matching is called "periodicity." Periodicity states that the accounting model-building process be constructed so as to produce documents depicting enterprise health at periodic intervals (usually on an annual basis). The periodicity concept or the notion of an annual accounting is one with which we are all familiar. Without periodic reports, the ability for investors to make comparative analyses would be severely curtailed and the taxation process would be impossibly cumbersome.

However, as we shall see later in this chapter, the method for aggregating all activity into a periodic profit or loss amount can lead to inappropriate interpretations of profitability when applied to individual activities or products which make up the final aggregated profit or loss figure. The point is that "profit" represents an externally oriented accounting convention largely dictated by the surrogate criteria of matching and periodicity; it is that amount which remains after costs have been subtracted from revenues. But the determination of those costs has required some procedures that, although "reasonable" from an inclusive, global or highly aggregated, detached or outside-oriented viewpoint, are nonetheless arbitrary and potentially irrelevant for particular problems or analyses.

A related consideration, although not actually a financial accounting criterion entity, is the influence of taxation laws on the accounting models of a firm. Most firms attempt to minimize their tax bill; in doing so they often use legitimate tax avoidance procedures which inaccurately portray the financial well-being of the company and also lead to cost data that are inappropriate for solving individual problems.

---

*Depreciation is the process used to allocate the cost of a long-life asset, such as a building or piece of equipment, to the various time periods in which that asset will be utilized.

Cost Accounting Systems

Many cost accounting systems have been designed in a partial attempt to overcome the highly aggregated outside orientation of financial accounting models. These systems typically divide the costs of a product into materials, labor, and overhead for the purposes of estimation and subsequent control. Overhead or burden comprises those indirect expenses, such as supplies, supervisory salaries, building depreciation, and other items that are difficult to associate directly with a particular task. The usual way in which the unit cost of a product or service is determined is to add an actual or "standard" cost of material, an actual or standard cost of direct labor, and a standard (predetermined) amount of factory burden or overhead which is expressed as a percentage of direct labor cost; standard amounts for general, administrative, and selling overheads may thereafter be added as percentages of the total cost comprised of materials, labor, and overhead or treated as a "period" or lump sum.

The process of determining the percentages or rates for factory burden, general, administrative, and selling expenses typically involve division of the total estimated expenses in the various categories for a year. Thus if in one year a company had a total in its direct labor account of $100,000 and the total of all the accounts comprising factory overhead or burden was $190,000 and conditions were expected to remain approximately the same for the next year, the factory burden rate would be set at 190%, i.e., for each dollar of direct labor expended in a product there would be a corresponding matched expense of $1.90 for factory overhead or burden.

There is an erroneous belief on the part of many designers that the final results from a cost accounting system must tie in with the financial accounting system of a company. Such a belief unfortunately means that cost accounting systems will generate cost data with a pattern of behavior driven by the same outside oriented criteria that drive the design of financial accounting models.

Cost Control

We have stated that a goal of cost-accounting systems is estimation and subsequent control and have discussed the concept of a "standard" cost for materials, labor, and overhead. Let us now examine the control process and the role of standards in that process. In this book, whenever we use the word *control* it will have the following meaning:

> Control is a three-step process involving (1) the determination of a standard, goal, or criterion; (2) the measurement and comparison of actual results with that standard; and (3) actions taken to correct deviations.

The control process is a very important one and necessarily involves the critical activities of obtaining a standard for comparison and measurement. Cost accounting systems must incorporate these standards in the measurement and comparison process. Since the standards are surrogate criteria, evolution should be expected and encouraged.

The establishment of cost standards for direct labor, materials and factory overhead allows for the computation of periodic variance analyses where actual performance can be compared with standard or estimated performance. Thus, for example, a company might have planned to build 1000 widgets in a month with material costs of $500. Suppose that 1100 widgets were produced and the actual material costs were $560. The total variance of $60 is comprised of a $50 volume variance (10% more output requiring 10% more input) and a $10 efficiency variance.

Variance reports and other periodically computed cost-accounting documents are primarily designed for routine or day-to-day control purposes. As such they can provide useful information for some specific problem areas. However, as is true for any model, it is quite possible to draw misleading inferences from these reports for other kinds of problems. Such reports unfortunately tend to develop a charisma without proper consideration given to the tailoring required for evolving problem statements and criteria. Although the assumptions of cost behavior are "reasonable," perhaps they are inappropriate for other analyses; for example, is there a causal relationship between direct labor and burden? Does each new dollar of direct labor *really* cause the firm to incur $1.90 in the factory overhead accounts? What happens when a cost versus benefit comparison for a particular job embraces the overhead causal assumption? The point is that routine day-to-day cost control procedures should not be allowed to dictate unique decisions in ways that are not appropriate for high order criteria of the firm.

A current trend in cost accounting practices is toward "responsibility accounting," where individuals are evaluated in terms of costs over which they exercise control. Although conceptually appealing, it is implied that individuals know exactly what is expected of them, that the reported cost criteria are appropriate surrogates for high order enterprise criteria, that the criteria are congruent and that evolution in criteria sets is not rapid.

A central tenet of this chapter is that unique data needs are dictated by particular problem formulations; criteria sets are imperfectly understood and evolution in criteria and data needs is to be expected. Serious errors are all too possible when data are obtained from data-generating models which assume rigid cost behavioral patterns. Let us now examine this issue in more detail.

PATTERNED COST BEHAVIOR MODELS

All accounting or record keeping systems presume a pattern of cost behavior. Within most accounting systems, a particularly appealing pattern of cost behavior is to assume that costs can be separated into those which are fixed and those which vary as a function of the volume produced or sold. The idea is that once such a separation has been made, various cost, volume, and profit relationships can be usefully analyzed. The best known model for this type of investigation is called breakeven analysis.

The Breakeven Model

The breakeven cost model assumes that all costs are fixed, variable, or semivariable as a function of sales volume. Semivariable expenses are further assumed to be capable of being divided into their fixed and variable components. There are also implied assumptions of causality. Thus if sales went up, it is assumed that variable costs would also go up, but the fixed costs would not change. The net result is a total pool of fixed costs, and variable costs which increase as volume increases. Sales volume is a direct function of the units sold. Figure 5.1 depicts a simple breakeven model.

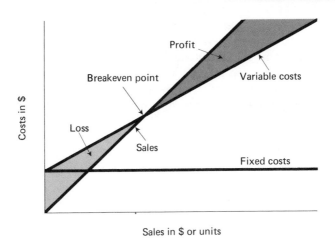

Figure 5.1 Breakeven model.

In Fig. 5.1 costs are plotted on the ordinate and sales on the abscissa. Sales can be plotted in either dollars or in units. If sales are plotted in dollars and the scale is the same for the abscissa as for the ordinate, the sales line will have a 45° slope; otherwise the slope of the sales line will be dependent upon the particular scale chosen. The breakeven point in units is calculated by solving for X in the following equation:

$$X \text{ (unit sales price)} = \text{Fixed cost} + X(\text{unit variable cost}).$$

Let us turn to a simple example. Suppose that at Westfall the fixed annual cost associated with chair manufacturing was $100,000. Let us further suppose that chairs sold for $25 each and the variable cost of producing a chair was $23. Substituting this data into the above equation:

$$25X = 100,000 + 23X,$$
$$X = 50,000.$$

Therefore, for this hypothetical data, the chair-building operation would reach its breakeven point at 50,000 units and it is assumed that sales levels above 50,000 chairs would be profitable. The model is supposedly useful for evaluating changes in costs and volume, but assumptions such as linearity of costs and sales, the relevant range of operations, a constant mix of variable costs, and sales equal to production make such evaluations questionable.

Fixed and Variable Costs

The idea of separating costs into fixed and variable components as a function of sales or volume is an appealing one. Unfortunately, however, for many kinds of costs this separation is difficult and the implied causality assumptions are tenuous. Many costs are variable but not as a function of sales. For example, in a given year how much does or should a company spend on repairs and maintenance for its equipment? on painting its building? on the employee picnic? Many of these kinds of expenses are quite variable depending upon circumstances such as the expected profits for the year; thus if it looks like a very profitable year some of the cost of painting the building can be borne with tax dollars. On the other hand, if it looks like an unprofitable year, the building can probably go without a coat of paint another year and equipment maintenance might be minimal. These kinds of costs are sometimes referred to as "decision" or "programmed" costs.

Another issue involved in the separation of costs into fixed and variable categories concerns a necessary frame of reference or level of aggregation. That is, the economists are fond of telling us that all costs are variable in the long run. For a particular problem, some costs that are normally considered variable may be fixed and vice versa. We will put forth some examples of just this sort of thing in our discussion of incremental cost models.

An Assessment

In assessing the usefulness of cost-volume-profit relationship models, one should consider what sorts of problems are better understood or solved through their use, and whether in certain circumstances the procedures lead to erroneous conclusions.

Cost-volume-profit relationships seem to be useful only in an extremely gross analysis of an autonomous operation (i.e., a high level of aggregation). Westfall might be considered in terms of overall annual volume, but we will see that the models are inappropriate for individual activities. Charles Horngren summed it up nicely: "The breakeven chart may be compared to the use of a meat-ax, not a surgeon's knife."* The model tends to break down for many common types of lower aggregation level problems such as for a one-job or one-product problem, because the causal assumptions indicate reductio ad absurdum cost behavior patterns. A significant loss in meaning tends to occur when cost-volume-profit relationships are assessed for subsystems such as individual products or product lines. Fixed costs must be determined by some allocation scheme; these allocations for breakeven analysis, as typically made in a cost accounting system, can be quite misleading. That is, overhead or burden items usually are allocated on the basis of direct labor hours or some other measure of output. Since fixed costs are allocated as a function of variable costs, do they therefore become variable? Let us consider the example shown in Box 5.2.

Suppose Westfall assumed the following cost behavior pattern for chair manufacturing: average direct labor cost = $2.50 per hour; factory overhead rate = 125% of direct labor cost; general, administrative, and selling overhead = 20% of total factory costs which include material, labor, and factory overhead. Suppose a job came along for 400 special chairs for a convention hall. The estimated unit material cost for these chairs is $9.00, estimated direct labor time is 2 hours, the sale price is $20.00, and a special chair assembly fixture will require 25 hours to construct.

Box 5.2

Let us now examine what will happen if we investigate the desirability of this job with the breakeven model.

First, which costs are to be considered fixed and which variable? One might be tempted to say that the only fixed cost for this job is the 25 hours required to make the special apparatus, so that the total fixed cost is therefore $62.50. It is entirely possible and indeed probable, however, that the labor expended on constructing specialized simple pieces of equipment or fixtures is accumulated into an account that is considered as a portion of factory burden. If so, then perhaps the way to determine profitability might be to consider the factory burden, general, administrative, and selling expenses as fixed, with material and direct labor as variable costs.

Variable costs per unit would be $14.00 (2 hrs. X $2.50 per hour + $9.00 material) and the combination of factory burden (125% of $5.00 =

---

*Charles T. Horngren, *Cost Accounting;* Prentice-Hall, 1967, p. 57.

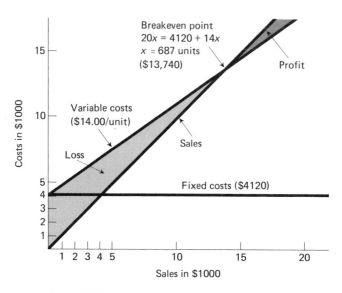

Figure 5.2

$6.25) and general, administrative, selling expense (20% of [$14.00 + $6.25] = $4.05) would yield a total fixed cost of $4120 [($6.25 + $4.05) × 400]. Figure 5.2 is a breakeven chart constructed on this basis.

There is, however, something rather strange about this sort of analysis. The process of finding fixed costs by using a percentage of variable costs times a constant amount (400 units) yields the "proper" fixed cost amount for 400 yet the abscissa of Fig. 5.2 shows sales varying and therefore the same fixed cost of $4120 at 0 sales or for any other sales volume, although our model for determining fixed costs yields different results for different sales volumes.

Different sets of assumptions, such as considering all the fixed costs as variable, yield different but equally strange results. One is forced to conclude that cost-volume-profit relationships do not yield meaningful insights into the desirability of individual job proposals when cost data are generated by models which incorporate allocation schemes. Let us now turn our attention to a class of models with an orientation more useful for such questions.

SITUATION-DEPENDENT COST MODELS

The notion of situation-dependence is intended to connote an orientation where evolving necessarily unique problem identifications lead to the specification of unique data needs. Such data usually cannot be found in suitable form within any record keeping system based upon assumed cost behavior patterns. When it is realized that unique data needs cannot be satisfied by *any* formal record keeping system, a freedom from constraints of existing or "hard data" can lead to more creative insightful problem identifications and solutions.

Incremental Cost Model

The concept of an incremental cost is an extremely important one for students of operations management. Simply stated, any cost is an incremental cost if it varies as a function of the alternatives considered, and any cost that does not vary among the particular alternatives considered is not an incremental cost. An incremental cost may be a fixed cost or a variable cost, and a variable cost does not necessarily have to be an incremental cost.

Many people believe incorrectly that the term "incremental cost" is synonymous with the accounting concept of variable cost. The belief is fundamentally incorrect because incremental costs are not based upon any assumed pattern of cost behavior that permits or requires classification. Accountants also use the term "direct cost" to identify that portion of a product's cost that is directly associated with the particular product such as materials and direct labor. Unfortunately, a recent trend in accounting circles is to use the term "marginal cost" for this concept. The accountant's marginal or direct cost still involves an assumed pattern of cost behavior as dictated by criteria of averaging, reasonableness, or fairness; it is not the same as the economist's concept of marginal cost, which is a nonpatterned, situation-dependent attempt to identify the net economic cost (including opportunity costs) of producing the *next* unit. It is the economist's concept of marginal cost that will be of interest to us: the particular use-oriented incremental or differential cost associated with the difference between two alternatives.

The term "incremental" or "differential" cost is best used when one also adds the term "analysis;" that is, one is concerned with making a differential or incremental cost analysis which carries with it the distinct recognition of a particular point in time. This is critical since a particular cost may be incremental to a decision at one time and not incremental to the same decision at a different time. Thus if the Westfall plant were offered additional chair business, an incremental analysis of the desirability of that business would include an assessment of the present unused chair-building capacity (if excess capacity could be utilized for these chairs the incremented costs might be limited to additional materials). At a different time that excess capacity could be quite different and the incremental cost associated with the two alternatives (to take or not to take the business) would be noticeably changed.

Since incremental costs are time or situation-dependent, it is not possible to design a record keeping system based upon them. Incremental costs are not averaged, fair in any abstract sense, or subject to the criterion of "reasonableness" from financial accounting. Incremental costs recognize a particular problem situation as unique and the costs associated with it as therefore unique. Any costs that are not changed as a result of a particular decision are regarded as being nonincremental to the decision; if such costs have already been incurred, they are regarded as being "sunk."

Examples

In order to see the complex nature of incremental costs in particular decisions, let us now return to the example examined previously in our discussion of breakeven analysis, where we were concerned with examining the desirability of the order for 400 extra chairs. The incremental cost approach to this problem begins by asking what costs will be incurred if this job is taken that will not be incurred if it is not taken. In our analysis above, for example, we assumed that direct labor was an important cost. The incremental approach asks: Is direct labor an incremental cost? That is, although the proposed job calls for 400 chairs at 2 hours of direct labor per unit, will we in fact have to contract for 800 additional direct labor hours? Is it possible that our particular plant presently is not working at a speed that would preclude getting this job done with the existing labor force? If we do require labor, what is the cost of that labor? It may not be appropriate to use the $2.50 average cost figure. For example, it could be that this particular job would be completed with the existing labor force working overtime. If so, the appropriate average cost is not $2.50 per hour but $3.75 per hour (assuming an overtime premium of 50% of direct labor). Also it very well may not be possible to buy exactly 800 hours of direct labor. It is necessary to hire whole men (not 2 7/8 men) and they are hired for "reasonable" periods of time. Whatever the best way is to obtain the required additional direct labor, it has a cost and that cost is the incremental cost for this decision.

The same kind of analysis is required for the material. The standard cost figure of $9.00 per unit for material may not be appropriate for our analysis. The cost could conceivably be zero. Perhaps we make another product now that has scrap material that could be used for this particular job. Alternatively, it might be that the material for these chairs must be ordered in certain large lots and that we must buy enough to make 600 units. If so, the $9.00 material cost again is inappropriate.

The same kind of analysis must be made of the burden accounts. Will this job require an additional man in factory supervision? Will it cause the company to incur greater costs for light and power? for heat? for supplies? for the president's salary? for selling expenses? for factory supplies? These questions must be answered and the resulting incremental costs carefully segregated.

The problem stated a need for 25 hours to construct a special piece of apparatus for this particular job. Whether or not that cost category is treated for accounting purposes as being part of the burden is irrelevant to our present analysis. The fact is that this activity will be incurred if the job is taken and it will not be incurred if the job is not taken; it is therefore potentially an incremental cost (it is also a fixed cost). The incremental cost associated with this 25 hours of work is dependent upon the particular circumstances that exist at this time in this company. That is, if a fixture maker now has unused time, it is possible that the incremental cost of constructing this apparatus is zero. Alternatively, if a new man has to be hired or the job has to be done on overtime, the appropriate incremental cost will have to be determined.

Let us say that the 25 hours required to construct this special apparatus will be done on overtime, that the standard labor and material estimates given above are correct and represent incremental expenses, and that no other additional expenses would be incurred if this job were taken. That means that there is an incremental fixed cost of $93.75 and an incremental variable cost of $14.00 per unit ($5.00 for direct labor + $9.00 for material). If a "breakeven analysis" were performed on this basis, the breakeven point would be at approximately 16 units ($20X = 93.75 + 14X$; $X = 15.6$).

One cannot say, however, that after 16 units the company is making a profit. We must remember that "profit" is an accounting convention; it is the subtraction of costs from revenues. A determination of these costs is made on a "reasonable" basis, and on that basis one cannot say that this particular job is making a profit after 16 units. What one can say is that after 16 units have been made, a contribution is being made toward profit and overhead. The division of this contribution into its profit and overhead components necessarily involves arbitrary allocations and will yield results from which improper inferences can easily be made; better inferences can be based on the undivided contribution.

The breakeven concept is still rather unappealing for this problem, primarily because the company is not going to make 16 units or 687 units, they are going to make 400 units or 0 units. A more useful analysis would be based upon the costs and benefits for the entire job.

Let us examine this same example under some differing assumptions. Suppose the sales price of this item were not $20.00 but $15.00. Should Westfall take this job under those circumstances? Will they make a profit if they do so? Under the same assumptions for incremental costs used above, the answers to these questions are: Yes, they should take the job;

and no, they will not make a profit—they will suffer a loss on the job. It may seem odd to advise a company to take a job on which it will lose money, but it is quite true that this is exactly what they should do.

The reason they will lose money is that the total cost of the chair is $24.30 comprised of $9.00 material, $5.00 direct labor, $6.25 factory burden, and $4.05 general administrative and selling expense (this analysis assumes that fabrication of the special apparatus is an overhead expense). They will, therefore, lose $9.30 on each chair. The reason they should take the job, however, is that although they lose $9.30 on each unit, losses are, like profits, an accounting convention (costs are matched with revenues). From an economic standpoint the firm is better off to "lose" $9.30 per chair than not to lose $9.30 per chair. This is so because of the incremental nature of the costs involved. Incremental costs as stated above are $14.00 per unit plus $93.75 as a fixed cost. The company will experience a net monetary inflow (in incremental terms) of $306.25 [400 units X 15.00 − (400 units X $14.00 + $93.75)]. This amount represents a contribution toward overhead and profit and is desirable even though the amount of the contribution is less than that which the accounting model would normally allocate as cost to such a job on a "fair" or "reasonable" basis.

Let us carry the example further. Suppose the sales price were not $15.00 but $14.50. Should the job still be taken? Here, the unit marginal contribution (sales price minus incremental cost) is $.50, for a total of $200.00; subtracting the $93.75 as a fixed cost still leaves a net contribution to overhead and profit of $106.25. And we could continue to cut the price down to less than $14.24 before our conclusion would change.

There is, however, another aspect to this analysis that students invariably want to consider as the price decreases. Typical reactions include those shown in Box 5.3.

What about the fact that if we take the job at a cheap price, we won't be able to take it later at a greater price? What if our other customers learn about this sort of price? What happens if we take these low paying chairs, tie up our production facilities, and therefore are not able to build more profitable chairs at a later time? Might we desire to take the job at less than $14.2344 in order to keep the work force together? How can we continue to stay in business if we lose money on each job? Must we not make a large amount of profit on some other job?

Box 5.3

These questions are all very reasonable. They do, however, have one thing in common; they all want to include other pertinent criteria. The inclusion of additional criteria means one thing—we have not considered all of the incremental costs in our analysis. Taking the chairs for a cheap price now instead of waiting until the customer is more desperate takes no account of the opportunity cost (perhaps adjusted by a probability estimate) of obtaining this job later on a more favorable basis. Ignoring the price effect of these chairs on our other work assumes that there will be no repercussions on our other customers; clearly in some sorts of marketing environments this is a very unrealistic assumption, and a better model should be constructed. Taking a low paying job that will tie up the facilities of the plant so that better jobs must be passed up indicates that there are not better alternatives or the assignment of a zero opportunity cost to this consideration; another way of viewing the zero opportunity cost assignment is to say that our forecast of future conditions is not good. Taking the job at less than $14.2344 per unit in order to keep the work force together merely means that we are assigning some incremental benefits to keeping the work force together that were not considered in the original incremental analysis.

The question about how one can stay in business and lose money on every job is particularly interesting. Students are often inclined to say that "cheap" jobs can only be taken if other "good" jobs are already being worked on so as to absorb all the overhead costs. The existence of good or bad jobs is basically irrelevant to the analysis, as is the question of whether or not the firm is making an overall profit. If the incremental costs have been properly stated, the decision is clear: Take the job at anything above $14.2344 per unit. If the company loses money and continues to lose money on this basis, it indicates that a mistake in deciding what business to enter was made. The mistake was, however, made at the time of *that* commitment. Those costs associated with going into business, setting up a factory, and building an organization are sunk. They are behind us; assuming that incremental costs and alternatives have been properly stated (there are no other alternatives that would be better), the alternative of taking this job at anything above $14.2344 per unit is better than the alternative of not taking this job.

A related consideration has to do with what price we should ask. The answer to that one is easy; the highest price we can get. Prices are simply not set on the basis of cost, and the only role cost should play in pricing is that the incremental cost should act as a lower bound on the acceptance of a particular job. Many arguments can be put forth against this proposition, but they seem invariably to involve a consideration of additional incremental features to the analysis rather than to repudiate the analysis itself. A good example is the argument that one cannot set an inordinately high price because there will be repercussions on other products or from the government. These potential repercussions may well be genuine; if so, they belong in the incremental analysis. Uncertainty about their existence is no excuse for their failure to be included. Many of the models presented in this course, as well as in quantitative method courses, are directly concerned with model building that includes such uncertainties.

Hard Data versus Soft Data

At the beginning of this section on situation-dependent cost models, we postulated an increase in creative problem identification based upon an elimination of hard-data constraints. Basically, hard data are those descriptors, representations, or models of systems that are readily available in objective form. Data generated by an accounting system are typically regarded as objective. The professionalization of financial accounting stresses objectivity; unfortunately, objectivity does not guarantee relevance, and man's natural desire for objectivity leads to a penchant for hard data that all too often are irrelevant.

Soft data are those descriptors, representations or models of systems that are subjective, individual, and less precise. However, they can be very relevant and more accurate (see Box 5.4).

The distinction between accuracy and precision can be seen by envisioning two scales which weigh a 100 pound weight 1000 times. The weights for the first scale average 100 pounds, but vary from 90 to 110. The weights for the second scale average 105 pounds, but vary from 104 to 106. The first scale is more accurate, the second more precise.

Box 5.4

For most problems, analyses based upon imprecise relevant data are vastly preferable to those based upon precise objective data that are irrelevant. Although few would deny this assertion in its abstract form, the preference for hard data often leads to *ipso facto* denial. The advocacy of using soft data might appear to contradict the position of Chapter 3 that more rigorous explicated models are to be preferred. Such is not the case; we want the most relevant data, irrespective of softness, and we will obtain superior results if those data are utilized in explicit models.

Our belabored chair example is a case in point. When the problem was formulated in an incremental cost model, a decision was reached: Take the job at any price greater than $14.2344 per unit; any price less than $24.30 per unit will result in a loss. It was only when this decision was reached that questions such as present price versus waiting, influence on other customers, tying up facilities, etc. were formulated. Data on these considerations are absolutely critical. The fact that these data will tend to be soft is not an acceptable reason for omitting them from the analysis. A significant strength of the incremental cost model is that it *forces* one to identify what data needs are truly relevant; the objectivity of patterned cost behavior models tends to act as a smokescreen to insightful analysis.

An Assessment

A situation-dependent cost viewpoint is the right one. It allows for the formulation of analyses that are in the best interest of the firm. It is a point of view that each student should attempt to adopt because it will come up again and again in your course in operations management, in other courses, in your careers, and indeed in making decisions about your everyday lives.

The major problem concerned with the incremental cost model lies in making sure that the proper alternatives have been included in the analysis. This is an important point and it is worth noting that it can never be done perfectly (as mentioned in Chapter 3, one cannot design the "perfect" model). The goal, however, is not perfection; it is for a model that is "good" or "better" than alternatives and that speeds the evolution toward improved problem identifications and more relevant data needs.

The noninclusion of relevant costs in analyses can make itself felt in unusual ways. One very relevant cost that many companies fail to consider is the cost to their organizations and executive talent of taking on what individually appear to be appealing alternatives, but collectively aggregate to a company whose name should be "Miscellaneous Ventures Incorporated." There are, however, companies that are keenly aware of this problem and have taken action accordingly. A good example is the Polaroid Corporation which for many years subcontracted the majority of its camera and film-making operations to other companies. Polaroid seemingly did not desire to use its executive talent in trying to meet day-to-day production schedules even though a cursory incremental cost analysis well might have indicated that internal production would be desirable. Rather they appear to have judged that their managerial skill was better spent in exploring the forefronts of technology and in obtaining sweeping patent protection for whatever discoveries could be made.

Such decision making does not mean that incremental analysis is wrong or "shortsighted." The company has identified an alternative action believed to be superior, and the alternative is based upon the inclusion of relevant but soft data. The problem, as with so many system design problems, lies in the criteria set; it is necessary to keep the major goals of the firm clearly in mind and to continually assess the congruity of lower order proximate criteria such as the reduction of objectively measured hard-cost data.

RELEVANCE—FROM WHAT POINT OF VIEW?

As stated at the outset, the goal of this chapter has not been to teach accounting nor to damn the accountant for his models. The financial accountant is concerned with a very worthwhile set of criteria; our goal is to create an increased awareness of these criteria, of the resultant outputs from systems and models designed under these criteria, and of some of the pitfalls awaiting the unwary.

It is worth noting that the outside orientation of financial accounting models is sometimes quite important to internal decision making. Management teams often are quite sensitive to stock prices, earnings, and other financial measures. This sensitivity sometimes leads to rather odd practices such as selling off timber lands at year end and rebuying them in the next year.

The goal in this section is to make each student a more sophisticated consumer of cost data; to create an awareness of the need for tailoring existing data and the need to build additional data generating models in terms of his own set of interests or criteria. In order to further develop this sophistication, this section will present some "war stories" that clearly illustrate the importance of the point of view or criteria set and show the kinds of possible misrepresentations when cost data are twisted to meet particular ends.

Ten Percent of Gross Inefficiency

A West Coast company manufactured small electric motors and related devices for military aircraft which performed such functions as actuating ailerons, retracting landing gear, moving armament into firing positions, and closing cockpit canopies. The ultimate customers for their products were the United States Armed Forces and to a lesser extent the air forces of countries which were equipped with American aircraft, but the company always acted in a subcontracting role with one of the major airframe companies. Contracts were awarded on the basis of bids but the bid information was tempered by the contractor's subjective feelings about a particular subcontractor in terms of many factors, most notably his prior cost overrun experience and his technical competence. The electric motor company was interesting in both regards. The company had a reputation for being able to solve problems that others could not solve; it also had a reputation for serious cost overruns.

A detailed exposition of governmental contractual arrangements is beyond the scope of this book. For this company, the usual procedure was a bid price followed up by a cost audit. The basis for the bid price was an estimate of materials, direct labor, factory burden (as a percentage of direct labor), general and administrative expense (as a percentage of total factory cost), and a profit rate of 10% of total cost. Government auditors concentrated on determining if the actual costs were in line with the estimated costs; they checked materials, direct labor hours, and the appropriateness of overhead rates. If serious discrepancies between actual cost performance and estimated cost performance were observed, the entire contract would be subjected to renegotiation and a price settlement.

The net result of operating within such an environment was quite interesting. The cost review procedure acted as a criterion entity in the day-to-day operations of the plant. At the factory operational level, the usual criterion of a desire for increased productivity was largely absent. In fact, some parts were fabricated in deliberately inefficient ways. The engineering side of the operation also led to inefficiencies; there were times when nonfunctional aspects of parts were held to ridiculously tight dimensional specifications. Both of these activities caused a higher than necessary direct labor cost.

Inefficient as the manufacturing operation was by itself, the direct labor inefficiencies were greatly enlarged by being thereafter subjected to a multiplicative factor for factory overhead and for general and administrative overhead. This particular company had a factory burden rate of 190% and a general and administrative burden rate of 20%; this meant that a dollar in direct labor became a total cost of $3.48. This sort of arithmetic led to an obvious desire to build up factory burden and general administrative expense rates.

The company employed an accountant who was "highly creative." A detailed exposition of how the various creative acts were performed, how the annual reports of the company were able to be certified, and how the company fared with audits from the Internal Revenue Service and other governmental agencies would be a textbook in itself, but a few amusing aspects of the operation are worth noting.

The company had annual sales of approximately $5 million; a government auditor was a bit amazed to find that an account titled "Miscellaneous Factory Expense" had an annual total of $900,000. When he inquired as to what was in it the accountant's typical creative reply was "Oh, a little of this and a little of that; you name it and you can have it." A review of factory supplies, including such items as repair parts, and expendable tooling (taps, dies, drill bits, carbide tip cutting tools, etc.) indicated that most items were carried in about a 15-year supply. These items were written off as current expense whenever they were purchased. It also seemed a bit odd to another auditor that a company of this size should have 23 company cars. Another interesting feature of the record keeping was that there were no raw materials inventories, a full warehouse on the premises notwithstanding. A particularly interesting application of the accountant's criterion of consistency was found in the nonexistence of physical inventory taking. Inventories for all accounting statements were "estimated." When asked how this could possibly be, the obvious answer was that it had always been done that way and they were very consistent.

Other intriguing aspects of the system could be described, but our goal is not merely to tell tales. To say that there was little in the formal accounting records of this company that could be utilized for operations management problems is a gross understatement. The company simply could not glean anything of a realistic nature from its formal record keeping system; relevant data either required a special study or were based on subjective opinion. The interdependencies of recording for various time periods as dictated by periodicity only compounded the problems. A tax avoidance procedure such as buying expendable tools for the future and expensing them currently only postpones the day of reckoning.

When a desire to increase expenses for Year One leads to purchase of tools for Year Two, what does one do at the end of Year Two? There seems to be little alternative but to buy tools for Years Three and Four. For the electric motor company, after 20 years of operation the only viable alternative open for cashing in the accumulated "expenses" seemed to be to sell the company.

It is tempting to conclude that this company was run by dishonest individuals. But, after all, they did not determine the rules of the game. They were acting within that set of rules or criteria and to some extent similar kinds of conditions exist in any organization where sales prices are based on cost. As an economist once nicely put it, "There certainly are a lot more carpets on the floors and pretty secretaries in the public utility companies than there are in New York clothing firms."

Individual Item Profitability

A company manufactured drill bushings which were largely sold through industrial jobbers.* The industrial jobbers who acted as the primary distribution outlet for the bushings were mainly small companies (average annual sales less that $500,000), and carried a wide range of goods such as repair parts for machines, drills, grinding wheels, wrenches, and industrial shelving.

In the United States, many firms of this size had been experiencing a profit squeeze as their costs of operation increased while they were not able to take advantage of the efficiencies available to larger firms, such as computerized paperwork procedures. To combat this trend, the industrial jobbers formed an association with the hope that collectively they could investigate better ways of doing business. They were joined in this association by their suppliers, whose interest in their well-being was obvious.

One of the studies undertaken by this association was an attempt to provide an analytical tool for each jobber to evaluate the individual items which collectively made up his line of goods. The study focused on a method for determining the profitability of each item, and the method selected was one which could be implemented by a company without data-processing equipment. Since profitability involved a computation of cost, some scheme for allocating fixed costs to the various items was necessary; the basis used was "a line of billing," or one line of an invoice. That is, the total overhead expenses were divided by the total lines of billing for a year and the resultant quotient was regarded as the allocated expense per transaction.

The drill bushing company was a progressive company and particularly interested in the well-being of their jobbers. When the new study on item profitability appeared, the company was anxious to see whether it should get involved in helping jobbers implement such a study. A pilot project led to some interesting revelations.

---

*A drill bushing is best thought of as a metal cylindrical doughnut that is heat treated and of very precise dimensions. Drill bushings are used in manufacturing to achieve precise alignments between drilled holes and for other kinds of positioning.

The study indicated that most industrial jobbers when dividing total fixed cost by the number of lines of billing would come out with a quotient of between $2 and $2.50. This meant that a $2 sale, even if the good were acquired for nothing, would not generate any profit and, therefore, would be undesirable. Similarly, a $5 sale with a 40% markup on sales price would not generate any profit. Although the drill bushings carried a high markup, they were usually sold in lots of one or two at a unit price of $2 to $3; thus, under this sort of analysis drill bushings would be deemed inferior. The study's recommended action for inferior products was either to drop them, to demand higher markups, or to decrease inventory and subsequent service provided for these products.

We have noted several times that profit is an accounting convention. As such, it requires some "reasonable" way to allocate cost. The allocation is necessary when we are talking about profit for a specific period or for an individual product. The scheme advocated for the industrial jobbers may perhaps pass the test of reasonableness. It emphatically is not, however, an analytical procedure which yields inferences in line with high order criteria of an industrial supplier. The procedure is arbitrary, and does not take account of actual cost behavior patterns. There is little or no causal relationship between the number of lines of billing processed in a year and the total fixed cost incurred by that company in the same year. To infer that each additional line of billing costs $2.25 or that each line of billing saved would save $2.25 is not only improper, it is misleading. In fact, it is so misleading that one could not help but wonder who was advocating such studies. A check indicated that prominent members of the committee who designed the study were affiliated with companies whose products sold for high prices. Under this particular allocation scheme, their products would look very good even without generous markups.

There are several lessons to be gleaned from this example. First, allocation schemes are basically arbitrary. Second, beware of the biases that absolutely *will* accompany an arbitrary allocation. Third, profit for individual items can be determined under some convention, but one must be so careful about the inferences drawn from individual item profit figures that it is perhaps better not to make such calculations. Profit is, after all, only a surrogate or proximate criterion entity which is used to judge enterprise well-being. When applied to individual products, it is highly possible and indeed probable that inferences will be drawn which will be disadvantageous for the firm, both in terms of a longer term profit calculation and in terms of criterion entities that are not so clearly reflected in the notion of profit.

An example of this latter kind of criterion entity or benefit was illustrated by another study at the drill bushing company. All bushing manufacturers published a catalog and there were approximately 30,000 "standard" sizes of bushings. Of these 30,000 sizes the vast majority of sales was accounted for by less than 100 sizes. Someone raised the question of whether the other sizes were profitable. The answer was that most of these sizes were not profitable, even on an incremental analysis of sales price versus only materials and direct labor.

Should the company then discontinue some of these sizes? The answer is no because the bushing company is not just selling standard sized bushings; their basic mission is to provide a service to their customers and that service is dependent upon customer confidence in the ability of the company to provide a high precision product for whatever need a customer might have. In short, you take the bitter grapes with the sweet.

Still another example of ultimate enterprise benefit as compared to usual short-run measures of effectiveness concerned the notion of "inventory control." One of the industrial suppliers (who had won awards for being among the ten best managed industrial jobbers in the United States) analyzed a particular line of taps and dies and thereafter made the following arrangement with the manufacturer. The jobber would buy a three-year supply of the goods and receive the appropriate quantity discount; he would pay for the goods with a noninterest bearing note payable one year from the date of purchase. The jobber sold the entire stock within six months!

The moral to this story: An almost universally held view that inventory is a necessary evil to be kept at the lowest amount possible is not always true—the existence of inventories can have interesting causal effects on sales. If the implications are interesting to those who sell from inventories, they should be even more interesting to their suppliers. An analysis based upon hard past sales data could not have predicted this outcome.

SUMMARY REMARKS

As stated before, this chapter is intended to increase awareness of how one views cost data. The importance of the point of view means both that one needs to specify data requirements based upon his own set of criteria and that one needs to identify the criteria set possessed by other analysts and thereafter assess the congruity of that criteria set with his own.

We have seen that one must be especially wary of allocation schemes; they are always essentially arbitrary and potentially irrelevant to particular problems. The kinds of errors illustrated by the use of percentage allocations in the breakeven, electric motor, and drill bushing examples clearly indicate the inherent bias in such schemes. A generalized adage is to always be wary of percentages. A further warning might be that when encountering percentages of percentages, start with the hypothesis that something will be misleading.

Financial accounting models are based upon a highly aggregated externally oriented point of view; this leads to cost-data behavioral patterns that can be noncongruent with particular internal problem identifications. A situation-dependent orientation would not be concerned with reasonableness or consistency, with what the firm has done before, or with what other firms are doing. Rather the emphasis would be on models which can provide data tailored to specific needs of specific individuals whenever desired. Many companies working in this direction call this kind of model building "management information systems;" reflected is a broader less patterned approach than that embodied by traditional cost-accounting systems. The design of such management information systems is particularly exciting when viewed from a dynamic or evolutionary viewpoint. As data reveal deviations from standards or expectations, problems are identified and system design efforts are mounted to deal with these problems. When these efforts are successful, the need for data about those areas decreases and other problem areas take on a relatively more important status which in turn calls for different informational needs. A user-oriented modeling environment will speed this evolutionary process.

REFERENCES

Anthony, Robert N., and J. S. Hekimiran, *Operations Cost Control,* Irwin, 1967.

Bierman, Harold, Jr., *Topics in Cost Accounting and Decision,* McGraw-Hill, 1963.

Horngren, Charles T., *Accounting for Management Control: An Introduction,* Prentice-Hall, 1965.

McFarland, Walter B., *Concepts for Management Accounting,* National Association of Accountants, 1966.

McRae, T. W., "Opportunity and Incremental Cost: An Attempt to Define in System Terms," *The Accounting Review,* (April 1970), pp. 315–21.

CHAPTER REVIEW

It may come as a bit of a surprise, but I really do not have anything against my colleagues in accounting departments. To paraphrase an oldie, some of my best friends are accountants. If you get fired-up by what is in this chapter, find inconsistencies with what you think other professors are saying, and engage in some heated discussions, the net result will be improved achievement of commonly shared pedagogical objectives.

It really is quite appropriate for us to be concerned with costs in your operations management course and to assess the proper surrogate relationship of a particular definition of cost to a particular problem. Attacking the criterion of cost minimization borders on heresy, but unquestioning acceptance of either the criterion or an established measurement of the criterion can result in very poor operations system designs.

OUTLINE OF THE CHAPTER

Introduction   (costs for particular criteria)

The financial accounting model   (model validity)

Criteria   (external, highly aggregated orientation)

Cost accounting systems   (disaggregated but external criteria retained)

Cost control   (evolving standards)

Patterned cost behavior models   (presumed patterns)

The breakeven model   (cost-volume-profit relationships)

Fixed and variable costs   (tenuous assumptions)

An assessment   (level of aggregation)

Situation-dependent cost models   (evolving unique data needs)

Incremental cost model   (net difference between decision alternatives)

Examples   (pertinent criteria)

Hard data versus soft data   (penchant for hard data)

An assessment   (proper alternatives)

Relevance—from what point of view?   (criteria)

Ten percent of gross inefficiency   (price versus cost)

Individual item profitability   (beware of allocation schemes)

Summary remarks   (match between data and criteria)

CENTRAL ISSUES

The primary goal of this chapter is to make you a sophisticated consumer of cost data; to better permit you to obtain costs that are relevant to particular decisions. The objective is a decision orientation, where it is the decision which acts as the criterion for dictating the cost. What is a relevant cost for one decision may be quite irrelevant for another.

A major tenet of this chapter is that a situation dependent orientation requires unique cost-data accumulation for each decision, and that it is not possible to keep cost records on an incremental cost basis. The dynamic nature of decision alternatives precludes approaches based upon rigid patterns of cost behavior. Patterned cost models are based upon assumptions that only seem to be appropriate for highly aggregated decisions.

The incremental cost approach can lead to the consideration of highly pertinent decision considerations. Many times data about these considerations tend to be quite soft; we all have a penchant for hard data that can lead to the use of models which obfuscate basic issues.

The ideas were illustrated with several examples including some "war stories" of how to bamboozle with numbers. I really believe that each of you should be aware of how these things can occur if you truly are to become "a sophisticated consumer of cost data."

ASSIGNMENTS

1. What are the annual costs to you as a student for a year of school? For a night school class?
2. The decision reached in the chair example was to take the job for 400 special chairs at any price greater than $14.2344. How many of these digits are significant?
3. An executive at the XYZ Radio and Television Fabricating Company has asked you to comment on the following memo from one of his industrial engineers.

FROM: ED MILLER
TO: A. H. HOWELL
RE: Performance Testing on the TD-47a

I have completed my analysis of the failure data for the TD-47a radio and now believe we should eliminate the final testing for this line. This conclusion is based on the following:

Standard time to test a TD-47a radio	2.3 minutes
Standard hourly wage cost	$2.90
Standard labor cost	.111
Overhead at 175%	.194
Total factory cost	.305
General and administrative at 15%	.045
Total cost for final testing	$.350

An analysis of rejections found by final testing indicates that approximately 3.9% of the radios assembled by this line are rejected by final inspection. Additional rejections due to customer complaints amount to approximately 0.8%.

Assuming that all 4.7% of the bad radios are returned, based upon our normal production of 150,000 units per year we will get back 7,050 radios per year.* Since it will cost no more to fix them when returned from customers than presently, the only incremental cost is for reshipment. The traffic department tells me that the average parcel post rate for this radio would be about $2.75.

Thus, you can see that we will save $.35 on each radio for an annual savings of $52,500 and only be faced with an offsetting cost of $2.75 x 7,050 = $19,387.50. A net savings of $33,112.50

4. The car you presently own is beginning to look a little shabby to you. What are the costs that might be relevant for trading it in on a newer model?

5. The O and R railroad has been setting its freight rates based on the fully allocated costs of its operations. They are faced with declining usage and many runs that show an accounting loss. What is a more rational price policy? What about the loss concept on a particular run? Under what conditions is this loss meaningful?

6. The Western Tool Co. has obtained approval as a supplier of widgets for the Bell system. The space required for production is more than that currently available at their Westwood plant. They intend to move another unrelated project, knuten valve assembly, to another building. They can lease this building for $8,000 annually including all maintenance and thereby free sufficient space at Westwood for widgets. The plant engineer estimates that the move itself will cost $2,500 but that subsequent knuten valve assembly will save the company $1200 to 1400 annually by eliminating inefficiencies in the present layout.

Manufacturing of the widgets requires additional equipment which will be leased at $15,000 a year. This machinery can produce from 20,000 to 50,000 widgets a year, depending on the number of operators. Each operator is capable of producing 5000 units a year and their annual wage averages $6,000. The maintenance crew servicing that part of the plant currently makes $8,000 a year. Each widget uses $1.10 in raw materials and sells for $3.50. Factory burden is allocated at 120% of raw material dollars.

Given that there is no other use for the capacity at Westwood and an expected demand for 35,000 widgets, how desirable is this contract? How vulnerable is Western if demand should drop?

---

*The 7,050 radio figure is probably conservative since some customers would not return a radio for defects not allowed by our inspectors.

CHAPTER 6

CAPITAL BUDGETING

Chapter 5 emphasized that cost data are necessarily determined by particular problems or criteria. We can now proceed to a related but somewhat more clear-cut problem: How to make appropriate adjustments for differences in the *timing* of pertinent costs (and revenues). The relevancy of cost data is important because the vast majority of problems involve cost criteria; the time patterns of those costs and offsetting revenues are also significant since so many system design efforts involve receipts and expenditures which occur over time.

This chapter is concerned with choices among alternatives on the basis of their expense and revenue time patterns. Let us stress again that the most significant aspect of investment decisions frequently lies in the creative determination of alternatives. We will return to this matter in Chapter 7; now we will concentrate instead on the subproblem of how to analyze a specified set of investment alternatives. Our goal is to provide a basic understanding of discounted cash-flow models that is necessary for the investigation of operations management problems. Many of these ideas will be expanded in other courses such as managerial economics and finance.

INVESTMENT DECISIONS

An investment decision involves the comparison of costs with either revenues, cost offsets (decreases in relevant costs), or alternative costs (more than one alternative for accomplishing the same function). These costs, revenues, cost offsets, or alternative costs are typically referred to as "cash flows"; the two most important attributes of these cash flows are their amounts and their timing. If all cash-flow timings were the same, we could make decisions based upon differences in amounts, and if all amounts were the same we could usually make decisions based solely on timings. Since timings and amounts are different, we will find it useful to develop a facility with models that account for differences in timing so that decisions can thereafter be based solely on resultant amounts.

The significance of differences in cash-flow timings is assessed by the concept of interest or discounting which represents the necessary incentive for which individuals or institutions are willing to postpone present uses of cash. The necessary incentive or interest rate is highly dependent upon the larger social system in which individuals or institutions find themselves, and it is not difficult to understand why in some countries the future is more heavily discounted than in others.

Cash Flows

A typical investment decision involves an initial expenditure for some piece of equipment which thereafter generates benefits (revenues or cost reductions). An example is the proposed conveyor for chair building at Westfall; let us assume that this investment would eliminate the need for two of the present workers. Suppose Westfall could buy this equipment at a price of $100,000, and that each of the replaced workers had an associated incremental cost of $8,000 per year. Is this a good investment?

In analyzing this investment, it is necessary to address ourselves to the second important attribute of cash flows, i.e., their timing. Specifically, for how many years will Westfall reap the benefits of this investment? What is the economic life of this asset? Clearly if the piece of equipment is to last for only one year, it does not seem to be a good investment; the longer it lasts the more revenues are generated and the more desirable the investment decision becomes. Let us say that the economic life of this piece of equipment is ten years. Figure 6.1 is a graphical model of the relevant cash flows for this investment decision. Note in Fig. 6.1 that the initial expenditure of $100,000 is shown as a negative cash flow in "year zero" and that the first positive cash flow of $16,000 occurs in period 1. This notation allows us to take into account the necessary passage of time after the investment is made until returns are realized from that investment. Figure 6.1 is, of course, a model of a fairly simple investment decision; the model however can readily accommodate a more complicated set of cash flows. Let us hypothesize an alternative conveyorized chair-building system with the same basic investment and cost-savings pattern but requiring an overhaul in the fifth year costing $20,000 and having a salvage value of $25,000 at the end of its economic life. These additional relevant cash-flow considerations can be readily reflected in the model (note that by convention only the *net* cash flow in each period is considered). Figure 6.2 depicts the alternative investment with the additional considerations.

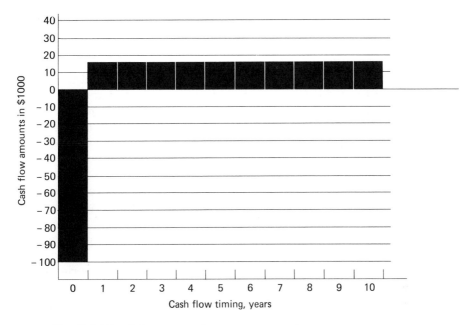

Fig. 6.1 Westfall conveyor investment.

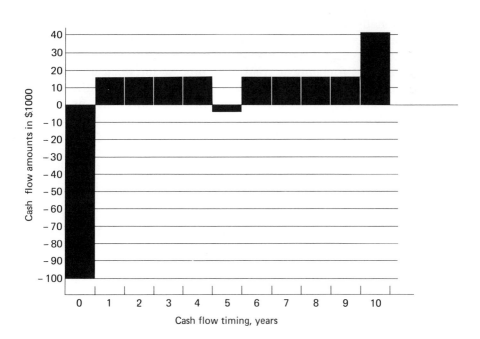

Fig. 6.2 Alternative conveyor investment.

Relevant Costs

Chapter 5 was devoted to an exposition of relevant costs, and those general ideas can now be made somewhat more explicit in terms of their influence on investment decisions. As the individual or unique aspects of each investment decision necessitate efforts being mounted to determine the appropriate incremental costs, we need to look beyond the data generated by financial accounting models to obtain cost information for investment decisions.

The notion of *sunk costs* is particularly germane to investment decisions. A cost is said to be sunk if there is no ability to recoup it. Thus for example, if the Westfall Furniture Company spent $80,000 to construct a new additional dry kiln, the $80,000 (minus some appropriate salvage or resale value) becomes sunk or unavailable to the firm immediately after being expended. This economic reality must be appropriately reflected in any subsequent investment decision. If after building a new dry kiln an alternative investment decision became available or known, the $80,000 expenditure should have no influence on that investment choice (naturally the *conditions* established by the $80,000 expenditure have a bearing on the additional investment choice—it is the new "norm" from which an incremental change is measured). The accounting model for depreciation, which is based on the two major criteria (sometimes conflicting) of reasonably matching costs to associated revenues and minimizing taxes within constraints established by taxing authorities, is simply not appropriate for recognizing the economic realities of sunk costs.

Suppose that a chemical treatment process for wood is developed which eliminates the need for dry kilns, and that the chemically treated wood costs $0.01 per bd. ft. more than untreated wood. Let us further suppose that the new kiln drys wood at a cost of $0.02 per bd. ft. and the old kilns at $0.03 per bd. ft. In what way does the $80,000 expenditure for the new dry kiln influence the decision to use chemically treated wood? The only way it does is in the determination of operating conditions. Moreover, the $0.02 per bd. ft. cost needs to be carefully scrutinized before comparing it to the chemical treatment alternative. Our interest is in only the direct or out of pocket cost. Any depreciation or other expenditures which will be unaffected by a change to chemically treated wood should not be included. Depending on how the costs have been calculated, it may still be more economically advantageous to use existing dry kilns or it may not be. In either case, the $80,000 expenditure has no direct relevance.

A consideration related to sunk costs is the opportunity cost associated with the periodic decrease in the resale or salvage value of an asset. The amounts of these decreases are usually not appropriately represented by accounting depreciation models; they are determined by the economic realities involved in particular situations. The anticipated decrease in resale value of a particular asset over the next time period should be considered as an opportunity cost of not selling the asset now. Thus, if one purchased an automobile for $2,000, could resell it for the same amount, and expected that a year later the automobile could be sold for only $1,500, there is a $500 opportunity cost involved in keeping the automobile for an additional year. A related opportunity cost concerns having potentially realizable funds tied up in a salable asset. If the car were sold for $2,000, that amount could be put into a bank to earn interest or be invested in some alternative investment choice (there are, of course, other considerations and costs associated with automobile purchases, e.g., anticipated repairs, comfort, style, status, etc.).

Models for estimating the fall in salvage or resale value for an asset may yield results that are at variance with actual conditions. But as noted in Chapter 5, however, a lack of hard data does not eliminate the need for considering such costs as relevant.

An appropriate consideration for determining relevant costs for particular investment decisions is economic life. Economic life is again a highly situation-oriented matter that is not necessarily related to the depreciation life used in the accounting model. Technological changes in assets and in uses of the assets, i.e., obsolescence or replacement for reasons beyond simple wear and tear, determine economic life. Social pressures for mass transportation systems, pollution free automobiles, clean rivers, etc., will cause many assets to be discarded before worn out. If two firms purchased identical fork lift trucks but one used the investment as a stopgap procedure until a conveyorized material-handling system was installed, clearly the economic realities and therefore the "economic lives" of these two investment decisions would be quite different. However, one cannot say that one of these companies has made a better investment choice than the other solely because the economic life is longer. The length of the economic life is but one consideration; the situation dependent decision must be based on the associated revenues or cost offsets as well as on the alternative possibilities.

PRESENT VALUE

Figures 6.1 and 6.2 depict the cash flow characteristics of two investment possibilities. In discussing these investments, we have yet to consider their desirability. Figure 6.1 involves an expenditure of $100,000 and an offsetting ten-year annual cost savings of $16,000. However, to simply compare $100,000 with $160,000 does not take account of the timing of these flows; there is no consideration given to the time value of money. The $16,000 to be received in year 10 simply does not have the immediate economic worth of the $16,000 to be received in year 1. The $16,000 to be received in year 9 also does not have the economic worth of the $16,000 to be received in year 1, although the year 9 cash flow is more valuable than the year 10 cash flow. Similar statements can be made about all 10 cash flows. And since the 10 cash flows differ in economic worth, it is not appropriate to add them together without making a transformation to a common economic base. The present value model is concerned with making this transformation.

The Model

Present value takes account of the economic reality of time varying cash flows by explicitly recognizing the time value of money through the concept of interest or discounting. Thus if we put $1.00 in a bank or savings and loan institution and leave it there for a year, we expect to get back more than $1.00 at the end of that year. Similarly if we want to have $1.00 at the end of the year, we need to invest less than $1.00 at present. If a bank pays 10% interest, $1.00 invested now would be worth $1.10 in one year and $1.21 in two years ($1.00 plus 10% of $1.00 plus 10% of $1.10). The general formula for calculating interest in this way can be expressed as:

$$S = P(1+i)^n.$$

where S is equal to the sum that is compounded or accumulated over time, P is the principal sum that is initially invested, i is the annual interest rate, and n is the number of years for which the principal is invested. Thus in our 10% interest example given above, the sum that would be available at the end of the first year is equal to the principal P($1.00) multiplied by $1+i$(1.1) raised to the nth (1) power. Thus $S = \$1.00 (1.1)^1$ or $S = \$1.10$. The $1.10 that would be available at the end of the first year could be considered as a new principal P reinvested at the end of the first period for one additional year and would therefore be multiplied by the same $(1.1)^1$ to achieve the $1.21 at the end of the second year. Such a procedure, however, is tedious and unnecessary; it does not take a great deal of mathematical sophistication to see that the same result would be achieved by multiplying the original principal P($1.00) by the $1+i$ term which has been squared (1.1 × 1.1 = 1.21). The fact that the term is squared reflects that the number of periods or years is two; corresponding power adjustments are made as n increases.

By simple manipulation the compound interest formula for a single sum given above can be restated as:

$$P = \frac{S}{(1+i)^n}.$$

This formula now expresses the present equivalent of a future sum rather than the future equivalent of a present sum. Thus for the 10% example, if we know we desire the sum S of $1.21 two years from today, we can solve for P (the amount needed for present investment) and come up with $1.00. If we desire $1.00 a year from today we can solve for its present equivalent ($1.00 ÷ 1.1) and come up with $0.9091. If we desire $1.00 two years from now, since we know that $0.9091 one year from now will be compounded into $1.00 the following year, we presently need some amount less than $0.9091 which when compounded by the 10% interest factor will yield $0.9091 one year from now. That amount is $0.8264 which is merely $0.9091 divided by 1.1 or multiplied by 0.9091 (which is 1 ÷ 1.1). Note also that as was true when calculating future sums, tedium can be avoided by first computing the n power term in the denominator; thus $1.00 ÷ (1+.1)^2 = 1 ÷ 1.21 = 0.8264.

We have examined two kinds of compound interest models. One is directed to finding the sum to which a known present investment would accumulate over a period of time; the other, to finding the present equivalent of a known future sum. Either of these approaches can be applied to investment decisions, but the more straightforward convention of discounting future cash flows to their present equivalents is widely used. That is, it is possible to compound each of the cash flows given in Fig. 6.1 to its equivalent amount at the end of the ten-year period, at which time the compounded $100,000 outlay can be compared with the sum of the compounded ten annual cash inflows. It is more straightforward, however, to make no adjustment to the present $100,000 initial cash flow that is being considered for investment, but instead to discount each of the ten future cash flows to its present equivalent. When all of the future flows have been discounted to their present equivalents, the comparison is made.

Another alternative that is sometimes used is to determine equivalent uniform annual costs. Thus if the $100,000 investment were made with funds "borrowed" at 10%, and the loan was paid back over the ten-year life of the asset, we will see that the annual payment would be approximately $16,275. The appeal of this method, however, is limited since actual cash flows rarely match the equivalent flows.

The act of discounting or of compounding involves a highly individualistic discount rate or rate of interest that implies an indifference to two alternatives. So if *your* rate of interest or discount rate is 10%, you would be completely indifferent to a proposal that you are to receive $0.9091 today, $1.00 a year from now, or $1.10 two years from now. If one of these three alternatives is more desirable to you than another, then 10% is not *your* rate. If $0.9091 today is more desirable than $1.00 one year from today, we can infer that your interest or discount rate is greater than 10%. If we now ask you whether you prefer $0.8333 today to $1.00 one year from today and you reply that you prefer $1.00 a year from today, we can infer that your rate of interest is less than 20%. If through a trial and error process we find that you are completely indifferent to $1.00 a year from today and $0.8772 today we can infer that your discount or interest rate is 14%.

Thus far we have limited our discussion to single payments. In making appropriate adjustments to the cash flows depicted in Fig. 6.1, we can discount each of the ten $16,000 future cash flows as an individual sum. At a 10% rate of interest, since $0.9091 is the present equivalent of $1.00 a year from today, the present equivalent of $16,000 one year from today is $16,000 multiplied by 0.9091 or $14,545.60. The second year's $16,000 cash flow is appropriately discounted by multiplying by 0.8264 (0.909 squared). Note that there is an assumption that the first year cash flows are all realized at the end or last day of the first year. We will come back to this assumption at the end of this major section.

It is not difficult to see that since $16,000 is being multiplied by two separate numbers (0.9091 and 0.8264) the sum of these two cash flows can be obtained by multiplying $16,000 by the sum of the two factors, 1.7355. Finding an equation to calculate the present value of a sum of uniform future cash flows involves a modest amount of algebraic manipulation to yield:

$$P = A \ \frac{(1+i)^n - 1}{i (1+i)^n}$$

where P is the present sum of a discounted series of uniform future payments of amount A, i is the interest rate, and n is the number of periods over which the uniform future cash flow is to be paid or received.

In actual practice, working with the present value formulas for either a single sum or a uniform series of payments would be tedious because of the necessity for raising $1+i$ to the nth power. To facilitate easy calculation of present values for single payments and uniform series, two tables of factors are presented as Appendix A and Appendix B at the end of the book. A perusal of Appendix A will show that for the 10% interest rate the factor for one period is 0.9091 and 0.8264 for two periods (expressed to four decimal places). These factors when multiplied by $1.00 yield the $0.9091 and $0.8264 in the previous examples. Appendix B at the 10% interest rate will show the first period factor as again 0.9091. The obvious reason that the two first factors are the same in the two tables is that for one period there is only a single payment. The second entry for the second period in Appendix B at 10% is given as 1.7355. This is the sum of the two factors given in Appendix A for periods 1 and 2 (minor differences in rounding will sometimes occur).

To obtain equivalent present values for either a single payment or uniform series, one need only go to Appendix A or Appendix B, select the proper rate of interest and the proper period, obtain the corresponding factor, and multiply that factor by the particular amount of the payment or payments.

Tables also exist for finding equivalent uniform annual amounts; entries in these tables are reciprocals of those in Appendix B. Thus the entry for 10%, ten years in Appendix B is 6.1446, and $1 \div 6.1446 = 0.16275$; when multiplied by $100,000 we obtain an annual amount of $16,275, as we indicated above.

Examples

Let us now finally evaluate the investment decision presented as Fig. 6.1. In that investment, $100,000 was to be expended for an annual saving of $16,000 over a ten-year period. The present value of the $100,000 is in fact $100,000, i.e., the appropriate multiplicative factor is 1.00. Thus the analysis may be as follows:

Cash Flows

Negative: Positive:

			P.V. Factor	
$100,000 x 1.000 = $100,000	Year	Amount	(Appendix A)	
	1	$16,000 x	0.9091 =	$14,545.60
	2	16,000 x	0.8264 =	13,222.40
	3	16,000 x	0.7513 =	12,020.80
	4	16,000 x	0.6830 =	10,928.00
	5	16,000 x	0.6209 =	9,934.40
	6	16,000 x	0.5645 =	9,032.00
	7	16,000 x	0.5132 =	8,211.20
	8	16,000 x	0.4665 =	7,464.00
	9	16,000 x	0.4241 =	6,785.60
	10	16,000 x	0.3855 =	6,168.00
		Total		$98,312.00

Negative Flows = $100,000
Positive Flows =   98,312
Net Loss*   = $ 1,688

---

*Although the term "loss" is used here, it should be recognized that we are not referring to losses with the required accounting convention as described in Chapter 5; perhaps a more appropriate term would be "disadvantage."

A much less tedious alternative is:

Negative Cash Flows:		Positive Cash Flows (using Appendix B):
$100,000 x 1.000 = $100,000	less	16,000 x 6.1446 = <u>98,313.60</u>
		Net Loss = $ 1,686.40

The difference between the $98,313.60 obtained by the alternative and the $98,312.00 obtained initially is due to rounding errors. This can be proved by summing the individual multiplicative factors used initially (total = 6.1445). The difference (0.0001) multiplied by $16,000 yields the difference between the alternative methods ($1.60).

By the above analysis the proposed conveyorized chair-building investment appears undesirable; it would seem, therefore, that the proposal should be turned down. The additional features of the alternative equipment choice as modeled by Fig. 6.2 ($20,000 overhaul cost in period 5 and $25,000 salvage value at the end of ten years) may or may not make this proposal more attractive. In investigating this question, each of the cash flows could be considered individually as above; alternatively, we need only consider the incremental aspects.

Incremental Cash Flows

Negative:	$20,000 x 0.6209 =	$12,418
Positive:	$25,000 x 0.3855 =	<u>$ 9,637.50</u>
Incremental net loss		$ 2,780.50

Thus even though the $25,000 salvage value appears at first glance to be more desirable than the $20,000 overhaul cost, when the timing of these two flows is taken into account it can be seen that the net result is an incremental loss of $2,780.50.

Let us turn to one further example. Suppose a firm is considering two different kinds of typewriters. One is an economy model costing $250 which is expected to last for 2 1/2 years and thereafter have no salvage value. The second more expensive model costs $600, has an economic life of 5 years, and is expected to have a $50 trade-in value at the end of 5 years. In addition, the second typewriter has certain features which seem to add to productivity, e.g., automatic carriage return. One estimate of the incremental value of the additional productivity features is $50 per year. Question: Which typewriter is more desirable if the company's discount rate is 8%?

One of the key aspects of this example is that the two alternatives cannot be compared without making some provision for the difference in their economic lives. Since the cheaper model typewriter has an economic life half that of the more expensive model, it is possible to compare one $600 typewriter to a series of two $250 typewriters. However, since the

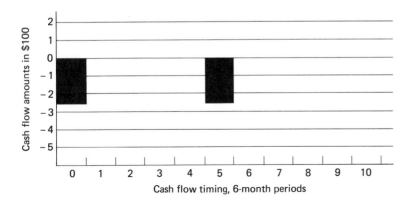

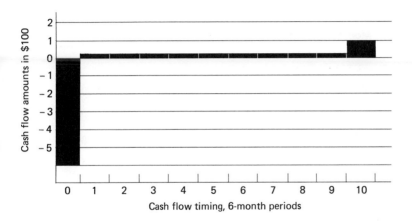

Fig. 6.3 Economy model typewriter (top), more expensive model typewriter (bottom).

second typewriter will not be purchased for 2 1/2 years, it is necessary to discount that second expenditure to its present equivalent. Another feature of this investment comparison is the fact that we are using half-year intervals. The simplest way to handle this complication is to express the annual interest rate of 8% as a semiannual rate of 4% for each half-year period, with the first typewriter having an economic life of 5 six-month periods and the second typewriter having an economic life of 10 six-month periods. Figure 6.3 depicts these two investments in diagrammatic form.

Note that the second expenditure of $250 for the economy model is shown in period 5. One might wonder whether this cash flow should be shown in period 6 since the typewriter is purchased after 5 periods. Remember, however, that the factors given in the table make the assumption that the flow occurs at the end of the period. Note also that the $50 operating advantage per year for the more expensive model is shown in Fig. 6.3 as $25 per period since each period is of six months duration. An analysis of the two alternatives follows:

Economy Model Typewriter

Negative cash flows:
Period 0: $250 x 1.0000 =	$250.00
Period 5: $250 x .8219 =	$205.48
Total outlay	$455.48

More Expensive Model Typewriter

Negative cash flow:
Period 0: $600 x 1.0000 =	$600.00

Positive cash flows:

Periods 1-10: $25 x 8.1111 =	$202.78	
Period 10: $50 x .6756 =	33.78	$236.56
Net outlay		$363.44
Net advantage — more expensive model over economy model		$ 92.04

Thus, it can be seen that the more expensive typewriter is a better investment opportunity than the economy model. It is worth noting, however, that this conclusion pivots on the incremental benefits associated with increased productivity. In the event that the viewpoint on the incremental nature of this benefit changes (perhaps there is a fixed amount of work for a secretary to do in a year and that amount will be accomplished with either typewriter), our conclusion about the relative desirability of the two typewriters would change.

An Assessment

The discounting of future cash flows to their present value equivalents allows one to compare diverse expenditure patterns on a common ground. The methodology is sound and conforms to the way most businessmen view their own situations in terms of interest or the costs of borrowing. Thus in any consideration of a conveyorized chair line at Westfall, the stream of benefits occurring over time needs to be properly compared to the initial cost of the line.

One "shortcoming" of the present value method as presented here concerns the assumption that all cash flows occur at the end of a year. In the typewriter example considered above this assumption was somewhat mitigated by using 6 month instead of one year periods. One can easily see the extension of this sort of thinking to monthly, daily, and hourly discounting periods. A logical extension is to go to what is called "continuous discounting," which is most often used in situations where small differences are important because of the large sums of money involved, such as for bonds. For the kinds of problems addressed in this book, such a level of sophistication is unnecessary; differences in analytical results will usually be large enough so that minor differences in discounting methods would not lead to different conclusions. When a choice of discounting model would change the analytical conclusion, it is usually desirable to appeal to the criteria system which recognizes discounted present value as but one surrogate criterion for assessing the worth of an investment; put another way, when the analytical results are close, conclusions should probably be based on other, perhaps qualitative, considerations.

Another problem with the present value method has to do with how one selects a particular interest or discount rate. Why did we use 10% for the Westfall Furniture Company examples? Why 8% for the typewriter example? Where did these numbers come from? Were the results of the first example ($100,000 outflow, $98,312 inflow) "close enough?" How do we tell? To a large extent, providing answers to these kinds of questions is beyond our present scope and are the sources of considerable discussion in managerial economics and finance courses. In a limited way, however, further insights are provided by the rate of return model to which we now turn our attention.

RATE OF RETURN

The rate of return model for evaluating investment decision is based on the same general concepts used for the present value model; future cash flows are discounted to their present equivalents. The major difference between the two models is that whereas the present value model starts with a given interest or discount rate, discounts all future flows back to their present equivalents, and thereafter judges one set of flows against another, the rate of return model does not take as input the interest or discount rate. Rather the rate of return model takes a given set of cash flows and finds that interest or discount rate which will equate the inflows with the outflows. That particular rate is said to be the "rate of return." This rate can thereafter be subjected to managerial scrutiny to ascertain the goodness of the investment decision in the light of the risks involved and other considerations.

It is sometimes felt that the informational content given by the rate of return model exceeds that given by the present value model. This is so because in strict application of the present value model, a particular investment possibility either passes or fails on the basis of the previously selected interest or discount rate. In such application, it is a go-no go procedure rather than one which assigns a variable measure of goodness to each particular investment possibility.*

The Model

Since the rate of return model utilizes the same concepts of discounting as present value, the formulae given above also apply to the rate of return model. Unfortunately there is no way to directly solve for a rate of return for a particular set of cash flows. There are some methods which zero in quickly on the appropriate rate, and there are existing computer programs which will give the rate of return for a particular set of cash flows. All of these procedures involve some "cut and try" and that method of attack can be utilized for the examples previously represented.

Let us start with the first example, the $100,000 initial negative cash flow versus a ten-year annual positive cash flow of $16,000 (Fig. 6.1). In evaluating this investment opportunity by the present value method, we discovered that a 10% discount rate produced a total positive cash flow of $98,313.60 versus a negative cash flow of $100,000. This means that the rate of return for this investment possibility is less than 10%. It does not appear to be a great deal less than 10%, however. Let us try an 8% rate. At the 8% rate, the appropriate present value factor for an annuity of 10 periods is 6.7101. When multiplied by $16,000 the result is $107,361.60. Since this sum exceeds the $100,000 outlay, we now know that the rate of return is more than 8% and less than 10%. We also can ascertain that since the 8% rate shows a difference of $7,361.60 and the 10% rate shows a difference of $1,686.40, the actual rate is closer to 10%. Solving for 9.5% yields a total discounted cash flow of $460.77 for the ten year annuity. The actual or equating rate of return is 9.61%.

The second example was the same as the first with the addition of a $20,000 negative cash flow in period 5 and a $25,000 positive cash flow in period 10. If we now look at this total package of cash flows (Fig. 6.2), we might again start by utilizing the 8% discount rate. If we do so, the present value for the annuity of $16,000 per year for ten years totals $107,361.60 as per above. The negative and positive cash flows in periods 5 and 10 respectively are discounted by the appropriate present value factors (0.6806 and 0.4632) to yield a net cash outflow of $2032 ($13,612

---

*Some authorities would disagree with this assessment, saying that net gain or excess discounted present value is the variable to be maximized. See for example, Harold Bierman, Jr., and Seymour Smidt, *The Capital Budgeting Decision*, 2nd Ed., Macmillan, 1966, p. 39.

– 11,580). This means that with the total set of cash flows discounted at the 8% rate, positive flows total $105,329.60; the rate is again greater than 8% but, as expected, not as high as previously (the equating rate is 9.53%).

Incremental Rates

Another way of viewing the second example is to find the incremental rate of return for that part of the investment which is different from the first example. That is, we know from the first example that the rate of return for that investment opportunity is 9.61%. Now the question becomes: what rate are we earning on the $20,000 outlay in period 5 which is offset by the $25,000 inflow in period 10? A cut and try approach finds 4% to be fairly close. The $20,000 outlay in period 5 takes on a present value of $16,438 whereas the $25,000 inflow at the end of period 10 takes on a present value of $16,890 (solving for a more exact rate yields 4.56%).

Through incrementally examining the rate of return, it is possible to better compare competing investment opportunities with differing cash flow patterns. Thus, if two alternative investment choices yield rates of 40% and 30% respectively, but the second involves a larger, sum (it is more desirable to make 30% of a dollar than 40% of a penny), it is possible to find the rate of return on the incremental or additional amount invested in the second opportunity. Although the rate will be below 30%, it well may be judged adequate, indicating that the second alternative with a rate of 30% is to be preferred to the first alternative with a rate of 40%.

Let us illustrate this with a concrete example. Suppose that Westfall was faced with two alternative ways to expand chair-building capacity. The first involved an expenditure of $20,000 that would yield a $7,000 annual return for five years. The second alternative was a larger scale change, costing $100,000 and yielding a $30,000 annual return for five years. Which one of these investment alternatives should Westfall take? The first investment alternative has a rate of return of approximately 22%; the second alternative, approximately 15%. Although the 22% rate of return seems more appealing, we should recall the warnings presented in Chapter 5 about using surrogate criteria based on percentages. The second alternative represents an incremental investment (over the first alternative) of $80,000 and an incremental annual return of $23,000. The rate of return on this incremental investment is approximately 13.5%, which well might be considered adequate or desirable (this return is *in addition* to the 22% return on the $20,000 investment).

In the comparison of the two typewriters by the present value method, we were able to say that the more expensive model was superior to the economy model when the interest rate was 8%. Since the analysis eliminated all revenues or positive cash flows that were the same for the two alternatives (not incremental to the decision), the kind of question we now ask is slightly different. Instead of solving for a rate of return that is thereafter judged for adequacy, we can solve for that interest or discount rate which will make us indifferent to the two alternatives. The judgment or managerial choice then becomes one of asking whether the situation warrants using such a high discount or interest rate. The higher the interest or discount rate used, the more current income at the expense of the future is favored; and therefore the decision will tend to favor the less expensive typewriter with its small initial outlay.

The rate of interest at which the decision shifts from favoring the more expensive model typewriter to the economy model typewriter is at slightly more than 16% (present value of the economy model cash flows equal $420.25, and more expensive model cash flows equal $409.10 for an annual rate of interest of 16%—the equating rate is 17.28%). The decision then is, if one's discount or interest rate is in excess of 17.28%, to buy the economy model; if one's discount or interest rate is less than 17.28% then the more expensive model should be purchased. If 17.28% appears to be about right, the decision should be made on the basis of other criteria. As a corollary, assuming that no other criteria were involved, we can make inferences about one's discount or interest rate based on the action taken on this particular investment choice.

An Assessment

Rate of return is a surrogate criterion entity often used for assessing economic performance. Unfortunately there are many ways of computing what is called "rate of return." The model presented in this chapter is also referred to as the yield method; by discounting all cash flows, it is a more appropriate model for investment decisions than those rate-of-return models which are based on averages or do not make adjustments for the time value of money.

Since the rate of return model is based upon the same concept of discounting or interest as that used in the present value model, information about investment decisions obtained by the two procedures tends to be somewhat similar. However, many decision makers prefer to know the equating rate of return so that it can be subjected to scrutiny rather than to state a rate before the analysis. Thus Westfall executives might deem the equating rate of return on an investment to be more important than knowledge that the investment has passed a specified present value test. They might feel that they have more information about the economic desirability of the investment. On the other hand, some executives are more inclined to use net present value. The choice is somewhat a matter of individual preference, but the overall objective is the same in either case: to appropriately assess economic realities with maximum information. We will see that the concept of "present value profile" provides even more information than either of the basic models.

As noted in our discussion of incremental rates, one has to be wary of stating the surrogate criterion as maximization of the rate of return. A related problem is that for some investment decisions there is more than one discounting rate of return which will equate the cash inflows to the cash outflows. This situation most typically happens when periods of net cash inflows are dispersed with periods of net cash outflows. Proper analysis of these nonconventional investment situations with the rate of return model is somewhat complex and beyond our present scope.

PAYBACK

The payback or payoff model for investment decisions is based on the appealing concept of finding the period of time necessary for an investment to be paid for from the savings it generates. Widely used in industry, the payback model is often used improperly. It is worthy of our study for both reasons.

The Model

The payback period in years is usually calculated by dividing the cost of the investment by the annual cost saving or revenue generated by that investment. Thus if a proposed piece of equipment costing $10,000 would generate a $2,000 annual savings over the present equipment, the proposal may be said to "pay for itself" in five years.

Analysis of the first of the three major examples we have been considering with the payback model is quite straightforward, with a payoff period of 6.25 years ($100,000 divided by $16,000). The second major example, where we add the negative cash flow in period 5 and a positive cash flow in period 10, is somewhat more cumbersome to analyze with this model. By referring back to Fig. 6.2, one can see an accumulated positive cash flow of $64,000 at the end of the fourth period. The $4,000 negative cash flow during the fifth period brings the accumulated total down to $60,000 at the end of the fifth year. Adding the $32,000 for the sixth and seventh years brings the total to $92,000. Half of the eighth year is required to accumulate the total $100,000. Therefore the second investment may be said to pay for itself in 8.5 years.

The third major example, the choice between alternative typewriters, is not well suited to analysis by the payback method since there is no cost saving or revenue function included (nonincremental to the decision). That is, the question we are concerned with is not whether there will be a typewriter, but which typewriter shall be purchased. It would be possible, however, to calculate some sort of incremental payback period based on the difference between the more expensive model and the cheaper model and the incremental operating advantage generated from the more expensive model, but such an analysis would produce results that are a bit obscure in terms of usual payback meaning. This analysis should also address the way in which the cash flows of periods 5 and 10 should be adjusted to account for the time value of money (At what rate should the flows be discounted?).

Unfortunately there are attributes of many investment decisions which require similar adjustments in order to permit evaluation by the payback method. The most notable of these is salvage value. If two alternative investments have the same cost, the same economic life, and the same associated revenue, but differ solely in that one has a terminal salvage value and the other does not, clearly the one with a salvage value is preferable on economic grounds and should, therefore, be favored by an investment decision model. The present value and rate of return models would have no trouble discounting that salvage cash flow. To be an acceptable model, the payback method should also discount that incremental cash flow and subtract it from the initial cost; to do so, however, requires a discount rate, and we will see that the most reasonable rate is based upon the rate of return.

Misuse

The payback method for evaluating investment decisions is, unfortunately, often misused. The misuse stems from the adoption of a standard or criterion for payback periods that does not take account of the economic life of the asset. Thus, for example, many firms make statements such as "all investments must payback in less than 3 years." This represents a misuse of the payback model because it is very possible under such a system to eliminate good investment possibilities and to accept bad investment possibilities. If an investment cost $1,000, generated savings of $500 per year, but only lasted for two years, it would be a poor investment although it pays back in two years. Similarly, an investment with a long economic life such as a building might be highly attractive but not able to be paid back by savings in three years. Although these examples are extreme, they are possible; less extreme cases can at least cause an improper ordering of priorities for investment decisions.

The way in which the payback method is properly used is to take explicit account of economic life through a calculation of the associated rate of return. This is most easily seen by returning to the first major example, where we found that the payoff period was 6.25 years. If we now turn again to Appendix B, the present value table for annuities, we can find the associated rate of return directly. The way this is done is to go down the lefthand column (periods) to the economic life of the asset, in this case ten years. In going across that row of numbers we will notice that 1% is 9.4713, 6% is 7.3601, etc. The numbers steadily decrease. If we keep going until the numbers reach 6.25 (the payback period) we will arrive at an associated rate of return of somewhere between 9 and 10%. The rate of return for that investment is in fact 9.6% as we have previously determined.

There should be no particular mystery about this procedure; in our desire to find the rate of return for this investment, we searched for a multiplicative factor to apply to the stream of ten annual $16,000 payments to yield a result of $100,000 (the initial cost). It is not suprising that dividing the $100,000 by the $16,000 will yield that multiplicative factor directly.

Perusal of any row of Appendix B will yield results that match our common sense. Continuing on the ten year row, we note that the shorter the payoff period, the higher the rate of return. Conversely, as the payoff period nears ten years (the economic life) the rate of return approaches zero.

Associated rates of return can be determined for other investment decisions as analyzed by the payback criterion, but a certain amount of bias will creep in as the cash-flow pattern tends to vary from that depicted in Fig. 6.1. We noted that the second investment showed a payout in 8.5 years. Using the Appendix B procedure, we ascertain that the associated rate of return is approximately 3%. The 3% rate of return calculation, however, is somewhat erroneous. In our discussion of the rate of return model above, we calculated that the rate of return for this investment choice was 9.53%. The difference can be largely accounted for by the peculiar payback feature of period 5 actually detracting from the payout condition and period 10 adding nothing to it.

Thus when payback is converted to an associated rate of return through the table of present value factors for annuities, distortion will occur when the cash flow pattern varies from the single initial negative cash flow and a subsequent uniform series of positive cash flows.

An Assessment

The payback period model for investment decisions is a proper procedure only if explicit recognition of the economic life and associated rate of return are considered. This can be done by adopting a rate of return (as per the present value method), and deriving the associated maximum payback periods for various economic lives from the table of present value factors for annuities; alternatively, associated rate of return can be determined by calculating the payback period for a particular investment choice, and using the table of present value factors for annuities with the particular economic life to determine the associated rate of return, which can thereafter be judged for adequacy (as per the rate of return method).

As we noted in our examples above, payback periods converted to associated rates of return through tables for present value factors for annuities will work well for uniform series, but they will yield odd results for investment decisions whose cash flow patterns vary significantly from the simple uniform series case. To some extent, the notion of payback only really makes sense for the uniform series case. That is, if an asset costing $5,000 returns nothing in 4 years and then returns $10,000 during the fifth year, we can calculate the payoff period as 4.5 years, but one wonders just what it means. It simply seems that the notion of payback is associated with funds coming in at somewhat of a uniform rate.

To the extent that payback is only properly considered when one derives the associated rate of return, it can be argued that perhaps the payback method should not be used and that investment decisions should be based on the rate of return model or present value model.

TAXES

Up to this point our discussion has omitted the effect of taxes on investment choices so that attention could be focused on the models themselves without confusing appurtenances. It is obviously important to know whether rates of return, present values, or payback periods are based on before or after tax considerations. It is also obvious that it is more realistic to make such calculations on an after-tax basis, since taxes represent significant cash flows. There is, however, no conceptual change in the way in which the models operate.

Depreciation

In order to determine after-tax flows, it is necessary to determine taxes; in order to determine taxes, it is usually necessary to refer to the financial accounting model which calculates depreciation of assets for tax purposes. The ways in which these calculations are made can dramatically affect the timing of net cash flows and therefore affect the relative desirability of investment choice.

To illustrate the impact of depreciation calculations on investment choices, let us examine the difference between double-declining balance depreciation and straight-line depreciation and how it influences tax timing and therefore cash flow characteristics and assessments. Let us return to our first major example and assume a ten-year depreciation life (it could easily be more or less than the economic life, but we will make them the same for this example). Let us further assume that there is no salvage value so that for a straight-line depreciation method the associated depreciation cost would be $10,000 per year. If the company were in the 50% tax bracket, it would pay a tax of $3,000 per year on the incremental increase in income for the ten-year period [50% (16,000 – 10,000)].

The after tax rate of return can now be calculated to be 5.08%. If, however, the company instead used double-declining balance depreciation, the following set of annual depreciation figures, taxes, and after tax flows would accrue:*

Year	Gross income	Depreciation	Tax	After tax cash flow
1	16,000	20,000.00	−2,000.00	18,000.00
2	16,000	16,000.00	0.00	16,000.00
3	16,000	12,800.00	1,600.00	14,400.00
4	16,000	10,240.00	2,880.00	13,120.00
5	16,000	8,192.00	3,904.00	12,096.00
6	16,000	6,553.60	4,723.20	11,276.80
7	16,000	5,242.88	5,378.56	10,621.44
8	16,000	4,194.30	5,902.85	10,097.15
9	16,000	3,355.44	6,322.28	9,677.72
10	16,000	2,684.35	6,657.82	9,342.18

The after-tax rate of return for this set of cash flows can be computed to be 4.8%. Thus one might be inclined to think that the straight-line depreciation method is superior since it results in a higher rate of return.

Present Value Profile

The conclusion comparing the two depreciation methods is only true for a company that judges its cost of capital to be in the vicinity of 5%. If the rate were lower, the straight-line depreciation method would be favored; if, as seems more likely, the company has a higher capital cost rate, the double-declining balance depreciation method will become favorable. A good way to see this is to compare the difference in net present values of the two alternatives over a range of discount rates. Such a comparison is called a present value profile. The added informational content for decision making is fairly obvious. For example, if we subtracted the after-tax flows from the straight-line method from those for the double-declining method, we would obtain the following cash flows.

---

*There are, of course, many alternative depreciation methods. Double declining balance with a change to straight line in later years would produce a higher after tax yield, but our interest is in exemplification, not in how to choose depreciation methods.

Year	0	$0
Year	1	5000.00
Year	2	3000.00
Year	3	1400.00
Year	4	120.00
Year	5	− 904.00
Year	6	−1723.20
Year	7	−2378.56
Year	8	−2902.85
Year	9	−3323.28
Year	10	−3657.82

The rate of return which equates this set of cash flows to zero is 7.20%. Figure 6.4 is a present value profile of this set of cash flows. It can be interpreted to mean that one will favor the double-declining balance method for depreciating this asset over the straight-line method for any discount or interest rate in excess of 7.2%. It is worth seeing that accelerated depreciation methods can be simultaneously "good" for a company with a high discount rate and a government with a low discount rate.

ADDITIONAL CONCERNS

Some of the ideas presented in this chapter will be expanded on in later chapters. For example, the interest or discount rate which we have taken somewhat as given will be examined in our studies of inventory control (What is the appropriate charge for having funds tied up in inventory?). To a great extent, however, the appropriate interest or discount rate is a matter beyond the scope of a course in operations management. Courses in managerial economics and finance typically devote significant amounts of time to this issue. Before we turn our attention back to issues that are more clearly within the operations management area, let us briefly note some of the additional concerns which call for changes, extensions, or tempering when using the basic models considered above.

Qualitative Factors

Properly discounted cash flow is but one surrogate criterion entity. It is very important to consider the many qualitative factors affecting an investment decision. The role of quantitative cash-flow model data may or may not offset other qualitative considerations; and as the quantitative aspects of investment choices become less clear-cut, the relative impact of qualitative criteria should become more dominant. As stated in Chapter 5, we must be wary of our penchant for hard data.

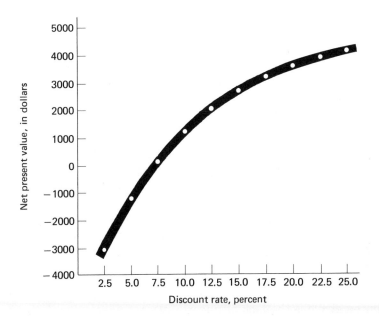

Fig. 6.4 Present value profile. Net difference in present value ($100,000 ten-year/asset) double-declining balance depreciation method minus straight-line depreciation as a function of discount rate.

Continuous Discounting

Continuous discounting involves no new conceptual problems; simply stated, it represents a better model of the real world and as such is preferable when the kinds of problems being considered call for this increase in modeling sophistication. To make such an assessment, we must again appeal to the criteria system which directs the model-building effort to find the proper level of abstraction or detail for our model. For most operations management problems, the need for continuous discounting will not be felt.

Other Models

The three major models for investment decisions presented above are obviously not the only models available. However, many of the other models are approximately the same. As noted before, the rate of return model presented here is sometimes referred to as a "yield" model where the yield from an investment is the rate of return. This model is not the only rate of return model; some models typically involve certain kinds of averaging assumptions which do not take explicit account of the particular individualistic pattern of cash flows for each investment decision.

Rates of return are computed for companywide financial analyses in still different ways [e.g., (net income ÷ total assets) or (net income ÷ stockholders' equity)]. Since rate of return is expressed as a percentage, the admonition in the summary remarks of Chapter 5 about being wary of percentages applies. When someone quotes a rate of return figure, it is wise to check the basis of calculation.

Multiple Return Rates

The possibility of more than one rate of return for a particular investment decision is more properly treated in a managerial economics or finance course. As noted above, for certain kinds of cash-flow patterns, it is possible that more than one rate of return will equate the positive and negative flows. This fact is a bit disquieting but is not cause for serious alarm. The condition most often occurs when there are several periods of net negative cash flows interspersed with periods of net positive cash flows.

Uncertainty

A more substantive issue in assessing the investment decision models presented above is the lack of uncertainty considerations in the models. In other words, the models are deterministic representations of what is actually an uncertain or stochastic real world situation. Thus, in our first major example we assumed with certainty that the initial cost would be $100,000 and that the revenue generated would be exactly $16,000 per year for exactly ten years. Clearly these flows are only estimates and those estimates are somewhat uncertain; the degree of uncertainty probably increases as the cash-flow timing becomes more distant from the present. Westfall executives very rightly should be quite concerned with the uncertainties in their estimates of costs and benefits of a new chair-building system. They would probably want to know the implications of various alternative outcomes.

To some extent, uncertainty can be represented in the choice of interest rate, and the desire for a stochastic model can be offset through sensitivity analysis. In our typewriter example presented earlier, we solved for that interest rate which made the two alternatives equally attractive. In this way, managers can assess their own individual feelings (including feelings about uncertainty) as to which side of the cutoff point they feel is appropriate. Similarly, the rate of return for the chair-building examples can be examined under differing conditions. Thus economic life, initial cost, annual positive cash flows, and changes in the annual cash flows over time can be investigated with the objective of finding the necessary conditions for a change in the outcome of the investment decision. Varying the discount rate to create a present value profile aids in coping with uncertainty. To do these things, however, again implies the need for some type of user-oriented modeling environment where many alternative hypotheses or conditions can be easily tested.

Estimating Procedures

Since negative errors in net cash-inflow estimates may reflect poorly on a particular individual, a conservative bias is often prevalent in estimates. The variations in this bias between individuals in the same firm and even in one individual from time to time represent a potential cost to the firm. Also for each individual, as well as collectively for the firm, the preference for, or aversion to cash flows is not linear with respect to amount. Thus for example, it has been found that individuals become more averse to entering a coin flipping gambling game as the amount of potential loss increases (when the payoffs are $1.00 or zero, most individuals are quite willing to pay $.50; when the payoffs are $10,000 or zero, few are willing to pay $5,000). Model-building efforts devoted to properly treating varying risk aversion in analyses are collectively referred to as utility theory and are typically treated in quantitative methods courses.

Costs Versus Benefits

Finally it is worth noting that many kinds of investment decisions involve investments where the costs are fairly easily determined but the benefits are not readily quantifiable. Thus it might be fairly easy to estimate the cost of photocopying equipment but difficult to explicitly state an associated benefit, revenue, or cost reduction. Another prevalent example involves investment in computer facilities; it is particularly difficult for many firms to quantify the benefit aspects of advanced computation systems. At an earlier time, a computer could be cost justified by making a comparison of computer operation with an existing situation where a large number of clerks were performing a fairly routine function. For many companies, however, the computer systems under present contemplation are not designed to replace an existing operation or way of conducting business. The benefits of such investment decisions become increasingly nebulous, albeit terribly important, and the investment decisions become increasingly similar to investments made for research and development. Chapter 7 is devoted to a model which will help resolve these kinds of problems.

SUMMARY REMARKS

It may seem that the additional concerns delineated above are pervasive enough to make one uneasy when using the basic models. Indeed it is true that in many ways our exposition of capital budgeting has been somewhat simplified. There is a considerable literature pertaining to capital budgeting models, and graduate seminars are often devoted to extensions and to an improved understanding of the pitfalls that accompany the use of various models. That this is so should be neither surprising nor alarming. Our discussion of models pointed out that all models are abstracted imperfect representations that are only valid for certain criteria. The models presented in this chapter are the most widely known. They attack the fundamental issues and do so in ways that are superior to rule of thumb and less rigorous approaches. Sophistication in their use is similar to sophistication in the use of any model—it can often lead to improved problem understanding and solution.

REFERENCES

Bierman, Harold, Jr., and J. Seymour Smidt, *The Capital Budgeting Decision,* 2nd ed., Macmillan, 1966.

Grant, E. I., and W. G. Ireson, *Principles of Engineering Economy,* 4th ed., Ronald Press, 1962.

Mayer, Raymond R., *Financial Analysis of Investment Alternatives,* Allyn and Bacon, 1964.

Reisman, A., and E. S. Buffa, "A General Model for Investment Policy," *Management Science,* VIII, no. 3, April 1962.

Terborgh, G., *Business Investment Policy,* Machinery and Allied Products Institute (Washington) 1958.

CHAPTER REVIEW

This chapter has had two related goals: (1) to stress the need to reflect differences in timings of costs and revenues; and (2) to develop an ability to use and understand three of the most widely used models for coping with investment decisions involving cash-flow timing differences.

Depending upon the school you are in and the sequence of classes you have taken, the materials presented in this chapter can range from being redundant to being quite difficult. If your instructor feels that a sufficient proportion of the class falls into the former category, he may decide to skip this chapter. If you have found the materials difficult, it may be encouraging to know that you will see these concepts again, probably in finance, managerial economics, and managerial accounting classes. My primary reason for including capital budgeting conepts in this book is because problems resulting in cash-flow patterns are very prevalent in operations management; it will be necessary for you to be able to cope with these problems, and an understanding of the basic concepts presented in this chapter will go a long way toward meeting that objective.

OUTLINE OF THE CHAPTER

Introduction	(goals of the chapter)
Investment decisions	(comparison of time-adjusted costs and revenues)
Cash flows	(time patterns of cost and revenue)
Relevant costs	(economic realities reflected)
Present value	(transformation to common base)
The model	(discounting)
Examples	(application of P. V. model)
An assessment	(matches business perceptions)
Rate of return	(discount rate determined, not given)
The model	(finding equating rate)
Incremental rates	(beware of percentages)
An assessment	(more potential information)
Payback	(widely used—often improperly)
The model	(time to recoup investment)
Misuse	(need to reflect economic life)
An assessment	(probably should not be used)
Taxes	(influence net cash flows)
Depreciation	(methods change timing and desirability)
Present value profile	(increased informational content)
Additional concerns	(limitations of the basic models)
Qualitative factors	(additional criteria)
Continuous discounting	(a minor sophistication)
Other models	(examine procedures for calculating)
Multiple return rates	(conditions leading to)
Uncertainty	(data are random variables)
Estimating procedures	(conservative bias)
Costs versus benefits	(hard versus soft data)
Summary remarks	(introductory scope)

CENTRAL ISSUES

The basic goal of capital-budgeting models is to make comparisons of costs and revenues with all values stated on a common base. Selection of an appropriate interest or discount rate permits cash flows in the future to be converted into their present equivalents. When the interest adjusted cash inflows are compared to the interest adjusted cash outflows, the model used is present value. The result of an analysis with the present value model is favorable when the adjusted cash inflows exceed the adjusted cash outflows.

The rate of return model is built upon the same discounting concepts as those used for present value. The essential difference between the two techniques is that present value requires an interest or discount rate input; rate of return solves for that rate which equates the adjusted cash inflows and adjusted cash outflows.

The payback or payout model finds the time required for the net unadjusted cash inflows to equal the original cash outflow. Interest adjustment to consider differences in timings of the flows is possible through wise selection of appropriate payback standards, but distortions can occur. The concept of an investment "paying for itself" is appealing, but the model can more easily lead to improper decisions than either present value or rate of return.

Recognition of the surrogate criteria relationships of capital-budgeting models to other criteria of the firm results in a need for further study of discounting concepts; the need is partially satisfied by an open-ended modeling environment which permits the sensitivity of investment decisions to be assessed.

ASSIGNMENTS

1. What is the present value of a single sum of $100 to be received six years hence with annual interest at 10%?
2. Prove your answer to problem 1 by taking that present value amount and compounding 10% interest annually.
3. You are considering purchasing six noninterest bearing notes. Three of them have face values of $100.00 and will come due one each at the end of years 3, 4, and 5. The other three have face values of $150.00 and come due one each at the end of years 6, 7, and 8. If your interest rate is 15%, what will you be willing to pay for these now?
4. How large a loan could you receive now for a single payment of $800 six years from now if interest is at 6%?
5. An investment alternative calls for an initial cash outflow of $2000. If the economic life is 8 years, how soon does the investment have to pay back if the interest rate is 4%?
6. At 6% interest, money will double itself in how many years?
7. An investment of $10,000 in packaging equipment is expected to provide a net cash savings of $1,000 per year for the next ten years. At the end of the tenth year the investment will have a cash salvage value of $4,000. What is the rate-of-return for this investment?
8. You have to decide between the following two opportunities.

	Opportunity I	**Opportunity II**
Annual income	$100 at end of each year	$50 at end of each year
Time span	Years 1 through 20	Years 1 through 40
Lump-sum income payments	None	$500 at end of year 10 $500 at end of year 40

At 10% which appears more favorable? At 4%? If there is any difference in your conclusions, how do you explain them? At what rate would you be indifferent?

9. At an interest rate of 12%, how much would you pay for an income of $10 per year starting at the end of year 1 for 20 years? For 50 years? Perpetually? (Hint—compute for 50%, 40%, 30%, and 20%.)

10. You are investing in a vending machine operation and have an alternative as to when you can collect your estimated commission on sales. It is expected to be about $120 per year for five years and you can receive it either at the end of the year or in equal installments at the end of each quarter. If your interest rate is 8%, how much less is the present value of the less desirable alternative?

11. An investment decision will have an effect on the operations of the company for the next 20 years. How important is an error of $1,000,000 made in the cash flow estimates for the years 1, 10, and 20, if the interest rate is 4%? 10%? 20%?

12. A hospital is considering two alternative X-ray machines. One is fairly inexpensive, but requires more expensive supplies and more frequent maintenance than the alternative more expensive piece of equipment. The expected cost characteristics are as follows:

	Equipment A	**Equipment B**
Original cost (installed)	$75,000	$105,000
Economic life	8 years	8 years
Salvage value	0	$20,000
Annual supplies cost	$8000*	$6,000**
Annual maintenance cost	$2400***	1,400

*Expected to increase at the rate of $400 per year after the first year.
**Expected to increase at the rate of $200 per year after the first year.
***Expected to increase at the rate of $150 per year after the first year.

The hospital administrator has asked you to determine which piece of equipment should be purchased. The cost of capital he has given you is 4% (The hospital in the process is floating some 4% bonds.)

13. The hospital administrator presented your analysis of problem 12 to the board of directors. One of the members, a prominent local businessman, took issue with the 4% cost of capital rate. He stated that in his business, a 20% rate was used even though he could borrow from the local bank at 7%. He also expressed some uneasiness over the Equipment A forecast for supplies expense which was admitted to be a "SWAG" (Systematic Wild Guess). The board decided to defer action until you could provide a more detailed analysis and the administrator would like you to do whatever you can.

14. A proposed office copying machine will cost $6000 but will save $.04 per sheet over present methods. Other data include:

Economic life	5 years
Depreciation term	6 years
Depreciation method	straight line
Incremental tax rate	50 percent
Copy volume	10,000 per month

Evaluate this investment both on a before and after tax basis with the present-value method using an interest rate of 10%.

15. Evaluate the investment choice presented in problem 14 with the rate of return model (before and after tax).

16. Evaluate the investment choice presented in problem 14 with the payback model (before and after tax).

17. A new supermarket cash register has the following cost characteristics:

Cost	$12,000
Salvage value (end of 10 years)	$4,000
Annual depreciation	$800
Desired before tax rate of return	15%
Annual savings	$2,500

Evaluate this investment choice with the present value model.

18. Evaluate the investment choice presented in problem 17 with the payback model.

19. Evaluate the investment choice presented in problem 17 with the rate of return model.

20. A company has compiled the following data on its fleet of cars:

Average cost:	$3000
Cost of capital:	10%
Average maintenance:	
Year 1	$100
Year 2	200
Year 3	325
Year 4	475
Year 5	650

Average trade-in allowance:

Year 1	$2300
Year 2	1900
Year 3	1550
Year 4	1250
Year 5	850

a) What is the best trade-in policy (on the average) for the company?

b) Car#113 is two years old, has relatively low mileage, and has only had a total of $35.00 in repairs. Assuming the trade-in allowance schedule given above, under what conditions should the company trade in the car?

c) Reformulate an answer to question (a) that is not based on averages.

21. Redo problem 20 with costs of capital from 6 to 20% in 1% intervals.

22. **Modern Furniture Inc.***

In January 1971, Roy and Harriet Chase learned of a technique for applying glass fibers to molded shapes. In the new process, resin impregnated glass fibers were sprayed onto a prepared mold by means of a specially adapted air pressure gun. The air jet sucked the hot impregnated glass fibers from a reserve tank into the air gun. A special fixture in the gun spun the fibers and hurled them against the mold with great force. The spray operation continued to apply layer after layer of the resin fiber until a complete fiber glass shell was built over the mold. When the shell had reached the desired thickness, it was first allowed to cool and then sprung from the mold.

During the spraying operation, the worker had to wear a breathing mask and goggles in order to protect himself from tiny glass filaments which were sometimes present in the air. The spraying operation was quite noisy because of the air jet, pumps, heating vats, and motors needed at the spraying site. In addition to his face mask, the worker had to wear a rubber suit to protect his clothing from glass particles. The spray room temperature was apt to be as high as 90 degrees on an average fall day. Periodically the work area had to be cleared of the resin fibers which had bounced off the mold or had missed it entirely while the edges of the mold were being sprayed. The operation required that the worker periodically move molds into position or reposition them. The worker had to stand during the actual spraying operation.

The Chases had been professional designers for over ten years. Recently Roy had been planning displays for a large department store which featured a modernistic motif. Harriet had been an artist with a local advertising agency and had been a highly successful amateur sculptress. For a number of years they had hoped to establish their own business designing and manufacturing modern furniture. Roy had been an art major in undergraduate school and later had taken an M.B.A. on a part-time basis. He and Harriet had saved $30,000 to invest in the business they hoped to establish. They doubted that they could borrow much more money if it were needed.

The fiber process seemed to offer an opportunity to produce a new kind of furniture with complete freedom of design. The resin spray process left

---

*This case was written by Professor J. Brian Quinn at the Amos Tuck School of Business Administration, Dartmouth College, and is used with his permission.

a shell of any desired color, including a woven appearance. A ⅛" shell was exceedingly strong and surprisingly light. A molded 36" x 18" x ⅛" shell could easily hold 500 pounds and weighed a little over two pounds. The surface of the shell next to the mold could be made perfectly smooth. The opposite surface could be dressed to the smoothness of a heavy fabric. Any shape could be molded provided it could be sprayed from one side.

The Chases became quite enthused about designing lightweight modern furniture constructed of impregnated fiber glass. They envisioned molded chairs, end tables, coffee tables, card tables, dining tables, special form bedroom, office, kitchen, and outdoor furniture. They felt that the new substance could be made to compete in all of the markets in which wood and molded plastics were then prevalent. Initially they intended to manufacture only special form chairs and tables. If these were successful, they would expand their line.

The Chases contacted the Harris Company, manufacturers of the resin-fiber spray equipment. The Harris Company salesman demonstrated the equipment at his plant. The process surpassed the Chases' greatest expectations. The material could be applied by unskilled labor. Such labor was available in the area for $2.50 per hour. The quality of the surface depended only on the mold finish and on the care with which the first layers of the shell were built up.

Time studies at the Harris Company had shown that 5 minutes of operating time were required for building up a shell with one square foot of surface ⅛" thick. Thirty minutes of cooling time were required on the mold after the last operation. An additional 48 hours of cooling and drying was desirable before trimming and dressing the reverse side of the shell. The cost of fiber and resin was estimated at 45¢ per surface foot. At the end of each day's operation, it was necessary to clean the equipment with a solvent. This cleaning required approximately 30 minutes. Once a week, a cleaning of the spray area was also desirable. The salesman suggested that it normally took about 2 hours to clean up the work area of one sprayer. The salesman said that the trimming and dressing operation normally took about ⅔ the spraying time for shells under 20 square feet of surface area. Trimming was a more skilled operation. Roy thought a man could be hired for about $3.50 per hour for this activity.

The salesman estimated the power and repair cost of operation at about $1000 to $1500 per year per machine. The salesman said that 130 square feet in a corner location were desirable for a single spraying operation. The equipment cost $3000 per complete unit. The Harris Company was willing to finance the Chases' purchase on a 8% basis, if they so desired. The equipment was expected to operate satisfactorily for about ten years. Roy knew of a small (1800-square-foot) abandoned plant he could rent for approximately $300 per month. Since the location was near a large city, Roy thought unit transportation costs to the wholesaler or to direct retail outlets would be negligible. Roy thought that two square feet of assembly and storage space would be needed for every one of spraying space.

Roy estimated the average cost of wrought iron legs for the molded furniture at $2.50 per set of four. He also estimated the investments in all other equipment and fixtures necessary to go into business at $3000 total. Harriet would quit her job and handle (1) mold design and construction and (2) the paper work of the business on a full-time basis. Assembly of legs to the molded forms was estimated at five minutes per leg. An average of four legs per piece were to be used. Unskilled labor could perform this function and prepare the furniture for shipment, an operation which Roy and Harriet thought would require another ten minutes per unit.

Roy and Harriet drew up some initial sketches of molded chairs and free form tables. The tables had about 15 to 18 square feet of surface. The chairs would require approximately 7½ square feet of surface. Roy felt the chairs could be successfully sold to either wholesalers or *large* retailers at about $15.00. The tables he thought could sell competitively at $20 to $25 to the trade. He thought that at these prices the business could sell as much as they could produce. He planned to let the wholesalers and retailers handle all promotion of the product in its early stages.

What would you recommend that Roy and Harriet do about this venture?

CHAPTER 7

ANALYSIS OF VALUE AND FUNCTION

The title of this chapter may lead one to think that it deals with some kind of mathematical analysis; however, it is not the mathematical connotation of function with which we will be concerned. This chapter presents a value model which can provide surrogate criteria that are better for fundamental enterprise objectives than those more common models based upon cost minimization. The major benefit of the functional analysis model is to foster a creative choice of alternative entities that are considered for inclusion in particular system design efforts.

In developing our functional analysis model, we will go beyond the usual notion of costs to include the concept of benefit or value which is not found in either financial or cost accounting models. Once value or benefit has been determined, it will act as a standard or criterion in the three step control process: (1) the determination of a standard, goal or criterion; (2) the measurement and comparison of actual results with that standard; and (3) actions taken to correct deviations. The value standard can be compared with the cost associated with a system which achieves that particular benefit or value.

Modeling procedures which include benefits or values in cost analyses are relatively new. A thoroughgoing historical summary of these analyses is beyond the scope of this book; but the functional analysis model presented here is an amalgam based on three major foundations which can be briefly enumerated. The first of these is value engineering or value analysis. The original work in this field has been largely attributed to Mr. Lawrence Miles of the General Electric Company. Value engineering/analysis has become quite popular with the United States Department of Defense, and most large defense contractors have a value-engineering group which is concerned with cost cutting. The activities of value engineers/analysts are somewhat akin to those of industrial engineers, although value engineers are not necessarily industrial engineers and vice versa.

The second foundation is called cost/benefit analysis. Cost/benefit analysis, as the name implies, is concerned with comparing the cost of some activity with the attendant benefit of that activity. Cost/benefit analysis again is a methodology associated with the U.S. Defense Department, and came into widespread use under the direction of Secretary of Defense Robert S. McNamara. Perhaps the major distinction between cost/benefit analysis and value engineering/analysis is the scope of problems considered. Thus while a value engineer might typically consider problems ranging from how to secure a wire to how to maintain appropriate oil temperature for an engine, a cost/benefit analysis might be concerned with trading-off costs of aircraft carriers or missiles in terms of benefits for overall defense for the country.

The third foundation for our present discussion is the "functional point of view" which is becoming increasingly popular in the behavioral sciences. There the concept of function has been adopted from physiology where researchers have been concerned with questions such as, what is the role or function of the thyroid gland in relation to the whole body? This view of function is concerned with considering the role of subsystems in fulfilling the criteria of the supersystem(s) in which they are embedded.

THE MODEL

The term functional analysis as used in this book refers to an examination process wherein the most basic feature, aspect, or function of a system is identified and its worth determined. The value of the function then acts as a standard or criterion by which existing or proposed system design efforts which accomplish the function can be evaluated. We will find our functional analysis model applies equally well to goods and services. The major goal of functional analysis is to objectively determine a particular function and thereafter assess the value of that function without regard to existing or proposed methods for achieving that function. This concept of function is quite similar to the discussion in Chapter 2 pertaining to the value of an entity or subsystem in a particular system design being determined by one or more attributes of the entity, not by any inherent worth of the entity itself. It was noted in that discussion that attributes only assume value in terms of a particular criteria set; that is, systems are designed for purposes and the entities or subsystems included in those systems are selected because they possess certain attributes which can be combined in ways to achieve the desired results. It is only by appeal to a particular criteria system that function can be determined, and the worth of any system-design effort can be assessed relative to alternative ways for achieving that function.

Function Value

The concept of function value is based on the belief that it is possible to state succinctly the inherent worth that a subsystem provides to the supersystem of which it is a part. For relatively simple systems where there is only one significant goal, it is often possible to state a function in terms of a single noun and single verb. Thus the function of a cigarette lighter is to "provide fire" (one might say that it is to provide sufficient heat to ignite a cigarette—thereby allowing for the inclusion of different entities into the design of a cigarette lighter). Similarly, the function of a belt might be to hold up trousers, a flowerpot to hold dirt, a sculptor's chisel to remove marble, a file cabinet to store documents, a plate to hold food, or an automobile to provide transportation.

All of these examples imply a use; that is, there is some supersystem which dictates a need which is fulfilled or satisfied by those entities. Those needs are highly individualistic in nature. A pipe smoker might define his need for fire (or sufficient heat) in a way that is somewhat different from the cigarette smoker which could in turn call for a different sort of device. For an ex-smoker, perhaps his cigarette lighter is used as a paper weight with the function "hold down paper." Similarly, for an authoritarian father the function of a belt might be "beating children;" for a miser, a flower pot might be "hiding money;" a student might see the function of a sculptor's chisel as "opening beer cans;" a mechanic might use a file cabinet for "storing tools;" an angry wife might use a plate for "clobbering husband;" or a conservationist might view an automobile as "creating smog." To some extent, these examples only reinforce the importance of criteria or the "eye of the beholder" in system design; remember that for mass manufacturing technology to be utilized, it is necessary for many "eyes" to "behold" in a somewhat similar manner. Box 7.1 provides an additional illustration.

A well-known mouthwash is advertised by a claim of killing germs by the millions. One individual replied, "Just the thought of having all those germs dying in my mouth is enough to make me sick!"

Box 7.1

Having established the particular criteria oriented notion of function, it is now necessary to turn our attention to that of "value." The way in which value is attributed to a given function is to contemplate and search for various alternative means of fulfilling the particular function at the lowest possible relevant cost. Thus fire might be provided by a match; trousers might be held by suspenders made of string; dirt might be held in a used tin can; marble might be quickly removed by sand blasting; documents might be stored on microfilm; food might be served on a piece of wax paper; and transportation might be provided by roller skates or a bicycle. Each of these alternatives has an attendant cost. If a reasonable search could not produce other alternatives with lower attendant costs, then the attendant costs of these alternatives would become the "values" attached to their respective functions.

For the examples dealt with above, one is concerned with more than merely fulfilling the most basic function. Thus a cigarette lighter should look good, a belt should be handsome, a flower pot should compliment the flowers, a sculptor's chisel should have a good heft, a file cabinet should blend with other furniture, a plate should be pretty, and an automobile should give status. It is to these issues that we now turn our attention.

Esteem Value

The basic notion of esteem value is that goods and services usually possess utility for consumers or users that is above and beyond the inherent basic function as identified in the preceding section. The goods possess attributes that appeal to other criteria within the user's criteria system. These attributes of a product or service make it more desirable and therefore more salable; those individuals who create products and services will therefore be interested in designing these extra or "esteem" characteristics into their products and services. A model based solely on a surrogate criterion of function fulfillment at minimum cost will lead to suboptimization. So, a given cigarette lighter design might be changed to include goldplating; the costs expended for the goldplating add nothing to the functional characteristics of the cigarette lighter but well might give the product esteem characteristics which more than justify their expenditure. Similarly, a belt might have a well polished buckle, a flower pot have a design on the side, a sculptor's chisel might have dark blue metal coloring on the blade, the file cabinet might have chromium decorations on the drawer fronts, the plate might have a flowered pattern and the automobile might have an emblem attached to the fender saying 300XXX-SUPER DUPER SPORT.

A new method for making shoes that is considerably less expensive than traditional methods is to extrude the soles. A necessary cutoff mark from the process is circled by one manufacturer and labeled "Mark of Excellence." Whether the product is indeed superior to shoes made with traditional construction means is open to doubt.

One should not minimize the importance of esteem value, particularly for consumer products and services. Indeed, for some consumer products the criterion of esteem value takes on such a significant role in the criteria set which drives the system design process, that the costs expended for esteem value are greater than those expended for function value.

Our model for functional analysis calls for the separation of product cost into the two categories of function value and esteem value. By separating total cost into that cost which provides a function and that cost which provides esteem characteristics one can more carefully assess the resultant system design outputs or attributes of function and esteem relative to their cost inputs.

One way in which total product cost may be separated into the two categories is to cost out the function value and arbitrarily assign the remaining cost to esteem value. For example, suppose that a cigarette lighter could be designed which would fulfill functional requirements (light reasonably often on the first try, last for a reasonable period of time before requiring refueling, and not leak if carried in a pocket) with a simple plastic molded case, a thin metal stamped part to hold the flint assembly and wick, the cheapest cotton for fuel retention, and a matching plastic cover which slips on and off (therefore requiring no threading), for a total cost of $.25. The $.25 could be regarded as function value for a cigarette lighter. If a proposed design had an estimated cost of $1.00, $.75 could arbitrarily be assigned to providing esteem value for that design. The immediate question that comes to mind when the esteem characteristics have been so costed out, is whether it would not be possible to achieve greater total esteem by spending $.75 per unit in a different manner, or whether the existing degree of esteem can be fulfilled for less cost.

A large camera manufacturer machined the outside diameters of all washers which were originally fabricated by a stamping or punch press operation. In terms of the functional requirements for the washers, a punch press could easily fabricate the part to within the design specifications for size. The only real reason for turning the washers was that machined washers were considered to be higher quality washers.

Box 7.2

As one considers esteem versus functional requirements, considerable insight in the design of products and services can often be achieved. A closely related question is what represents quality in a product? We will deal with that question in a later chapter, but in the context of our present discussion it is worth noting that product components that are manufactured with "high quality" should be scrutinized in terms of the final users' and consumers' quality criteria. Box 7.2 illustrates this issue.

Who considers the washers to be of higher quality? Would the average camera buyer know the difference? Were the washers placed in the camera where the camera buyer would in fact even see them?

Evolution

The arbitrary division of total cost into functional and esteem categories provides surrogate criteria which more clearly define the attributes desired in a product or service and assess the propriety of system design entities required to achieve those attributes. In the process of identifying the inherent function and thereafter assigning all nonfunctional cost to esteem characteristics, one often finds shortcomings in the original functional definition. Thus for example, for the belt's original function of holding up trousers we postulated that a piece of string crisscrossed over the shoulders would serve the function (let us assume that such a piece of string would cost $.02). If a proposed belt cost $.80 we would therefore assign a cost of $.78 to esteem characteristics. However, our $.02 string suspenders would not be very comfortable on a man's shoulders, nor would it be convenient continually to tie and untie the ends of the string (which would become frayed) to the tops of trousers, nor would the string suspenders have a product life equal to that of a leather belt. These additional functional criteria or constraints can be added and a new function value established (perhaps stouter string with felt shoulder pads and chrome plated steel hooks which go through the belt loops in trousers).

For our flower pot example a tin can might not be as satisfactory for holding dirt as a flower pot because it is subject to rust which both limits its life and contaminates the dirt. A paper bag would also hold dirt but would be subject to even more rapid aging. So, perhaps an explicit recognition of product life is required. But one might reasonably ask whether it is necessary that the product life be greater than that of the flowers which are planted in a pot rather than taking the life of existing devices for holding dirt as the standard or criterion.

These examples imply an evolution in the statement of function. This evolution represents improved understanding and subsequent design of the criteria system which drives, directs, or controls the system design process itself. That is, our functional analysis model is directly concerned with the criteria system since the cost attribute of the succinct statement of function is intended to act as the sole surrogate criterion by which system design efforts are to be judged. But as noted in other discussions, all models are imperfect abstractions that can be improved upon or evolved. The evolution requires appeal to still higher criteria sets; our functional analysis model facilitates this evolution by its blatant attempt to depict a complex set or system of criteria by one single functional statement. In the process of assessing the single surrogate criterion, considerable insights can be gleaned; this is particularly so as additional criteria entities or functional constraints are added and the necessary incremental costs to achieve incremental functional features are examined.

EXAMPLES

The literature in the field of functional analysis is largely a literature of examples. Although most of these examples are "hardware" or goods oriented, the model provides equally good if not better insights into system design activities that are more of a service nature. In this section we will use our functional analysis model for a series of increasingly ill-defined situations with the goal of further reinforcing the model as a part of our growing repertoire of approaches to operations management problems.

Wood Drying Shed

Westfall is interested in reducing their inventories of raw lumber and the time required for air drying lumber. The most significant source of extra time required is due to the continued redrying from rain and snow moisture. John Hughes, the assistant plant manager, has contacted several vendors in the area; the most economical alternative appears to be a corrugated steel building of simple design (Fig. 7.1). The vendor for this kind of structure has given John a firm quotation of $200,000. Would you as an outside analyst advise them to accept the quotation?

There is a particularly interesting and somewhat insidious aspect to the way the preceding question has been framed; there are only two possible actions which are being considered—go or no-go on a particular specific design. This particular style of question is one that is very prevalent in industry. Answering the question requires determination of the benefits which will accrue to Westfall from reduced lumber inventories and drying time, and a comparison of those benefits with the attendant cost of achieving the benefits. The relevant cost and benefit data can then be fed into an appropriate capital-budgeting model which will produce a result such as an expected rate of return for that particular investment opportunity. The typical procedure then calls for an assessment of the capital-budgeting model output (and perhaps an assessment of the inputs to the model) and then a decision.

Unfortunately this process of analysis could easily lead to a result which justifies the $200,000 expenditure but is an inappropriate decision because the benefits provided by the particular design could be achieved by an alternative design with far less cost. Breaking out of the typical

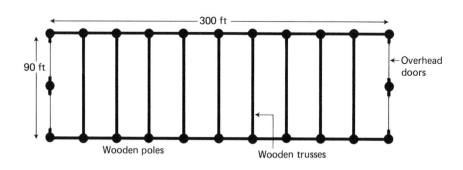

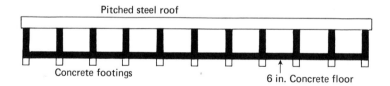

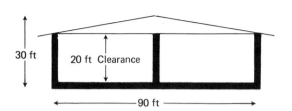

Figure 7.1 Westfall drying shed

analytical procedure for assessing such investment decisions involves a consideration of alternative ways of achieving the benefits to the Westfall operation derived from the wood-drying shed; alternatively (but far less imaginatively) it involves a consideration of the various ways in which the cost of constructing a drying shed could be reduced.

Aside from the unfortunate tendency of the capital investment decision process to grind on to a conclusion without considering alternatives, in considering alternatives to a proposed design we may be severely limiting the scope of our thinking. Our desire for the wood-drying shed has nothing to do with the shed itself—it is for a particular attribute associated with that shed, namely, ability to keep moisture from the wood. We simply do not know how good (in terms of the criterion of cost) the proposed design is in providing that benefit relative to some unknown "optimum" way of achieving the desired benefits.

Cost reduction activities, although potentially beneficial (the costs saved exceed the costs spent on cost-saving activities), usually tend to be severely handicapped or limited by proposed designs. For example, supposing a cost study is made of the proposed design and the concrete floor of the shed was deemed to be unnecessary. Let us also suppose that if the floor were eliminated from the design, a saving of $40,000 or 20% could be achieved. Most individuals would be quite happy with a saving of $40,000 or 20% in total cost for a particular project. The issue which has not been considered, however, is whether a 20% saving on a base of $200,000 is really good or whether one ought to be able to achieve a 90% saving.

It is exactly to this issue that functional analysis is directed. The goal is not to be limited in thinking by the existence of a proposed design. What we are really interested in is not an entity called a wood-drying shed, but some particular attributes which a wood-drying shed possesses, i.e., the function of a wood-drying shed for the existing set of problems at the Westfall plant, which is primarily to allow reduced inventories and drying times for raw lumber. This in turn should lead to reduced costs. If we wish to restrict our thinking solely to eliminating the absorption of precipitation during air drying, we still can broadly state the inherent function of the wood-drying shed very simply as "keep out rain and snow." Given that function we can then attempt to conjure up the cheapest possible way one might be able to keep out rain and snow, and to assign a cost or value to that function. This function value can then serve as a goal, standard, or criterion by which we can judge any proposed design that is intended to fulfill the function.

Thus for this example, one fairly obvious way of fulfilling the function of keeping out rain and snow would be to wrap each load in a plastic cover and continue to leave the loads outside. Let us assume that a sufficient number of reusable tarpaulins could be purchased for less than $10,000. Using our arbitrary rule of assigning the difference between proposed design cost and function value to esteem value, we would come up with

$190,000 or 95% for esteem features in the proposed design. Since it is quite doubtful that Westfall is interested in spending large sums of money to build prestigious drying shed facilities, we have identified a potentially large cost reduction.

At this point, however, it is appropriate to review the existing set of functional specifications with an eye toward evolution based upon the inclusion of additional functional constraints or criteria. The first of these that comes to mind is that we want the wood to give off its natural moisture as well as not absorb moisture from rain and snow, i.e., we want the wood to dry. Unfortunately, covering the wood with tarpaulins will tend to restrict air drying.

Adding this constraint leads to suggestions such as a drying shed with no walls or doors or floor; (approximately $60,000) or perhaps to individual roof like devices that could be placed on top of each wood pile (air circulation would be better but some moisture would be absorbed); or perhaps to large tents.

Our present objective, however, is not to speculate on what constitutes the "ultimate weapon" for wood-drying procedure at the Westfall Furniture Company. We are illustrating the functional analysis model and showing how it is often possible to achieve a desired set of attributes with system designs that are not limited by proposed or existing problem approaches or solutions.

Boat Gasoline Tank

Suppose a boat manufacturer were designing a new boat, that because of the desired attributes of this boat a 100 gallon gasoline tank were required, and that a proposed stainless steel tank were estimated to cost $500. The issue facing the boat builder: Yes or no to the proposed design. Supposing he said no (based on what criteria?) and a cost reduction effort eliminated $75 from the cost. The typical procedure would now be to submit the $425 proposed redesign to a yes-no decision.

Using our functional analysis model, however, we disregard the proposed design and start by asking or defining the function of a gasoline tank. A reasonable initial functional description of a gasoline tank might be "holds gasoline." In searching for ways in which the function of holding gasoline could be achieved, one might reasonably identify two standard sized 55 gallon drums as being possible candidates for the function of holding 100 gallons of gasoline. If standard 55 gallon drums could be purchased for $15 each, it would seem that the function value for holding 100 gallons of gasoline is $30; or, the original design costing $500 can be broken down into about 6% for function and about 94% for esteem. Clearly a sizable cost reduction seems possible.

Additional function constraints may now be added to this example. Thus two 55 gallon drums take up more space than the boat designer is willing to allocate for fuel storage, and since the boat is to be used in salt water, a standard 55 gallon drum with no corrosion resistance would not be acceptable. However, 55 gallon drums can be covered with a corrosion resistant material and it may well be possible to design a 100 gallon compact drum-like container made of ordinary sheet steel with some sort of corrosive resistant coating. Such a container could be designed to require minimal machining and welding requirements and perhaps be purchased for about $50 to $75. It might also be possible to use the boat itself as an integral container (particularly with Fiberglass construction) or to put plastic bags inside the hull.

It is worth noting that the gasoline tank is only one subsystem in a larger supersystem. That supersystem (the boat), also performs a set of functions and the achievement of those functions is what dictates the needs for various subsystems. Functional analysis can and should be applied to each of the subsystems and to the largest supersystem, namely the boat. That is, if a boat were designed to haul supplies to an offshore oil drilling rig, it is possible that alternative ways of achieving the function or some larger function in which this subfunction is embedded can be found, (e.g., helicopters).

A highly significant benefit of the functional analysis model is its usefulness in a supersystem design effort for identifying those subsystems which have a large cost reduction potential and therefore deserve the kind of creative system design effort necessary to achieve such reductions. Rather than having cost saving talent expended on an "across the board" approach, subsystems with truly significant potential reductions can be studied intensively.

Wristwatch

Moving now to more of a consumer product, we find that the desirability for esteem value being carefully built into the product becomes much more prominent. Perhaps the most basic function of a wristwatch may be defined as "tells time." However, when one starts conjuring up the various ways to tell time in a simple manner, possibilities such as a cheap sundial come to mind. Since sundials are not noted for portability, for use on cloudy or rainy days, for use inside buildings, for use at night, or for great accuracy, some additional functional specifications are in order. Accuracy in a device for keeping time is a relative matter depending upon user criteria; however, for the majority of consumers a portable time-keeping device which keeps time to within two minutes per day, would be accurate enough. Pocket watches costing about $3 will maintain this desired accuracy.

With the establishment of a $3 function value for a wristwatch, our functional analysis model attributes 70% of the cost of a $10 wristwatch to esteem value. Similarly, a $100 wristwatch is $97 for esteem value and $3 for function value. Are these assessments of esteem value reasonable? What about the convenience of having a timepiece strapped to the wrist? What about increased accuracy claimed by more expensive watches (one well-known brand guarantees the accuracy of their watch to within one minute per month)? What about having a watch with a luminous dial that can be read in the dark? or a calendar watch which also gives the days of the month? What about a watch with an alarm? a watch that requires no winding? that has 17 jewels? 21 jewels? What about a watch whose tick is almost imperceptible? or that hums insteads of ticks? What about a watch that is solid gold or platinum or diamond studded?

Whether any of the above timepiece attributes should be added to the list of functional requirements or constraints can only be resolved by appealing to the criteria sets of the users. As noted many times before, these criteria sets are unique; thus it is possible that a consumer would include a platinum case as a functional requirement if his skin was allergic to other kinds of metals. For the manufacturer, the question is which of these and other attributes might be considered as functional requirements by a large segment of the population. Clearly some of these attributes such as the convenience of having a timepiece strapped to the wrist are more universally considered as basic or essential than others.

A good many of the items in the above list of attributes simply cannot be reasonably interpreted to be functional requirements. Whether a watch has 17 jewels or 21 jewels is a matter which most people could not verify; in fact the majority of the population probably do not even know the function or purpose of jewels in a watch. Clearly the claims of economy through longer life do not stand up in the face of analysis. A $10 watch discarded at the end of two years represents an annual cost of $5; a $100 watch, even without considering the time value of money, would require a 20-year life with no repairs or maintenance to compete. Thus one is left to the conclusion that attributes such as how many jewels, or hums instead of ticks, or accuracy above and beyond what one requires in daily living, are not widely held functional requirements. Rather these attributes represent surrogate or proximate criteria for other user desires perhaps summed up in the word status—in short, these attributes provide esteem characteristics to the product.

In viewing esteem characteristics for the product, one should not overlook the important effect of advertising and promotion on identifying or creating esteem characteristics. Consumers don't inherently have a desire for hums instead of ticks; similarly, the emphasis on product desirability being enhanced by a watch with many jewels has recently been nicely reversed by a company which stresses a decreased number of moving parts.

In applying the functional analysis model to a wristwatch, we have concluded that a large portion of the cost is devoted to providing esteem characteristics to the product. This conclusion, however, should not carry any sort of value judgement about the property of various product choices. "Goodness" or "badness" should not be assigned to products on the basis of some assessment of function value relative to esteem value. A wristwatch is an inherently esteem-oriented product and that is true because consumers desire esteem characteristics in wristwatches. What one might question, however, is the way in which a particular manufacturer designs esteem characteristics into his product. Men's wristwatches look so surprisingly alike that about the only way one can tell a $10 wristwatch from a $100 wristwatch is to get close enough to read the brand name. It would seem that design efforts oriented toward greater product differentiation might yield benefits.

From the point of view of functional analysis, the wristwatch example illustrates the way in which product attributes and their attendant costs can be separated into the two categories of function and esteem. Once such a separation is made, it is often possible to identify improvements in either area and/or make significant cost reductions.

Field Warehouse

Many companies typically manufacture their products in factories and distribute them to their customers via field warehouses which are located near the customers. Using our functional analysis model we can ask: What is the function of a field warehouse? One might start by defining the function as "holds goods;" that is, a field warehouse is an inventory which allows large economical production runs to be doled out according to customer needs. Although this "decoupling" of production from sales is indeed provided by a field warehouse, it is also provided by other inventories; and we shall see in later chapters that this particular decoupling function could be better fulfilled by a policy which kept the inventory in a centralized location such as at the factory.

Inventories located at the factory, however, do not possess the attribute of closeness to customers and therefore do not provide the same degree of customer service as field warehouse inventories. If we broaden our set of functional constraints or criteria for a field warehouse inventory to include providing customer service, we can usefully quantify what we mean by customer service; for example we may desire to provide 12 hour delivery for our products after receipt of a customer order. But there are alternative ways of providing the function of 12 hour delivery. Do we really need field warehouses? What about air freight? Is 12 hour delivery an average time or need? Do some customers need even speedier delivery? speedier delivery on some items at some times? For some items do we really know who our customers are and might we provide them with the service that they desire in other ways? For example, could we keep part of our inventory on their premises? What is it that these customers really want? Is it possible that the requirements for short delivery times are brought about by somewhat artificial means such as payment terms where customers order at the last minute so they will have the maximum time before they have to pay their account?

The answers to these questions are dependent upon particular situations or criteria: for instance, how do particular users utilize a particular product or service? What represents reasonable time delays in particular instances? Time delays of one hour might be excessive for a life-saving drug or repair part for a large computer system; but for a bookstore to replenish its supply of a particular book, several days or a week might not be unacceptable.

The field warehouse is only one possible entity in a system of physical distribution that fulfills the function of getting goods from production to consumption. A good example of how the inherent function can be achieved in far more effective ways is provided by changes in physical distribution methods made at Baumritter (see Box 7.3).

At one time there were approximately 40 retail outlets for Ethan Allen furniture in the greater New York metropolitan area. These outlets each maintained their own inventories based upon individual predictions of demand, space available for storage, and financial ability to carry inventory. The total inventory held by the 40 firms averaged about $3,000,000, but the probability of completely satisfying large orders was small (approximately 0.25). Each retailer tended to carry fast moving items, but large orders often included one or more slow moving items from the extensive product line. By creating a regional warehouse, one inventory of about $700,000 could be carried which would have a much higher probability (approximately 0.8) of satisfying any individual order.

Box 7.3

In this example, individual retailers would no longer carry inventory themselves; from the customer's point of view, however, it was as if each retailer had a significantly higher inventory. The cost of carrying the $700,000 inventory was added to the delivered cost of the furniture, but the net cost to the retailer was reduced since he no longer had to carry his own inventory.

The benefits were achieved by considering the basic function or need, and not being constrained by enterprise ownership boundaries. Twelve additional field warehouses were established in other U.S. metropolitan areas with similar benefits. Interestingly, in 1971 Baumritter closed one field warehouse and was giving serious thought to closing several others. The reason? Because the basic function could be fulfilled from four major factory warehouses, once reliable production schedules could be met at the various plants.

It took courage to close the field warehouse. Some of those warehouses had been in operation for less than three years, and to the casual observer closing looked like an admission of failure. As noted in several other places, however, the goal is *evolution;* we have to crawl before we can walk, and it is terribly important not to get personal prestige criteria structured in a way that impedes progress.

THE CRITERIA SET

In several places in this chapter, we have noted that the functional analysis model is oriented toward the criteria set and evolution in the surrogate criteria used for evaluating system design efforts. In this section, we will expand on this criteria orientation by examining two related concepts that can usefully augment one's understanding of operational criteria and the influence of using surrogate criteria.

Dysfunctionalism

The concept of dysfunctionalism expands on the "eye of the beholder" notion by noting that system performance is only functional in terms of a criterion or set of criteria and that virtually any system is functional for *some* criterion or criteria. Identifying those criteria for which various levels or types of system performance are functional can often lead to significant understanding. Thus if workers on a conveyorized chair-building line were paid a straight hourly wage, work stoppages become regarded as "free" rest breaks and are functional to worker criteria. Similarly, if employees are paid on the basis of output, although poor quality is dysfunctional in terms of Baumritter criteria, it might become functional in terms of the individual employees' criteria. This conflict in criteria well may be serious enough to call for a redesign of the criteria system to make individual employee criteria and enterprise criteria more congruent. Box 7.4 further illustrates this point.

An employee working in a crating department asked if he could take home the wood scraps to burn in his fireplace. After this request was granted, the following observation was made: At about 3:00 P.M., the employee would check the amount of wood scrap; if the amount was not sufficient for his needs, he would cut up whole boards into scrap pieces.

Box 7.4

In viewing the performance of any system it is often quite useful to attempt to specify the kinds of criteria for which various performance levels would be deemed functional and other performance levels deemed dysfunctional. As one popular authority nicely put it, "Competence, like truth, beauty and contact lenses, is in the eye of the beholder."*

By specifying the goals satisfied by different system performance levels, conflicts in criteria of the kind described in Box 7.4 may be more readily recognized and may result in a redesign of the criteria system or perhaps a change in design of the system directed by the criteria so that the probability of congruent system performance levels is increased. Thus if Westfall employees were partially remunerated on the quality and quantity of furniture shipped, system performance levels deemed desirable by all parties might be achieved.

Multiple Causality

A concept related to the notion that system performance is always desirable in terms of some criterion is the complexity of assessing *why* a particular system performance level has occurred and how short-run actions affect long-run conditions. This is a very perplexing matter and involves the notions of feedback which will concern us throughout our studies of operations management.

A standard example for illustrating multiple causality is that based on the study of a wilderness area by an ecologist. Suppose he finds that the mountain sheep population is decreasing. A rather simple cause-effect relationship is to establish that wolves eat sheep and therefore that the "solution" to this problem is to introduce a bounty for wolves. Such a solution, however, does not take account of the other many interrelated factors. The sheep themselves need food and perhaps the problem is due to a diminished supply of plant life caused by a drought. Notice also that in the preceding statements we have let ourselves ascertain that in fact a "problem" actually exists. Who says so? On what basis do we determine

*L. J. Peter and R. Hull, *The Peter Principle,* Bantam Books, 1969, p. 26.

that a decrease in the mountain sheep population represents a problem? What are the criteria for which a decrease in sheep population is dysfunctional? functional? This is no small matter, but let us for the moment brush it aside and think of a diminished sheep population as a problem.

Since wolves eat sheep perhaps a bounty on wolves represents a good solution to this problem. However, wolves not only eat sheep, they eat other animals such as jackrabbits. A bounty on wolves would tend to increase the jackrabbit population. Since the jackrabbit population eats some of the same forage as sheep, our "solution" may in fact worsen the "problem." Moreover, if the sheep population is too large relative to the natural supply of forage, perhaps the best long-run solution to insuring that a healthy sheep population exists (is that the surrogate criterion or is it pure numbers of sheep alive at one accounting period or point in time?) is to not only let, but to encourage the wolves to eat the weaker animals.

From the systems point of view, there are three major points to be gleaned from this example. First, the subsystem problem that we have identified is embedded in a larger supersystem; solutions to a subsystem problem will affect that supersystem. In our example, help to the sheep represents help to the jackrabbits which worsens the problem for the sheep in the long run. Also, other subsystems have an effect on our analysis—natural forage and rainfall, for example.

Second, and perhaps even more importantly, we must come back to the role of the investigator in the problem solution, particularly in terms of criteria. If the "study" were done by sheep hunters, the criteria are rather obvious; but for an ecologist, exactly why should sheep be favored? Why not the wolves, or the jackrabbits, or even the natural forage? Clearly if the sheep did not need the grass, it would have a chance to spread more rapidly.

Third, the analysis did not explicitly deal with a time or discounting dimension; a long run "solution" for sheep might be their present elimination in order to establish a better natural forage. The point is, that we have implicitly established a criterion that says that the present population of sheep is in some way better than wolves, jackrabbits, grass, or future populations of sheep.

The need for detached analysis that does not casually adopt evaluative criteria is fairly obvious for an ecologist, and the same notions apply in subtle ways to operations management problems. Unfortunately, operations management problems are much more difficult to see and view in a detached way; one can be considerably more detached about sheep and wolves than about people and existing methods of operation. Nevertheless, surrogate criteria and one's point of view dominate analyses of any sort.

The recognition that problem formulations and analyses will shift as criteria change will lead to better system design efforts. We can see at Westfall that a change in chair-building methods can have a profound influence on both the operations that succeed chair building (e.g., finishing) and on those that precede chair building (e.g., parts manufacture); moreover, a change can strongly influence the personal objectives or criteria of the individual employees. We also have implicitly assumed that increased chair production is "functional." Part of our analysis ought to include an assessment of criteria for which increased chair production would be dysfunctional. An obvious example would be if the demand for chairs was not consistent. Less obvious examples might include conditions imposed upon other plant operations such as a better capability to build tables to go with the chairs. We might also inquire whether increased chair output will be achieved from improvements in the surrogate criterion of increasing chair-building capacity or whether increased capacity will go unutilized because of other problems which will come up such as limitations on chair finishing.

The furniture industry is rife with complex feedback problems. The industry structure is such that entry can be achieved by a relatively unsophisticated manufacturer. The entering firm requires a very limited marketing organization, because broad exposure to retailers can be achieved at "furniture markets" held several times each year in certain cities. If the firm is successful at the furniture markets, it immediately faces the problem of trying to minimize the costs of physical distribution. These costs will tend to be high for a new firm since the firm will tend to possess a limited product line and therefore be required to market in a wide geographic area. A related force on the firm will be to expand its product line. This force will partially arise from satisfied customers and partially as a solution to the physical distribution cost problem.

Unfortunately, a broadened product line tends to cause manufacturing cost inefficiencies; the most visual of these derive from amortization of setup costs over smaller lot sizes. The solution is to manufacture in large lot sizes which, unfortunately, leads to poorly constituted finished goods inventories, back orders, and resultant poor customer service. The backlash from customers results in expediting and other stopgap actions, when these problems should be recognized as symptomatic.

Furniture industry protocol makes efficiency hard to achieve. Furniture is subject to rapid style changes which the manufacturer hopes will allow him to achieve product differentiation, and the retailer hopes will stimulate consumer buying. Style changes are relatively easy to accomplish with a production organization based on nonstandardized parts and are regarded as appropriate reasons for not standardizing parts.

Sales at furniture markets lead manufacturers to a near-sighted view of the retailer as the final consumer. Because of existing retailing practices and rapid style changes, retailers frequently hold sales to reduce inventories. The manufacturers in turn offer special sales concessions to dealers which result in retail inventory buildups. The result is a volume orientation based on the appeal of low prices, and the orientation of retailing personnel tends to be toward unloading at a "bargain" price; the consumer has little aid in basic need identification and fulfillment. As a result, consumers tend to have a reduced satisfaction in home furnishings relative to other consumer durables and the industry does not achieve substantial growth rates.

The lack of manufacturing identification with the final consumer because of his policy of selling at furniture markets leads to the retailer making the link to the final consumer, which leads to the lack of consumer identification with manufacturing brands, which leads to retailer dominance of the manufacturers, which in turn leads to the ability to enter the market easily. The effect is that many firms working to what they perceive as their individual interests do so at their collective cost.

SUMMARY REMARKS

In this chapter we have presented a model which can broadly be called functional analysis. This model concerns itself with identification and subsequent costing of the inherent function of either a good or service. The resultant cost acts as a surrogate criterion for system design effort. The function values established by the model allow one to make relative efficiency assessments of various subsystem design efforts. Through such an assessment, those subsystems which have the greatest potential for cost reduction can be identified. By the establishment of esteem value we explicitly note and identify that portion of a product or service's cost which does not add to the functional utility of the product or service. Such a statement of esteem cost or value does not carry with it some global assessment of goodness or a normative connotation, it is merely a descriptive measure. Given that descriptive measure, the operational problem or issue is how to achieve more esteem value with a given dollar cost or how to achieve the same amount of esteem with a reduced dollar cost.

The functional analysis model is directly oriented toward the criteria system and in achieving improved evolutionary speed in the design of that system. By starting with a single criterion and subsequently examining incremental criteria entities or functional constraints, it may be possible to design products and services more profitably and competitively in terms of basic customer needs.

Although functional analysis has been used for improved cost effectiveness in the design of physical goods, the inherent ideas are also applicable to services, and the potential payoffs there well may be many times larger than for functions that are more hardware oriented. To some extent the artificiality of differentiating between "hardware" and "software" or goods and services is highlighted by the model treatment of the inherent function of any good as actually a service; the inherent function of all of the examples considered in this chapter are best considered in terms of the services they provide to users.

The functional analysis model involves concepts that can be difficult to apply in particular circumstances, and the resultant data produced by the model tend to be imprecise and somewhat soft; it nonetheless is worthy of our attention as an emerging model to aid in the design of operational systems and the criteria systems which direct those system design efforts. To whatever extent this is possible, we will want to utilize the model in later chapters of this book and in our evolving understanding of operations management problems.

REFERENCES

Budnick, A. S. "Value Engineering—A Form of Industrial Engineering," *The Journal of Industrial Engineering,* Vol. XV, no. 4, July–August 1964.

Greve, John W., editor, *Value Engineering in Manufacturing,* Prentice-Hall, 1967.

Miles, L. D., *Techniques of Value Analysis and Engineering,* McGraw-Hill, 1963.

Miller, Stanley S. "How to Get the Most Out of Value Analysis," *Harvard Business Review,* January–February, 1955.

Ridge, Warren F., *Value Analysis for Better Management,* American Management Association, Inc., 1969.

CHAPTER REVIEW

I think that this chapter is one particularly worth the trouble for you to understand. The sequence of ideas is likely to be quite different from those you will find in other places. You can obtain important insights into many kinds of problems with the functional analysis model, and the approach can provide a useful structure to creative problem delineation and solution.

In some ways, the ideas in this chapter are most like those in Chapter 3, especially the role of criteria and the establishment of proper surrogate relationships. In other ways, this chapter builds on the notions of relevant costing presented in Chapter 5. The functional analysis model further attempts to push us away from the penchant for hard data; it does so by providing an approach for assessing and improving surrogate criteria.

OUTLINE OF THE CHAPTER

Introduction	(foundations)
The model	(generates alternatives)
Function value	(single surrogate criterion of use)
Esteem value	(all cost beyond use)
Evolution	(multiple use criteria)
Examples	(concepts applied)
Wood drying shed	(yoke of a proposed design)
Boat gasoline tank	(comparative subsystem evaluation)
Wristwatch	(high esteem nature)
Field warehouse	(function varies—even in same company)
The criteria set	(improved surrogate criteria)
Dysfunctionalism	(functional for what criteria?)
Multiple causality	(complex feedback relationships)
Summary remarks	(emerging useful model)

CENTRAL ISSUES

This chapter is concerned with costs and benefits. Rather than having benefit or value determined by cost, determination is based upon situation dependent *use*. The functional analysis model is useful in problem delineation as well as problem solution; it not only critically examines existing or proposed system designs, but forces examination of the relative roles played by subsystems in terms of supersystem criteria.

When the model has been applied to many subsystems which make up a supersystem, those with the greatest reduction potential are highlighted. Creative system design efforts can be directed to the areas of highest expected payoff.

The approach of the model is to tersely define the basic function or use provided by (or desired in) a system, think of the cheapest possible way to achieve the stated function, adopt the cost of that way as function value, and use that cost as the sole surrogate criterion for assessing proposed or existing means of achieving the function.

The audacious adoption of tersely stated function value as the single surrogate criterion often leads to inclusion of additional functional criterion entities. However, each of these new criterion entities has to "pass muster" on the way into the criteria system. If use cannot be clearly validated, the criteria must be integrated into the concept of esteem. The creative design of esteem characteristics is fostered by analysis which explicitly attempts to separate use from esteem features.

Several examples are presented in the chapter including use of the model for a wood-drying shed at Westfall. We will pick up this example again in Chapter 8 when we consider some models for implementation and control of a designed system. The diversity of the examples is intended to illustrate the use commonality of the functional analysis model. In particular the distinction between "good" and "service" is seen to be not genuine.

The concepts of dysfunctionalism and multiple causality point out the differences that exist in criteria orientation and the complex feedback relationships between criteria and system performance. Establishment of a surrogate criterion always opens up the possibility of suboptimization and actions taken in the light of perceived criteria have a way of leading to other perceived criteria which may or may not be congruent.

ASSIGNMENTS

1.   **Andrews Tool and Hardware Company***

On September 11, 1971, the executive planning board of the Andrews Tool and Hardware Company met for the first of a series of important meetings. The company, one of the larger industrial and consumer tool manufacturers in the country, had enjoyed a large share of the consumer tool market for a number of years. Recently, however, increasing imports of foreign-produced tools had cut rather deeply into their market share, and this series of meetings had been called to discuss what action should be taken to meet this threat.

John Maggard, vice-president for marketing, opened the meeting with these remarks: "As we all know, many of our hand tools, particularly in the consumer market, are meeting stiff foreign competition. In the last year, I estimate that our market share has dropped at least 5 percent, and I hardly think that it will stop there. Many of my district sales managers have interviewed hundreds of their wholesalers and retailers, and the consensus is this —there is no advantage in stocking our tools rather than imported stuff. Nearly every one of our sales features has been copied in one form or another by foreign manufacturers, and side by side there is little difference between competing products. The trade can purchase foreign stuff at better

*This case was written by Professor J. Brian Quinn at the Amos Tuck School of Business Administration, Dartmouth College, and is used with his permission.

than twenty per cent below our prices and still net higher margins. Gentlemen, I feel that some drastic changes are in order."

Mike Miller, advertising director, retorted quickly, "John, I really can't see how this problem has developed. We offer the consumer a full line of tools, from nail sets all the way up through power tools, and much of our line is interchangeable. Most of this import stuff is a one-shot proposition, which the buyer may never be able to match or replace. The full line is what we've stressed in our advertising, and I think more emphasis on it might do the trick."

"Mike, that's just the problem," replied Maggard. "It seems that the typical consumer-tool buyer, the home handyman, is only interested in one tool at a time. When he sees our product for, say $3.50, and an import for $2.98, and they appear basically identical; he picks the lower priced tool. He doesn't care about a full line, nor is he concerned about replacement parts —all he's interested in is the particular tool he's buying at the moment."

Dave Smith, president of Andrews Tool, broke in, "John, according to the last batch of sales figures you issued, some of our worst losses seem to be in the hand-drill line. From what you've found in the interview data, do you feel the same problems exist here as with the rest of the consumer tools?"

"Dave, generally speaking, the hand drill situation is a typical example of our problems. We've always tried to produce a quality drill—one that would stand up well both in the market and also in use. And I think the production boys have done a damn good job on our present model. But as I said before, I think we're overpriced in the market—our costs have to come down so we can compete favorably with the imports. I don't mean that quality has to go out the window, but something has to give."

Smith then turned to Jerry Hitchcock, vice-president for production, and asked, "What's your opinion on this, Jerry?"

"Dave, we've tried to produce this drill, to quality specifications, as cheaply as possible. Several major changes have been made in manufacture and assembly in the last couple years, and I think cost accounting will verify that we have shaved off every penny in production costs that is possible with our present design. We've tried to hold to reasonably standard machines for producing the drill, so that slack in its demand can be taken up by producing another item. I think that the production department has gone as far as it can without a major design change."

Bob Egeran from engineering design spoke up next, "Jerry, you infer that design hasn't made it easy enough for your men to drop the cost a few cents now and then. At your request, we've made several changes in the design of the drill. Last January we simplified the gear housing casting and found enough shortcuts in design to lower costs about eight cents per unit! We also reshaped the handles so that production could be increased 30 units an hour! We've tried to design a hand tool that will stand up as well as any on the market and still achieve this at a minimum of production cost. Frankly, although I haven't seen many imports, I think that ours is the best on the market—regardless of price—and that alone should sell it."

Smith broke in again quickly with, "O.K., let's not get hot over this. I think the design question deserves a lot of thought, but we're not meeting here to find a scapegoat. Personally, I think that Jerry may have put us on the right track; perhaps design modifications will provide the cost-cutting answer. John?"

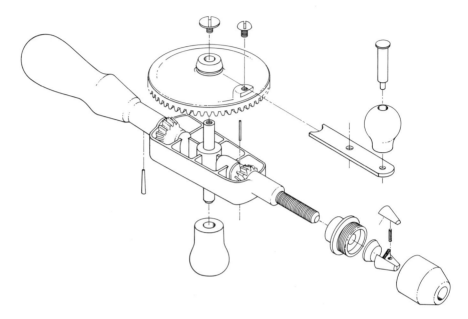

Figure 7.2 Andrews hand drill

"Dave, while we're on the question of design, I think we should consider not only production cost but also marketability. As I said earlier, there is little to differentiate our product from the foreign competition when they're side by side on a shelf. If we worked at this, perhaps we could design in something—and I'm not sure what it might be—that would make our product stand out. I realize we're trying to cut costs, but couldn't the drill be made more salable without a manufacturing price increase?"

"John, I don't know. Your idea definitely has merit, and perhaps changes can be made that would cut our costs and also differentiate the product. I've had a design consultant in the office a few times lately, and we've been talking over problems like this. Let me see what he has to say on this matter, and perhaps his firm can get us a report on the drill by our next meeting. I think we can agree that design changes which will facilitate manufacture—and also increase the marketability of the product—are what we're looking for here."

You are the design consultant for the Andrews Tool Company. Dave Smith has called you in after the executive meeting and described the previous conversation. Come to class prepared to present your recommendations (Fig. 7.2 shows the present drill).

2. For the Modern Furniture Company, Problem 22 in Chapter 6, identify the basic "operations" function. How can the functional analysis model be applied?

3. The president of the Baumritter Corporation has stated that Baumritter is not really in the furniture business; rather their goal is to help the homemaker create a pleasing environment for her family. In what ways might the distinction be important?

4. Apply the functional analysis model to the problem of selecting a college. Reconsider your answer to Problem 4 of Chapter 4.

5. Look again at your answer to Problem 4 of Chapter 5. Sort the costs that you considered relevant into those for function and those for esteem. Do any additional possibilities come to mind?

CHAPTER 8

PROJECT MANAGEMENT

The functional analysis model in Chapter 7 can be a mind-expanding device to identify important changes for an organization. Achieving those changes, however, is not always a simple matter. Many companies find themselves with no shortage of good ideas, but unable to implement the ideas fast enough. Similarly, many consulting reports contain cost-saving proposals which are not implemented. This chapter presents some models which are particularly useful for the design and implementation of major projects.

Project or network planning models are most widely used for governmental research and development contracts. However, as is typical with many techniques used by the government, the few relatively simple ideas on which the models are founded have become somewhat lost in bureaucratic procedures. Our interest in this chapter is to show how a complex project can be subdivided into a number of component tasks, the division of labor required to accomplish those tasks, and some reporting and control procedures for monitoring accomplishment of the tasks.

THE BASIC PERT MODEL

PERT (Performance Evaluation and Review Technique) is a model for planning and controling complex jobs; it divides the total job into a series of subjobs or tasks which are viewed as a network. The objective is to reduce the time required to accomplish large jobs or projects. The name PERT is the best-known acronym for the network planning process, and this chapter will be primarily devoted to an exposition of PERT models. However, the Critical Path Method (CPM) is also in fairly wide usage and we will briefly examine this model after the basic PERT model is presented.

Sequential Constraints

The easiest way to understand a PERT model is by example. In Chapter 7, a wood-drying shed was proposed for the Westfall Furniture Company. Let us suppose that the total job has been broken down into the set of tasks or activities presented as Table 8.1.

	Activity or task	Preceding activities	Time estimates (days)
a	Start	—	0, 0, 0
b	Purchase poles, trusses, and overhead doors	a	10, 10, 25
c	Purchase roof and walls	a	3, 3, 3
d	Purchase electric lights	a	1, 1, 1
e	Remove lumber now on site	a	1, 2, 3
f	Fill and grade to level surface	e	5, 7, 8
g	Excavate and pour pole footings	f	2, 3, 4
h	Set wooden poles	g, b	4, 5, 15
i	Set wooden trusses	h	3, 4, 8
j	Install roof	c, i	2, 4, 6
k	Install walls	c, i	2, 3, 3
l	Install overhead doors	j, k	4, 6, 10
m	Pour concrete floors	h	3, 3, 3
n	Install electric lights	d, j	2, 4, 5
o	Finish grade and landscape	l, m	5, 7, 9
p	Finish	n, o	0, 0, 0

Table 8.1 Wood drying shed activities

As noted in Table 8.1, the first task or activity is to start the project; immediately thereafter, we can issue purchase orders for poles, trusses, overhead doors, roofing materials, walls, and electric lights. These purchases are divided into three categories, since they involve different vendors. We also can immediately start on the project by removing lumber presently stored on the site where the building is to be constructed. The other activities are fairly self-explanatory.

In the second column of Table 8.1, precedence, or sequential requirements are presented. That is, it is necessary to accomplish activity e (removing lumber now stored on the site) before starting activity f (filling and grading the area to a level surface). Similarly, we need to complete the grading in activity f before activity g (excavating and pouring the footings) can be started. Activity h, setting the wooden poles in place, requires both the completion of pole footings and the purchase of poles. Note, however, that activities j (install roof) and k (install walls) have the same sequential requirements; this means that these two activities can proceed simultaneously.

The third column of Table 8.1 contains three estimates for the time required to accomplish the activities. We will see later why three estimates are required. For now, the center estimate may be regarded as the most likely time requirement.

Activities and Events

In PERT terminology, the subtasks necessary to accomplish a project are called activities. The completion of an activity is regarded as a milestone or event. The milestone nature of events is in keeping with sequential constraints which prohibit start of an activity until its predecessors have been completed. An event may represent the completion of more than one activity when start of a subsequent activity is dependent upon completion of more than one predecessor activity. Several cases in point are illustrated in Table 8.1, and we shall see shortly that depiction of this kind of event relationship is often facilitated by "dummy activities."

The basic PERT model portrays activities and events as a network, commonly called a PERT chart, arrow diagram, or directed graph. Figure 8.1 is a PERT chart for the wood-drying shed project.

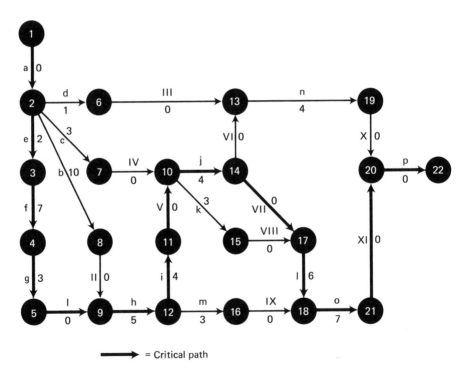

Fig. 8.1 PERT chart for the wood-drying shed project.

The activities labeled a through p in Table 8.1 are shown as arrows on the PERT chart. Completion of an activity is represented by a circle or node. Starting with node 1 we see that activity a culminates in node 2 which represents the completion of activity a. Since activity a depicts the start of the project, it may seem a little odd to have an event which depicts the completion of starting. This convention and a similar one for finishing are required by some computer programs, and they make comparison of PERT and CPM somewhat more straightforward. From event 2, activities b, c, d, and e are initiated resulting in events 8, 7, 6, and 3 respectively. If we follow the path based upon activities e, f, and g resulting in events 3, 4, and 5, we now desire to schedule activity h which follows activity g. However, activity h requires more than is depicted in the event or milestone numbered 5. Our sequential constraints require that activity h, setting the wooden poles, requires footings as well as poles. Event 9 is included in Fig. 8.1 to represent the completion of both activities b and g. This event is achieved by two dummy activities labeled I and II in the diagram and having zero associated times.

Dummy Activities

There are 11 dummy activities shown in Fig. 8.1. For ease of exposition, whenever two activities necessarily precede another, completion of each activity is shown separately with two dummies depicting completion of both activities. An exception is seen in the event numbered 18. Activity o must be preceded by activities l and m. Note that event 16 signifies completion of activity m, and event 18 depicts completion of both activities l and m without a separate completion on l. We see that it is possible to depict the correct precedence relationships in more than one way.

Figure 8.1 could be constructed with substantially fewer dummies. Figure 8.2 simplifies Fig. 8.1 by eliminating 9 of the 11 dummy activities and reducing the total number of events to 13.

Note that whereas in Fig. 8.1 activity h required a separate milestone for the completion of both activities b and g, we show that condition in Fig. 8.2 with event 7. However, event 8 in Fig. 8.2 still requires a dummy activity. This is so because activity n requires the completion of both activities d and j, whereas activity l requires j (and k) but not d. The other dummy activity shown in Fig. 8.2 derives from activity l requiring the completion of both activities j and k, but they both begin with the same milestone, event 5. The condition shown as Fig. 8.3 is not permissible; since computer programs identify activities by pairs of event numbers, both activities j and k would be represented as 5-9 in this case.

In the balance of our discussion of the wood-drying shed, we will use Fig. 8.2, although in many ways the extra dummy activities used in Fig. 8.1 clarify the basic PERT structure.

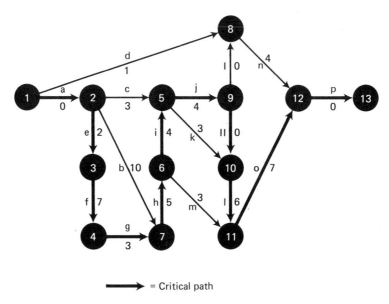

Fig. 8.2 PERT chart for the wood drying shed project (Simplified).

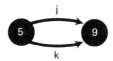

Figure 8.3   Parallel activities (incorrect)

The Critical Path

The critical path is that set of dependent sequential relationships which results in the longest time from start to finish of the project. Ascertaining the critical path involves calculating the longest cumulative time for each possible path through the network. We can see from Fig. 8.2 that one path goes from event 1 to event 8 to event 12 to event 13, but this path only requires the completion of activities d, n, and p.

In Table 8.1, the last column is titled "Time estimates" and includes three numbers for each activity. Let us for the moment only concern ourselves with the middle estimate, which is the most likely time estimate for each activity. These times are shown next to the activity letters in Fig. 8.2.

We see that activity a requires zero time so that event 2 is achieved at time zero. Event 3 is achieved at the end of the second day, and event 4 is achieved seven days later at the end of day 9. Event 7 is achieved at the end of day 12 insofar as this event depicts the completion of activity g and its predecessors. However, event 7 also depicts the completion of activity b which can occur at the end of day 10. Since the event signifies completion of both b and g, it is achieved at the end of day 12. Similarly, event 5 is achieved at the end of day 21 even though activity c could have been completed at the end of the third day. Event 10 is dominated by activity j and its four-day time requirement over activity k's three-day requirement, and is achieved at the end of day 25. Similarly, event 11 is achieved at the end of 31 days even though activity m can be completed at the end of 20 days. Thus the critical path through the network is events 1, 2, 3, 4, 7, 6, 5, 9, 10, 11, 12, 13. The total time required to reach event 13 is 38 days.

Slack

For those activities which are not on the critical path, it is possible for delays not to adversely affect the scheduled time of 38 days. Note that event 12 will be reached at the end of the 38th day. Since activity n precedes event 12 but is not on the critical path, it could be started as late as at the end of the 34th day. Since both of its predecessor events, d and j (j dominating) will be completed by the end of the 25th day, nine days of slack exist.

Table 8.2 shows the slack available for the activities comprising Fig. 8.2.

Note that although the critical path is long and somewhat involved, encompassing many activities, there still is substantial slack on some aspects of the project. For example, there seems to be no hurry to purchase the roofs, walls, and electric lights. Similarly, the concrete floor can be scheduled with considerable flexibility.

In some projects, the slack report is the most important document. It defines how much tolerance remains on noncritical path activities before they too will become critical. The existence of slack on some projects infers that certain work centers, resources, or manpower are being underutilized. It is sometimes possible to shift resources from one activity to another, thereby expediting critical activities and the entire completion time cycle. In fact, it should be quite clear that one of the major benefits of the PERT model is to know where expediting will achieve the greatest payoffs. For the wood-drying shed example, there is little point in speeding up the purchase of certain components. On the other hand, we will soon see that although the purchase of poles, trusses, and overhead doors is not on the critical path as presently calculated, it nevertheless is worthy of our concern.

Activity	Expected completion date (T_E)	Latest allowable completion date (T_L)	Slack ($T_L - T_E$)
a	0	0	*
b	10	12	2
c	3	21	18
d	1	34	33
e	2	2	*
f	9	9	*
g	12	12	*
h	17	17	*
i	21	21	*
j	25	25	*
k	24	25	1
l	31	31	*
m	20	31	11
n	29	38	9
o	38	38	*
p	38	38	*
I	25	34	9
II	25	25	*

* Critical path

Table 8.2 Available slack

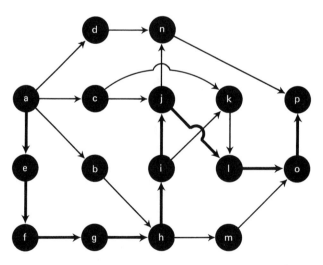

Fig. 8.4 CPM chart for the wood drying shed project.

Relation to Critical Path Method (CPM)

The basic PERT model described above is very similar to the Critical Path Method with one major change. Whereas the arrows in a PERT diagram represent activities and the nodes represent completion of the activities, in CPM the nodes represent both activities and events; the arrows merely show the sequential requirements of the activities. As a result, the use of dummy activities is not required. Any concrete preference for one technique over the other is usually based on personal criteria; some people find one structure more suitable to their problems than the other, and often the presence of a computer program dictates the choice. There are also some differences in terminology between the two techniques, but they seem more of an academic than a practical interest. Figure 8.4 shows our woodshed example with the CPM model.

Two other differences between CPM and PERT and a PERT cost approach which we will consider later in the chapter, and the use of probabilistic time estimates in PERT to which we now turn our attention.

PERT PROBABILITIES

Treatment of the time requirements for activities as deterministic, i.e., known with certainty and no variability, is not in keeping with our understanding of time requirements. That is, how did we find out that it will take ten days to purchase poles, trusses, and overhead doors for the wood drying shed? Surely these times tend to be random variables, and a model which reflected the uncertainties well might be considered more "valid."

Three Time Estimates

The PERT model considers the time for each activity as having a probability distribution, and paths through the network are calculated using these probability distributions. In Table 8.1 the last column has three time estimates separated by commas. In our analysis up to this point we have used only the middle estimate. The three estimates are obtained from people most intimately involved with accomplishing the activities or tasks, and are stated as the optimistic, most likely, and pessimistic estimates.

The three time estimates are combined by assuming that the distribution of activity times is well modeled by the beta distribution. The probabilistic PERT model is based upon the following methods for calculating the mean, variance, and standard deviation for activity times:

$$t_e = (a+4m+b)/6$$

$$\sigma = (b-a)/6$$

$$\sigma^2 = [(b-a)/6]^2$$

where

  a = optimistic time estimate

  m = most likely time

  b = pessimistic time

  t_e = mean or expected time

  σ = standard deviation

  σ^2 = variance.

The beta distribution allows for phenomena to be represented by distributions that are symmetrical or are skewed either to the right or to the left. Figure 8.5 shows these three kinds of probability distributions. The first distribution is symmetrical, so that m (most likely time) = t_e (mean). This distribution describes the time estimates for events e, g, j, and o on our example. The second probability distribution shown in Fig. 8.5 is skewed to the right so that the mean or expected time is greater than the most likely time. This distribution might be used to describe activities h, i, and l. The opposite condition is shown in the third probability distribution of Fig. 8.5 where the mean time is less than the most likely time. This phenomenon exists for activities f and n.

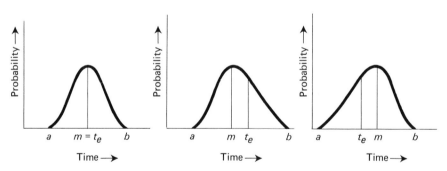

Fig. 8.5 Beta distributions for PERT times.

The three distributions given in Fig. 8.5 do not describe all of the time estimate distributions for the activities given in Table 8.1. Activities a, c, d, m, and p are shown as having no variability. Ignoring the start and finish activities, activities c, d, and m appear to be routine activities which are not subject to the same kinds of uncertainties as the others. Thus for example, the purchase of electric lights may be a simple matter of going to the local electrical supply store and picking them up.

Activity b reflects considerable uncertainty. Purchase of these materials takes 10 working days unless the supplier is out of stock; a back order necessitates shipment from the factory and an extra three weeks (15 working days). Although this distribution would be skewed to the right, it is not depicted in Fig. 8.5 since the optimistic and most likely times are equal. The opposite case exists for activity k where the most likely and pessimistic times are equal.

Outputs

The time estimates for the wood-drying shed activities can now be recalculated on the basis of expected values or mean times. Table 8.3 makes this calculation as well as recalculating the expected completion dates for the individual tasks and the overall project.

Activity	Mean time (t_e)	Expected completion date (T_E)	Latest allowable date (T_L)	Slack (T_L-T_E)
a	0	0	0	*
b	12.5	12.5	12.5	*
c	3.0	3.0	23.5	20.5
d	1.0	1.0	37.0	36.0
e	2.0	2.0	2.67	0.67
f	6.83	8.83	9.5	0.67
g	3.0	11.83	12.5	0.67
h	6.5	19.0	19.0	*
i	4.5	23.5	23.5	*
j	4.0	27.5	27.5	*
k	2.83	26.33	27.5	0.83
l	6.33	33.83	33.83	*
m	3.0	22.0	33.83	11.83
n	3.83	31.33	40.83	9.5
o	7.0	40.83	40.83	*
p	0	40.83	40.83	*
I	0	27.5	37.0	9.5
II	0	27.5	27.5	*

*Critical   path

Table 8.3 Expected value activity times

A comparison of Table 8.3 with Table 8.2 indicates that the expected completion date is no longer at the end of the 38th day; rather, we now expect to complete the project at day 40.83. The "extra" time derives from the time estimates themselves. More times are skewed toward pessimistic times than are offset by times skewed toward optimistic. This is particularly notable in activities b and h which together account for an expected increase of three days.

It is also interesting to note that basing the activity time for b on the expected value rather than the most likely estimate results in a change in the crictical path. Returning to Fig. 8.2, the critical path is no longer found from events 1-2-3-4-7 etc., it now follows the path of events 1-2-7 etc. Activities e, f, and g no longer are on the critical path, and Table 8.3 shows these three activities as having 0.67 days of slack.

An additional kind of output from a PERT system (particularly one that is computerized) presents probabilistic estimates of completing the project within certain times. Probabilities are computed by finding the total variance associated with all activities on the critical path. This is found by calculating each variance as indicated above and summing variances along the critical path. The assumption is made that the resulting distribution is normal, that its mean is the sum of the mean times for individual activities, and that its variance is the cumulative variance for these activities. Standard one-tail normal distribution tests can thereafter be made. For example, the data in Table 8.3 indicate an expected completion date of 40.83 days; tests could be made to find the probability of completion in 41 days, 45 days, 50 days, and so on.

An Assessment

There have been several criticisms of the PERT probabilistic methods in the literature. Specific criticisms include validity of the Beta distribution assumptions, the ability for people to consistently estimate what is meant by optimistic and pessimistic times, the psychological pressure to complete a task on schedule associated with a single time estimate, and the possibility of playing insidious games by clever estimating.

In many ways, PERT is the epitome of SWAG—Systematic Wild Guessing. The probabilistic procedures systematically combine wild guesses. However, as stated in a prior chapter, SWAG is a lot better than WAG. The probabilistic features can potentially be used to better represent the inherent uncertainties associated with many kinds of activities.

The probabilistic features can often be quite revealing. In our example, we saw how a change in critical paths took place as well as a change in expected completion date. Another kind of probabilistic feature comes about from the proper incorporation of the uncertainties. If the time estimates for activity g were increased from 2, 3, 4 to 3, 4, 5 we would see just such a result. The critical path would remain as indicated in Fig. 8.2, and the expected completion date would be increased from 40.83 days to 41.16 days. If a probabilistic test were now run for this critical path for completion on, say day 42, we would find that the probability for completing the project at the end of day 42 had increased, even though the critical path had also increased.

The removal of activity b from the critical path has a strong influence on the calculation, since it has the highest variance of any activity in the network. MacCrimmon and Ryavec discuss this phenomenon.* They show how critical paths can have competition from other paths which are almost critical and how the cumulative variance along the "almost critical paths" should not be ignored.

PERT/COST

PERT/COST is a logical extension of the basic PERT model; the criterion of cost has now been added to that of time. The addition of costs to the network concept once again forces us to reorient our thinking about the ways in which cost data should be collected. We now must build our costs around jobs and projects designed to accomplish a functional set of criteria. Our prior discussions of cost relevance will also be germane to determining proper levels of detail, allocation procedures, and related issues.

Objectives

The fundamental objectives of PERT/COST are to achieve more realistic estimates of the costs associated with activities and to provide means for control of a project so that interim cost results can be better understood. PERT/COST is largely used for governmental contracts, where a related goal is to reduce the size of cost overruns. Still another objective relates to achieving the best possible tradeoffs between time and cost. Typically the critical path for a project needs to be shortened, but this can be accomplished in more than one way; the PERT/COST methodology attempts to achieve time reductions in the most economical manner. To the extent that data imputs are relevant, time and cost tradeoffs are better understood.

To illustrate the basic ideas behind PERT/COST, let us turn to Fig. 8.6 which shows a budget for our wood-drying shed project.

The point C_B on the ordinate represents the total budget in dollars for the project and T_B on the abscissa represents the budget in time. The budgeted expenditure rate is not a linear connection of the origin and the intersection of points C_B and T_B. Almost any function conceivably could connect these points, but the one shown in Fig. 8.6 is based upon the fact that initial costs are fairly high as components are purchased with the

---

*K. R. MacCrimmon and C. A. Ryavec, "An Analytical Study of the PERT Assumptions," *Operations Research,* **12** no. 1 (January-February 1964): 16–37.

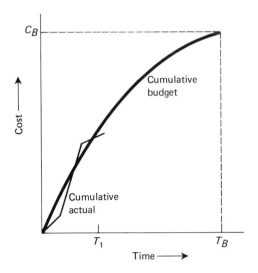

Fig. 8.6 Wood drying shed budget.

rate of expenditure decreasing toward the end of the project. The particular function chosen is illustrative of the wood-drying shed, and certainly
is not intended to have any normative connotations.

Also shown with a dotted line is the actual expenditure rate on the
project. At time T_1, cumulative actual expenditures are less than cumulative budgeted expenditures. We might conclude, therefore, that good cost
control is being achieved on this project and there is a high probability
of completing the total project within budgeted cost.

However, the approach used in Fig. 8.6 lacks one terribly important
ingredient, namely, performance data. The conclusion that the project is
in control assumes that results are being achieved on schedule. This may
or may not be the case.

The PERT breakdown of a total task into component activities allows
us to go beyond the model depicted in Fig. 8.6 to include performance
criteria; by budgeting costs for each of the subtasks, we also can make cost
comparisons more routinely and have better estimates for outcomes of the
total project. Let us say that point T_1 is the end of the third week or
fifteenth day. If we return to Table 8.3, we note that we expect to have
reached the milestones or events associated with the completion of activities a, b, c, d, e, f, and g. Let us assume that we have cost estimates for
each of these activities, and that the management report shown as Table
8.4 is provided.

Activity	Expected completion date	Actual completion date or present percent complete	Budgeted cost	Cost to date	Final overrun (underrun)
a	0	0	0	0	—
b	12.5	75%	$50,000	$65,000	$15,000
c	3.0	0%	25,000	0	
d	1.0	0%	10,000	0	
e	2.0	1.3	5,000	$ 3,000	($2,000)
f	8.83	12.0	15,000	$33,000	$18,000
g	11.83	15.0	8,000	$ 8,000	—
h	19.0	5%	12,000	$ 1,000	
i	23.5	0%	10,000	0	
j	27.5	0%	8,000	0	
k	26.33	0%	5,000	0	
l	33.83	0%	12,000	0	
m	22.0	0%	20,000	0	
n	31.33	0%	10,000	0	
o	46.83	0%	10,000	0	
p	40.83	0%	0	0	
_	27.5	0%	0	0	
ll	27.5	0%	0	0	

Table 8.4 Wood-drying shed: progress report—day 15.

Although the total budgeted for activities a through g is $113,000 and the total costs expended to date have been $110,000, the detailed progress report shows that the project is in trouble from both a cost and time standpoint. The cost for purchasing wooden poles, trusses, and overhead doors was estimated to be $50,000. The actual cost is $65,000 for a net cost overrun of $15,000 (30%). Also, it appears that the uncertainty associated with this activity was warranted; we expected the material to arrive at day 12.5, and they are not on the site at the end of day 15. The progress report of 75% complete indicates that these materials are expected at day 20; this in itself will push back the scheduled completion date by 7.5 days.

The favorable cumulative cost versus cumulative budget comparison shown in Fig. 8.6 comes about because the purchases of roof, walls, and lights have been delayed since they are not on the critical path. Of the remaining activities, activity 3 (remove lumber now on site) was accomplished in 1.3 days instead of the expected 2.0 days with a cost savings of $2,000. On the other hand, activity f (fill and grade to level surface) seems to have been seriously underestimated in terms of both required time and expense. Activity h (setting the wooden poles) is listed as being 5% complete with a $1,000 expenditure. Apparently, someone is trying to make the job go faster once the poles are received.

> This overlapping phenomenon is often possible in PERT networks. That is, the sequential constraints are not always as hard and fast as the model indicates, and sometimes sequential constraints can be eliminated by larger expenditures or different ways of accomplishing a task.

Work Packages

The information contained in Table 8.4 potentially represents very powerful information for management control purposes. Achieving this information, however, is another matter. Our discussions of cost data naturally led to cost accounting systems, and PERT/COST progress reports appear to be capable of construction from basic cost accounting information. Unfortunately, most cost-accounting systems are not set up in a way that such reports can be generated. Being dictated by financial accounting criteria (and convention), cost-accounting systems group costs by organizational areas, flows of materials, and time periods; PERT/COST data are associated with activities and events.

In order for PERT/COST data to be accumulated into reports such as that shown in Table 8.4, it is necessary for cost data to be gathered on the basis of the particular activities and events which make up a particular project. In essence, a cost-accounting system has to be designed for each project. This implies a unique chart of accounts so that costs can be accumulated on the same basis as the activities which measure progress towards the overall objective.

If we consider that an account exists for each activity in a network, we still might like to further subdivide costs which go into that account on bases such as material, labor, and overhead. In making these kinds of decisions, it seems appropriate to again fall back upon user oriented criteria sets. That is, what kinds of control might exist for these projects, or what kinds of managerial actions might be taken as a result of certain conditions.

It is my opinion that if the PERT/COST model is truly to be used as a management control device, then there is little need for overhead allocations. If a manager could be given up-to-date information on only those cost items over which he has some control, the possibility of his taking the correct action seems enhanced. Moreover many individuals who might be intimately involved with managing specific tasks in a project have limited understanding of accounting systems and therefore will find overhead allocations both difficult to understand and difficult to translate into concrete actions. In fact, overhead allocations can easily lead to the kinds of problems we discussed in Chapter 5.

Building an accounting system around a PERT chart brings us back to a recurring issue in operations management: the level of aggregation problem. The example we have been considering is intentionally short for illustrative purposes. When one is concerned with a PERT chart with hundreds or even thousands of activities, it is clear that some aggregating seems appropriate. Just what the proper level of aggregation is for a particular project cannot be stated as an ironclad rule. It obviously depends upon user criteria. The following defense department story illustrates the point rather well:

> Two system analysts were discussing the capabilities of a third systems analyst in rather disparaging terms. One especially critical remark was, "the trouble with that guy is that he throws around billions like they were mere millions."

The level of aggregation problem is different for managers concerned with different levels of activity within the project. If a large company had twenty or thirty projects going on simultaneously, it would seem appropriate for top management to be concerned with only the overall progress on each project. On the other hand, middle managers might be concerned with major system components in a project, subcomponents which make up major components, or smaller divisions of activities down to perhaps individual activities. We find ourselves, therefore, with a further design criterion for the accounting system. It should be capable of aggregating events into groups of events, groups of events into larger or different groups, *etc.,* on any basis consistent with managerial interest. Insufficient detail will not allow the manager to pinpoint responsibility consistent with the kinds of corrective actions open to him, and too much detail either wastes his time or causes him to disregard the information.

Within defense department applications, events are typically grouped into work packages which become the basic building blocks for the reporting and control system. There are three primary guides to the placing of events within work packages:

1. The events should be of a similar type or involve use of similar resources

2. The work packages should contain events with timings so that final accountings on packages are fairly frequent; if long periods of time elapse before outcomes are known, the value of the cost breakdown system deteriorates

3. Work packages should be fairly similar in dollar amounts

These general guidelines are often expressed in defense department applications in work packages not generally exceeding three months duration or $100,000 in cost with typical work packages ranging from $10,-000 to $50,000. Specific rules are difficult to set up. One defense department application simply was too large for existing computers to handle. A delightful editorial by Andrew Vazsonyi suggests that the final resolution for large PERT systems is a "Shredmaster Conveyor 400" that has the incredible ability to gobble up and shred into pulp 2500 pounds of computer printout per hour.*

Crashing

One major goal in the use of PERT/COST models is for better understandings and tradeoffs of time and cost. Frequently when a project is divided into activities and the critical path determined, the resultant expected time is longer than desired. Decreases in time require expediting or "crashing" of critical path activities. There are usually several activities which can be crashed and the cost-time tradeoffs well may differ. Thus Fig. 8.7 shows three hypothetical activities and associated cost versus time relationships.

Activity Y is depicted as having a u-shaped cost function which is minimized if the activity is accomplished in the time corresponding to the bottom of the u. Activity X has a rather peculiar looking cost function.

---

*Andrew Vazsonyi, "L'Histoire de Grandeur et de la Decadence de la Methode PERT," *Management Science,* **16,** no. 8 (April 1970,): 455.

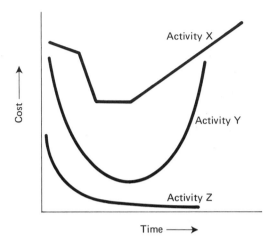

Fig. 8.7   Cost-time tradeoffs

For a certain range of times the cost does not vary, but upper and lower limits are reached where linear increases in cost as a function of time are experienced. The rate of linear cost increase is shown as being discontinuous at one point. Hypothetical activity Z is a cost-time tradeoff such that cost continually decreases as time increases.

Any of these or a myriad of other cost-time functions might represent some particular activity in some particular project. Although such functions are conceptually appealing, they can be extremely difficult to find in practice. PERT/COST is largely used for government contract work, and the author's personal experience leads to the cynical view that on government contracts any change of any kind always leads to an increase in cost; costs never go down. It is necessary to continually assess the criteria system, and one is sometimes forced to conclude that a major criterion for government contract cost-accounting systems is to justify increases in cost.

These kinds of issues pervade the use of PERT and PERT/COST. Nevertheless, although one should not casually accept minimization of relevant costs as the sole criterion, a model can indeed permit this goal to be better achieved, especially when good data are provided. Let us return once more to our wood-drying shed example. Suppose we accept the data presented in Table 8.3 as to critical path and project completion dates but are dissatisfied with completion in 40.83 days. We need to have the job completed in 38 days, and would like to crash activities along the critical path to achieve that deadline. With this objective in mind, the following crashing suggestions were obtained:

1. A special order placed for activity b which would cut two days off the expected time at a cost of $5,000

2. One additional day could be gained on activity b at a cost of $4,000

3. For activity h, setting the wooden poles, use of a local contracting firm could reduce time up to three days at $3,000 per day

4. There does not seem to be any way to reduce time requirements for setting the wooden roof tresses (activity i)

5. For activity j, extra manpower can be devoted to installing the roof. The cost will be $7,000 to save two days

6. For activity l the overhead doors can be installed in two days by bringing in a special door hanger from Boston. The net cost would be $20,000

7. Grading and landscaping (activity o) can be started sooner but certain aspects will necessarily have to be done over. The net result would be to cut up to two days at a cost of $3,000 per day

Although we need to cut 2.83 days from the expected data, for simplicity let us work with a three-day reduction. The cheapest place to reduce costs is through possibility number 1. This only allows for a two-day reduction, however, so an additional day must be picked up through alternative 3 or alternative 7. The net-time reduction of three days is achieved at a cost of $8,000. If we found ourselves into the project as we did in the progress report presented as Table 8.4, a reduced set of alternatives would be available to us and we would not be able to achieve a three-day saving for $8,000.

An interesting side issue is whether one should crash the schedule early in the project irrespective of cost so that later crash possibilities are still available if actual times are longer than anticipated. Thus for example, if we were depending on alternative 7 to cut one of the three days we only have one additional day left in that alternative as a hedge against uncertainties. It would seem more appropriate to reduce the expected completion date by alternative 3 keeping alternative 7 in reserve.

It may also be, of course, that reductions on the critical path can lead to different paths becoming critical. The expected time for activity b of 12.5 days is only slightly greater than the cumulative time associated with activities e, f, and g. Event 7 is reached in 11.83 days for that path. This means that when the time for activity b is reduced below 11.83, it will have no effect on the critical path unless activities e, f, or g are also crashed. It would seem then that our decision to accept alternative 1 may be somewhat shortsighted. On the other hand, the competition from alternative paths is not strong for activities h, l, and o. The crashing of activity j beyond 1.17 days will interfere with activity k.

These examples show the complexity of interrelationships between time and cost. One must be extremely wary of looking at any one activity in isolation from the rest. The PERT/COST model recognizes the inherent complexities and permits a much more rational tradeoff of time and cost for the entire project as an integrated effort.

Resource Allocation

A related cost issue involves the availability of resources when dictated by the project schedule and use of those resources when not dictated by the project schedule. It is quite possible and indeed probable that a PERT model will call for more people of a particular kind in some time period than are available. Various models for allocating resources to balance loads have been developed.*

The assumption of unlimited manpower and resources is clearly untenable for many projects. By starting some activities earlier than indicated and others later than indicated, some load leveling can often be achieved. The ease with which such leveling is achieved is dependent upon a particular project. The extent to which schedules for activities with slack can be changed before becoming critical is a major factor.

THE PROJECT MANAGEMENT CONCEPT

The chapter has so far been almost completely devoted to an exposition of the basic PERT model and extensions to include cost. Additional refinements could be added, but they are beyond our present scope. At this time, it is more useful to consider application of the ideas which underlie PERT models. A considerable amount of hoopla has been connected with PERT and PERT/COST. Defense department alphabet soup, make-work projects for computers, and defense contractor image-making have contributed to oversell and obfuscation of what are essentially a few sound but simple ideas. Andrew Vazsonyi illustrates this well in his description of a skeptical visitor to a defense contractor's two-story lecture hall for the display of PERT charts. It seems that after hearing of all the wondrous things accomplished in this specially designed room, the skeptic investigated the log book of all people using the room. He found that the primary

---

*A survey of these models can be found in E. W. Davis, "Resource Allocation in Project Network Models—A Survey," *The Journal of Industrial Engineering,* **17,** no. 4 (April 1966):177–88.

users were employees to update the PERT charts, that project managers only entered the room with visiting firemen, and that the chief engineer had never entered the room.*

All of this is enough to make one skeptical, and a healthy skepticism is a very useful commodity. On the other hand, one should guard against letting his skepticism go to the point where the baby is thrown out with the bath water. There are some fairly simple fundamental concepts such as breaking a job into subtasks or activities, assessing alternative ways to accomplish those activities, recognizing milestones or events which must be reached before subsequent activities can take place, finding those activities whose times affect the completion date and those whose times can be altered without affecting the final completion date, visualizing the entire process as a network, and making intelligent cost-time tradeoffs.

Let us now turn to an examination of how these fundamental ideas were used in a modest-sized company.

The ABC Company

The author was called in as a consultant to a manufacturing company (herein called ABC) which mined and converted a raw material into a consumer product. The company perceived an inadequate return from its manufacturing sector, but the exact definition of the assignment was kept open-ended and broad in nature to avoid artificial roadblocks to fundamental understanding. An important part of the consulting relationship involved problem delineation, which steadily evolved during the consultation period.

The study focussed initially on a manufacturing audit and the identification of potential cost reductions. Two major varieties of cost reduction seemed possible: across the board increases in worker productivity with the existing set of methods or technology, and significant changes in the methods themselves. The latter attack was taken with major cost reduction projects sought.

As major projects became identified, some broader issues became apparent. Perhaps the most fundamental observation was that there was no lack of perceived cost reduction potentials within the company. In fact, many of the specific cost-saving proposals suggested by the consulting study later seemed to have been previously identified by manufacturing personnel. The problem as seen by the middle managers in the manufacturing function was a lack of manpower to study and implement the cost-saving proposals. These middle managers also felt that there was insufficient direction from top management as to the priority of cost-reduction projects.

---

*Vazsonyi, *op. cit.* pp. 453–54.

At this point, the focus of the consulting study shifted from the identification of potential cost reductions to the *process* of implementing improvements within the company, to causes of sluggishness, and to ways in which the implementation process might be improved.

One of the main reasons for failure to implement improvements was that the line organization could not carry out improvement projects while taking care of day-to-day activities.

This situation seemed to require staff support for operations improvement projects in two major areas: in the technical or engineering area, and in managerial-project planning. Present improvement projects were accomplished largely by line managers whose technical talents were limited and who were clearly occupied with many other activities. Projects were undertaken without use of techniques such as PERT; few projects were finished on schedule, substantial cost overruns were frequent, and the number of projects which could be tackled was limited. A project management concept was recommended for major capital appropriation items and for problems which crossed funtional authority boundaries.

Project Authority

Just as normal accounting systems in a firm are not easily adaptable to projects, normal organizational systems are not easily adaptable to accomplishment of projects. The talents required come from people in different areas who are responsive to different sets of criteria. The essence of the project management concept is a different approach to authority delegation and placing of responsibility. The concept involves vesting of a special kind of authority for the accomplishment of the specific task.

The project management concept specifically charges a task force with accomplishment of a clearly delineated task. A proposal is made stating the resources required, and allocation of the resources to the project implies authority over the use of those resources that will not be circumvented for other needs. With authority comes responsibility.

The major benefit derived from the project management approach is the task orientation and delineation of authority for the specific project that cuts through formal layers of authority in the organization. A side benefit is the establishment of a goal that can be completed instead of a continuing issue such as profitability that can always be improved.

The task delegation of authority and concrete goal tend to make projects an enjoyable experience for team members. A true sense of accomplishment is often experienced which is quite different from the day-to-day frustrations of coping with ongoing operations. However, the *esprit de corps* and authority of the project team is partially gained at the expense of line operations and can be resented by those who are not on the team or who have given up the authority.

The authority of the task force on a specific project must be of a temporal nature. There should be a termination date after which authority is no longer vested in the project. Although the project management concept cuts through the formal layers of authority of an organization, one should not casually accept those monolithic layers of authority as necessarily bad. The authority delegation accomplishes the ongoing goals of the enterprise, and we must be careful that cutting through these layers for the accomplishment of specific tasks does not undermine the structure in some fundamental way.

Consideration of Alternatives

One of the most valuable aspects of the project management process is the structure provided for accomplishing some objective. Our prior discussions of the systems approach indicated that objectives are always capable of being stated in ways that are more fundamental to the enterprise. Evolution in stated objectives was clearly experienced on the initial ABC Company project as well as on subsequent projects. The selection of members for project teams as well as a deliberate attempt to spend time in freewheeling activities led to synergistic benefits.

All activities or project tasks can and should be questioned, and the statement of objectives for the overall project should also be subject to review. In many ways, this questioning process will be frustrating, particularly to action oriented line managers. The systems approach encourages more and more encompassing problem definitions which are increasingly in line with enterprise objectives, but which are also increasingly difficult to understand and solve.

The Project Concept at ABC

A particular project was to be selected by ABC manufacturing people from several which reasonably might be done within six to twelve months. A project team was set up to plan, evaluate, and coordinate this and a project manager was appointed. The team included the plant manager, chief engineer, supervisor directly responsible for the area in which the improvement was planned, purchasing agent (during the early stages), and project manager. The total job was broken down into component parts or activities. A PERT chart and schedule of resources required was thereafter prepared.

The project management concept had the approval and commitment of top management. This meant that resources needed for this project would have priority over alternative uses. This was most important in manpower resources, particularly engineering manpower. The project required one engineer's time for almost six months. Because this time was made available with other uses for this man's time receiving lower priority, the project was completed within a reasonable time period.

When the detailed list of required technical activities was finalized, the project team seemed rather surprised. The improvement project called for purchase of a new piece of capital equipment, and at the outset it was felt that only a minimal amount of engineering talent would be required. As it turned out, however, installation of the equipment required design of concrete footings, changes in handling systems for very heavy materials, structural steel designs for some auxiliary equipment, major changes in the electric power system, and redesign of a system for pumping abrasive materials.

Accomplishment of improvement projects within the ABC Company prior to the establishment of the project concept saw financial resources being committed, but not manpower resources with the same commitment. As a result, many projects seemed to not have someone clearly responsible for completion of specific tasks at specific times as well as someone clearly responsible for coordinating activities between different individuals and/or departments who might accomplish those tasks.

Although at the date of this writing the ABC Company has not established a formal cost-accounting system for project control, the size of projects considered are not of the magnitude discussed in the defense department literature. The ABC Company has annual sales of approximately $10 million, and the initial improvement project represented an expenditure of about $125,000. Nevertheless, the need for project control implies that accounting systems need to be constructed so as to accommodate this control. For the ABC company, a duplicate record-keeping system was established that ignored all overhead allocations and kept strict track of direct costs.

The project management concept at ABC resulted in the first project being completed within 10% of estimated cost, with cost savings that were greater than those stated at the outset, but with a slippage in final time schedule of two months from the anticipated seven months. Although the two-month slippage was unfortunate and potentially avoidable in future projects, the company felt that the overall timing was extraordinarily good and that without the close control and integration of all activities which the project management concept provided for, the actual time would have been at least doubled and probably tripled.

Several other projects were subsequently attacked, and good results were achieved. At the time of this writing, the project management concept is becoming an increasingly important part of ABC approaches to improved company operations.

Staff Support

The need for engineering staff support of improvement projects at the ABC company was described above. Two other kinds of necessary staff support were for the project management process itself and for relationships with outside vendors, i.e., purchasing with a broad definition of the term.

The need for someone within the organization to be continually concerned with the project management process derives from a preoccupation with results on the part of project team members. This is particularly so for those team members whose line operations will be affected by the project improvement. A good part of the benefits from the project concept come from consideration of more alternatives, as well as the relationships among alternative activities. It is necessary to keep action-oriented individuals from charging off with the first alternative which appears to be feasible.

Another kind of staff support of the basic project management process concerns construction of PERT charts and capital appropriations requests. In the ABC company, line managers tended to submit capital appropriation requests which were not well documented, and they regarded any delay in acceptance of their proposals as evidence of managerial stodginess.

In the course of evaluating the initial project at the ABC company, the author was impressed with the number and complexity of contacts with outside vendors of one kind and another. What initially seemed to be a fairly straightforward purchase of capital equipment involved a good deal of evolution in design specifications and the selection of a vendor who was not even considered at the outset. Although in a total sense the final piece of equipment did not vary greatly from that conceived initially, important choices were made in components and operating features. Integration of these design specifications into the final piece of equipment involved substantial interactions between ABC engineers and the capital equipment vendor. However, the number of contacts and the complexity of those contacts with other suppliers of resources was surprising. A relocation of material-handling facilities required a special crane to be brought from several hundred miles away. Electric equipment changes involved substantial coordination with the local power company. Weather conditions affected the ability of subcontractors to work on outside portions of the job. The inability of one subcontractor to perform what had been expected required the use of ABC maintenance personnel. Maintaining delivery schedules for purchased components required constant vendor contacts. Most important of all, a healthy feedback between design specifications and capabilities of many vendors led to important evolutionary improvements in understanding of the actual equipment needs.

SUMMARY REMARKS

In this chapter, we started with the basic PERT model which provides a structure for dividing a complex job into manageable subtasks or activities, understanding the sequential relationships or constraints among the activities, and knowing where controls will be most needed to achieve desired goals. The analysis was expanded to include cost considerations and alternative means for achieving ends; we found ourselves once again returning to the questions of cost relevance first proposed in Chapter 5 and continued into Chapter 7 where a model for better understanding basic objectives was presented. In Chapter 8, we have examined a model for achieving stated objectives and found that use of the model can have evolutionary feedbacks to the stated objectives.

The PERT and PERT/COST models have been presented in this chapter at a fairly basic level. Increasing complexities can be added, and more rigorous modeling procedures such as linear programming to determine cost-time tradeoffs have been proposed in the literature. However, it is the author's opinion that excursions into these methodologies tend to become somewhat academic. Underlying the models are some fairly simple yet powerful concepts which can lead to important enterprise benefits if utilized within the proper organizational framework.

REFERENCES

Evarts, Harry F., *Introduction to PERT,* Allyn and Bacon, 1964.

Levin, Richard I., and C. A. Kirkpatrick, *Planning and Control with PERT/CPM,* McGraw-Hill, 1966.

Miller, Robert W., *Schedule, Cost, and Profit Control with PERT,* McGraw-Hill, 1963.

Modev, Joseph J., and C. R. Phillips, *Project Management with CPM and PERT,* Reinhold Publishing Corp., London, 1964.

Wiest, Jerome D., and F. K. Levy, *A Management Guide to PERT/CPM,* Prentice-Hall, 1969.

CHAPTER REVIEW

This chapter completes our series of chapters explicity devoted to costs. However, you will find us returning again and again to cost considerations in the balance of the course. Cost is almost always an important surrogate criterion entity in the system design process. I hope that you now will be better able to assess the surrogate relationships and be a more sophisticated consumer of cost data.

There are three related major goals that I would like to see you gain from this chapter. First, I hope you have gained a basic understanding of PERT and related models; I also hope you will be able to see the proper role of extensions to these models.

Second, I believe it is valuable for you to understand how to use these models at the detailed level; although you may forget the details later, you will not forget that you have done the analysis before and that with a few hours study you could do it again. The combination of the first and second objectives means that if you are employed by a company that desires to use, or is using one of these models, you could do the detailed analysis or ask the right questions of those doing the analysis.

Third, I hope that you have gained some appreciation for the project management concept. Cutting through the formal layers of authority for a clearly defined objective can result in important enterprise benefits.

OUTLINE OF THE CHAPTER

Introduction   (models for achieving project objectives)

The basic PERT model   (project time-planning and control)

Sequential constraints   (which tasks necessarily precede others)

Activities and events   (PERT chart—tasks and milestones)

Dummy activities   (when essential)

The critical path   (longest cumulative time through network)

Slack   (activities not on critical path)

Relation to CPM   (nodes represent both activities and events)

PERT probabilities   (data are random variables)

Three time estimates   (optimistic, most likely, pessimistic)

Outputs   (expected value approach)

An assessment   (potential increase in informational content)

CENTRAL ISSUES

The basic PERT model divides a clearly defined objective or project into component tasks or activities. The sequential relationships of the activities can be shown by the PERT chart. The nodes of the chart represent milestones or events, and the arrows represent the tasks or activities necessary to achieve the events. The critical path is that route through the network or PERT chart which requires the longest time. Slack time exists for those activities not on the critical path. Slack is the amount of time by which those activities can be delayed before becoming part of the critical path.

By adding three time estimates (optimistic, most likely, pessimistic) to the basic PERT model, a probabilistic approach can be taken to project time control. The expected value for the total project completion date will vary from the sum of most likely times for critical path activities when the probability distributions for those times are skewed. The extent of variability in individual task time estimates determines the probability distribution of time required for the overall project.

PERT/COST adds the criterion of project cost control to project time control. The model requires a cost-accounting system to be tailor made for each project. Tradeoffs between time and cost typically need to be considered so that the expected completion date will be achieved with higher probability at the lowest additional cost.

The project management concept stresses the problem environment for which PERT-type models are appropriate. A case study of a real company was presented. Their basic problem was a lack of concentrated effort being devoted to the accomplishment of specific project type problems. Capital improvement projects involved many people within different parts of the organization; no single thread of authority for the project existed. The result was long completion times, cost overruns, and a limited ability to undertake significant cost reduction programs.

ASSIGNMENTS

1. A total job has been broken into 16 component tasks. The component tasks, sequential constraints, and time estimates follow:

Tasks	Preceding tasks	Time estimates (days)		
		Optimistic	Pessimistic	Most likely
A	—	10	20	15
B	A	5	7	7
C	A	6	12	8
D	A	9	9	9
E	B	14	20	17
F	B	9	10	10
G	C	12	30	20
H	C,D	3	3	3
I	D	15	20	15
J	E,F	7	8	8
K	F,G	15	40	18
L	H	9	12	10
M	H,I	7	8	7
N	J,K,L	6	9	8
O	L,M	5	5	5
P	N,O	2	2	2

Determine the critical path, slack, and expected duration for this project using PERT or CPM.

2. A project has 11 component tasks that can be accomplished either by one man working alone, or by several men working together. The tasks, sequential contraints, and time estimates follow:

Task	Predecessors	Man days required
A	—	10
B	A	8
C	A	5
D	B	6
E	D	8
F	C	7
G	E,F	4
H	F	2
I	F	3
J	H,I	3
K	J,G	2

You have up to five men that you can assign on a given day. A man must work full days on each project but the number working on a project can vary from day to day. Prepare a daily assignment sheet so as to finish the project in minimum time.

How many days could the project be compressed if unlimited manpower were available each day?

3. A company has divided a project into the following component tasks with associated time estimates, sequential constraints, and "crash" costs:

			"Crash" data	
Tasks	Preceding tasks	Time (days)	Possible # of days	$ per day
A	—	4	1	100
B	—	5	2	60
C	—	2	0	—
D	A	4	1	70
E	B	1	0	—
F	B,C	2	1	110
G	D,F	3	1	240
H	G	2	0	—
I	E	2	1	50
J	H,I	3	1	300

CHART
N,W
C,P
IMPROV

Determine the critical path and the slack for each element in the project.

4. Reconsider Problem 3:
   A. How would you reduce the completion date by 2 days? What is the cost?
   B. How would you reduce the completion date by 3 days? What is the cost?
   C. How would you reduce the completion date by 4 days? What is the cost?
   D. How would you reduce the completion date by 5 days? What is the cost?

5. For the 18-task project below, determine the critical path and slack associated with each task. Use the most likely estimate alone as the length of each task.

		Time Estimates (weeks)		
Task	Preceding tasks	Most likely	Optimistic	Pessimistic
A	—	5	5	5
B	A	6	5	7
C	A	9	9	10
D	B	6	5	6
E	C	7	5	10
F	C	4	4	5
G	C,D	1	1	1
H	E	9	7	10
I	F	18	18	20
J	H,I	7	5	15
K	F	12	10	20
L	J	5	4	7
M	J,K	4	4	8
N	L,M	9	7	10
O	G	20	10	40
P	O	18	12	24
Q	N	3	3	4
R	P,Q	6	5	8

Contract length 70 weeks

6. Repeat assignment 5 using the three time estimates and the formula given in the chapter. What difference does the consideration of variance make on your analysis?

7. The project (assignment 5) has been broken down into five job centers to facilitate control. The centers are as follows:

I	II	III	IV	V
B	A	F	I	N
D	C	K	J	Q
G	E	M	L	R
O	H			
P				

At the end of 30 weeks you receive the following report. Evaluate the status of the project and each job center.

	Budget	Spent	%Complete
A	10,000	11,000	100
B	10,800	10,500	100
C	18,500	18,400	100
D	10,500	10,500	100
E	14,400	15,000	100
F	10,400	10,400	100
G	1,800	2,000	100
H	17,600	16,800	85
I	55,000	30,300	60
J	21,400	0	0
K	32,500	15,400	55
L	15,500	0	0
M	10,000	0	0
N	44,000	0	0
O	37,800	14,200	40
P	32,400	0	0
Q	15,800	0	0
R	30,800	0	0

8. A penalty clause in the contract for this project (assignment 5) assigns a cost of $20,000 per week for every week or fractional part past week 70 that delivery is delayed.

Considering the condition in week 30 (assignment 7), what actions if any should be taken to accelerate the program? The cost of crashing and the limits on the tasks that can be accelerated are given below.

	Cost/wk	Limit (wks)
L	1,500	2
M	1,250	1
N	2,500	1
O	900	1.2
P	900	2
Q	2,500	.5
R	2,500	1

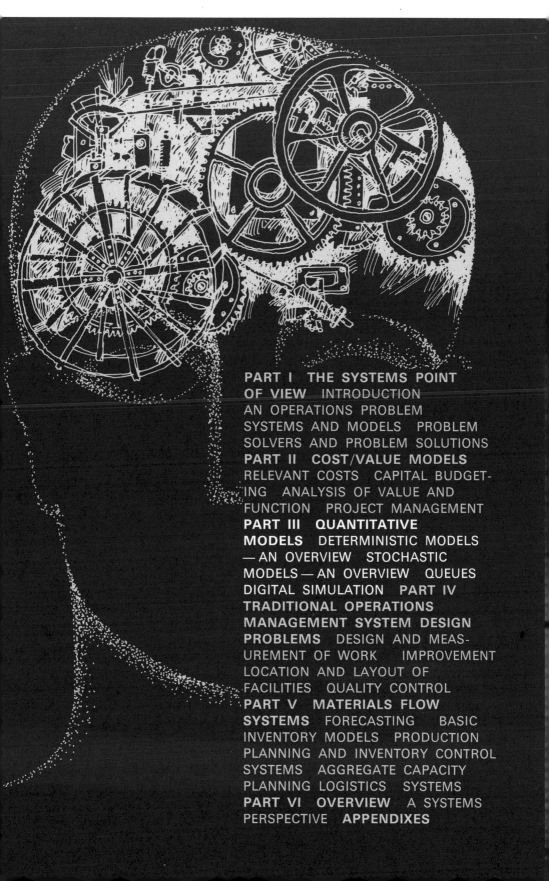

INTRODUCTION
TO PART III

The major goal of Part III is to foster your appreciation and under-standing of how quantitative models yield results to real world problems that are superior to results obtained from less rigorous approaches. For many of you, the kinds of problems used to illustrate techniques learned in quantitative analysis courses were too abstract; it takes time to appreciate the relevance of drawing balls from urns or estimating horse race results with statistical theory (if it worked, why wasn't the author at the track making his fortune instead of writing a book?).

There are many real world operations management problems which can be attacked with quantitative techniques and digital computation power. I believe that your acquiring a working knowledge of these techniques requires an exposure and commitment that goes beyond what we can reasonably accomplish in the basic operations management course. However, the course neither can nor should be considered in isolation. The design of a curriculum is an interesting system design problem to which your evolving understanding of the systems approach can be applied. Courses should be designed in terms of congruent surrogate criteria; the pragmatic nature of operations management can increase your interest in potential benefits obtained from quantitative courses, and prior grounding in quantitative techniques allows the operations management course to concentrate on applications.

Chapter 9 is a brief overview of deterministic models. The intent is to show what kinds of operations management problems lend themselves to solutions by these methods, and to illustrate the flavor of the analytical process when these deterministic models are used. The key aspect that you should see is the potential "richness" of the analysis; how through sensitivity analysis and postoptimality analysis it is possible to examine many kinds of "what if" questions and thereby derive a great deal of insight into the kinds of managerial action that are appropriate. An important distinction you should pick up in Chapter 9 and see reinforced in Chapter 10 is that between systems and models. Even though a particular problem may have stochastic elements, it is often possible to derive important insights from models which ignore the stochastic features.

Chapter 10 is a brief overview of stochastic models. In this chapter, the kinds of variability and uncertainty which exist in operations management problems are described, as well as some quantitative techniques used to determine proper managerial actions to cope with uncertainties. A major section of the chapter is devoted to an overview of decision theory and how the act-event consequence viewpoint can yield insight into complex problems.

Chapter 11 presents a way of looking at operations management problems where stochastic interactions dominate the character of the system. You will find that one of the most pervasive issues in operations management is the flow oriented or queuing nature of problems. It is essential for you to understand the ways in which information, materials, money, and other entities flow through a system, and you will find that flow-oriented or queuing models provide solutions to problems involving these entities that are quite superior (and often contradictory) to mental, intuitive, or nonflow oriented models.

Chapter 12 builds on the flow orientation to operations management problems with the consideration of a form of model building that is particularly felicitous to open-ended, user-oriented analyses: digital simulation. The use of digital computation power to investigate real world business problems is growing rapidly and for good reasons. The kind of modeling environment that can be established allows for analysis with poorly designed and improperly understood criteria sets. You will be able to see how the analysis of problems considered in Chapter 11 is made much richer with digital simulation models.

CHAPTER 9

DETERMINISTIC MODELS
— AN OVERVIEW

Models are often divided into the categories of deterministic and stochastic. In the deterministic case, the assumption is that all data required are known exactly without uncertainty or variability. Stochastic models, on the other hand, regard data requirements as probability distributions and the models are concerned with interactions or cascading influences of uncertain events. Since most business and economic phenomena appear to be of a random or stochastic nature, one's usual expectation is that deterministic models have very little applicability in the real world. Such is not the case.

It is useful to distinguish between problems and solution procedures for those problems. Problems may have uncertainties but solution procedures which ignore the uncertainties can often produce good results. Abstract arguments about deterministic versus stochastic models have little meaning. The distinction only seems pertinent in regard to individual problems; for a particular problem the basic question is whether or not uncertainty is the essence of the problem or whether the uncertainty reflects a limited knowledge about a few problem aspects. In some important operations management problems the former situation is true. For many other kinds of problems, however, we will find that uncertainties can be adequately examined with sensitivity analyses.

The distinction between stochastic and deterministic models can become quite academic. As more and more sensitivity analyses are performed with a given deterministic model, the resultant total analysis approaches being stochastic. It is quite possible that a particular model might be considered deterministic by one individual and stochastic by another. One test often used is whether a model will always produce the same result from the same starting conditions, or whether random interactions yield a distribution of final conditions. Our purpose in this chapter is not to define exact dichotomies. Rather it is to understand the basic flavor of deterministic analyses and why these models can yield important insights. In Chapter 10 we will briefly consider stochastic models, and Chapters 11 and 12 will expand the understanding to some important operations management considerations.

MATHEMATICAL PROGRAMMING MODELS

The most widely used deterministic models fall into the general category of mathematical programming with linear programming being the most popular. Although not all problems fit the conditions necessary for mathematical programming models, the techniques are continually being applied to a wider range of real world problems with important benefits resulting.

Linear Programming

Linear programming is a methodology for optimally allocating scarce resources among competing uses according to some criterion. Examples of linear-programming use include determination of types and quantities of products produced from a set of resources so as to maximize profitability, blending of ingredients to achieve certain outputs such as cattle feed to meet minimum nutritional constraints mixed from many available grains with different nutrient values and prices, scheduling of production in the face of seasonal demand patterns, the shipment of goods from several production or warehouse facilities to satisfy demands with minimum transportation costs, the constitution of inventories with limited funds in order to achieve minimum stockout conditions, optimal use of production facilities when alternative production methods are possible, minimization of material losses such as cutting of paper sizes from a large roll, and make-buy analyses to effectively utilize capacity.

A basic concept in mathematics is the solution of simultaneous equations when there are at least as many equations as unknowns, with the result being values for the unknowns which simultaneously satisfy the conditions of all equations. Linear programming is essentially a methodology for solving certain problems where there are more unknowns than linear equations. The result is an area of solution space where values for the unknowns will satisfy all the constraints reflected in the equations; linear programming methodologies perform an efficient search of that space to find the particular set of values for the unknowns which will result in minimization or maximization of some objective function. Let us consider a simple example to show how this process takes place.

Suppose that the monthly capacity for chair building and table building at Westfall were 14,000 units and 9,000 units respectively. Let us further suppose that the rough and finish mills can produce up to 15,000 units of either chairs or tables or any combination thereof. Let us also

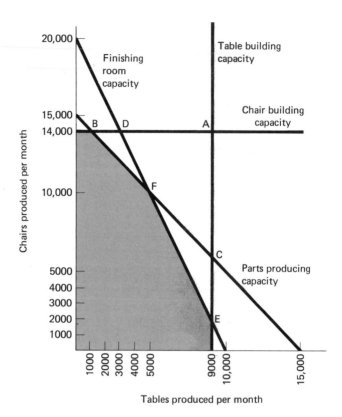

Fig. 9.1 Chair and table building capacities.

suppose that the finishing room could accommodate up to 20,000 chairs or 10,000 tables or any combination thereof. At what level should chairs and tables be produced? Figure 9.1 shows the production capacity constraints.

As shown in Fig. 9.1, the chair-building capacity is 14,000 units irrespective of the number of tables produced; similarly, the absolute capacity of tables is 9,000 per month irrespective of chair-building capacity. If it were possible to make parts enough for 14,000 chairs and 9,000 tables, we would do so. That is, we would produce at point A in Fig. 9.1. However, point A is not a feasible alternative. The constraint of parts-producing capacity is set at either 15,000 chairs or 15,000 tables or some combination of the two. The line depicting this constraint narrows the solution space or number of feasible alternatives; if 14,000 chairs are built only 1,000 tables can be produced and if 9,000 tables are made, only 6,000 chairs could be produced, (points B and C). The constraint of finishing room capacity also prohibits production at point A. If 14,000 chairs are run through the finishing line, only 3,000 tables can be run through, and if 9,000 tables are produced, only 2,000 chairs could be finished (points D and E).

The interaction of these two additional constraints further reduces the range of feasible solutions. The finishing room capacity constraint does not permit point C to be a feasible alternative, and the parts-producing capacity prohibits point D as a feasible alternative. The remaining solution space of feasible alternatives is bounded by points B, F, E, 9,000 on the abcissa, and 14,000 on the ordinate, (the shaded area in Fig. 9.1). 9.1).

We are still faced with the question of how many chairs and how many tables to make. The underlying theory of linear programming proves that the best solution will be at an extreme point in the feasible solution space. The casual observer might suggest point F but this implies something about profitability. If the relative profitability of chairs and tables is such that one chair yields more profit than one table, then point B is the optimum production mix. If chairs yielded $11.00 per unit and tables $10.00 per unit, production would yield a total profit of $164,000 ($11 × 14,000 + $10 × 1,000). Production at point F would yield only $160,000. If the contribution for chairs and tables was equal, then any point along the line between B and F would be equally desirable. Point E would become desirable when the slope of a line depicting relative profitability was steeper than that connecting points F and E.

The problem depicted in Fig. 9.1 is obviously oversimplified, but the basic form of analysis can be expanded to incorporate much more complex situations. Additional constraints such as minimal numbers of tables and chairs, or table-chair combinations are easily added, and analysis of more than two products simply means that graphical solutions cannot be employed. The ideas, however, are the same. A solution space of feasible alternatives is found and extreme points of that solution space are systematically searched with an objective function which expresses the relative desirability of alternatives. Linear programming methodologies permit one to know when the optimal solution is achieved as well as which direction to take toward optimality from a non-optimal solution.

Finding an optimal solution to a linear programming model is often the smallest part of the job, particularly with the availability of computer programs. Frequently, a much more interesting and demanding part of the analysis involves postoptimality studies. Various kinds of sensitivity analyses can be performed, usually based upon changes of assumptions such as the value of relaxing each constraint to determine the marginal benefit of that relaxation. Even in our simple example described above, we can see that if point F is the optimal solution, then increases in chair-building or table-building capacity are of no value; similarly, if point B is the optimum solution, then it is only chair-building capacity and parts-producing capacity that keeps us from earning greater profits. If the profit contribution line were parallel to the line connecting B and F, then increasing profitability is only achieved by increasing our ability to produce parts. If again the optimum point was point B, depending upon the slope of the profit line, marginal changes in chair-building capacity versus marginal changes in parts-producing capacity can be evaluated.

Similar analyses for more realistic problems often result in the most important benefits from the linear programming approach. As the complexity of the problem increases, the ability to intuitively understand the kinds of marginal tradeoffs involved in postoptimality analysis decreases sharply. Also, it should be clear that analysis of constraints implies an ability to change them; once again, we find ourselves concerned with a user-oriented model-building approach, since it is users who know *how* to achieve relaxation of the constraints.

Extensions

Linear programming assumes that constraints and criteria can be stated in linear relationships. That is, our parts-producing capacity can be divided into chairs and tables in some constant ratio. There are many problems which cannot tolerate the linear axioms. However, linear programming often provides insight into some of these problems that can be quite profound. Constraints that are not linear over their entire range may be "close enough" in pertinent sections, and the insight offered from postoptimality analysis still can lead to the right decisions being made in the real world situation.

Extensions of linear programming methodologies include the restriction of solution values to integer numbers for the variables. For example, it is doubtful that we would make 11,247.39 chairs and 3,752.61 tables. Solution of integer programming problems implies a great deal more than mere rounding of linear programming solution values, since the problems are combinatorial in nature.

Other extensions include quadratic programming, other approaches with nonlinear objective functions, and parametric linear programming where extensive sensitivity analyses are performed.

The complexity of solution procedures for extensions to basic linear programming models can be quite profound. As a result, many problems which do not really satisfy the assumptions of linear programming are formulated in nonlinear terms but solved with linear programming methodologies. The resultant problem solutions are often "good enough" for real world problems.

OTHER DETERMINISTIC MODELS

Many other kinds of mathematical analyses are primarily of a deterministic nature. A list would necessarily include things as diverse as *pro forma* income statements, Gantt bar charts for scheduling, the classical economic order quantity (EOQ) model, and the linear decision rule for aggregate capacity planning which we will consider in Chapter 20. It is neither feasible nor desirable to construct an exhaustive list. In the balance of this chapter, the goal of understanding benefits from deterministic model formulation perhaps is best served by a brief description of dynamic programming, then an exposition of heuristic and simulation approaches to problems of increasing complexity.

Dynamic Programming

Dynamic programming is a technique which allows a large problem with many variables to be split into subproblems, each with only a few variables. Solutions to the series of subproblems are relatively much easier to compute. The structure of dynamic programming is particularly useful for problems which involve a set of interactive decisions made over time. For example, production scheduling decisions made in one month affect the resultant end of the month inventories which in turn affect the production requirement for the following month.

If at the beginning of a year we considered all production scheduling strategies for each of the 12 ensuing months, the resultant problem would be enormous. The dynamic programming approach allows us to begin by only considering the schedule for the last month, solving that relatively simple problem, next solving the schedule for the next-to-last month with knowledge of the last month's schedule, etc.

Dynamic programming is applicable to many time-oriented problems, such as periodic maintenance of equipment decisions and other problems which can be structured as "decision trees." A major section in Chapter 10 is devoted to this kind of problem structure. As was true for linear programming, the most important benefits of the dynamic programming formulation are often achieved through extensive sensitivity analyses. Since decisions made in different time periods interact, it is even more difficult to intuitively understand the effects of various alterations in constraints.

Heuristics

For many kinds of deterministic problems, particularly those that are combinatorial in nature, formulation in mathematical programming terms is possible, but the resultant computational burden of solution is infeasible. In Chapter 15, we will see several of these models that have been proposed for dealing with the plant layout problem. We will also see

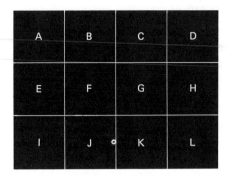

Fig. 9.2   1 2-department layout problem.

heuristic procedures for the balancing of assembly lines and plant location analyses.

For our purposes, the word *heuristic* may be defined as "an appealing
rule of thumb." To illustrate, let us turn to Fig. 9.2 which is a simple
12-department layout problem.

In this problem the objective is to place each department relative to
the other departments so that flow of material among the departments
(given) is moved over a minimum distance. In Chapter 15 we will see that
no feasible procedure exists for finding an optimum solution to this problem. For example, the problem can be formulated as an integer linear
program, but solution is computationally infeasible.

"An appealing rule of thumb" approach to this problem is to start
with some existing solution and to thereafter examine the incremental
effects of exchanging pairs of departments. If this pairwise exchange
heuristic is applied iteratively until no further pairwise exchanges will
reduce the summed flow-distances, the resulting solution is quite good
(but not necessarily optimal).

In Chapter 15 we will examine other heuristic procedures for this
problem. In our present context, it is worth noting that heuristic approaches represent a powerful way to achieve good solutions. The pairwise exchange heuristic will produce results for the 12-department layout
problem in about five seconds of computer time (Honeywell—General
Electric 635). Moreover, the final results achieved are within a few percentage points of the optimum.

Problem approaches based upon these appealing rules of thumb often
have similar properties. When properly devised, they can achieve quite
good solutions at moderate computational costs by iteratively attacking
pieces of the problem in a "reasonable" way.

Simulation

In Chapter 12 we will discuss simulation primarily as a technique for investigating stochastic problem situations. However, deterministic simulations can also be made. For many problems a mathematical representation can be constructed, but solution of those mathematical representations is beyond the power of formal mathematical analysis. In Chapter 21 we will examine the industrial dynamics model-building approach. Industrial dynamics is essentially a deterministic simulation, although elements of uncertainty can be added through sensitivity analyses and noise functions.

Still another approach to solving complex problems for which formal mathematical analysis is inadequate is with computer search methodologies. Thus linear programming algorithms allow for very efficient "searching" of the solution space of feasible alternatives; for many kinds of problems, such as those with important nonlinearities, search "heuristics" are used to find good solutions with, again, no guarantee of optimality. These search procedures almost invariably rely on the massive computational power of digital computers.

SUMMARY REMARKS

In this chapter we have attempted to briefly examine the kinds of problems which might be attacked with deterministic models, and the underlying strategy or approach of some of these models. When the essence of particular problems involves interactions of random events, deterministic models tend to become invalid and we are forced to use stochastic models. On the other hand, for many situations the uncertainties are only reflected in a few parameters which can be adequately explored through sensitivity analysis. When this is the case, significant reductions in modeling efforts are often experienced. Many times even though the underlying problem has uncertainties associated with it, a solution method which ignores the uncertainties can produce important insights.

It is important for future business executives to understand some of the more basic deterministic models and the fundamental approach embodied in those models. The final solutions provided from the models are only inputs into executive decision-making. The model reliance upon criteria which do not represent the entire criteria system implies that user interaction will be required. Moreover, we have seen that some of the more important outputs from these models indicate possible directions for executive action. We would expect a feedback as additional actions are conceived by executives; the proper modeling environment can provide very important insights into the desirability of such actions.

REFERENCES

Ackoff, Russell L., and Maurice W. Sasieni, *Fundamentals of Operations Research,* Wiley, 1968.

Bowman, E.H., "Production Scheduling by the Transportation Method of Linear Programming," *Operations Research,* vol **4,** no. 1 (Feb. 1956): 100–103.

Driebeck, Norman J., *Applied Linear Programming,* Addison-Wesley, 1969.

Stockton, R. Stansbury, *Introduction to Linear Programming,* Irwin, 1971.

Wagner, Harvey M., *Principles of Operations Research: With Applications to Managerial Decisions,* Prentice-Hall, 1969.

CHAPTER REVIEW

Chapters 10 and 11 are both short. I really do not see how it is possible for us to spend the time for an in-depth treatment of quantitative techniques in your operations management course and still cover other important materials. My sole goal in both of these chapters is to increase your belief in the value of studying quantitative materials; for you to see that the techniques are useful in the real world.

OUTLINE OF THE CHAPTER

Introduction	(problems *versus* models)
Mathematical programming	(growing use)
Linear programming	(search of feasible solution space)
Extensions	(L.P. axioms *versus* real world)
Other deterministic models	(diversity)
Dynamic programming	(series of subproblems)
Heuristics	(appealing rules of thumb)
Simulation	(computer power)
Summary remarks	(models and users)

CENTRAL ISSUES

Although real world problems often have uncertainties, models which do not incorporate uncertainty attributes often provide better insights for decision-making than alternative models. Although the assumptions of linear programming might not agree with the real world, for the range of decision alternatives available, an L. P. model might be "good enough."

The solution of mathematical models can quickly become computationally infeasible. Solution cost criteria make heuristic and other approximation procedures very appealing for many kinds of problems.

CHAPTER 10

STOCHASTIC MODELS
— AN OVERVIEW

We concluded Chapter 9 with the belief that future business executives should be able to understand some of the basic deterministic models and the kinds of modeling environments which can make use of those techniques. We now briefly turn our attention to stochastic analyses used for important operations management problems; the underlying models will be based largely upon probability theory and statistics (classical and Bayesian). We will start by identifying some problems in operations management and approaches useful for understanding those problems. Thereafter an overview of the decision theoretic approach to problems will be presented. The objective of the chapter is to reinforce the necessity for students to understand basic models for coping with uncertainty. Applications of this understanding will be developed in subsequent chapters.

VARIABILITY IN OPERATIONS MANAGEMENT

We saw in Chapter 8 that PERT models typically use three time estimates: most likely, pessimistic, and optimistic. Since actual times will always tend to vary somewhat from estimates, one is inclined to feel more comfortable with the three estimate technique which incorporates uncertainty. At the same time, it was noted that many applications use PERT or CPM in a deterministic manner without the three time estimates. This seeming inconsistency in fact illustrates the fundamental distinction between systems and models that we noted in Chapter 9: Problems may have uncertainties, but solution procedures which ignore the uncertainties can often produce good results. Whether the results are "good enough" depends upon the particular problem, available models, and criteria. Let us now attempt to more fully appreciate the ubiquitous variability that pervades operations management problems.

Cost Data

In our discussions of relevant cost data, we noted the inherent difficulty of establishing which costs were pertinent to particular decisions. At least in the case of past decisions, the costs are capable of being known. For future decisions costs must be estimated; the kind of model used for PERT time estimates would seem to offer better insights than models based purely on best guesses or extrapolation.

In the realm of financial accounting, the generation of *pro forma* statements for expected future operating results is a common practice. Such statements can be generated with sales and cost components being extrapolated, but surely most interested parties would like to see analyses indicating sensitivity of final results to variations in the estimates.

Our discussions of capital-budgeting models did not incorporate uncertainty except in passing reference. The expected cash flows are point estimates of what are more properly viewed as probability distributions. Uncertainties as to proper discount rates also exist and we noted the increased model usefulness of the present value profile approach.

A more fundamental kind of uncertainty in capital-budgeting models involves expected success of an investment. That is, many capital-budgeting decisions are risk oriented. Moreover, timings of the risk decisions often make them ideally suited to decision tree analyses. A good example is seen in the choice of drilling projects by an oil company. As actual experience is obtained, uncertainties are resolved (dry holes or productive wells); subsequent activities may depend quite heavily upon which way the uncertainties are resolved.

Queues

In Chapter 11 we will present a widely applicable approach to operations management problems which are based upon interactions of uncertain events. Queuing models are based upon a flow orientation to problems. The flows can be materials in manufacturing, such as furniture parts flowing through the Westfall factory; customers entering, going from place to place, and leaving a retail store; money transferred in and out of a firm's accounts; or water arriving via rain and snow melting to a series of rivers, dams, and lakes.

Any delay or stoppage in a flow represents an inventory or queue. For many flow-oriented systems, the criteria are intimately involved with these stoppages. Westfall would like to reduce work in process inventories, but also wants to obtain good machine utilization. They would like to decrease the time required for an item to be manufactured, but desire steady working hours and labor productivity. Retail stores attempt to minimize customers waiting times, but do not wish to have idle personnel. During a sale in one department, additional personnel may need to be transferred from a less intensively utilized department or temporarily hired. A firm desires to utilize funds in income-generating ways, but does not want to get caught short. And decisions made in river systems involve flood control, irrigation, drinking water, navigation, power generation, and pollution control.

For many of these flow-oriented problems, timings of events affecting the inventories or queues are uncertain; modeling approaches which incorporate the uncertainties will yield more fundamental insights into the kinds of managerial actions required than models based upon a deterministic view of the flows. The goal of Chapter 11 is to provide an understanding of basic models for flow systems with uncertainty. Chapter 12 will expand the understanding to show how digital simulation models can relax many of the limiting conditions associated with the more basic queuing models.

Work Measurement

In Chapters 13 and 14, we will be concerned with the design and measurement of work. The amount of output that results from the process will vary from day to day and hour to hour. Estimating this output for some operations management problems will require a probabilistic approach (e.g. required areas for work-in-process inventories).

One of the functions of a work measurement system is to estimate output for wage payment plans. A fair day's pay for a fair day's work is the goal. Estimates of fair times are often based upon observations of actual work requirements. An interest in having those estimates fairly reflect long term operating conditions calls for estimates to be based upon many observations. On the other hand, the cost of making estimates goes up as the number of observations increases. The net result is a statistical problem in sample size determination.

Sample sizes for work measurement problems are determined on the basis of required accuracy and precision in the estimates and by the inherent variability in the process observed.

Other statistical models used in work measurement include means of classifying attributes of potential employees (e.g., height, arm-reaching ability, finger dexterity), the concept of normal or required pace, and random sampling of various work activities.

Line Balancing

In Chapter 15 we will discuss models for the design of assembly lines. Examples include the proposed conveyorized chair-building procedure for Westfall, the rough mill, and the finishing room. In assembly line problems, the total job is split into component tasks (requiring work measurement models), and the work flows through sequential operations. The balance of these assembly lines is a nontrivial problem, especially when many tasks are performed such as in automobile assembly.

Assembly line problems are properly viewed in a queuing context since the required time for each task is a random variable and the interaction of these random variables gives rise to waiting lines and idle work stations.

In practice these problems are usually examined with deterministic models. The resultant assembly line design often requires considerable fine tuning in order to achieve the predicted output. A good example is seen in a new large finishing room designed for one of Baumritter's factories. After nine months of operation, the finishing room had only achieved about one half of the designed output rate; idle stations existed due to lack of material, and some items had to be removed from the conveyor because inadequate room existed to store the queue. A digital simulation study to make improvements in the layout of equipment and to identify better ways for loading the conveyors was designed by a consulting firm.

Quality Control

Variability exists for any production or conversion activity such as the size, weight, number of defects per square inch, etc. Tolerances on interchangeable parts are established so that a specified degree of variability can be accommodated. Statistical quality control models monitor production as it occurs. Closely related models are used to analyze lots or batches of material after production, such as in the case of purchased parts. The statistical models test hypotheses for critical dimensions and variability in those dimensions. Based upon sampling theory, plans are devised which specify the sample size and features which result in either acceptance or rejection of the hypotheses. The plans are designed so that specified error probabilities are not exceeded.

The underlying theory for quality control models is statistical hypothesis testing based upon the normal, binomial, and Poisson probability distributions. An understanding of the kinds of real world situations properly represented by these probability distributions is basic to statistical quality control. It is also necessary to be able to perform standard analyses based upon these distributions and to understand other probability concepts such as the central limit theorem.

Forecasting

In Chapter 17 a distinction is made between forecast and prediction where the former is based upon extrapolation of past data and the latter includes intuitive factors. Forecasting of the future based upon the past is a statistical process. Although regression and correlation models are often used for this purpose, in this book we will develop a different approach, exponential averaging or smoothing. Exponential averaging, although different from the more normal means of averaging, achieves results for many real world problems that are superior to those achieved through averaging procedures. Responsiveness of the average to new data is parameterized so that whatever level of stability-responsiveness is called for in a particular situation can be accommodated. The procedure is also computationally superior to the more usual averaging methods.

As an averaging procedure, exponential smoothing is a statistical process. The measure of central tendency can be subjected to hypothesis tests; tests are also made for variability in the process. Hypotheses about allowable forecast errors can be routinely tested in a computerized forecasting system. Other kinds of statistical tests are also performed. The goal is a procedure for routinely forecasting many items where exceptions based upon the rejection of hypotheses can be highlighted for managerial action.

Inventory Control

We noted above that inventories are queues; we will see that the major function of an inventory is to decouple successive stages in the production-distribution-consumption chain. Clearly the demand for most items is random, forecasts for expected demand will be in error, and the way to hedge against stockouts is to carry extra inventory. The amount of extra inventory carried is determined with statistical models where the probability of a stockout specified by management will not be exceeded.

Statistical approaches are also used to contend with variability in times required to replenish inventories, and in variability of usage during the replenishment or lead time period.

In most inventory control models, the underlying probability distribution is normal. However, we will see in Chapters 18 and 19 that it is necessary not to accept casually the assumption that variations in usage are adequately modeled by the normal or Guassian distribution. We will see that use of a statistical approach is valid when the underlying phenomena are well represented as a random process; the underlying demand for component parts, on the other hand, is often dictated by assembly schedules which are not properly viewed as random processes. When these essentially deterministic data are treated as stochastic, poor inventory control decisions can result.

Production Scheduling

The scheduling of production involves considerable uncertainty. The time to complete a job can be estimated by work measurement methodologies; all aside from the statistical nature of those estimates, actual times are strongly influenced by worker assignments and other phenomena. Whether equipment is ready when called for by the production schedule is another probabilistic matter. A selection of which job to run next from those waiting to be processed on a given piece of equipment results in variability in total time for a job to be completed. Moreover, the actual needs of the production line will vary from the forecasted needs and a commitment to the production schedule must usually be made before actual demands are known.

All of these random events mean that actual output will vary from scheduled output; even if actual output did not vary from scheduled output, actual needs are usually different from scheduled needs. A degree of imbalance between needs and availabilities in one period affects the production schedule for the next period over which we have control. The production scheduling process is therefore one of constant updating as actualities replace expectations.

In Chapters 19, 20, and 21, we will see that variabilities associated with production scheduling are not independent of other enterprise subsystems. The kind of job done in the market place influences both the absolute amount of production requirements and the mismatch between expectations and actualities. The ability to accurately forecast required work components makes estimates of productive output more reliable. Reduction of work-in-process inventories allows the production function to react more quickly. One needs to not only understand statistical models which can be used to represent underlying production scheduling phenomena, but to understand how to change the basic character of those phenomena.

DECISION THEORY MODELS

Let us now turn from specific operations management problems that are well investigated by stochastic models to an approach to problems which is stochastic in nature—decision theory. In a general way, decision theory fulfills two useful functions: the first is clarification and synthesis of the decision-making process, and the second is an operational tool for formal analysis. The structure of the procedure allows one to break down a problem into appropriate decision stages. It also encourages a better choice of system entities, because its act-event consequence way of thinking naturally leads to consideration of a wider choice of alternatives. Once a problem has been structured in a decision theoretic framework, means exist for formal analysis of the problem. The resultant solutions obtained can lead to important understanding of particular uncertainties and the managerial actions needed to cope with those uncertainties.

The basic structure of decision theory is built upon a set of alternative acts available to a decision maker and a set of possible events which may take place. The combination of some acts and some events results in outcomes that the decision maker finds favorable, while other combinations result in unfavorable outcomes. The consideration of a problem in terms of act-event consequences is often a mind-expanding experience. Different possible events are considered, leading to the consideration of more alternative acts, which in turn lead to still more possible events, etc. Let us briefly examine how this process might be applied to the Westfall conveyorized chair-building proposal.

The Decision Matrix

Let us start with a very simple set of alternatives and possible outcomes. The decision is to either build the conveyorized chair assembly line or not build it, and the possible events are that conveyorized chair building works or it doesn't work. Figure 10.1 shows these two acts and these two events.

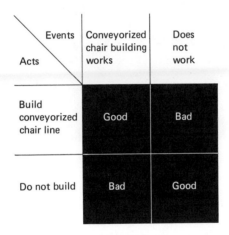

Fig. 10.1 Conveyorized chair-building decision matrix.

Figure 10.1 shows that if we build the conveyorized chair line and it works, in some way this will be "good" for the organization. On the other hand, if we build the conveyorized chair line and it does not work, this will be "bad." Similarly, if we choose not to build the conveyorized chair line and it would have produced desired results we will have made a mistake not building it, and if we do not build and it would not have worked we will have made the right choice.

The use of "good" and "bad" to categorize outcomes is not terribly informative. Also, the notion of the conveyor either working or not working like a light bulb seems a bit far-fetched. Suppose we could build a conveyorized chair-building line for the total process and that the incremental cost of this system is $50,000; also suppose the properly discounted stream of labor savings might be either –$25,000, $0, $50,000, $75,000 or $100,000. Let us assume that a partially conveyorized chair line could be built for $25,000. Figure 10.2 shows this expanded decision matrix and resultant outcomes.

Acts \ Events	Labor cost increases $25,000	Labor cost remains the same	Labor cost decreases $50,000	Labor cost decreases $75,000	Labor cost decreases $100,000
Build totally conveyorized chair line ($50,000)	– $75,000	– $50,000	$0	$25,000	$50,000
Build partially conveyorized chair line ($25,000)	– $50,000	– $25,000	$25,000	$50,000	$75,000
Do not build ($0)	– $25,000	$ 0	$50,000	$75,000	$100,000

Fig. 10.2 Expanded decision matrix.

If one were to look only at the outcomes depicted by the boxes, he might be tempted to pick the third act since in only one possible event out of five will this result in a net cash decrease. Moreover, in that case the other acts also result in even further net cash decreases. The missing ingredient is probability. That is, the chances of achieving a labor cost decrease of $100,000 by relying on existing chair-building methods do not seem very likely. Further, the probability of achieving various reductions is directly dependent upon the feasibility of the two proposed designs. The ability to achieve labor cost decreases through conveyorized chair building implies an understanding of models for the design and measurement of work, for the balancing of assembly line operations, and for the scheduling and coordination of chair building activities with the rest of the Baumritter organization. Decision theory provides the structure for the overall analysis. Models from operations management (and other areas) are used to estimate the outcomes of act-event consequences as well as to stimulate the inclusion of better acts and events into the analysis.

The Decision Tree

Figures 10.1 and 10.2 provide a structure for analysis, but they lack the sequential nature of many act-event decision situations. The decision tree overcomes this limitation and improves on the surrogate criteria used for evaluation.

Let us assume that the possible labor cost savings discussed above reflect output changes; that is, no men will be hired or fired in chair building, the output from the line will either decrease, remain the same, or increase in proportion to the labor savings. In discussions of conveyorized chair building in earlier chapters, we noted that increased production implied an ability to increase capacity in the chair-finishing operation as well as an ability to sell the increased volume. Figure 10.3 is a portion of the tree diagram associated with these acts and events.

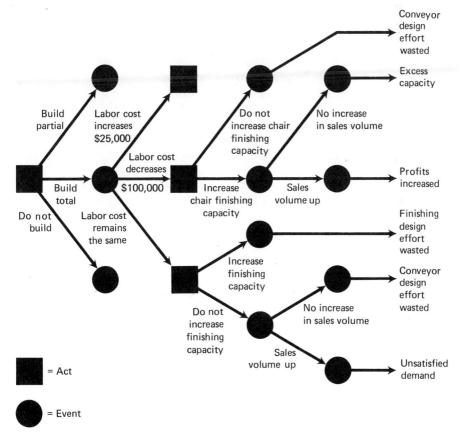

Fig. 10.3 Conveyorized chair-building decision tree.

Figure 10.3 more clearly shows the sequential nature of acts and events. We start with the same three possible acts shown in Fig. 10.2, but only three of the five possible events for the first act of Fig. 10.2 are shown. Note that based upon the outcome of our attempts to build a totally conveyorized line we are faced with another decision, namely, whether or not to increase finishing capacity. In Fig. 10.3, this is shown as an act without any chance events associated; clearly this could be revised if the problem involved uncertainties. That is, perhaps a decision is made to increase finishing capacity but the actual increase either does not result or should be viewed as a probability distribution. Note that the decision not to increase finishing capacity results in a terminal act-event combination where the conveyor design effort has been wasted. If finishing capacity is increased, then we need to know whether sales volume will also increase. If there is no increase in sales volume, we are faced with excess capacity. If sales volume goes up, profits for the company should be enhanced.

In the lower portion of Fig. 10.3, we have built the totally conveyorized line, but no increase in output has occurred. The decision whether to increase the finishing capacity or not seems fairly clear. An increase will only result in excess capacity in finishing with wasted design effort.

The sequential nature of the decision depicted in Fig. 10.3 indicates that the decision about increasing finishing capacity can be postponed until after the outcome from the earlier decision is known. Clearly in many kinds of situations this is not the case. However, for many decision situations partial information can be obtained at periodic intervals which allows for shifts in the decision strategy. For example, the decision to drill an oil well may imply the design of a tank collection system, but purchase of the items might be delayed pending analysis of core drill samples.

It should be clear from Fig. 10.3 that decision trees can become quite complex. Decision trees, like the process they model, are combinatorial in nature. The decision tree approach provides a logical structure for the real world complexities that exist in many decision problems. Fortunately, analysis of many such problems can be accomplished with dynamic programming methodologies.

Benefits and Use

Because decision theoretic models can accommodate the complexity of large interrelated decision problems, a better structure among the attributes of decision entities can be obtained. Sequential constraints, the value of subsequent information, and possible combinations of chance events are highlighted by these models and permit both improved insight into the problems as well as decisions which in the long run should be better than those based on rule of thumb.

A key aspect of the structure provided by decision theory models is the possibility of better communication between individuals who understand various pieces of the total decision problem. For example, the decision on the Westfall conveyorized chair-building line would involve many individuals in the company. An analysis which fostered the creative abilities of these individuals to identify new acts and events and to better assess their implications has a distinct chance of providing a better final solution than less rigorous approaches.

Although use of the models of decision theory is not extensive at this time, a rapid growth seems to be occurring; the author knows of many companies using the technique to evaluate the introduction of new products. It should be, however, noted that use of these models does not guarantee that favorable events will always occur. Professor Paul Vatter once expressed this very eloquently in a seminar the author attended. After a long buildup replete with German phrases, he summed it up something like, "all battle preparations are for naught if the angel of mercy spits on your flintlock."

Criteria

The criterion for evaluating the decision in Fig. 10.2 was net cash contribution. When we recognize the necessity of including probabilities, the result implies that the criterion is maximization of expected monetary value. Although expected value is a widely used criterion, the concept of utility plays a role in many analyses. Individuals and firms differ in their predisposition towards risk when amounts get high, with the relationship between expected monetary value and fundamental objectives becoming invalid. Most of us are less willing to flip coins for $1,000 than for $1.

A related issue has to do with feelings about optimism and pessimism. When the events include not only acts of nature but competitive forces which can be assumed hostile, then the criterion of always maximizing the minimum possible payoff or minimizing the maximum possible loss is often used (the so-called maximin criterion). Conversely, a criterion of optimism will ignore probabilities and always pick the act with the largest possible payoff (the so-called maximax criterion). Still another criterion is concerned with after-the-fact regret; the decision-maker attempts to select a strategy so that malevolent nature will produce results with his "might have beens" minimized (the so-called minimax regret criterion). Other criteria that differ from expected value are also used, as well as mixtures of criteria.*

---

*For a more complete discussion, the interested reader should see D. W. Miller and M. K. Starr, Executive Decisions and Operations Research, 2nd Ed. Prentice-Hall, 1970, Chapters 4 and 5.

The Role of Probability

One of the attributes of an event is its probability of happening. We saw above that these probabilities were critical to analysis of decision theory models. To achieve the benefits of decision theory, it is necessary for at least one of the model users to understand fundamental probability concepts; moreover, it is necessary for all users to at least believe in probability theory. This is well illustrated by one of the author's students who once had a very short job interview with an exploration executive of a major oil company; the student was prepared to perform sophisticated analyses, but the executive stated, "we don't believe in any of that highfalutin probability stuff here."

A proper user-oriented modeling environment will be quite helpful in establishing better communication among those who make subjective probability estimates and conceive new acts and events. There is, however, an analytical role to be played. The ways in which subsequent information is used to update probability estimates, the manipulation of prior distributions to posterior distributions, a facility with dimensional analysis, the ability to account for utility preferences, and the ability to perform sensitivity analyses all imply a level of analytic expertise. Again, there is also an implication that communication exists between those with the expertise and those who understand the problems.

SUMMARY REMARKS

Aspects of uncertainty pervade almost all operations management problems. It is valuable to understand the basic approaches to uncertainty, and to develop an appreciation for when and under what conditions models which do not reflect the uncertainties will yield good problem solutions. Moreover, when uncertainties are undesirable, or models are unable to indicate actions which adequately cope with the uncertainties, the character of the uncertainty can sometimes be changed by managerial action. Insight is provided into corrective actions by knowing what kinds of uncertainty *can* be accommodated.

Managerial actions can often be usefully structured into a decision theoretic model. Decision theory allows problems to be broken down into component parts and the interrelationships among the component parts can be better structured than with rule-of-thumb approaches. Although a significant learning investment is required for the student to adequately perform the detailed analyses, the investment is a worthwhile one. More and more problems are being structured with decision-theory approaches, and the results for these problems tend to be superior. It makes sense for prospective executives not only to be able to cope with these kinds of analyses, but indeed to foster growth in their use.

REFERENCES

Churchman, C. West, Russell L. Ackoff, and E. Leonard Arnoff, *Introduction to Operations Research,* Wiley, 1957.

Schlaifer, R., *Probability and Statistics for Business Decisions,* McGraw-Hill, 1959.

Simone, Albert J., *Probability: An Introduction with Applications,* Allyn and Bacon, 1967.

Springer, Clifford H., R. E. Herlihy, R. T. Mall, and R. I. Beggs, *Probabilistic Models,* Irwin, 1968.

Starr, Martin K., *Product Design and Decision Theory,* Prentice-Hall, 1963.

CHAPTER REVIEW

I stated the goal of this chapter at the end of Chapter 9; basically, my sole objective is for you to increase your awareness of real-world problems which can be studied with rigorous modeling procedures. Some stochastic models of particular relevance to operations management problems will be considered in Chapters 11 and 12.

OUTLINE OF THE CHAPTER

Introduction	(goals of the chapter)
Variability in operations management	(pervasive uncertainty)
Cost data	(estimates inexact)
Queues	(flow orientation)
Work measurement	(statistical models)
Line balancing	(cascading uncertainties)
Quality control	(statistical monitors)
Forecasting	(exponential averaging)
Inventory control	(safety stocks)
Production scheduling	(interacting random events)
Decision theory models	(structure for decision-making)
The Decision matrix	(act-event consequence)
The Decision tree	(sequential decisions)

Benefits and use	(rapid growth occurring)
Criteria	(alternative values)
The role of probability	(analytical ability)
Summary remarks	(understand models)

CENTRAL ISSUES

The pervasive nature of variability in operations management is illustrated by briefly describing some of the uncertainties associated with cost estimates, flows of materials, labor requirements, line balancing, product characteristics, demand estimates, replenishment cycles, and production scheduling. A thoroughgoing understanding of probability and statistics provides a context for viewing these and many other problems.

Decision theory models are presented as a structure for decision processes. The act-event consequence viewpoint acts as an incentive to the creative consideration of additional alternatives. The sequential nature of decision-making is modeled by the decision tree. There is a growing use of these models, and forward-looking future business executives will be proficient in their use.

CHAPTER 11

QUEUES

This chapter presents a widely applicable way of viewing and modeling operations management problems. Problem situations usually involve various flows such as materials, customer orders, people in and out of retail stores, or money in and out of a bank. Any delay or stoppage in these flows is a queue, frequently the cause of one's interest in flow-oriented problems. Thus one might be interested in a steady flow of chairs on a conveyor, in increasing the flow of customer orders, in having shorter waiting times in a retail store, or in keeping bank balances to a level that minimizes the probability of overdrafts but uses the maximum amount of money in productive or interest-bearing ways. By recognizing the common flow-oriented aspects of these situations, it is often possible to structure a particular problem situation in a flow-oriented or queuing model which will yield significant insights, not only into "good" solutions, but also into the problem identification area and into the appropriate design of a criteria set for a flow-oriented problem. There are a great many different kinds of flow-oriented or queuing problems, and there are many flow-oriented or queuing models which depict these situations, but they all have a few important common properties. This chapter will describe these common properties, present a few explicit queuing models, and depict some important issues in formulating or building specific queuing models.

FLOW SYSTEMS

In Chapter 3 we noted that some individuals find it useful to consider a system as a black box which transforms inputs into outputs. Those who view systems as universally possessing inputs and outputs by definition view all systems as having flows. We will see that a flow-oriented viewpoint of systems is widely applicable, and that an investment in understanding the common aspects of flow-oriented systems can be beneficial.

Delays or stoppages in a flow system are called queues; thus any inventory is a queue, an order backlog is a queue, or customers waiting to be serviced represent a queue.

Parameters

All flow-oriented or queuing systems involve four major features which define or describe the important flow characteristics of that system. The four major parameters of our general queuing model are arrivals, service, discipline, and criteria. Each of these will be discussed in detail.

The first of these features or parameters is the general notion of "arrival." The notion is necessarily broad enough to encompass such "arrivals" as loads of parts at the chair-building area, individual chairs arriving at each station on the conveyorized chair-finishing line, breakdowns occurring or arriving at some repair facility, customers arriving at a store, orders arriving at an order desk, rain arriving at the ground and later arriving via rivers at a dam, and fire alarms arriving at a fire station.

The second major feature or parameter of a queuing system is the notion of "service" which again must be considered in a very broad sense. Thus the parts which are brought to the chair-building area are assembled or serviced, the chair which arrives at the first lacquer station is sprayed or serviced, the breakdowns that occur are repaired, the retail customers are waited on, the orders are processed, water is released from the dam for generating electricity or irrigation, and the fires are put out.

The third feature or parameter which describes queuing systems is referred to as the "queue discipline." The queue discipline is a rule or set of rules which describes the order in which arrivals will be serviced. One simple queue discipline is first-come first-served; another is to always service the arrival from those waiting to be served with the shortest expected processing or service time (the so-called shortest operation next rule).

A fourth feature or parameter of a queuing system is the criterion or set of criteria that drive the design and operation of a queuing system. Thus if one's objective were to minimize the number of customers waiting in line, a queue discipline of shortest operation next would yield results that are superior to a queue discipline of first-come first-served. However, such a queue discipline would tend to push customers with large demands continuously back in their spot in the queue with resultant high waiting times. Criteria frequently are associated with delay or waiting times, as well as with the number of arrivals waiting to be served.

Both the arrivals and services have a time dimension. Specifically we will consider the times between arrivals and the times for service. Both of these times tend to be somewhat variable, and the extent of the variations affects various criteria of the queuing systems with which we will be interested, such as the expected time that an arrival will have to wait before being serviced and the number of arrivals that are usually waiting for service. To understand flow-oriented situations we will use models of a statistical nature in order to reflect variations in interarrival and service times. Thus a particular interarrival time may be thought of as having been drawn from a population of possible interarrival times, and a particular service time belongs to a population of possible service times.

We will see that when the populations of interarrival and service times can be approximated by common statistical distributions, it is easier to make predictions about queuing systems.

Utilization

The interaction of arrivals and services (with a queue discipline) gives rise to measures of effectiveness which the criteria system deems important. One of these measures of effectiveness is the extent to which the server is utilized, or conversely the extent of server idle time; this measure is commonly referred to as the "utilization factor" or "traffic intensity factor." Because of variability in the times between arrivals and/or service times, it is necessary for the average time between arrivals to be greater than the average service time; expressed in terms of rates (rates are the reciprocal of times—mean service time of ten minutes or 1/6 hour is a mean service rate of 6 per hour), it is necessary for the service rate to be greater than the arrival rate. Clearly the number of chairs arriving per hour at the chair finishing area cannot exceed the average number serviced per hour. The need for the service rate to exceed the arrival rate can be borne out somewhat by intuition: if the mean time between arrivals were less than the mean service time, the waiting line or queue would continue to build; if the average time between arrivals were equal to the average service time, the randomness or variability in arrivals and services would also cause the queue or waiting line to grow.

We noted in Chapter 10 that for some kinds of problems the stochastic features dominate. This condition is particularly true for queuing problems, and the only hedge against the uncertainties is to build in slack or idle time—the *average* service rate must be greater than the *average* arrival rate in order to tolerate variability around the averages.

The extent to which the service rate must be greater than the arrival rate depends heavily upon the amount of variability in interarrival and service times. For a given amount of variability or randomness in the service and arrival rates, as the arrival rate approaches the service rate, we can expect both the average waiting time and the number of arrivals waiting to be served to increase. The ratio of arrival rate to service rate is the utilization or traffic intensity factor and is commonly denoted by the Greek letter ρ.

We noted that the necessity for ρ being less than 1 is due to the interaction of the randomness or variability of arrivals or variability of services. It, therefore, follows that improvements in measures of effectiveness such as average waiting time can be obtained by decreasing ρ (one might normally increase the service rate rather than decrease the arrival rate but such a choice would obviously be dictated by criteria) or by decreasing the variability or randomness in arrivals and/or services. Thus the number of customers waiting to be served in a retail store can be decreased by providing faster service (e.g., a better checkout method in a self service store), by decreasing the number of customers (e.g., hire surly clerks), by inducing the customers to shop more uniformly throughout the day and week (e.g., give more trading stamps at "off" hours), or by decreasing variability in the time to serve the customers.

Categorization

Flow-oriented or queuing situations are often categorized as to whether they are single channel-single service, single channel-multiple service, multiple channel-single service, or multiple channel-multiple service. Figure 11.1 depicts these four kinds of queuing systems.

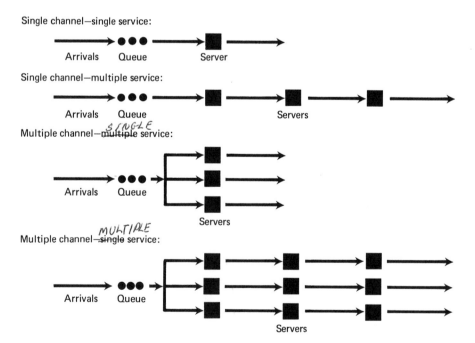

Single channel—single service:

Arrivals   Queue   Server

Single channel—multiple service:

Arrivals   Queue   Servers

Multiple channel—~~multiple~~ *SINGLE* service:

Arrivals   Queue

Servers

Multiple channel—~~single~~ *MULTIPLE* service:

Arrivals   Queue

Servers

Fig. 11.1 Queue categories.

The single channel-single service queuing situation may be exemplified by customers arriving at a single checkout stand in a supermarket. The single channel-multiple service kind of queuing situation depicts one's usual conception of an assembly line and also may be illustrated by a checkout counter at a supermarket with a checkout clerk, a person for bagging the groceries, and a person for taking the groceries to the customers' cars. The multiple channel-single service queuing system may be exemplified by a supermarket with several checkout counters with just a checkout clerk and the multiple channel-multiple service by the supermarket with multiple checkout counters, each having packaging and carryout personnel. Since each of these four kinds of queuing systems is possible in a supermarket, both the initial design (how many checkout counters to put in, ability to use two or three personnel) and the ongoing operation of a supermarket system (under what conditions to add or delete a channel or service point) are interesting examples.

EXAMPLES

Let us look at some examples and explicitly identify the features or parameters of arrivals, services, queue disciplines and criteria. In doing so, we will see the consequences of flow stoppages or queues and the ways in which a queue or flow orientation leads to particular problem solutions that can differ widely from intuitive feelings about those problems.

Westfall Furniture Plant

Let us start with the flow of materials within Westfall. We may think of that flow as beginning with logs "arriving" at a stock pile based upon buying decisions and delivery characteristics. The log stock pile is a queue which is "served" by sawing the logs into boards. The queue discipline would probably not be strict other than to achieve some rotation of the stock. The criteria for this queuing system are primarily to support continuous sawing (ρ of 1.0), to minimize the inventory investment (the queue of money), and to take advantage of favorable buying conditions.

The outputs from sawing represent arrivals to the air drying queue which also receives arrivals from lumber buying. Although all of the lumber inventory is "serviced" by the dry kilns, the lumber varies in thickness and the service time is partially dependent upon the thickness. Furthermore, the output from dry kilns has to be of thicknesses required by subsequent services. We can see that the material flow tends to become increasingly less homogeneous as logs are cut into particular thicknesses, boards are cut into particular lengths, lengths are glued into particular panels, panels are machined into particular parts, parts are held or allocated to particular items, and items are held for particular customers or distribution channels. We will see that queues or inventories allow quasi-independent operation of successive production and distribution stages; to whatever extent homogeneity can be built into the needs of a flow system, important improvements can be achieved. Thus if glued panels can be standardized, one "queue" of a standard size can support several subsequent needs.

The tempering shed queue between dry kilns and cutoff saws is to allow for mismatches in kiln output and cutoff saw needs. The criteria affecting the size and composition of dried board inventories at Westfall are related to the need for mismatches in kiln and cutoff saw production rates; thus, although sawing production hours can be extended or curtailed, the kilns operate 24 hours per day, 7 days per week. If annual kiln capacity is close to annual dry lumber needs, variations in cutoff sawing rates can only be achieved through dried board inventories. Conversely, the limited space available in the present Westfall tempering sheds indicates that sawing rates and kiln output rates are closely coordinated; the desire for changes in production levels is accommodated by excess kiln capacity and by inventories held after sawing.

All of the work in process inventories within Westfall (e.g., sawed boards, glued panels, semifinished parts, white goods, and subassemblies) serve a decoupling function similar to that of the tempering shed. That is, they permit quasi-autonomous operation of successive production stages. Furthermore, the larger these inventories, the greater the potential autonomy or degree of mismatch and the greater the ability to satisfy surrogate criteria that are local to the individual product creation stages (e.g., machine utilization and individual productivity).

Although larger work in process inventories permit potential increases in measures of local criteria, they also cost money and can lead to confusion when their physical presence impedes operations (this condition frequently occurs in the finish mill at Westfall). The objective is to strike a balance; to carefully constitute the work in process inventories so that maximum autonomy is achieved with a minimum total work in process queue and to more fully support those operations where autonomy is most valuable. Achieving this objective is a formidable task that is beyond our present scope. Part V of this book is devoted to materials flow system design.

Before leaving this brief flow-oriented view of Westfall operations, it is worth stating explicitly what may be intuitively obvious: All of the individual flow-oriented operations are interrelated in that the output of one stage becomes an arrival to a successive stage. Changes in any stage almost invariably affect the pattern of output from that stage which can often have a profound influence on the next stage or conversion process. Thus we have noted that a completely conveyorized chair-building line at

Westfall will have serious ramifications on chair finishing unless chairs are queued at the end of chair building or unless the process of chair finishing is changed to tolerate the input flow conditions established by chair building. Within the chair-building operation itself, the most serious flaw with conveyorized chair building is the lack of autonomy provided to individual operations.

Doctor's Office

Let us now consider the flow of customers or patients through a doctor's office as a queuing problem. A doctor's criteria might be thought of as maximizing revenue through seeing the largest number of patients consistent with providing adequate medical attention. A doctor might also feel under some constraint with regard to the amount of time that his patients have to wait, but some of us have empirical experience that many doctors set this constraint fairly high (a similar example relates to the cost implicitly associated with student waiting time for registration). To some extent, patient waiting time influences revenue determination through feedback mechanisms. Thus if experience leads to expected long waits, one may be less inclined to go to the doctor or perhaps be more inclined to seek out competitive sources of medical attention. A related cause-effect linkage or feedback mechanism might be utilized to advantage in terms of the doctor's criteria. Perhaps patients who are unpleasant or hypochondriacal should be subjected to long waiting times.

If patients represent arrivals into the system and times spent in consultation with the doctor represent servicing, we would expect variability both in the times between arrivals for the patients as well as in the servicing times because of variations in particular patient needs. The doctor in attempting to maximize his income will attempt to work with a ρ or utilization factor close to unity. He will want to be busy as much as possible. But as we have noted above, as utilization factors approach one, expected waiting times and the average number of people waiting grow dramatically.

One might reasonably question the ability of a doctor to increase his utilization factor when such an increase implies an ability to substantially increase the arrival rate. Does the doctor have more potential patients than he can presently handle? It very well may be, however, that a doctor with a given number of patients might wish to schedule his appointments with those patients in an intensive way so that he might have time unhindered by appointments to use for other pursuits such as research, hospital visits, or golf.

The effect of appointment-making by the doctor has some interesting queuing aspects. We have noted that waiting times and queues are partially determined by the variability or randomness in arrival patterns.

The only way one can design a system to cope with wide variability in arrival patterns (or in service patterns) is to accept a relatively lower utilization factor, ρ. However, for a retail store example we noted that increased performance (for the stated criteria) could be obtained by inducing the customers to shop more uniformly and thereby reduce the variability of times between arrivals. An appointment schedule does just that. Although variability and randomness such as emergencies and missed appointments still are to be expected, the amount of variability is substantially reduced; this means that for an expected level of waiting time or people waiting, an increased utilization of the facilities (the doctor, his offices, etc.) can be realized.

Another intriguing aspect of the doctor example is the appropriate queue discipline. Should it always be first come-first served? If a patient shows up an hour early should he be taken ahead of his scheduled appointment time and thereby make other people wait? If a doctor is through with a patient before the next scheduled appointment, should he start another consultation? Should that consultation only be with the person who has the next appointment? Answers to these questions can only be found by appealing to the set of criteria. That is, one has to trade off the criteria of increased utilization of the doctor with patient unhappiness over being treated in a way they regard as unfair vis-à-vis waiting.

A final interesting aspect of this example has to do with the customer perception of waiting. We have implicitly assumed (a) that customers do not like to wait and (b) that customers know how long they are waiting. Both of these assumptions are not necessarily correct. Box 11.1 illustrates the point rather well.

It seemed that upon completion of a large office building the tenants were extraordinarily unhappy about elevator service. Long waiting times were frequently cited. The owners of the building called in a prominent operations research team who studied the demand pattern in order to ascertain whether some scheme might be designed to reduce waiting time such as certain elevators being express only at various times of the day, having nonstop elevator service to particular floors, or perhaps increasing the speed of the elevators. After considerable study, they came to the conclusion that the only viable alternative for providing better service was to add two more elevators to the existing set. Adding two elevators to the existing building represented an incredible cost and the owners of the building were desperate to find some alternative solution. They called in a psychologist who knew nothing of queuing problems and cared less. After several days of wandering about the building and listening to conversations, he proposed a solution: Install full length mirrors in the elevator waiting areas. His proposal was implemented and the complaints stopped; people spent their time looking in the mirrors checking hairdos and neckties—they did not mind waiting.

Box 11.1

Fire Department

An interesting example of the way in which different criteria call for quite different system performance levels can be seen by viewing a fire department in a queuing context. Fires may be regarded as arrivals and the servicing as required times for extinguishing fires. A major criterion or objective is directly related to the expected waiting time; namely, it is quite undesirable to have someone call up and report a burning house and have to reply that there are two other houses ahead of his. In terms of the queue discipline, one might expect that first come-first served would be the rule; but hard and fast rules usually require exceptions, priorities, or tempering. For example, if the fire department were putting out a fire in a single family dwelling and the local hospital suddenly caught fire, it would seem appropriate to shift resources to the hospital even if it meant permitting the single family dwelling to burn to the ground.

In considering the operation of a fire department, it is indeed appropriate to do so in a queuing context. Thus if one studied work patterns in a fire department, found that firemen played pinochle 80% of the time and concluded that the town needed fewer firemen, he would be incorrect. In a queuing context, to offset a concern for waiting lines represented by fires, we must accept a fire department operation with a small value for ρ; that is, we desire to have the firemen unoccupied most of the time so that they will be available when an "arrival" occurs.

A similar kind of analysis holds for maintenance of expensive equipment. If a piece of equipment has a high cost of being down due to breakdowns, it follows that a repair crew may stand idle most of the time in order that when needed they will be able to get the equipment running again in a very short period of time.

In considering queuing cost tradeoffs, we must appeal to incremental costing. If a task can be identified that firemen can do in their idle time which can be immediately dropped when a fire occurs, that task has zero incremental cost. Perhaps that is why fire engines and fire fighting equipment are always so well polished. It also explains why firemen have the time to repair second hand toys for needy children and perform other services for the community.

An interesting example of this incremental cost phenomenon was presented during a hospital "field trip." When visiting an intensive care unit, the tour guide (head nurse) observed a nurse shaving a patient. The head nurse was quite apologetic for using such high paid talent for what seemed like a fairly menial task which could be carried out by a less highly trained person. Such an approach, however, does not take account of the queuing or incremental aspects of the situation. The nurse represents a server and the arrivals to that server are represented by extremely sudden patients needs. It follows for that nurse, just as for the firemen, that she should have a low utilization factor; that is, the cost of waiting time for such sudden requests is very high. And a task such as shaving a patient which can be abandoned when an "arrival" occurs, carries with it zero incremental cost.

Supermarket

Let us now return to the supermarket example where we were concerned with checkout stands. In viewing the criteria for both the initial design and subsequent operation of a supermarket checkout system, it is necessary to address the question of how checking out ties in with the overall objectives or criteria of the supermarket; specifically, what surrogate measures of system performance we would deem as "good," and to what extent we are willing to trade off dollars of capital or labor for improved service. Perhaps an appropriate way to proceed would be to use the functional analysis model developed in Chapter 7 and ask, what is the function of a checkout system? If the function is described as "receive proper payment," then various alternatives come to mind for the initial design stage, such as a system of encoding prices on goods so that they might be read with an optical scanning device placed beneath a conveyor belt; or a system where customers entering the store are issued a coded card which would actuate automat type chutes for the various purchases with a computer keeping a running tally (such a system would require no individual marking of items and could be extended to a monthly billing for coded cards issued permanently to customers with good credit ratings).

Coming away from the rather esoteric possibilities for the initial design of a checkout system and limiting our alternatives to the design of an operating system for a typical or existing checkout system, we seem to be faced with determining a set of policies or decision rules for how to employ various checkout alternatives.

It is interesting to note the positions of user and designer in undertaking such an investigation. If the role we are playing is that of outside experts coming in to "solve" the checkout problem, a typical expectation would be that the user specify a level of service such as desired average waiting time per customer. The analysis would then attempt to find the least cost way of obtaining that objective. However, average waiting time per customer is a surrogate or proximate criterion entity for the more important and encompassing criteria of customer service and customer satisfaction and these in turn are surrogates for enterprise well-being. The "average" waiting time might be a poor surrogate criterion by itself; thus for example, customers might have different expectations about waiting time for different times of the day and different days of the week and year.

In addition, we must not forget the message pertaining to elevators in Box 11.1. Perhaps waiting in checkout lines can be made pleasant by providing free coffee, or by having checkout of the goods performed without the customers presence (shopping carts might be attached to some form of tow line conveyor) and many pleasant ways for the customers to pass the time could be considered. Also, there is the difference between actual waiting time and perceived waiting time, and the difference between waiting time that the customer deems arbitrary or avoidable and waiting that is deemed as unavoidable, i.e., "the people are doing as well as they can." Perhaps a supermarket should employ a man with a tendency toward profuse perspiration who nervously runs back and forth around checkout counters helping in whatever ways he can and wearing a coat that says MANAGER.

A user oriented modeling environment for this problem should yield benefits because the user's set of criteria is bound to evolve. That is, even if a user specifies a desired level of average waiting time, he should be concerned with knowing about various kinds of incremental choices available to him. Checkers, checkout stands, bag boys, and perspiring managers come in integer quantities (we cannot hire 2.3 checkers); and part-time workers require some degree of advance notice and stability in their employment patterns. Other criteria also come into play so that a manager might have some preference for an extra checker over bag boys so that an adequate supply of trained checker personnel is maintained over time. Or conversely, a manager might feel that part-time employment for high school students represents an important community service.

In formulating the checkout counter problem in a queuing model, we would be concerned with arrivals of customers to the checkout area, service times under various types of operating conditions such as a checker who checks and packages versus a checker with a bag boy, various queue disciplines such as ten items or less going through an express line, and whether the criterion of average waiting time per person should include additional objectives or constraints.

In Chapter 5, we noted the need to add data collection to our evolutionary approach to problem solving. The design of a system for collecting arrival and service time data under various operating conditions is itself a formidable problem. At this stage, before reading any further, you as a student should assume the task of designing a set of decision rules for operating a checkout system and issue a directive for data collection. Specifically, you should address the following questions (you will gain from putting your directive in writing): (1) Exactly what data would you like to have for your analysis? and (2) How will you go about collecting that data?

Student directives often state a desire for information on waiting times and therefore suggest that an observer in a store gather waiting time data. Such an approach will not be very useful. Waiting times are a residual that occur because of the interaction of the arrival time pattern or distribution of arrivals and the service time pattern or distribution of service times. Not only do we not need to observe waiting times directly, if we did so we would be unable to answer various kinds of "what if" questions that revolve around changes in arrival and service time distributions.

In collecting data on arrival patterns, it would be necessary to observe the time between arrivals at a checkout area. This data could be usefully summarized in some sort of cumulative probability distribution. In fact, one distribution would again be inappropriate. There are actually many distributions or arrival patterns which are dependent upon the time of the day, day of the week, and day of the year (e.g., holiday weekends). Since the real world arrival pattern is so strongly influenced by these time-oriented buying patterns, it is probably necessary (a matter of criteria!) for whatever model we select to represent these time pattern dependencies.

To a lesser extent, perhaps service time patterns are also influenced by time-oriented buying patterns; that is, housewives tend to purchase large quantities on Thursday and Friday when they do the major buying for the coming week. It would seem that service time requirements might be a function of the number of items purchased; the adequacy of such a relationship might be established by the use of a linear regression model. It might also be established that total dollar amount of cash register receipts would yield an adequate predictive value of the necessary service or work content. Further modeling efforts (we will consider these in our chapters devoted to work measurement and improvement) could yield estimates of the various service times associated with particular values of work content under differing operational conditions such as box boys or no box boys.

Once basic data for arrival patterns and service times are available, modeling efforts (we will see in the next chapter that a digital simulation model would provide a felicitous environment) could examine the effect on various measures of effectiveness such as waiting time and checker idle time for different sets of policies or decision rules such as:

1. Call a second checker when the waiting line gets to 3, 4, or 5.

2. Proceed as per number 1 but call a third checker when the total of the two lines gets to 10.

3. Call a bag boy(s) under various kinds of conditions.

4. Open an express line at certain times of the day, days of the week, or particular operating circumstances.

The incremental costs and benefits of these alternative strategies or decision rules could then be subjected to managerial scrutiny. Perhaps a particular set of operating policies would immediately emerge as dominant, but a more likely outcome would be to encourage those in a managerial role (users) to identify other kinds of strategies, policies, or sets of decision rules that they would like to see examined by the model and perhaps to postulate different kinds of operating conditions for which they would like to see the results tested (such as "what happens if the demand—expressed in terms of customer arrivals—increases by 20%?").

ANALYTICAL MODELS

The so-called analytical queuing models derive their name from a practice in operations research of only applying the term "analytical" to models where a mathematical optimum can be proved. Since this is not true for many kinds of models (notably simulation models), these models are not considered to be "analytical" by operations researchers. Let us now turn our attention to some queuing models for which optimum conditions can be mathematically proved. However, as is true for all models, these analytical models are abstractions that may or may not well represent a real world system. There is a definite set of assumptions that is attached to the use of any model and that necessary for the analytical queuing models will be found quite limiting for many of the examples that were identified in the preceding section. We will find that the analytical models only apply to a subset of the queuing problems in which we will be interested. Although we will later show how some of the assumptions can be relaxed, our initial assumptions for analytical queuing models include:

1. That the only category of queuing situation we can model is the single channel-single service variety.

2. That the queue discipline is first come-first served.

3. That it is possible for the length of the waiting line to grow infinitely long.

4. That the distribution of arrivals per time period is appropriately modeled by the Poisson distribution.

5. That the distribution of service completions per time period is well modeled by either the Poisson distribution or by a constant.

It can be seen from these limiting assumptions that the scope of real world situations which can be appropriately modeled by analytical models is quite limited. Thus the supermarket example does not appear to be appropriately modeled by these techniques because of its multiple channel-multiple service nature, its violation of a first come-first served queue discipline by express lines, and the fact that infinite waiting lines indeed are not possible because people will just leave; and we have not even begun to consider the appropriateness of modeling arrival and service rate patterns with Poisson distributions (a constant service time clearly seems inappropriate).

The queuing problem of patients arriving at a doctor's office might not be overly constrained by an assumption of single channel-single service or by an assumption of a first come-first served queue discipline. However, an infinite line seems unreasonable because people would leave and because of a finite size waiting room. The service completion time pattern conceivably might be adequately modeled by the Poisson distribution, but the distribution of arrival rates is variable with seasons, weather, and holidays (people tend to not get sick before holidays); a model of this arrival pattern seems inappropriate if the probability of a long time between arrivals remained constant.

For some questions of interest to the operation of a fire department, it might be possible that all of the above assumptions are adequately met; however, for a metropolitan city the situation would be multiple channel-single service and a quite significant design question might be concerned with the number of channels.

For Westfall, we would find it difficult to accept the possibility of any waiting line to grow infinitely long. A conveyorized chair-building line would not be single channel-single service, and we have noted that many reasons exist for violating a first come-first served queue discipline in the finish mill area (e.g., short list requirements).

Since the above set of limiting assumptions seems to be rarely satisfied completely, one might wonder why we bother with these models. There are several good reasons. First, when the assumptions are met, the resulting analysis is quite simple and therefore relatively inexpensive. A second reason for using these models is that the degree of necessary fit between the limiting assumptions and the real world situation is a matter of criteria; for some questions the answers obtained with analytical models whose assumptions are somewhat invalid are good enough. A third reason is that new analytical models are being continually developed to deal with increasingly complex questions; we will discuss some of these extensions in a later section.

Poisson Arrivals

Although delving deeply into probability theory is clearly beyond the scope of this book, a brief description of the Poisson probability distribution will aid us in assessing its value as a model of arrival and service rates; what follows is intended for those students with a limited mathematical background.

There are many kinds of probability distributions. Perhaps the best known theoretical probability distributions are the normal and binomial.

The normal distribution with its familiar bell shaped curve represents a good model of many real world phenomena and is therefore quite useful in many kinds of problem solving; we will rely on it extensively in other chapters of this book, most notably in our discussion of quality control, forecasting, and inventory control. We say that the normal distribution is a two parameter distribution because if we know the arithmetic mean and the standard deviation of a process that is modeled by the normal distribution, we know all we need to know for analytical purposes.

The binomial distribution is also a two parameter distribution but is a discrete probability distribution (as opposed to a continuous distribution such as the normal) where probabilities come in "chunks" rather than in infinitesimally small pieces. Thus the number of heads in 5 coin flips can only be 0, 1, 2, 3, 4, or 5 (not 4.6). The binomial distribution represents a useful model for situations with two outcomes and independent trials such as yes/no, either/or, on/off, or acceptable/unacceptable. As such, we will find it appropriate for certain kinds of quality control procedures.

The normal distribution is not a very appropriate distribution for modeling times between arrivals, arrival rates, service times, or service rates. This is largely so because the normal distribution encompasses values from plus infinity to minus infinity; neither times nor rates can be negative. The binomial distribution, although not encompassing negative values, is also not well suited for queuing situations.

There are other theoretical probability distributions which do not go negative and, therefore, might represent useful models for particular real world patterns of arrival or service rates. However, the Poisson distribution is blessed with one outstanding attribute, namely that it is a distribution that is completely described by one parameter; it is therefore easy to manipulate mathematically. Whereas the normal distribution requires both the mean and standard deviation and the binomial requires the number of trials and the appropriate proportion, the one parameter (usually expressed as the Greek letter λ) of the Poisson distribution is both its mean and its variance.

The Poisson distribution (named for a Frenchman who established its mathematical properties) does not include negative values. It has been called the distribution of rare events, and mathematicians have found certain rather esoteric statistical data to be extraordinarily well modeled by a Poisson distribution. Thus it is said that the number of Prussian soldiers in a particular war who died per day as a result of horse kicks is modeled almost perfectly by the Poisson distribution; and a study indicated that for a bakery the number of raisins per raisin cake was also modeled very well by the Poisson distribution. It can be seen from these two examples that the Poisson distribution is a distribution useful for considering phenomena that are expressed as rates; that is, so many

X's *per Y.* Since arrival rates are expressed as the number of arrivals *per* some unit of time, a Poisson distribution will be a good model for *some* real world arrival rate patterns.*

In discussing the Poisson distribution, it is also appropriate to briefly consider the negative exponential distribution. The negative exponential distribution can be useful for modeling "times." The Poisson distribution is a discrete distribution; that is, the number of arrivals per time period cannot be noninteger. But since time can be measured as finely as desired, it is understandable that the probability distribution which models time should be a continuous distribution. Interestingly, the negative exponential distribution and the Poisson distribution are closely related. We have noted that time is the reciprocal of rate (a time of fifteen minutes is a rate of four per hour); if a set of times is modeled well by the negative exponential distribution, we can say that the rates associated with those times will be modeled well by the Poisson distribution. Figure 11.2 shows the general shapes of the Poisson and negative exponential distributions.

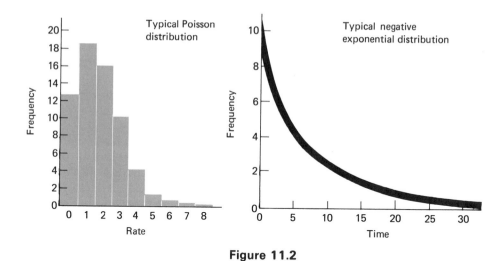

Figure 11.2

Poisson Service Rate Models

Let us consider the following hypothetical problem: A one-man barbershop is interested in examining the effect on waiting time of a new high-speed clipper which will reduce the time to give a haircut. The barbershop

---

*Many real world queuing problems have indeed been found to have arrival rate patterns that closely resemble the Poisson distribution.

is in a busy airport, is open 24 hours a day, 7 days a week, and an earlier study indicated that the demand pattern was uninfluenced by the time of day or day of week. An enterprising business administration student spent several days at the barbershop collecting information. Data for the time between arrivals for 200 customers are summarized in Fig. 11.3. For comparative purposes, a negative exponential distribution which attempts to model these data is also presented.

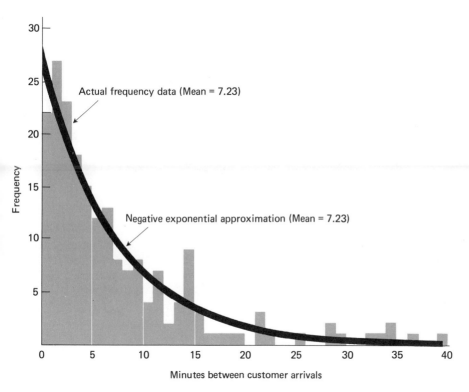

Fig. 11.3 Barbershop Arrival Data (200 arrivals) and Negative Exponential Approximation (frequency of 22 for 0-1 minutes indicates that 22 of the 200 customers arrived less than 1 minute after the previous arrival).

Suppose we decide that the theoretical negative exponential distribution (represented by the solid line in Fig. 11.3) is an appropriate model of the real world data. Since the two distributions have the same mean time of 7.23 minutes between arrivals, we can say that the mean arrival *rate* is $1 \div 7.23 = 0.1383$ customers per minute or 8.3 customers per hour and that the Poisson distribution with a value of λ (mean and variance) = 8.3

is an appropriate model for the arrival rate pattern in this particular problem.

If the distribution of service times is modeled by some negative exponential distribution, the service rate may also be modeled as a Poisson process (the single parameter for the Poisson process modeling service rates is commonly denoted by the Greek letter μ); and we can determine some important attributes of the queuing system directly through the following set of formulae:

Utilization or traffic intensity factor—

$$\rho = \frac{\lambda}{\mu}; \quad \text{since} \quad \mu > \lambda, \quad 0 \le \rho < 1. \tag{11.1}$$

Mean number in the system, including the one being serviced—

$$L = \frac{\lambda}{\mu - \lambda} \qquad S = \frac{\lambda}{\mu - \lambda} = Q + \frac{\lambda}{\mu}. \tag{11.2}$$

Mean number in the queue—

$$Q = \frac{\lambda^2}{\mu(\mu - \lambda)} = S - \frac{\lambda}{\mu}. \tag{11.3}$$

$W = \frac{1}{\mu - \lambda}$ Mean time in the system including the service time—

$$T_S = \frac{1}{\mu - \lambda} = T_Q + \frac{1}{\mu} = \frac{S}{\lambda}. \tag{11.4}$$

Mean waiting time—

$W_Q = W - \frac{1}{\mu}$

$$T_Q = \frac{\lambda}{\mu(\mu - \lambda)} = T_S - \frac{1}{\mu} = \frac{Q}{\lambda} \tag{11.5}$$

Probability of n units in the system—

$$P_n = \left[1 - \frac{\lambda}{\mu}\right]\left[\frac{\lambda}{\mu}\right]^n \tag{11.6}$$

Percentage of time that the service facility is idle—

$$I = P_{(0)} = \left[1 - \frac{\lambda}{\mu}\right]\left[\frac{\lambda}{\mu}\right]^0 = \left[1 - \frac{\lambda}{\mu}\right] = 1 - \rho \tag{11.7}$$

Returning to the barbershop example where the mean arrival rate λ was determined to be 8.3 customers per hour; if the average service time were six minutes per customer, then the mean service rate, μ, is 10 per hour. Let us also say that the other necessary assumptions enumerated earlier (page 259) have been met, and we can therefore use the formulae to investigate some questions about the system.

Starting with the first equation, we see that the utilization or traffic intensity factor,

$$\rho = \frac{\lambda}{\mu} = \frac{(8.3)}{10} = .83.$$

That is, we would expect the barber to work 83% of the time and to be idle 17% of the time. Equation 11.2 tells us that on the average we would expect to see S people in the system, including the one being serviced where

$$S = \frac{\lambda}{(\mu - \lambda)} = \frac{(8.3)}{(10 - 8.3)} = 4.88 \text{ customers.}$$

The average number of customers waiting to be serviced is expressed as

$$Q = \frac{\lambda^2}{\mu(\mu - \lambda)} = \frac{(8.3)^2}{10(10 - 8.3)} = 4.05 \text{ customers.}$$

Notice that the difference between the expected number of customers in the system including the one being serviced and the expected number of customers waiting in line is not 1.0 for the customer being serviced. It is less than 1.0, because at some times the service facility will be idle and there will not be a customer being serviced. The difference is 0.83 which happens to be the traffic intensity factor. This has intuitive appeal since as the traffic intensity factor approaches 1, the server will tend to be continuously busy and the difference between the mean number in the queue and the mean number in the system including the one being serviced will approach 1.0.

Using Eq. 11.4, the expected average time that a customer will spend in the system including the time for service, is

$$T_S = \frac{1}{(\mu - \lambda)} = \frac{1}{(10 - 8.3)} = 0.59 \text{ hour.}$$

Using Eq. 11.5 to solve for the mean waiting time we find that

$$T_Q = \frac{\lambda}{\mu(\mu - \lambda)} = \frac{8.3}{10(10 - 8.3)} = 0.49 \text{ hours.}$$

Note here that the difference between the expected time in the system and the expected waiting time is simply the average time for service $1/\mu$.

The probability of n units in the system can be solved for various values of n so that if, for example, we were interested in knowing the probability that four customers would be in the barbershop, we could solve

$$P_{(4)} = \left[1 - \frac{-\lambda}{\mu}\right]\left[\frac{\lambda}{\mu}\right]^4 = \left[1 - \frac{8.3}{10}\right]\left[\frac{8.3}{10}\right]^4 = 0.0807$$

That is, we would expect that if we observed the shop conditions many times, about 8 times per 100 observations we would find four customers in the shop. Turning finally to our last formula for the percentage of time that the service facility is idle we find that

$$P_{\eta} = (1-\rho)\rho^{M} \qquad P_{(0)} = \left[1 - \frac{\lambda}{\mu}\right]\left[\frac{\lambda}{\mu}\right]^{0} = \left[1 - \frac{8.3}{10}\right]\left[\frac{8.3}{10}\right]^{0} = 0.17$$

which is the same result as obtained in the formula $1-\rho$.

Now that we have illustrated how the basic formulae work, let us start investigating some questions which might interest our hypothetical barber. Suppose the new kind of clipper will reduce the average time required for giving a hair cut from 6 to 5 minutes (let us assume that the distribution of service time will still be adequately modeled by the negative exponential distribution). How much is the device worth to the barber? Going back to our model, we can easily calculate the changes that will occur in the various measures of effectiveness for this queuing system with the proposed change in μ. Thus for example, expected average number of people waiting in line for a haircut will be reduced from 4.05 to 1.56 and the expected waiting time would be reduced from 0.49 hours to 0.19 hours. At face value, an expected reduction in the average number of people waiting and the average waiting time seems desirable; however, unless the barber attaches some kind of economic loss to customer waiting time or some kind of economic gain to increasing his own idle time (which increases from 17% to 31%), then the device has no value since it does not increase his business.

We would expect that the barber's main interest will be in increasing λ since an increase in the average arrival rate represents an increased number of customers arriving over the day and an increased total revenue. If the barber became convinced that the new device would lead to an increase in the number of customers coming into his shop, then the clipper is worth the value associated with the incremental revenue. For example, if λ were to increase from 8.3 to 9.3 and haircuts were $3 each, the barber would experience an incremental gain of $3 per hour which could be used to offset the cost of the clipper.

Constant Service Rate Models

Models have also been analytically derived for dealing with situations where the arrival rate pattern is appropriately modeled as a Poisson process and the service times are more properly regarded as being constant rather than varying in accordance with a negative exponential distribution. Of the seven formulas given for the Poisson service rate models, Eqs. 11.1 and 11.7 do not change; the appropriate formulae for the mean number in the system, mean number in the queue, mean time in the system, and mean waiting time follow:

Mean number in the system, including the one being serviced—

$$\hat{S} = \frac{\lambda(2\mu-\lambda)}{2\mu\,(\mu-\lambda)} = \frac{\lambda^2}{2\mu\,(\mu-\lambda)} + \frac{\lambda}{\mu} = \hat{Q} + \frac{\lambda}{\mu}\,.$$ (11.8)

Mean number in the queue—

$$\hat{Q} = \frac{\lambda^2}{2\mu\,(\mu-\lambda)} = \frac{Q}{2}\,.$$ (11.9)

Mean time in the system including service time—

$$\hat{T}_S = \frac{\lambda+2\,(\mu-\lambda)}{2\mu\,(\mu-\lambda)} = \frac{\lambda}{2\mu\,(\mu-\lambda)} + \frac{1}{\mu} = \hat{T}_Q + \frac{1}{\mu}\,.$$ (11.10)

Mean waiting time—

$$\hat{T}_Q = \frac{\lambda}{2\mu\,(\mu-\lambda)} = \frac{T_Q}{2}\,.$$ (11.11)

In examining the differences between the constant service rate models and the Poisson service rate models, we can derive an improved appreciation of the way in which the measures of effectiveness are influenced by randomness in both the arrival and the service patterns. Our intuition tells us that if we reduce some of the randomness in a queuing system, we should have less interference and therefore less waiting times. That is, if there were no randomness in the time between arrivals (a constant, unchanging time) and no time variance in service times, there would be no waiting line as long as the service rate were greater than or equal to the arrival rate, nor would there be waiting time, and the number of units in the system would never exceed 1. Since this is so, the service rate could be set equal to the arrival rate thereby reducing idle server capacity to zero. In queuing systems, however, it is precisely because of variations in interarrival and service times that waiting times and queues occur and why it is necessary to have the service rate exceed the arrival rate to keep waiting times and queues to reasonable amounts. Thus we would expect that by eliminating the variability in the service rate we will decrease waiting times and queues; Formulas 11.9 and 11.11 clearly illustrate this since they correspond to Formulas 11.3 and 11.5 being divided in half. Formulas 11.8 and 11.10 also show reductions where the relationships of mean number in the system to mean number in the queue, and mean time in the system to mean waiting time remain as before

$$(S = Q + \frac{\lambda}{\mu}; \; T_S = T_Q + \frac{1}{\mu})\,.$$

Equation 11.6, the probability of n units in the system, will also change when the service rate is represented as a constant. The general nature of the change will be for higher probabilities for lower numbers in the queue and reduced probabilities for higher numbers in the queue. The exact mathematical relationship is more difficult to derive.

In our barbershop example, if instead of an assumption of service times being modeled by a negative exponential distribution we considered the service times to be constant, the expected number in the queue drops from 4.05 to 2.03 and the expected waiting time would decrease from 0.49 hours to 0.24 hours. Similarly, if the new clipping device achieved a constant time for haircuts, then its benefits would be enhanced. The moral to the story seems clear: Decreases in variability of service times can be as beneficial as decreases in the service times themselves. Queuing problems largely derive from interacting stochastic processes.

Extensions

Thus far we have only considered analytical queuing models that satisfy the assumptions of single channel-single service, first come-first served queue discipline, infinite population, Poisson arrival rates, and Poisson or constant service rates. There are other analytical models that have been developed which relax some of these assumptions. Thus the single channel-single service assumptions can be relaxed to cover multiple channel-single service situations. These models retain the other assumptions but do allow one to consider the effect of incremental additions in channels which is a kind of problem that is prevalent in the real world. Examples include the checkout counter problem, additional toll booths at a toll road, additional clerks at an airline reservation desk, or additional personnel at a tool crib in a factory.

The relaxation of Poisson or constant probability model assumptions has also been accomplished to a limited extent. There are a few other distributions with mathematical properties that are amenable to analytic manipulations and adequately represent some real life situations. Of particular interest is the Erlang family of service distributions.

There has also been a relaxation of the assumption that infinite waiting lines are possible. A book entitled *Finite Queuing Tables** presents a set of tables which allow one to assess the various attributes of queuing systems when the possible number of arrivals is limited. For example, if a tool crib serviced finish mill machine operators at Westfall and there was a total of 75 such operators, it is clear that the waiting line could never exceed 75 and some correction would have to be made to a set of formulae which assumed that the waiting line could possibly grow to infinity. The tables are given for finite populations of 4 to 250 with the

---

*L. G. Peck and R. N. Hazelwood, Wiley, 1958.

feeling being that above 250 infinite assumptions will not cause serious distortions.

Another kind of "finite" queuing situation that has received study involves "turn-away," which means the process of arrival generation does not change, but the length of the queue is constrained by some maximum value. A real world example might be a theater with a finite number of seats.

An Assessment

Analytic queuing models have been used in a number of real world applications; however, because of the necessary assumptions for using the models, they are only applicable to a small subset of the total population of problems that can be usefully thought of in a queuing or flow-oriented context. Even for that subset, the analysis becomes quite cumbersome when one goes beyond the basic assumptions to encompass more complicated real life problems, and we will find it expedient to use alternative solution methods for many problems that could be investigated with complex analytical queuing models.

A good example of the inability of analytic queuing models to deal with complicated situations is seen in the "job shop" problem which has had a great deal of attention in the literature of operations research (the Westfall finish mill is a typical job shop). A job shop problem is probably best categorized as multiple channel-multiple service; with a series of jobs each requiring different amounts of work in different work centers or machines. Behind each work center is a queue of jobs to be processed which in turn will go to other centers until completion. The usual question is in what order should the jobs behind each work center be run? Criteria are typically stated as minimum time for a set of jobs to be completed or maximum utilization of the work centers. Analytic solutions to this problem are only available for the two work-center case unless severe limiting assumptions are made. Problems larger than two work centers (except for a special case of the three center problem) require solutions by "nonanalytic" means—namely digital simulation. In Chapter 12 we will examine this methodology in detail. The appeal of this modeling approach will become obvious for the simplified barber shop problem; but more importantly, the approach accommodates investigations of more complex problems which are so prevalent in the real world.

SUMMARY REMARKS

In this chapter we have examined the pervasive nature of flow-oriented systems and looked at one kind of modeling approach for better understanding and designing such systems. Although the limiting assumptions of the analytic queuing models makes them appropriate for investigating only a subset of the flow oriented or queuing problems in the real world, some general impressions can be gained and the limiting assumptions can be removed when using digital simulation models.

Perhaps the most significant appreciation gained from viewing problems in a queuing context is to become keenly aware of the influence of randomness or variability in arrival and service rates on waiting lines and waiting times. Box 11.2 clearly illustrates the point:

It seems that at the outbreak of the Korean war munitions were to be shipped from San Francisco. Apparently the shipments of munitions by train into San Francisco were set at a level so that the average train arrival rate was equal to the average ship loading and departure rate. It was heard that at one point box cars were lined up outside San Francisco for 25 miles.

Box 11.2

One might say that such an outcome was obvious and that it proves an earlier adage of being wary of averages. However, there is a distinct difference between being "wary" and having explicit modeling capabilities for predicting real world, flow-oriented-system conditions under various policies and conditions.

Although analytic queuing models are limited in their applicability, our interest is more broad than the simple problems amenable to analytic solution. Our systems orientation is toward ever increasingly more inclusive problem formulations. By viewing the flows of materials, information, men, and money, we gain an important overview of the firm. The stochastic interactions of these flows and queues in a dynamic sense is what gives rise to many organizational problems and opportunities. A large portion of the remaining chapters in this book are devoted to developing a flow orientation to problem identification and solution.

REFERENCES

Bhatia, A., and A. Garg, "Basic Structure of Queueing Problems," The *Journal of Industrial Engineering,* Vol. 14, no. 1, January-February, 1963.

Morse, Philip M., *Queues, Inventories, and Maintenance,* Wiley, 1958.

Panico, Joseph A., *Queuing Theory,* Prentice-Hall, 1969.

Paul, Robert J., and R. E. Stevens, "Staffing Service Activities with Waiting Line Models," *Decision Sciences,* **2,** no. 2, (April 1971):206–18.

Saaty, T. L., *Elements of Queuing Theory,* McGraw-Hill, 1961.

CHAPTER REVIEW

The primary goal of this chapter is for you to develop a flow orientation to operations management problems. This orientation recognizes the effects of cascading uncertainties, the kinds of systems which must be designed to cope with these uncertainties, the benefits from system designs which reduce uncertainty, the differences in system design that derive from changes in flow-oriented criteria systems, and the counterintuitive aspects of solutions to flow oriented problems.

You should not regard the analytical models presented in the chapter as definitive; rather, the models should be considered primarily as illustrative. By changing parameters, it is possible to rapidly understand the consequences implied by changes in service rates, arrival patterns, variability, and so on. Although most real world problems violate the assumptions of the analytical models, the underlying approach remains valid when constructing more appropriate models.

OUTLINE OF THE CHAPTER

CENTRAL ISSUES

There are many kinds of flows in an organization, such as materials, money, people, orders, etc. Any stoppage in a flow results in an inventory or queue. Some of these queues are desirable and others not, depending upon criteria. The size of the queues and length of time spent in queues depends upon the variability and rate of arrivals, the rate and variability of service, and the order in which arrivals are served. Utilization of servers (people, machines, etc.) is often an important criterion; increased utilization can be achieved by longer queues and/or decreased variability in arrival or service rates.

Several examples are given to illustrate the flow orientation and the shifts resulting from different criteria. The overall flow of material at Westfall results in many queues, and actions taken in one area affect others. A doctor's criteria of efficiently utilizing himself can lead to large expected waiting times, but partial elimination of randomness in interarrival times can be achieved with an appointment schedule. Considering a fire department in a queuing context illustrates that many situations call for low utilization of the servers.

The analytical models presented are based upon assumptions of single channel-single service, first come-first serve queue discipline, infinite line length potential, Poisson arrival rate, and either negative exponential or constant service times. Models are given for expected length of the waiting line, utilization rate, expected waiting time, and other system conditions. Partial relaxation of assumptions is discussed, with more complete relaxation and improved user involvement promised in Chapter 12.

ASSIGNMENTS

1. Describe the flows, flow stoppages, and flow-oriented criteria in the following:

    a) A chair-building line
    b) A conveyorized chair-building line
    c) The Westfall finish mill
    d) The Westfall Furniture Co. (materials)
    e) The Westfall Furniture Co. (money)
    f) The Baumritter Corporation
    g) A refinery
    h) A manufacturing concern
    i) A bank
    j) A hospital

2. Describe some Westfall flow situations not mentioned in the chapter that fit the following queuing categories:

    a) Single channel-single service
    b) Single channel-multiple service
    c) Multiple channel-single service
    d) Multiple channel-multiple service

3. Describe two additional non-Westfall examples for each of the categories in problem #2.

4. Automobiles arrive at a single toll booth at a mean rate of 1 per minute in a manner that has been regarded as being adequately modeled by the Poisson distribution. The times to service these automobiles average 15 seconds with a distribution that may be approximated by the negative exponential.

   a) Determine the traffic intensity factor.
   b) Determine the mean number of automobiles in the system.
   c) Determine the mean number of automobiles in the queue.
   d) Determine the mean time in the system.
   e) Determine the mean waiting time.
   f) Determine the probability of five automobiles in the system.
   g) Determine the percentage of time that the server will be idle.

5. How would your answers to problem #4 change if the service times were more properly considered to be constant?

6. A college registrar's office experienced an average arrival rate of 25 students per hour (Poisson) and an average service time of 2 minutes (negative exponential).

   a) What is the average waiting time?
   b) What is the average number of people waiting in line?
   c) For two particular weeks in September, the average arrival rate increases to 100 and the average service time is decreased to 45 seconds. What is the effect on waiting time and queue length?
   d) What factors might mitigate the September conditions?

7. A New York hair stylist schedules 3 appointments per hour and the actual arrival rate pattern is closely approximated by a Poisson process. The present average service time is 15 minutes and the distribution of service times is adequately modeled by the negative exponential distribution. The average contribution to profit and overhead (sales price less out-of-pocket expense) is $4.00 per customer. Business is very good and the hair stylist has been under considerable pressure from customers who want more frequent appointments. He is extremely reluctant to increase customer waiting time; however, a proposed additional chair, two additional hair dryers, and one additional helper should allow him to reduce the average service time to 10 minutes (still negative exponentially distributed) while maintaining adequate quality standards. How desirable is the proposed change in operations?

8. Consider problem 3–4 which is essentially a flow problem. Pattern this system as a queuing problem and describe what might be considered arrivals, service times and queue disciplines. Unlike the other examples given in this chapter it will probably be useful for you to consider the service rates being dependent on arrivals.

CHAPTER 12

DIGITAL SIMULATION

In Chapter 11 we identified and studied the flow-oriented aspects of ongoing or proposed operations management systems. We noted, however, that the assumptions of analytical models tend to restrict their application to only a small subset of all flow-oriented or queuing situations, and that a modeling procedure which was more general and more readily adaptable to unique user-perceived needs would have significant value. Since digital simulation models can possess many of these desirable features, this chapter provides an elementary knowledge and appreciation of this important modeling procedure.

THE MODEL

The term "simulation" is unfortunately very broad and vague; one could say that any representation is a simulation and that the word itself, therefore, becomes a synonym for "model." Such a use is not really wrong or inappropriate. That is, one could say that he has a mental model of Westfall chair building which he uses to "simulate" the effect of some change in chair-building methods. Nevertheless, we will find it beneficial to restrict the use of the word "simulation" to that involving simulation with digital computers. This definition is still very broad, however, as it would encompass any sort of problem solving with a digital computer. Thus a student could use the digital computer to "simulate" the effect on his $10 cash balance of spending $5 for a football ticket. However, such a simulation is somewhat inefficient since great skill in the use of mental models is not required to predict the solution. Put another way, the cost/benefit relationship of using a digital simulation model for this particular problem does not appear to be very favorable relative to competing modeling mechanisms.

As the student's problem gets more complicated, however, the relative desirability of digital simulation increases; thus if our student invests his money in the bank at 5% interest, calculation of his cash balance becomes more difficult. If the interest is compounded quarterly or daily, the calculations become complex and the attributes of a simulation model become even more desirable. If the student chooses not to invest his money in a bank but to "invest" it in a poker game, the problem situation is more uncertain; a realistic problem definition and concomitant modeling environment should depict this uncertainty. The model well might become quite complex if the problem definition now becomes concerned with *how* the student is to "invest" in the poker game. Should he bluff? When should he call? Should he drop in a "Jacks or better" game when another player opens and he does not have a pair?

The term "digital simulation" can be used to encompass a broad class of computer representations or models. The term "Monte Carlo simulation" is often applied to a subset of digital simulation models based on random or stochastic processes. Since queuing problems are generally formulated on the basis of interacting random arrival and service patterns, we will find Monte Carlo simulation models appealing for the study of many flow-oriented problem situations.

Empiricism

Digital simulation models in general, and Monte Carlo simulation models in particular, represent an orientation toward problem solving different from that embodied in analytical or mathematical models. Rather than being a somewhat detached analysis based on mathematical rigor, digital simulation models rely on an empirical trials process. For example, one appealing way to study the operations of a supermarket checkout counter would be simply to observe the effects of varying entity choices, policies, or sets of decision rules at a store.

As noted in our discussion of model building in Chapter 3, however, using the real world system for experimentation can be time-consuming, costly, and possibly dangerous. It would take a considerable amount of time to observe each supermarket entity choice or set of decision rules before the "character" of that choice or set of decision rules could be adequately understood; and since a large number of entity choices and sets of decision rules would warrant investigation, a great deal of time would be involved. It would be extraordinarily hard to insure that each set of entity choices or decision rules were carried out under similar conditions; if for no other reason, this would be true because customer behavior (including the arrival rate) is influenced in a feedback manner by past system performance characteristics. The costs involved in trying out various policies could be large, and bizarre sets of entities or rules might involve costs that are high enough to be considered dangerous, or in fact to incur actual physical danger. Nevertheless, the possibility of trying out various choices through empirical experimentation is very appealing, particularly when considered from an evolutionary viewpoint where empirical results lead to an improved delineation of criteria and subsequent experimental and real system changes. Simulation models possess this appeal by replicating the important aspects of system components in a modeling environment whose performance can be empirically observed.

One authority states that "the distinction between a simulation model and a mathematical model is essentially the same as that encountered in any physical science between prediction by the use of a mathematical model and by physical experimentation. The distinction is perhaps less clear in the present (simulation) case because the experimentation is performed on an abstract model rather than a physical model but it is not less real."*

Decision Rule Character

It was stated above that one is interested in ascertaining the "character" of a set of entities or decision rules. Let us briefly examine these terms within the framework for system design and model building presented in Chapter 3. There a system was defined as a collection of entities and the relationships among the attributes of those entities. For a flow-oriented or queuing problem situation such as a checkout counter, entities include customers, checkout counters, bag boys, cash registers, and conveyor belts. Another terribly important set of entities is the less tangible organizational entities representing the policies or decision rules for the operation of the checkout system, such as, "Call another checker when the number in the waiting line reaches 5." Both the tangible and less tangible entities have large numbers of attributes; but our flow-oriented "fake" system, representation, or model will depict only those attributes or characteristics of each entity that are deemed significant by the criteria set.

The relationships of the various entity attributes give rise to attributes which are more properly associated with the system as a whole (such as the interaction of arrival time patterns and service time patterns to yield waiting times). These system attributes are commonly referred to in digital simulation models as "system states." System design and model-building criteria are typically concerned with these states, and since this concern almost invariably incorporates a time dimension (the behavior pattern of a system over time), a desirable digital simulation model output is a time series of system states which is often referred to as a "state history."

---

*Richard W. Conway, "Digital System Simulation," Unpublished paper, January 20, 1958, p. 7.

An interest in the "character" of a system infers an overall examination of digital simulation model state histories. The examination of character is used in the model validation process (to be discussed later in this chapter) and in the assessment of alternative model-building and system design choices. One reason for the use of the term "character" is that digital simulation models, unlike analytic models, do not provide answers which can be proved optimal. Simulation models test a set of decision rules for some period of simulated history, and the results for that simulated history are considered against alternative entity choices for the same simulated history. Whether or not the results are "good enough" must be resolved in terms of particular user criteria.

Even when dealing with problems capable of being solved by optimum producing analytic procedures, there is often much to be said for viewing the overall character of a state history. For example, in viewing a simulated state history, a user might find that his interests or concerns (appropriate surrogate criteria) are oriented toward extreme rather than average conditions.

Criteria

Although the matter is more fully dealt with in the discussion of model validation, it is worth reiterating the point made in Chapter 3 that the criteria for model building are critical for assessing the degree of model representation goodness, and that the assessment necessarily is highly individualistic and comparative.

The individualistic nature of a set of criteria plays a strong role in the kind of modeling procedure chosen and in the choice of model attributes to be studied. In digital simulation models, the determination of which system-state descriptions are to be depicted as a time series and thereafter studied can be made only by appealing to the set of criteria which has dictated a particular model design effort.

In discussing individualized criteria sets it will again behoove us to recall the evolutionary orientation of the user-designer concept; perceived user needs lead to individualized models to yield individualized inferences, and it is quite appropriate that users (who have the criteria) be involved in the model-building efforts. Unfortunately, many large scale simulations have not had intimate user involvement during the model-building stages; these efforts often eventually prove themselves to be only very interesting examples of digital simulation model building that are unable to answer significant user questions. Moreover, because of the inherent flexibility of digital simulation models, the final model configuration is more difficult to predict than for more rigorous models, and a continuing need for appeal to the user criteria will be felt.

In our discussion of criteria in Chapter 3, we noted that most systems of interest were driven or directed by more than one goal or criterion, and that therefore a system of criteria exists. We also examined the need for good design of this criteria set and the inherent difficulty involved in criteria system design. Analysis of digital simulation model results through the "character" of those results thus involves not only the difficulty of making assessments but also a set or system of criteria whose relationships and relative importance are difficult to establish. Indeed, one of the major goals of a simulation design effort is often the design of a model in which an evolving set of criteria is "reasonably" satisfied and congruent.

Level of Aggregation

The level of aggregation problem is concerned with the detail with which system entities should be represented in a model. Thus all workers on a proposed conveyorized chair-building line could be represented in terms of speed by the standard time from industrial engineering estimates, individual differences in speed among different workers could be represented, or differences based on fatigue levels at various times of the day and days of the week could be included. Clearly, each of these extensions well might yield improved predictions of chair-building performance. Whether or not such improvements in predictive ability are worthwhile can be ascertained only by again appealing to the criteria system.

Similarly, in studying service times at checkout counters in order to know whether one should be concerned with predicting times for making change, opening bags, checking soap powders or cans of beans, or closing the cash register drawer, one must return to the problem statement or question under consideration. That is, exactly what is the particular problem? For that particular problem, what is the appropriate degree of aggregation in our model? Clearly the level of aggregation that is appropriate for one question or problem well might not be appropriate for another. The extent of the inappropriateness can be significant, and a recognition of the evolutionary aspects of problem identification, model formulation, and problem solution enforces the need for intimate user involvement in the model-building process.

The Computer

Simulation does not necessarily require a computer; this method of solving problems has indeed been known for centuries. Rapid growth in the use of simulation as a problem-solving technique, however, has been a fairly recent trend. To some extent this growth is due to the steady evolution toward more general models that was cited in Chapter 3. Yet the primary reason for growth in use of digital simulation models is the computational economies made available through digital computers. Figure 12.1 illustrates that dramatic nature of the cost reductions which have been made. Note that the cost per calculation in a twenty-year period has been reduced by a factor of 100,000! An important result of this computation cost reduction is that the relative efficiency of "analytic" methods has decreased sharply. Equally significant is the increasing availability of the benefits obtained from mathematical rigor without the costs involved in obtaining mathematical sophistication. Digital simulation concepts, methods, and practice are becoming increasingly easy to master. Much of this increasing facility and user-orientation is due to the decreasing cost curve depicted in Fig. 12.1; computer modeling environments (e.g. INF*ACT) can "afford" to substitute "inefficient" use of the computer for increased user orientation.

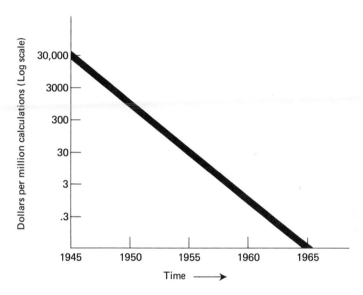

Figure 12.1 From Forrester, Jay W., Advanced Industrial Dynamics Course, Massachusetts Institute of Technology, Summer, 1965

An important feature of economical computerized simulation is the ability to easily perform controlled experimentation where all aspects of a situation are held constant with variations tested in sequential fashion. In this way, various sensitivity analyses can be performed and the "what if" questions that are so relevant to rapid evolution in perceived user needs can be answered. Thus our supermarket example might have identified a "good" set of policies or decision rules for when to use various combinations of checkers, box boys, etc. An important kind of "what if" question might be concerned with the "goodness" of these rules for changes in the demand pattern, e.g. 10% increase, or double trading stamps on Wednesday.

CONSTRUCTING A MONTE CARLO SIMULATION MODEL

Constructing a simulation model which will replicate an existing or proposed real world system need not be a huge undertaking. The methodology for representing queuing or flow-oriented situations in a Monte Carlo simulation is very straightforward and commonsensical. Let us now return to the barbershop example which we considered in Chapter 11, first as a simulation without a computer and then using the computer.

The Barber Shop Revisited

Figure 11.3 presented a histogram or frequency distribution of the various times between arrivals of customers at the barber shop (a solid line repre-

Minutes between arrivals	Frequency	Percentage or probability of occurrence	Cumulative probability	Associated random numbers
.5	22	.11	.11	000-109
1.5	27	.135	.245	110-244
2.5	23	.115	.36	245-359
3.5	18	.09	.45	360-449
4.5	15	.075	.525	450-524
5.5	12	.06	.585	525-584
6.5	13	.065	.65	585-649
7.5	8	.04	.69	650-689
8.5	7	.035	.725	690-724
9.5	8	.04	.765	725-764
10.5	4	.02	.785	765-784
11.5	7	.035	.82	785-819
12.5	2	.01	.83	820-829
13.5	4	.02	.85	830-849
14.5	9	.045	.895	850-894
15.5	3	.015	.91	895-909
16.5	1	.005	.915	910-914
17.5	1	.005	.92	915-919
18.5	1	.005	.925	920-924
19.5	1	.005	.93	925-929
21.5	3	.015	.945	930-944
22.5	1	.005	.95	945-949
25.5	1	.005	.955	950-954
28.5	2	.01	.965	955-964
29.5	1	.005	.97	965-969
32.5	1	.005	.975	970-974
33.5	1	.005	.98	975-979
34.5	2	.01	.99	980-989
36.5	1	.005	.995	990-994
39.5	1	.005	1.00	995-999

Table 12.1

sented the negative exponential distribution model of the data). Table 12.1 expresses those frequency data so that percentages or probabilities of occurrence can be determined.

In the first two columns we find the data previously presented in graphical form as Fig. 11.3 of Chapter 11. The third column converts the frequency data to percentages or probabilities in order to follow the convention of probabilities of mutually exclusive exhaustive sets of events summing to unity. The fourth column converts the individual probability data to a cumulative probability distribution so that deriving a set of associated random numbers will be facilitated.

A similar procedure could be used to determine a set of associated random numbers to represent or model observed service time data. To simplify our present discussion, however, let us assume that the service rate given before ($\mu=10$ per hour) is a constant.

Since the data on arrivals presented above are given as percentages or probabilities which add to 1.000, we can take 1000 pieces of paper for arrivals and associate appropriate times with each piece of paper. Thus for example, we have 110 pieces of paper associated with an arrival time of 0.5 minutes after the arrival of the previous customer and 135 pieces of paper associated with an interarrival time of 1.5 minutes. The one-thousand pieces of paper representing different interarrival times can be put into a hat; thereafter, the simulation procedure is merely to artificially create an arrival by drawing a piece of paper from the arrival hat and determining the corresponding time that has elasped before this hypothetical customer has entered our barber shop model (each paper is returned to the hat after recording information).

A number of various schemes could then be used to keep track of whether the service facility was idle or occupied when an arrival occurred, the number of people waiting in line, and the length of time that each customer has to wait for service. Thus, supposing we draw (individually and replace before subsequent draws) ten pieces of paper with the following numbers: 3.5, 19.5, 2.5, 10.5, 12.5, 1.5, 0.5, 7.5, 13.5, 2.5. Since our hypothetical barber takes a constant six minutes for a haircut (he must have been trained in the U.S. Army), we can investigate our barber shop with Table 12.2.

We can see from the above data that the first customer arrived with a simulated interarrival time of 3.5 minutes, which is the equivalent of saying he arrived 3.5 minutes after the previous customer. Similarly, the second customer arrived 19.5 minutes later, etc. We also see that the barber was idle for the first 3.5 minutes, after which time he started working on customer number 1, finishing at time 9.5. He was then idle for 13.5 minutes until time 23, when customer number 2 came in and was immediately served.

Customer #	Simulated interarrival time	Cumulative arrival time or "clock"	Waiting time	Service "clock"	Service activity
1	3.5	3.5	No	0.0- 3.5 3.5- 9.5 9.5-23.0	Idle Customer #1 Idle
2	19.5	23.0	No	23.0-29.0	Customer #2
3	2.5	25.5	3.5	29.0-35.0 35.0-36.0	Customer #3 Idle
4	10.5	36.0	No	36.0-42.0 42.0-48.5	Customer #4 Idle
5	12.5	48.5	No	48.5-54.5	Customer #5
6	1.5	50.0	4.5	54.5-60.5	Customer #6
7	0.5	50.5	10.0	60.5-66.5	Customer #7
8	7.5	58.0	8.5	66.5-72.5	Customer #8
9	13.5	71.5	1.0	72.5-78.5	Customer #9
10	2.5	74.0	4.5	78.5-84.5	Customer #10

Table 12.2

When the barber's idle time is totaled, we find that he is idle for a total of 24.5 minutes out of the total simulated study time of 84.5 minutes (29%). We can also see that customers 3, 6, 7, 8, 9, and 10 had to wait 3.5, 4.5, 10.0, 8.5, 1.0, and 4.5 minutes respectively. The total waiting time for these 6 customers is 32.0 minutes or an average waiting time per customer of 3.2 minutes. Since 6 customers had to wait, and for portions of the time when customers number 7 and 8 were in the barber shop 2 customers were waiting, a minute-by-minute check of the waiting line status would find it at 2 for 6.5 minutes (50.5 - 54.5 plus 58.0 - 60.5), at 1 for 19.0 minutes (25.5 - 29.0 plus 50.0 - 50.5 plus 54.5 - 58.0 plus 60.5 - 66.5 plus 71.5 - 72.5 plus 74.0 - 78.5), and at 0 for the remainder of the study. Since the "eleventh arrival" has not been generated and we do not know whether he would wait, the study may be considered complete at time 78.5

and average length of the line can be computed to be [(2 × 6.5)+(1 × 19.0)+(0 × 45.5)] ÷ 78.5 = 32.5 customer minutes ÷ 78.5 minutes = 0.41 customers (note that the numerator in this calculation works out to be the total waiting time).

A computer simulation model of the barber shop example could be constructed in the same way as the hand simulation, with a similar lack of elegance. It is, however, necessary to be slightly (though not outstandingly) clever to know how to substitute arithmetic operations for pieces of paper, hats, and tally sheets. Just as for the hand simulation there were many ways of keeping track of the queuing model states, there are also many possibilities for designing a computer simulation which will produce desired results. A computer program written in Dartmouth BASIC is appended to this chapter (Appendix A) which represents *one* digital simulation model of the barber shop problem; wherever possible, the coding has been purposely done in an elementary manner. A few additional refinements are also presented, but a thoroughgoing exposition of methodology is clearly beyond our present scope.

One such useful addition or refinement is methodology for using "standard" probability distributions. Appendix A will briefly treat the use of several of these distributions. It is also worth noting that although Appendix A is written in BASIC, languages such as SIMSCRIPT and GPSS (General Purpose Systems Simulator) have been specially designed for simulation.

Clocks

For both the hand simulated and the computer models, clocks are utilized so that various system states can be observed over time. Since we are usually interested in some sort of summary statistics, we must keep track of various system states. In the hand simulated exercise, we could have observed the conditions of server utilization, waiting time, and length of the waiting line by performing a minute by minute check of the status of these conditions over the simulated time. In a computer simulation, this method of "sweeping" across selected entities to examine their states at periodic time intervals is one way to collect system state data. However, in order to minimize the effect of sampling errors, it would be necessary to make "sweeps" between small intervals of time. An alternative method which is referred to as the "next event" procedure advances the clock used for the simulation to the next "status disturbing event" rather than advancing clocks by some fixed time interval. Thus with a computer model of the barber shop example, a status disturbing event is represented by a customer arrival or by the completion of a haircut. Since system states change only when there is a status disturbing event, clocks change abruptly from one clearly definable state to another and summary

statistics are kept accordingly. The next-event clocking strategy eliminates problems with sample size considerations for collecting summary
statistics and also provides for substantial economies in computing time.

In some large simulation models where many causes for a status
disturbing event exist, "sweeping" is used. Industrial dynamics models
programmed in DYNAMO are a case in point, and one issue facing the
model builder is the choice of sampling interval.

AN ASSESSMENT

Digital simulation models represent an increase in sophistication over
mental, verbal, written, and graphical models. They enjoy the rigor of
mathematical models yet do not require the traditional investment to
obtain mathematical prowess. By relying on numerical and logical relationships to represent subsystems or entities, the behavior of larger
systems which are comprised of these subsystems or entities can be investigated.

One digital simulation enthusiast has stated that investigations
based upon digital simulation can represent a logical extension of the case
method of teaching*; a brief exposition of how this is so should be informa-
mative. In our discussions of the Westfall Furniture Company case many
kinds of operations policies and problems were examined. Thus at various
times we examined a conversion to conveyorized chair building, the influence of short lists on day-to-day operations, and a shelter to facilitate air
drying of lumber. For all of these problems, typical case discussions are
built upon relatively intuitive, nonrigorous models. For these discussions
simulation models could be developed that would explicitly examine various methods for conveyorized chair building, the operation and staffing
requirements for different chairs being produced on a conveyor, the decrease in short list requirements brought about through various finished
good inventory policies, and the interaction of air drying capacity with
seasonal buying of lumber. The recommendations based on these explicit
models have potential for being of significantly better quality than those
based on "armchair," "mental" or "black cigar (Fig. 3.2)," models. We will
attempt to document this potential with the assignments 12 through 17
at the end of the chapter.

Digital simulation models can be designed to parallel very closely
evolving individualized analyses. They represent a class of models with
the ability to incorporate various kinds of complexity and uncertainty;
these elements are almost universally present in interesting operations

---

*Jay W. Forrester, "The Structure Underlying Management Processes," paper
presented at the Academy of Management Meeting, Chicago, December 1964.

management problems. As is true for any procedure, however, proper use is not guaranteed and trouble awaits the unwary. We will now consider briefly some of the more important questions facing users of digital simulation models.

Tactical Problems

One of the most significant tactical problems facing a user of digital simulation models concerns the effect of startup or transient conditions. For example, in our hand simulation of the barber shop problem we started with an idle barber who had no probability of occupation until the "first" customer arrived. Although the effect of this 3.5 minute run-in or transient period might not be deemed to be terribly significant for a problem that is single channel-single service, if the problem situation were single channel-multiple service, multiple channel-single service, or multiple channel-multiple service, the time of transient or nonequilibrium conditions could increase dramatically. An awareness of this phenomenon should be an essential part of one's approach to problem solving with digital simulation. Even for the relatively simple barber shop problem, another transient condition can be observed in our hand-cranked simulation; note that 4 out of the first 5 customers did not have to wait while all of the next 5 waited. The results of the simulation also bear out the transient influence. The analytical model of Chapter 11 produces an expected waiting time of 14.7 minutes (the simulation model in Appendix A produces an average waiting time of 16.3 minutes for 10,000 simulated arrivals), while our hand simulation yielded 7.85 minutes.

A related problem is concerned with the proper sample size or length of a simulation run. Since digital simulation models rely heavily upon the representation of random phenomena through random number generation, one is always in the position of making assessments based on partial information. Longer simulation runs add to the credibility of simulation results but carry the added cost of increased computer time.

The problem of proper starting conditions is often ameliorated by larger sample sizes, by discarding the initial portion of a simulation run, by initiating the run with more reasonable states than "empty and idle," or by some combination of the three. Adequate sample size determination is usually assessed by determining statistical measures of precision and confidence for digital simulation results. Since one is very often interested in comparing various system designs (e.g., one set of decision rules versus another), it is usually easier to evaluate results on a relative rather than on an absolute basis. This is accomplished by using the same set of random numbers for comparative simulation runs.

The problems of transient conditions and proper sample sizes for digital simulation models make absolute statements of model results difficult. Our present goal is merely to note the problem. Those who design large scale digital simulation investigations will want to understand these issues in a way that is quite beyond our present scope.*

Validation

In our discussion of models in Chapter 3, we noted that the goal of model building is not to replicate or exactly duplicate the operation of an entire system in all its detail. Rather, model building attempts to include representation of the essence while ignoring, truncating, or aggregating nonimportant aspects of the real system. The notion of importance implies a criterion of what is "good" or "valid;" and a digital simulation model that is good or valid for one purpose is not necessarily good or valid for other goals, criteria, or purposes. Thus we see that the criteria system which was depicted as a large cloud overhanging the model-building process in Chapter 3 dominates any assessment of model building. It is only by appealing to the criteria system that one can select appropriate levels of aggregation, readily judge the adequacy of model run or sample sizes, and ascertain what represents a good or valid model. The audacious step of making inferences about a real world system based upon model results is always dangerous, yet the danger must be viewed in relative terms; inferences made from a simulation with a "short" run length or with "inadequate" attention having been given to transient conditions still may be superior to inferences based on a mental model. And whether or not a more sophisticated model is justified can only be determined by examining the user's criteria.

The notion of the validation or adequacy of a digital simulation model in some abstract sense is difficult to define. Adequacy or validation almost always comes back to a matter of criteria. Thus one set of authors judges adequacy on the basis of whether or not state histories produced by a simulation model compare favorably to state histories produced by the system modeled. As such a statement leads quickly to a definition of "favorable," the authors necessarily return to the purposes or criteria possessed by a researcher.† The notion of "who" the researcher is, and from where his criteria come, is a matter of no small concern; our discussion of the user-designer concept must be kept in mind.

One other test of validation has to do with validating model components. That is, particularly for systems which do not exist, models of the entire system are more difficult to judge for adequacy than the models of

---

*For a more detailed consideration of these matters see Richard W. Conway, "Some Practical Problems in Digital Simulation," *Management Science,* 10, no. 1, October 1963.

†George W. Evans, G. F. Wallace, and G. L. Sutherland, *Simulation Using Digital Computers,* Prentice-Hall, 1967, p. 9.

system entities or the subsystems which comprise the larger system being represented. A useful validation procedure is to subject model components to tests of "adequacy" with the expectation that a system designed with good or valid components has significant probability of being itself good or valid. Conversely, the validity of models based upon highly tenuous components is open to question even when the state history produced by such a model compares favorably with a state history produced by an actual system. Thus individuals should rightfully be wary of basing inventory decisions on a model that predicted past behavior very well by examining the batting averages of three New York Mets players.*

Data Collection

Digital simulation models with their distinctively empirical flavor seem almost naturally to involve some amount of data collection. The design of a data collection system, however, is a significant problem in terms of both the extent and timing of data collection activities. It is this author's opinion that those who use digital simulation models should resist the temptation to initiate extensive data collection activities at an early stage of model development. This is true for several major reasons. First, without specifying the appropriate level of aggregation in the model, it is not possible to know the corresponding appropriate level of aggregation in data collection; data which are too disaggregated lead to excessive data collection costs, and extremely aggregated data may be useless.

The second reason for not initiating premature data collection activities concerns the general notion of sensitivity analysis. It is quite possible to construct a model with hypothetical data and to make final decision choices or draw inferences from the model that are highly insensitive to the actual values of the data. In fact, the insensitivity may cover a broad enough range that the subjective judgment of those having a knowledge of the data values would indicate that the actual values of the data will not fall outside the insensitive range. Conversely, sensitivity analyses may indicate that a very meticulous data collection procedure is called for. This means that model builders will find it useful to initially design their models on the basis of hypothetical data or data that represents subjective opinions.

It is important to note that when one becomes accustomed to building digital simulation models based on subjective opinion data, it is possible

---

*An interesting study of the problems inherent in an abstract approach to verification of simulation models is found in Thomas H. Naylor, and J. M. Finger, "Verification of Computer Simulation Models," *Management Science,* 14, no. 2, October 1967; a critique of this article by James L. McKenney in the same issue; another critique by William E. Schrank and Charles C. Holt, also in the same issue; and several letters to the editor in subsequent issues.

to include considerations or entities that are deemed terribly important in the systems being modeled but that are often omitted from the model-building effort because "hard" data cannot be collected. One authority strongly advocates the inclusion of these subjective opinions in digital simulation models.*

A third major reason why data collection activities should not be entered into hastily concerns the evolution in problem identification, model formulation, and problem solution which not only can be expected to be a part of any investigation using digital simulation models, but indeed which should be fostered. An evolutionary user-oriented modeling approach is quite compatible with the use of digital simulation models, as the methodology is almost totally open-ended and devoid of the limiting structure that is so prevalent in analytical or mathematical models. If rapid evolution in perceived user needs is to be achieved, it is important that a study not become bogged down in data collection "coolie" work. When data needs are perceived, significant advances in data specifications (including elimination of needs) can frequently be obtained by making believe that a set of data exists and asking questions such as: What will I do with the data? What kinds of analyses will I perform? What kinds of decisions or actions will I take based on different data values? What is the next problem to be identified after analysis of this data is completed?

SUMMARY REMARKS

Digital simulation models are particularly user oriented because they facilitate evolution from mental models to explicit quantitative models with large attendant benefits. One of the most important of these benefits is the experience or understanding of a real world system gained through the process of designing a computerized simulation model. Many times the mere process of explicitly quantifying relationships leads to significant understanding, useful inferences, and subsequent design changes in real world systems.

Digital simulation potentially represents a user-oriented methodology, and because a user orientation implies evolution both in system design and the criteria system, digital simulation models well may be preferable to alternative modeling procedures based on analytic or mathematical formulations yielding "exact" answers.

One reason for a preference for digital simulation models over analytic models is of course tied to the evolutionary aspects of system design, since the digital simulation model is more capable of alteration in highly

---

*Jay W. Forrester, "Modeling of Market and Company Interactions," *Proceedings,* American Marketing Association, 1965 Fall Conference.

individualistic ways. Another is concerned with the transference of global criteria such as customer service into surrogate or proximate criteria such as average waiting time. That is, perhaps *average* waiting time is an appropriate measure for some kinds of situations such as service procedures for toll booths, but an inappropriate measure for waiting times in exclusive dress shops. Perhaps the critical concern is represented by the tails of these probability distributions for waiting time; "excessive" (as viewed by the customer) waiting time may lead to lost customers where each customer accounts for significant contributions to overhead and profit. As already noted in several earlier chapters, it is extremely difficult for a user to adequately specify a fixed set of proximate criteria by which he would judge more global criteria. However, since he will be able to evolve his specification of these proximate criteria through an interaction with a properly designed modeling environment, it follows that a model which fosters user interaction is preferable to one which does not.

Techniques such as analytic queuing models that yield results based only upon long run steady state expectations may not yield insights comparable to state histories or time series obtained from an empirically oriented model. Before one views such evidence as supportive to analytic models, it is worth noting that it is quite possible that the real world system never reaches the steady state; our dress shop well might open its doors at 9 with servers in an "empty and idle" state and refuse to admit further customers after 5. Clearly a model which reflected these conditions might be useful (and more "valid").

An additional consideration in the use of digital simulation models is the cost of using such models. Proponents of analytical models are prone to quote the substantial costs in computer time that can accompany simulation model investigations. The computation cost to achieve comparable results for a queuing situation examined by the two models is typically found to be significantly greater for the simulation model. However, the relative efficiency of analytic models decreases as we move down the cost per calculation curve depicted in Fig. 12.1. Also, computer costs well may not be the relevant cost to minimize. Although many digital simulation models involve substantial efforts, some useful digital simulation models can be formulated quite quickly, and lead to rapid evolution in perceived user needs.

It is also important to remember that digital simulation models can be applied to a class of problems much greater than that amenable to analytic or mathematical solutions. One particularly prevalent business problem situation which can only be adequately handled by simulation is that concerning feedback. In Chapter 21 we will see how this form of model building can permit powerful insights into broadly defined operations management problems.

REFERENCES

Evans, George W., II, G. F. Wallace, and G. L. Sutherland, *Simulation Using Digital Computers,* Prentice-Hall, 1967.

McMillan, Claude, and R. E. Gonzales, *Systems Analysis: A Computer Approach to Decision Models,* Rev. Ed., Irwin, 1968.

Meier, Robert C., William T. Newell, and Harold L. Pazer, *Simulation in Business and Economics,* Prentice-Hall, 1969.

Mize, Joseph H., and J. G. Cox, *Essentials of Simulation,* Prentice-Hall, 1968.

Kaczka, Eugene E., "Computer Simulation," *Decision Sciences,* **1,** nos. 1&2 (Jan.-Apr. 1970): 174–92.

Withington, Frederick G., *The Use of Computers in Business Organizations,* Addison-Wesley, 1966.

CHAPTER REVIEW

In some ways, this chapter builds naturally on the flow orientation presented in Chapter 11. We see the same example treated with a digital simulation model, and the expanded insights into the problem obtained thereby. We also see how some more complex problems, such as those attendant to conveyorized chair building, can be understood with a digital simulation model.

In other ways, however, this chapter gets into some detailed aspects of a particular model that is somewhat inconsistent with our approach to linear programming and other methodologies. I feel comfortable in this because you are more likely to see linear programming in other courses; if you also already understand simulation, then the chapter may be somewhat repetitious. In any event, emphasis on digital simulation in a broad context is consistent with our interest in user-oriented models for implementing the systems approach.

OUTLINE OF THE CHAPTER

Introduction	(builds on Chapter 11)
The model	(digital computer representation)
Empiricism	(experimental flavor)
Decision rule character	(system state history)
Criteria	(necessity for user involvement)
Level of aggregation	(based on criteria)
The computer	(dramatic cost decrease)

Constructing a Monte Carlo simulation model	(straightforward process)
The barbership revisited	(trial and error approach)
Clocks	(sweeping *versus* next event)
An assessment	(logical progression in rigor)
Tactical problems	(transient conditions and sample size)
Validation	(user criteria)
Data collection	(try to minimize)
Summary remarks	(user-oriented models)
Appendix A	(program, results, generators)

CENTRAL ISSUES

Representation of operations management problems in a digital computer model allows for an empirical, experimental, or cut-and-try approach to understanding of complex phenomena and interactions. Replication of important entities permits understanding similar to observation of the real world. By evaluating the queues or other system states over-time, it is possible to derive improved sets of policies or decision rules.

The rigor of mathematical analysis results in clear perceptions of how subsystems operate, and the resulting interactions of those subsystems. User involvement is desirable for all the reasons stated in earlier chapters; it is fostered by the explicitness of this form of model building, and it is not discouraged by a need for mathematical sophistication.

Constructing a Monte Carlo simulation is a straightforward task, one easily mastered by students of average ability. The approach is a logical step in rigor and sophistication from mental models, to verbal models, to written models, to graphical models (flow chart), to computer models.

Although there are some technical problems to consider, such as transient conditions, I conclude that even when used in unsophisticated ways, the approach can yield profound insights into problems; one necessarily must compare the results with those obtained from mental or verbal models, not with those possible from the "ultimate" model.

ASSIGNMENTS

1. A coal mining company is considering opening some additional coal mines on land it holds. There are uncertainties associated with finding exploitable coal deposits, however, and an engineering consultant has provided the following data:

Approximate cost to open a new mine = $100,000
Approximate present value of a successful attempt = $500,000
Present cash available for these ventures = $200,000
A one-half interest in each success will be sold for $300,000 which
  can be reinvested in opening additional mines
Present demand limits the need for new mines to five.

Simulate ten histories of this investment by flipping two coins where two heads is considered a success. What would you recommend to the company?

2. Repeat problem 1 using a table of random numbers.
*3. Repeat problem 2 in a compuiter for a simulation of 1000 trials.
*4. Repeat problem 3 varying the present cash available from $100,000 to $1,000,000 in $100,000 increments. In what way would you modify your recommendations?
*5. Identify and test two additional "what if" questions or extensions to the analysis.
6. A college dean has the following appointment schedule for next Monday morning:

Time	Individual	Expected time required
9:00	Rich alumnus	20 minutes
9:15	Poor alumnus	5 minutes
9:30	Homecoming queen	40 minutes
10:00	Militant student group	30 minutes
10:45	Company recruiter	5 minutes
11:00	Professor	15 minutes
11:15	Student	15 minutes

After examining his past records, his secretary estimates that for any given appointment the following probabilities will apply:

Arrival times

1 chance in 10 that the individual will be 20 minutes early.
2 chances in 10 that the individual will be 10 minutes early.
5 chances in 10 that the individual will be just on time.
1 chance in 10 that the individual will be 10 minutes late.
1 chance in 10 that the individual will not show up.

Appointment durations

1 chance in 10 that it will take 80 percent of the expected time.
2 chances in 10 that it will take 90 percent of the expected time.
2 chances in 10 that it will take 100 percent of the expected time.
2 chances in 10 that it will take 110 percent of the expected time.
2 chances in 10 that it will take 120 percent of the expected time.
1 chance in 10 that it will take 130 percent of the expected time.

Two months ago, the dean accepted an invitation to address a luncheon meeting of the New York Sanitation Workers on this Monday. In order to be on time, he must leave his office by noon.

a) Develop a random number assignment scheme to reflect the appropriate arrival time and appointment duration probabilities.
b) Explicitly state the rules by which the dean will operate.
c) With a random number table, simulate five histories of the dean's Monday morning.

*7. Repeat problem 6 in a computer for a simulation of 1000 histories.
*8. What changes could be made in 6(b) to increase the probability of making the luncheon?
*9. For the barbershop problem generate exponential interarrival times (mean = 7.23) and examine the effect of varying the average service time from 5 to 7 minutes in increments of 0.1 minutes (for both constant and exponential).
*10. For the barbershop problem, replace the distributions for interarrivals and service times with normal distributions (constrain the values of X generated to nonnegative numbers) with the same means (7.23 and 6 minutes respectively). For tests of 100 arrivals, what happens as the standard deviations vary from 0 to 10 minutes in 1/2-minute increments?
*11. What conclusions do you draw from problems 9 and 10?
*12. For a particular chair, the standard time for assembly (up to but not including staining) is 10 minutes. If the job is divided into 5 operations of 2 minutes each, determine how many chairs will be produced per 8-hour day under the following conditions:

a) No variability in the 2 minute operation time;
b) The mean time for each operation is 2 minutes, exponentially distributed, and there are no queues between operations—that is, operator 1 cannot begin a new chair until operator 2 has completed the previous chair; operator 2 cannot begin until operators 1 and 3 have completed their operations, operator 3 similarly for operations 2 and 4, operator 4 similarly for 3 and 5, and operation 5 cannot begin until operation 4 is completed;
c) Same as (b) except that one chair may be queued between each operation if desired;
d) Same as (c) with possible queue size of 2;
e) Same as (c) with possible queue size of 3;
f) Same as (c) with possible queue size of 4;
g) Same as (c) with possible queue size of 5.

*13. Repeat problem 12 where the standard time for operation 3 is 2.1 minutes instead of 2.0 minutes.
*14. Repeat problem 12 where the standard time for operation 3 is 2.0 minutes, normally distributed (constrained to positive values), and the standard deviation is 0.5 minutes.
*15. Repeat problem 14 with:

a) Standard deviation = 1.0 minutes;
b) Standard deviation = 2.0 minutes;
c) Standard deviation = 3.0 minutes.

*16. Repeat problem 12 where instead of five 2-minute operations, the task is divided into:

    a)   two 5 minute operations;
    b)   three 3⅓ minute operations;
    c)   four 2½ minute operations;
    d)   ten 1 minute operations.

*17. What conclusions about assembly operations do you draw from problems 12–16?

APPENDIX A TO CHAPTER 12

The following program written in Dartmouth BASIC is not intended to be a simulation model which makes efficient use of the computer. In fact, I have a strong belief that novice programmers should not try to produce efficient computer coding—they should use anything that works, bearing in mind the KISS principle (Keep It Simple, Stupid). Computers operate at high speed so that inefficient coding usually results in neglible incremental costs. Also, many times coding that appears to be efficient is not. The surrogate criterion of minimizing the number of statements is a good case in point. After the barbership program is presented, an alternative, more elementary way to generate interarrival times is presented. This alternative more than doubles the length of the program, but the computer running time is reduced.

Let us now turn our attention to the program (Fig. 12.2 is a flow chart). The first major section (between lines 100 and 270) is an initialization section. In line 120, several variables are initially set to zero:

A will be associated with interarrival times
$A1$ is the clock on accumulated interarrival times
B is the accumulator for waiting time
N is the accumulator for the number of arrivals
$S1$ is the clock on departures after servicing and waiting (if necessary)
$S2$ is the accumulator for actual service times
X will be associated with random numbers.

As noted in line 130, the variable $N1$ (the number of arrivals) is set to 1000. We will find this use of a variable to be convenient if we later desire a different run length. This is done where results are given. By changing the 130 to read, "LET $N1 = 10000$," conditions are tested over a larger sample.

```
100 '******************************************************************
110 'LINES 120 TO 260 ARE FOR INITIALIZATION PURPOSES
120 LET A=A1=B=N=S1=S2=X=0
130 LET N1=1000          'WE WILL SIMULATE THE ARRIVAL OF 1000 CUSTOMERS
140 DIM C(30),P(30)
150 FOR I=1 TO 30        'LOOP TO READ IN TABLE OF THE 30
160 READ C(I)               'OBSERVED INTERARRIVAL TIMES
170 NEXT I
180 DATA .5,1.5,2.5,3.5,4.5,5.5,6.5,7.5,8.5,9.5,10.5,11.5
190 DATA 12.5,13.5,14.5,15.5,16.5,17.5,18.5,19.5,21.5,22.5
200 DATA 25.5,28.5,29.5,32.5,33.5,34.5,36.5,39.5
210 FOR I=1 TO 30        'LOOP TO READ IN TABLE OF THE CUMULATIVE
220 READ P(I)               'PROBABILITIES ASSOCIATED WITH
230 NEXT I                  'THE INTERARRIVAL TIMES
240 DATA .11,.245,.36,.45,.525,.585,.65,.69,.725,.765
250 DATA .785,.82,.83,.85,.895,.91,.915,.92,.925,.93
260 DATA .945,.95,.955,.965,.97,.975,.98,.99,.995,1.0
270 '******************************************************************
280 'LINES 290 TO 370 ARE THE MAIN PART OF THE PROGRAM
290 GOSUB 450             'BRANCH TO GET SIMULATED ARRIVAL
300 IF N>N1 THEN 560      'PROGRAM COMPLETED?
310 GOSUB 400             'BRANCH TO GET SERVICE TIME
320 IF S1<A1 THEN 360     'TEST--NEXT EVENT=SERVICE OR ARRIVAL?
330 LET B=B+S1-A1         'ACCUMULATED WAITING TIME
340 LET S1=S1+S           'ARRIVAL LEAVES SYSTEM S(SERVICE TIME)
350 GO TO 290                'MINUTES AFTER THE PREVIOUS DEPARTURE
360 LET S1=A1+S           'DEPARTURE S MINUTES AFTER ARRIVAL
370 GO TO 290
380 '******************************************************************
390 'LINES 400 TO 420 ARE A SUBROUTINE FOR DETERMINING THE SERVICE TIME
400 LET S=6              'CONSTANT SERVICE TIME OF 6 MINUTES
410 LET S2=S2+S         'ACCUMULATED SERVICE TIME
420 RETURN
430 '******************************************************************
440 'LINES 450 TO 530 ARE A SUBROUTINE FOR DETERMINING INTERARRIVAL TIME
450 LET N=N+1           'COUNT OF NUMBER OF ARRIVALS
460 LET X=RND           'RANDOM NUMBER BETWEEN ZERO AND ONE
470 FOR I=1 TO 30       'LOOP TO ASSOCIATE AN INTERARRIVAL TIME
480 IF X>P(I) THEN 510      'WITH A RANDOM NUMBER SO FREQUENCIES
490 LET A=C(I)              'APPROXIMATE THOSE OF EMPIRICAL DATA
500 GO TO 520
510 NEXT I
520 LET A1=A1+A         'ACCUMULATED INTERARRIVAL TIME
530 RETURN
540 '******************************************************************
550 'LINES 560 TO 660 ARE TO PRINT OUT THE FINAL RESULTS
560 PRINT TAB(5);"MODEL INFORMATION AFTER"N1"SIMULATED ARRIVALS"
570 PRINT TAB(5);"--------------------------------------------"
580 PRINT
590 PRINT TAB(5);"MEAN TIME BETWEEN ARRIVALS =";A1/N1
600 PRINT TAB(5);"MEAN SERVICE TIME ="S2/N1
610 PRINT
620 PRINT "UTILIZATION FACTOR=";S2/A1
630 PRINT "MEAN NUMBER IN THE SYSTEM =";(B+S2)/A1
640 PRINT "MEAN NUMBER IN THE QUEUE =";B/A1
650 PRINT "MEAN TIME IN THE SYSTEM =";(B+S2)/N1
660 PRINT "MEAN WAITING TIME =";B/N1
670 END
```

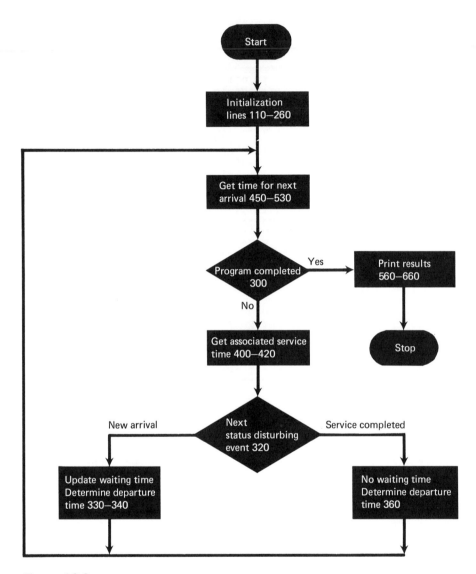

Figure 12.2

Line 140 merely sets aside computer storage space for two 30-element vectors or subscripted variables named C and P. Lines 150 to 200 fill the first vector with the 30 interarrival times, and lines 210 to 260 fill the second vector with the 30 associated cumulative probabilities for the various interarrival times. The data in lines 180 to 200 and 240 to 260 are the same as those presented in columns 1 and 4 of Table 12.1.

Lines 290 to 370 are the main part of the program where arrivals are associated with service times and where waiting times are determined. Line 290 sends the computer to a subroutine where an interarrival time is generated, and line 310 does essentially the same thing for an associated service time. By using subroutines or separate models for arrivals and services, changes can be readily made. Thus the subroutine for service is only 2 lines since we are working with a constant service time, but line 400 could be replaced with other lines to generate other kinds of service time patterns.

The test performed in line 300 is to see whether enough arrivals have been generated. When 1000 have been processed, N will come back from the interarrival time subroutine as 1001 and the program will be terminated.

The test made in line 320 is to find out what is the next status disturbing event. If $S1$ (the time the previous customer departed) is less than $A1$ (the arrival time of the present customer), then the departure time $(S1)$ of the present customer will be S (service time) minutes after he arrives $(S1 = A1 + S)$. If, however, the present customer arrives before the previous customer has departed (i.e. $A1 < S1$), then accumulated waiting time (B) will be increased by the amount $(S1 - A1)$ and the present customer arrival will depart S minutes after the previous customer departs $(S1 = S1 + S)$.

The subroutine between lines 430 and 540 generates interrarrival times in a way similar to the hat used in the hand-cranked model. Line 450 merely advances the count of arrivals each time the subroutine is entered so that the test of line 300 can be made. Line 460 gets a random number between zero and one and assigns it to the variable X.

In line 470, we enter a loop where X is successively tested against the cumulative probability data contained in the vector P until a value of P is found that is not less than X. At this point, the index or subscript I associated with the successful value of P is used to associate an appropriate interarrival time from the C vector to A (the simulated interarrival time). Then the loop is left (the probability of going all the way through the loop is only 0.005), the accumulated interarrival time is determined, and the program returns to line 290.*

Lines 560 to 660 print out the final results after the test in line 300 indicates that the required number of customers have been simulated. In line 590, the mean time between arrivals is computed to be the accumu-

---

*For the student who finds this arrival time determination hard to comprehend, start with the alternative method presented on page 333; it is essentially the same without using subscripted variables.

lated interarrival time divided by number of arrivals. Similarly, in line 600 the mean service time is computed, although the result of the calculation is obvious with a constant service time. If, however, our evolving analysis called for a change in that assumption or condition, we would only need to replace line 400 as indicated earlier.

Line 620 determines the utilization factor as $S2$ (accumulated actual service time) divided by $A1$ (accumulated interarrival time). In lines 590 and 600 we divided both of these variables by $N1$ to get average interarrival and service times. Our present calculation of the utilization factor (ρ) is therefore the same as that used in Chapter 11 (times instead of rates).

The mean waiting time computed in line 660 is quite straightforward, with the total waiting time (B) being divided by the number of customer arrivals $(N1)$. Since the mean time in the system is always made up of service plus waiting, it can be seen that line 650 is the addition of the two factors computed in lines 600 and 660.

We have noted earlier in the chapter how the mean number in the queue works out to be determined by dividing the total waiting time by the elapsed time of the study. Line 640 accomplishes this by dividing B by $A1$ (the arrival time for the $N1+1$ or 1001 customer). It might be argued that $S1$ (the departure time for the $N1$st customer) should be used; either one has a slight bias, but with a large enough sample size the choice will be unimportant.

The mean number in the system (line 630) is again computed by a relationship established in Chapter 11, where the expected number in the queue plus the utilization factor (expected number being serviced) equals the expected number in the system.

If we now run the program, we will get the following results:

```
MODEL INFORMATION AFTER 1000 SIMULATED ARRIVALS
--------------------------------------------------

MEAN TIME BETWEEN ARRIVALS = 7.3835
MEAN SERVICE TIME = 6

UTILIZATION FACTOR= 0.812623
MEAN NUMBER IN THE SYSTEM = 3.17316
MEAN NUMBER IN THE QUEUE = 2.36053
MEAN TIME IN THE SYSTEM = 23.429
MEAN WAITING TIME = 17.429

TIME: 1.561 SEC.
```

By changing one line in the program, we can increase the sample size to 10,000 and get slightly different results:

1.30 LET N1 10000

```
        MODEL INFORMATION AFTER 10000 SIMULATED ARRIVALS
        ------------------------------------------------

        MEAN TIME BETWEEN ARRIVALS = 7.25425
        MEAN SERVICE TIME = 6

    UTILIZATION FACTOR= 0.827101
    MEAN NUMBER IN THE SYSTEM = 3.07296
    MEAN NUMBER IN THE QUEUE = 2.24586
    MEAN TIME IN THE SYSTEM = 22.292
    MEAN WAITING TIME = 16.292

    TIME: 13.309 SEC.
```

A highly useful validation check is to compare the results from the simulation to those we get using the analytic models from Chapter 11. There we found the actual empirical interarrival data to have a mean value of 7.23 minutes (8.3 per hour); if we use the models based upon assumption of Poisson arrival rate pattern and constant service time of 6 minutes (10 per hour), we obtain the following:

$$\rho = \frac{\lambda}{\mu} = \frac{8.3}{10} = 0.83$$

$$\hat{S} = \frac{\lambda\,(2\mu - \lambda)}{2\mu\,(\mu - \lambda)} = \frac{8.3\,(20 - 8.3)}{20\,(10 - 8.3)} = 2.856 \text{ customers}$$

$$\hat{Q} = \frac{\lambda^2}{2\mu\,(\mu - \lambda)} = \frac{(8.3)^2}{20\,(10 - 8.3)} = 2.026 \text{ customers}$$

$$\hat{T}_S = \frac{\lambda + 2\,(\mu - \lambda)}{2\mu\,(\mu - \lambda)} = \frac{(10 + 2\,(10 - 8.3)}{20\,(10 - 8.3)} = 0.344 \text{ hrs.} = 20.6 \text{ min.}$$

$$\hat{T}_Q = \frac{\lambda}{2\mu\,(\mu - \lambda)} = \frac{10}{20\,(10 - 8.3)} = 0.244 \text{ hrs.} = 14.6 \text{ min.}$$

Note that the simulated results indicate longer waiting lines and times even though the simulated mean time between arrivals is slightly longer. By referring back to Fig. 11.3, this result might be explained by the relatively poor negative exponential approximation to the empirical data in the tails of the distributions.

Perhaps the most complicated aspect of the program involves the generation of interarrival times. An alternative procedure which accomplishes the same results is easier to understand, but requires more computer coding. We delete all but the first two lines of the initialization section (lines 140–260) and replace the arrival subroutine (lines 440–530) with the following, which will produce results identical to those produced previously (we also need to renumber lines 550 to 670).

QUEUE4   02/20/70 16:42

```
440 'LINES 450 TO 1360 ARE A SUBROUTINE FOR DETERMINING INTERARRIVAL TIME
450 LET N=N+1
460 LET X=RND
470 IF X>.11 THEN 500
480 LET A=.5
490 GO TO 1350
500 IF X>.245 THEN 530
510 LET A=1.5
520 GO TO 1350
530 IF X>.36 THEN 560
540 LET A=2.5
550 GO TO 1350
560 IF X>.45 THEN 590
570 LET A=3.5
580 GO TO 1350
590 IF X>.525 THEN 620
600 LET A=4.5
610 GO TO 1350
620 IF X>.585 THEN 650
630 LET A=5.5
640 GO TO1350
650 IF X>.65 THEN 680
660 LET A=6.5
670 GO TO1350
680 IF X>.69 THEN 710
690 LET A=7.5
700 GO TO 1350
710 IF X>.725 THEN 740
720 LET A=8.5
730 GO TO 1350
740 IF X>.765 THEN 770
750 LET A=9.5
760 GO TO 1350
770 IF X>.785 THEN 800
780 LET A=10.5
790 GO TO 1350
800 IF X>.82 THEN 830
810 LET A=11.5
820 GO TO 1350
830 IF X>.83 THEN 860
840 LET A=12.5
850 GO TO 1350
860 IF X>.85 THEN 890
870 LET A=13.5
880 GO TO 1350
```

```
890 IF X>.895 THEN 920
900 LET A=14.5
910 GO TO 1350
920 IF X>.91 THEN 950
930 LET A=15.5
940 GO TO 1350
950 IF X>.915 THEN 980
960 LET A=16.5
970 GO TO 1350
980 IF X>.92 THEN 1010
990 LET A=17.5
1000 GO TO 1350
1010 IF X>.925 THEN 1040
1020 LET A=18.5
1030 GO TO 1350
1040 IF X>.93 THEN 1070
1050 LET A=19.5
1060 GO TO 1350
1070 IF X>.945 THEN 1100
1080 LET A=21.5
1090 GO TO 1350
1100 IF X>.95 THEN 1130
1110 LET A=22.5
1120 GO TO 1350
1130 IF X>.955 THEN 1160
1140 LET A=25.5
1150 GO TO 1350
1160 IF X>.965 THEN 1190
1170 LET A=28.5
1180 GO TO 1350
1190 IF X>.97 THEN 1220
1200 LET A=29.5
1210 GO TO 1350
1220 IF X>.975 THEN 1250
1230 LET A=32.5
1240 GO TO 1350
1250 IF X>.98 THEN 1280
1260 LET A=33.5
1270 GO TO 1350
1280 IF X>.99 THEN 1310
1290 LET A=34.5
1300 GO TO 1350
1310 IF X>.995 THEN 1340
1320 LET A=36.5
1330 GO TO 1350
1340 LET A=39.5
1350 LET A1=A1+A
1360 RETURN
1370 '************************************************************
```

Another alternative for determining interarrival times is to randomly generate them from a negative exponential distribution. To do so, we can replace the previous long subroutine (lines 450–1360) with the following.

```
450 LET N=N+1
460 LET A=-LOG(RND)*7.23
470 LET A1=A1 +A
480 RETURN
```

This subroutine produced the following results which can be compared with the analytic results on page 00:

```
MODEL INFORMATION AFTER 10000 SIMULATED ARRIVALS
------------------------------------------------

    MEAN TIME BETWEEN ARRIVALS = 7.2842
    MEAN SERVICE TIME = 6.04173

UTILIZATION FACTOR= 0.829429
MEAN NUMBER IN THE SYSTEM = 4.76181
MEAN NUMBER IN THE QUEUE = 3.93238
MEAN TIME IN THE SYSTEM = 34.686
MEAN WAITING TIME = 28.6443

TIME: 27.264 SEC.
```

Still another alternative is to change the service time distribution from constant to negative exponential as follows:

```
400 LET S=-LOG(RND)*6
```

Adding this subroutine to the preceding produced the following results:

```
MODEL INFORMATION AFTER 10000 SIMULATED ARRIVALS
------------------------------------------------

    MEAN TIME BETWEEN ARRIVALS = 7.21475
    MEAN SERVICE TIME = 6

UTILIZATION FACTOR= 0.831629
MEAN NUMBER IN THE SYSTEM = 2.95834
MEAN NUMBER IN THE QUEUE = 2.12671
MEAN TIME IN THE SYSTEM = 21.3437
MEAN WAITING TIME = 15.3437

TIME: 17.742 SEC.
```

The appropriate analytic models from Chapter 11 yield:

$$\rho = \frac{\lambda}{\mu} = \frac{8.3}{10} = 0.83, \qquad S = \frac{\lambda}{\mu - \lambda} = \frac{8.3}{10 - 8.3} = 4.88$$

$$Q = \frac{\lambda^2}{\mu(\mu - \lambda)} = \frac{(8.3)^2}{10(10 - 8.3)} = 4.05$$

$$T_S = \frac{1}{\mu - \lambda} = \frac{1}{10 - 8.3} = 0.59 \text{ hr.} = 34.4 \text{ Min.}$$

$$T_Q = \frac{\lambda}{\mu(\mu - \lambda)} = \frac{8.3}{10(10 - 8.3)} = 0.49 \text{ hr.} = 29.4 \text{ Min.}$$

Thus we see how it is possible to readily change our model to accommodate changes in assumptions. Obviously, many of those assumption changes would be identified by particular users (who have criteria). The ease of investigating many kinds of assumption changes is enhanced by using "standard" probability distribution generators which merely call for a change in parameters (e.g. a 10% faster service rate).

To facilitate the use of such "standard" probability models, the balance of this appendix presents 12 of the most popular probability models in the form of a subroutine that can be appended to simulation programs.*

```
10000' <><><><><><><><><><><><><><><><><><><><><><><><><><><><><><>
10001'THIS SUBROUTINE WILL DELIVER A SAMPLE DRAWN FROM ANY ONE OF
10002'TWELVE PROBABILITY DISTRIBUTIONS.
10003'
10004'APPENDING THIS PACKAGE TO A SIMULATION PROGRAM WILL ALLOW
10005'THE DRAWING OF A SAMPLE BY SIMPLY SPECIFYING THE DISTRIBUTION
10006'DESIRED AND THE APPROPRIATE PARAMETERS.
10007'
10008'THE DISTRIBUTION IS SPECIFIED BY ASSIGNING A VALUE TO (H0).
10009'PARAMETERS ARE ASSIGNED AS (H2),(H3),ETC.
10010'THE SAMPLE VALUE IS  RETURNED AS (H1).
10011'
10012'USE OF THIS PACKAGE PREEMPTS THE VARIABLES (H0),(H1),....,(H9).
10013'
10014'       -----  ------------------------------------------
10015'       H0=1   CONTINUOUS UNIFORM DISTRIBUTION
10016'              FROM (H2) TO (H3).
10017'       H0=2   DISCRETE UNIFORM DISTRIBUTION
10018'              FROM (H2) TO (H3) INCLUSIVE.
10019'       H0=3   POISSON DISTRIBUTION
10020'              (H2) MEAN AND VARIANCE.
10021'       H0=4   NORMAL DISTRIBUTION
10022'              (H2) MEAN AND (H3) STANDARD DEVIATION.
10023'       H0=5   LOG-NORMAL DISTRIBUTION
10024'              (H2) MEAN AND (H3) STANDARD DEVIATION.
10025'       H0=6   BINOMIAL DISTRIBUTION
10026'              (H2) TRIALS WITH AN (H3) PROBABILITY OF SUCCESS.
10027'       H0=7   NEGATIVE BINOMIAL DISTRIBUTION
10028'              (H2) SUCCESSES WITH AN (H3) PROBABILITY OF SUCCESS.
10029'       H0=8   GEOMETRIC DISTRIBUTION
10030'              (H2) PROBABILITY OF SUCCESS.
10031'       H0=9   EXPONENTIAL DISTRIBUTION
10032'              (H2) MEAN.
10033'       H0=10  ERLANG DISTRIBUTION
10034'              (H2) EVENTS WITH AN (H3) MEAN.
10035'       H0=11  BETA DISTRIBUTION
10036'              (H2) EVENTS IN RATIO TO (H3) EVENTS.
10037'       H0=12  HYPERGEOMETRIC DISTRIBUTION
10038'              (H2) TRIALS WITH AN (H3) PROBABILITY OF SUCCESS,
10039'              DRAWN FROM A POPULATION OF (H4).
10040'       -----  ------------------------------------------
```

---

*Description of these process generators is beyond our present scope. See Thomas H. Naylor, J. L. Balintfy, D. S. Burdick, and K. Chu, *Computer Simulation Techniques,* Wiley, 1966, Chapter 4.

```
10041'
10042'<><><><><><><><><><><><><><><><><><><><><><><><><><><><><><><>
10043 IF ABS(HO-6.5)<6 THEN 10046
10044 PRINT "HO OUT OF RANGE. HO=1 ASSUMED."
10045 LET HO=1
10046 IF HO>6 THEN 10048
10047 ON HO GOTO 10100,10200,10300,10400,10500,10600
10048 ON HO-6 GOTO 10700,10800,10900,11000,11100,11200
10049'<><><><><><><><><><><><><><><><><><><><><><><><><><><><><><><>
10100'<><><><><><><><><><><><><><><><><><><><><><><><><><><><><><><>
10101'CONTINUOUS UNIFORM DISTRIBUTION FROM (H2) TO (H3).
10102          LET H1=H2+RND*(H3-H2)
10103          RETURN
10200'<><><><><><><><><><><><><><><><><><><><><><><><><><><><><><><>
10201'DISCRETE UNIFORM DISTRIBUTION FROM (H2) TO (H3), INCLUSIVE.
10202          LET H1=INT(H2+RND*(H3-H2+1))
10203          RETURN
10300'<><><><><><><><><><><><><><><><><><><><><><><><><><><><><><><>
10301'POISSON DISTRIBUTION WITH (H2) MEAN AND VARIANCE.
10302          LET H1=0
10303          LET H3=1
10304          LET H3=H3*RND
10305          IF H3<EXP(-H2) THEN 10308
10306          LET H1=H1+1
10307          GOTO 10304
10308          RETURN
10400'<><><><><><><><><><><><><><><><><><><><><><><><><><><><><><><>
10401'NORMAL DISTRIBUTION WITH (H2) MEAN AND (H3) STANDARD DEVIATION.
10402          LET H1=H2+H3*1.414214*SQR(-LOG(RND))*SIN(6.2831852*RND)
10403          RETURN
10500'<><><><><><><><><><><><><><><><><><><><><><><><><><><><><><><>
10501'LOG-NORMAL DISTRIBUTION WITH (H2) MEAN AND (H3) STANDARD DEVIATION.
10502          LET H4=SQR(LOG((H3/H2)^2+1))
10503          LET H5=LOG(H2)-H4^2/2
10504          LET H1=EXP(H5+H4*SQR(-LOG(RND)*2)*SIN(6.2831852*RND))
10505          RETURN
10600'<><><><><><><><><><><><><><><><><><><><><><><><><><><><><><><>
10601'BINOMIAL DISTRIBUTION OF (H2) TRIALS WITH AN (H3) PROBABILITY
10602'OF SUCCESS IN EACH TRIAL.
10603          LET H1=0
10604          FOR H4=1 TO H2
10605          IF RND>H3 THEN 10607
10606          LET H1=H1+1
10607          NEXT H4
10608          RETURN
10700'<><><><><><><><><><><><><><><><><><><><><><><><><><><><><><><>
10701'NEGATIVE BINOMIAL DISTRIBUTION OF (H2) SUCCESSES WITH  AN
10702'(H3) PROBABILITY OF SUCCESS IN EACH TRIAL.
10703          LET H1=1
10704          FOR H4=1 TO H2
10705          LET H1=H1*RND
10706          NEXT H4
10707          LET H1=INT(LOG(H1)/LOG(1-H3))
10708          RETURN
10800'<><><><><><><><><><><><><><><><><><><><><><><><><><><><><><><>
10801'GEOMETRIC DISTRIBUTION WITH (H2) PROBABILITY OF SUCCESS.
10802          LET H1=INT(LOG(RND)/LOG(1-H2))
10803          RETURN
10804'<><><><><><><><><><><><><><><><><><><><><><><><><><><><><><><>
```

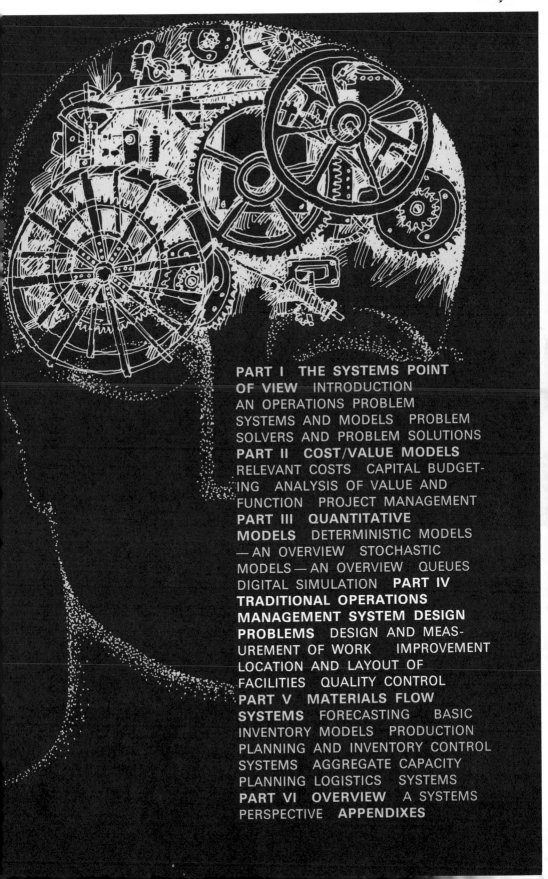

INTRODUCTION
TO PART IV

Part IV is devoted to some of the classical problems that have been investigated in operations management, as well as to some of the more prominent models used to investigate those problems. Although the scope of our studies will of necessity be limited, I believe that you should be able to derive sufficient understanding to interact meaningfully with people having more detailed knowledge; you should also have a sufficient overview of topics such as work measurement, facility location and layout, and quality control to appreciate where additional approaches fit in. You will not be intimidated by the work factor method for time standards or by complex tables for quality control procedures, even though we will not study these particular techniques. By knowing that you once understood the basic issues and basic strategy for coping with these issues, you will know that a small amount of study will bring your knowledge up to the required level.

Of even greater importance than knowing that you can cope with models for these problems at a detailed level is the critical appreciation you will derive from your evolving appreciation of the systems concept. The strengths and weaknesses of various techniques and problem definitions need to be subjected to scrutiny in terms of assumptions about surrogate criteria. As a future executive, you will need to do this, and you will find that practitioners familiar with detailed models are often unable adequately to see the forest for the trees. In fact, having the ability to see particular problems in proper perspective is often the factor which separates executives from those lower in the organization.

Part of your systemic view of these models will be based upon insights obtained in other courses. Organizational behavior classes often discuss the sociotechnical aspects of work measurement systems, and I believe that your overall appreciation of the issues is enhanced by a clear understanding of the models used. In a similar way, accounting courses discuss standards and variance reports where the basic input data are generated by work measurement models; your knowledge will lead you to question the validity of those data. As we noted in the introduction to Part III, your work in quantitative analysis will augment your understanding of variability in these traditional operations management problems, and vice versa.

Chapter 13 considers issues involved in the design and measurement of work. The design of work methods should precede work measurement, and a set of motion economy principles has been developed over the years to aid in job design. Work measurement involves some technical issues as well as some philosophical issues. If your assignments include one of the projects at the end of the chapter, you will understand these matters well. As one of the few concrete measurement systems used in business, it is interesting to discover how necessarily arbitrary the procedures are.

Chapter 14 examines this arbitrariness. A critical investigation of some of the underlying axioms of work measurement leads to the same conclusion reached in Chapter 4: Evolution is to be expected; any job design is capable of being improved. The fact that this evolution has been widely disregarded in industrial engineering practice is partially responsible for gold bricking practices which pervade many industries. An improved model for estimating output in an evolutionary context is presented.

Chapter 15 is devoted to two related problems, the location of facilities (plant location) and the layout of facilities (plant layout). The criteria systems for both problems tend to be complex, and available models tend to focus on one or a few surrogate criteria. We will examine the surrogate relationships, and also briefly delve into the design of some models. Although a detailed technical comparison of layout and assembly line balancing models is beyond our present scope, you should find the process of how some of these models were formulated to be of intellectual and perhaps practical interest.

In Chapter 16 you will develop an appreciation for the issues and models used in quality control. I apologize for the length of the chapter, but my experience has been that students either do not adequately learn or else forget statistical hypothesis testing. If you understand these materials, you will be able to read the chapter fairly quickly. We will initially attempt to define the issues of quality control. Quality is a difficult commodity to quantify, and improvements in quality involve personnel and motivational issues. Surrogate quality criteria need to be assessed in terms of overall company goals. As the detailed models are presented, you should try to consider the applicability of quality control models to other kinds of problems. The notion of preestablished limits that signal corrective action has value beyond that of statistical processes. We will also see statistical applications of these ideas in Chapters 17 and 18.

CHAPTER 13

DESIGN AND MEASUREMENT
OF WORK

We start our section on operations management system design problems with a traditional problem area that has received a great deal of attention since the end of the last century. Design and measurement of work was then the central problem area which concerned the scientific management movement and continues to this day to represent the major occupation for industrial engineers. The history of work design and measurement makes fascinating reading and includes some stormy labor disputes and a congressional investigation of scientific management; unfortunately, our present scope precludes such a history. However, partly because of the continuing controversy associated with the design and measurement of work in many current labor disputes, it should be beneficial to gain an appreciation of the methodologies or models involved and their inherent assumptions and weaknesses.

JOB DESIGN

Job design is concerned with the efficient use of human resources. It attempts to find very good methods of accomplishing tasks. Workers and other possible system entities have attributes that are included and structured. Suppose Westfall considered use of a 20-year-old, 200 pound man and other entities to move cartons in the warehouse. They might consider the man's inherent lifting ability associated with his physiological cost of lifting various amounts of weight in a working day of a specified length. Figure 13.1 represents a crude model of what the energy expenditure in weight lifted for Westfall's hypothetical 20-year-old man might be.

We will see, however, that an interest in weight moving involves considerably more than a mere substitution of horsepower or physiological energy for pounds. The amount carried per trip, the method of carrying or moving, the length of the trip, the way in which resting time periods are designed, and the criteria sets of laborers are all significant variables.

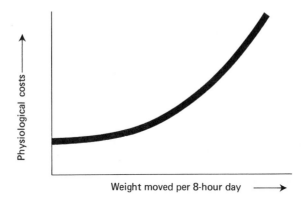

Figure 13.1

Criteria

The goals or criteria for job design are relatively easy to state. The dominant criterion is simply to accomplish work in the most economical way —to use that combination of human and mechanical inputs which minimizes the cost of achieving some specified task with a specified or desired output rate. Additional criteria in the set are concerned with individual dignity; although they tend to mitigate against a "commodity" viewpoint of labor, we will see how improvements in the design of the criteria system can result in both increased worker satisfaction and decreased task cost.

In Box 13.1, two early applications of scientific management illustrate the potential returns from improved design and measurement of work:

In 1899 Frederick W. Taylor undertook a study of pig iron handling at the Bethlehem Steel plant in South Bethlehem, Pennsylvania. The job involved the transportation of "pigs" of iron from a storage area into freight cars (a pig of iron weighs 92 lbs.); workers typically carried a pig up an inclined ramp into the freight car where the pigs were stacked. Taylor made his studies by finding a particular worker (identified in the literature as Schmidt) who worked a 10-hour day, 6-day week handling pig iron and was observed trotting a mile to and from his home to the Bethlehem yards. This individual was accepted by Taylor as what he deemed a "first class man." At the offer of a significant increase in wages (60%), Schmidt agreed to engage in the experiments in work methods that Taylor desired. Taylor's experiments concerned the identification of the significant variables involved in the job and the subsequent varying of each variable individually while holding other variables constant. When Taylor started his investigations, the average man transported about 12 ½ tons of pig iron per day; in the new method, about 47 ½ tons were transported per day for a net increase of about 300%. This method involved an enforced series of resting times totaling 57% of the working day. Taylor was thereafter able to recruit and train other individuals to work at the desired output rate and make the 60% bonus.

Frank Gilbreth, a contemporary of Frederick Taylor (and with his wife the hero and heroine in the novel *Cheaper by the Dozen*), went to work for a building contractor at age 17. One of Gilbreth's first jobs involved brick laying where he noticed that brick layers had 3 distinct ways of laying bricks; there was a fast method, a slow method, and a method used when teaching someone else how to lay bricks. Each of these methods utilized a different set of hand and body movements. From this experience (and other similar experiences) Gilbreth formulated the notion of what he called the "one best way"; that is, Gilbreth believed that a best or optimum method for performing any task should be able to be identified. When Gilbreth started to study brick laying methods the average output was less than 120 bricks per man hour; Gilbreth was able to increase this output to 350 bricks per man hour and in the process started his own construction firm and became fairly wealthy. There is one further interesting statistic that should be added: Frank Gilbreth achieved the output rate of 350 bricks laid per man hour in about 1910; the official union scale for the number of bricks laid per *day* in one U.S. metropolitan city is currently reputed to be 400.

Box 13.1

System Boundaries

As noted in our discussion of the system design process in Chapter 3, the inclusion or bounding of a system, although necessary, is always somewhat artificial; the systems approach indeed achieves its benefits by continually looking for the most artificial aspects of the bounding process. Bounding artificialities are particularly germane to "standard" problems since all problems tend to become increasingly unique as they are defined in a way which more closely resembles the overall character and goals of a particular unique organization.

For the job design problem, the major kind of potential suboptimization attributable to bounding comes from the acceptance of a specified task. That is, the process of dividing a total job or task into individual segments or subtasks may severely limit the ability to design job methods for the subtasks; when the total required activities for the creation of a product are broken down into tasks for subsequent job design, opportunity costs of designing work methods solely within prescribed job task specifications can be significant.

One of the strong influences in job content or task specification has been the principle of labor specialization; a division of labor where continual subdivisions lead to increased specialization historically has been found to yield efficient use of human resources. In following this principle to extremes, however, no account is taken of the interactions with the systems both of human beings considered individually in terms of their own personal goals or criteria of social systems. In recent years, some investigators have indicated that perhaps an approach based on *increasing* work content can lead to increased worker interest and satisfaction which in turn can lead to significant enterprise benefits; this approach has come to be called "job enlargement."

The interaction between task specification and the determination of work methods for those specified tasks has been succinctly identified by Buffa, who differentiates between "job content" and "job methods."[*] He identifies the following factors as influencing job content or task identification:

1. The drive to gain the advantages of division of labor
2. The limitations specified by product designs and existing processes
3. The limitations specified by production quotas
4. The limitations specified by layouts and pacing effects of machines and conveyors
5. The limitations specified by the desire to make skill requirements uniform within jobs
6. The drive to gain the advantages of worker satisfaction through job enlargement

He also identifies the following six factors as influencing job methods for the design of a specified task:

1. Physical and economic limitations
2. Control of the working environment
3. Physiological data
4. Psychological data
5. Arrangement and flow of work and study of the motions and time required
6. Fatigue and work schedules

Motion Study

In the next major section we will turn our attention to the determination of a time standard for a specified task. However, motion study is a very important step which should precede time study. One should determine the best method before establishing a time standard. Thus for the two applications presented in Box 13.1 it is clear that before one could determine a reasonable time expectation for laying bricks or for carrying pig iron, it was necessary to determine the best methods for performing those tasks.

The responsibility for determining the proper methods should not be placed on the workers. There are several reasons why this is so. First, each

---

[*]Elwood S. Buffa, "Toward a Unified Concept of Job Design" *Journal of Industrial Engineering*, **11**, no. 4 (1960): 346–51.

worker will tend to do things in a somewhat different way; it should be possible to find the best ways for doing various segments of the job and to synthesize a method based on individually attractive segments. It does not seem reasonable or fair to ask workers to make such syntheses—they are concerned with a feasible method, not an optimal one.

Second, if a good synthesis is to be used, it will be necessary to have an explicit or written model of the job design. This will be necessary for educational purposes as well as for incorporating improvements. Evolution should be expected, and the descriptive models must correspondingly evolve in an orderly manner.

Third, if a group is solely directed to the study of proper methodology for work, it should be able to make comparative observations and from these observations evolve some standardized methods which are superior. That is, evolution in job methods should be fostered by transplanting efficiencies discovered in one method to another.

Fourth, a process which leads to rapid evolution of superior methods should be capable of professionalization so that superior work methods become standardized or known to a group of experts or professionals whose orientation is solely devoted to the methodology of work. From these standard methods for working conditions, it might even be possible to evolve a set of principles with which one views a particular work activity; such a set does indeed exist and over the years the following set of 22 principles of motion economy has been codified:*

Use of the Human Body

1. The two hands should begin as well as complete their motions at the same time

2. The two hands should not be idle at the same time except during rest periods

3. Motions of the arms should be made in opposite and symmetrical directions and should be made simultaneously

4. Hand and body motions should be confined to the lowest classification with which it is possible to perform the work satisfactorily

5. Momentum should be employed to assist the worker wherever possible, and it should be reduced to a minimum if it must be overcome by muscular effort

6. Smooth continuous curved motions of the hands are preferable to straight-line motions involving sudden and sharp changes in direction

*Copyright 1963 © by John Wiley & Sons, Inc. (From *Motion and Time Study: Design and Measurement of Work,* R. M. Barnes. By permission of John Wiley & Sons, Inc.)

7. Ballistic movements are faster, easier, and more accurate than restricted (fixation) or "controlled" movements

8. Work should be arranged to permit easy and natural rhythm wherever possible

9. Eye fixations should be as few and as close together as possible

Arrangement of the Work Place

10. There should be a definite and fixed place for all tools and materials

11. Tools, materials, and controls should be located close to the point of use

12. Gravity feed bins and containers should be used to deliver material close to the point of use

13. Drop deliveries should be used wherever possible

14. Materials and tools should be located to permit the best sequence of motions

15. Provisions should be made for adequate conditions for seeing. Good illumination is the first requirement for satisfactory visual perception

16. The height of the work place and the chair should preferably be arranged so that alternative sitting and standing at work are easily possible

17. A chair of the type and height to permit good posture should be provided for every worker

Design of Tools and Equipment

18. The hands should be relieved of all work that can be done more advantageously by a jig, a fixture, or a foot operated device

19. Two or more tools should be combined wherever possible

20. Tools and materials should be prepositioned whenever possible

21. Where each finger performs some kind of specific movement such as in typewriting, the load should be distributed in accordance with the inherent capacity of the fingers

22. Levers, crossbars, and hand wheels should be located in such positions that the operator can manipulate them with the least change in body position and with the greatest mechanical advantage

Anthropometric Data

Although the principles of motion economy listed above have been distilled from many years of industrial engineering experiences and are quite valuable as general principles, they lack the rigor of some explicit models or statements that might be derived from experimentation of a laboratory nature. Anthropometry is concerned with providing more explicit models of the characteristics of the human body so that jobs may be designed in better accordance with human abilities. Thus motion economy principle number 16 states that the "height of the work place and the chair should preferably be arranged so that alternative sitting and standing at work are easily possible." But for one designing a work place, the obvious question is, precisely what height should the table be? Precisely at what height should the chair be? A related issue concerns the desired outputs or models of worker characteristics provided by anthropometry: We not only want to know the *average* worker characteristics which then indicate such considerations as the *average* height for tables, we need to know the *distribution* of characteristics for the population that we wish to employ in a particular occupation.

A good deal of this more basic research has been done by physiologists, psychologists, and engineering academics. Interdisciplinary activity between members of these groups is sometimes referred to as "human engineering." One fairly recent project in anthropometry involves the determination of a set of data for handicapped individuals; as greater advances are made in life-saving medical practices, the number of people in the population possessing such characteristics as partial paralysis from a stroke has increased substantially. The design of jobs as well as the design of everyday living devices which can be operated by these individuals is therefore of increasing importance.

One ongoing research activity in anthropometry is related to the physiological cost of performing work. This research involves ascertaining energy expenditures based on oxygen consumption or heart beat patterns. Although this research is still at a fairly preliminary level, studies have yielded insights into the proper amounts of rest or fatigue allowances required for high energy-consuming activities.

Some of the more important inputs to job design that have evolved from anthropometry include the normal reach dimensions for arm movements which do not require movements of the body trunk; chair and table heights; strength requirements for legs, arms, and hands; finger dexterity; the effects of prepositioning; design of dials for increased readability; and the effects of varying temperature, noise, and light. Work on this last area, the ways in which job performance is influenced by various illumination levels, led to the interesting results briefly described in Box 13.2.*

---

*For a fuller description, see Elton Mayo, *The Human Problems of an Industrial Civilization,* Viking Press, 1960; and F. J. Roethlisberger and W. J. Dickson, *Management and the Worker,* Harvard University Press, 1940.

An outside research group carried on a series of experiments over several years at the Western Electric Company's Hawthorne works during the 1930s. One group of experiments was devoted to developing an explicit model for the effect of illumination levels on work performance. For these experiments, a sample work group was selected to perform their normal work in a specially designed room where illumination levels could be varied. The task they were performing was a manual assembly with a well defined standard method, and a production history; a control group was operating in a normal working environment. The experiments went on over several months and some very encouraging correlations between performance levels and illumination levels were observed. These encouraging correlation coefficients seemed to indicate that it would be possible to make predictions in the effects of changes in illumination levels. The experimenters were very happy with their results, but one day decided to change the experimental conditions. On this day, the employees were told that the light intensity was increased when in fact it was decreased; the interesting result was that performance levels increased to the level expected for the higher announced illumination level. Succeeding experiments had similar results; performance measures correlated very well with announced illumination levels but had very little correlation with actual illumination levels. On reflection, it became obvious that these employees, either consciously or unconsciously, were very happy to have research groups interested in their well-being; they responded to this happiness with performance levels that they considered desirable in terms of the research team's criteria. The same general phenomenon was observed in a subsequent series of experiments devoted to the design of rest periods and the length of the working day. Again, performance was judged to be increased mainly because of motivational factors. This phenomenon is now referred to as the "Hawthorne Effect" and we will find it to be a very interesting potential causal factor in other areas of investigation in this book.

Box 13.2

Models for Motion Study

Over the years a number of models have been developed to aid in the conservation and better use of human resources in performing specific tasks. One of the early techniques developed by Frank Gilbreth involved the use of a low film speed time exposure of a repetitive task performed with small lights attached to the hands. Analysis of the subsequent movement patterns indicated possible economies. A more easily implemented procedure that is widely used involves a detailed specification of the functions performed by each hand during a job cycle. Figure 13.2 is a left hand-right hand chart for a very important task performed at a "well-known small Eastern school"—opening cans of beer.

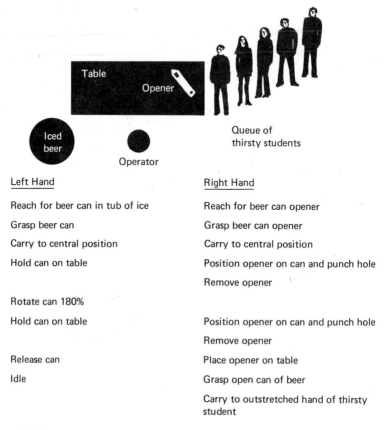

Figure 13.2

A more detailed model for analyzing hand movements involves the use of special high speed motion picture equipment that takes pictures at the rate of 1,000 frames per minute. A detailed analysis of each frame (.001 minutes) enables the hand movements to be meticulously timed and broken down into elements which are called "therbligs" (therblig is Gilbreth spelled backwards with the t and h transposed). All hand motions are categorized as one of the following 17 therbligs:

1. Search—locate an object visually or by groping for it
2. Select—choose one part from among several
3. Grasp—close the fingers around a part
4. Transport empty—motion of the empty hand
5. Transport loaded—motion of the hand while carrying object
6. Hold—manual support or control of an object
7. Release—relinquish manual control

8. Position—locate an object in specific position
9. Preposition—orient object correctly
10. Inspect—compare object with standard
11. Assemble—unite mating parts
12. Disassemble—disunite mating parts
13. Use—manually implement production procedure
14. Unavoidable delay—idle beyond operator's control
15. Avoidable delay—idle for which operator is responsible
16. Plan—mentally determine next action
17. Rest to overcome fatigue—a periodic delay due to operator fatigue

With both left hand-right hand and micromotion models, inefficient uses of the hands are highlighted. Analysts particularly look for idle time, long or unnecessary transports, and use of the hands for functions which could be fulfilled by jigs or fixtures. Thus, holding is a function which can be fulfilled by a jig or fixture; use of a hand to hold violates the 18th principle of motion economy.

The man-machine chart is a model for those problem situations involving a man and machine interaction or the interaction of several man and/or machine cycles. Such an interaction will almost invariably involve some randomness in the cycle times of the men and/or machines; to the extent this is so, it is preferable to treat such problem situations as "queuing" problems. Figure 13.3 depicts a typical man-machine model for a Westfall employee who applies a special clear silicone "paint" to drawer sides and bottoms to facilitate ease of opening and closing. In this job, the operator uses a spray gun and two fixed-cycle drying ovens where it takes two minutes to "paint" the drawer, one minute to put it into the oven (first removing the preceding dry drawer), and seven minutes to dry.

Job Enlargement

Job enlargement is a term that has been coined for the process of improved job design through increasing the scope and complexity of each individual worker's assigned task. Job enlargement runs counter to the direction indicated by specialization of labor. How can this be? One answer is suggested in our preceding section on system boundaries for job design. That is, the assumption that individual and social system criteria are outside the boundaries of the job design system is artificial; the effect of that artificiality can, in some situations, lead to marginal reductions in productivity that are greater than the marginal increases in productivity associated with the benefits derived from further labor specialization. Thus the decrease in pride of individual craftsmanship associated with individual or two-man chair-building teams may more than offset the benefits of specialization gained in assembly line chair building at Westfall.

HANO CHART

Time (min)	Man	Oven #1	Oven #2
1	Paint drawer		
2	Put drawer in oven #1	Necessary idle	
3			
4	Paint drawer		
5			
	Put drawer in oven #2		Necessary idle
6			
7	Idle	Dry	
8			
9	Paint drawer		Dry
10			
	Put drawer in oven #1	Necessary idle	
11			
12	Paint drawer		
13			
	Put drawer in oven #2		Necessary idle
14			
15	Idle	Dry	
16			
17	Paint drawer		Dry
18			
	Put drawer in oven #1	Necessary idle	
19			
20	Paint drawer		
21			
22	Put drawer in oven #2		Necessary idle
23	Idle	Dry	
24			
25	Paint drawer		Dry
26			

Figure 13.3

There have been several reported examples where job enlargement benefits were obtained; they include an original study at IBM Corporation where machine operators assumed a much greater role in the setup and inspection operations, a pump assembly at the Maytag Company where an assembly line of five to seven highly specialized workers was exchanged for a series of complete individual assembly stations (workers' names were put on the pumps), and various office jobs where greater responsibilities led to decreased error rates and employee turnover.

Some attempts have been made to quantify the effects of job enlargement on employee performance, but conclusive results have not been obtained. Although job enlargement plans often lead to improved productivity measures and improved employee satisfaction, we should not ignore the influence on morale as depicted by the Hawthorne studies: Are the improved measures due to some inherent change in the job design itself, or are they due to positive employee feelings toward increased managerial interest in their welfare?

There are those who will say that it does not make any difference as long as the benefits do in fact accrue, but it is worth thinking about the long-range difference between a change in job design that leads to an inherently superior use of human resources versus what is essentially a morale-building activity. The former should be more capable of being sustained and should be equally amenable to a properly designed morale-building effort. Morale-building efforts, however, should be carefully analyzed in terms of the hidden costs of achieving increases in morale, the ability to sustain increased morale over an extended time horizon, and the effects of cascading various kinds of morale-building programs. Thus for example, if a job enlargement plan involves the board chairman or corporation president talking to workers about their jobs, what is the opportunity cost associated with utilizing highly paid executives in this capacity? And if the president is a necessary ingredient to the implementation of these plans, what proportion of his time will be spent in this way? Finally, how do workers respond to a series of morale-building programs, particularly when these programs approach the theatrical? A type of quality control program that will be examined in more detail in Chapter 16 has involved striped-shirted executives riding through factories on fire engines with Dixieland bands.

Participation of the workers should be considered in the design of jobs. It has been found that some assembly lines could achieve much greater production over an 8-hour day by turning the control of the assembly line speed over to the workers rather than having the speed decided by specialized expert job designers. Participation is very much oriented toward the process of implementing change. As such, it is somewhat similar to the user-designer concept but typically does not include either the conscious design of a user-oriented modeling environment or the goal of rapid evolution in perceived user need. Participation such as that involved in the assembly line speeds, for example, utilizes the real system instead of any model and is dominated by the criterion of output per day;

in addition, it is worth noting that the example most often described in the literature was engaged in *after* the system had been completely designed by experts and that system did not perform to design specifications.

STOPWATCH TIME STUDY

Although it may sound from our discussion of job design that there are so many complicating factors that the task is hopeless, such is not the case. Jobs do get designed, but because of many of the aspects described above, they are often far from perfect and evolutionary improvements are possible. This evolution is dealt with explicitly in Chapter 14; for now let us turn our attention to the goals and methodology for measuring the work content of a specified job design or task.

Criteria

The basic goal or criterion of time study is to provide a standard to which output can be compared; or, to determine what represents "a fair day's work for a fair day's pay." The notion of "fair" is an important one because we would like to have the standards comparable for all jobs, having been established by a reasonable and consistent detached analytical process rather than by historical circumstance. The desire for formally determined standards rather than informal standards based upon past performance recognizes the undesirability and inequity of standards (such as those used in budgets) that are based upon varying past efficiencies.

In actuality, time standards are rarely determined for anything but fairly routine repetitive tasks. This is true because the methodology involved in determining an objective time standard for less well-defined activities is not appealing in terms of its degree of objectivity. Nevertheless, if one has an interest in controlling operations it is necessary to have standards of some sort; the absence of well-defined methodology simply cannot be accepted as an excuse for not establishing standards.

Remember that control is a three-step process of (1) establishing a standard, criterion, or objective; (2) measuring against that standard or objective, and (3) correcting for deviations. Without the first step, standard determination, one simply cannot "control."

The Model

The stopwatch time-study model for the estimation of required labor inputs can be described as a series of eleven discernible steps:

1. Determine the proper method for the task
2. Divide the job or task into elements
3. Select an appropriate operator for study

OBSERVATION SHEET

ELEMENTS	UPPER LINE : SUBTRACTED TIME / LOWER LINE : READING															AV. TIME	SELECTD TIME	OCC. PER CYCLE	EFFORT RATING	NORMAL TIME
	1	2	3	4	5	6	7	8	9	10	11	12	13	14	15					
Get beer can and opener	.04	.05	.03	.04	.04	.04	.04	.04	.04	.03	.04	.04	.04	.04	.03	.038	.038	1	90	.034
	.04	.17	.21	.42	.56	.68	.81	1.20	1.72	1.86	1.98	2.11	2.25	2.37	2.49					
Open can (2 holes)	.05	.04	.08	.07	.05	.06	.32*	.03	.07	.05	.05	.07	.04	.06	.09	.075	.075	1	115	.086
	.09	.21	.35	.49	.61	.74	1.13	1.23	1.79	1.91	2.05	2.18	2.29	2.45	2.58					
Give to thirsty student	.03	.03	.04	.03	.03	.03	.03	.15**	.04	.03	.04	.03	.04	.03	.04	.061	.034	1	80	.027
	.12	.24	.39	.52	.69	.77	1.16	1.68	1.83	1.94	2.07	2.21	2.33	2.46	2.62					
Total Normal Time																				.147
Allowances (10%)																				.016
Standard Time																				.163

FOREIGN ELEMENTS :
* Operator dropped opener
** Operator drank this can of beer

TOOLS, JIGS, GAUGES, PATTERNS, ETC. :
Beer can opener

Figure 13.4

4. Observe and record the elemental times
5. Performance rate each element
6. Calculate the required sample sizes
7. Obtain any additional data indicated
8. Determine the selected time
9. Calculate the normal time
10. Determine appropriate allowances
11. Calculate the standard time

Figure 13.4 represents a completed time study of the beer can opening task modeled with a left hand-right hand chart in Fig. 13.2. Let us now turn to a discussion of the procedures and assumptions involved in the 11 steps, using Figs. 13.2 and 13.4 for exemplary purposes.

Proper Method

The process of job design is devoted to the determination of the proper method for a specified task. It therefore follows that job design precedes time study and that there is limited value in a time estimate for a poorly designed task. However, in our discussion of job design we noted that evolution will probably occur; the net effect of this evolution is increasingly to erode our confidence both in the appropriateness of job methods and also in required time estimates or forecasts of labor inputs for those jobs. This evolutionary phenomenon and concomitant erosion of faith in time estimates has wide ranging ramifications in the operating system of a company, particularly in the interaction and suboptimization of enterprise goals and individual employee goals; Chapter 14 is largely devoted to consideration of these issues. A chapter-end problem is addressed to possible improvements in the job method utilized for Figs. 13.2 and 13.4.

Division into Elements

A key step in establishing a standard time by stopwatch time study methods is the division of the job into a set of elements or components that are individually timed. There are several major reasons why timing individual elements has an advantage over merely timing an entire job cycle. First, by breaking a job down into its logical elements it is possible to better assess the job design or method for each component of a job; for example, in our beer can opening example there was a larger degree of variation in the time for the second element than for the first; this well could be a cause for scrutiny of the job design for that element, although the variation is not as discernable in the total time for the operation. Also, one might like to use a "functional analysis" approach to each element —perhaps such an analysis would indicate that on a relative basis far too much time was being expended on opening the cans. A related problem that is highlighted by a division into elemental times is inconsistency in working conditions; thus if a variation in elemental times for an assembly element was due to an inconsistency in the ease of putting together mating parts, remedial action such as a change in quality standards might be initiated.

A second major reason for breaking a job down into elements relates to a desire to easily change a standard when only one element has changed or to create a new standard for a job that is similar in all regards except for one or two elements. Thus if our beer opening operator were now faced with aluminum topped cans which are easier to open, or 16 oz. cans which are somewhat more awkward, or cans with pop tops, the method and time study analyses could be directed toward only those elements which had changed. Another benefit exists in performance rating each element individually, rather than attempting to determine some "average" rate of performance for a task where the operator is inherently more facile in some aspects than in others. Thus our beer can opener appears to be more adept at the second element than the other two; perhaps better training would be valuable. This notion seems particularly appropriate when certain aspects of the job are determined by a machine cycle. For the Westfall silicone drawer painting example with a fixed oven drying cycle, an operator might work at a very fast pace for the element for putting items into the dryer and be quite slow during the painting element since he is constrained in output by the fixed cycle oven drying process. It is important to not interpret the operator's slow pace during the fixed machine cycle as a lack of initiative.

Having established the major reasons for dividing a job into elements, let us consider the *process* of such a division. There is not one "correct" way to divide a job into elements. The process is somewhat of an art, and is necessarily influenced by individual company conditions. If Westfall were establishing a standard for drilling a ¼" hole in a piece of ½" maple, the division into elements might be done in a particular way if many such holes of various diameters were drilled through various thicknesses of different kinds of wood. There are, however, some practical considerations for elemental division imposed by the method of observation. Since an analyst must note the end of an element and read a stopwatch simultaneously, clear-cut beginnings and endings are important; in some cases a sound such as a completed unit being discarded or the end of a machine cycle can be heard while observing the stopwatch. Another kind of practical consideration involves the analyst's limited ability to record observations; if elements are too short, accurate timings cannot be made.

Appropriate Operator

The selection of an appropriate operator to perform the specified task is not intended to imply that only the best man should be timed. There is a distinct difference between Frederick Taylor's "first class man" and an "appropriate" operator. Taylor believed very strongly in the notion of selective employment where only those individuals who were ideally suited to a particular task should be hired for that task. He believed that one man in five or perhaps even fewer were suited for consideration as "first class men" for particular tasks.

This notion has lost a great deal of its applicability as the amount of strenuous manual activity has decreased, as the average age of the work force has increased, and as societal values toward worker rights to retain employment have shifted. Today a frequently stated standard is that jobs are to be designed to enable 95% of the individuals who consider themselves qualified for this kind of activity to do the job at an acceptable pace daily throughout their entire working lives. An appropriate man to study for a given task could be *any* individual from this population of workers.

The connotation of an appropriate worker does, however, carry with it an appropriate training period. That is, the appropriate operator should be facile enough with the task so that he is working in a manner not substantially different from the one he will use for the entire job. In actual practice, operations are rarely timed until conditions have been fairly well stabilized; the actual time period before time studies are initiated may vary from several hours to several weeks and would depend upon the complexity of the job, its length, and the amount of attention placed on prior job design (some "job designers" unfortunately do not use models— they design the actual system and experiment with it).

Differences in speed among various operators are not a problem; it is the time study analyst's responsibility to make performance ratings which adjust for differences in operator speeds. The analyst also has the responsibility for assessing a related consideration, the "baloney" factor. Some operators can put on magnificent theatrical performances designed to cause an overestimation of the necessary time for the task they are performing. On the other hand, there are operators who like to be considered as fast, good, or cooperative who try to impress observers even if it is necessary to engage in unsafe work practices.

Observation and Recording

The actual observation and recording of elemental times involves the use of a stopwatch and a time study form similar to that presented as Fig. 13.4. The watch and form are typically mounted on a clipboard which is designed to allow observation of the task and watch simultaneously. Figure 13.5 is an example of such a stopwatch and clipboard (note that the watch is calibrated in decimal minutes rather than seconds).

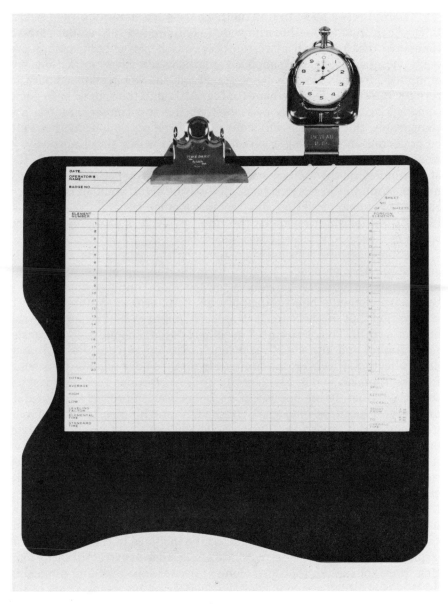

Fig. 13.5 Courtesy of Meylon Stopwatch Corporation, New York, New York.

There are two basic timing methods used for stopwatch time study. In the "continuous" method the watch is allowed to run, actual elapsed times are recorded, and after the observation period subtractions are made successively; in the "snapback" method successive subtractions are eliminated by each element being timed and the watch snapped back to zero for the subsequent element timing. Although there have been some comparative studies which indicate that the two timing methods are comparable, this author firmly believes that the continuous method is to be preferred. In observing a job and reading a watch simultaneously, it would be very easy to consistently misread the watch by perhaps 1/100 of a minute; in the continuous method, this error becomes relatively unimportant, but in the snapback method the error would exist for each reading or element and therefore assumes a much larger degree of importance. Also, for short elements the time involved in snapping back the watch can become relatively significant.

A more serious consideration involves the role of the time study analyst. In the snapback method, direct gathering of elemental time might bias an observer's reading toward more uniform timings. If 9 successive elements had timings of 0.15, 0.16, or 0.17 minutes, a tenth observation that was between 0.19 and 0.20 might well be regarded by the analyst as 0.19. This is so since "good" job design should yield a "consistent" timing and also since variations in timing will call for increased data collection. However, the time study methodology must be somewhat imperfect, and it is not fair to cover up imperfections through overt or covert activities by the analyst. If a job has been improperly designed, if an operator has been improperly trained, if matching parts don't match, if an elemental breakdown incorporates divisions that are not clearcut and therefore difficult to observe, or if the operator is varying his performance level; the model which depicts this job should depict the variances so that appropriate remedial actions such as improved job design or increased data collection can be instituted.

A related "fairness" has to do with the treatment of "foreign elements." A foreign element is defined as something which is not a part of the normal job and therefore should not be included in the calculation of required time for a job. Thus, in cycle 8 of Fig. 13.4 an extraordinarily long time was required for the third element because the operator stopped to drink a beer. If we assumed that this beer drinking was not part of the "quality control procedure," then the time for this element can be discarded from the calculation of required time (the selected time for element 3 is based on the average time for the remaining 14 elements). However, note that in cycle 7 the time required for the second element was also quite long. The explanatory note states that the opener was dropped; it then had to be rinsed off and dried. Is this to be considered a foreign element? Was the beer can opener dropped because the operator was inept or not properly trained in his job? Or was it because a certain amount of beer squirts on the opener from time to time and the opener becomes slippery? One can think of many reasons why this particular event might have happened; the important point is, however, that the event *did* happen and the continuous method of timing required that the event be chronicled and judged. The snapback method allows the analyst to possibly thumb the watch until the next cycle occurs.

Performance Rating

Performance rating involves an adjustment by the analyst to account for differences in operator speed. Thus if one operator is working at a pace that is considered adequate or "normal" and another operator is working twice as fast, the performance ratings for these two individuals are 100% and 200% respectively. When the analyst times either of these operators the resultant normal time will be the same when the observed times are multiplied by the performance ratings.

The problem involved with such a procedure, however, is to establish just what it is that represents an "acceptable" or "normal" pace. How are we to decide? Does it vary from analyst to analyst? If so, how much does it vary?

In any measurement system some standard of comparison must exist, and work measurement is no exception. Also, in any measurement system actual or observed measurements will vary from the "real" value. Therefore, in addition to establishing a standard or norm, we are also faced with assessing the degree of error associated with actual practice.

In ascertaining what represents an acceptable level of performance or norm, a rather global criterion common to work measurement systems is the following statement: The pace should be one that 95% of the population who consider themselves qualified for a given task, should be able to meet day in-day out, year in-year out with no adverse effects on their health. This criterion entity, needless to say, is difficult to apply to particular situations. A surrogate set of criterion entities involves the establishment of "bench marks" for acceptable performance levels. The most widely known of these bench marks is the statement that a man should be able to walk 3 miles per hour. Since much work does not involve walking, however, other bench marks have been established. Thus, a man is supposedly able to deal 52 cards into 4 equal piles in 0.5 minutes and a "standard" board with 30 holes can be filled with pins (2-handed method) in 0.41 minutes.

These bench marks still are not specific enough for usual work measurement problems. Therefore, a set of norms for typical manual operations was required. The Society for the Advancement of Management filmed a set of 24 factory and clerical operations performed at various paces and had these films rated by experienced time and motion study analysts. Ralph M. Barnes has a set of films showing 25 operators working at a total of 80 different speeds which have been rated by thousands of individuals. The results were pooled and the average ratings for each task at each speed have been established as norms. The films are generally available, and most time and motion study analysts view these or similar films several times each year in order to continually adjust their own concept of normal or required performance to that agreed upon by a community of their peers.

To those who would paraphrase Voltaire's depiction of history as "a lie agreed upon," the time study analysts can reasonably demand that critics come up with a better alternative. As noted in our earlier discussion of anthropometric data, some efforts are being made to objectively measure work in terms of physiological cost, but such studies are in their infancy and the amount of work that requires significant physical expenditure continues to diminish. In any measurement system, some standard of comparison or norm is essential as illustrated by the "Vermonter" story in Box 13.3.

A summer visitor asked a Vermonter if his wife was better. The Vermonter's answer: "Than what?"

Box 13.3

Although the establishment of a norm is very important for all kinds of work, it seems particularly important when workers are remunerated on an incentive basis. Thus most incentive wage schemes state that a worker who performs at 125% of standard will receive 125% of his nominal wage. Unfortunately, depictions of worker abilities and norms are sometimes grossly misrepresented because of a feedback loop which "rewards" outstanding performance levels by increasing the amount of work expected as a base or norm. This is a very significant problem and we shall devote a large part of Chapter 14 to its consideration.

Required Sample Sizes

The sample size question is one to which we have alluded at several previous points. Basically, the issue is to establish some desired level of confidence in our estimates of required time and to time enough observations or cycles so that the desired confidence is achieved. Since the number of cycles to be timed is influenced by variability in the data, it is necessary to establish some measure of data variability. The typical procedure involves timing 10 to 15 cycles and thereafter determining whether enough data have been gathered. Appendix A to this chapter describes the methodology involved in making these calculations.

Obtain Indicated Data

The methodology described in the appendix for calculating required sample sizes has to be applied to each element. That is, specified confidence and precision levels lead to a sample size calculation and that sample size calculation should be made for each element; the result is that the element with the largest degree of variability will determine the number of observations required. And as noted in our previous discussions on timing methods, if the resultant indicated number of observations would require that a time study analyst make observations for two weeks duration, so be it (the beer can opening example would require more than 1000 observations). If the degree of variability in a job indicates such a sample size requirement, the only reasonable alternatives seem to be to gather the data or to spend additional time on the job design itself. Any other alternative either reduces the confidence in the time standard produced and /or involves spurious methodology.

Selected Time

The selected time for an element is that time which will subsequently be performance rated to determine the normal time. In most works on the subject, a selected time is defined as the "average" time; however, although to most students of business administration today the term "average" is translated into arithmetic mean, to some people this is not so: averages are equated with medians or with modes. Without going into a detailed exposition of statistics, it should be fairly evident that since the arithmetic mean utilizes the actual values of all sample observations (whereas neither the median nor mode do so) the arithmetic mean is a "more powerful" statistical measure. More powerful simply implies that it better describes (in one single summary number) all observed data than do alternative single descriptors or statistics. Yet there are those who advocate using the mode as the selected time since it is that time value that is most expected.

Use of modes or medians, however, introduces a bias similar to inadequate sample sizes; both fail to adequately account for extreme observations. If an occasional long element time is an inherent part of the operation (such as our slippery beer can opener), its influence on calculating "fair" time should not be disregarded. If the resultant time standard is judged to be too high (perhaps through the use of functional analysis), further job design efforts may be warranted. In Fig. 13.4 arithmetic means are used (element 3 had a foreign element removed) for calculating selected times.

Normal Time

The calculation of normal time is merely an arithmetic operation where selected times for each element are multiplied by performance ratings and summed into one normal time for the task. Thus for beer opening selected elemental times of 0.038, 0.075, and 0.034 were multiplied by the attendant performance ratings of 90%, 115% and 80% to produce normal times of 0.034, 0.086, and 0.027, respectively.

Appropriate Allowances

Allowances are typically added to normal time for delays that are not the fault of the operator, for personal time, and for fatigue. Although some efforts are being made to determine fatigue allowances based on energy requirements and available energy reserves, most fatigue allowances are based upon rules of thumb similar to performance norms that have evolved over extended periods of industrial engineering practice. Personal allowances again have little analytical basis, but a fairly widely accepted minimum is 5%. Delay allowances are extended to workers to allow for decreases in productivity beyond their control. The extent of these decreases is, of course, situation oriented; estimating appropriate unavoidable delay allowances can be accomplished by extended time studies or, as is more often the case, through work sampling which we will discuss later in this chapter. Often, allowances for delays, fatigue, and personal times are established on a departmental or companywide basis and are influenced by negotiations with labor unions; that is, allowances are often more a matter of bargaining than a matter of objective study.

Standard Time

The calculation of standard time is also merely an arithmetic operation where appropriate allowances are added to normal times. However, the *way* in which these allowances are added is important, and without proper attention placed on methodology serious consequences can occur. The following is the proper formula for calculating standard time:

Standard time = Normal time ÷ (1-Total percentage allowances)

Thus the normal time for opening beer cans is 0.147 minutes and the total allowances are 10%; the standard time is .147÷ (1-.1) or 0.163 minutes. This is a quite different result than would be obtained if standard time were calculated as normal time plus 10% of normal time (0.147 + (0.10X.147)) or 0.162 minutes. The difference brings to mind a statement made in Chapter 4 regarding percentages; the question one should always ask is "percentage of what?"

$$\frac{.147}{1-(.10)} =$$

070

If we tell our workers that they receive a 10% personal and fatigue allowance and that allowance is thought of as 10% of the working day (48 minutes per 480 minute day), then we expect them to work $480 - 48 = 432$ minutes per day. The 432 minutes represents total normal time for the day; if the 10% allowance is computed on normal time, one gets a result of 43 minutes per day rather than 48 minutes per day. When the result of this miscalculation is discovered and a union bargaining team requests back pay for ten or fiteeen years at 5 minutes per day, the result can be embarrassing to say the least.

ALTERNATIVE TIME STANDARD MODELS

Although the stopwatch study model for estimating reasonable time standards is the most widely known model, alternative modeling procedures exist, some possessing attributes that are desirable in certain situations. Let us now consider some of these alternatives.

Elemental Data Systems

Elemental data systems are a logical extension of stopwatch time study methods; the basic idea is to systematically perform step two of the time study model described above (divide the job or task into elements) so that the description or designation of elements is comparable from job to job. With such comparability established, a set of elemental times becomes available which can be used like building blocks to assemble time standards for subsequent tasks. As we mentioned above, it would be desirable to have such data to adapt an existing standard to a new job where only one or two elements are changed since such an adaptation would require substantially less time study input. The argument for this desirability can be readily extended from a simple change of one element to the combination of elements to establish a completely new work standard.

Consistency between time standards can be considerably enhanced through the elemental data approach. The elemental data model allows for comparative analysis of elemental times; inconsistencies in elemental times will be more apparent than the inconsistencies that could be observed by assessing the adequacy of an aggregated standard time for a complete task. From a functional analysis point of view, one might derive interesting inferences by comparing the relative labor expenditures for performing functions such as transporting, holding, or making holes. Such comparisons might indicate the most significant potential substitutions of equipment for labor.

In considering the advantages of elemental data systems, two additions should be considered. First, a system of elemental times will be extremely useful for establishing standards on short-run jobs. In some companies, by the time a standard is established through the stopwatch time study procedures, the job has long since been completed; and an important criterion entity for judging a work measurement system is related to speed—employees should be able to calculate their earnings as they accrue rather than being informed after the fact. The second additional advantage is also time-oriented. For many jobs it is desirable to carefully estimate the required labor cost and time long before actual experience has accrued. Some of the problems for which such time estimates are required include pricing decisions, alternative designs, establishment of production schedules, and manpower budgets.

An important potential for elemental data systems lies in an evolutionary feedback into job design. If jobs are described by, or made up from, a common base of widely used elements, it should be possible (particularly if work measurement data are kept in machine readable form) not only to upgrade other method specifications when improvements are made, but in fact to calculate on a companywide basis the amount of labor expended for various elements or groups of elements. Thus, although drilling holes in one furniture part may not appear to have great potential savings, perhaps the total amount of drilling for Westfall and all other Baumritter plants represents a substantial labor expenditure. Viewing this resultant sum well might provide a source for potential savings that would warrant much larger investments in job design and equipment improvement than could be justified on an individual job basis. It is very important to note, however, that improvements in work methods represent a very sensitive area for potential strife between management and labor. Improvements can come in ways that run counter to personal or group criteria. We will consider this much more explicitly in Chapter 14.

One advantage sometimes cited for elemental data systems is that standards can be determined without performance rating. Such a statement, although accurate, is somewhat misleading; although performance rating is not required, it is inherent since it was used to obtain the original data for the data base. All subsequent data rely on those performance ratings and implicitly accept the concept of normality used in obtaining those elemental times.

There has been some question as to the validity of standards determined by elemental data systems. However, since this questioning is applicable to time standard models which are based on smaller (micro opposed to macro) building blocks as well, we will take up the question of validity in the following section.

Methods Time Measurement

An alternative to elemental time data systems based on data from a particular company, is to use one of several available synthetic data systems that have been developed for smaller or micro work components.

A number of these micro time systems have been developed, and certain consulting firms specialize in adapting these systems to a given company's needs. The trade names for some of these systems include Work Factor, Basic Motion Time Study, and Methods Time Measurement. The latter, usually referred to as MTM, is the most popular of these micro time systems and we will only describe it explicitly although alternatives do exist.

The MTM system divides a job into the motions of reach (R), move (M), turn (T), apply pressure (AP), grasp (G), position (P), release (RL), disengage (D), eye travel time (ET), eye focus (EF), and various body, leg, and foot motions. Each of these motions is described in terms of the variables which influence the necessary times to accomplish the motion. Thus reach (R) is characterized by the distance involved and the quality of the object or location reached to; move (M) is similar to reach in that distance and exactness of location partially determine the necessary time, but required time is also dependent upon the weight of the object moved.

MTM was developed from films so that the motions involved in a task or job could be divided into very small segments. The time units used in MTM are 0.00001 hours or 0.0006 minutes; these increments are called time measurement units (TMU). The time values given in the tables presented as Fig. 13.6 are stated in TMU's.

In order to better understand how to use the MTM model, let us now look at Fig. 13.7 which is an MTM analysis of the beer can opener example previously described in Figs. 13.2 and 13.4.

When considering Fig. 13.7, one of the first observations to be made is that the MTM description or model is a more explicit or exact statement of how the beer can opening job is to be performed than that depicted by either the left hand-right hand model or the stopwatch time study model. An attendant benefit of this explicitness is a natural tendency to view each individual MTM motion with an eye toward economies. Thus for example, the distances moved to get unopened cans and to give opened cans to thirsty students appear to be excessive.

In comparing the time standard of Fig. 13.7 with that obtained in Fig. 13.4, we notice standard time results of 0.114 and 0.163 minutes respectively; the rate set by MTM happens in this case to be about 30% lower than that by stopwatch time study. The immediate question that comes to mind is how this might be so and whether this discrepancy will always occur.

In determining the beer can opening time standard with the stopwatch time study model, we had one foreign element which was eliminated and another "odd" element which was judged to be an inherent part of the job. In our subsequent discussions of sample sizes, we found it necessary to observe about 1000 observations to adequately account for

Reach—R

Distance Moved Inches	Time TMU				Hand In Motion		CASE AND DESCRIPTION
	A	B	C or D	E	A	B	
¾ or less	2.0	2.0	2.0	2.0	1.6	1.6	A Reach to object in fixed location, or to object in other hand or on which other hand rests.
1	2.5	2.5	3.6	2.4	2.3	2.3	
2	4.0	4.0	5.9	3.8	3.5	2.7	
3	5.3	5.3	7.3	5.3	4.5	3.6	
4	6.1	6.4	8.4	6.8	4.9	4.3	B Reach to single object in location which may vary slightly from cycle to cycle.
5	6.5	7.8	9.4	7.4	5.3	5.0	
6	7.0	8.6	10.1	8.0	5.7	5.7	
7	7.4	9.3	10.8	8.7	6.1	6.5	
8	7.9	10.1	11.5	9.3	6.5	7.2	C Reach to object jumbled with other objects in a group so that search and select occur.
9	8.3	10.8	12.2	9.9	6.9	7.9	
10	8.7	11.5	12.9	10.5	7.3	8.6	
12	9.6	12.9	14.2	11.8	8.1	10.1	
14	10.5	14.4	15.6	13.0	8.9	11.5	D Reach to a very small object or where accurate grasp is required.
16	11.4	15.8	17.0	14.2	9.7	12.9	
18	12.3	17.2	18.4	15.5	10.5	14.4	
20	13.1	18.6	19.8	16.7	11.3	15.8	
22	14.0	20.1	21.2	18.0	12.1	17.3	E Reach to indefinite location to get hand in position for body balance or next motion or out of way.
24	14.9	21.5	22.5	19.2	12.9	18.8	
26	15.8	22.9	23.9	20.4	13.7	20.2	
28	16.7	24.4	25.3	21.7	14.5	21.7	
30	17.5	25.8	26.7	22.9	15.3	23.2	

Move—M

Distance Moved Inches	Time TMU				Wt. Allowance			CASE AND DESCRIPTION
	A	B	C	Hand in Motion B	Wt. (lb.) Up to	Fac-tor	Con-stant TMU	
¾ or less	2.0	2.0	2.0	1.7	2.5	0	0	A Move object to other hand or against stop.
1	2.5	2.9	3.4	2.3				
2	3.6	4.6	5.2	2.9	7.5	1.06	2.2	
3	4.9	5.7	6.7	3.6				
4	6.1	6.9	8.0	4.3	12.5	1.11	3.9	
5	7.3	8.0	9.2	5.0				
6	8.1	8.9	10.3	5.7	17.5	1.17	5.6	
7	8.9	9.7	11.1	6.5				
8	9.7	10.6	11.8	7.2				
9	10.5	11.5	12.7	7.9	22.5	1.22	7.4	B Move object to approximate or in-definite location.
10	11.3	12.2	13.5	8.6				
12	12.9	13.4	15.2	10.0	27.5	1.28	9.1	
14	14.4	14.6	16.9	11.4				
16	16.0	15.8	18.7	12.8	32.5	1.33	10.8	
18	17.6	17.0	20.4	14.2				
20	19.2	18.2	22.1	15.6				
22	20.8	19.4	23.8	17.0	37.5	1.39	12.5	
24	22.4	20.6	25.5	18.4				C Move object to ex-act location.
26	24.0	21.8	27.3	19.8	42.5	1.44	14.3	
28	25.5	23.1	29.0	21.2				
30	27.1	24.3	30.7	22.7	47.5	1.50	16.0	

Fig. 13.6 MTM tables. Copyrighted by the MTM Association for Standards and Research. No reprint permission without written consent from the MTM Association, 9-10 Saddle River Road, Fair Lawn, New Jersey, 07410.

Turn and Apply Pressure—T and AP

Weight	Time TMU for Degrees Turned										
	30°	45°	60°	75°	90°	105°	120°	135°	150°	165°	180°
Small— 0 to 2 Pounds	2.8	3.5	4.1	4.8	5.4	6.1	6.8	7.4	8.1	8.7	9.4
Medium—2.1 to 10 Pounds	4.4	5.5	6.5	7.5	8.5	9.6	10.6	11.6	12.7	13.7	14.8
Large— 10.1 to 35 Pounds	8.4	10.5	12.3	14.4	16.2	18.3	20.4	22.2	24.3	26.1	28.2

APPLY PRESSURE CASE 1—16.2 TMU.   APPLY PRESSURE CASE 2—10.6 TMU

Grasp—G

Case	Time TMU	DESCRIPTION
1A	2.0	Pick Up Grasp—Small, medium or large object by itself, easily grasped.
1B	3.5	Very small object or object lying close against a flat surface.
1C1	7.3	Interference with grasp on bottom and one side of nearly cylindrical object. Diameter larger than ½".
1C2	8.7	Interference with grasp on bottom and one side of nearly cylindrical object. Diameter ¼" to ½".
1C3	10.8	Interference with grasp on bottom and one side of nearly cylindrical object. Diameter less than ¼".
2	5.6	Regrasp.
3	5.6	Transfer Grasp.
4A	7.3	Object jumbled with other objects so search and select occur. Larger than 1" x 1" x 1".
4B	9.1	Object jumbled with other objects so search and select occur. ¼" x ¼" x ⅛" to 1" x 1" x 1".
4C	12.9	Object jumbled with other objects so search and select occur. Smaller than ¼" x ¼" x ⅛".
5	0	Contact, sliding or hook grasp.

Position*—P

CLASS OF FIT		Symmetry	Easy To Handle	Difficult To Handle
1—Loose	No pressure required	S	5.6	11.2
		SS	9.1	14.7
		NS	10.4	16.0
2—Close	Light pressure required	S	16.2	21.8
		SS	19.7	25.3
		NS	21.0	26.6
3—Exact	Heavy pressure required.	S	43.0	48.6
		SS	46.5	52.1
		NS	47.8	53.4

*Distance moved to engage—1" or less.

Figure 13.6 (Continued)

Symetrie
SI. "   "
NOT "   "

Release—RL

Disengage—D

Case	Time TMU	DESCRIPTION
1	2.0	Normal release performed by opening fingers as independent motion.
2	0	Contact Release.

CLASS OF FIT	Easy to Handle	Difficult to Handle
1—Loose—Very slight effort, blends with subsequent move.	4.0	5.7
2—Close — Normal effort, slight recoil.	7.5	11.8
3—Tight — Considerable effort, hand recoils markedly.	22.9	34.7

Eye Travel Time and Eye Focus—ET and EF

Eye Travel Time $= 15.2 \times \dfrac{T}{D}$ TMU, with a maximum value of 20 TMU.

where T = the distance between points from and to which the eye travels.
D = the perpendicular distance from the eye to the line of travel T.

Eye Focus Time = 7.3 TMU.

Body, Leg, and Foot Motions

DESCRIPTION	SYMBOL	DISTANCE	TIME TMU
Foot Motion—Hinged at Ankle.	FM	Up to 4″	8.5
With heavy pressure.	FMP		19.1
Leg or Foreleg Motion.	LM —	Up to 6″	7.1
		Each add'l. inch	1.2
Sidestep—Case 1—Complete when leading leg contacts floor.	SS-C1	Less than 12″	Use REACH or MOVE Time
		12″	17.0
		Each add'l. inch	.6
Case 2—Lagging leg must contact floor before next motion can be made.	SS-C2	12″	34.1
		Each add'l. inch	1.1
Bend, Stoop, or Kneel on One Knee.	B,S,KOK		29.0
Arise.	AB,AS,AKOK		31.9
Kneel on Floor—Both Knees.	KBK		69.4
Arise.	AKBK		76.7
Sit.	SIT		34.7
Stand from Sitting Position.	STD		43.4
Turn Body 45 to 90 degrees— Case 1—Complete when leading leg contacts floor.	TBC1		18.6
Case 2—Lagging leg must contact floor before next motion can be made.	TBC2		37.2
Walk.	W-FT.	Per Foot	5.3
Walk.	W-P	Per Pace	15.0

Figure 13.6 (Continued)

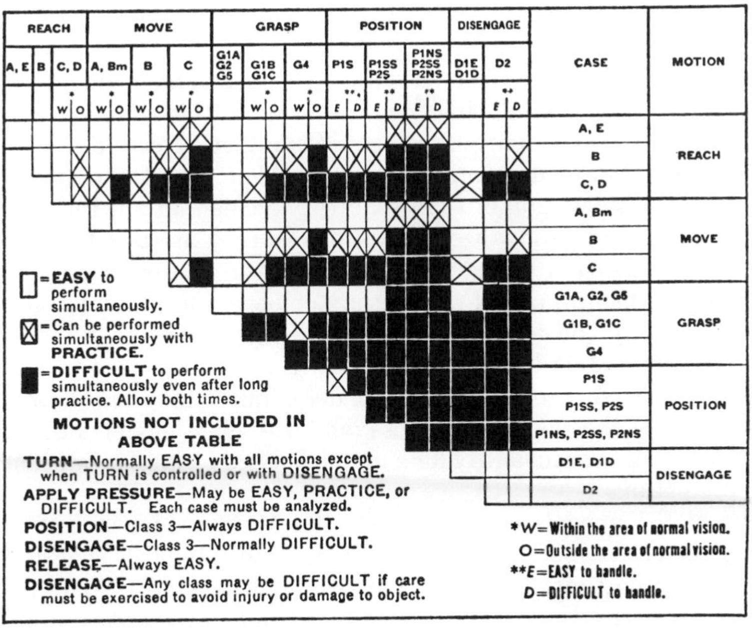

Simultaneous Motions

REACH			MOVE			GRASP			POSITION				DISENGAGE			
A, E	B	C, D	A, Bm	B	C	G1A G2 G5	G1B G1C	G4	P1S	P1SS P2S	P1NS P2SS P2NS	D1E D1D	D2	CASE	MOTION

The body of this figure is a triangular matrix of cells (□ = EASY, ◫ = with PRACTICE, ■ = DIFFICULT) arranged against the following row CASE labels:

CASE	MOTION
A, E	REACH
B	REACH
C, D	REACH
A, Bm	MOVE
B	MOVE
C	MOVE
G1A, G2, G5	GRASP
G1B, G1C	GRASP
G4	GRASP
P1S	POSITION
P1SS, P2S	POSITION
P1NS, P2SS, P2NS	POSITION
D1E, D1D	DISENGAGE
D2	DISENGAGE

Legend:

□ = **EASY** to perform simultaneously.

◫ = **Can be performed simultaneously with PRACTICE.**

■ = **DIFFICULT** to perform simultaneously even after long practice. Allow both times.

MOTIONS NOT INCLUDED IN ABOVE TABLE

TURN—Normally EASY with all motions except when TURN is controlled or with DISENGAGE.

APPLY PRESSURE—May be EASY, PRACTICE, or DIFFICULT. Each case must be analyzed.

POSITION—Class 3—Always DIFFICULT.

DISENGAGE—Class 3—Normally DIFFICULT.

RELEASE—Always EASY.

DISENGAGE—Any class may be DIFFICULT if care must be exercised to avoid injury or damage to object.

*W = Within the area of normal vision.

O = Outside the area of normal vision.

**E = EASY to handle.

D = DIFFICULT to handle.

Figure 13.6 (Continued)

Motion description	MTM description	Time (TMU)
Reach for beer can and beer can opener	R24C	22.5
Observe location of next can to open	ET & EF	27.3
Grasp can and opener	G1A	2.0
Move can and opener to central position	M24A	22.4
Position opener on can	P2S	16.2
Open one side of can	TM90°	8.5
Remove opener from can	TS75°	4.8
Turn can around	TS180°	9.4
Open second side	TM90°	8.5
Remove opener from can	TS75°	4.8
Move opener to location on table	M12B	13.4
Put opener on table	RL1	2.0
Move can and right hand together	M6A	8.1
Grasp can in right hand	G1A	2.0
Move open hand to thirsty student	M18A	17.6
Giver beer to student	RL1	2.0
Total Time (TMU)		171.5

Normal time $= 171.5 \times 0.0006 = 0.1029$ Min.

Standard time $= 0.1029 \div (1-.1) = 0.114$ Min.

Figure 13.7 MTM analysis of beer can opening.

the variability in element 2. If the "odd" time for cycle 7 of element 2 were eliminated, the standard time for the operation would drop from 0.163 minutes to 0.143 minutes and the variation between the two models to about 15%.

One should not, however, casually decide to eliminate the "odd" elemental time observed during the time study. If that activity has been judged to be an inherent part of the existing method, it should be included in the time standard determination. Our MTM model simply did not include any consideration of time required to clean off slippery tools; it is a model based upon idealized conditions as they are perceived by the analyst in a somewhat detached environment—they are based upon observations of a mental model rather than on observations of a real world operating system. The detachment has significant strengths in that methods are determined and analyzed in a way that is not biased by existing "poor" practices. At the same time, the detachment may lead to an inaccurate model of the real world; those who use MTM models necessarily must assume the responsibility for a match between actual conditions and model predictions.

One of the appeals often cited for the MTM model is that it is a detached, objective method for establishing time standards that does not require the subjectivity inherent in stopwatch time study. There is some truth in this statement; because the technique is so widely used, the method should be fairly uniformly applied from situation to situation, company to company, and industry to industry.

However, one should not fall back upon a quasi-scientific procedure and thereby abdicate the responsibilities that are necessarily an integral part of any work measurement system. First, it is worth noting explicitly that the MTM model will not be used in the same way by all analysts. Two analysts well might come up with different time standards for the same job both using MTM analysis. Also, as we observed in our comparison of the standard determined for the beer can example by MTM to the standard determined by stopwatch time study, discrepancies between the results achieved by these models can and do occur. A second aspect of using the MTM model which must be reckoned with is the ability of the workers to understand the way in which their job standards, and hence their pay, are determined. Anything which makes these calculations difficult is invariably viewed by the workers as a "snow job." A very critical third aspect of using MTM analysis relates to the concept of normality; although MTM analysis does not require performance rating, the issues involved in performance rating still exist and are potentially swept under the rug without adequate consideration by merely accepting the MTM group's opinion of what constitutes normality, adequate work levels, or a "fair day's work."

In practice, unfortunately, there is a certain "authenticity" attributed to synthetic data systems that can mask improper analyses. The authenticity is very much like the awe with which many individuals view computer analysis; one often hears the statement "it must be right, it came out of the computer." The same kind of awe is often held for MTM analyses because of their detached scientific flavor. This is unfortunate because almost all of the underlying assumptions of stopwatch time study also pertain to standards determined through the MTM model. And all aside from the model used to establish a time standard for a specified or given task, we must never forget that job design is a prerequisite; the objectivity of MTM analyses must not be allowed to substitute for inadequate attention to principles of motion economy and appropriate task specifications. Box 13.4 clearly illustrates the kind of MTM misuse which is possible.

A manufacturer of chain saws utilized a large grinding machine to insure flatness and parallelism of the major part protruding from the engine over which the chain rides. The amount of grinding required and the way in which the grinding had to be done varied because of both the amount of material remaining to be removed and the degree of parallelism possessed by the parts prior to grinding. Variations in prior machining methods and heat treating were the primary causes of this variability. Thus a warped part would first be placed on the grinding table with the bulge up for a light cut in order to achieve some degree of flatness which could then be placed down on the table to machine the other side; depending upon the degree of warpedness and the amount of material remaining, several such reversals might be necessary in order to assure a flat parallel part of desired thickness. When asked about how a time standard could be determined for such a job (it would seem that the inherent variability would necessarily call for a very large sample size) the head of the industrial engineering department replied that extensive stopwatch time studies had been attempted over a duration of several days without being able to achieve adequate results; thereafter a time standard was quickly determined using MTM analysis.

Box 13.4

Both MTM analysis (and competitive systems) and elemental data systems represent potentially valuable adjuncts to the stopwatch time study model for determining labor time standards. We have seen, however, that neither is a panacea that eliminates the inherent problems in the design and measurement of work. As noted in Chapter 3, models are abstractions which may or may not be good for particular situations or criteria; a match of the criteria used to establish a system of elemental data or MTM with a given problem environment must be made.

Use of these systems does not require performance rating, but some concept of rating and normality are inherent and should be assessed relative to individual experience and values. Although the building block concept is an appealing one, the question of whether the time for a complete job can be properly synthesized by adding elemental times is open to some question. The bias introduced by an assumption of additivity is potentially more serious for elemental data systems since part of the design of such systems is in fact building block specification; the ease of simultaneous motions and the ease with which one kind of motion follows another are but two of the questions involved in assessing the additivity bias. Finally, the art involved in specifying a task as the synthesis of a set of elements or motions should not be understated.

Work Sampling

Another alternative to the time study model for measuring work is work sampling. The basic idea behind work sampling is that significant informational content for measuring work may be obtained by a sampling approach to analyzing work patterns. Suppose we were interested in measuring worker idle time due to a lack of material for a chair-building line at the Westfall Furniture Company. One way such a measurement might be obtained would be to observe the building operation over an extended period of time, keeping track of the number of minutes spent in idle time due to lack of material and number of minutes spent in other activities (the activities must be mutually exclusive and exhaustive). An alternative measurement method is to sample—to make a number of observations of this activity and categorize as previously stated; this alternative measurement method is called work sampling, although both measurement methods are actually based upon a sample or subset of the total population of Westfall chair-building worker activity.

If "significant informational content" is to be obtained from work sampling, it is essential that we have a criterion or set of criteria to establish "significance." Operationally, the issue is how to trade off greater precision in our estimate or measurement obtained by larger sample sizes with the costs of obtaining sample information; resolution obviously has to fall back upon the criteria set.

To illustrate the methodology, let us turn to Fig. 13.8 which is a minute by minute account for one chair-building line over a three week time period, where the activity has been divided into the two categories of idle due to lack of material and not idle due to lack of material.

A direct measurement of Fig. 13.8 leads to idle time due to lack of material of 10%. It is worth noting that this three-week period is only a subset of the total chair building activity. For the purposes of discussion, however, let us consider it as a "population" and examine various estimates of the population gained through sampling.

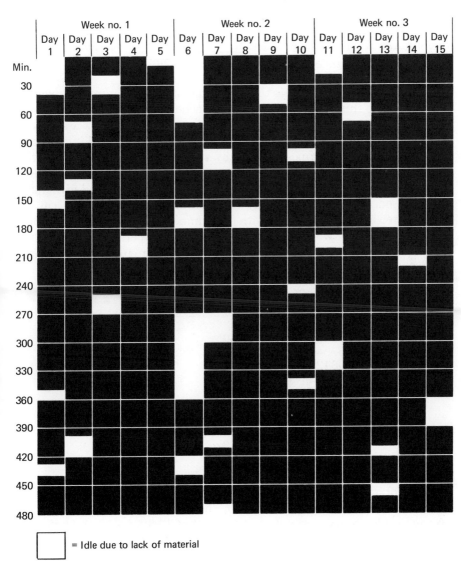

= Idle due to lack of material

Fig. 13.8 Idle due to lack of material.

One "sampling plan" is simply to observe the activity only once; but the estimate of the population parameter would necessarily be either 0 or 100% with a rather high error potential. An alternative is to observe the activity every hour on the hour for the 15-day period (120 observations assuming we begin to observe at minute 60); such a result yields a measure of 17/120 or 14.2%. Doubling the sample size and making observations at half-hour intervals gives a result of 33/240 or 13.7%;

15-minute intervals yields 59/480 or 12.3%. An appealing alternative is to not make observations with equal time intervals between observations but to randomize the time interval while keeping the same number of observations.

One way to randomize is to use a table of random numbers such as Appendix C to this book, along with some scheme to associate time observations with the numbers drawn. For example, if we draw a series of five-digit random numbers, each minute in a 480-minute working day can be associated with two possibilities by the first three digits where the numbers 961-999 (and 000) are discarded (e.g., 001 and 002 = the first minute in the day, 003 and 004 = the second, etc.). Fourth and fifth digits can be used to designate the day for each of the 15 days; each can be represented by six possibilities with the numbers 91-99 (and 00) discarded. (6 X 15 = 90. Since two digits have 100 possible numbers, we must discard 10.) The following illustrates the procedure if we were to draw ten random numbers:

Random numbers	Minute of the day	Day
10097	50	discard
37542	188	7
08422	42	4
99019	discard	4
12807	64	2
66065	330	11
31060	155	10
85269	426	12
63573	318	13
73796	369	discard

The author applied such a procedure for the same number of observations as obtained from an every hour on the hour procedure (8 per day times 15 equals 120 observations), he got a result of 12.3% based on one set of random numbers. Increasing the sample size to 240 gave a result of 10.9%; 480 observations gave a result of 9.6%.

As expected with both the sampling plan based on a constant time interval between observations and the randomized plan, the results obtained through sampling plans with greater numbers of observations tend to approach the results of the total three week subpopulation. As also expected, the incremental costs, as measured in terms of necessary additional sample information, increase for adding additional degrees of precision. It is customary for work sampling plans to start with a specified level of precision and a specified confidence interval, and thereafter solve for the required number of sample observations. Methodology for making such calculations is included in Appendix A to this chapter.

Work sampling can be used to establish time standards as well as to make estimates about working and idle time proportions. To establish a standard by work sampling methods, we use the information obtained from the work sampling study as to the proportion of time the worker was engaged in the designated job, the total time of the study, the number of units completed or produced during the study period, and an estimate of the average performance rating when the worker was engaged in productive activity. Normal time is then equal to:

$$\frac{\text{Total time of the study X Work proportion X Performance rating}}{\text{Number of completed units}}$$

Standard time is computed in the same way as for other modeling mechanisms. Advocates of work sampling claim that standards can be set for many kinds of jobs to which stopwatch time study models would be exceedingly difficult to apply such as maintenance and clerical jobs which involve diverse activities.

There are many pros and cons to work sampling, but like all modeling procedures it is better suited to some situations than to others. Since the number of observations required is often quite large (Appendix A indicates that for a desired precision level of plus or minus 1% and 95% confidence, for a proportion of 20% the required sample size is in excess of 6,000 observations), one can make favorable use of work sampling for grouped activities rather than single operators or machines. Although work sampling may be used for jobs involving considerable variety, job methods are often not carefully described in a work sampling study; the result is that improper attention to job design is possible and that significant changes in methodology may not be detected.

A kind of work sampling plan that has been receiving considerable interest, most notably in defense-oriented plants, is a plantwide sampling system with admittedly small sample sizes where departments or groups are rated relative to each other and relative to themselves over an extended time horizon. There are various names for these systems, TEMPO and PACE being two of the better-known plans. The basic idea is that a trained industrial engineering group will make random observations of each department or group in a company; for each observation a count will be made of the people in the department and a performance rating assigned to the group as a whole. On this basis, comparative evaluations between departments or groups can be made and the performance of individual departments or groups can be charted over a period of time. Although the statistical validity of these procedures is open to some question, they do seem to serve an important function; in the terms of Chapter 3, an explicit model has been formulated and substituted for an intuitive model—management was making comparative evaluations previously, but those evaluations are now based upon an improved model. The model can and should evolve as norms or expectations for the behavior of specific groups become better understood; thus for example, a group of computer programmers well might spend a great deal of their time away from their normal location for good reasons.

SUMMARY REMARKS

In this chapter we have considered the important relationships between the design of systems for accomplishing tasks and the measurement, evaluation, or estimation of labor inputs required to accomplish specified tasks. In the consideration of the various models, both for job design and work measurement, many perplexing questions were raised and left unresolved such as the interaction of job design systems, work measurement systems, and systems involving individuals and groups with their associated personal criteria sets. Many of these issues revolve around notions of system evolution and an unfortunate lack of evolutionary viewpoint that is inherent in most job design and work measurement models. In the next chapter we devote our attention to an evolutionary viewpoint.

REFERENCES

Abruzzi, A., *Work Measurement,* Columbia University, Press, 1952.

Barnes, Ralph M., *Motion and Time Study,* 6th Ed., Wiley, 1968.

Davidson, Harold O., *Functions and Bases of Time Studies,* American Institute of Industrial Engineers, 1957.

Paul, Robert J., "Performance Standards for the Non-Manual, Non-Repetitive Activity?" *The Journal of Industrial Engineering,* **19,** no. 12 (Dec. 1968): 612–17.

Taylor, Frederick Winslow, *The Principles of Scientific Management,* Harper and Brothers, 1911.

CHAPTER REVIEW

I hope that you come away from this chapter with an understanding of design and measurement of work problems. I also hope you understand some of the basic models proposed for solving these problems and have an appreciation both of the match between the problems and the models, and the advantages offered by additional models which might be proposed.

In a practical sense, understanding of design and measurement of work will be valuable to you for assessing any manual activity, whether it be manufacturing, assembly, or clerical; you should be able to recognize good and bad designs and methods for checkout in a supermarket or service in a restaurant. Making these assessments and contemplating how improvements could be made will sharpen your abilities.

A good lesson in implementation can be gained from observing your wife, husband, mother, father, child, or close friend; see what happens when you tell them you have ideas for making their task easier. Try various ways to frame the question ranging from "you don't know what you are doing," to "I wonder if you could help me understand the application of some models for studying work?" Think about the implications for the design of a proper modeling environment.

OUTLINE OF THE CHAPTER

Introduction   (historically important problem area)

Job design   (good methods)

Criteria   (productivity)

System boundaries   (task specification)

Motion study   (principles of motion economy)

Anthropometric data   (physiological capacities)

Models for motion study   (detailed techniques)

Job enlargement   (worker satisfaction)

Stopwatch time study   (measurement methodology)

Criteria   (fair day's work)

The model   (eleven steps)

Proper method   (job design first)

Division into elements   (analysis of subactivities)

Appropriate operator   (competent in that job)

Observing and recording   (continuous timing)

Performance rating   (adjust for operator speed)

Required sample sizes   (confidence-precision)

Obtain indicated data   (account for variability)

Selected time   (arithmetic mean)

Normal time   (selected X performance rating)

Appropriate allowances   (rules of thumb and bargaining)

Standard time   (proper calculation

Alternative time standard models   (other techniques)

Elemental data systems   (building blocks)

Methods time measurement	(smaller building blocks)
Work sampling	(for more varied work)
Summary remarks	(need for evolutionary approach)
Appendix A	(sample size formulas)

CENTRAL ISSUES

As noted in the title, this chapter is concerned with design and measurement of work. The former logically precedes the latter. We should find or design a good method for accomplishing a task before determining the time required for the task. Job design almost always involves division of a job or task into smaller subtasks or steps. The division process needs to be examined carefully, because subsequent job designs are constrained by it.

Models for job design include principles of motion economy which act as a checklist for evaluating proposed designs, anthropometric data which essentially inventory human capabilities and their associated physical costs, and specific techniques such as micromotion analysis (high speed motion pictures), left hand-right hand chart (work done by each hand), and man-machine chart (machine cycle and operator).

Measurement of work can be made with several models, but the most widely known is stopwatch time study. The goal is an objective system for determining expected output levels. The methodology involves a check for proper method, division of the task into elements for timing, selection of an adequately trained operator, observing and recording the times for each element, performance rating each element, a calculation of required sample sizes, obtaining any additional data indicated, determining the selected or average time for each element, calculation of normal times with performance ratings, determination of appropriate allowances (personal needs, fatigue, delays, etc.), and calculation of the standard time which includes the allowances.

Alternative models for measuring work have the same underlying foundations as stopwatch time study. Elemental data systems are an attempt to synthetically construct new time standards from existing standards either by extrapolating (drilling a 1/2" hole instead of a 1/4" hole) or by a building-block approach (positioning time from job A plus machining time for job B to get time for job C).

Methods Time Measurement and alternative synthetic data systems carry the building-block concept further. These systems divide work into very small motions such as reaching which are parameterized by distance and other factors. The resultant times are combined to construct time standards. It is important for the user of such systems to be sure that the actual job method and conditions match those idealized in the synthetic data system.

Work sampling attempts to measure work by randomly sampling worker activity over a more extended time period than that used for stopwatch time study. The technique is particularly useful for measuring work with considerable variety. Questions of confidence and precision in the estimates involve determination of appropriate sample sizes. In some applications relatively small sample sizes are used which do not result in high degrees of confidence and precision; however, the technique is superior to having managerial opinion based on "looking around." In other words, SWAG (systematic wild guessing) is better than WAG (wild guessing).

ASSIGNMENTS

1. Examine the beer can opening example:

    a) What principles of motion economy are not being adequately considered?
    b) What improvements can you suggest?
    c) Construct a new left hand-right hand chart for your improved design.
    d) Calculate a new work standard using the MTM model.

2. A work measurement study of a bank teller's operation was concerned with the required time to count out $100 comprised of six $10 bills, seven $5 bills, and five $1 bills. A **continuous** stopwatch time study yielded the following data:

				Cycle time in minutes							Performance rating
Element	1	2	3	4	5	6	7	8	9	10	
(1) Count 6—$10	.12	.75	1.41	2.05	2.70	3.46	4.07	4.71	5.37	6.18	110
(2) Count 7—$5	.27	.90	1.55	2.19	2.85	3.60	4.23	4.86	5.52	6.33	105
(3) Count 5—$1	.37	1.02	1.64	2.31	2.96	3.68	4.33	4.98	5.65	6.42	100**
(4) Count $100	.57	1.21	1.85	2.51	3.15	3.88	4.54	5.18	6.00*	6.62	120
(5) Give to "customer"	.64	1.29	1.93	2.58	3.23	3.95	4.60	5.25	6.06	6.69	90

  *Operator had to recount this $100.
  **Difficult to assess because $1 bills were new — others used.

    a) Calculate the required sample sizes (95% confidence, ± 5% precision).
    b) Calculate the normal time for the above specified way of counting $100.
    c) Assuming total allowances equal 15%, calculate the standard time.
    d) How would you treat the two footnoted remarks?

3. If the bank's interest were to determine necessary service time for teller station staffing decisions, what recommendations would you make in regard to an elemental data system? How would you go about elemental specification?

4. The work sampling study of a laboratory technician over a one-week period (40 hours) yielded the following data: total blood samples analyzed = 590, idle time = 30%, performance rating = 90%.

    a) Determine the required number of samples in order to obtain 95% confidence level and a ±5% precision level.
    b) If allowances for this particular type of work total 10%, determine the standard time per blood sample.

5. An operator worked on a job with a standard time of 2.5 minutes. At the end of a 9-hour day he had produced 300 parts. The operator is paid $3.50 per hour with time and one half for time in excess of 8 hours per day and works on a 100% premium wage incentive plan with guaranteed base wage. What are his total earnings for the day?

6.

Elements	Cycle									
	1	2	3	4	5	6	7	8	9	10
(1)	.1	.09	.1	.08	.11	.08	.09	.19	.13	.09
(2)	.05	.05	.05	.05	.07	.06	.06	.06	.05	.05

For the 2-element task above calculate the required sample size for each element to obtain a precision of ±5% with 95% confidence.

The following three problems (7–9) are projects which involve actual job design, the development of time standards for the method derived, and the making of cost estimates.

For each of the following problems you are to assume that bulk quantities of materials will be available at the assembly station and that a material handler will periodically take away complete assemblies from whatever large receptacle you utilize for this purpose. The use of a simple jig or fixture will be allowed except that any expenditures for such devices cannot exceed $10.

Prepare a written report not exceeding five pages plus five exhibits. Selected groups will demonstrate their procedures to the class using fresh components.

7.   Socketome Connector Company

The Socketome Connector Company has hired you to design an assembly process for their connectors.

Specifically, you are to design a single station hand assembly method for the connector comprised of the following parts: main housing, notched nut, wire clamp, and 2 screws. (Fig. 13.9)

Socketome has a uniquely designed quality control program. Periodically our inspector takes a handful of completed connectors from each assembly worker's supply, places them in a large bag, shakes the bag vigorously for thirty seconds, and checks to see that all connectors have remained assembled. Rejects are attached to the assembly operator's toes until visible pain accrues. Any operator who accumulates more than ten rejects in a day is sent home (unless he has more than ten toes).

Assembly workers are paid $2.00 per hour plus a $1.00 per week quality control soap allowance (for clean toes). Overhead is usually charged at 150% of direct labor.

8.   Screw Ball Pen Company

Due to a recent large increase in the number of papers being written by college students the Screw Ball Pen Company has been unable to satisfy demand for their product (Fig. 13.10). Their part capacity is sufficient but they would like you to design a hand assembly method for use until new automated assembly machines can be brought on line.

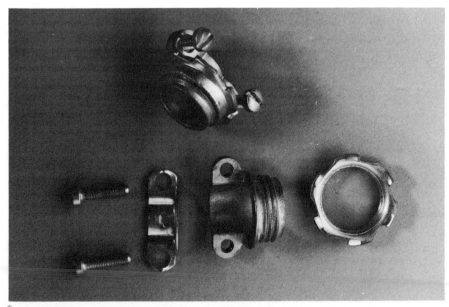

Figure 13.9

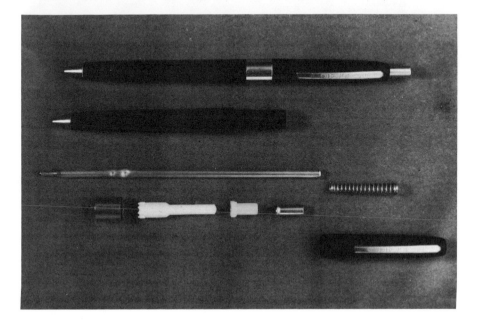
Figure 13.10

Assembly workers are paid $2.50 per hour and manufacturing overhead has been allocated at 100% of direct labor. Screw-ball would like your proposal including cost estimates as soon as possible.

9.   **The clothespin caper**

The Organization of American Spring Wood Clothespin Manufacturers and Assemblers (OASWCMA) has a problem. One of its members has requested immediate consulting assistance due to a breakdown of automatic assembly equipment. You are to provide the consultant services.

The assembly equipment breakdown has created an urgent situation in the member's production system. The assembly department is bottlenecking the entire system as orders continue to pour in. The member has therefore requested recommendations for a single station, hand assembly method for the three part clothespin (Fig. 13.11). For control and planning purposes the member must have time standards for all operations of the assembly method. No redesign of parts or materials is desired.

OASWCMA has requested your recommendation as soon as possible. You must be prepared to present estimates of assembly cost per 1,000 clothespins. Assembly workers are paid a straight wage of $2.00 per hour. Assembly overhead is allocated at $1.00 per direct labor hour.

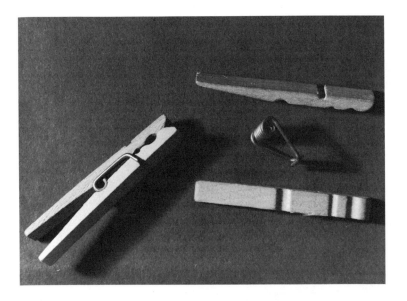

Figure 13.11

APPENDIX A TO CHAPTER 13

SAMPLE SIZE DETERMINATIONS

A detailed presentation of the statistical reasoning behind the calculation of adequate sample sizes would necessarily involve us in a discussion of the normal probability distribution, the law of large numbers, and the central limit theorem. Although these matters are better left to your courses in quantitative analysis, we will want to consider them explicitly for their influence on several important operations management models, most notably quality control and forecasting. However, since use of these statistical measures is more intimately involved in quality control than in work measurement, we will defer detailed discussion of sample sizes until Chapter 16.

Stopwatch Time Study

Adequate sample sizes may be determined by using the following formula and associated set of sample size factors which are based upon desired confidence and desired precision levels:

$$N = \left[\frac{TSSF\sqrt{n\Sigma X^2 - (\Sigma X)^2}}{\Sigma X} \right]^2$$

where:

N = necessary sample size
$TSSF$ = time study sample size factor
n = number of cycles
ΣX = sum of elemental times
ΣX^2 = sum of each elemental time squared
$(\Sigma X)^2$ = square of sum of elemental times

Time study sample size factors (TSSF)

		Desired precision	
		±5%	±10%
	90%	33.0	16.5
Desired	95%	39.2	19.6
confidence	97%	43.4	21.7
	99%	51.6	25.8

Returning now to our beer can opening example, let us check out the indicated necessary sample sizes. To facilitate calculations, let us restate the elemental times as given in Fig. 13.4 in the following way.

Elements

	1			2			3	
Cycle	Time (X)	X^2		Time (X)	X^2		Time (X)	X^2
1	.04	.0016		.05	.0025		.03	.0009
2	.05	.0025		.04	.0016		.03	.0009
3	.03	.0009		.08	.0064		.04	.0016
4	.03	.0009		.07	.0049		.03	.0009
5	.04	.0016		.05	.0025		.03	.0009
6	.04	.0016		.06	.0036		.03	.0009
7	.04	.0016		.32	.1024		.03	.0009
8	.04	.0016		.03	.0009		.04	.0016
9	.04	.0016		.07	.0049		.03	.0009
10	.03	.0009		.05	.0025		.04	.0016
11	.04	.0016		.05	.0025		.03	.0009
12	.04	.0016		.07	.0049		.04	.0016
13	.04	.0016		.04	.0016		.03	.0009
14	.04	.0016		.06	.0036		.04	.0016
15	.03	.0009		.08	.0064			
15 (n)	.57 (ΣX)	.0221 (ΣX^2)	15 (n)	1.12 (ΣX)	.1512 (ΣX^2)	14 (n)	.47 (ΣX)	.0161 (ΣX^2)

Turning to the first element, we see that the number of cycles *(n)* is 15, the sum of elemental times is .57 (ΣX), and the sum of elemental times squared is .0221 (ΣX^2). Substituting into our equation, we get the following:

$$N = \left[\frac{39.2\sqrt{(15)\ (.0221) - (.57)^2}}{.57} \right]^2$$

$$= \left[\frac{39.2\sqrt{.3315} - .3249}{.57} \right]^2$$

$$= \left[\frac{39.2(.08)}{.57} \right]^2 = (5.54)^2 \approx 31$$

The above calculation for the sample size N is based upon a desired confidence level of 95% and a desired precision level of ±5%. These levels are the ones most commonly used for time study and mean that we have a 95% probability that the elemental time computed will not be in error by more than 5% of the true element time with the desired sample size N. If we desired to be 99% confident of our estimate of the true population parameter or element time, the appropriate time study sample size factor (TSSF) would necessarily be changed from 39.2 to 51.6; the resultant sample size indicated would be approximately 53. The table of time study sample size factors matches our intuition about the required sample sizes; that is, the multiplicative factors increase as more confidence or more precision is desired.

As noted in the chapter, the times associated with element 2 are the most variable and will therefore lead to high sample sizes. Using the 95% confidence interval and desired precision level ±5%, we see that the required sample size for element 2 is computed as follows:

$$N = \left[\frac{39.2\sqrt{(15)\ (.1512) - (1.12)^2}}{1.12} \right]^2$$

$$= \left[\frac{39.2\sqrt{1.0136}}{1.12} \right]^2$$

$$= \left[\frac{39.2(1.007)}{1.12} \right]^2 = (35.39)^2 \approx 1250$$

As can be seen, the required sample size N is about 1250 observations. This is largely due to the long time associated with cycle 7 for this element. Reducing the desired confidence interval to 90% still only reduces the necessary sample size to about 900. If the time for element 7 is eliminated from the calculations (this should *not* be done casually or merely because the result is fewer observations), the required sample size is then reduced to approximately 100.

Work Sampling

The calculation for desired sample sizes in work sampling is based upon the binomial distribution. To determine appropriate sample sizes, the following formula and associated work sample size factors (WSSF) can be used.

$$N = WSSF\ \frac{(1-P)}{P}$$

where:

N = necessary sample size
$WSSF$ = work sample size factor
P = proportions of time spent in activity to be estimated

Work sample size factors (WSSF)

		Desired precision ±5%	±10%
	90%	1049	272
Desired	95%	1536	384
confidence	97%	1884	471
	99%	2663	666

In ascertaining the appropriate sample size for a work-sampling study, it is necessary to know the proportion of time spent in the activity to be estimated. The way this proportion P is typically determined is to obtain some sample data and estimate P and thereafter estimate the sample size; when the proper sample has been taken a further determination of adequacy is made.

Turning to some examples, for the proportion of idle time due to lack of material for the Westfall chair-building operations, an initial study might indicate that P is approximately 10%; substituting for P in the above equation yields a multiplier of 9 for each work sample size factor depending upon the desired confidence and precision levels. Thus if we desired to maintain a 95% confidence level and ±5% precision, we would need a sample size of about 13,825.

It is worth noting that the desired precision levels utilized in the formula and work sample size factors given are based upon "relative" precision rather than "absolute" precision. That is, remembering our warnings about percentages given in Chapter 5, we must ask, "Percentages of what?" The distinction is that when estimating a proportion of say 5%, and desiring a precision level of ± 5%, the "relative" precision means 5% *of* the 5%; that is, we desire to have our confidence interval run from 4.75% to 5.25%. That is quite different from the desire to be within an "absolute" ± 5%; that is, a desire to be from 0% to 10%. Formulas also exist for desired precision on an absolute basis and, as expected, the necessary sample sizes tend to be smaller.

CHAPTER 14

IMPROVEMENT

At several points in Chapter 13 we alluded to the need for viewing the standards determined by work measurement models in an evolutionary context. We have talked of evolution throughout this book; for operations management problems there are few, if any, optimal solutions which we cannot expect to see improved upon over time. In this chapter we will consider mismatches between labor standards determined by work measurement models and output potentials, causes for these mismatches, a model for reducing the mismatches, and some attendant implications of using the model.

WORK STANDARDS—A REASSESSMENT

An evolutionary point of view leads us to believe that no method is incapable of improvement. However, the work standards developed through the models described in Chapter 13 tend to be regarded in a static or nonimprovable fashion. The assumption is that once a method and associated standard have been determined, there is little or no subsequent need for reevaluation. That is, at Westfall for example, once the standard time to assemble a captain's chair has been set, it would be extraordinary to change it. Many individuals believe that evolution, learning, or improvement is an inherent attribute to any task. Thus one authority states, "The learning curve, I believe, is an underlying natural characteristic of organized activity, just as the bell-shaped curve is an accurate depiction of a normal or random distribution of anything, from human I.Q.'s to the size of tomatoes."*

If an evolutionary viewpoint is a more inherently accurate depiction or model of the real world than a static or nonvarying model, an approach to work standards which utilizes learning will be more "valid" than the models described in Chapter 13.

---

*Winfred B. Hirschmann, "Profit From the Learning Curve," *Harvard Business Review,* January–February, 1964, p. 125.

Model Validity

In our discussions of validity (see particularly Chapters 3 and 12), it has been maintained that validity is a highly individualistic, necessarily comparative assessment made in terms of particular criteria sets. On this basis, one might argue that inferences drawn from work measurement models are "valid" since they yield better estimates of labor time requirements than subjective opinions; that is, they represent systematic wild guesses (S.W.A.G.s) rather wild guesses (W.A.G.s). However, one should not make such comparisons with a straw man. Are there alternatives which will stand up better over time?

In assessing whether alternative procedures are better, we necessarily must come back to highly individualized sets of criteria (recall the Vermonter's reply to the question of his wife being better in Box 13.3). One is often interested in making work requirement predictions, but an insidious aspect of using this interest as a validation procedure results in a feedback loop between predictions and outcomes. That is, the work measurement models presented in Chapter 13 are considered "valid" because they produce labor time estimates that are quite close to subsequent actual times observed. However, it is very important to note that the labor time estimates produced by work measurement models are thereafter used as criteria or standards in the 3-step control process; deviations of actual results from standards call for control or remedial actions. When actual results closely match anticipated conditions, no control or remedial activities are indicated and the predictive models are assumed to be good or valid. Such a conclusion, however, may be quite incorrect when assessing higher order enterprise criteria. That is, we will see that surrogate criteria established for a work measurement or industrial engineering group often relate to the reliability of estimates; unfortunately these labor time estimates may be made more reliable by restricting output (in terms of its potential).

Dysfunctionalism

In our Chapter 7 discussion of functional analysis, we noted that system performance levels are only functional in terms of criteria or sets of criteria, and that virtually any system performance level is functional for *some* criterion or set of criteria. A cursory examination of work measurement systems, particularly those which embody incentive wage payment plans, would lead to the conclusion that increased performance levels or output would be congruent with enterprise as well as individual employee criteria sets. Unfortunately, however, ever increasing output rates are not typically observed in ongoing work measurement systems. Rather, output levels tend to rise to a certain point and then stabilize; industrial engineering zealots view such stabilized production or output levels as supportive to validation of their model-building efforts. Those who have observed actual working conditions, however, know differently; output levels are very often restricted to levels where industrial engineering predictions will still be regarded as "valid." The validity check is made not only by industrial engineers but also by higher level management assessments of actual performance levels. Thus if performance levels continue to increase, typical managerial responses are that the industrial engineering estimates are too "loose" or that the industrial engineers are being too "easy" in setting standards; this kind of opinion is particularly prevalent when ordinary laborers on incentive wages start earning more than middle-management and executive salaries.

What happens when performance levels become "too high?" A typical procedure calls for "tightening the screws" or pushing the performance levels back down; there are many degrees of subtlety to the way in which decreased performance levels can be achieved. A related question has to do with the extent to which actual performance measurements or levels vary from potential levels. Box 14.1 relates the author's introduction to the problem.

The author grew up around machine tools and started to run a lathe in his father's machine shop at age 8. At age 18, he took a job as a machinist in a well-known camera manufacturing plant (this particular company is known for extremely good employee-employer relationships). Since the author had gone in as an 18 year old with "10 years of experience" he felt that he was regarded with considerable skepticism and that he would have to work hard to merit continuing employment. Although he was informed in rudimentary terms of the existence of an incentive wage plan, he did not understand it and was used to working for his father where the rule was "go like hell." The company was working 2 hours overtime each day (a 10-hour day) plus 8 hours overtime on Saturday.

On the first day, an orientation meeting for new employees consumed 2 1/2 hours. At the end of the day a lead man helped count the number of parts produced and prepare the daily performance ticket based upon a 10-hour working day. When the author came to work the following morning, he was greeted by considerable confusion and unhappiness. It seemed that for the 10-hour day, he had turned in a 237B hour (the company used the Bedaux system where 60B's = 60 minutes of work = 100%) or approximately 400%. At a nominal or base wage rate of $1.50 per hour, he had earned more than $65 the first day. The natural assumption that a mistake in count had been made led to more and more people gathering around as the count was checked and rechecked; the next natural question led to complete inspection of the entire day's output, but no rejects could be found. By 9 A.M., it was decided that the time standard was in error since it had been computed for a different method; a new standard cut the rate by more than half.

> About 10:30 one of the older workers came over and said, "Son, let's you and me go get a cup of coffee." Over coffee it was explained that due to the author's stupidity a good job had now become a tough job. The rate on that job had been in existence for five years and the job ran several times per year; yet up to that time, no one had turned in more than an 85B hour on that job. The job now represented more than twice as much work for the same amount of money. The older worker stated that performance levels in excess of 85B's always led to rate reductions and that one tried to stay in the 80 to 85B hour range all the time. He also stated that fellow workers did not appreciate seeing rates driven down. It was explained that a fellow who used to work there who had been piggish, seemed to have a lot of trouble with his car while it was parked in the parking lot.
>
> The author learned fast and edged his average performance level up to almost 90B's. In turning in a 90B hour for the 58 hour week, the typical procedure was to work only during the hours that the foreman (who would spy on the workers) was present; the foreman worked a 40 hour week. In addition, an extra 3/4 of an hour was taken for lunch so that a long pinochle game could be played, and about ten coffee breaks per day was the rule. On Saturday, all the parts for the day had been previously made during the week and stored in a tool box so that 8 solid hours of pinochle could be played.

Box 14.1

Humorous (or horrifying) as this "war story" may be, it serves to illustrate the extent to which pegged or restricted output exists. It is functional for workers to soldier or restrict output in terms of their long-run and joint interests; to produce at full potential, although functional in terms of immediate return, leads to a feedback where more work is expected and required for the same amount of pay. The situation is at least as bad in those places where informal standards have been established, and the soldiering phenomenon should not be construed as only applicable to "blue collar" workers.

Many industrial engineers say that standards are not changed in their company; such a statement, however, is typically followed by, "Unless there is a change in the method." Unfortunately, the methods used to determine a great many time standards are described in very loose, imprecise terms. Thus, one can almost always identify some "change" in method and high performance levels are *ipso facto* "proof" of a method change. One cynic pointed out that if all else failed, the part itself could be redesigned.

An interesting three-part question to ask industrial engineers is:

a) What is the average performance index in your company?
b) What is the highest performance index that anyone ever turns in?
c) What would you do if someone turned in one that was significantly higher?

One head of an industrial engineering department for a large company answered that the average performance index was 125% and the highest that he had seen was 135%; when asked what he would do if someone turned in a level of say, 150%, he said that he would go out and investigate to find out what was wrong. The same man said his company never changed standards unless there had been a method change. Box 14.2 illustrates the problem as it exists at Westfall. Let us thereafter turn to a more thoroughgoing analysis of the underlying or contributing factors that seem invariably to lead to restricted output rates.

Some students were taking a field trip through the Westfall plant. Their tour guide was an industrial engineer. At one point, they observed a woman driving two dowel pins into one end of a 20 inch long part with a hammer, then turning the part end for end and driving two additional dowel pins into the other end. After observing for a few minutes, the industrial engineer told the operator: "I am going to walk on ahead. Show the boys how you can do it when I am not around." After he left, she stacked up 10 parts, placed dowel pins with both hands, put a board over the lot; and drove them all in at once. She then turned them end for end all together and repeated the process.

Box 14.2

CONTRIBUTORY FACTORS

The major contributory factor to the existence of restricted output levels has been identified above; formal and informal control procedures view increasing performance levels as evidence of poorly designed standards, and neither industrial engineers nor individual workers find it functional to identify what are regarded as "poor" standards. Let us now move our analysis down to a lower level of aggregation and consider some important individual contributory factors which lead to this dysfunctionalism in terms of enterprise output objectives.

Methods Evolution

We noted in Chapter 13 that work standards are established for a particular method, that there is a fair degree of art involved in determining the "best" method, that almost any method should be capable of being improved, and that time standards are only guaranteed for a particular method. The extent to which a specified method can be improved is obviously dependent upon the skill of those who designed the original method. To blithely assume, however, that the specified method is in fact the "best" completely discounts the existence of any methods improvements skills possessed by workers. Clearly, workers do have the ability to see certain kinds of efficiencies, and they certainly have the ability to transplant efficiencies learned in one job or another. Many times a labor-saving device constructed for one job can be used in others, and industrial engineering departments do not or cannot comprehend all possible uses for new devices. Rarely do formal programs exist for cross referencing methods improvements, although in Chapter 13 we noted the potential benefits from such cross referencing.

Many companies believe that the discovery of a methods improvement by a worker will become part of the formal job specification, because the worker will submit a suggestion to an appropriate committee which makes rewards (sometimes quite substantial ones) for cost-saving suggestions. However, all too often suggestions are hidden or not reported because although a methods improvement suggestion might lead to benefits to that employee who submitted it, many improvements are not the product of one single identifiable worker; even if they are, the social system comprised of all the workers often regards payments for such rewards as due to the group itself.

Many "small" shortcuts are identified by lead men or foremen who although supposedly managerial personnel, nonetheless identify with the workers and feel that their own job is made easier by having a little "cushion" in the system. Any worker who turned such a suggestion into a suggestion system would not be highly regarded by his fellow workers. In addition, workers typically do not like to admit that one of their peers is inherently more clever; almost any kind of suggestion tends to be regarded as "finking."

Another course of potential method improvements often comes about because initial methods are purposely designed in an inefficient manner. Many methods are determined by foremen, lead men, or setup men who design a "baloney" factor into a job so that when timed the job will require significantly more time than it will later take. Thus the author remembers a job at the camera factory where three extra tools were mounted on the machine to be used only when the time study man was around; a fourth tool performed its function as well as the function of the other three very nicely. Again, one must ask whose "side" the setup man is on. Is it realistic to assume that he will determine job methods in such a way that his friends will have to work hard?

Worker Variability

An important consideration in viewing performance measures is the underlying variability or distribution of worker capacities or abilities. That is how much faster can one man work than another? Time and motion study authors usually accept the position that, with rare exceptions, the range for most physical and mental capacities is such that the best performance is twice as good or fast as that of the worst. If we took the phrase "with rare exceptions" to mean a ±3 standard deviation range (we will see that this is the range used for quality control), and the statement that 95% of the working population should be able to operate at a 100% level, we can construct the following normal curve depiction:

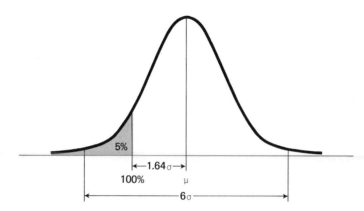

Figure 14.1

As noted in our discussion of queuing problems, since the normal curve runs from -∞ to +∞, it may not be a good model for depicting rates such as output in parts per hour (which cannot be negative). In Fig. 14.1, we unfortunately do not know what the value of μ (average performance level) should be. Industrial practice indicates that the average performance level for workers on incentive wages is somewhere around 125%. If we accept a value for μ of 125%, σ becomes about 15.2% and the upper limit becomes about 170%. That is, we would expect 95% of our workers to have performance levels in excess of 100% with the average about 125% and the best about 170%.

Unfortunately, in most work measurement systems output rarely gets to the 170% range. Rather, it is usually held to under 135% (80–85B's), as noted previously. The distribution of worker output is not well modeled by Fig. 14.1; Fig. 14.2 is more typical.

A well-known system for estimating worker speed is called the Westinghouse Rating System. Under this system, operators are rated on the basis of four factors—skill, effort, conditions, and consistency. Each of these factors is divided into 6 or 12 categories; descriptive phrases and

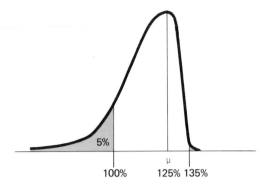

Figure 14.2

concomitant speed or effort-rating factors are given. It is interesting to note that if the ultimate in every category is assigned we have:

Factor	Descriptor	Rating
Skill:	Superskill	= +15%
Effort:	Excessive	= +13%
Conditions:	Ideal	= + 6%
Consistency:	Perfect	= + 4%

Thus a person with super skill working under ideal conditions with perfect consistency at an excessive rate of effort can achieve only a performance rating of 138%!

If Fig. 14.2 has the appearance of an unusual model of a real world phenomenon, an equally strange model can be observed by plotting individual or group performance levels over time.

In Fig. 14.3, we see a leveling off of performance or speed; we will see that the learning curve model would predict otherwise. When a company observes this phenomenon, it probably can conclude safely that pegged production is the cause. If the plot is on a companywide basis and the company is on incentive wages, the effects of selective employment (where good or fast workers are encouraged) should additionally contribute to an increasing average performance level.

Industrial Engineering Training and Tradition
To some extent, the existence of pegged production levels must be blamed upon a rather dogmatic posture of industrial engineering. Frank Gilbreth

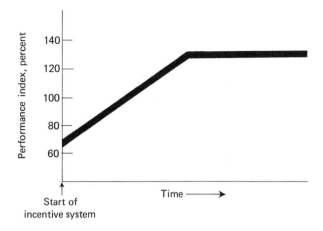

Figure 14.3

stated that one best way could be found; unfortunately, many industrial engineers not only believe this but assume that whatever method they are using for a particular job *is* the one best way. To a large extent, the authenticity of standards determined by the models examined in Chapter 13 has been oversold. A related shortcoming is the above-mentioned underestimation of variations in worker capacities or abilities.

A set of shibboleths has evolved which do not adequately depict real world actualities. Improvements, however, involve changes at the basic assumption or axiom level of industrial engineering. To make such changes involves not only an admission of past errors, it involves issues such as collective bargaining disputes where industrial engineering "hard" data have played significant roles. It also involves a different philosophy on the part of industrial engineers, workers, and management toward the use of industrial engineering data.

One significant problem in many work measurement systems is inadequate training given to time and motion study personnel. These individuals often have little training in the operations they are to study and are therefore susceptible to being "conned." Once conned, we find ourselves in the insidious feedback loop where model validation is judged on the basis of prediction adequacy as described above. In Chapter 13 we noted mechanical problems such as elemental divisions and performance rating. When these features are coupled with the large degree of talent or art required to determine a good method, the net result is a need for a highly skilled, carefully trained investigator.

THE LEARNING CURVE

The existence of restricted output levels and some of the possible causes for this restriction have been presented above. The simple truth is that any model which assumes a static world devoid of evolution has to be shortsighted. Improvements are possible in the way any task is performed, whether it be playing golf or assembling chairs at Westfall. A model which attempts to understand how this improvement comes about and how it might be fostered will surely be better than those which assume a constant rate of productivity or effectiveness.

The Improvement Phenomenon

The term "learning curve" is the most widely used and general term to describe the phenomenon of improving efficiency as a function of time or increasing output. However, some authors prefer to use other terms such as manufacturing progress function, improvement curve, or experience curve; the distinction is that learning implies improvement in the time required to perform a specified task, but our scope will encompass method changes, equipment changes, design improvements, and significant amounts of managerial talent to continually refine and implement improved functional analyses of the kind described in Chapter 7.

The characteristic curve of improvement depicts a constant percentage reduction of labor per unit as a function of cumulative units produced. Figure 14.4 presents an 85% learning curve, plotted on the left on arithmetic scales, and on the right on logarithmic scales (85% is a parameter for the constant percentage reduction or slope of the curve).

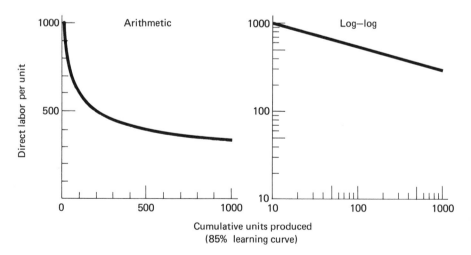

Figure 14.4

The first reported use of the learning curve was in the manufacture of airplanes. The airframe industry continues to be a major user; present applications include aerospace, evaluation of subcontractors, estimation, and reporting to the Defense Department. Other applications described in the literature are for increasing yields from refineries as a function of the number of barrels produced, for maintenance as a function of the number of times a particular activity has been performed, for machine shops, for various assembly operations, for wiring, and for construction projects.

Although the learning curve model has never been formally applied at the Westfall Furniture Company, the universality of the improvement phenomenon is supported by several observations. Thus for example, the number of board feet dried per year in an existing kiln continues to increase each year, trim losses at the cutoff saws appear to be going down, losses of material from improper panel gluing have decreased, and the overall productivity of the plant has shown a steady increase. It is worth noting that each of these examples involves a measurable activity and hence a surrogate criterion; we will consider the influence of criteria and the expectation of progress more fully in a subsequent section.

Learning curves have been applied (and misapplied) to a variety of problem situations. The technique's associations with the airframe industry and military contracts has led to considerable usage in cost estimating, pricing, contract negotiation, labor and facility planning, and for estimating the implications of major changes in design. Although the basic flavor of the approach is applicable to almost any activity, we will see that the continuous nature of the curves shown in Fig. 14.4 are best approximated at a level of aggregation which smoothes out the inherent discreteness associated with changes in individual operations. Thus Conway and Schultz state: "Carrying the function into use as a detailed labor control device seems to be stretching experience too far. . . . Applying it to individual operations as a control is justified by no known data which the authors have seen."[*]

The Model

As noted previously, the learning curve model is based upon a constant percentage reduction in required inputs or a function of constant percentage increases in outputs. These reductions are most typically expressed in terms of the effect of doubling the output quantity. Thus Fig. 14.4 is based upon a constant percentage reduction of 15% whenever the cumulative units produced is doubled. Such a curve is referred to as an 85%

[*]Richard W. Conway and Andrew, Schultz, Jr., "The Manufacturing Progress Function," *The Journal of Industrial Engineering* **10**, no. 1 (January-February 1959):50.

learning curve; if the 10th unit requires 1,000 direct labor hours, then the 20th unit requires $(1,000 \times .85) = 850$ direct labor hours, the 40th unit requires $(850 \times .85) = 722.5$ direct labor hours, the 80th unit requires $(722.5 \times .85)$ direct labor hours, etc. This relationship can be expressed mathematically in the following way:

$$A_i = A_1 \times i^{-b},$$

where

A_i = the direct labor hours required for the ith unit;

A_1 = the direct labor hours required for the 1st unit;

i = count of cumulative units produced;

b = reduction parameter or slope of the learning curve.

If any two values of i are stated so that $i_2 \div i_1 = 2$. then we see that we are looking for the power to which 2 must be raised in order to achieve our desired learning curve percentage. Thus, $2^{-.2345} = 0.85$, and a curve for which $b = .2345$ is an 85% learning curve.

The logarithmic transformation of our basic equation yields:

$$\log (A_i) = \log (A_1) - b \times \log (i),$$

which is a linear equation with slope $(-b)$. Raw learning curve data plotted on an arithmetic scale will resemble the lefthand side of Fig. 14.4; if logarithmically transformed, they would approximate a straight line on the same arithmetic scales. The more usual procedure, however, is to accomplish the same result by plotting the raw data on a log—log scale as shown on the right in Fig. 14.4.

In our discussion up to this point, we have been emphasizing the comparison of inputs to outputs on a unit basis as opposed to making the comparison on an average unit basis. Some individuals feel that the cumulative average hours per unit is a more desirable relationship to study; cumulative average data may be computed by summing individual data and dividing by the count of cumulative units produced:

$$\overline{A}_j = \frac{\sum\limits_{i=1}^{j} A_i}{j}$$

where

$\overline{A}_j$ = the average direct labor for the 1st to the jth unit;

A_i = unit direct labor as above;

i = count of units produced as above.

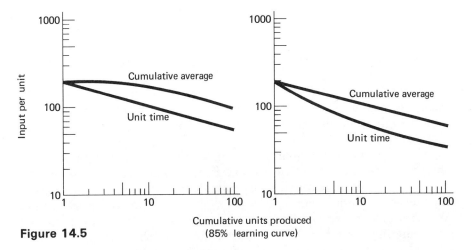

Figure 14.5

Cumulative units produced
(85% learning curve)

Figure 14.5 depicts two alternative relationships between the unit time and the cumulative average time. In either case, since the time for the first unit is both the unit time and the average time, the two curves intersect at the ordinate. In the left-hand side of Fig. 14.5, it is the unit curve which is considered to be linear over all ranges with the cumulative average curve becoming asymptotically parallel to it. In the curve shown on the right in Fig. 14.5, the opposite formulation holds; the cumulative average curve is considered to be a log-linear over all ranges with the unit time curve becoming asymptotically parallel to the cumulative average curve. Since the two curves are essentially parallel over the interesting ranges in either case, the choice largely revolves around ease of calculation and one's inherent interest or criteria.* If the cumulative average approach (Fig. 14.5, right) is taken, the unit time can be obtained by the following formula:

$$A_i = i \times \overline{A}_i - (i-1)\overline{A}_{i-1}$$

A perusal of Fig. 14.5 is somewhat interesting since both the curves start with the same time for the initial unit; clearly, however, the formulation on the left which depicts log-linear unit time results in substantially higher costs. An alternative way to construct Fig. 14.5 would be to equate both sides at the point where the curves become parallel (after

---

*Conway and Schultz show how the cumulative average formulation can mask significant deviations which will be illustrated by the unit time formulation. The masking occurs because of the smoothing influence of past data on the depiction of more recent data. See Conway and Schultz, *op.cit.,* p. 41, 48.

roughly 20 units). Such a formulation, however, would result in differing times for the initial unit of production.

What is clearly illustrated by considering Fig. 14.5 in this regard is that extrapolations based upon the required inputs for the initial unit are dangerous if for no other reason than the difference in formulation possible. Indeed, however, there are in fact more fundamental reasons why embryonic conditions which are so largely affected by preplanning, goodness of engineering design, availability of materials, etc. should not dominate construction of the model.

A more reasonable approach involves time requirements on either the unit time or cumulative average time at some point after the two curves have become parallel. This point, along with the anticipated learning curve percentage can be used as a pivot to estimate future results. Whether or not past results fit the curves it is clearly not as important as predicting the future. The required inputs at the pivot point can be either estimated or actual; in either case, it would seem to represent a more reliable base for extrapolation than the actual or estimated inputs required for the 1st unit.

The curves depicted in Fig. 14.4 and 14.5 are based upon a continuous uniform improvement rate. Other kinds of situations have been empirically observed. Figure 14.6 depicts three such situations. In the left hand side of Fig. 14.6, the data point to a substantial disruption of the learning phenomenon at about the 150th unit; thereafter, the learning process continues along a pattern roughly parallel (but above) that initially established. This situation is referred to as a "scallop" and usually occurs when a major interruption in a program occurs such as by stopping operations for some time period, moving to a new facility, or making substantial design changes. Note that the distance between the parallel lines of the old learning curve and the learning curve established after the interruption can represent a very substantial unplanned cost overrun. One of the major aircraft manufacturers attributed a multi-million dollar loss to just such a scalloping problem.

Also depicted on the left in Fig. 14.6 is a phenomenon at the end referred to as a "toe-up." It is not unusual toward the end of a job or contract for the rate of improvement to level off, stop, or even reverse itself. For one thing, the expected advantages from method changes and other improvements are not going to be amortized over a large number of units. In addition, as actual phasing out conditions begin it is fairly common to see employment patterns changed with concomitant inefficiencies. The last segment of the curve depicted on the left in Fig. 14.6 shows just such a phenomenon.

The curve on the right in Fig. 14.6 shows a definite plateau. This condition could occur for many reasons, including the development of an

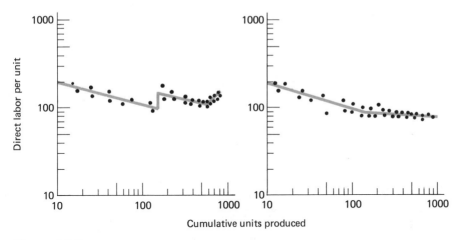

Figure 14.6

informal standard, a lack of improvement oriented resources being de-voted, or the emerging dominance of a fixed machine cycle time.

Transient Conditions

Figure 14.5 pointed out two different ways of viewing the initial condi-tions prior to the time when the cumulative average and unit time curves become parallel. A more general problem concerns the whole startup period which can easily result in nonlinearities. Startup penalties of one kind or another, poor planning, disrupted deliveries, process modifica-tions, and other kinds of transient problems can vary greatly from one job to another. The pivot point idea which essentially discounts early empiri-cal data is useful for eliminating the bias that is associated with ex-trapolating from highly variable early data.

The pivot point concept illustrates an interesting danger associated with utilizing transient information. In Fig. 14.7, an estimate has been made that it will take 50 man hours to produce the 100th unit and that the rate of learning on this task will be 80%. Actual data are plotted which indicate that the 100th unit is indeed produced in approximately 50 hours. The question that an analysis of the data leads to, however, concerns the validity of the 80% curve. That is, Fig. 14.7 shows that the actual data seem to be well approximated by a 90% curve with the 50 hour/100 unit pivot. If indeed the 90% curve is correct and the expected length of the job is 500 units, then a 4,200 hr. cumulative variance in required manpower will result. On the other hand, it may very well be that the early data merely reflect good preplanning and efficiencies. It seems absurd that more inefficiency in the production in the first 100

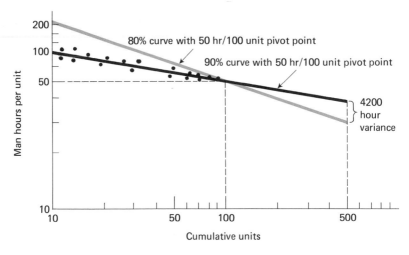

Figure 14.7

units would lead to a better fit with the 80% curve which naturally has a higher point of interception with the ordinate (104.9) than the 90% curve (70.95).

Appendix A to this chapter presents some useful tables for calculating time estimates with various progress functions. Use of the tables is based upon the pivot point concept where a time value (estimated or actual) is given for some unit or average. The tables are based upon multiplicative factors to apply to that pivot point. For example the first column in Appendix A gives factors for a 70% learning curve. Naturally, the factor associated with 100% of the pivot is 1.0000 and the factor associated with 200% is 0.7000. If a time of 5 hours were given for the 50th unit of production, then the time for the 5th unit (10% of the pivot) would be 3.2702 X 5 hours = 16.351 hours. If we wanted to estimate the expected time for the first unit, we could not do so directly from the table (no factor given for 2%). However, we could estimate the time for the 5th unit as we did above, regard it as a new pivot point, recognize that 1 is 20% of 5, and multiply 16.351 hours by 2.2891 to get an estimate of 37.429 hours for the first unit.

Implementation

Although the evolutionary features captured in the learning curve model are an inherent part of any activity, nonetheless achievement of the benefits requires offsetting investments of time and resources. Employees want to know what is expected of them; regardless of whether the standards are determined by objective or formal means, we need to overcome many strong traditions to establish a policy of ever increasing expectations that does not become regarded as attempted exploitation.

The influence of criteria cannot be set aside. Adoption of the learning curve model leads to expectations or forecasts of future performance levels. Those expectations or forecasts naturally become goals, with someone responsible for the achievement of those goals. With an assumption of equality between authority and responsibility (one cannot be reasonably held responsible for something without sufficient authority to make it occur), resources will be devoted to the fulfillment of the objectives and the "validating" of the forecasts. When individuals take it upon themselves to provide the kinds of improvement demanded by the learning curve, expectations tend to become reality; the proportion of the improvement that comes about from the Hawthorne effect as opposed to system of changes and methodology and design may vary substantially from case to case, but there is little doubt that when a preconceived plateau is established as a goal, improvements well may cease when that goal is reached.

There has been some attempt made to understand the rate of learning which is inherently possible in certain situations, and to identify those features of a job which determine the inherent susceptibility to improvement. The original work by Wright proposed an 80% learning curve as universally applicable. Subsequent researchers have found learning curve rates varying between 65 and 95%. One authority lists the following factors affecting the rate of learning:*

1. Man-machine ratio—as the percentage of machine-dominated work increases, the inherently possible rate of improvement decreases

2. Degree of skill or mental effort applied in the task—high skill requirements imply an extended learning period

3. Extent of tooling—more sophisticated tooling reduces the need for worker skill and effort

4. Quality of organization and supervision—increased organizational and supervisory efforts lead to better job conditions as well as improved morale

5. Methods improvement activity—increased learning requires investments in methods improvement

6. Incentives—a proper incentive system can foster high learning rates

7. Extent of preproduction planning—poor preproduction planning can artificially generate initial learning rates that appear to be very desirable

---

*J.H. Holdham, "Learning Curves—Their Applications in Industry," *Production and Inventory Management,* 4th Qtr, 1970, pp. 43–46.

8. Sensitivity of work to error—error sensitive work appears to require longer periods of time to achieve significant improvement

9. Morale—worker morale has a strong impact on the rate of learning

An Assessment

By now it should be apparent that the learning curve model could be dangerous indeed, if applied without committing the required resources to achieve expectations. It should also be clear that deceptive games can be played with the model if one's criteria are oriented toward deception. Nonetheless, it is the author's strong conclusion that the learning curve model represents an improved and potentially very useful view of any good or service-producing activity. It is superior to alternative normative models of expected results, and it has the potential for making significant improvements in the set of surrogate criteria used to evaluate subsystem performance.

Let us now postulate a commitment to proper use of the learning curve model. With that commitment established, we need to consider how one might properly collect data so that a user-oriented approach to the model can be obtained. The need for user involvement should be obvious; supervisory personnel who will be asked to accomplish a job with decreasing resource inputs simply have to know what is expected of them and believe that such expectations can be met. The implications for decreased labor requirements for the accomplishment of a given task clearly have to be considered in the planning for long-range staffing requirements. In addition, as improvement-oriented activities are aggregated over many jobs, there is a resultant implied requirement for methods improvement personnel, design engineers, etc.

The predictions coming from the learning curve model should be better than those coming from alternative predictive mechanisms (including SWAG—Systematic Wild Guessing). Nevertheless, in each situation there will be some variability from the prediction or "sample error." A user orientation implies that the learning curve model be available in such a way that interested individuals can assess the implications of various errors, e.g., what are the implications of assuming a 70% learning curve when in fact we can only achieve 75%? 80%? What empirical data must we observe to conclude that a different learning rate is in effect? What will an error in the assumed learning curve parameter mean for staffing and costs? What sorts of resources need to be deployed in order to get a particular project back on the desired overall learning curve rate? What is the proper planning and timing for those resources? Is our desired end attainable without major equipment changes? without significant design changes? Conversely, what are the payoffs associated with moving a particular activity from a 75% learning rate to a 70% learning rate? What are the implied resources that we must commit to achieve this increased rate of learning?

It would seem desirable to collect learning curve data and formulate a learning curve model for every operation and employee in an organization. Such an undertaking, however, would involve massive amounts of data collection and standard determination; discontinuities due to discrete method and design changes would tend to make a fit between the data and the model tenuous. As data from different operations or individuals are aggregated, the fit will improve, but at some point we will find ourselves concerned with aggregating what are essentially apples and bananas. That is, if the factors which affect the rate of improvement are greatly different from one operation to another (e.g., one is largely machine-based and the other is not), a combination of these activities which are diverse in their inherent susceptibility to improvement could lead to objectives which are increasingly difficult to achieve.

At least one key to the level of aggregation problem might be to look to the natural subsystem classifications within an organization which are usually based upon similar working activities. Thus for example, within Westfall one ought to be able to collect data on board feet of lumber cut per man hour, board feet through the rip saws per hour, board feet of panels gluded per hour, productivity in the finish mill, or the number of chairs assembled per man hour. Once the concept of expected improvements in the inputs required to achieve specified or common outputs is established, the implications on the surrogate criteria system for those who manage these subsystems is clearly established. Comparative evaluations of supervisory personnel should be improved, and the way in which improvement-oriented resources should be allocated will be more in line with enterprise objectives.

Use of the learning curve model for ongoing day-to-day operations with all of its implications for the surrogate criteria operating within a firm has a major ramification for the operations of an enterprise and the concomitant individual criteria and behavior patterns of people within the firm. In order to implement a system of continually increasing expectations, a certain spirit of integrity and concern for the worth of an individual must pervade the operations of the company. Let us now turn our attention to this matter.

A SPIRIT OF HEARTY COOPERATION

My experience in the camera plant is not atypical of industrial practice. The learning curve model supports the inherent evolution toward improved efficiency reflected in that experience. Moreover, we have seen that proper use of the model might drive or speed the evolution in efficiency. The costs of restricted output and undeveloped potential are enormous. It is probably quite conservative to state that output in most companies could be increased by at least 50% and perhaps by 100% or more. Many workers strongly dislike artificial restrictions on their earnings and would like very much to increase their salaries by 50 to 100%. Or, if their salaries were to remain the same for the same amount of output, they would like to have the leisure time associated with achieving the same output in fewer hours (I could have achieved my 6 days of work in the camera factory in 3). From the company point of view, an increase in output of 50 to 100% represents an increase in plant capacity at very little incremental cost. If a way can be found to reduce restricted output levels and undeveloped potential, it should be possible for employees to earn substantially larger sums of money, for companies to earn greater returns while competing vigorously, and for whole societies to benefit.

Criteria Congruence

If the many benefits that are possible to achieve through increased productivity are to be obtained, it will be necessary to establish an organizational environment that is not based upon the traditional conflict pattern of labor versus management. Frederick Taylor expressed it well in his third principle of scientific management where he stated a need for "a spirit of hearty cooperation" between management and labor. Simply stated, an enterprise criteria system should be designed so that it is in the interests of all employees to work at maximum efficiency; the result should be substantial improvements in individual as well as company criteria. Organizations where noncongruent criteria sets lead to restricted output have a great potential for improvement.

Achieving this improvement requires the establishment of a spirit of hearty cooperation. Since Frederick Taylor first suggested the idea over 50 years ago, instituting a spirit of hearty cooperation is not a trivial undertaking. However, neither is it a Utopian dream. A few isolated instances such as the Lincoln Electric Company do in fact exist. Employees in that company earn substantial incomes (Approximately twice the average income paid by manufacturers in the same general industry), extraordinary fringe benefits exist, and there is a long waiting line of people wishing employment in the company; moreover, the company is financially sound and able to compete vigorously in the electric welding equipment market.

Personal Suggestions

The establishment of a spirit of hearty cooperation is necessarily a long range project where many existing attitudes must be changed. How this might be accomplished is clearly beyond the scope of this book, let alone this chapter, and what might be appropriate for one organizational situation would not necessarily be right for another. Nevertheless, it is perhaps useful to look at a few personal opinions as to how one might evolve toward a more cooperative environment.

First of all, I believe it to be absolutely essential for all levels of management, but particularly top management, to fervently believe in and make a commitment to the principle of hearty cooperation. Employees will (with some justification) regard cooperative efforts as a "snow job." Not only is it necessary to overcome hostile feelings based upon past antagonisms, to a large extent one is faced with overcoming the history of industrial organization. It certainly will not be done overnight, nor can it be done by fiat. A considerable degree of soul searching will be required in the process. Moreover, since the enterprise will have to largely exhaust its "believability" quota, the costs of failure may be high. If management wants to establish the spirit of hearty cooperation, it will be necessary to continually "turn the other cheek" and thereby reaffirm corporate and personal dedication to the undertaking.

One of the key subgoals in the design of an improved working environment is an open channel of communication through which expressions of opinion and concrete suggestions can be moved. The establishment of some sort of ombudsman who would listen to any and all points of view might be the best way to achieve this goal ("he" might be a detached third party or some democratically selected group). In addition to pure communication of opinions and ideas, the user-designer concept seems appropriate; that is, management should strongly desire to not have their efforts regarded as placation. It is assumed that people involved in specific jobs have ideas that would prove valuable if a proper modeling environment existed so that they could be tested. Thus, operating in conjunction with a communications channel would be a technical or staff capability to create appropriate modeling environments for the participative study of particular problems.

As particular problems are identified, studied, and solved, I would expect certain individuals to emerge as being especially creative and innovative. These individuals should be valuable additions to the staff or technical capabilities which support and foster evolution in methods, design, equipment, morale, training, etc. It is my opinion that a large degree of untapped potential resides in employees and that important support well may grow from unexpected sources.

In terms of specific suggestions, the "cooperation committee" might start by critically examining many traditional "control" procedures that simply do not stand up in the fact of functional analysis given the commitment and belief in a cooperative spirit. It well might be useful to initially select improvement areas that demonstrate managerial goodwill. Thus one might ask why time clocks exist, or why some individual work patterns might not be tailored to meet individual need patterns. For example, if the function of an accounts payable clerk is to prepare the necessary papers for paying a specified set of invoices, why is it necessary for that individual to be in the office for exactly 40 hours each week from exactly 8 to 5 each day with one hour off for lunch? Why isn't it possible for employees to work hard enough so that an occasional 3 or 4 day weekend can be taken? Should it not be possible for an individual employee through working hard or through working longer hours to "earn" 2, 3, or 4 vacations per year? Is it not possible for us to organize work patterns and activities so that more individualistic work schedules can be achieved?

The above issues may appear to be somewhat tangential to the basic goal of getting the same amount of output from a production facility at reduced cost or greater output for the same cost. Nonetheless, they are important to individual criteria sets, and efforts put to such improvements well may facilitate an atmosphere that fosters cooperative efforts. Significant changes in efficiency are possible; unfortunately, great changes in efficiency usually seem to occur only when it is a matter of company survival. There have been several reported instances of companies faced with competition severe enough to force liquidation; subsequent arrangements with workers (some involving profit sharing features) permitted the companies to not only survive but in fact to prosper.

SUMMARY REMARKS

In this chapter we have subjected the models presented in Chapter 13 to critical analysis. Labor estimates based upon industrial engineering standards are widely regarded as one of the few enterprise problem areas for which highly accurate models exist. We found, however, that the validation procedure has an important flaw, namely, actual conditions are strongly influenced by the predictive process. The result is restricted output and suboptimization of enterprise as well as individual goals. The extent of the mismatch between actual and possible grows over time as natural forces of evolution foster efficiency. The evolution is described by the learning curve model, and can be accelerated by proper design of the surrogate criteria set for evaluating performance.

Achievement of substantial progress in efficiency as dictated by the learning curve model requires a commitment and spirit of cooperation beyond that present in most organizations. The means of providing a cooperative spirit has involved presentation of perhaps the most subjective and opinionated materials in this book. As I see it, the potential payoffs in the economic well-being of the country and world are too great to not try.

REFERENCES

Cochran, E.B., "Learning: New Dimension in Labor Standards," *Industrial Engineering* (Jan. 1969), pp. 38–47.

Carlson, John G., "How Management Can Use the Improvement Phenomenon," *California Management Review,* **3,** no. 2 (Winter 1961).

Conway, R.W., and Andrew Schultz, Jr., "The Manufacturing Progress Function," *The Journal of Industrial Engineering,* **10,** no. 1 (Jan.-Feb. 1959): 39–54.

Gottlieb, Bertram, "A Fair Days Work Is Anything You Want It To Be," *The Journal of Industrial Engineering* **19,** no. 12 (Dec 1968): 592–99.

Hirschman, Winfred B., "Profit From the Learning Curve," *Harvard Business Review,* **42,** no. 1 (Jan.-Feb. 1964): 125–39.

Holdham, J.H., "Learning Curves-Their Applications in Industry," *Production and Inventory Management,* (4th Qtr. 1970), pp. 40–55.

CHAPTER REVIEW

This chapter reinforces the central role of evolution in system design. By providing you with an explicit model of the evolutionary *process,* you hopefully should be better able to anticipate system design improvements and take the actions necessary to achieve them. It is a normative model that you should attempt to apply for assessing your own efforts as well as those of subordinates.

We presented the learning curve model primarily in the context of a reconsideration of work measurement models. The most common work measurement models tend to be applied to repetitive operations at a low level of aggregation. The learning curve is well applied to higher levels of aggregation, and to less well structured work designs. Thus you might reasonably expect (and take actions to obtain) improvements in your score at some sport, a steadily increasing productivity from studying as you go through college, a reduction in the average time it should take to check out groceries in a supermarket, or a continuing ability for you or your subordinates to accomplish any specified task in less time.

OUTLINE OF THE CHAPTER

Introduction	(evolution in time requirements)
Work standards—a reassessment	(static approach invalid)
Model validity	(restricted output)
Dysfunctionalism	(noncongruent criteria)

Contributory factors	(additional factors)
Methods evolution	(worker improvements)
Worker variability	(unrealistic assumptions)
Industrial engineering training and tradition	(no one best way)
The learning curve	(model of evolutionary process)
The improvement phenomenon	(continuous improvement)
The model	(calculations and use)
Transient conditions	(pivot point concept)
Implementation	(relation to individual criteria)
An assessment	(proper model—use it)
A spirit of hearty cooperation	(necessary ingredient to use)
Criteria congruence	(can be achieved)
Personal suggestions	(total organizational commitment)
Summary remarks	(benefits worth seeking)
Appendix A	(computational factors)

CENTRAL ISSUES

A reassessment of work standards finds them to be less evolutionary than our evolutionary expectations of the tasks they model. Work measurement models are often considered valid because actual results comply with model predictions. However, the compliance is all too frequently achieved by restricted output on the part of the workers. The workers find it dysfunctional to increase output because the increases are interpreted as validity rejection of the work measurement models; the result is new standards or more work for the same pay.

It is entirely reasonable to expect evolution or improvements in worker productivity. Employees learn to work faster and more efficiently, methods improvements are found or transplanted from similar activities and selective employment encourages retention of employees most gifted for particular tasks (particularly if wage incentives are paid).

A good part of the mismatch between evolutionary expectations and results is due to industrial engineering traditions, and the ways in which industrial engineering is viewed within a company. The extent of worker variability has been underestimated, one best way of doing a job has been oversold, and the exactness of work measurement models has been overstated.

The learning curve incorporates a steady expectation of evolution. The model is parameterized by a percentage improvement factor which indicates the expected time when the quantity doubles. Thus an 80% curve with 10.0 hours for the first unit would expect 8.0 hours for the second, 6.4 for the fourth, 5.12 for the eighth, etc. A set of factors presented as Appendix A permits calculation of intermediate values, e.g., 7.021 hours for the third unit (80% curve, 300% of pivot = .7021).

The model is capable of misuse, and the underlying criteria of those using the model need to be carefully considered. When use is for bargaining with governmental agencies for contract renegotiations, we need to consider again the relevant costing considerations presented in earlier chapters. I conclude, however, that the model is of great potential usefulness; it should be used because it is superior to alternatives and because the resultant operations should become more congruent with overall enterprise objectives.

Full implementation of the model requires a spirit of hearty cooperation between management and workers. Those who are affected by expected improvements in their operations need to believe in the practicality of achievement, and they want to be assured of not being personally hit in the pocketbook during transient periods. The levels of improvement possible can result in benefits which can be shared by all employees. It is not unreasonable to expect output to double, prices to be reduced, profits to increase dramatically, and wages to increase by 50% or more.

ASSIGNMENTS

1. The Blow-Me-Down Bomb Co. has been asked to bid on a new anti-anti-bomb-bomb called the Piece Maker Special. The company estimates that it will take 20 hours to construct the 50th unit and that an 80% learning curve will be experienced.

    a) What is the expected average time for the first four units?
    b) What is the approximate estimated time for the 500th unit?
    c) Repeat A and B with a rate of learning of 85%. 75.%

2. A historical learning rate of 82% seems appropriate to an operation your firm is considering. Engineering estimates that the 20th unit will require 430 direct labor hours. What do you expect to be the unit requirements for the first unit? the 10th? the 100th? the 1000th?

3. The following times were taken from a pilot run of 50 units on a new procedure. Estimate the rate of improvement.

Unit	Unit time (hours)
5	43.5
10	37.4
15	35.0
20	33.2
25	31.8
30	30.6
35	30.0
40	28.8
45	28.0
50	27.6

4. The time required to assemble the first unit of a new product was 47 hours. You expect a learning rate of 82%. What percentage decrease do you expect in required assembly time by the 5th unit? Suppose an expected decrease of 37% over the first five units was only 30%. What would you infer about the progress of the job? Why?

5. a) Given an expected curve of 70% and 861 hours required for the first unit, how many labor hours do you expect in total for the first 10 units?
   b) How much time do you expect the 100th unit to require?

6. a) The following times are from the first 1000 production units of a new product. What is the apparent rate of learning?

Unit	Time (hours)
100	80
200	58
300	48
400	42
500	38
600	35
700	32
800	30
900	29
1000	27

   b) Can you expect this rate indefinitely? Why or why not?

7. You have developed a hand assembly method for widgets and are considering bidding for a contract to assemble 500 of them.
   During trial runs you found that assembly times ran as follows:

Unit	Time (minutes)
1	65.6
10	36.5
20	30.2
30	27.4
40	26.3
50	23.9
60	23.0

Assuming your total cost is $2.30 per direct labor hour and you desire a margin of 10%, what price would you bid for the contract? Make all assumptions explicit and consider the sensitivity of your answer to errors in learning rate estimations.

APPENDIX A TO CHAPTER 14

UNIT FACTORS FOR PROGRESS FUNCTIONS

% PIVOT	70 %	72 %	74 %	76 %	78 %	80 %	81 %	82 %	83 %	84 %	%
5	4.6717	4.1362	3.6743	3.2743	2.9266	2.6232	2.4861	2.3577	2.2374	2.1245	5
10	3.2702	2.9780	2.7190	2.4884	2.2827	2.0086	2.0130	1.9333	1.8570	1.7846	10
15	2.6544	2.4574	2.2799	2.1194	1.9739	1.8418	1.7802	1.7214	1.6653	1.6116	15
20	2.2891	2.1442	2.0120	1.8913	1.7628	1.6789	1.6311	1.5853	1.5413	1.4991	20
25	2.0408	1.9290	1.8262	1.7313	1.6437	1.5625	1.5242	1.4872	1.4516	1.4172	25
30	1.8581	1.7693	1.6871	1.6107	1.5597	1.4734	1.4430	1.4116	1.3822	1.3537	30
35	1.7164	1.6447	1.5778	1.5154	1.4869	1.4021	1.3768	1.3506	1.3261	1.3022	35
40	1.6024	1.5438	1.4889	1.4373	1.4213	1.3431	1.3212	1.3000	1.2793	1.2592	40
45	1.5082	1.4600	1.4146	1.3716	1.3620	1.2931	1.2747	1.2569	1.2394	1.2224	45
50	1.4286	1.3889	1.3514	1.3153	1.3078	1.2500	1.2346	1.2195	1.2048	1.1905	50
55	1.3609	1.3275	1.2965	1.2662	1.2600	1.2122	1.1993	1.1867	1.1743	1.1623	55
60	1.3006	1.2739	1.2484	1.2242	1.2155	1.1787	1.1680	1.1575	1.1472	1.1371	60
65	1.2482	1.2265	1.2058	1.1860	1.1751	1.1488	1.1399	1.1313	1.1228	1.1144	65
70	1.2015	1.1842	1.1676	1.1517	1.1380	1.1217	1.1145	1.1077	1.1006	1.0939	70
75	1.1595	1.1461	1.1331	1.1206	1.1086	1.0970	1.0914	1.0859	1.0804	1.0750	75
80	1.1217	1.1117	1.1018	1.0924	1.0833	1.0749	1.0702	1.0660	1.0618	1.0577	80
85	1.0872	1.0801	1.0731	1.0665	1.0600	1.0537	1.0506	1.0476	1.0447	1.0417	85
90	1.0557	1.0512	1.0468	1.0426	1.0385	1.0345	1.0325	1.0306	1.0287	1.0269	90
95	1.0267	1.0246	1.0225	1.0205	1.0186	1.0167	1.0157	1.0148	1.0139	1.0130	95
100	1.0000	1.0000	1.0000	1.0000	1.0000	1.0000	1.0000	1.0000	1.0000	1.0000	100
105	0.9752	0.9771	0.9790	0.9809	0.9827	0.9844	0.9853	0.9861	0.9869	0.9878	105
110	0.9521	0.9558	0.9594	0.9630	0.9664	0.9698	0.9714	0.9731	0.9747	0.9763	110
115	0.9306	0.9359	0.9411	0.9462	0.9511	0.9560	0.9584	0.9608	0.9631	0.9655	115
120	0.9105	0.9172	0.9239	0.9304	0.9367	0.9430	0.9461	0.9491	0.9522	0.9552	120
125	0.8915	0.8997	0.9076	0.9154	0.9231	0.9307	0.9344	0.9381	0.9418	0.9454	125
130	0.8737	0.8831	0.8923	0.9013	0.9103	0.9190	0.9233	0.9276	0.9319	0.9361	130
135	0.8569	0.8675	0.8778	0.8880	0.8980	0.9079	0.9128	0.9177	0.9225	0.9273	135
140	0.8410	0.8526	0.8640	0.8753	0.8864	0.8974	0.9028	0.9082	0.9135	0.9189	140
145	0.8260	0.8386	0.8510	0.8632	0.8753	0.8873	0.8932	0.8991	0.9050	0.9108	145
150	0.8117	0.8252	0.8385	0.8517	0.8647	0.8776	0.8840	0.8904	0.8967	0.9030	150
155	0.7981	0.8125	0.8267	0.8407	0.8546	0.8684	0.8752	0.8821	0.8889	0.8956	155
160	0.7852	0.8003	0.8153	0.8302	0.8450	0.8596	0.8667	0.8741	0.8813	0.8885	160
165	0.7729	0.7888	0.8045	0.8202	0.8357	0.8511	0.8586	0.8664	0.8741	0.8817	165
170	0.7611	0.7777	0.7942	0.8105	0.8268	0.8430	0.8510	0.8591	0.8671	0.8751	170
175	0.7498	0.7671	0.7842	0.8013	0.8183	0.8352	0.8436	0.8520	0.8603	0.8687	175
180	0.7390	0.7569	0.7747	0.7924	0.8100	0.8276	0.8364	0.8451	0.8539	0.8626	180
185	0.7287	0.7471	0.7655	0.7839	0.8021	0.8204	0.8294	0.8385	0.8476	0.8567	185
190	0.7188	0.7378	0.7567	0.7756	0.7945	0.8133	0.8228	0.8322	0.8415	0.8509	190
195	0.7092	0.7287	0.7482	0.7677	0.7871	0.8066	0.8163	0.8260	0.8357	0.8454	195

% PIVOT	70 %	72 %	74 %	76 %	78 %	80 %	81 %	82 %	83 %	84 %
200	0.7000	0.7200	0.7400	0.7600	0.7800	0.8000	0.8100	0.8200	0.8300	0.8400
210	0.6826	0.7035	0.7245	0.7455	0.7665	0.7876	0.7981	0.8086	0.8192	0.8298
220	0.6665	0.6882	0.7100	0.7319	0.7538	0.7759	0.7869	0.7980	0.8090	0.8201
230	0.6514	0.6739	0.6964	0.7191	0.7419	0.7648	0.7763	0.7879	0.7994	0.8110
240	0.6373	0.6604	0.6837	0.7071	0.7307	0.7544	0.7664	0.7783	0.7903	0.8024
250	0.6241	0.6477	0.6716	0.6957	0.7201	0.7446	0.7569	0.7693	0.7817	0.7942
260	0.6116	0.6358	0.6603	0.6850	0.7100	0.7352	0.7479	0.7607	0.7735	0.7864
270	0.5998	0.6245	0.6496	0.6749	0.7004	0.7264	0.7394	0.7525	0.7657	0.7790
280	0.5887	0.6139	0.6394	0.6652	0.6914	0.7179	0.7313	0.7447	0.7583	0.7719
290	0.5782	0.6037	0.6297	0.6560	0.6828	0.7099	0.7236	0.7373	0.7511	0.7651
300	0.5682	0.5941	0.6205	0.6473	0.6745	0.7021	0.7161	0.7302	0.7443	0.7586
310	0.5587	0.5850	0.6117	0.6389	0.6666	0.6947	0.7090	0.7234	0.7378	0.7524
320	0.5496	0.5762	0.6033	0.6310	0.6591	0.6877	0.7022	0.7168	0.7315	0.7464
330	0.5410	0.5679	0.5953	0.6233	0.6518	0.6809	0.6956	0.7105	0.7255	0.7406
340	0.5327	0.5599	0.5877	0.6160	0.6449	0.6744	0.6893	0.7044	0.7197	0.7351
350	0.5249	0.5523	0.5803	0.6090	0.6382	0.6681	0.6833	0.6986	0.7141	0.7297
360	0.5173	0.5449	0.5732	0.6022	0.6318	0.6621	0.6775	0.6930	0.7087	0.7246
370	0.5101	0.5379	0.5665	0.5957	0.6256	0.6563	0.6718	0.6876	0.7035	0.7196
380	0.5031	0.5312	0.5599	0.5894	0.6197	0.6507	0.6664	0.6823	0.6985	0.7148
390	0.4964	0.5247	0.5537	0.5834	0.6139	0.6452	0.6612	0.6773	0.6936	0.7102
400	0.4900	0.5184	0.5476	0.5776	0.6084	0.6400	0.6561	0.6724	0.6889	0.7056
410	0.4838	0.5124	0.5418	0.5720	0.6030	0.6349	0.6512	0.6677	0.6843	0.7012
420	0.4779	0.5066	0.5361	0.5665	0.5979	0.6300	0.6464	0.6631	0.6799	0.6970
430	0.4721	0.5009	0.5307	0.5613	0.5928	0.6253	0.6418	0.6586	0.6756	0.6929
440	0.4665	0.4955	0.5254	0.5562	0.5880	0.6207	0.6374	0.6543	0.6715	0.6889
450	0.4612	0.4903	0.5203	0.5513	0.5832	0.6162	0.6330	0.6501	0.6674	0.6850
460	0.4560	0.4852	0.5153	0.5465	0.5787	0.6118	0.6288	0.6460	0.6635	0.6812
470	0.4510	0.4803	0.5106	0.5419	0.5742	0.6076	0.6247	0.6421	0.6597	0.6775
480	0.4461	0.4755	0.5059	0.5374	0.5699	0.6035	0.6207	0.6382	0.6559	0.6740
490	0.4414	0.4709	0.5014	0.5330	0.5657	0.5995	0.6168	0.6344	0.6523	0.6705
500	0.4368	0.4664	0.4970	0.5288	0.5616	0.5956	0.6131	0.6308	0.6488	0.6671
550	0.4159	0.4458	0.4769	0.5092	0.5428	0.5776	0.5958	0.6138	0.6324	0.6513
600	0.3977	0.4278	0.4592	0.4919	0.5261	0.5617	0.5800	0.5987	0.6176	0.6372
650	0.3817	0.4118	0.4435	0.4766	0.5112	0.5474	0.5661	0.5851	0.6046	0.6245
700	0.3674	0.3976	0.4294	0.4628	0.4978	0.5345	0.5535	0.5729	0.5927	0.6129
750	0.3546	0.3848	0.4167	0.4503	0.4857	0.5227	0.5420	0.5616	0.5818	0.6024
800	0.3430	0.3732	0.4052	0.4390	0.4746	0.5120	0.5314	0.5514	0.5718	0.5927
850	0.3325	0.3627	0.3947	0.4286	0.4644	0.5021	0.5217	0.5419	0.5625	0.5837
900	0.3228	0.3530	0.3850	0.4190	0.4549	0.4929	0.5127	0.5331	0.5540	0.5754
950	0.3140	0.3441	0.3761	0.4101	0.4462	0.4844	0.5044	0.5249	0.5460	0.5676
1000	0.3058	0.3358	0.3678	0.4019	0.4381	0.4765	0.4966	0.5172	0.5385	0.5604

	98 %	96 %	94 %	92 %	90 %	89 %	88 %	87 %	86 %	85 %	x PIVOT
5	1.0912	1.1929	1.3066	1.4339	1.5767	1.6548	1.7376	1.8256	1.9191	2.0186	5
10	1.0694	1.1452	1.2282	1.3191	1.4191	1.4727	1.5291	1.5882	1.6504	1.7158	10
15	1.0569	1.1182	1.1845	1.2564	1.3342	1.3757	1.4189	1.4640	1.5110	1.5602	15
20	1.0480	1.0994	1.1545	1.2136	1.2772	1.3107	1.3456	1.3818	1.4194	1.4584	20
25	1.0412	1.0851	1.1317	1.1813	1.2346	1.2625	1.2913	1.3212	1.3521	1.3841	25
30	1.0357	1.0735	1.1135	1.1558	1.2008	1.2244	1.2486	1.2737	1.2995	1.3262	30
35	1.0311	1.0638	1.0982	1.1346	1.1730	1.1930	1.2136	1.2348	1.2566	1.2791	35
40	1.0271	1.0554	1.0852	1.1165	1.1494	1.1665	1.1841	1.2021	1.2206	1.2397	40
45	1.0235	1.0482	1.0739	1.1008	1.1290	1.1437	1.1587	1.1740	1.1898	1.2059	45
50	1.0204	1.0417	1.0638	1.0870	1.1111	1.1236	1.1364	1.1494	1.1628	1.1765	50
55	1.0176	1.0358	1.0548	1.0746	1.0951	1.1057	1.1166	1.1276	1.1389	1.1505	55
60	1.0150	1.0305	1.0467	1.0634	1.0807	1.0897	1.0988	1.1081	1.1176	1.1272	60
65	1.0126	1.0257	1.0392	1.0532	1.0677	1.0751	1.0827	1.0904	1.0983	1.1063	65
70	1.0105	1.0212	1.0324	1.0438	1.0557	1.0618	1.0680	1.0743	1.0807	1.0872	70
75	1.0084	1.0171	1.0260	1.0352	1.0447	1.0496	1.0545	1.0595	1.0646	1.0698	75
80	1.0065	1.0132	1.0201	1.0272	1.0345	1.0382	1.0420	1.0459	1.0498	1.0537	80
85	1.0047	1.0096	1.0146	1.0197	1.0250	1.0277	1.0304	1.0332	1.0360	1.0388	85
90	1.0031	1.0062	1.0095	1.0128	1.0161	1.0179	1.0196	1.0214	1.0232	1.0250	90
95	1.0015	1.0030	1.0046	1.0062	1.0078	1.0087	1.0095	1.0104	1.0112	1.0121	95
100	1.0000	1.0000	1.0000	1.0000	1.0000	1.0000	1.0000	1.0000	1.0000	1.0000	100
105	0.9986	0.9971	0.9957	0.9942	0.9926	0.9918	0.9910	0.9902	0.9894	0.9886	105
110	0.9972	0.9944	0.9915	0.9886	0.9856	0.9841	0.9826	0.9810	0.9795	0.9779	110
115	0.9959	0.9918	0.9876	0.9833	0.9790	0.9768	0.9746	0.9723	0.9701	0.9678	115
120	0.9947	0.9893	0.9839	0.9783	0.9727	0.9698	0.9669	0.9640	0.9611	0.9582	120
125	0.9935	0.9869	0.9803	0.9735	0.9667	0.9632	0.9597	0.9562	0.9526	0.9490	125
130	0.9924	0.9847	0.9769	0.9689	0.9609	0.9569	0.9528	0.9487	0.9445	0.9403	130
135	0.9913	0.9825	0.9736	0.9645	0.9554	0.9508	0.9462	0.9415	0.9368	0.9321	135
140	0.9902	0.9804	0.9704	0.9603	0.9501	0.9450	0.9398	0.9346	0.9294	0.9241	140
145	0.9892	0.9784	0.9674	0.9563	0.9451	0.9394	0.9338	0.9281	0.9223	0.9166	145
150	0.9883	0.9764	0.9645	0.9524	0.9402	0.9341	0.9280	0.9218	0.9156	0.9093	150
155	0.9873	0.9745	0.9616	0.9487	0.9356	0.9290	0.9224	0.9157	0.9091	0.9024	155
160	0.9864	0.9727	0.9589	0.9450	0.9311	0.9240	0.9170	0.9099	0.9028	0.8957	160
165	0.9855	0.9709	0.9563	0.9415	0.9267	0.9193	0.9118	0.9043	0.8968	0.8892	165
170	0.9847	0.9692	0.9537	0.9382	0.9225	0.9147	0.9068	0.8989	0.8910	0.8830	170
175	0.9838	0.9676	0.9513	0.9349	0.9185	0.9102	0.9020	0.8937	0.8854	0.8770	175
180	0.9830	0.9660	0.9489	0.9317	0.9145	0.9059	0.8973	0.8886	0.8800	0.8713	180
185	0.9822	0.9644	0.9466	0.9287	0.9107	0.9018	0.8928	0.8837	0.8747	0.8657	185
190	0.9815	0.9629	0.9443	0.9256	0.9071	0.8977	0.8884	0.8790	0.8697	0.8603	190
195	0.9807	0.9614	0.9421	0.9228	0.9035	0.8938	0.8841	0.8744	0.8648	0.8551	195
200	0.9800	0.9600	0.9400	0.9200	0.9000	0.8900	0.8800	0.8700	0.8600	0.8500	200
210	0.9786	0.9573	0.9359	0.9146	0.8934	0.8827	0.8721	0.8615	0.8509	0.8403	210

% PIVOT	85 %	86 %	87 %	88 %	89 %	90 %	92 %	94 %	96 %	98 %
220	0.8312	0.8424	0.8535	0.8647	0.8759	0.8871	0.9095	0.9320	0.9546	0.9773
230	0.8226	0.8343	0.8459	0.8576	0.8693	0.8811	0.9047	0.9284	0.9521	0.9760
240	0.8145	0.8266	0.8387	0.8509	0.8631	0.8754	0.9001	0.9248	0.9498	0.9748
250	0.8067	0.8193	0.8319	0.8445	0.8572	0.8700	0.8956	0.9215	0.9475	0.9737
260	0.7993	0.8123	0.8253	0.8385	0.8516	0.8648	0.8914	0.9182	0.9453	0.9725
270	0.7923	0.8057	0.8191	0.8326	0.8462	0.8599	0.8874	0.9152	0.9432	0.9715
280	0.7855	0.7993	0.8132	0.8271	0.8411	0.8551	0.8835	0.9122	0.9412	0.9704
290	0.7791	0.7932	0.8074	0.8217	0.8361	0.8506	0.8798	0.9093	0.9392	0.9694
300	0.7729	0.7874	0.8020	0.8166	0.8314	0.8462	0.8762	0.9066	0.9374	0.9685
310	0.7670	0.7818	0.7967	0.8117	0.8268	0.8420	0.8728	0.9039	0.9355	0.9676
320	0.7613	0.7764	0.7916	0.8070	0.8224	0.8380	0.8694	0.9014	0.9338	0.9667
330	0.7559	0.7712	0.7868	0.8024	0.8182	0.8341	0.8662	0.8989	0.9321	0.9658
340	0.7506	0.7663	0.7821	0.7980	0.8141	0.8303	0.8631	0.8965	0.9305	0.9650
350	0.7455	0.7614	0.7775	0.7937	0.8101	0.8266	0.8601	0.8942	0.9289	0.9641
360	0.7406	0.7568	0.7731	0.7896	0.8063	0.8231	0.8572	0.8920	0.9273	0.9634
370	0.7359	0.7523	0.7689	0.7856	0.8026	0.8197	0.8544	0.8898	0.9258	0.9626
380	0.7313	0.7479	0.7648	0.7818	0.7990	0.8164	0.8517	0.8877	0.9244	0.9618
390	0.7268	0.7437	0.7608	0.7781	0.7955	0.8131	0.8490	0.8856	0.9230	0.9611
400	0.7225	0.7396	0.7569	0.7744	0.7921	0.8100	0.8464	0.8836	0.9216	0.9604
410	0.7184	0.7357	0.7532	0.7709	0.7888	0.8070	0.8439	0.8817	0.9203	0.9597
420	0.7143	0.7318	0.7496	0.7675	0.7857	0.8040	0.8415	0.8798	0.9190	0.9590
430	0.7104	0.7281	0.7460	0.7642	0.7826	0.8012	0.8391	0.8779	0.9177	0.9584
440	0.7065	0.7245	0.7426	0.7609	0.7795	0.7984	0.8368	0.8761	0.9164	0.9577
450	0.7028	0.7209	0.7392	0.7578	0.7766	0.7957	0.8345	0.8744	0.9152	0.9571
460	0.6992	0.7175	0.7360	0.7547	0.7737	0.7930	0.8323	0.8727	0.9141	0.9565
470	0.6957	0.7141	0.7328	0.7517	0.7709	0.7904	0.8302	0.8710	0.9129	0.9559
480	0.6923	0.7109	0.7297	0.7488	0.7682	0.7879	0.8281	0.8693	0.9118	0.9553
490	0.6889	0.7077	0.7267	0.7460	0.7656	0.7854	0.8260	0.8678	0.9107	0.9547
500	0.6857	0.7045	0.7238	0.7432	0.7630	0.7830	0.8240	0.8662	0.9096	0.9542
550	0.6705	0.6901	0.7100	0.7303	0.7508	0.7718	0.8146	0.8589	0.9045	0.9515
600	0.6570	0.6771	0.6977	0.7187	0.7399	0.7616	0.8061	0.8522	0.8999	0.9491
650	0.6448	0.6655	0.6866	0.7081	0.7301	0.7524	0.7984	0.8461	0.8956	0.9469
700	0.6337	0.6548	0.6764	0.6985	0.7210	0.7440	0.7913	0.8406	0.8917	0.9449
750	0.6235	0.6451	0.6671	0.6896	0.7127	0.7362	0.7848	0.8354	0.8881	0.9430
800	0.6141	0.6361	0.6585	0.6815	0.7050	0.7290	0.7787	0.8306	0.8847	0.9412
850	0.6055	0.6277	0.6505	0.6739	0.6978	0.7224	0.7731	0.8261	0.8816	0.9395
900	0.5974	0.6200	0.6431	0.6668	0.6911	0.7161	0.7678	0.8219	0.8786	0.9380
950	0.5899	0.6127	0.6362	0.6602	0.6849	0.7103	0.7628	0.8180	0.8758	0.9365
1000	0.5828	0.6059	0.6296	0.6540	0.6790	0.7047	0.7581	0.8142	0.8732	0.9351

CHAPTER 15

LOCATION AND LAYOUT
OF FACILITIES

The location of an enterprise system or subsystem is a decision which connotes and possibly denotes an extended commitment to a pattern of operations; one which both takes advantage of local conditions and at the same time is limited by them. The layout or physical arrangement of facilities within an organization also involves a time commitment and is conceptually similar to the location problem; both involve placements of activities and relationships among attributes of those activities, but the layout problem is usually considered at a given or specified location. Moreover, although buildings are sometimes constructed around layouts, more often facilities have to be arranged within an existing or slightly modified building configuration.

Within the Baumritter Corporation, location decisions include the purchase or construction of additional factories, expansion of existing factories, additional orbit or regional shipping centers, field warehouse changes, new franchised stores, termination of relationships with independent retailers, and moving the corporate headquarters. Layout decisions involve activities such as rearrangement of finish mill equipment at Westfall, movement of the panel gluing area to allow larger inventories of glued panels, addition to the Westfall finishing room, arrangements of inventories within the regional and field warehouses, placement of rooms and items (furniture, rugs, wallpaper, accessories, etc.) in franchised stores, and the placement of offices and other facilities in the new corporate headquarters. This chapter is devoted to an exposition of the ways in which such location and layout problems are analyzed, and the models which are available to aid in this analysis.

LOCATION PROBLEMS

We have stated many times that there is no such thing as "the _____ problem"; in our present context, fill in the blank space with "location."

The diverse nature of location problems is clearly illustrated by the kinds of problems Baumritter faces. Moreover, analysis of a "location problem" can and often should include a thoroughgoing investigation of basic functions fulfilled by the entities to be located. Perhaps the function provided by a warehouse can be fulfilled by alternative entities and the "location problem" solved by not locating anything. The unique nature of these decisions means that even within a specified industry or firm, location decisions are necessarily tailored to the particular criteria of an enterprise at a particular time.

Objective criteria for facilities location include initial costs, operating costs, and marketing implications. Subjective criteria also seem to be important for many location choices. The dynamic nature of location decisions is particularly well illustrated by the consideration of foreign locations. Each location change creates implications for balance among all the entities in the system.

Initial Cost Criteria

The initial costs of a location change obviously include land, construction, and equipment. Less tangible costs include legal fees, executive talent expended in closing the deal, travel expenses, training of a new work force and other start-up costs, and the overall adjustment that must be made within the company. The purchase of an additional factory has always involved Baumritter's president, executive vice-president and vice-president of manufacturing in lengthy negotiations with the seller. To a man, these individuals have stated that no matter how much time they anticipate will be required for negotiations, it never is enough. The provision of sufficient legal protection necessitates a painstaking attention to detail that is time consuming and expensive. One particular furniture factory purchase with which the author was intimately involved resulted in an agreement on January 11th; the contract was consummated on about April 1st with an approximate expenditure of one man year of executive talent. Moreover, there was nothing particularly unusual about the deal.

Another initial or investment cost involves work-in-process. It is not at all unusual for a medium-sized furniture factory ($5 million per year output) to have $2 million tied up in work-in-process inventories; the raw lumber inventory at Westfall alone is often in excess of $1 million. Similar work-in-process inventory is required in any manufacturing concern with a long processing or lead time.

The costs of training a new work force with all the attendant features of the learning curve often represent a major location cost. One of the primary reasons Baumritter has purchased existing furniture factories has been to capture existing work forces which can more readily adapt to the manufacture of their product than could untrained personnel. Clearly for some enterprises this cost is much more significant than for others. Electronic assembly required for television sets inherently requires less training than machine tool manufacture; location alternatives available to the former are considerably greater than those available to the latter.

The initial cost is borne by the enterprise in making the adjustment to a new location. This is particularly true within Baumritter and other multifactory companies when an additional factory is added to the system. Transportation costs and methods necessarily must change, standardized methods of operation including quality control procedures and furniture construction methods must be instituted, and the division of activities among the now larger set of factories must be rebalanced.

Operating Cost Criteria

Within the general classification of operating costs, one typically needs to consider labor wage rates, productivity indices, supplies, utilities, support activities, raw materials, and transportation costs. These factors have to be considered with a time dimension. Thus for example, in the 1950s many furniture, textile, and other kinds of manufacturing firms migrated toward the southern part of the United States based upon the attraction of cheaper labor. To determine whether the labor cost was indeed going to be lower necessitated an adjustment for productivity. Even so, labor costs in the south were attractive at that time; but the labor cost advantage eroded through the 1960s as more and more firms moved south. At the present time, Baumritter feels that their unit labor costs in the south are roughly comparable to those in Vermont.

On the other hand, genuine differences in labor costs do exist. The author knows of an electric equipment manufacturer in California who was able to cut the cost of assembling circuit breakers 30% by shipping the parts to Puerto Rico. The same firm later moved a portion of its manufacturing operation to Mississippi. In both cases, the major criterion was reduced operating costs, but the initial cost aspects of the move were also desirable; large tax savings, free land, and very favorable bonded indebtedness were provided by governmental development units.

An availability of suppliers and supporting companies can also be a significant location factor. A major corporation can often draw suppliers, but a furniture manufacturer in Wyoming might find it difficult to subcontract and to receive professional services from suppliers of finishing materials or tool manufacturers. Lack of supplier support could be fatal; at a minimum, extra supplies and longer lead times would be required.

The availability of raw materials in close proximity is another potentially major location criterion. An additional reason for the southern migration of furniture companies was the availability of large timber resources. However, this availability was more important to some firms than to others, particularly those using large amounts of core wood for veneer construction.

To a large extent, nearness to raw materials is a surrogate for transportation costs. Clearly a heavy or bulky raw material which is converted to a relatively much less heavy or bulky material would call for a location near the source of supply. For some products this is not the case; oil refining can be near the market since little volume is lost in the refining process.

The costs of transporting manufactured goods to the final consumer often represent 20% or more of the total cost. Clearly this cost is affected by the location of facilities. Although location of the manufacturing plant itself influences this cost, the location of various warehouses, wholesalers, and retailers has an even more profound influence. Within Baumritter, the existence and location of orbit or regional warehouses and field warehouses are partially based upon transportation and related cost issues; but equally important criteria for warehousing in the company are related to marketing considerations.

One of the more important functions provided by warehouses in some enterprises is that of "mixing." A multifactory company often achieves shipping economies by pooling decentralized factory outputs in one or more warehouses which in turn ship orders that are larger than those possible direct from the factories to customers (we will see in Chapter 18 that mixing is the most important function provided by a wholesale grocer).

Marketing Criteria

An analysis of the transportation cost minimization criterion leads naturally to the third major category of location issues—marketing implications. Location of manufacturing facilities in close proximity to market needs is exemplified by oil refining, automobile assembly, and the upholstered goods portion of the furniture industry. Although the transportation economies of shipping automotive parts as compared to completed automobiles is obvious, an additional reason for location near to final demand is based upon the ability to react quickly to changes in demand. In the oil industry, Middle Eastern crude oil could be refined in the Middle East and shipped to the United States as refined products, but location of refineries on the East Coast allows for immediate shifts in the supplies of refined products to meet market needs, e.g., an extended cold period requiring greater fuel oil supplies. Similarly, the automobile assembly plant can produce green cars when green cars are selling well, and the upholstered furniture plant can custom match fabrics to specifications.

Proximity to market is important to many manufacturing concerns; it is vital in the location of retail facilities and for some facilities designed to support retail operations. For the majority of manufacturing companies, contact with the ultimate consumer must be located near that consumer. It is necessary to identify who the consumers and potential consumers are, where they are concentrated, where a facility can best satisfy their needs, and how such a facility should be designed. Clearly the location of Baumritter's Ethan Allen Showcase stores demonstrates an attempt to design a superior contact with the ultimate consumer. Automobile agencies, gasoline stations, drug stores, banks, and an almost endless number of other multiple retailing and industrial supplying firms are located in ways to support and encourage marketing goals.

Warehouses and other channels of physical distribution used to support contacts with final consumers similarly are influenced strongly by marketing criteria. However, it is terribly important to view these entities in functional terms, rather than to assume that necessary support can only be provided by one configuration of supporting entities.

Subjective Criteria

Many of the factors discussed above will require subjective judgments as to their anticipated future values. Thus for example, the operating cost advantage of lower wage rates can disappear if enough competition comes in, or low real estate taxes might be based upon a present paucity of community services. Subjective estimates are almost always required for expectations about the supply of labor, local attitudes toward the firm, or the extent of labor unrest. Factors influencing the desirability of a particular location insofar as moving people in include availability of housing, appearance of the area, recreational possibilities, and proximity to cultural activities.

A more basic subjectivity can also have a profound impact on location decisions. If the corporation president is fond of Colorado, the firm is apt to be located in Colorado. Baumritter's president talks of an early love for Vermont, and the majority of Baumritter's production comes from that state. Another executive in the company has wanted to purchase a plant somewhere in Maine. Although this may make location decisions sound as if they are solely based on "black cigar" models, this is not the case. I doubt whether Baumritter would consider building a plant in Nevada no matter how much someone in the company likes the desert air. The more objective criteria delineated above tend to create a solution space or range of possible alternatives, and when those alternatives are somewhat equal, decisions can be based upon increasingly subjective criteria.

For Baumritter, a new factory must be located in some reasonable proximity to an existing regional shipping center, it would be desirable to be located along the route of a back haul, the site should facilitate visits by staff personnel to more than one factory per trip, and the basic components of production (labor, lumber, machinery, supplies) must be readily available. The net result coupled with a desire to minimize initial investments, usually means that the number of choices open to Baumritter for the purchase of a new plant is not large.

As location decisions approach the marketplace, e.g., regional warehouses and field warehouses, actual choices tend to be made on even more objective criteria. The "buy 'em cheap" approach is not as possible, operating costs are less subjective, and locations tend to be based upon hard data such as the movement of goods between origins and final destinations, and a specified level of customer service.

Foreign Locations

The basic reasons for considering foreign locations are not different from those stated above. However, additional opportunities and constraints come into being, and the dynamic nature of some opportunities serves to better illustrate the location decision process. Foreign location is largely based upon the economic law of comparative advantage. One naturally envisions ten-cent-per-hour laborers in Asia or some far corner of the world, and such places do exist (a former student from the small island of Mauritius in the South Indian Ocean was interested in attracting industry with that approximate wage scale). However, wage rates in many countries that historically have been low (e.g., Japan) have increased substantially over the last decade.

Low wage rates are not the only variable to be considered. Substantial differences in productivity are common and must be reconciled. Also, labor cost is obviously only one factor in production. Foreign locations naturally tend to favor labor-intensive commodities with a low relative cost of transportation. We all recognize transistor radios and other electronic devices as representative, but recent possibilities include computer key-punching; Baumritter purchases carved wooden panels, leaded glass and rush seats from foreign suppliers.

Foreign manufacture for United States consumption typically necessitates increased lead times and work-in-process inventories. In Chapter 19 we will examine the impact of such increases on manufacturing operations.

Up to this point we have considered foreign location for the manufacture of goods to be consumed in the United States, and no distinctions were made between purchasing from the foreign supplier and ownership of a foreign subsidiary. Many foreign location decisions are based upon marketing criteria and an interest in profitability based on consumption rather than production at the foreign location. The opportunities attendant to developing markets in foreign countries often are superior to those in the United States. Examples include the market for central heating equipment in England, the Western European market for appliances, and foreign business use of computers.

Many foreign markets are appealing for the use of equipment which has become technically obsolete in the United States. The DC 3 may still be the best aircraft for many developing countries, even though nationalistic pride often calls for jumbo jets.

Problems connected with ownership of a foreign subsidiary can be significant. Countries vary in their receptiveness to United States foreign investments; Japan is quite reluctant to permit outside investment with a maximum allowed foreign ownership of 49% in any company. Mexico is also tight with many legal conditions necessary before entry is approved. Other countries such as Costa Rica are very receptive to foreign investments.

Operations in Western Europe, Japan, or South Africa tend to be quite different than those in less developed countries. Different legal codes, inflationary currencies, and the specter of expropriation are some of the hard facts involved in undertaking foreign operations. Softer facts that can be even more devastating center around differing cultures, or the environmental assumptions which have been transplanted from the American value system. Examples range from the frequent number of holidays in Italy and the lack of the Protestant ethic to tales related by my colleague Wayne Broehl of fishing fleets which quickly became used for smuggling instead of fishing.

A somewhat less spectacular example of poor environmental assumptions involved a Baumritter purchase of English made furniture; lack of central heating in England leads to an 18% relative humidity standard which results in severe cracking in American homes. The moral to the story seems to be that important foreign opportunities exist and profitable multinational firms may become plentiful, but mistakes are sure to be made along the way.

A Systems Context

The location of an enterprise system or subsystem can be quite dynamic. What represents the best combination to satisfy the criteria at one time well may not be the best combination at a later time. It is difficult for a firm to know of location possibilities; the kinds of encouragement offered by regional commissions and individual areas change, are not well publicized, and are often subject to some negotiation. It is for these reasons that many enterprises contemplating location decisions employ consulting firms who specialize in location. Similarly, some areas employ consultants to find firms whose operations are particularly well suited to their advantages.

In a more subtle sense, there is the whole process of location problem cognizance. For most firms, the benefits from location changes can go unrecognized for long periods of time. It is simply easier to stay with an existing pattern, especially when no personnel have been budgeted to consider changes in location.

Although reasons for location changes can be dramatic such as the discovery of a labor supply in Mauritius or extremely favorable conditions in a new plant in the Ozarks, the location problem is affected by many of the decisions within the firm. Changes in the amount of customer service or support given to retailers by a manufacturing firm can lead to implied changes in distribution and the locations of various activities within the distribution system. Since one of the major functions of a distribution system is to provide place utility, movement of the manufacturing operation into closer proximity to the market might be an alternative solution to the provision of improved customer service.

Another major function served by the distribution system is to provide time utility. That is, there is an inherent time dimension to the provision of goods to the ultimate consumer. Entities in the distribution system often exist because of this time dimension; e.g., Baumritter field warehouses were established to provide delivery to final consumers within a week after purchase instead of eight to twelve week delivery from a factory. The important point to note about this problem solution, however, is that our interest is in the customer service criterion of one week delivery rather than in having field warehouses per se.

By changing the methods of production planning and inventory control, it is sometimes possible to achieve important changes in customer service criteria without some typical distribution system entities. Locations of production activities and subsequent distribution channels should not be considered independently. The consideration can be enhanced by an understanding of the basic materials flow from raw material to final consumer and the kinds of criteria which are pertinent to this flow. Materials flow is the subject of Chapters 17 to 21, and we will see location of facility issues being considered again at that time in the light of an improved perspective.

LOCATION MODELS

There is no model which can accommodate all of the issues described above in a rigorous manner. The number of issues tends to be large, and tradeoffs of criteria such as local attitudes toward the firm with worker training costs are difficult to make. Rigorous location models tend to focus upon the more objective data, with check list approaches used for subjective considerations. In this way, rank on objective measures can be determined and thereafter the other considerations can be assessed in a qualitative way.

In the determination of objective cost measures, many firms find themselves evaluating only a small number of possibilities, so that hand calculation of each alternative is feasible. For example, if a publishing firm contemplating a Western warehouse narrowed the choice down to Los Angeles, San Francisco, Salt Lake City, or Seattle, many of the expected cost ramifications could be calculated by hand.

On the other hand, as the scope of analysis increases, we will find that representation in a computer will be more desirable. If our "simple" warehouse location decision described above included the evaluation of different assumptions or volume changes over the years, it would be desirable to not evaluate those assumptions by hand. If we relaxed the choice of actual locations somewhat, we might like to evaluate many more cities (e.g., Fresno, California or Las Vegas, Nevada). Complicating our analysis still further are decisions as to whether all West Coast orders flow through the facility or whether some large orders are filled directly from the factory. When the scope of the problem includes not just one factory and one additional warehouse but many factories and many warehouses, the complexity goes up substantially and the benefits of a digital simulation model increase.

The Heinz Company Simulation

A pioneering effort in the use of digital simulation models for location decisions by Shycon and Maffei describes a consulting assignment at the H. J. Heinz Company.* The approach used in this study has since been applied to many firms with multiple factories and/or multiple warehousing operations.

The Heinz operations involve geographically dispersed factories near major growing areas and warehouses located to serve national consumption patterns. During the 1950s Heinz faced changes in those consumption patterns for typical reasons such as shifts in population; a more fundamental change derived from a rapid growth of independent grocery wholesaling firms which replaced direct deliveries to stores from firms such as Heinz.

As a result of these forces, the pattern of orders experienced by Heinz had grown toward fewer but larger orders and a total increase in volume. By 1960, more than 95% of domestic sales were accounted for by approximately 4,000 distributors, chains, and institutional suppliers. The company reduced the number of warehouses from 68 to 43 between 1957 and 1959, and thereafter called in a consulting firm to assess further changes. A digital simulation model was designed to evaluate the feasibility of various warehouse location patterns. The final recommendation was to go to a network of 32 warehouses, some in existing locations and some in new locations. The expected annual cost savings were approximately $250,000.

---

*Harvey N. Shycon, and R. B. Maffei, "Simulation—Tool for Better Distribution," *Harvard Business Review* **38**, no. 6 (November-December 1960): 65–75.

The Heinz Model

The model was used to evaluate ten alternative warehouse location patterns. The ten patterns were specified by Heinz users and were not determined by the computer model. The model could, however, be used to evaluate "what if" questions such as might be based upon moving a Texas warehouse to New Orleans.

In order to make the evaluations, it was necessary to collect data on customer orders; their size, pattern, frequency, mix of products, and type of delivery mode. It was also necessary to estimate transportation and warehousing costs and to establish the originating factory for shipments of various commodities to particular warehouses and customers.

Patterns of customer orders were developed as a function of the type of business performed by the customer and his location; all customers in a given geographical area and type of business were assumed to have a consumption pattern that was independent of annual purchases. Transportation costs were estimated on the basis of linear distances between factories, warehouses, and customers; and the type of transportation means and cost for that particular geographic region. Warehousing costs were estimated for each warehouse as a function of the dollar volume of sales serviced; a fixed plus variable linear relationship was established based upon historical company data.

The final model was validated by predicting total distribution costs for previous years and warehousing configurations with small percentage errors (1.5% for the previous year and 3.5% for the last year with 68 warehouses). Our normal diligence to percentage calculations, however, is again appropriate; the expected $250,000 annual saving is less than 2% of total distribution costs.

Use of the model is not described in the published report. Heinz received a working program that presumably could be used to evaluate many patterns of warehouse locations. In a Harvard Business School case describing the simulation, it is stated that Heinz management felt it necessary to make adjustments for circumstances not reflected in the model such as inadequate trucking service for one recommended location, special tax and labor considerations, and instances where linear cost assumptions for trucking rates were substantially in error.* There is no structural reason why the model should not allow for these kinds of conditions to be added and subsequently evaluated.

Extensions

The Heinz Company situation in some way is less complex than that faced by other firms. Catsup made from California grown tomatoes is very likely

---

*H. J. Heinz Company Simulation, ICH 9M78, Intercollegiate Case Clearing House, Boston, Mass.

to be manufactured in California. For other firms, choices on the location of factories and allocations of items to be made within factories is much more capable of being changed.

The model used for the Heinz company simulation readily permits one to examine changes in factory and warehouse locations. For an example, the author was told that the model clearly demonstrated large payoffs from catsup manufacturing on the East Coast.

At a more fundamental level the basis of predicting customer ordering patterns ignores the ability of a company like Heinz to influence those ordering patterns. The general methodology used in the simulation is to categorize customers on the basis of dollars of sales per year, number of orders per year, and product diversity ordered. In Chapter 19, we will see that firms such as those who order from Heinz do so with computer systems which result in orders that are highly influenced by supplier discount structures. It would be interesting to undertake an investigation of what operating costs and benefits are associated with different kinds of ordering patterns, and thereafter attempt to identify possible Heinz policies that would result in those order patterns. The fact is, Heinz has considerable control over the character or pattern of orders received, and the importance of this feedback should be recognized. In Chapter 21 we will consider a modeling approach which recognizes the extent to which a firm can control matters of this kind and in a larger sense its own destiny.

All of these extensions and any implied criticisms of the Heinz simulation study necessarily must be tempered by recognizing the intervening time between the 1970s and 1959 when the study was completed. Let us now turn to the descendant of the original Heinz model.

The LOGISTEK Model*

The Heinz Company study was the first of many location studies carried out by Harvey Shycon and various associates. In the course of these subsequent studies, a natural evolution has occurred in the underlying methodology. The model is now called LOGISTEK.

The most important evolutionary change has been to an adaptive model. That is, where the Heinz model was primarily concerned with the laborious calculations of evaluating a fixed set of location choices, the LOGISTEK model also iterates in an adaptive fashion to find good location patterns.

The typical procedure for LOGISTEK is to start with perhaps 100 warehouses when the expected number is somewhere around 30. The

---

*The author is grateful for descriptions of this model and its applications furnished by Harvey N. Shycon and Robert L. Schuldenfrei of Applied Decision Systems, Inc., Wellesley Hills, Massachusetts.

model can assign customers to warehouses in several ways, but for ease for exposition let us say that minimum distance from warehouses to customers is used. Let us express these distances as a matrix of the distances between warehouses and customers. When all customer orders for the period under study have been assigned to particular warehouses, the total cost can be computed. This cost will involve transportation costs as well as variable warehousing costs, but will also involve an allocation of fixed costs. When the total volume for each warehouse is computed, the fixed cost in that warehouse can be allocated to this volume.

The distance matrix given above can now be recalculated as a cost matrix. Each cell will contain the total cost of serving each customer from each warehouse. Because of efficiency differences in warehousing as well as differences in volume, the minimum cost way to ship may not be the minimum distance.

The model now repeats the assignment process but uses the minimum shipment cost as the criterion for assigning customers to warehouses. After all customers have again been assigned, new warehouse total volumes result and new allocations of fixed costs are made. The result is an updated total shipping cost matrix that once more can be used to allocate customers to warehouses.

The iterative process is continued until a convergence upon a warehouse location pattern is established. As shipping volume is taken from one warehouse and given to another, the unit cost of the former tends to increase since fixed costs must be allocated over fewer units. Conversely, the unit cost of the latter tends to go down as more volume is handled. The result is for some warehouses to be driven out of existence and for others to increase in size until some pattern is reached where shipping cost and warehousing cost tradeoffs are quite good.

At the end of this process, a final location pattern has still not been achieved. What has been achieved is the establishment of the approximate number of warehouses needed for this particular firm. If 100 warehouses were reduced to say 25, we still do not know whether we have the *right* 25. Furthermore, since the minimum cost combination will be at the bottom of a rather flat U-shaped curve, some deviations can be accommodated with small incremental costs.

In actual practice, the LOGISTEK model is usually run for about 12 different initial combinations of many warehouses which are reduced to a lesser number. At that point, the 25 or so remaining warehouses in each of the 12 runs need to be carefully scrutinized by users in order to suggest alternative possibilities. For example, in one case a Miami warehouse was continually closed down in favor of a New York warehouse and a New Orleans warehouse; the primary reason was that the Miami warehouse was not close to any demand except in Miami, but establishment of a warehouse in Tallahassee was a good choice.

In actual company situations, about 20 or 25 more computer runs are required after the initial 12 or so which identify the basic location patterns. It is essential for users to be intimately involved in this stage of the analysis, since it is at this stage that cost and customer service criteria can be traded off. For example, in one study it was found that although a Houston warehouse was more expensive than satisfying Houston demand from Dallas, the difference was only $5,000 per year but with a marked improvement in delivery time and customer support.

Although the iterative feature of the model is an important advantage, like all models it has inherent dangers. In one example, warehouses existed in both Baltimore and Washington. Both warehouses were shut down in favor of a New York warehouse, but a single warehouse between Baltimore and Washington was even better. The model has to be tempered by judgment and requires user involvement. We also must be quite careful that allocated fixed costs represent potentially incremental costs. Nevertheless, the model is a powerful tool that permits much more sophisticated tradeoffs of important logistics costs.

The cost understanding gained with the model can be quite significant. Marginal cost data similar to linear programming shadow prices highlight differences in public versus private warehouses, economies of scale, fixed versus variable cost tradeoffs, etc.

An additional interesting application of the LOGISTEK model is to take the resultant set of warehouse locations and feed them to an existing, proposed or purely hypothetical set of factories. The same kind of production fixed and variable cost structure will result in adaptive assignment of warehousing needs to factories. The process of assigning customers to warehouses and thereafter warehouses to factories can feedback on warehousing choices. The net result is a model which begins to examine the overall product movement in a company. In Chapter 21, we will see how important such an examination can be.

LAYOUT PROBLEMS

As noted above, the layout problem conceptually is similar to the location problem in that both involve placement of facilities, and that placement is dependent upon the relative location of other facilities which interact with the facility to be placed. As typically specified, the layout problem tends to be more interactive but less global in criteria considered than the location problem. That is, layout problems usually involve simultaneous interactions among many facilities, but do so on the basis of a set of criteria which presumes a set of products or services, methods for creating those products or services, sales volumes for the products or services, manufacturing capacities, and other important operations management activities which are related.

Job Shops versus Assembly Lines

A distinction is often made between two basic production strategies, the job shop and the assembly line. In job shop production, like activities are grouped together, such as all lathes in one department or the molders at Westfall being located in close proximity. Assembly line production, on the other hand, involves placement of equipment wherever needed for the subsequent conversion stage of a product; examples include Westfall's proposed conveyorized chair-building line, the rough mill, the finishing room, and automobile assembly lines. As can be seen from the Westfall case, most companies tend to have mixtures of the two basic production strategies, and the mixtures tend to reflect the different kinds of criteria sets which operate for the two approaches. Each of these basic production approaches implies a method of layout, and job shop, process, or functional layout is contrasted with assembly line, flow, or product layout.

Job shop layout with its groupings of similar machines allows for more diverse products to be manufactured since any part can be sent to as few or many conversion stages as required. The job shop also allows for each machine to be utilized somewhat independently of other machines; this in turn permits a lower investment in equipment. Job shop layout also permits better utilization of manpower and the development of more general capabilities since the man is not tied to a fixed rate of production and a relatively fixed task. Proper utilization of manpower and equipment in job shops, however, requires work-in-process inventories so that each operation can be quasi-independent of the others; cost of inventories and resultant long manufacturing lead times need to be traded off against better utilization of productive capacity.

Line or product layout, on the other hand, results in reduced work-in-process, reduced handling of material, shorter manufacturing lead times, more limited production scheduling and supervisory efforts, greater job specialization, the possibility of reduced training and less expensive labor, and possible reductions in damage. The line layout achieves these benefits at the cost of flexibility, and potential inefficiencies in the use of individual men and/or machines. Achievement of balanced resources becomes the major criterion.

The job shop approach to production tends to be used for more diverse products, and where intensive utilization of equipment offsets the disadvantages associated with long lead times, larger work-in-process inventories, etc. These tradeoffs are clearly seen in furniture production. The finish mill at Westfall is essentially a job shop; considerable diversity in configuration of wooden parts is achieved by repetitive operations on a few basic types of machines. On the other hand, as soon as items are assembled, they are put into the finishing room and completed on an assembly line basis. Diversity of product configuration influences the times for finishing operations such as applying stain, wiping, etc., but the *sequence* of steps is the same for all items. The same thing can be said about the rough mill portion of the factory. Although different parts are being cut, all parts pass through the same series of operations from cut off saw, to rip saw, to panel gluing; it is only at the finish mill stage that the flow of each part becomes determined by the desired final configuration.

It is also worth noting that the Westfall finish mill is where the most expensive equipment is required; utilization of these machines and their operators is relatively more important than in assembly and finishing areas where much less expensive equipment and less highly trained employees are used.

Both of the major types of layout involve movement of materials to men and machines. Although the vast majority of production conversion processes are based on these two layout types, it is worth noting that other possibilities exist; moving men and machines to material in a fixed position such as for building a ship represents another kind of production strategy, but one that is relatively rare and that typically does not involve complex layout decisions.

JOB SHOP LAYOUT MODELS

Several models have been proposed for the relative location of facilities or work centers in a job shop. Applications include not only machine shops, but motion picture studios, maintenance areas, banks, hospitals, and offices of many types. The objective function is typically stated in terms of minimization of some cost that varies as a function of the distances between system components and the flows which must travel those distances. We will begin our investigation by examining these terms as they might apply to Westfall; subsequently, we will be able to see how they apply to other examples, most notably offices.

The Westfall Finish Mill

Table 15.1 is a list of activities performed in the finish mill and the associated areas for those activities.

Figure 15.1 shows a block layout of the ten rough mill activities. If data were collected on the flow of material between each activity or department, we could attempt to locate each department so that those

Table 15.1

Activity	Area (sq.ft.).
A Dovetailing	300
B Mortising	450
C Drills	600
D Sharpers	500
E Lathes	1625
F Band saws	875
G Double end tenoners	1350
H Board and panel inventory	1400
I Planers	1750
J Molders	1050
Total	9900

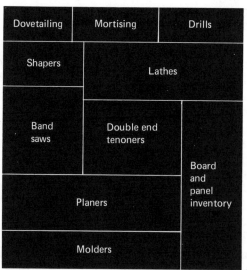

Fig. 15.1 Layout of the Westfall Finish Mill.

with greatest flow between them would be adjacent, while departments without significant flow were separated by greater distances.

The CRAFT Model*

The Computerized Relative Allocation of Facilities Technique (CRAFT) is designed to aid in the analysis of layout problems of the job shop variety. The complexity of such problems is determined by the number of activities or departments and the relationships among those departments. Even with only ten departments, good solutions to the Westfall finish mill layout problem are difficult to achieve without an evaluative model. Moreover, the model must be more than a technique to evaluate all possibilities; for only ten departments, a high speed computer would require several days running to exhaustively examine all possibilities; when the number of departments is increased to twenty or thirty all the computers in the world working for one hundred years could not enumerate the possibilities.

The CRAFT model takes as inputs a spatial array similar to Fig. 15.1, a matrix of flow between all departments, and a matrix of cost to reflect differences in material handling methods when significant. The program begins by calculating the centroids of each department and measuring the distances between pairs of centroids on rectangular coordinates (the assumption being that products and people move in aisles or corridors rather than directly over the straight line distance). The matrix of flow is weighted by the cost matrix, and the resultant cost weighted flow matrix is multiplied by the matrix of distances previously calculated. Summation of the resultant matrix yields the estimated material handling cost for the initial or starting block layout.

The model attempts to make improvements in the cost by testing the implications of exchanging pairs of departments. For example, what would happen to total cost if the lathe department was located where the present double end tenoner department is located and vice versa?

The model examines all pairwise exchanges (ten departments = 10 $\times 9/2 = 45$ possibilities) and picks the largest indicated cost reduction. The model then switches the locations of the indicated departments, and if an actual cost reduction is indeed made, the exchange is permanently made. The program then recalculates the distance matrix and repeats the evaluative process. Iteration after iteration is performed until no pairwise exchange is expected to reduce total cost.

The model can also consider three-way exchanges with a small increase in computation time; the possibilities considered in each iteration

*E. S. Buffa, G. C. Armour, and T. E. Vollmann, "Allocating Facilities with CRAFT," *Harvard Business Review*, **42**, no. 2 (March-April 1964): 136–158.

Fig.15.2 CRAFT initial layout of the Westfall Finish Mill.

$= N \times (N-1) \times (N-2)/(2 \times 3)$. Up to forty departments can be accommodated, and computer run times are often less than one minute.

An additional feature allows for any department or departments to be fixed in location and not moved irrespective of indicated materials handling cost savings. The feature allows shipping and receiving docks to not be placed in the middle of a plant, for equipment located in special areas (e.g. high bay or overhead crane) to remain in those areas, and for the incremental costs of subjective constraints to be sequentially evaluated.

Figure 15.2 is a CRAFT representation of the Westfall finish mill. When the model was given this initial block layout and matrices of flow and cost data (not shown), the cost was estimated to be $2524.68.

When this layout was evaluated by the CRAFT model, four changes or iterations were made to reduce the cost. The final layout is shown as Fig. 15.3.

```
 1  A A A A B B B B B B B E E E D D D D D
 2  A     A B           B E   E D       D
 3  A A A A B B B B B B B E   E D       D
 4  I I I I I I E E E E E     E D D D D D
 5  I     I E                 E G G G G G
 6  I     I E                 E G         G
 7  I     I E             E G             G
 8  I     I E             E G             G
 9  I     I E E E E       E G             G
10  L     I C C C C E     E G             G
11  I     I C         C E E G             G
12  I     I C         C E E G             G
13  I     I C         C E E G   G G G G
14  I     I C C C C C E E G G H H H H
15  I I I I I I I I I I I I I I H H H H
16  I F F F F F F F F F H H H H H     H
17  F             F H                 H
18  F             F H                 H
19  F F F F F F F F F F H H H H H     H
20  J J J J J J J J J J J J J J J H   H
21  J                         J H     H
22  J J J J J J J J J J J J J J H H H H
TOTAL COST    1847.90
```

Fig. 15.3 CRAFT final layout of the Westfall Finish Mill.

CRAFT has been applied to many real world problems and is used by industrial engineering departments and consulting firms. However, as is true with all models, one must be wary of the assumptions underlying the model. Let us now examine some of these.

Layout Configuration

The CRAFT model assumes that all flow within a department originates at the centroid of that department. The problems that can result from this assumption were dramatically illustrated when a group of students was given the Westfall finish mill problem as an assignment. Specifically, they were asked to find a good layout without the CRAFT model and told that grades for the assignment would be based upon their layouts as evaluated by CRAFT. Most solutions were not as good as the CRAFT solution given above as Fig. 15.3, but some were slightly better and a few were spectacularly better. Out of 84 student solutions, 6 had cost values of $766.68,

```
 I  E  E  E  E  C  I  I  G  G  G  G  H  H  H  H  H  J  J
 2  E           E  C  I  I  G        G  H  H        H  J  J
 3  E           E  C  I     I  G     G  F  B  H  H  J     J
 4  E           E  C  I     I  G  G  F  F  B  H  H  J     J
 5  E           E  C  I     I  G  G  F  F  B  H  H  J     J
 6  A  E        E  C  I     I  G  G  F  F  B  H  H  J  J  J
 7  A  E  E  C  C  I     I  G  G  F  F  B  H  H  J  D  D
 8  A  E  E  C  I        I  G  G  F  F  B  H  H  J  D  D
 9  A  E  E  C  I        I  G  G  F  F  B  H  H  J  D  D
IO  A  E  E  C  I        I  G  G  F  F  B  H  H  J  D  D
II  A  E  E  C  I        I  G  G  F  F  B  H  H  J  D  D
I2  A  E  E  C  I        I  G  G  F  F  B  H  H  J  D  D
I3  A  E  E  C  I        I  G  G  F  F  B  H· H  J  D  D
I4  A  E  E  C  I        I  G  G  F  F  B  H  H  J  D  D
I5  A  E  E  C  I        I  G  G  F  F  B  H  H  J  D  D
I6  A  E  E  C  I        I  G  G  F  F  B  H  H  J  D  D
I7  A  E  E  C  C  I     I  G  G  F  F  B  H  H  J  J  J
I8  E           E  C  I     I  G  G  F  F  B  H  H  J     J
I9  E           E  C  I     I  G  G  F  F  B  H  H  J     J
20  E           E  C  I  I  G     G  F  F  B  H  H  J     J
2I  E           E  C  I  I  G        G  H  H        H  J  J
22  E  E  E  E  C  I  I  G  G  G  G  H  H  H  H  H  J  J
TOTAL COST    766.68
```

Fig. 15.4 Strip layout.

$985.62, $987.50, $1073.33, $1073.33, and $1086.40, respectively. There was no other solution below $1600.00.

The low cost layouts all followed a common approach. All departments were represented as either long strips or dumbbell shapes; all department centroids were located in close proximity. Figure 15.4 shows the lowest cost layout.

I do not think that the layout shown in Fig. 15.4 repudiates the validity of the CRAFT model. It does, however, illustrate a potential weakness that users should understand. The final result as measured by the objective function is simply not independent of the configuration of the subdepartments; as the subdepartments become increasingly different from perfect squares, the approximation of all movement as originating at centroids tends to lose validity. Let us now turn to some even more fundamental issues.

Surrogate Criteria

The sole criterion of evaluation used in CRAFT and most other job shop layout models is the minimization of materials handling cost which is assumed to be a linear function of the distance between departments or groupings of similar activities. Some heroic assumptions are involved in using this sole criteria for evaluation of layout "goodness." Other criteria affect layout decisions, the basis for grouping individuals or machine tools tends to be somewhat arbitrary, the incremental nature of materials-handling cost is open to question in many layout investigations, the data used are typically historical rather than anticipated, the interaction of the layout problem with other organizational issues and operations management problems tends to be ignored, and empirical investigation indicates that most decisions are made on a piecemeal basis rather than on the basis of a thoroughgoing analysis of the total layout of the organization.

Additional criteria include any forces for relative or absolute placement, from the desire to separate inflammable painting materials and welding to the president's wish for the corner office overlooking the lake. Some empirical work done by the author in a defense contracting plant lead to the realization that the major layout criterion was image—all new equipment was placed where visiting generals would see it. A beautification program involved building a sculptured cement block wall in front of large doors to the maintenance area, so that these "ugly" doors would not be seen from the street; in the six months that followed, an interior wall had to be removed twice to get equipment into the area.

In other situations, use of the materials-handling cost criterion can be inappropriate because these costs cannot be assigned to particular product movements except arbitrarily. Also, materials-handling cost that varies as a function of the distance between system components may not be significant relative to other enterprise costs, and the weightings used to reflect existing methods of materials handling may be improperly constraining future materials-handling methods.

Problems with data other than cost also exist. The flow of materials is typically gathered from operations sheets which show the sequential nature of each part or product conversion. Unfortunately, organizations typically have operation sheets for products made in the past and the assumption that future product mixes will be the same can be tenuous. Moreover, the sequence data thus accumulated tend to be based upon routing conventions that are often possible to change, and the source of these data all too often is from a low-level clerical operation within the company.*

*For a more thoroughgoing exposition of these issues, see Thomas E. Vollmann and E. S. Buffa, "The Facilities Layout Problem in Perspective," *Management Science* 12, no. 10 (June 1966): B450–B468.

Additional Models

Other models for the job shop layout problem have been proposed in the literature; the CRAFT model, however, is the most widely used at this time. Most of the others tend to be more of interest to academic research, and a thoroughgoing comparison of these techniques is beyond the scope of this book.*

A brief discussion of some of these alternative solution procedures, however, will permit an increased understanding of heuristic problem approaches. It will also allow us to better understand a model that is consistent with user-oriented approaches to problem solving as well as our interest in models useful for nonmanufacturing technologies.

Although the CRAFT model does not produce optimum solutions, as noted in our Chapter 3 discussions of optima, the term is reserved for those situations where it is possible to prove that the very best solution has been obtained. The CRAFT model is a heuristic procedure, and the word heuristic may be defined as "an appealing rule of thumb." The appealing rule of thumb in CRAFT is to make pairwise exchanges (and/or threeway exchanges) that reduce cost; at each iteration the greatest cost-reducing exchange is made until no further cost-reducing exchange can be made. Although the final result from the CRAFT model is quite good, there is always the possibility that an exchange of four or perhaps five departments simultaneously would reduce costs further.

Some work has been done which indicates that final solutions from heuristic procedures such as CRAFT tend to be within a few percentage points of the optimum. There are, however, other heuristics that can be used. Research indicates that these heuristics can produce results not essentially different from those based on pairwise exchanges, but can do so with significantly reduced costs of computation.

Although we earlier stated that many CRAFT runs could be made with less than one minute of computer time, the computation cost grows sharply as the number of departments is increased. Thus for a standard problem set, the heuristic embodied in CRAFT required approximately 40 seconds for a 20-department problem, 250 seconds for a 30-department problem, and 1050 seconds for a 40-department problem (Honeywell-General Electric 635). The author and some colleagues were interested in a real world problem with 121 departments; a more efficient heuristic was required.

Essentially, the best pairwise exchange heuristic is a brute force technique that does not make efficient use of information. The procedure creates a ranked table of all pairwise exchanges which might reduce cost, and then only utilizes the first entry in the table; for the next iteration,

---

*The interested reader should see C. E. Nugent, T. E. Vollmann, and J. Ruml, "An Experimental Comparison of Techniques for the Assignment of Facilities to Location," *Operations Research,* **16**, no. 1 (January-February 1968): 150–73.

the entire table is recomputed even though entries in the former table have high probability of being included in the subsequent table.

A heuristic suggested by Seehof and Evans does not go to the trouble of making tables of pairwise cost reductions and taking the largest entry in the table first; whenever any exchange is uncovered which will reduce costs, it is made.* Use of this heuristic results in many more exchanges being made, but the computation cost per exchange is low enough that results comparable to those based on the best exchange heuristic are achieved in substantially less time (12 seconds, 57 seconds, and 125 seconds for the 20, 30, and 40 department problems respectively).

Another heuristic proposed by Hillier and Connors utilizes problem information to obtain a subset of possible pairwise exchanges that are more likely to yield benefits. It determines the relative desirability for a department to unilaterally move to the right, to the left, up, or down from its present location. The procedure yields results that are again comparable, and with computation times substantially less than the best pairwise exchange heuristic but not as good as those obtained with making any improvement as it is discovered (23 seconds, 105 seconds, and 285 seconds for the 20, 30, and 40 department problems).

By combining the notion of a carefully collected subset with better utilization of calculated information and the use of a "quick and dirty" procedure after the major part of the cost reduction potential has been achieved, a new heuristic called ranked product was developed which again achieved solutions comparable to those of the other heuristics with reduced computation times (10 seconds, 35 seconds, and 85 seconds for the 20, 30, and 40 department problems respectively). When applied to the 121 department empirical problem, the heuristic achieved final solutions with approximately eight minutes of computer time.

Before going on to the 121 department empirical problem and the lessons implied, let us briefly return to the pursuit of optimum solutions and understand why the heuristic approach appears to be the only feasible real world alternative. The assignment of facilities to locations (layout) problem can be formulated in mathematical programming terms, but the resultant problem is computationally infeasible. Another alternative is to use a semienumerative or branch and bound method. This approach evaluates only a small subset of all possibilities, by calculating boundaries which indicate that major groups of solution possibilities cannot be better than one already known. The author and a colleague have developed such a model which can achieve optimum solutions for the 12-department problem in a small fraction of the time required for total enumeration. Unfortunately, the small fraction is still a large amount of computation

---

*J. M. Seehof and W. O. Evans, "Automated Layout Design Program," *The Journal of Industrial Engineering,* **18,** no. 12 (December 1967): 690–95.

time; total enumeration would require approximately one year and the branch and bound algorithm produces the optimum solution in approximately 7,000 seconds (the heuristic methods described above require less than five seconds). The algorithm was applied to 1/15 of the 15-department problem (an "easy" 1/15); solution required more than 200,000 seconds of computer time. At the commercial billing rates then in effect for that computer, the computation cost would be $80,000; if we assume that the other 14/15 would require equal time, it is fairly clear that the real world application of this approach is infeasible. The moral to the story is quite clear: the enormity of combinatorial problems is such that very small subsets are still very big problems, and heuristic procedures seem here to stay.

An Office Layout Model

The criterion of material-handling cost which is utilized in the job shop layout models can be broadened to encompass any linear measurement of desired proximity. In an office, a good analog can be found in the relative placement of people and equipment so that walking times are minimized and so that people who need to communicate to accomplish their jobs are located in close proximity.

If we collect data on the face-to-face contacts initiated by each individual in an office with each other individual and with significant pieces of equipment, e.g., Xerox, files, safe, or supply room, these data can be combined into a "flow matrix." A cost-weighting factor can be added for differences in wages. If a "block layout" is added, we now have the input data required for the CRAFT model. Unfortunately, however, distances in the CRAFT model are calculated on rectangular coordinates which would seem to require people walking through walls. Moreover, the CRAFT model cannot handle multiple stories.

The office layout model overcomes these problems by inputting a distance matrix rather than having distances computed internally. One can obtain distances from architectural drawings using a map mileage reader, and movements between floors can be accommodated. The model accepts a given set of locations for offices and makes changes in the assignment of people to offices so as to reduce total cost expressed in terms of personnel movement.

The original use of the model was for two office layouts, one with 33 "departments" (people and significant pieces of equipment) and the other for 121 departments. Significant savings were indicated in both cases, and the model is currently being used by architectural firms and layout consultants.*

---

*A more complete description will be found in T. E. Vollmann, C. E. Nugent, and R. L. Zartler, "A Computerized Model for Office Layout," *The Journal of Industrial Engineering,* **17**, no. 7 (July 1968): 321–27.

An interesting aspect of this initial application concerned the interactions between users and designers. The users were management personnel within the companies studied, as well as architects who were designing new quarters for prospective lessees of office space. The management personnel were quite interested in a model which made changes in office space less subjective; they also liked the idea of a layout based upon their own highly individual internal communication needs. The architectural firm used the model to augment their understanding of the organization's needs and the best layout to satisfy those needs.

The architects prepared layouts for prospective clients of the lesser based upon what the architectual firm thought the lessees needs would be. Use of the model clearly indicated that the architects' perception was often incorrect. In one case the architects reserved a corner office for a particular executive; the model consistently moved that man to a more central location, and "fixing" his location in the corner office always led to substantially higher costs. The architects thereafter redesigned the layout with a more commodious office placed centrally. Other improvements included several changes in the design of a secretarial and central file keeping area.

The end result was an interaction between model users and designers based upon an evaluative model which led to better understanding of the organization and its needs for facilities.

An Assessment

Those who use job shop layout models should understand the inherent assumptions and limitations of the models. Nevertheless, the layout of physical facilities can be enormously complex, and models which cope with this complexity can be terribly useful. Almost any layout problem will involve subjective criteria and considerations not represented in the formal layout model. For this reason, it is important to again consider the total modeling environment and evolution driven by user criteria. Formal layout models often can allow a user to sequentially examine the effects of various subjective changes, so that tradeoffs of incremental cost and subjective improvement criteria can be accomplished.

DETAILED LAYOUT MODELS

The job shop layout models considered above are concerned with the relative location of departments or grouped activities, not with the detailed placement of components within the department. Within each department, each facility must be placed within the total prescribed area.

Two-Dimensional Templates

The most commonly used model for detailed layout is the two-dimensional template. Use of this model is basically the same whether arranging the

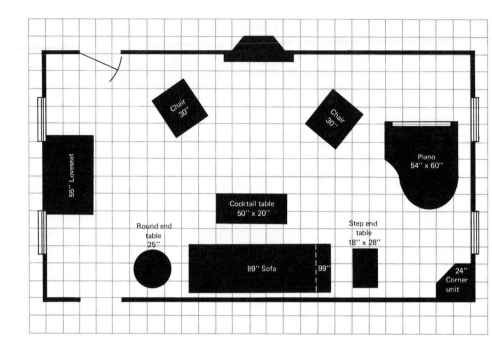

Fig. 15.5 Ethan Allen decorating templates.

molders in Westfall's finish mill or placing furniture in a living room. Those of us with ambitious mothers grew up with firsthand knowledge of one way to attack the problem: trial and error. A better method is found in the back of Baumritter's 350 page catalogue, the *Ethan Allen Treasury of American Traditional Interiors.*

Pages of graph paper where one fourth inch equals one foot can be used to draw the boundaries of any room, and two-dimensional templates for Ethan Allen furniture can be arranged within the room. Figure 15.5 shows this approach applied to the author's living room.

Similar models are used by the interior decorating specialists at Baumritter for the placement of furniture within coordinated room plans for Ethan Allen showcase stores. In these models, an additional feature is the use of small pieces of sample fabrics pinned to the rooms so that color coordination can be enhanced.

Two-dimensional templates on standard scales are available from equipment manufacturers, with widespread use for placement of machine tools. Templates for machine tools often include added dimensions to insure adequate spacing for parts of the equipment which extend such as tables on a milling machine.

At one time, two-dimensional templates were the most sophisticated modeling procedure used in the analysis of layout problems. Today, however, the relative placement of major departments, machine centers, or personnel are usually studied with the aid of analytic procedures before actual detailed layout.

LINE LAYOUT MODELS

Detailed layout procedures similar to those illustrated in Fig. 15.5 will be useful for arranging facilities in an assembly line layout. However, the relative location of facilities or block layout problem does not exist as it does for the job shop. The placement of facilities is dominated by the sequence of operations necessary to accomplish the objectives of the line. The suspension system for an automobile is installed before the body, a cafeteria customer picks up a tray before selecting food, and ladder-back chairs have the cross slats or "rungs" installed before the seat.

The primary problem in line layouts is balance; how to partition the total job into subtasks that are sufficiently equal in time to effectively utilize employees and achieve the desired output.

Table 15.2 Required tasks for ladder-back chair assembly

Task	Standard time (minutes)	Required preceding tasks
A	0.4	—
B	0.5	A
C	0.2	A
D	1.0	A
E	0.9	B
F	0.6	B
G	0.3	B
H	0.1	C
I	0.5	D
J	0.6	E
K	0.1	F,G
L	0.2	H,I
M	0.5	J
N	0.1	K
O	0.2	K
P	0.1	L
Q	0.1	M,N
R	0.5	O
S	2.6	P
T	0.1	Q,R,S
Total	9.6 minutes	

The Line-Balancing Problem

In Chapter 2 we examined chair building at the Westfall Furniture plant
and a proposal that these chairs be made on a production line basis. Table
15.2 represents a breakdown of the total building process for ladder-back
chairs into 20 subtasks. The required times for the subtasks would necessarily come from a work measurement system; actual variability in these
times and our understanding of the learning phenomenon will obviously
influence the actual times observed. However, let us begin by putting
these issues aside and considering the time estimates as accurate.

The last column in Table 15.2 represents the precedence or sequence
requirements; tasks B, C, and D must be preceded by task A, etc. Notice
also that the total time for all tasks is 9.6 minutes. Figure 15.6 is a
diagrammatical representation or precedence chart that looks very much
like the PERT models considered in Chapter 8.

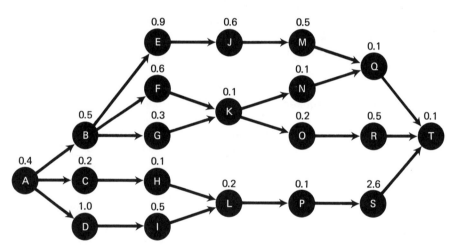

Fig. 15.6 Precedence chart of the required tasks for ladder-back chair assembly.

The line balancing problem is to divide the total task shown in Fig.
15.6 into stations so that the desired output rate is achieved. Thus if our
interest was in producing one chair every two minutes, we would hope to
accomplish the total task with five assembly stations, each station assigned no more than 2.0 minutes of work to accomplish on each chair that
comes by. In looking at Fig. 15.6, we see that task A has a required time
of 0.4 minutes, task B has a required time 0.5 minutes, task C has a
required time of 0.2 minutes, and task E has a required time of 0.9
minutes, for a total of 2.0 minutes. Since task E can be performed after

Table 15.3 Ladder-back chair assembly line balancing

Solution for five stations (2.0 minute cycle time)

Station	Tasks	Time (minutes)	
1	A, B, C, E	$0.4 + 0.5 + 0.2 + 0.9 =$	2.0
2	D, F, G, H	$1.0 + 0.6 + 0.3 + 0.1 =$	2.0
3	I, J, K, L, M, P	$0.5 + 0.6 + 0.1 + 0.2 + 0.5 + 0.1 =$	2.0
4	N, O, Q, S	$0.1 + 0.2 + 0.1 + (2.6 \div 2) =$	1.7
5	R, S, T	$0.5 + (2.6 \div 2) + 0.1 =$	1.9

Solution for four stations (2.4 minute cycle time)

Station	Tasks	Time (minutes)
1	A, B, E, F	$0.4 + 0.5 + 0.9 + 0.6 = 2.4$
2	C, D, G, H, I, K, L	$0.2 + 1.0 + 0.3 + 0.1 + 0.5 + 0.1 + 0.2 = 2.4$
3	J, M, S	$0.6 + 0.5 + (2.6 \div 2) = 2.4$
4	N, O, P, Q, R, S, T	$0.1 + 0.2 + 0.1 + 0.1 + 0.5 + (2.6 \div 2) + 0.1 = 2.4$

Solution for three stations (3.2 minute cycle time)

Station	Tasks	Time (minutes)
1	A, B, C, D, G, H, I, L	$0.4 + 0.5 + 0.2 + 1.0 + 0.3 + 0.1 + 0.5 + 0.2 = 3.2$
2	E, F, J, K, M, N, O, P, Q	$0.9 + 0.6 + 0.6 + 0.1 + 0.5 + 0.1 + 0.2 + 0.1 + 0.1 = 3.2$
3	R, S, T	$0.5 + 2.6 + 0.1 = 3.2$

Solution for ten stations (1.0 minute cycle time)

Station	Tasks	Time (minutes)	
1	A, B	$0.4 + 0.5 =$	0.9
2	D		1.0
3	C, H, I, L	$0.2 + 0.1 + 0.5 + 0.2 =$	1.0
4	E		0.9
5	F, G, K	$0.6 + 0.3 + 0.1 =$	1.0
6	J, N, O, P	$0.6 + 0.1 + 0.2 + 0.1 =$	1.0
7	M, R	$0.5 + 0.5 +$	1.0
8	S	$(2.6 \div 3) =$	0.9
9	Q, S	$0.1 + (2.6 \div 3) =$	1.0
10	S, T	$(2.6 \div 3) + 0.1 =$	1.0

task B, but does not require task D to precede it, we can combine tasks A, B, C, and E into our first assembly station. The second assembly station can be made up of tasks D, F, G, and H for again a total time of 2.0 minutes; alternatively, the second station could be comprised of task D, F, G, and K but not D, G, I, and L because task H must precede L. Table 15.3 gives solutions for five assembly stations, four stations, three stations, and ten stations.

Note that in the solution for five stations, the first three stations each have 2.0 minutes of work to perform whereas station four has only 1.7 minutes and station five 1.9 minutes of work. The output from the system is obviously dependent upon the longest single station time, and the operators in stations four and five would have idle time (in a real world system, the idle time might be absorbed by placing the least qualified worker at station four or by having the last two workers help in other ways with the operation). In the solution for four stations, it is possible to balance the total job exactly so that each station requires 2.4 minutes, which conceptually results in no idle time cost. The same result is achieved for three stations (2.4 × 4 = 3.2 × 3 = 9.6). Cycle times of 4.8 minutes with two stations could be achieved by combining the tasks performed in stations one and two into one station and doing the same thing for stations three and four in the four-station solution.

In both the five-station and four-station solution, the desired cycle times are less than time required for task S. The way this problem is handled is to have task S performed by more than one station or individual. This does not mean that task S has been subdivided into two subtasks, but that each of the indicated stations will perform task S on every other ladder-back chair. That is, for the five-station solution the operator at station four performs tasks N, O and Q on each chair but task S only on alternate chairs. Similarly, the operator in station five performs tasks R and T on all chairs but S on those not done by operator four. This means that the time required for station four will be only 0.4 minutes on one chair and 3.0 minutes on the next chair; similarly, the times for station five will be 0.6 minutes for chairs that have task S already completed and 3.2 minutes for those requiring task S. Although the average time for station four will be 1.7 minutes and 1.9 minutes for station five, an underlying implication is that one or two chairs are inventoried in front of stations four and five. That is, the variability in actual cycle time will be reflected in an inventory rather than on the output of the line; if this were not so, output of the line would again be limited by the longest operation time of 2.6 minutes.

If the desired output from the line is one chair every minute, we require ten stations and the balancing problems might be more severe. This turns out to not be the case for this example, and a solution is provided in Table 15.3. However, if the times for tasks A and J were exchanged as well as the times for tasks C and M, it would not be possible to achieve the desired output of one chair per minute with ten stations; eleven would be required. The small time values required in the problem as presently formulated allow for good combinations of activities to be made. As these combinations become more troublesome and as sequential constraints are added, the difficulty of achieving desired output rates with the minimum possible number of stations increases.

The assembly line balancing problem given here is relatively trivial compared to those faced daily by automobile assembly plants and other firms. In addition, the days of making automobiles in the historic Henry Ford manner where "you can have any color you like, as long as it is black" are gone forever. Constant changes in the product mix, changes in desired output rates, and new models provide a good source of employment for operations researchers, practical engineers, and operating men on the line; they probably also do a lot for stimulating sales of aspirins and antacids.

Models for Line Balancing

The approaches used in building models for line balancing are conceptionally quite similar to those used for the job shop layout problem. The problem again is combinatorial in nature so that total enumeration is infeasible. Optimal producing methods include formulating the problem as an integer linear program, a dynamic programming approach, and a branch and bound procedure. To date, it appears that the optimum producing methods cannot cope with problems as large as those frequently encountered in the real world; just as was true for the job shop layout problem, we find ourselves using heuristic approaches for practical problems.

Many heuristics have been proposed for the line-balancing problem. If we consider the process used to balance the ladder-back chair assembly lines, we can see how one might build a heuristic procedure. If we start at the initial station, we might add tasks to each station sequentially until we reach the desired cycle time. One heuristic which will be useful in deciding how to add tasks is to always add that task from the subset of those possible (sequential constraints) that has the largest processing time.

Let us apply this heuristic to our five-station assembly line problem. We start with task A, to which we can add either task B, C, or D; we add task D, and can now add task B, C, or I. We pick either task B or I (they are tied—let us say we pick B) for a total station time 1.9 minutes. With A, D, and B in station one, we can add C, E, F, G, or I; all of these additions would bring the total over the maximum allowable so we go on to station two. Station two begins by selecting task E since it is the task with the largest processing time. The tasks possible to now add are C, F, G, I, and J; F and J are tied so we will take F for a total time of 1.5 minutes. Adding J would violate the 2.0 minute requirement, but the next largest time for a task, I, results in a station of 2.0 minutes. At this point, J becomes the first task included in station three; it is followed by M, G, C, H, L, and K for a total station time of 2.0 minutes. Application of the heuristic to task S which exceeds our desired cycle time requires some sort of special treatment, but it should be clear that it is relatively easy to combine the remaining tasks into two stations that will satisfy the constraints. Note that the strategy employed in the heuristic was to hold back small times for use when needed; task C waited a long time to be placed in a station, and we had many small times remaining as we neared the end of the process.

Other heuristics take account of the largest number of immediate followers, the times associated with the immediate followers, backtracking when desired results are not achieved, and other "appealing rules of thumb." Another approach uses a biased sampling scheme to generate possible solutions.*

An Assessment

Once again, there is little doubt that formal models for line balancing can be of significant aid to the consideration of real world problems. The answers that result from these models, however, have to be regarded with the same kind of care we found necessary for the job shop layout models. The process of breaking a total job into tasks is not trivial, and often both the process of partitioning and the sequential constraints are somewhat arbitrary with redefinitions possible. Similarly, the use of standard times ignores the kinds of phenomena we saw in Chapter 2 where some workers were much more highly skilled and faster than others. We have already noted the influence of the learning phenomenon, and we have yet to consider the problem from a stochastic or probabilistic point of view.

The formal models are still useful for assessing balance conditions and for obtaining a solution which can thereafter be subjected to other considerations. A standard rule of thumb is that only 90% of the cycle time is to be assigned to a particular worker. A formal model can accommodate these kinds of constraints and encourage fruitful interaction with users, in this case experienced engineers, who can usually improve a starting solution by redefining tasks, relaxing sequential constraints, etc.

---

*For a detailed exposition of assembly line balancing models, see Edward J. Ignall, "A Review of Assembly Line Balancing," *The Journal of Industrial Engineering,* **16**, no. 4, pp. 244–54.

Stochastic Analysis

All of the models generally used for line balancing are based upon deterministic estimates of required times. In actuality the times required for tasks are random variables, and the entire process should be viewed within a queuing context.

In Chapter 11 we discussed queuing models and the general applicability of these models to what in this chapter we have called line-balancing problems. In Chapter 12, problems 12 through 17 are in fact stochastic analyses of the ladder-back chair line balancing problem considered in this chapter. Problem 12 assumes a five-station assembly line with two-minute cycle times and asks for the expected output per eight-hour-day under conditions of no variability in the two-minute cycle time, exponential distributions for the cycle times with various queues between operations permissible, and normally distributed cycle times with varying standard deviations and possible queue sizes.

The first question asked is the expected daily output with an assumption of constant times; a steady state model would yield 240 units per day, but beginning with an empty and idle condition results in 236. This result is, of course, not affected by allowable queues between assembly stations. When the two-minute average time is generated from a negative exponential distribution for each time and no queues are permitted between assembly stations, we find that the stations are idle slightly more than 50% of the time and the expected output for one simulation run dropped to 114.4 units. The same run with an allowable queue of one unit between stations increases the expected daily output to 143.6; for a possible bank of two, the expected output increases to 158.0, for three, to 173.3, for four, to 178.8, and for five, to 184.6.

Other aspects of the problem set in Chapter 12 pertaining to chair assembly consider the influence of greater variability in the times through use of a normal distribution with specified mean but differing standard deviation. The results are as expected; for any given queue length the expected output decreases as more variability in station time is experienced.

The effects of considering required station times as random variables should not be surprising. Nor should it be surprising that the addition of queues, banks, or in-process inventories between stations results in increased output. In Chapter 18 we will formally state the function of an inventory as decoupling successive stages in a production-distribution chain. It is exactly that function which a bank fulfills in an assembly line. It allows for variations in the time required to complete a task to not be reflected in output by the weakest link in the chain principle; rather, variations are reflected in the inventories, so that long times for one cycle are balanced by shorter times for another, and the mean time for the required tasks more closely represents the expected output of the entire assembly line.

Another way this variability in cycle times can be compensated for is in the concept of "time availability." The concept is well illustrated by considering a variable speed conveyor belt with products spaced differently. If the belt is running at ten feet per minute with parts spaced ten feet apart, one part will pass an operator every minute. However, if the operator can reach 2.5 feet in either direction up or down the conveyor belt from where he is positioned, the time available to work on a product coming by is one-half minute. If the speed of the conveyor belt is cut in half and the spacing between products is also cut in half, the same number of products pass the operator per day, but the time available to the operator is doubled. This doubling of the time available serves the same function as a bank; it permits greater variability in individual cycle time and a long-run output approaching the longest mean cycle time for any station on the line. Another real world example of time availability is exhibited in certain kinds of assembly lines where operators ride the conveyor belts. This approach is often used for the assembly of major appliances, and the effect is somewhat the same. Operators normally ride only a certain distance but the length of the ride can be lengthened or shortened according to variations in cycle times.

SUMMARY REMARKS

In this chapter we have examined a class of problems which represent relatively long-run commitments to modes of operation. Both the location problem and the layout problem need to be formulated in terms specifically applicable to a given company at a given time for a given set of circumstances.

The models examined in this chapter are potentially useful for these kinds of decisions. Like all models, however, they have limitations that we must understand if we are not to be led down primrose paths. Nevertheless, the location problem, the job shop layout problem, and the line balancing problem tend to grow very complex in the real world. Intuitive or "black cigar" models simply cannot be expected to yield benefits competitive to those possible with more rigorous models. The user-designer concept must again be considered so that the establishment of a modeling environment which fosters understanding of the problem is encouraged.

To a large extent, location and layout problems are strongly dependent upon other considerations in the firm, most notably production planning-inventory control and the overall nature of materials flow both within the company and to ultimate consumers. It is to these issues that Chapters 17 through 21 are devoted.

REFERENCES

Buffa, Elwood S., *Operations Management: Problems and Models,* 2nd ed., Wiley, 1968.

Lipton, Paul, and John Cabrera, "Plant Location–An Integer Programming Application," *Production and Inventory Management,* **12**, no. 1, (First Qtr. 1971): 32–41.

Muther, Richard, *Systematic Layout Planning,* Industrial Education Institute, Berlin, 1961.

Reed, Ruddell, Jr., *Plant Location, Layout, and Maintenance,* Irwin, 1967.

Techniques of Plant Location: Studies in Business Policy, No. 61, National Industrial Conference Board (New York) 1953.

Webster, L., and M. D. Kilbridge, "Heuristic Line Balancing: A Case," *The Journal of Industrial Engineering,* XII, no. 3, May–June 1962.

CHAPTER REVIEW

When I started to write this book, I made a commitment to exclude materials that are of academic but little real world interest. I think Chapter 15 comes closer to breaking that covenant than any other; I am somewhat apologetic for indulging my interests in the location of facilities problem. I have tried to make the treatment brief and to focus on real world aspects.

On the other hand, although development of new layout heuristics or branch and bound algorithms are tangential to a survey of operations management, your overall education is probably well served by *briefly* following one such tangent. There are many real world problems that are combinatorial in nature; the kinds of heuristic approaches used for layout and line balancing are applicable. You should now have a better feeling for how such solution procedures are constructed, and you hopefully should recognize again our continuing concern with surrogate criteria relationships and the need for *users* to assess those relationships.

OUTLINE OF THE CHAPTER

Introduction	(placement of enterprise activities)
Location problems	(unique criteria)
Initial cost criteria	(hard and soft data)
Operating cost criteria	(time dimension)
Marketing criteria	(functional approach)
Subjective criteria	(solution space)
Foreign locations	(costs and markets)

CENTRAL ISSUES

The location problems faced by an enterprise are unique to that firm and dynamic. New opportunities are continually becoming available and known for product (or service) creation, for product sale, and for product distribution. The opportunities interact with the criteria system of the firm, and with the existing set of systems designed to fulfill product creation, sale, and distribution.

Models for location studies were at one time almost completely qualitative; recently developed models permit improved understanding of objective data (e.g., shipping costs) and tradeoffs of objective and subjective considerations. Simulation approaches such as that used in the LOGISTEK model can lead to a modeling environment where users better understand locational decisions and issues such as customer service; these user-oriented approaches also lead to increased control over the environment faced by the firm as the influences of decision alternatives are examined.

Layout problems are divided into two major types, job shop and assembly line. The two types represent differing production strategies; the first being more flexible, and the second potentially being more economical. The job shop layout problem is concerned with the relative location of facilities, so that the flows of materials between departments travel over minimum distances. Computer models such as CRAFT obtain good solutions to these problems by heuristic problem-solving techniques. Again, insights into the influences of subjective criteria are facilitated by a user-oriented approach. The models work well for problem situations where the "material flow" is people or communications; office layout is well-suited to these techniques.

The assembly line layout problem is basically one of balancing the work required at each station. For many firms, the balancing problem has to be solved often to achieve changes in output volumes. Models for line balancing are similar in approach to the heuristic models used for job shop layout. Treatment of station times as deterministic ignores the inherent queuing nature of the assembly line. In actual practice, work in process inventories, loading to less than 100% of expected times, and other techniques are used to offset stochastic properties.

ASSIGNMENTS

1. If you were employed by a major oil company to locate filling stations, what measures of effectiveness would you consider important? What data would you collect and evaluate prior to choosing among alternatives?

2. In what ways does the location problem of an upholstery furniture manufacturer differ from that of a case goods or dining room furniture manufacturer?

3. Draw the layout for a restaurant or cafeteria with which you are familiar. What criteria are reflected in the design as it stands? Can you make any improvements? Be sure to specify what the criterion is that each "improvement" better satisfies.

4. The following assembly problem is to be performed on a four-man line. Assign the tasks so that the line is balanced.

Task	Time	Precedents
A	1.2	—
B	.8	A
C	5.3	A
D	1.6	B
E	.5	B
F	.7	C
G	1.8	C
H	1.0	E,G
I	.6	D,F
J	1.3	I,H

5. Solve problem 15-4 for a three-station assembly line.

6. Use the line balancing heuristic presented in the chapter to assign the following tasks to each station on a 5 man assembly line.

Task	Time	Precedents
A	.3	—
B	1.0	—
C	1.1	B
D	.5	B
E	1.1	A
F	1.2	D
G	.5	F,C
H	.4	G
I	.6	H
J	.8	I,E
K	2.0	J
L	.4	J
M	.9	L
N	.3	K,M
O	.7	N

7. The trust department of a small bank is remodeling and they have come to your firm for advice. After several weeks of study and observation of trust operations you have obtained the following information:

Initial layout

1 Board room	2 Accounting	3 Data processing
4 Tax accounting	5 Filing	6 Estates
7 Trust officers	8 Receptionist	9 Vice-president

The files located in the center of the building can only be moved at great expense and are therefore considered to be permanent.

Face-to-face contacts

From \ To	1	2	3	4	5	6	7	8	9
1	—	1	0	0	6	10	20	6	40
2	0	—	230	180	270	90	25	3	0
3	0	235	—	195	380	60	30	0	1
4	1	130	205	—	175	180	18	0	2
5	10	160	330	190	—	75	110	20	30
6	4	10	0	265	45	—	50	6	5
7	15	20	0	5	38	20	—	65	45
8	25	0	0	0	0	15	120	—	80
9	75	1	2	0	10	15	60	85	—

Hourly wages

1	$20.00
2	3.50
3	4.00
4	3.60
5	2.20
6	8.00
7	10.00
8	3.80
9	16.00

Use a computerized heuristic to find a better solution than the current layout.

8. The trust department in assignment 8 has grown and they are adding a mutual fund group that is to have their own offices. The entire department is moving to a new building which is to be L shaped as shown below.

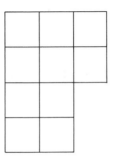

The total interaction between the new department and the others is expected to be as follows:

1 2 3 4 5 6 7 8 9

0 10 40 25 50 3 2 0 2

The wages in the new department average $3.80. Use a computerized heuristic to find a good layout. (Hint: Add two departments to make the building square, make all the cost-flow entries for these departments zero and freeze them in the corner of the building.)

9. A layout study was made in the engineering office of the Sandy-Gale Aircraft Company, Ltd. of Canada. Initially, the study focused on the flow of work through the system, but it was difficult to generate meaningful cost data on this basis. The search for realistic measures of effectiveness finally narrowed down to the relative location of people in the company as required by their face-to-face contacts with others at Sandy-Gale. It was finally decided to collect data on face-to-face contacts initiated by each person for the month of March, and to accumulate this data in the form of the matrix of Table 15.4. The entire department was divided into twelve groups or areas as indicated by Table 15.4. A floor plan of the engineering office of Sandy-Gale is presented in Fig. 15.6. Each cell in Table 15.4 indicates the number of face-to-face contacts initiated by that group, for example 15 from (1) to (2).

The management of the engineering department decided that each of the groups required about the same amount of floor space. In addition, management had foreseen the need for flexibility and had installed movable partitioning for office walls. For all practical purposes, management stated that any group would probably work effectively almost anywhere in the engineering department. There was but one exception to this. Because of the location of the foyer, the bay windows, the water cooler, and the rest rooms, management decided that the area for supervision could not be moved from its present location.

Table 15.5 presents the average hourly wage per employee in each of the groups of the engineering department.

Determine if the present layout could be improved upon using the criterion of face-to-face contacts. If so, present an improved office layout.

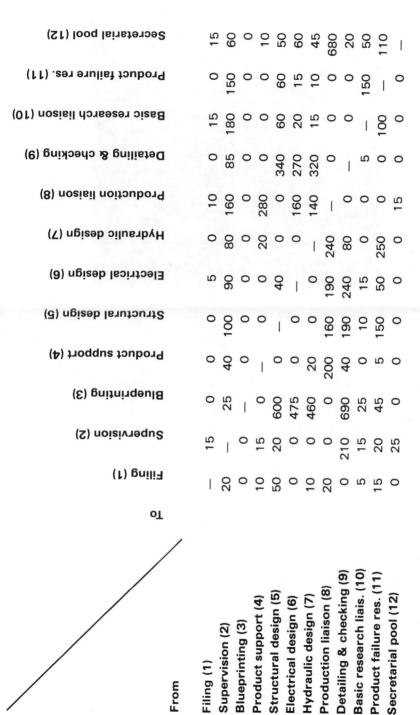

From \ To	Filing (1)	Supervision (2)	Blueprinting (3)	Product support (4)	Structural design (5)	Electrical design (6)	Hydraulic design (7)	Production liaison (8)	Detailing & checking (9)	Basic research liaison (10)	Product failure res. (11)	Secretarial pool (12)
Filing (1)	—	15	0	0	0	5	0	10	0	15	0	15
Supervision (2)	20	—	25	40	100	90	80	160	85	180	0	60
Blueprinting (3)	0	0	—	0	0	0	0	0	0	0	150	0
Product support (4)	10	15	0	—	0	0	20	280	0	0	0	10
Structural design (5)	50	20	600	0	—	40	0	0	340	60	0	50
Electrical design (6)	0	0	475	0	0	—	0	160	270	60	60	60
Hydraulic design (7)	10	0	460	20	0	0	—	140	320	20	15	45
Production liaison (8)	20	0	0	200	160	190	240	—	0	15	10	680
Detailing & checking (9)	0	210	690	40	190	240	80	0	—	0	0	20
Basic research liais. (10)	5	15	25	0	10	15	0	0	5	—	150	50
Product failure res. (11)	15	20	45	5	150	50	250	0	0	100	—	110
Secretarial pool (12)	0	25	0	0	0	0	0	15	0	0	0	—

Table 15.4 Sandy-Gale Aircraft Company—face-to-face contacts.

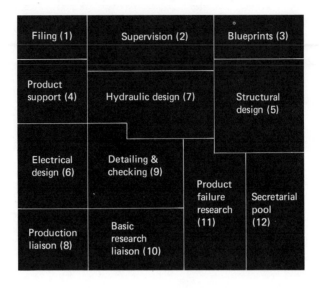

Figure 15.6 Sandy-Gale Aircraft Company *plant layout, present.*

1) Filing	$1.80
2) Supervision	$5.00
3) Blueprint	$2.10
4) Product support	$2.70
5) Structural design	$4.50
6) Electrical design	$4.50
7) Hydraulic design	$4.50
8) Production liaison	$2.70
9) Detailing and checking	$3.60
10) Basic research liaison	$3.10
11) Product failure research	$4.20
12) Secretarial pool	$2.40

Table 15.5 Sandy-Gale Aircraft Company—*mean wage per worker.*

CHAPTER 16

QUALITY CONTROL

At several points in this book we have defined control as a three-step process involving (1) determination of a standard, goal, or criterion; (2) the measurement and comparison of actual results with that standard; and (3) actions taken to correct deviations.

Although quality control programs necessarily must be concerned with all three steps of the control process, most of the models proposed for quality control tend to be associated with step two. That is, *given* a specified standard and regardless of what corrective action will be taken, models built upon probabilistic concepts attempt to make important inferences about production or conversion processes and the outputs from these processes. Before turning to these models for quality control, however, we would be remiss if we did not examine the process by which both quality standards and corrective actions are determined.

PRODUCT QUALITY

The process of translating enterprise objectives into surrogate quality criteria will almost surely involve some suboptimization. The basic needs of the ultimate consumer which are served by the product or service must be understood and translated into concrete specifications for component parts and means of product creation. The continuing achievement of these quality objectives for many products requires constant attention to quality. The attention often is directed more appropriately toward motivation of workers whose actions result in quality achievement, rather than toward the inspection function as a sensor to measure resultant quality. The phrase, "Quality must be built into the product—not inspected in," is familiar throughout industry.

The Nature of Quality

What is quality? How does a product become regarded as high quality or low quality? Is a Rolls Royce automobile of higher quality than a Chevrolet Vega or a Ford Pinto? Does satisfaction of a large market need by these lower priced automobiles in some way constitute quality? If so, does this mean that any television program widely watched is of high quality?

Our functional analysis model from Chapter 7 is helpful in the pursuit of answers to these questions. Let us say that we can identify the functional and esteem value characteristics desired in a product or service. Existing products or services which provide those functional and esteem characteristics better than competing products or services are in a real sense "high quality." One of the most interesting aspects of defining quality in this way is that quality becomes a relative matter, and there is no such thing as a fundamental quality standard which is unvarying over time. Moreover, quality does not have to be perceived in the same way by all individuals, or universally agreed upon.

Since *perception* of product quality is so important, marketing efforts to change perceptions can be important. The kind of "high quality" image associated with Rolls Royce automobiles is created for many products. A case in point is a firm manufacturing two brands of vodka, one of which has a well-known national brand name and high quality image; according to a company employee, the only fundamental difference between the two products is the price.

Understanding quality in relative terms takes cognizance of competitive realities. Analyses in *Consumers' Report* reflect this comparative nature, but the analyses necessarily are oriented largely toward functional characteristics rather than esteem values. Definitive answers to which car looks better or the value of daisies appliquéd on the front of a refrigerator necessarily have to be made on the basis of individual preferences.

Quality is very much an evolutionary concept. Competitive pressures tend to force firms into devoting increasing attention to quality, and advertising feedbacks can change consumer perceptions of what constitutes good quality. Even with a specified design, there is evolution in quality. Thus many people believe that automobiles produced near the end of the model year tend to be better cars than those produced at the beginning of the same model year. Cost and quality tradeoffs tend to be different as the learning phenomenon allows a specified task to be performed in less time; more time can therefore be devoted to insuring that the job is done right.

It is useful to think about quality in relation to the sales price that can be charged for an item, and the cost of producing the item. Clearly, if a product is of higher quality its sales price can also be higher. If the quality is increased, the cost of production may also increase. Figure 16.1 depicts these general relationships.

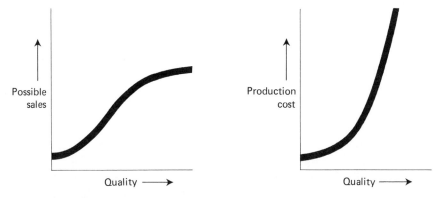

Fig. 16.1 Relationship of quality to price and cost.

The curve depicting quality and possible sales indicates that increases in quality generally lead to the ability to charge a larger sales price, but that at some point additional quality features either cannot be passed along in sales price increases or that the size of the market for goods in that quality range is limited. Figure 16.1 shows the general relationship between quality and production cost. It will be generally true that higher quality costs more money and that decreasing returns will be experienced as we approach the limits of ways to increase product quality. Figure 16.2 combines the two curves from 16.1.

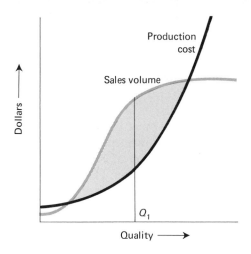

Fig. 16.2 Quality strategy.

By combining the two relationships from Fig. 16.1, we see that there are quality levels that are infeasible as well as those that are feasible. The shaded area between the two curves represents a solution space of feasible quality strategies, and Q_1 indicates the point where the difference between sales and cost maximizes the return.

In order to see how these general ideas of product quality nature are applied more specifically, let us now examine quality in furniture manufacture and see how these ideas affect Baumritter.

Furniture Quality

The assessment of quality in a piece of furniture is very much an individual matter. Some people like colonial, some like Mediterranean, and others like modern. Within any of these general styles, there are great differences in what is perceived as quality. High lustre finishes are generally considered high quality, but the open grain look of some woods finished only with linseed oil is pleasing to some consumers. Within the colonial or American traditional style of furniture, birch and maple pieces are knot- and defect-free; whereas pine furniture has many knots to be judged of high quality.

Consumers desire their furniture to be serviceable for extended periods of time and for products to maintain good appearance. These general objectives tend to be translated into some structural features, but even many of these tend to be more emotional than real. A good example is dovetailed drawers. Over the years people have come to regard dovetailed drawers as being of high quality. It is not at all unusual to see prospective furniture buyers walk up to a chest, open the drawers, and look at the sides to see whether indeed they are dovetailed. Dovetailing is one acceptable means for good drawer construction, but there are certainly others, particularly with the technological advances recently made in adhesives. Nevertheless, if the public thinks that dovetailed drawers are of high quality, firms like Baumritter will not only make all drawers dovetailed, they will advertise this fact and contribute to the belief that dovetailed drawers represent high quality.

Substantial differences do exist between brands of furniture. A factory that was making a well-known (and more expensive) brand of colonial furniture shifted to production of Ethan Allen furniture and found the quality standards more demanding. The sanded surfaces before finishing had to be more accurate (both in terms of flatness for flat surfaces such as table tops and desired smoothness to properly absorb stains); application of stains and finishing materials was more rigorous; rubbing requirements were more strenuous; and the wood selected for individual panels had to be matched much more carefully.

In a real sense, the Ethan Allen quality image represents an important marketing asset to the Baumritter corporation. The design of each piece of furniture tends to be slightly more complex than competing brands, and the quality is not only better, it is consistent. The consistency is important since the product line is based upon an open stock policy. It is necessary for all plants to produce to uniform quality standards that are maintained over time. The establishment of the Ethan Allen brand name backed up by consistent quality and designs which tend to be hard to produce go a long way to achieving brand loyalty; it also makes it more difficult for competitors to enter the market and copy.

Quality Motivational Program

As we noted in the introduction to this chapter, achievement of product quality necessarily includes the people who build quality into products. Although proper motivation for employees is a subject above and beyond quality control, many firms continually emphasize quality in motivational programs for their employees.

Motivational programs for instilling a continuing emphasis on product quality vary from the mundane to the spectacular. The former variety includes signs posted in the shop emphasizing quality, and in the latter we find programs such as "Zero Defects." In all of these motivational programs, however, there is a need for credibility. This is well illustrated by Box 16.1.

The author was going through a particularly dirty factory which had a history of poor employee relations. Throughout the factory someone had very recently placed pristine signs that read "TEAMWORK POWERS PROGRESS." Every part of the plant seemed to be festooned with these signs. Finally the author came to one area where the sign had been removed, turned over and on the back of it printed, "B.S. BAFFLES BRAINS."

Box 16.1

Zero defects programs have a primary objective of employee motivation to accomplish error-free performance. Widely used by military and defense contractors, the original zero defects program was initiated in 1962 at the Martin Company in Orlando, Florida. The concept of zero defects implies infinite quality, and one wonders if such a level of quality resides within the shaded solution space of profitable quality strategies in Fig. 16.2. Those who have designed zero defects programs tend to regard the efforts as successful with appropriate statistics to back up their beliefs. The statistics, however, often are stated in percentage terms and one wonders about claims such as "A 100% reduction in the number of errors punched on IBM cards in support of the vehicle maintenance program."*

Zero defects programs may achieve results, but the theatrical nature of many such programs strongly hints of "B.S. Baffling Brains." The idea of having the president of a large corporation ride through a factory on a fire engine with a Dixieland band seems somehow ridiculous. Although an employee might be amused and even impressed the first time he got a zero defects cake to take home, the third or fourth time his wife might prefer a case of beer. Claims that "now workers are going to get the proper tools to do their job" make one wonder why they didn't have proper equipment before.

The design of an enterprise to manufacture a product is a complex task requiring managerial talents. Slogans and campaign gimmicks cannot replace necessary hard work, and real dangers from a credibility gap can develop.

On the other hand, employee motivation and the development of healthy work attitudes is an important part of the managerial task that requires constant attention. Perhaps the real danger in a zero defects program is oversell. If the employees are motivated to believe that something will be different, it is incumbent upon those who propose such a scheme to carry it through. Maintaining the momentum and the proper degree of seriousness is critical; concrete results should not be confused with number games where the goal is to maximize the number of suggestions or create an opportune base for percentage comparisons.

Although negative aspects of a zero defects program can be strong, these programs have nonetheless led to some important benefits. One major reason for these benefits is the establishment of a methodology for encouraging employee participation in the design of product creation. Every employee has some ideas about how operations might be improved and those ideas should be solicited. Motivational programs can encourage the kind of communication implied in solicitation of such ideas.

Another kind of communication involves a better understanding of customer needs or marketing criteria on the part of individual workers who create the product. Some programs post all customer complaints and praise in the plant where those who created the good or bad features will see them. Selected production workers sometimes visit sites where their products are being used and discuss use of the products with the customer. This seems particularly valuable for expensive industrial products such as machine tools.

---

*Donald E. Newnham, "Zero Defects—Do it Right the First Time," *The Journal of Industrial Engineering,* 17, no. 1, (January 1966): 3.

Pride of workmanship, self-identification with the product, and an increased interest in one's job can lead to important quality improvements and a resultant competitive advantage in the marketplace. Baumritter achieves some of these benefits by encouraging tourists to visit their factories. Tour guides escort groups through the factories and show off the craftsmanship that goes into each piece of Ethan Allen furniture. All aside from marketing implications of such visits, the production workers derive a great deal of pride from seeing consumers of their efforts appreciate the skill and devotion they give to the products.

The difference in output quality between a plant with this kind of pride and one without it can be profound. This is well seen by reading how many workers on automobile assembly lines feel about their jobs. For many of them, heavy use of drugs seems to be the only way to get through the day. Stories of empty bottles being deliberately placed inside door panels to rattle, engines that are not bolted to the transmissions, and numerous other quality problems have to be at least partially due to poor employee motivation. The costs are high for necessary inspection and for jobs designed to preclude such poor output; the effects of poor output reaching the marketplace are presently being felt in an increasing lack of consumer faith and more militant consumer, governmental, and legal actions.

STATISTICAL CONTROL MODELS

As noted in the introduction to this chapter, quality control models are largely concerned with the second step in the quality control process. With only a partial understanding of the marketplace and the evolving nature of the company and market interaction, somehow manufacturing must decide what will be produced and what specific quality standards will be established. Once these specifications for products and component parts are determined, statistical quality control models can be established to check whether the standards are being achieved or whether corrective action is required. Statistical control models have been developed for two basic situations. The first is as an ongoing control for production as it is happening. The second is concerned with assessing the output from a production process after the fact, for example, the purchase of components in a batch. We will be primarily concerned with the first situation, control of production output as it is being produced.

Product Variability
Variability is an inherent fact of life. Just as there are no two snowflakes exactly alike, there are no two parts produced by a production process that are exactly alike. There will always be a difference, even though

measuring devices available for monitoring the difference may not be able to detect it. In many ways, the history of production and the Industrial Revolution were intimately involved with control over production variability. Before the advent of standardized parts, products were created by fitting each part individually to the others. Standardized parts and standardized manufacturing methods allowed for parts interchangeability and decreased costs; at the same time, tolerances on individual parts had to be tightened so that part matching would be insured.

In large measure, statistical control models for monitoring production are concerned with variability and insuring that the variability stays within boundaries specified so that functional features of the end product will be insured. Choices of productive equipment are often largely made as a function of variability. More expensive devices tend to be capable of producing to tighter tolerances than less expensive devices. More expensive machinery tends to be worth the investment when tighter tolerances are required.

The degree of variability that can be tolerated is quite different for some products than for others. It also is quite different for components within products. Although standard woodworking tolerances tend to be expressed in eighths and fourths of an inch, there are some dimensions in a piece of furniture which are less critical and some that are considerably more critical. The diameter of the decorative part of a pedestal table is not critical since no parts fit to it; on the other hand, the diameter of a chair leg which is glued into a hole must fit precisely if the chair is to hold together. Similarly, although the *widths* of drop-leaf dining room table leaves may not seem critical, it is critical that the leaves be of the same *length* as the main part to which they are attached.

Once product specifications have been translated into detailed sizes, tolerances for individual parts are determined and choices are made as to which parts to make on certain pieces of equipment; statistical models can be used to assess whether the desired specifications are being met. The basic underlying theory for these models is statistical hypothesis testing. Variability is inherent in manufacturing, and the primary question that the statistical hypothesis models address is whether variation observed in a sample is due to chance or to some assignable cause. That is, the test will be on some parameter of a process such as its mean, and sample evidence will either support the hypothesized value of the parameter or cause the hypothesis to be rejected.

Control Charts for Variables
Let us suppose that a twenty-three inch drawer front is being cut on the double-end tenoner machine, that we desire to hold a tolerance of ±.010 inches, that we have a device capable of measuring to within .001 inches, and that we do not know whether this machine is inherently capable of

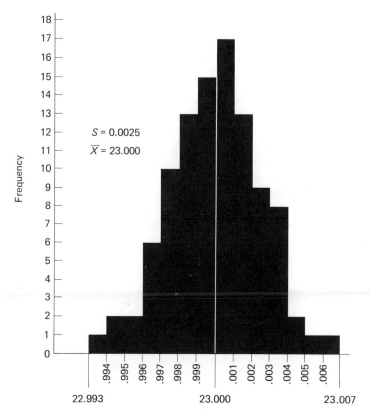

Fig. 16.3 Sample of 100 drawer fronts cut on double-end tenoner.

producing parts consistent with our desired specifications. (To illustrate calculations, we will carry decimal places beyond this measurement capability.) In an attempt to understand the capabilities of the double-end tenoner machine, the machine was set up for a run of these parts. Figure 16.3 is a histogram of 100 drawer fronts cut on the double-end tenoner.

The abscissa of Fig. 16.3 is read in increments of .001 inches; it would seem that this machine is capable of maintaining the desired tolerances. The largest variation observed is only .007 inches away from the nominal dimension and the tolerance is .010 inches.

If we accept the data in Fig. 16.3 as representative of this machine, we can calculate the mean and standard deviation which are 23.000 inches and .0025 inches respectively.* Let us also for the moment assume

---

*There are some problems associated with basing estimates on samples. See Duncan, Acheson, J., *Quality Control and Industrial Statistics,* 3rd Ed., Richard D. Irwin, 1965, p. 385.

that the shape of Fig. 16.3 allows us to assume that the underlying probability distribution of parts cut on this machine is normal (we will soon see how use of the central limit theorem allows us to relax this assumption). Figure 16.4 shows the normal approximation of the data in Fig. 16.3 with the curve rotated ninety degrees. Note that we have also shown two upper and lower limits labeled UNTL and LNTL. These are the natural tolerance limits based upon plus and minus three standard deviations from the mean.

The basic idea of a statistical quality control chart can be illustrated with Fig. 16.4. We hypothesize that the underlying process or machine for cutting the 23" dimension on drawer fronts is in control. If the process is in control we would expect to see parts produced with dimensions following the distribution depicted in Fig. 16.4. If we inspect a part coming from this machine with a length less than 22.9925 inches or greater than 23.0075 inches, we will reject the hypothesis that the underlying mean of the distribution is 23.000 inches.

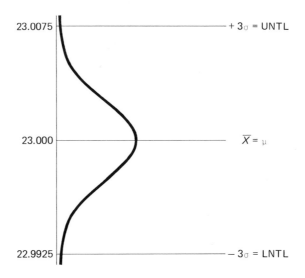

Fig. 16.4 Normal approximation of drawer fronts cut on double-end tenoner.

Rejection of the hypothesis is a conclusion that the variation from the nominal dimension observed cannot be due to random causes, but is due to some assignable cause which has changed the underlying parameter (mean) on which the hypothesis is based.

Figure 16.4 shows that the normal distribution does not have all of its area between the plus and minus three standard deviation range; the table of areas under the normal curve gives the cumulative probability as 0.9973. This means that 27 times out of 10,000 a result outside the plus and minus three-standard-deviation range would be observed when the true mean was 23.000 inches. In those instances, our conclusion that the process is out of control would be incorrect.

The underlying concepts of statistical quality controls are reflected in the methodology used above. However, actual methodologies employed are more complex for two related reasons. The first is a reluctance to assume normality for the distribution of sizes coming from each and every process, and the second is due to the fact that a normal distribution is described by two parameters, the mean and the variance or standard deviation. Our concern is not only with central tendency, it is also with variability of the process. Use of the central limit theorem will support the normality assumption, and a separate control chart for process variance will satisfy the other requirement.

In your basic statistics course, you learned that if repetitive samples of size n are drawn from a normal population with mean μ and standard deviation σ, the resultant distribution of sample means is normal with mean μ and standard deviation $\sigma/\sqrt{n}$. That is, if we took one hundred pieces of paper which represent the observed results from our drawer front example, and put them into a hat which we regarded as the "population," our assumption of normality for this problem in essence says that if we were to draw from this population samples of size 1, note the result, and return the observation to the population hat, the resultant distribution would look very much like Fig. 16.4 (our inability to measure to infinite decimal places would mean that the distribution would not be continuous, but the histogram would tend to approximate the continuous normal distribution).

If we instead take samples of size 4 from the "distribution hat," calculated the mean for each sample, regard each mean as an observation, return the four pieces of paper to the hat, plot the resultant distribution of sample means as a histogram, and perform the process repetitively, the resultant distribution will be normal with the same mean as the mean of the population and with a standard deviation equal to the population standard deviation divided by the square root of the sample size ($\sigma_{\overline{x}} = \sigma_x \div \sqrt{n}$). For our drawer front example, the resultant distribution of sample means would have a mean of 23.000 inches and a standard deviation of $0.0025 \div \sqrt{4} = 0.00125$.

You also learned in your basic statistics course that even when the original population is not normal, the distribution of sample means approaches normality as n becomes large. Just how quickly this process occurs is well illustrated by Fig. 16.5, which shows four radically different underlying or population distributions and resultant distributions of sample means for various sample sizes.

In each of the four population cases shown in Fig. 16.5 it is also clear how the dispersion of sample mean distribution shrinks as the size of

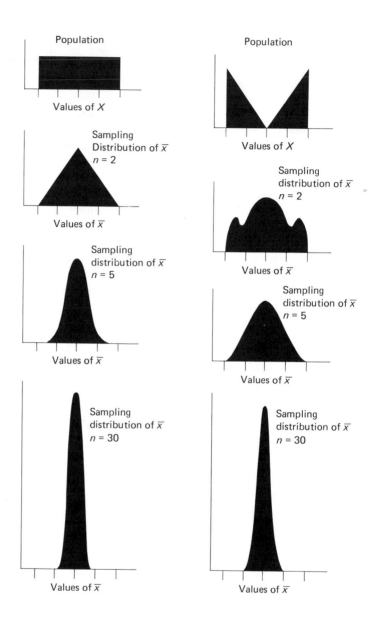

Fig. 16.5* Sampling distributions.

*Reproduced with permission from Kurnow, Ernest, G. J. Glasser, and F. R. Ottman, *Statistics for Business Decisions,* Richard D, Irwin, Homewood, Illinois, 1959.

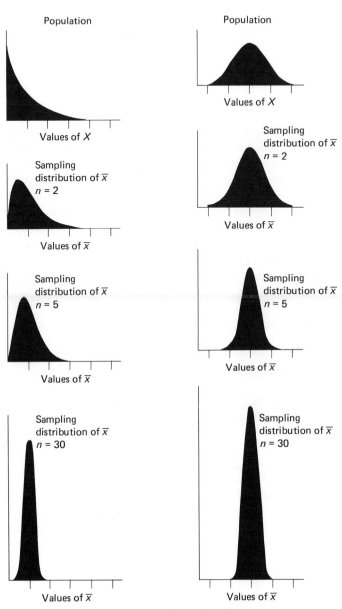

Fig. 16.5 (continued)

samples increase. If we construct a control chart for sample means similar to Fig. 16.4, the three σ limits will also shrink. If the sample size is 4, the standard deviation of sample means will be $0.0025 \div 4 = 0.00125$, and the three σ limits will be $\pm.00375$. If the sample size $n = 9$, then the three σ limits equal $\pm.0025$, and if $n = 25$ then $\pm 3\sigma = \pm.0015$ inches.

Figure 16.6 shows the relationship between the information given in Fig. 16.4 and a set of three σ limits for samples of size 4.

The top line of Fig. 16.6 labeled UDS specifies the upper design specification; similarly the bottom line LDS is the lower design specification. Both are based upon the nominal dimension 23.000 inches $\pm$ .010 inches. The next pair of bands is the upper natural tolerance limit, UNTL, and lower natural tolerance limit, LNTL, shown in Fig. 16.4. These represent the normal variability range of the process; also shown is the normal curve which approximates this underlying distribution. The closest pair of lines to the mean of the distribution is the UCL, upper control limit, and LCL, lower control limit. This band represents three σ limits for the distribution of sample means where the sample size = 4. The normal distribution for these sample means is also shown.

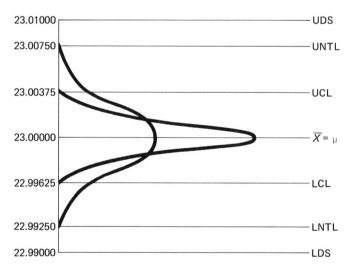

Fig. 16.6 Control chart (sample size = 4).

We now can state an explicit decision rule for quality control of the drawer front: go to the machine, take a sample of four parts, measure each part, compute the arithmetic mean of these four parts, and conclude that the process is in control if the arithmetic mean falls between 22.99625 inches and 23.00375 inches. If the arithmetic mean for the four parts is outside of these control limits, conclude that the process is out of control and institute corrective action.

Note that it is quite possible to conclude that the process is out of control even if all four parts are within the design specifications or even within the natural tolerance limit band. We will see later why we nonetheless would conclude that the process is out of control.

Another feature of the control process is to consider the horizontal axis of Fig. 16.6 as a time dimension. Individual observations of sample means are plotted as they are made at periodic intervals so that trends in nominal dimension can be observed (see Fig. 16.8 for an example).

In actual practice, only the UCL and LCL are drawn on control charts. This is both for simplicity and to keep employees from "second guessing" the statistical theory which underlies the control chart.

The Dynamic Control Chart

One of our original questions was whether the double-end tenoner machine was inherently capable of producing drawer fronts to the design specifications. We found that the drawer fronts could be produced with this machine. In fact, as shown in Fig. 16.6, the upper and lower natural tolerance limits fall within the upper and lower design specifications. If the natural tolerance limits were outside of the design specifications, we would usually conclude that this machine was not inherently capable of achieving the desired output. There would be more than a 0.0027 probability that parts produced would be outside of the design specifications.

Because the underlying variability in the process or machine is less than that required in the finished product, we do not necessarily have to set up the machine so that the nominal dimension is 23.000 inches. If we were interested in saving lumber, for example, we might like to set up the mean of the process so that all parts will be within the design specifications, yet will be made with the smallest possible amount of lumber.

Although this may be a rather bizarre example when considering lumber, it is not at all bizarre when considering steel or other valuable materials. If a steel mill could roll steel to much tighter tolerances than those which specify the steel, more pieces of 1/16 inch steel can be rolled from a ton if each piece is slightly thinner.

Another reason why the average dimension of the process might be set different from the nominal dimension given in the specifications is because some kind of predictable wear takes place in the tools as the process goes on. By setting the process average above or below the nominal dimension (depending upon which way the tool wear goes) the length of time between changes due to tool wear can be increased. For example, if our drawer front machine used tooling which wore as a function of the number of parts processed we would expect the average dimension to increase over time. By setting the initial average dimension lower than 23.000 inches, we could cut more drawer fronts before having to adjust the machine.

What is the lowest point at which the average dimension can be initially set? When asked this question, students often say that the process can be established so that the lower control limit and lower design specification are the same. This would mean establishing the initial mean at 22.99375 inches. This is incorrect. Returning to Fig. 16.6, it can be seen that such a procedure would result in the lower natural tolerance limit being outside the design specifications; a significant portion of the output would be outside of the design specifications. The answer is to set the lower natural tolerance limit equal to the lower design specification, which results in the mean being set equal to 22.99750 inches. We can now reconstruct Fig. 16.6 as Fig. 16.7.

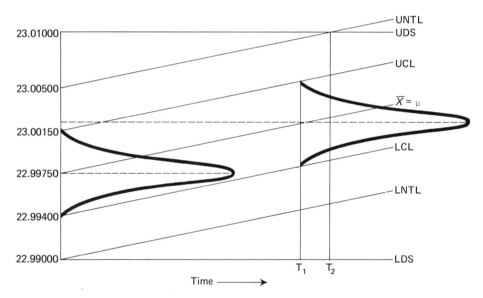

Fig. 16.7 Dynamic control chart (sample size = 4).

Figure 16.7 shows the upper and lower design specifications as non-changing over time. The lower natural tolerance limit, lower control limit, mean, upper control limit, and upper natural tolerance limit, however, do vary with time. The slope of these parallel lines indicates the rate at which we *expect* tool wear to increase the size of the boards over time. It is important to note that we must expect such a shift and know the slope if we are to use the dynamic control chart model. One should not establish after the fact a set of lines for past data; it is necessary to predict the situation ahead of time. Note that a value of 23.002 inches for a mean of sample size 4 would be judged outside of the control limits at the start of the process, but not outside the control limits at time T_1. Also note that the same underlying normal distribution for sample means is used for the control limit process. The only difference is that the underlying expected distribution is shifting over time. This can be seen by the depiction of two normal curves showing the underlying distribution at the outset as well as at time T_1.

The time T_2 indicates the point at which tool wear has increased to such an extent that the nominal dimension plus the inherent process variability causes the upper natural tolerance limit to coincide with the upper design specification. This point is reached at time period T_2. At that point, the underlying process no longer meets design specifications and adjustment of the machine is required. The expected mean of the process at Time T_2 is 3.00250 inches.

The Range Chart

We noted that the normal distribution is a two-parameter distribution; in order to describe a normal process we need both parameters, the mean as well as the variance or standard deviation. The mean is the measure of central tendency and the variance or standard deviation is the extent of variability in the distribution. For example, in looking at Fig. 16.6 we see two normal distributions with the same mean but with different standard deviations.

Our objectives in a quality control procedure relate to both the measure of central tendency and the measure of variation in the process. That is, all of our control chart discussions so far have been based upon the underlying variability in the double-end tenoner machine. Our measure of variability was based upon a sample of one hundred parts shown as Fig. 16.3. For those one hundred sample observations, we computed the standard deviation to be approximately 0.0025 inches. In subsequent construction of the control charts we assumed that this sample standard deviation, s, was in fact the population standard deviation, σ.

In reality we need to control both the measure of central tendency or the average length of the drawer fronts as well as the variability or standard deviation of these drawer fronts. We accomplish this objective by constructing a range chart as well as the $\overline{X}$ or mean chart.

A control chart could be constructed for standard deviations, with sample standard deviations from our periodic observations compared to upper and lower control limits for the standard deviation of the process. Our objective, however, is not to control the standard deviation; rather, it is to control the inherent variability in the process. There are several statistics or measures of variability which might be used to control a varying process, the better known including the standard deviation, variance, range, and interquartile range. The choice of the range in statistical quality control is based upon a very important feature, namely, it is very easy to compute. You don't need to be a mental giant to subtract the value of the smallest observed part from that of the largest in the sample. The use of computers for quality control may overcome computational burdens.

The range, however, is not as "powerful" a statistic as the standard deviation. By powerful we mean that, although the range is a measure of variability, it is influenced by only two observations in the sample. For example, suppose we took two samples of five observations from some process. The first sample yielded results of 6, 7, 8, 9, and 10 respectively. The second sample had observations of 6, 10, 10, 10 and 10 respectively. Although the range is the same for both samples, the underlying variability is quite different. The standard deviation would more accurately reflect this variability, since all observations are weighted in the measure of process variability.

The net result of using the range as our measure of process variability is that there are times when one could say that the process variability is out of control if such a test were made on the standard deviation or variance when such a statement cannot be made with the range. That is, the control limit band for variability with the range is inherently wider than it is with the standard deviation. We are more likely to conclude that the process is in control when indeed it is not.

Since the range and standard deviation both measure process variability, it should not be surprising that one measure can be approximated with the other. A standard set of quality control factors can be used to make conversions between standard deviations and ranges, but these conversion factors are based on normality assumptions. In practice, these factors are used in the initial establishment of control charts so that standard deviation calculations are not required. Appendix A to this chapter provides these factors. Apropos of our discussion of statistical power, however, we will see that control limits for the mean or $\bar{X}$ chart based upon estimates of product variability measured by the range will tend to be wider than those based upon the standard deviation.

Control Chart Construction

Supposing that instead of the sample of one hundred drawer fronts taken to construct Fig. 16.3, we collected ten samples of four parts each. Alternatively, we could regard the one hundred pieces of paper representing drawer fronts as a "population" and draw ten samples of four with replacement. Table 16.1 gives ten samples of four parts each.

Table 16.1 Ten samples of four drawer fronts

	1	2	3	4	5
	23.0025	23.0005	23.0005	22.9995	22.9965
	23.0005	23.0005	23.0005	22.9965	23.0035
	23.0015	23.0035	23.0015	23.0015	22.9975
	22.9955	22.9965	23.0055	23.0005	22.9995
$\bar{X} =$	23.0000	23.00025	23.0020	22.9995	22.99925
$R =$	.007	.007	.004	.005	.007

	6	7	8	9	10
	23.0005	22.9965	23.0025	23.0005	22.9975
	23.0005	23.0005	23.0005	23.005	22.9985
	22.9965	23.0045	23.0005	22.9985	23.0035
	22.9975	23.0025	22.9965	23.0005	22.9965
$\bar{X} =$	22.99875	23.0010	23.0000	23.0000	22.9990
$R =$	.004	.008	.006	.002	.007

$$\bar{\bar{X}} = 22.999975 \approx 23.0000$$
$$\bar{R} = .0057$$
$$s = .00251$$

The summary statistics at the bottom of Table 16.1 indicate that the grand mean $(\bar{\bar{X}})$ for all forty pieces of data is 22.999975 inches which we can easily round off to 23.0000 inches. The average range for the ten samples $(\bar{R})$ is 0.0057 inches. The sample standard deviation (s) for the forty pieces of data is 0.00251 which again is quite close to the sample standard deviation used previously.

An empirical justification for the relationship of $\sigma_{\bar{X}}$ to σ_X can also be drawn from the ten samples, although the dangers of sampling error should not be overlooked. If each X for the ten samples is regarded as an observation, a standard deviation can be computed from these pieces of data as approximately 0.00096. Use of the $\sigma_X = \sigma_X \div \sqrt{n}$ formula with the addition of a small population correction factor results in an expected standard deviation of 0.00116.

Calculation of standard deviations is a tedious process. By use of the quality control factors given in Appendix A, we can construct control charts directly from the mean and range. The upper control limit is equal to $\bar{\bar{X}} + A_2\bar{R} = 23.0000 + (0.729 \times 0.0057) = 23.00416$ inches. The lower control limit is calculated as $\bar{\bar{X}} - A_2\bar{R} = 23.0000 - (0.729 \times 0.0057) = 22.99584$ inches. Note that the multiplication of A_2 times $\bar{R}$ represents our expected three standard deviations. An estimate of $\sigma_{\bar{X}} = (A_2\bar{R}) \div 3 = (0.729 \times 0.0057) \div 3 = 0.001385$. Note again that this estimate is larger

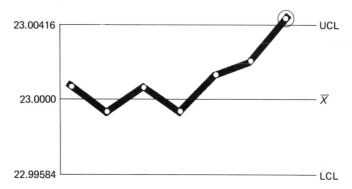

Fig. 16.8 Drawer front $\overline{X}$ control chart based upon quality control factors.

than that obtained by dividing the actual standard deviation for the forty samples (0.00251) by $\sqrt{n}$. Figure 16.8 shows the resultant chart with some illustrative data plotted (the circled observation indicates that the process is then out of control).

Construction of the $\overline{R}$ control chart is also straightforward with the quality control factors. The expected range, $\overline{\overline{R}}$, is equal to $H \times \overline{R} = (0.961)$ X (0.0057) = 0.00548. The lower control limit = $D_3 \times \overline{R} = 0 \times 0.0057 = 0$. The upper control limit = $D_4 \times \overline{R} = 2.282 \times 0.0057 = 0.01301$. The resultant $\overline{R}$ chart is given as Fig. 16.9, again with some illustrative data plotted.

The $\overline{R}$ chart is based upon the same concepts as the $\overline{X}$ chart. There is an expected or underlying distribution of ranges associated with a specified level of variability in the machine or process. Figure 16.9 results in the decision rule that if we observe a range greater than 0.01301 inches,

Fig. 16.9 Drawer front $\overline{R}$ chart.

we will reject the hypothesis that the underlying variability in the process is as we expected it to be.

The notion of a lower control limit on $\overline{R}$ is interesting. As noted in Appendix A, the D_3 factor for samples of 3, 4, 5, and 6 is equal to 0. Thereafter it increases gradually. A lower control limit on $\overline{R}$ means that it is possible to reject the variability hypothesis when the range is too low. It may seem slightly odd to conclude that the process is out of control when the variability is being controlled better than expected. However, even though the resultant output may be quite good, we have an expectation as to the variability in the process, and a range that is lower than the lower control limit on the $\overline{R}$ chart indicates that the hypothesis about variability is not valid. Once again, we note the distinction between the second step in the three-step control process and the third; our model is based upon a comparison of actual results with anticipated results—corrective action depends upon the situation.

The upper and lower control limits for the range are based upon variability in that statistic. It is sometimes hard for students to think about variability in a statistic which itself measures variability, but reference to Table 16.1 shows that the actual ranges observed will indeed vary over time. If the distribution expressing that variability is assumed to be normal, we can apply the same kind of three-σ-limit quality control chart ideas used in the $\overline{X}$ chart. The D_3 and D_4 statistics accomplish this procedure. An alternative would be to observe many ranges, calculate the average range, and determine the standard deviation of ranges. Upper and lower control limits could be established accordingly. Although the ten samples of four drawer fronts is probably too small for this purpose, we nonetheless could compute the variation around the average range ($\overline{R} = 0.0057$). The standard deviation is approximately 0.0018 inches, yielding an upper control limit of $0.0057 + 0.0054 = 0.011$ inches, and a lower control limit of $0.0057 - 0.0054 = 0.0003$ inches.

Other Control Charts

The $\overline{X}$ and $\overline{R}$ charts are probably the most widely used control charts in industry. Two other types of control charts, although not as widely used, are worthy of our consideration. This is primarily so because, although the major emphasis in this chapter is upon models for quality control, we will see in subsequent chapters how control chart ideas are valuable in other applications (e.g., in monitoring hypotheses underlying statistical forecasting models).

The p chart is a control chart for "attributes" instead of a control chart for variables. It is useful in those situations where the output from a process is easily characterized as either good or bad. Examples include electric light bulbs that either work or do not work, books examined to see whether any pages are missing, employees in a department as either there or not there, or an automobile engine that either starts or does not start at the end of the assembly line. Alternatively, we can consider items for which variability can be measured as either good or not good. That is, for example, instead of measuring the drawer fronts in terms of their exact lengths, we could determine the proportion of drawer fronts examined which meet the desired specifications. Such a procedure will sometimes be less expensive to utilize than the $\bar{X}$ and $\bar{R}$ charts, but it will not be as sensitive or diagnostic a procedure.

The p chart is based upon the binomial distribution which is parameterized by the population proportion, p, and the sample size, n. When the expected proportion defective is either stated or observed from past sample information, the estimate of error or variation is computed as:

$$\sigma_p = \sqrt{\frac{\bar{p}\,(1-\bar{p})}{n}}.$$

Control charts based upon plus and minus three standard deviations are drawn in the usual way. Figure 16.10 is a p chart for the drawer front example if we expect 5% defectives, and samples of size two hundred are drawn. Some illustrative data are plotted.

As shown in the calculations for Fig. 16.10, our procedure would be to draw a sample of size 200, calculate the proportion defective in that sample, and reject the hypothesis if the proportion is less than 0.0038 or greater than 0.0962.

Still another kind of control chart is the c chart; whereas the underlying probability distribution for the $\bar{X}$ and $\bar{R}$ charts is the normal, and the

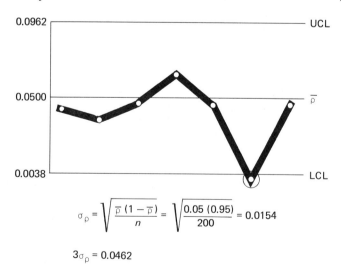

Fig. 16.10 p chart for drawer fronts (5% defective).

p chart is based upon the binomial distribution, the c chart is based upon the Poisson distribution. Recalling our discussion in Chapter 11 the Poisson distribution is useful for describing rare events where the events are described as a rate, such as so many raisins per raisin cake or arrivals per hour. The c chart is used to monitor defects per item such as blemishes per automobile paint job, defects in cloth per yard, or the number of blemishes in the finish of a piece of furniture.

Construction of the c chart is again based upon three standard deviation limits. In Chapter 11 we noted that the Poisson distribution was a single parameter distribution, with the mean equal to the variance. This means that the standard deviation is equal to the square root of the mean $(\sigma_c = \sqrt{\bar{c}})$. Our three standard deviation control limits are then determined by the average or expected number of defects $(\bar{c})$, $\pm 3\sqrt{\bar{c}}$.

The primary problem in the use of c charts is the definition of what constitutes a defect. Considerable judgment seems to be involved. Also, not all defects are the same. A finish blemish in the top of a dining room table is more important than one in a less noticeable place. A 1" scratch may not only be worse than a 1/8" scratch, it may be worse than eight of them.

Type I and Type II Errors

At several points in our discussion, we have made passing reference to errors. Statistical quality control procedures involve two basic kinds of errors for each hypothesis. Let us examine these errors for our drawer front hypothesis that the average length is 23.000 inches. Four things can happen when we test a hypothesis: (1) we can reject a true hypothesis; (2) we can accept a false hypothesis; (3) we can accept a true hypothesis; and (4) we can reject a false hypothesis.

Numbers 3 and 4 are what we would like to do all of the time, whereas numbers 1 and 2 are errors. Since we are working with samples, we run the risks of numbers 1 and 2 which can now be called type I error and type II error. That is, if we inspected each and every part, then we would be able to calculate the actual drawer front mean (as well as the actual drawer front standard deviation). Our sampling plan means that there are times when we will conclude that the process is out of control when indeed it is not and there are also times when it is possible for us to conclude that our process is in control when indeed it is not in control.

Type I error is sometimes referred to as the producer's risk, and type II as the consumer's risks. Implied are the risk that a producer will take corrective action when he doesn't need to and the risk that a consumer will accept defective output or corrective action will not be initiated when it should be.

The three standard deviation limits that underlie the statistical quality control procedures imply a certain probability of type I error. As noted above, the area under a normal curve contained within ± three standard deviations is 99.73%. By definition, the probability of type I error is 0.0027. That is, 27 times out of 10,000, three-standard-deviation quality control procedures will reject a hypothesis when the actual observed situation was due entirely to chance.

The probability of committing a type II error is more difficult to assess. In our prior discussion of control charts we simply ignored it. The reason that it is harder to assess is because we are less likely to accept a false hypothesis when the false hypothesis is quite different than if the false hypothesis is quite close to the expected or tested hypothesis. For example, the probability that we would accept the drawer front mean hypothesis of 23.000 inches is much lower if the actual mean of the process is 30.000 inches than if the actual mean of the process is 23.001 inches.

The extent to which the hypothesis can be wrong is a managerial decision. Representation of type II errors is more easily seen through the operating characteristic (OC) curve, to which we now turn our attention.

OPERATING CHARACTERISTIC CURVES

The operating characteristic curve for any particular control chart approach (or acceptance sampling plan) shows how well the approach discriminates—it shows the probabilities associated with type I and type II errors. Let us first look at the operating characteristic curve for variables, and then see how OC curves for attributes are constructed.

The OC Curve for Variables

We have seen that by changing the size of the sample in an $\bar{X}$ control chart the control limits change. In all of the $\bar{X}$ charts considered, we have used 3σ limits, which means that the probability of a type I error is the same, irrespective of sample size. Let us return to the drawer front example to see what varying sample size infers for the probability of committing a type II error. Figure 16.11 illustrates the problem.

The normal curve with the mean labelled $\bar{X}_1$ at 23.000 inches represents the hypothesis we have been testing. Our upper and lower control limits are 23.00375 inches and 22.99625 inches respectively. A small area on either side of the control limits coming from the normal curve with mean $\bar{X}_1$ is depicted. This combined area represents the probability of type I error of 0.0027. If the actual mean of the process is shifted from 23.000 inches to 23.003 inches, the probability that a type II error will be committed is depicted by the area to the left of the upper control limit coming from the normal curve with mean $\bar{X}_2$. This shaded area (including the solid black lower righthand corner) is more than half of the area under the curve. Using a standard normal curve area table, we find the

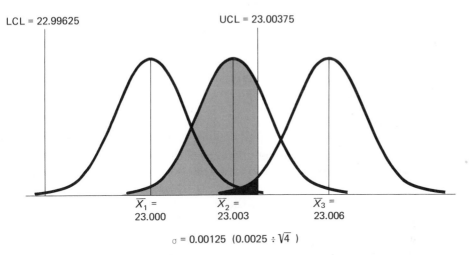

LCL = 22.99625   UCL = 23.00375

$\overline{X}_1 =$ 23.000 $\overline{X}_2 =$ 23.003 $\overline{X}_3 =$ 23.006

$\sigma = 0.00125$ $(0.0025 \div \sqrt{4}$)

Fig. 16.11 Drawer front example with different process means (n=4).

probability of committing a type II error to be 0.7257 if the underlying mean of the process has shifted to 23.003 inches.

If the mean shifted to 23.006 inches, we would expect to see the distribution of sample means as shown in the curve depicted with the mean $\overline{X}_3$; a small lefthand portion of this curve goes below the upper control limit of 23.00375 inches. The solid black area represents the probability of accepting the hypothesis that the mean is 23.000 inches when the mean is actually 23.006 inches. Using our normal curve area table, we find that the probability of a type II error is 0.0359 when the underlying mean has shifted to 23.006 inches.

The probabilities of type II errors associated with means of 23.003 and 23.006 are two points on an OC curve for the drawer front problem. We will construct an entire OC curve soon. Before we do so, however, let us examine two more fundamental ideas of operating characteristic curves.

First, suppose that a decision maker views the situation depicted in Fig. 16.11 and is unhappy with the magnitude of type II error associated with the shift in mean to 20.003 inches. He is happy to not be rejecting true hypotheses very often but is unhappy with the 0.7257 probability of accepting a false hypothesis. If the three-standard-deviation upper control limit were reduced to a two-standard-deviation control limit, the UCL would be placed at 23.0025 inches. This would reduce the probability of a type II error associated with mean $\overline{X}_2$. The reduction would, however, be offset by an increase in type I error from the present level of 0.00135 (right tail) to 0.0278. The fundamental idea is that type I error can be traded off for type II error; however, with a given sampling plan it is impossible to achieve a lower probability of one error without some offsetting increase in the probability of the other error.

A second fundamental idea pertains to the sample size. Figure 16.11 like all of our prior control chart studies of the drawer front example is based upon a normal distribution of sample means when the sample size is four. If we increase the sample size, we can achieve reduction of the probability of type II error without increasing the probability of type I error or achieve simultaneous reduction of both errors. To illustrate, let us redraw Fig. 16.11 based upon samples of size 25. Figure 16.12 then is basically the same as Fig. 16.11, except that the tighter normal distributions are for sample means where the sample size is 25.

As shown in Fig. 16.12, if our distributions of sample means are now based upon sample size 25, a marked shrinkage occurs. Keeping with our three standard deviation limits, we recalculate the upper and lower control limits as 23.0015 inches and 22.9985 inches respectively. Note that this calculation results in the same probability of type I error for Figs. 16.11 and 16.12. The probability of type II error, however, is drastically reduced. If the true mean were to shift from 23.00 inches to 23.003 inches,

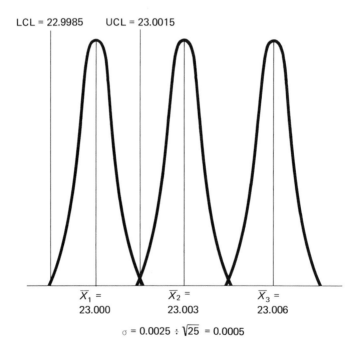

LCL = 22.9985   UCL = 23.0015

$\bar{X}_1 =$ 23.000

$\bar{X}_2 =$ 23.003

$\bar{X}_3 =$ 23.006

$\sigma = 0.0025 \div \sqrt{25} = 0.0005$

Fig. 16.12 Drawer front example with different sample means ($n=25$).

the probability that we would observe a sample from this distribution which fell within the control limit is 0.00135. Note that 23.003 inches just happens to be 3 standard deviations above the upper control limit, whereas 23.000 inches is 3 standard deviations below the upper control limit. This is the reason the two curves intersect the upper control limit at the same point. The probability of type II error associated with a shift in the process mean to 23.006 inches for this sampling plan is too small to find in most tables of the normal curve area. It is that area beyond nine standard deviations from the mean.

We see then that for a particular sampling plan, reductions in the probability of a type I error can only come at an increase of the probability of type II error and vice versa. Decreases in the probability of both errors or in one error without an offsetting increase in the other can be achieved by increasing the sample size. The larger the sample, the less likely the mean of that sample is to vary from the true mean of the distribution; larger samples do a better job of discriminating. Let us now plot the two OC curves which completely describe the probability of type II errors associated with sample sizes of four and 25 for our drawer front example.

Figure 16.13 clearly demonstrates the phenomena we have seen in Figs. 16.11 and 16.12. As the sample size increases, the distribution of sample means will get ever tighter until a single spike is approached which represents 100% inspection.

Although in Fig. 16.13 it looks as though the probability associated with 23.000 inches is 1.00, this is not so. At 23.000 inches, the probability of accepting the hypothesis is 0.9973, since there is a 0.0027 probability of rejecting this hypothesis (type I error).

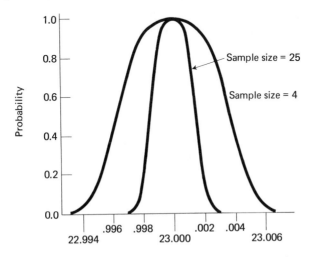

Fig. 16.13 Operating characteristic curves for the drawer front example.

The OC curves shown in Fig. 16.13 as well as the discussion leading up to those curves are based upon the assumption that we know the inherent variability of the process and that that variability is constant. That is, we assumed that σ was known and nonvarying. OC curves can be constructed for $\bar{X}$ charts when σ is varying, but the resultant OC function must be represented as a surface, not a curve. In actual practice, the assumption of a known constant variability in the process is not damaging, since an $\bar{R}$ chart will be used to control variability. The $\bar{R}$ chart itself has an underlying OC function which describes how well it discriminates. It gives the various probabilities associated with sample ranges that fall within the range control limits when indeed the underlying variability is different from that hypothesized.

OC Curves for Attributes

Just as there are control charts for attributes (go-no go, or good-bad) there are OC curves for attributes as well as variables. Although construction of these curves sometimes seems more complex, the underlying approach is exactly the same as that for variables. We have type I and type II errors and the only way that one can simultaneously decrease both errors is by increased sample sizes.

OC curves for attributes continue to have probability plotted on the ordinate as done in Fig. 16.13. The abscissa similarly denotes some underlying population parameter, but in this case the parameter is percent defective.

In Fig. 16.10, we constructed a p chart for the drawer front example; we expected 5% defectives, and our decision rule was to take a sample of size 200, calculate the percentage defective, and conclude that the process was in control if that percentage defective was between 0.38% and 9.62%. The lower control limit being set at 0.0038 implies the same kind of phenomenon we saw in a lower control limit above zero for range charts. That is, if we took a sample of size 200 and found no defectives we would conclude that the process is not generating defectives at a 5% rate. In the real world, people are more often worried about the upper control limit (especially in acceptance sampling). Let us simplify the decision rule in Fig. 16.10 to "take a sample of size 200, and reject the lot if there are more than 20 defects." Figure 16.14 shows the OC curve for this decision rule. Note that the allowable number of defects is labeled c; in the literature this is referred to as the acceptance number.

Rejecting on 19 defects would be more in keeping with the 9.62% UCL. Use of 20 will later allow us to make some interesting comparisons. The effect would be to decrease the type I error beyond the 3 σ limits.

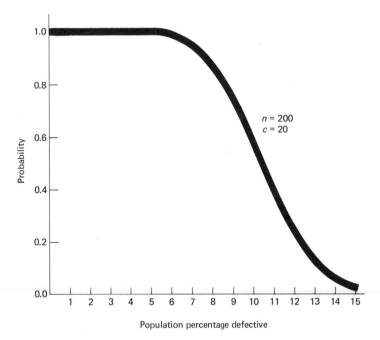

Fig. 16.14 Operating characteristic curve (n=200, c=20).

Specifically, setting LCL at 0 and UCL at 0.10 in Fig. 16.10 would result in a type I error probability of about 0.0012.

In Fig. 16.14 the probability that we would conclude the process is in control is essentially 1.0 until 5% defectives are observed. At that point the probability of accepting is 1.0 minus the type I error. From there on, the curve tends to fall rather rapidly with only a small probability of accepting the underlying hypothesis ($\bar{p} = 0.05$) when the actual population percent defective becomes as high as 15%.

The steepness of the OC curve shown in Fig. 16.14 is the analogue to the tightness to the OC curves in Fig. 16.13. The ideal OC curve for Fig. 16.14 would drop from 1.0 minus the type I error level at 5% to a probability of zero immediately thereafter. That is, the OC curve would be essentially a discontinuous step. Again, this might be achieved with 100% inspection.

The n of 200 and c of 20 in Fig. 16.14 is the ratio of 1 in 10. To again illustrate how increased sample size provides better discrimination, let us turn to Fig. 16.15 which shows four additional OC curves with the same ratio, but with smaller sample sizes.

Figure 16.15 is plotted on the same scale as Fig. 16.14. Note that when $n = 10$ and $c = 1$ the probability of accepting the hypothesis of $\bar{p} = 0.05$

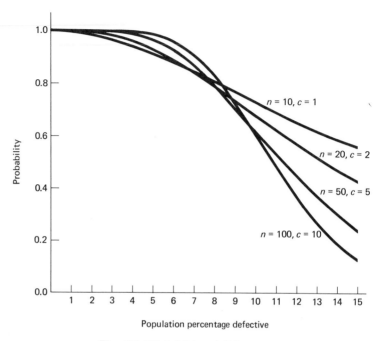

Fig. 16.15 Additional OC curves.

remains at more than one half when the actual population percent defect is 15%. Note also that at 5% defective, this sampling plan has about a 10% probability of a type I error (area between the top of the OC curve and 1.0). As the sample sizes increase, the probability of type I error tends to decrease as well as the probability of type II error. It is also worth noting that all 4 OC curves perform about equally well when the actual population percentage defective is in the 8 to 9% range.

The OC curves depicted in Figs. 16.14 and 16.15 were constructed using the Thorndike Chart which is given as Appendix B to this chapter. To construct any OC curve, one merely multiplies the percentage of defective figures along the OC curve abscissa by the sample size, looks up these values on the abscissa of the Thorndike Chart, and reads off the corresponding probabilities from the curves depicting different acceptance numbers.

ACCEPTANCE SAMPLING MODELS

Early in this chapter, we made a distinction between models for the control of production, and models for assessing a given lot or batch of production after the fact. Let us now turn our attention to the second group of models which are commonly referred to as acceptance sampling procedures. The underlying statistical techniques for acceptance sampling are the same as those used in statistical control models. For a manufacturing firm, both models would tend to be used; control charts for items manufactured in house and acceptance sampling techniques for purchased items.

The basic task in acceptance sampling is to design a decision rule such that a sample will be drawn from the total lot of material; based upon information from that sample, the entire lot will be accepted, the entire lot will be rejected, or further sampling might be called for.

Acceptance Sampling by Variables

Having established the concepts of type I and type II error and OC curves which show how a given sampling plan will affect type II error when type I error is specified, we can now go on to the design of sampling plans to achieve the desired results. The basic objective is to find a combination of sample size and control limits which will satisfy the desired results. Since increased sample sizes imply increased costs, we will be anxious to find that plan which will achieve the desired results at the lowest possible cost.

In order to construct a sample plan, we need to have certain managerial inputs. We need to know the tolerable levels of type I and type II errors, and we need to have some specified levels for the population parameter under consideration that management finds undesirable.

To illustrate, let us once again return to Figs. 16.11 and 16.12. If management interest was in the mean dimension of the drawer fronts being 23.000 inches, and the permissable level of type I error were given with the 3 standard deviation limits, then the curve labelled $\overline{X}_1$ in Fig. 16.11 depicts this situation. We noted, however, that the probability of a type II error associated with a population parameter of 23.003 inches ($\overline{X}_2$) is 0.7257. If management established 23.003 inches as the critical level, and they were willing to tolerate the probability of type II error at 0.7257, then a plan based upon samples of size 4 would achieve the desired results.

For most problems, a type II error probability of 0.7257 would be too high for the critical value. If, however, the critical value were not $\overline{X}_2$ but $\overline{X}_3$ (23.006 inches) then the probability of a type II error is only 0.0359 (shown as the solid black left tail of curve $\overline{X}_3$ in Fig. 16.11).

If our critical value was 23.003 inches, and three standard deviation limits expressed the desired type I error, and management was unwilling to tolerate a 0.7257 probability of type II error, then the only way to satisfy the situation is by increasing the sample size. In Fig. 16.12, we see that a sample size of 25 results in the probability of type II error of only 0.00135 when the population parameter is 23.003 inches.

If the permissible type II error is higher, say 0.10, then some sample size greater than four but less than 25 will achieve the desired results.

Figure 16.16 shows the situation and the resulting calculations to arrive at a sample size of 13.

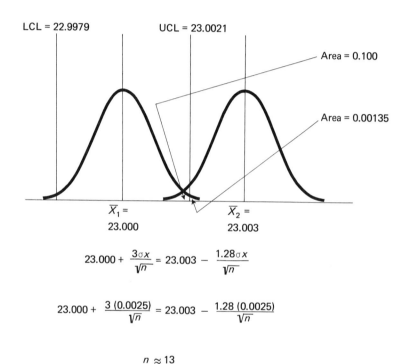

$$23.000 + \frac{3\sigma x}{\sqrt{n}} = 23.003 - \frac{1.28\sigma x}{\sqrt{n}}$$

$$23.000 + \frac{3\,(0.0025)}{\sqrt{n}} = 23.003 - \frac{1.28\,(0.0025)}{\sqrt{n}}$$

$$n \approx 13$$

Fig. 16.16 Sampling plan for drawer front example, where permissible limits for type I error are set at $\pm 3\sigma$, and for type II error, at 0.10.

As noted in Fig. 16.16, the necessary sample size to satisfy the requirements is 13. This is obtained by knowing that the underlying variability of the process as reflected by the standard deviation is 0.0025 inches. Using the formula $\sigma_X = \sigma_{\bar{X}} \div \sqrt{n}$ and the normal table to find the number of standard deviations away from the mean which leaves 10% of the area (1.28), allows us to solve for n.

In actual industrial situations, these calculations would be tedious. Standard sets of tables exist for various combinations of type I and type II error.

Let us briefly sum up the situation and resultant decision rule: For the drawer front example, instead of control as production is occurring, we are judging a completed lot of drawer fronts (perhaps purchased from a subcontractor). We are willing to tolerate a type I error based on usual 3σ limits. We want to guard against the mean of the drawer fronts being 23.003; we want to keep the probability of accepting a lot with this quality at 0.10 (type II error). The decision rule is to randomly select 13 drawer fronts from a batch or lot, calculate the mean for those 13 parts, and accept the hypothesis that the mean dimensions for all of the parts in the lot is 23.000 if the sample mean falls between 22.9979 and 23.0021 inches.

It is worth noting that this procedure as applied to acceptance sampling conceptually could also be applied to the control chart approach. This is not usually done because three-standard-deviation limits are set without any real thought given to the type I-type II error tradeoff or the critical values to guard against through the design of a sampling plan. Moreover, there are some good arguments for more frequent samples of 4 or 5 when the process is ongoing and the desire is to quickly detect problems.*

Acceptance Sampling by Attributes

Acceptance sampling by attributes is essentially the same problem as that for variables. We need to find an OC curve that satisfies the conditions established by management. These conditions are typically stated as the allowable probability of the type I error (producer's risk), the allowable type II error (consumer's risk), the equivalent of the mean in variables sampling which is now called the acceptance quality level (AQL) and the analogue to the critical dimension in variables sampling which is that percentage defective for which we are willing to tolerate the type II error called the "lot tolerance percent defectives" (LTPD). Let us refer back to the OC curve given in Fig. 16.14. If the probability of type I error is given as 0.01, we see from our Thorndike Chart that with $n = 200$, $c = 20$, the probability of a type I error is 0.01 at a population percentage defective of 6% ($pn=12$). If the allowable type II error probability is 0.07 and the critical level is 14%, *then* the OC curve drawn in Fig. 16.14 fits our requirements and the indicated sample size and acceptance numbers are $n = 200$, $c = 20$.

If the critical population percentage defective or LTPD were less than 14%, with the same allowable type II error probability, then the OC curve would have to be more discriminating (steeper) which would call for a larger sample size. The same thing would be true if the LTPD were

---

*Acheson, J. Duncan, *op. cit.* pp. 396–97.

maintained at 14% but the allowable type II error were decreased. The OC curves shown in Fig. 16.15 show sampling plans for less rigorous requirements.

Solving for the exact sample size in attributes sampling is somewhat more difficult than for variables sampling. A trial and error procedure with the Thorndike Chart can be used, but again extensive tables exist in industry for finding the sample size which will provide the desired features.

Just as was true for control charts for attributes and control charts for variables, sampling plans based upon attributes can always be substituted for sampling plans based upon variables. Instead of measuring an item to find out its exact size, it can be categorized as good or bad. However, attributes sampling plans require larger samples to achieve corresponding levels of type I error, type II error, and critical values. Duncan states that a p chart may require a sample of about 50 against a sample of about 10 for an $\overline{X}$ and $\overline{R}$ Chart.*

The sampling plans we have discussed so far are based upon a single sample where the result is either to accept some hypothesis or to reject the hypothesis. (Specific actions might be to reject a lot of incoming materials.) An alternative is to use double sampling. In double sampling a preliminary sample may be extreme enough to call for no further sampling either because one can conclude that the underlying quality is either very good or very bad. For example, suppose a single sampling plan called for sample size of 200 and decision rule of no more than 20 defective; if 100 parts were inspected without an error, it does not seem intuitively reasonable to inspect the additional 100. This is easily seen in the OC curves in Fig. 16.15. A sample of $n = 10$, $c = 1$ is quite adequate if the percentage defective is only 1%.

If the data from the initial sample do not allow us to discriminate in this way, then a second sample is taken which increases our ability to discriminate. In sequential sampling the notion is to continue sampling until either a concrete rejection or concrete acceptance can be achieved.

Because the initial sample is smaller than that required for a single sampling plan, sequential sampling plans can result in smaller samples being taken and reduced inspection costs. Sequential sampling plans allow for sampling to cease whenever discrimination, either good or bad, can be achieved.

The design of specific sequential sampling plans is beyond our present scope, but the same ideas of type I and type II errors and critical levels apply. Again, standard tables exist for construction of such plans to achieve desired results.

---

*Acheson J. Duncan, *op. cit.* p. 399.

EXPLICIT COST MODELS

We started our chapter by accepting the standard industrial criterion of ±3 standard deviation control limits. In our discussion of the operating characteristic curve, we broadened our understanding to encompass the notions of type II error and tradeoff between the probability of rejecting a true hypothesis and the probability of accepting a false hypothesis. We then asked for managerial inputs as to the values for those probabilities as well as critical levels of difference between population parameters. In many ways the managerial input approach tends to dodge the basic issue. The primary objective is to tradeoff type I and type II errors with sampling cost, and the overall objective is to minimize cost in some global sense. That is, there is cost associated with type I errors, cost associated with type II errors, and cost associated with larger samples.

Error Costs

In many real world situations, the existence of a tradeoff between the cost of type I errors and type II errors goes unrecognized by the general population. A good example is the development of drugs to combat disease. A concern with not putting a drug on the market which may have side effects until very extensive testing is accomplished, must be balanced against the expected benefits which are not achieved by keeping the drug from those who need it. Although calculation of these costs is difficult and the data tend to be soft, the problem nonetheless exists and solution of the problem is not aided by ignorance of the basic tradeoff.

Similar difficult tradeoffs exist in many fields. A concern with ecological damage led to pesticides not being used against the Gypsy Moth in 1970, but the summer of 1971 saw an infestation which seriously weakened trees in New England. What is the cost of having a defective automobile sold? Clearly a defect in the paint job is less important than a defect in the steering mechanism, but how much less important? Who decides? How are the costs felt by the manufacturer?

The Basic Model

In Fig.16.16 we were given managerial input as to allowable probabilities for type I and type II errors as well as critical levels in the underlying population parameter to be controlled. We then solved to find the necessary sample size which would permit these criteria to be met. Implied in that analysis is a managerial understanding of the tradeoff between type I type II error, but little if any attention is given to the cost of sampling. It happens that when the critical area to be guarded against is set at 23.003 inches, the sample size was 13; however, if the critical level had been set at 23.001 inches, the necessary sample size would be greater than 100. Since the cost of measuring each part is significant, or if the testing procedure destroyed the parts, clearly sampling cost has to be included in the overall cost minimization tradeoff. Thus a very general cost model might be:

where
$$TC = (p_I c_I) + (p_{II} c_{II}) + (c_i n)$$

TC = the total cost to be minimized

p_I = the probability of a type I error

c_I = the cost of a type I error

p_{II} = the probability of a type II error

c_{II} = cost of the type II error

c_i = unit cost of inspection

n = sample size

Additional factors can be added to the basic model including the frequency of inspection for a process, cost of making corrective changes in production methods, and lost production due to time spent on inspection.

Knowledge of the process itself (mean and standard deviation or percentage defective) is also assumed. For many kinds of processes, the form of this knowledge is better considered as a prior distribution; the use of Bayesian analysis to generate posterior probabilities in the light of additional information becomes especially useful.

Procedures to tradeoff costs of type I and type II errors with sample information in light of prior and posterior probabilities are simply beyond our present scope.* Our present purposes are sufficiently satisfied by at least noting that the industrial practice of blindly adhering to plus and minus three standard deviation limits cannot readily be defended in terms of the more important goals of the firm.

SUMMARY REMARKS

In this chapter we have attempted to expand our understanding of quality as a surrogate criterion for enterprise well-being. We found that a concrete definition of quality is extremely difficult and that translating objectives manifested as quality in the market place into specific measurable criteria for manufacturing is not a straightforward process. Considerable suboptimization is possible. Nonetheless, from a hazy understanding of what is desired in the marketplace as well as what actions might result

---

*The interested reader should see Robert D. Fetter, *The Quality Control System,* Richard D. Irwin, 1967 and Robert Schlaifer, *Introduction to Statistics for Business Decisions,* McGraw-Hill, 1961.

from production changes, a set of specific measurable objectives somehow results (usually from the engineering function of the firm).

We also examined the means for assuring that actual output of productive processes matches the desired specifications. The basic underlying models for quality control procedures are statistical in nature. Tests of hypotheses are formulated and evaluated on the basis of the underlying probability distributions appropriate to particular situations. The normal distribution is used for variables, and the binomial distribution underlies statistical models for proportion defectives.

The quality-control chart/test-of-hypothesis approach is useful beyond the control of factory operations. Conceptually, the upper and lower control limit notions are appropriate to the control of expenses and other enterprise phenomena. For many of these phenomena, we will find the statistical nature of quality control models to also be appropriate. In these cases the models developed in Chapter 16 will be even more readily transferable.

REFERENCES

Cowden, Dudley J., *Statistical Methods in Quality Control,* Prentice-Hall, 1957.

Duncan, Acheson J., *Quality Control and Industrial Statistics,* 3rd Ed., Irwin, 1965.

Fetter, Robert B., *The Quality Control System,* Irwin, 1967.

Grant, Eugene L., *Statistical Quality Control,* McGraw-Hill, 1964.

Starr, Martin K., *System Management of Operations,* Prentice-Hall, 1971.

_____, *Product Design and Decision Theory,* Prentice-Hall, 1963.

CHAPTER REVIEW

Chapter 16 is the longest chapter in the book. This fact is slightly disconcerting to me because I frankly do not think the subject matter is the most important part of your course in operations management. It is not that the area is unimportant, but there are several other problem areas that are at least as critical to the goals of the firm. Moreover, the major development of models for quality control occurred about 30 years ago; topics such as production planning and inventory control systems have greater potential application at this time.

To some extent this chapter reinforces your course work in statistics and quantitative methods. It has been my experience that most students have a hard time understanding the value of statistical hypothesis testing. An understanding of these models is basic to classical statistics, and many of you will better comprehend the approach in the context of quality control.

An understanding of statistical quality control will provide you with a useful frame of reference as we move into the next major section of the book. For example, models for forecasting will yield results that are subject to error; we will want to make continuing assessments of whether the error is random or due to invalid modeling procedures.

OUTLINE OF THE CHAPTER

Introduction	(control = standard, measurement, correction)
Product quality	(consumer criteria)
The nature of quality	(costs *versus* benefits)
Furniture quality	(competitive advantage)
Quality motivational programs	(zero defects)
Statistical control models	(actual *versus* standard)
Product variability	(random variation *versus* underlying change)
Control charts for variables	(3 standard deviation limits)
The dynamic control chart	(predictable drift)
The range chart	(variability hypothesis)
Control chart construction	(quality control factors)
Other control charts	(*p* charts and *c* charts)
Type I and type II errors	(reject true, accept false)
Operating characteristic curves	(type I & II error probabilities)
The OC curve for variables	(type I *versus* type II *versus* sample size)
OC curves for attributes	(sample size, acceptance number)
Acceptance sampling models	(assessment of a lot or batch)
Acceptance sampling by variables	(design of sampling plan)
Acceptance sampling by attributes	(AQL and LTPD)
Explicit cost models	(error cost *versus* sampling cost)
Error costs	(type I and II error cost tradeoffs)
The basic model	(probabilities *versus* costs)
Summary remarks	(approach useful for other problems)

CENTRAL ISSUES

The nature of quality is an interesting issue; consumers view quality in terms of functional and esteem characteristics, and manufacturers design and create products with imperfect knowledge of those criteria. Defining detailed quality standards for products such as furniture is very difficult, and usually done somewhat arbitrarily. Motivational programs such as zero defects can instill an improved quality consciousness on the part of the workers, but medicine-show theatrics can lead to letdowns and a credibility gap.

The measurement of any characteristic or attribute of a set of parts or products will result in variability of the measurements. Statistical quality control procedures set up hypotheses about this variability; when actual data indicate rejection of a hypothesis, the conclusion is that the process creating the characteristic is out of control. Limits on statistical control charts are typically set at plus and minus three standard deviations. Hypotheses for variables are made for both the mean or measure of central tendency and the range or measure of variability. Control charts can also be constructed for good-bad assessments or for the number of defects per unit. Construction of actual control charts is facilitated by tables of quality control factors which can be applied to sample data.

The three standard deviation limits result in a probability of 0.0027 of rejecting a hypothesis when the hypothesis is indeed correct. This kind of mistake is called a type I error (rejecting a true hypothesis). A type II error is committed when a hypothesis should be rejected, but is not (accepting a false hypothesis). The operating characteristic curve depicts the probabilities of committing type I and type II errors. A different OC curve is associated with different sampling plans; larger sample sizes discriminate more effectively.

Acceptance sampling is concerned with after-the-fact passing on the worth of an entire batch of an item, as opposed to controlling the production of that item while it occurs. The underlying methodologies are the same, but the objective is to determine the sample size and decision rules in order to insure compliance with stated type I and type II error probabilities.

Explicit cost models go beyond specification of type I and type II error probabilities. The relative costs of these errors in specific situations and the costs of sampling are traded off to achieve a minimum cost plan. An ongoing process of incorporating data as it is collected leads to formulation of the problem in a Bayesian framework.

ASSIGNMENTS

1. The mean diameter of a lot of bushings is 2.0034 inches and the standard deviation 0.0065 inches. What are the probabilities that a single bushing will be above the upper design specification of 2.02 or below the lower design specification of 1.98?

2. a) What is the probability that a canning machine filling cans to a mean weight of 4.502 ounces with a standard deviation of 0.13 ounces will produce outside the 4.4 to 4.6 ounce limit set by management?

b) What is the probability that the mean of a 4-can sample will be outside the same tolerance?

c) What is the probability associated with a 25 can sample?

3. Set up an $\overline{X}$ control chart for problem 2b.

4. A knuten valve manufacturer has enlisted your aid in deciding which of his four gdunk machines to use for a particular valve stem. He also wants you to prepare the appropriate quality control chart.

Data

Engineering specification—length: no problem
Engineering specification—diameter: 1.500 in. ± 0.0010 in.
Sample size: 9

Gdunk machine #1
    Capacity: 0.5 inches to 2.5 inches
    Standard deviation on diameters: 0.0001 inches
    Per hour billing charge: $10.50

Gdunk machine #2
    Capacity: 0.0625 inches to 1.75 inches
    Standard deviation on diameters: 0.00015 inches
    Per hour billing charge: $9.00

Gdunk machine #3
    Capacity: 1.00 inches to 3.00 inches
    Standard deviation on diameters: 0.0002 inches
    Per hour billing charge: $8.00

Gdunk machine #4
    Capacity: 1.25 inches to 2.00 inches
    Standard deviation on diameters: 0.00035 inches
    Per hour billing charge: $6.00

5. a) The diameter of parts produced on all four machines in problem 4 tend to increase with the number of parts produced due to tool wear. The rate of increase has been estimated at 0.0001 inches per hundred parts. If you were using machine number 3, what would be the initial setting and how many parts would you expect to produce before readjustment became necessary?

b) If the machines all produce 100 valves per hour and cost approximately $40 to readjust, which machine would offer the most economic operation? Prepare a dynamic control chart for samples of 4 and indicate the initial setting and expected number to be produced before readjustment becomes necessary.

6. It should be obvious that the strategy used to answer problem 5 depends on the variability of the machines remaining constant. Construct an R control chart for machine number 2 in 16-4 with sample size 4.

7. Construct $\overline{X}$ and $\overline{R}$ control charts for the following 9 samples of 4 items. Use the Quality Control Factors in Appendix A of this chapter.

1	.2732	.2703	.2748	.2800
2	.2728	.2749	.2720	.2738
3	.2758	.2759	.2767	.2709
4	.2779	.2769	.2781	.2796
5	.2747	.2754	.2753	.2776
6	.2710	.2696	.2706	.2708
7	.2726	.2760	.2768	.2747
8	.2749	.2763	.2755	.2761
9	.2725	.2714	.2750	.2767

8. Acme Pencil Co. purchases crates of 10,000 erasers. Acme intends to inspect 1% of each crate. For the purpose of establishing an expected proportion defective a complete inspection was done on one crate turning up 383 defective erasers. Construct a p chart for use in the proposed inspection plan.

9. Using the Thorndike Chart, construct OC curves for Acme Pencil. Assume that they will continue to use a sample size of 100. Try acceptance numbers of 0, 2, 5, and 10. What are the probabilities of type I errors for each of these acceptance numbers if the population percentage defective is 5%.

10. At the construction site of a high-rise apartment building you are responsible for accepting precut and drilled steel beams. Lengths must be held to a tolerance of ±0.10 inches, 99% of the time. The beams are shipped in lots of 20. The standard deviation of beam lengths measured from past experience is 0.05 inches. Your superior has decided that a permissible type I error is 0.2 and type II error is 0.05. What would be a suitable sampling plan?

Miller Company*

The Miller Ballbearing, Inc., was a fairly small manufacturer of ballbearings. Nevertheless, it produced more than 1000 different ballbearings to fulfill the particular needs of its customers.

Ballbearings consist of 4 major parts. The outer ring, the inner ring, the balls, and a device which separates the balls. Production of ballbearings begins simultaneously at several different stations. Balls are first stamped into rough shape from steel wire. The flanges and burrs are then removed on a rough abrasive wheel that dresses the balls to a diameter which is approximately 0.01" oversized. The balls then go through a series of abrasive tumblers. In each successive tumbler the abrasive becomes finer. The balls are left in each tumbler a prescribed period of time to remove a certain amount of metal. The fineness of the abrasive determines the smoothness of finish. The length of time in the tumbler determines the amount of metal removed. As one engineer said, "We don't quite know why, but each ball comes out round. All we worry about is its size and finish. Once the balls enter the tumblers, human hands only touch them to inspect them and to move them to the next tumbler."

*This case was written by Professor J. Brian Quinn at the Amos Tuck School of Business Administration, Dartmouth College, and is used with his permission.

After tumbling is complete the balls are put through a series of screens containing holes of the desired size ± 0.001″. Successive screening and tumbling can hold the balls to ± 0.0001″ (exact, oversized and undersized). With special care, a few balls of ± 0.00001″ may be selected from a lot.

The rings (or races) are cut from bar stock or tubing on automatic screw machines which hold tolerances of ± 0.002″. Once the machines are set up, no human touches the ring until the machine drops it complete onto an oil filter screen. From the screw machines the rings go to heat treat where the stresses induced by machining are removed.

A scale is picked up by the metal during heat treat. This scale is removed by shot blasting and washing. The rings are then ready for grinding.

The races are ground on Heald automatic grinders. Once properly set up the Heald machines will hold desired tolerances to ± 0.0001″ on all dimensions. By means of a second grind and hand dressing with a special abrasive cloth, tolerances of ± 0.00001″ can be held with surface fineness of microinch tolerances. Tolerances of ± 0.0001″ can be read on air gauges. Surface finishes in microinches can be measured on an electronic gauge. Contour conformity can be read on a "shadow graph."

Dimensions on the ball separators are not critical. These are made of bakelite or stamped metal parts. Tolerances of several hundredths are allowable for all but a few applications. Some ballbearings do not even use separators.

Assembly is performed by hand. Balls of selected tolerances are matched with each set of rings. The balls are placed loosely in the race using a jig. The inner-ring is cooled and the outer-ring is placed over the assembly. The entire unit is then cooled to room temperature. Grease is added, if needed, and the units are sent to final inspection before packing.

Applications for Miller ballbearings vary considerably. Three examples will illustrate this variation. One ballbearing is used for roller skates. Another is used in aircraft propellers. A third is used for the inertial guidance systems of experimental rockets. The roller skate bearings are made in lots of several thousands. Propeller bearings are normally made in lots of a few hundred. Guidance system bearings are produced in various quantities from units to hundreds depending upon the degree of development of the missile.

To maintain the quality expected of the product the company has established a centralized quality control department. The department has complete responsibility for all aspects of quality control in the company's 3 plants. George Miller, the president's brother, heads up this department.

Mr. Miller expressed his department's job this way. "We don't try to inspect quality into a product, we see that it is built in. Everyone must be quality minded to produce our kind of product at the lowest possible cost. So we try to keep quality uppermost in everyone's mind.

"Take our new race manufacturing plant. Nothing like it in the whole country. It's temperature and humidity conditioned throughout. Working conditions are identical in a blizzard or in midsummer. The entire plant was painted with new 'Eye-ease pastels'. We have electronic circuits to brighten and dim the overhead lights depending upon changes in outside lighting conditions. If a cloud shuts out the sun the lights get brighter. Morning and evening light conditions are the same as at midday. It's the greatest thing I ever saw.

"Not only that, we have probably the best housekeeping plant in the United States. No grease or sawdust on floors around here. That keeps accidents down too, you know. That's another one of my jobs—safety supervisor. If the employee has to worry about whether he's going to slip down he can't watch his job. We vacuum every department twice per shift and mop the whole place down everynight. We figure our extra housekeeping costs us about $7,000 a year, but it's worth it. Boosts morale. Makes people proud of the place where they work. This pride carries over to their product. Some of the workers are downright offended if any of their work is rejected.

"We try to select people who want to produce a quality product. As you know this is an old mill town and the people here have a tradition of fine craftsmanship. They also seem to inherit a tremendous dexterity and interest in machines. I don't think we could find as many good people anyplace else in the country. Give me a good old New England worker any day. Everyone of our people is given a battery of tests before he is hired. We look for a basically contented person, not a driver. He has to have the eye–hand facility to suit him to the job, but we actually prefer people who have never worked in other ballbearing plants. Then we can train them our way. 80% of our employees are women. They are better precision workers.

Since we pay only hourly wages—the best in the area incidentally—we depend on social pressures to get the girls to work. We put a new girl on a 3-month probation. During that period we watch her closely. If she doesn't get along with her group, we either move her or let her go. Most of our girls are good workers, so they expect a new girl to hold up her end. We have a merit-rating system which lets us pay our better people a premium wage. We don't need time standards. The foreman can see whether a girl is working hard enough. If we were unionized, we probably couldn't do this. But the workers have voted down the union 7 times now. The highest the union ever got was 20% of our employees. They know they have a good thing here. You notice all the girls sit down at their jobs in specially fitted chairs. We think that keeps them from getting tired. We make them stop work 5 minutes every hour and give 15 minute breaks in the morning and afternoon. Keeps life from getting too dull.

"We say our place is human engineered. We have a game room and auditorium for employees. Did you know a lot of them stay for a while after work almost every day. I guess their homes aren't as comfortable as the plant. Every worker has his own locker and is expected to pick up his work area at the end of the shift. We give them 10 minutes just for that. You can't expect a man to start the day with his eye on quality if his workplace looks like a pig pen.

"Wherever possible we let the worker do his own set up and testing. We try to keep each batch of work identified by who worked on it, right up till the time we ship. This way we can make life uncomfortable for anyone who doesn't catch his own mistakes. On the continuous operations—like screw machines or grinders—we use control charts. Our men watch those like hawks. If they see a machine drifting out beyond one sigma, they stop it and readjust the tooling. The workers know this and watch the charts themselves. We have even offered prizes for the machines with the lowest reject rates during the year and you should have seen them scramble for that.

"The other operations are all hand operations, so we inspect everything

100%. Balls, rings, separators, and final assemblies are all brought into the central inspection room to the gages where our central group of 30 inspectors are. Our gages are checked against a master before each shift. We throw out gages if they can't hold 1/10 of the desired tolerance. Master gages are kept in a temperature controlled box which is completely dust free. Our master gages are so sensitive that some of them will detect the effect of an extra fingerprint on a surface.

"We do such a thorough job on quality control that we have had only one customer complaint in five years. There the problem turned out to be an internal flaw in one of the balls. As you know a failure in an aircraft engine bearing could cost us and our customers plenty. In a missile, 10-million dollars may ride on every gyro bearing working correctly. But we think our bicycle and roller skate bearings are just as important. They carry our name to the public. We give all bearings the same quality attention. It keeps our people from getting into sloppy habits. Granted, our tolerances aren't as tight for the cheaper bearings, but we hold to them just as rigorously. If you let up on an easy job, workers won't be able to readjust when it really counts.

"You might be interested in our equipment policy. Every major machine is torn down once a year, and all worn parts are replaced. Preventive maintenance, like this, is costly as hell, but we figure we gain three ways. We have very few machine breakdowns, so other repair expense is held to a minimum. We are able to schedule our production more accurately, so we eliminate almost all bottlenecking costs and provide our customers better service. Finally, we figure that we can schedule machine maintenance labor better so it only costs us three extra men anyway. We have tried to figure how much we save in resetup costs because of better machine control, but haven't been able to come up with a figure.

"We normally replace all major equipment on a rotating basis every five years or whenever the machine will not hold at least 1/10 of the tolerances pieces made on it require. We arrived at this policy after an elaborate statistical analysis by our engineers. They figured the average obsolescence time for our equipment is about five years. This means we ought to look at every operation that frequently and see whether or not there aren't better ways to do the job. In nine out of ten cases we have decided, both for quality and cost considerations, to replace existing equipment. The workers like this too. They know they have the best tools available to work with. There's none of that "chewing gum and string" philosophy here. We replace about a million dollars worth of equipment each year.

"Did I tell you about our incoming materials control? As you can see, materials cost is not a very great percentage of our total cost, but we think quality materials are essential to a quality product. We have a full time chemist who takes a sample out of every incoming batch of material (bar stock, tube, wire and Bakelite). We test its chemical content, tensile shear and bearing strength, and give it a visual check for flaws. On some missile work, we even X-ray the materials for internal flaws. Our vendors have been carefully selected. Our engineers have drawn up careful specifications and have visited every vendor's plant. They must be convinced of the vendor's ability to do the job before we place an order. As a result, our reject rate of vendor material is infinitesimal. In the last five years we haven't had to return more than a couple thousand dollars worth of stuff.

"All this may sound a little elaborate for a 10-million dollar business, but we have built a reputation for quality and there is only one way to hold it. Besides, with 80% of our business being government work, we can pass these costs along to our customers. In a lot of our markets, being able to build a few special bearings when they are needed is our bread and butter. When the volume gets very big we sometimes lose out to the big boys. In the roller skate business we only sell to a local manufacturer who makes skates for the pros. Our bicycle bearings go into the best-known bicycle in the area. Our automobile bearings are strictly for the top lines of cars. We couldn't touch New Departure in that small car stuff.

"Let me show you a couple of our specific control techniques." Mr. Miller then began to explain how balls were tested for size. Each ball is put through a series of screens with increasingly finer holes. Each set of balls is automatically screened to the nearest 0.001. For special purposes balls can be rescreened, by using a screen with reamed holes to 0.0001 (oversized and undersized). For special applications, ball gages can check on diameter tolerances (roundness) of the ball. Usually, tumbling roundness is assumed to be accurate enough. Sample balls from each batch are checked for hardness and grain structure.

A control chart is kept on each machine. For example, in the case of the ring grinder which finish grinds the O.D. outer-rings to 1.0000 ± 0.0001, immediately following the last complete setup the following samples of 4 items were taken in a half-hour period.

		Item		
Sample	**1**	**2**	**3**	**4**
1.	.3	.6	−.4	.1
2.	.2	−.3	0	−.5
3.	.1	.8	−.3	−.4
4.	.8	.4	0	.4
5.	−.6	−.1	.2	−.3
6.	.3	−.9	.3	−.1
7.	.5	.1	.3	−.5

The table entries are in 0.0001 minus one inch (i.e., sample 1, item 1 = 1.00003)

When it has been established that a machine is in control, samples of 4 items are taken at half-hour periods. Following the previous 7 samples from the ring grinder, the following results were obtained for 16 four-item samples in an 8-hour period.

	$\overline{X}$ (ins)	R (.0001')		$\overline{X}$ (ins)	R (.0001")
1	1.000008	1.3	9	1.000043	.5
2	1.000007	.1	10	1.000052	1.5
3	1.000019	.8	11	1.000051	1.0
4	1.000022	1.5	12	1.000065	1.7
5	1.000021	.7	13	1.000062	2.1
6	1.000029	.9	14	1.000067	.5
7	1.000035	1.7	15	1.000068	1.9
8	1.000037	1.3	16	1.000068	2.0

These points plotted on the control chart show clearly that the machine is producing parts well within specification limits.

Bakelite separators are stamped and drilled by a nearby machine shop, using jigs provided by the Miller Company. As these units come in they are inspected on a sample basis for overall dimensions, ball hole size, and radical spacing of drilled holes. Chemical content and strength inspection have already been described. Miller Company does not consider the tolerances of separators a critical quality factor in most bearings. Consequently, if no more than 2% of each 50-unit sample is defective, the company accepts the order. If 2% to 6% are defective, they sample again and reject according to Miller Standard 105A tables. If over 6% are defective, they reject the order, or if delivery is a crucial matter, they 100% inspect the lot and reject only bad units. Most defective separators will be caught visually at assembly anyway because they affect the spacing and fit of balls in the races. Reassembly of a bearing only costs 50 cents, inspection costs 5 cents, and it costs $10 to reject a lot, including the cost of repacking and handling within the plant and the possibility of having a material shortage.

The company has kept careful records of the quality of each lot received, and has found the following distribution of percentage good to be typical:

% Good	Relative frequency
100	.1
98	.2
96	.4
94	.2
92	.1

11. a) Be prepared to comment on this company's quality control program. Are the specific techniques of control described adequate for the purpose?

b) Prepare a control chart for the data on the previous page.

APPENDIX A TO CHAPTER 16

QUALITY CONTROL FACTORS

Type of chart	Central line	Lower limit	Upper limit
Average, $\overline{X}$	$\overline{\overline{X}}$	$\overline{\overline{X}} - A_2\overline{R}$	$\overline{\overline{X}} + A_2\overline{R}$
Range, R	$\overline{R} = H\overline{R}$	$D_3\overline{R}$	$D_4\overline{R}$
Fraction defective, p	$\overline{p}$	$\overline{p} - 3\sqrt{\dfrac{\overline{p}(1-\overline{p})}{n}}$	$\overline{p} + 3\sqrt{\dfrac{\overline{p}(1-\overline{p})}{n}}$
Count of defects, c	$\overline{c}$	$\overline{c} - 3\sqrt{\overline{c}}$	$\overline{c} + 3\sqrt{\overline{c}}$

n	A_2	H	D_3	D_4	d_2	n
3	1.023	0.938	0	2.574	1.693	3
4	0.729	0.961	0	2.282	2.059	4
5	0.577	0.970	0	2.114	2.326	5
6	0.483	0.975	0	2.004	2.534	6
7	0.419	0.978	0.076	1.924	2.704	7
8	0.373	0.980	0.136	1.864	2.847	8
9	0.337	0.982	0.184	1.816	2.970	9
10	0.308	0.983	0.223	1.777	3.078	10

THORNDIKE CHART

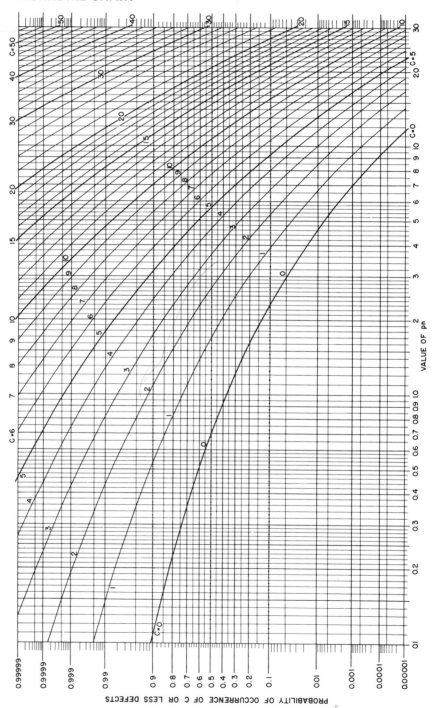

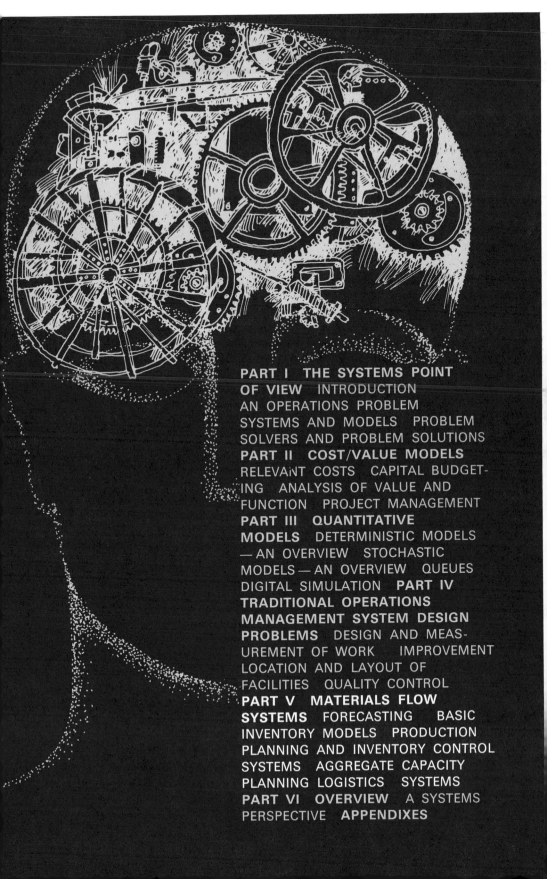

INTRODUCTION TO
PART V

Part V is to me the most interesting part of the book, and it well may be the most enjoyable part of your course in operations management. The problems and models presented in this part currently are receiving special attention in the business world, and significant improvements in company operations are possible. The knowledge you gain in this part will give you an opportunity to take an active role in achieving those improvements.

In Part V you will probably derive the greatest understanding of the benefits of the systems approach. You will see that integration of subsystems and the design of those subsystems in terms of higher order criteria are needed; that the proper surrogate criteria for subsystems are often counterintuitive, and that a primary reason for improvement potential is due to disjoint approaches where "reasonable" criteria for subsystems have been used. You will also see that implementation of counterintuitive system designs calls for careful attention to the notions embedded in the user-designer concept.

The plan of attack will be to start with some of the most straightforward materials, basic models and the criteria sets appropriate to use of those models. We will then add continuing real world complexities, and you will see how surrogate criteria shift and how improved subsystem design runs counter to intuitive and historical approaches. The strategy is bottom-up rather than top-down, because I believe that your overall understanding will be enhanced by first understanding some of the basic ideas (that are fairly straightforward in isolation) and then seeing why application of some of these basic ideas can be inappropriate.

Chapter 17 is concerned with forecasting. There are many possible methods or models for forecasting, including such diverse approaches as collective opinion and regression. We will be almost exclusively concerned with exponential smoothing, which is particularly well suited to repetitive routine forecasting of many items. Exponential smoothing is a highly technical sounding term for what is inherently a fairly simple and commonsense concept. The presentation in Chapter 17 is somewhat more terse than that in most of the previous chapters. The goal is for you to understand this approach to forecasting in detail; strengths and weaknesses are better discussed in subsequent chapters when we take up proper *use* of forecasting results. The use issue is very interesting. Many businessmen will tell you that they need better forecasts (you will be equipped to provide them); by the time you get through Part V, you should realize that many times the real problem is what is being *done* with forecast data rather than with the accuracy of the data. It is usually possible to design a system that is not very sensitive to forecast errors.

With a basic understanding of forecasting methodology under your belt, you will be ready to tackle the design of basic inventory control systems. Chapter 18 starts with the basic models for buying and producing in batches, considers hedging against uncertainty in terms of forecast errors, and builds up to a computerized set of routine decision rules for inventory control. The set of decision rules is used in many companies which have criteria systems congruent with the underlying strategy.

Chapter 19 is devoted to your understanding why the strategy of the decision rules developed in Chapter 18 is quite inappropriate for companies which must react in the manufacturing function to outputs generated by a set of decision rules based solely on inventory criteria. Chapters 17 and 18 only consider the Baumritter case tangentially, because use of the basic models must be severely tempered by a much more global criteria set. In Chapter 19 you will see how manufacturing criteria associated with utilizing manpower and capital equipment capacities change the role of inventories to a residual rather than a force which drives the system. A model used for Baumritter factories will be discussed; development and implementation of a "good" set of routine decision rules required a user-oriented modeling environment to facilitate evolution in problem delineation and solution.

Chapter 20 takes up a vital concern which was taken as a given in Chapter 19—the establishment of aggregate capacities. In Chapter 19 we found our criteria system largely concerned with utilizing capacities, but you now need to consider the medium- to long-range planning process which results in capacity changes. Some models for coping with these issues will be presented, as well as the approach which is currently being attempted for Baumritter.

One of the key themes running through Chapters 19 and 20 is a change in the company orientation from reaction in the face of economic conditions to a posture where more control over one's own destiny is achieved. Chapter 21 carries the materials-flow orientation beyond the factory into the distribution system and an interface with the marketing function. You will see how control over the distribution system can be terribly valuable to a manufacturing firm, and how improved decision rules can be developed which result in improvements in the flow of goods from raw materials to final consumption. A proper division of labor and congruent sets of decision rules among separate firms in the logistics system can result in overall benefits which can be equitably divided. When considering an entire logistics system, the kinds of subsystem decision rules which are congruent with overall objectives are difficult to establish and they can be quite counterintuitive. Industrial dynamics models are directly concerned with the design of those decision rules, and you will find the flavor of this modeling environment potentially useful for the design of logistic systems as well as for other problems in "enterprise design."

CHAPTER 17

FORECASTING

The goal of this chapter is to provide a working knowledge of certain forecasting procedures, most notably exponential smoothing. This working knowledge is necessary in the design of materials-flow systems as well as for other aspects of enterprise system design.

THE FORECASTING PROBLEM

Simply stated, the forecasting problem is to achieve a "good" estimate of future conditions. As noted in other chapters, the notion of "goodness" infers a set of objectives or criteria for making such an assessment. Although any estimate of future conditions might be deemed a forecast, we will restrict our use of the term "forecasting" and focus our present attention on a subset or class of forecasting models which can be potentially applied to many kinds of estimation problems. For expository purposes we will consider here sales or demand forecasting.

Although we will follow a common practice of loosely equating "sales" and "demand," it is worth noting that sales is only *one* observed indication of underlying desire or demand.

Forecasts versus Predictions

Some authors like to distinguish between predictions and forecasts so that estimates of future demand can be segregated into (1) the causal factors that generated past demand, and (2) the new causal factors that are expected to come into play in the determination of demand. The actual demand for a product is generated by a complex interaction of many factors. Moreover, it is very difficult to adequately understand and model all of these many factors such as the effects of competition, strength of the economy, or advertising expenditures. There is considerable appeal to saying that we will attempt, in an aggregative fashion, to identify some past basic demand level generated by this complex set of known and unknown factors; by doing so, we can separate our future estimating efforts into two categories of models, one for estimating the future aggregative basic demand level, and another which is concerned with better assessments of the influence of additional or new causal factors on a given or basic demand level. Efforts of the first category (forecasts) can be largely associated with statistical measurements based upon sound statistical theory; efforts of the second category (predictions) are much more intuitive or judgmental. Predictions must be made on many occasions, such as when substitutes for an existing product are coming on the market, when a change in economic conditions would indicate that a sizable change in demand will occur, or when demand estimates are required for new products for which no past demand performance data exist. Thus when Baumritter added a new line of Ethan Allen oak dining room furniture, predictions were required both for the new item sales and for the influence on existing item sales.

Forecasting, on the other hand, may be usefully defined as being based upon the projection of the past into the future where the past is assumed to represent a series of unknown or random interactive conditions that will be maintained in the future. It is necessary to carefully select or screen past data to obtain an appropriate forecasting base; just as "nonrandom" conditions are incorporated into future demand estimates as predictions, past demand actualities that are to be used for forecasting are often appropriately screened to eliminate the effect of "nonrandom" conditions. Thus, if one were interested in obtaining an estimate of weekly demand for a restaurant in a college town, he would be well advised to eliminate football home game weekends, graduations, etc. from his base for forecasting and to use such data for the predictive components of his estimate. Similarly, the influence of a major promotion must be segregated to ascertain base level sales in Ethan Allen Showcase Stores.

The selection or screening of past data implies that some underlying behavioral model exists that permits the forecaster to judge "nonrandomness." Making this judgment is a part of the highly individualistic model validation process that we considered in Chapter 3 and in other application areas.

As the title of this chapter indicates, the major emphasis here will be upon forecasting rather than on prediction. Since prediction is primarily a judgmental matter that is highly situation oriented, few explicit models are available. We will, however, see that our forecasting methodology will attempt to identify instances where predictive or judgmental inputs are required.

Criteria

As noted above, forecasters are interested in obtaining a good estimate of future demand. Our past use of the term "good" to infer a relative measure that is something less than optimal or best is applicable to this situation. We will also find pertinent our prior notion of evolution in both "goodness" and how goodness is assessed.

The goodness of a forecast is dependent upon how it is to be used; the cost of forecast errors is situation oriented, and one should ideally design a forecasting methodology that takes into account explicit recognition of the relevant costs. Thus for example, as analogous to the costs of type I and type II errors considered in our treatment of quality control, the cost of underestimating sales might be enough higher than the cost of overestimating sales that a consistent upward bias should be included in the forecasting model.

Unfortunately, a decision-oriented cost function implies a unique forecasting model for each decision, even when separate decisions are based upon forecasts of the same phenomenon. This is clearly seen in sales forecasts used by both marketing and production functions. The former have an air of hopefulness and an incentive or goal for sales people; the latter require commitments in men, materials, machines, and money. Clearly the costs of error in the two functions can be quite different.

One way out of this conundrum is to adopt a somewhat detached forecasting methodology that attempts to minimize forecast errors, with *use* of the forecast being a separate matter. Thus we will see in later chapters how inventories are designed to cope with sales underestimations. Deciding which forecasting methodology does *in fact* minimize the forecast error, however, is not a simple matter. Agreement on which of several alternative models achieved the minimum forecast error over a set of past data requires agreement on the measure and the method of measurement; two common measures are the average error and the average squared error, and the appropriate number of periods and period weightings to make up the average will also lead to different "errors." Even more difficult is the assessment of how error is to be minimized in the future. We will want to maintain "current" measures of forecast reliability so that model changes or judgmental inputs can be made when indicated.

Deciding when such changes are indicated is not a simple matter; involved are the situation-dependent relevant costs of rejecting appropriate models and not rejecting inappropriate models. In assessing forecasting model goodness, there are two conflicting surrogate criteria that reflect these costs. First, the models should produce forecasts which are stable and unaffected by random fluctuations. That is, if the "real" demand for a particular chair was 10 units per week, a forecasting model which viewed one weekly demand of 11 units as indicative of product growth might forecast 12 units for the next week; this model would produce results that are erroneous more often than a forecasting procedure which was oriented toward estimating the long-run average. On the other hand, the second conflicting surrogate criterion states that a forecasting model should be responsive to "genuine changes" in demand. The model based upon estimating the long-run average will consistently yield demand estimates that tend to be below actual demands if a true growth pattern in sales occurs.

The notions of "real" demand and "genuine changes" in demand again reflect on the implied underlying behavioral model of the demand generating process. At one extreme is the belief in some hypothetical "stone tablet" which is inscribed with *the* function for generating demand. Our focus will be much more adaptive, reflecting the continuing possibility or expectation of change, for reasons both within and beyond the firm's control.

A very important criterion is tied to the notion of use, purpose, or function. What use will be made of the estimate? For some kinds of problems, decision alternatives are quite sensitive to variations in demand estimates. Further, some kinds of problems require substantially different levels of aggregation. Thus, although a clothing manufacturer might make shirts in various colors, he also makes them in various sizes; for production planning and inventory control purposes it is necessary to deal with nonsubstitutable stock keeping units (SKU's). In essence a size 9 red cannot be substituted for a size 12 red or for a size 9 blue.

An additional criterion entity which is related to purpose concerns forecast speed or cost. Since the number of SKU forecasts required for a particular production-planning and inventory control operation can easily run into the hundreds of thousands, forecasting models which require fewer calculations will be favored, even when computers are involved. A related consideration has to do with required data files; we will see that the exponential smoothing model requires considerably less data storage than other common forecasting models.

The Forecasting Interval

Before one can start to forecast, it is necessary to ask what the forecasting or data collection interval should be. The use of demand estimates will determine whether a daily, weekly, monthly, quarterly, or yearly forecast is required. In Chapters 18, 19, 20, and 21, we will see that various kinds of material-flow system components require quite different time horizons; thus for the determination of an economic order quantity, an annual demand forecast might be appropriate, while a weekly forecast might be required to keep production scheduling within acceptable limits.

For most materials management problems, a frequent objective is to forecast demand over a time period long enough for a replenishment order to be received or manufactured, i.e., what we will call the "lead time." However, the lead time will tend to be different for different items; a forecasting system that worked successfully with different time intervals would tend to be cumbersome. For this reason, companies such as Baumritter typically select one forecast interval for all products and make appropriate adjustments in forecasted demand and expected forecast error for individual lead-time periods. Choice of a forecast interval is situation or use dependent; one frequent consideration is utilization and turn around time on the computer; another concerns the potential bias in using monthly data that vary in the number of days, but more importantly the number of working, selling, or weekend days. Many companies have adopted a four-week forecasting interval which leads to a 13 "month" year.

Extrinsic versus Intrinsic Forecasts

Forecasting methodologies are sometimes divided into two categories—extrinsic and intrinsic models. As the names imply, extrinsic forecasts have an outside, external orientation, while intrinsic forecasts are based upon internal circumstances. Extrinsic forecasts are formulated upon associations such as sales of appliances and disposable personal incomes, sales of door handles and housing starts, or sales of alcoholic beverages and teachers' salaries. For each of these three examples one can find a strong association; it is often possible to make estimates based upon leading indicators such as the demand for door handles several months hence, as a function of present housing starts. Extrinsic forecasts are usually based upon regression analyses; a study of this material is best left to courses in quantitative analysis and managerial economics. It is worth noting here, however, that extreme care is required in the interpretation of statistical association to infer that cause-effect relationships exist. Thus the association of teachers' salaries and alcoholic beverage sales may very well be due to their joint relationship to a third factor—national income.

One will usually find an extrinsic forecast more useful for forecasting sales at a level of aggregation higher than the SKU. Thus, although the Baumritter Corporation might be able to forecast sales on a companywide basis nine months into the future, based upon an extrinsic model of housing start data, they would be less able to do so for sales of ladder-back chairs. Forecast errors for sales of individual items will tend to be smaller when such forecasts are made with an intrinsic model. Nevertheless, although we will now turn our attention to the development of intrinsic models, the relationship of individual SKU models to a model for predicting overall company sales should not be neglected. That is, the summation of individual item sales is equal to the overall company sales, and a model which predicted overall company sales well might be used as an influence or factor to adjust the estimates of individual item sales.

One additional feature of the relationship between global or total company sales models and individual item sales models is worthy of consideration. Building an aggregate or global model involves the analysis of total company sales, and the development of both a forecasting model and an underlying theory of behavior or pattern for those sales. Unfortunately, a theory which passes empirical validation tests in the aggregate may prove to be grossly inadequate for individual item sales. The most common mismatch comes from a clearly recognizable trend in overall company sales that is primarily due to price increases or increases in the product line; individual item sales on a unit basis may be steady or in fact even decreasing! More subtle mismatches arise from the assumption of a universally applicable seasonal influence which may not apply equally to all items; at Baumritter, special promotions of a few items often account for a significant share of seasonal sales.

COMMON FORECASTING MODELS

As noted above, forecasting (as opposed to prediction) is estimation of the future based upon the past. Thus a naive forecasting method would be to estimate or guess that demand in the next time period will be equal to demand in the most recently observed time period. Let us turn to Fig. 17.1 to examine the performance of this forecasting scheme. (Although the data presented as Fig. 17.1 are hypothetical, they are representative of sales data for many Baumritter items.)

To forecast monthly sales for the year starting January 1970, sales for the first month (January) are estimated or forecasted to be equal to December 1969 sales (110); it can be seen that a forecast error of 20 occurs. Similarly our forecast of February sales based upon the 90 units sold in January is off by 5 units, the March and April forecasts are correct, and the May and June forecasts are off by 5 units each. The forecast errors for the rest of the year are 0, 10, 5, 10, 10, and 0 respectively. Total forecast error is 70 units or 5.8 units per month on the average.

Smoothing

In assessing the above forecasting method, it becomes fairly clear that what appear to be random fluctuations in monthly sales have played a large role in achieving the forecast error. An intuitively pleasing ap-

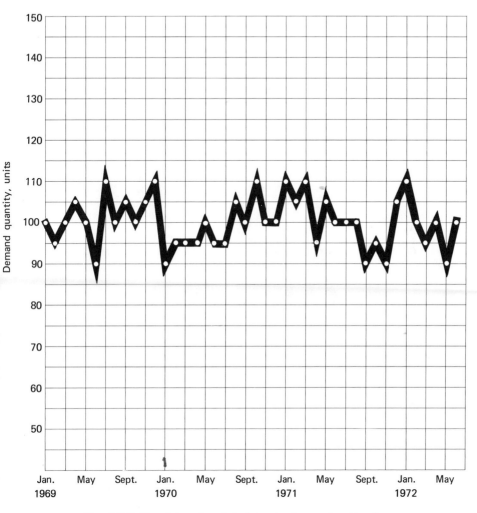

Fig. 17.1 Monthly sales data (steady demand pattern).

proach would be to draw a line of best fit through the demand points of Fig. 17.1 and use it for a forecast. That is, we desire to damp or smooth out random fluctuations (the term smoothing is synonymous with averaging). Let us forecast the same 12 periods of demand with a model based upon the average demand. For the first forecasting period (January 1970) our estimate is equal to the average demand for 1969 or 101.7. The forecast error is 11.7. In estimating February, our model tells us that the demand will be 100.8; the forecast error is 5.8 units. The demand estimate for March is 100.4 and the forecast error is 5.4 (which happens to be

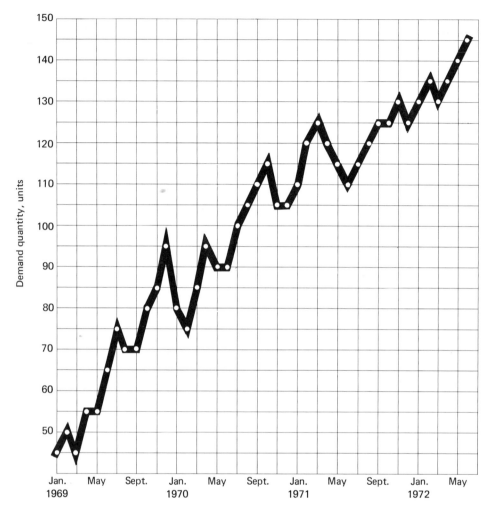

Fig. 17.2 Monthly sales data (growth pattern).

greater than the forecast error using the naive model). The forecast errors for the months of April through December are 5.0, .3, 4.7, 4.4, 5.7, .5, 10.5, 0 and 0 respectively. The total forecast error has been reduced to 48.6 or 4.1 on the average (a reduction in error of 22 to 30%).

Thus we see that the forecasting model based upon average or smoothed demands is superior to the naive forecasting scheme, which made no attempt to smooth out random fluctuations. The forecast errors associated with demand estimates being made on the basis of the long-run average will in fact tend to be minimized as more and more demand observations are included in the long-run average. This is, however, true only for situations which exhibit a steady demand pattern such as that depicted in Fig. 17.1. Let us now turn to Fig. 17.2.

The demand in Fig. 17.2 exhibits a clear growth or trend pattern. Applying a forecasting scheme based upon the long run average to the 12 months of 1970 yields forecast errors of 14.2, 8.1, 17.5, 26.8, 19.7, 18.5, 27.5, 31.1, 34.5, 37.9, 21.1, and 20.2 respectively (average monthly error equals 23.1). If we use the naive model based solely upon the prior month actual demand, the forecast errors are 15, 5, 10, 10, 5, 0, 10, 5, 5, 5, 10, and 0 respectively for an average monthly forecast error of 6.7.

The reason that the naive model is so clearly superior to the forecasting scheme based upon the long-run average for the situation depicted in Fig. 17.2 is that the long run average is inherently unresponsive to changes in demand. That is, in predicting the last demand period (December 1970), the actual demand for January 1969 shares equal weight in the calculation with that of November 1970. It is clear that a scheme based upon long-run averages will always tend to lag a significant change in demand. The model based solely upon last month's demand has smaller forecast errors because it has discarded the older information with its strong bias toward underestimation of the trend.

However, just as a straight line could be fitted to the data in Fig. 17.1, one can be fitted to the data in Fig. 17.2; and we can consider the variability around either line as randomness or "noise." The extent of the noise or randomness around either line will contribute to forecast error; we are looking for a forecasting procedure which smooths out error while still remaining responsive to significant changes in demand patterns.

Moving Averages

One fairly common type of forecasting technique is the moving average. The moving average attempts to eliminate obsolete data through an averaging or smoothing of only the most recent n observations. As n (the number of observations to be included in the moving average) grows larger, the forecasting model will tend to do a better job of smoothing or damping out noise; on the other hand, as n grows larger, older data are included and the forecasting model becomes less responsive to changes in demand patterns. This is illustrated by Fig. 17.3, which shows the forecast errors associated with 1 through 12 month moving averages for the sales data presented as Fig. 17.1 and Fig. 17.2.

As you can see, the forecast error associated with the sales data presented as Fig. 17.2 increases as the number of months used in calculating the moving average increases. For the Fig. 17.1 demand data there is a tendency for smaller forecast errors to be associated with the inclusion of a greater number of months in the moving average, although it appears that any model except a one-month moving average will yield fairly consistent forecast errors.

The data plotted as Fig. 17.3 are based upon forecasts and associated errors for 30 months, January 1970 through June 1972 (1969 data are used for initialization). The particular patterns of demand on which these forecasts are based necessarily contain some sampling errors in terms of the estimates of long-run monthly forecast errors associated with moving averages of various periods; the effect of these sampling errors should not be minimized. Thus the data plotted in Fig. 17.3 are based upon two particular demand situations, one with a clear trend and one which remains remarkably steady. Since the real world often yields demand situations that change from one to the other, or are somewhat of a hybrid nature, relative assessments of forecast model goodness can be difficult to make. Moreover, as we noted before, the idea of fundamental change in a demand pattern has implications for the underlying theory or model of behavior which generates the demand.

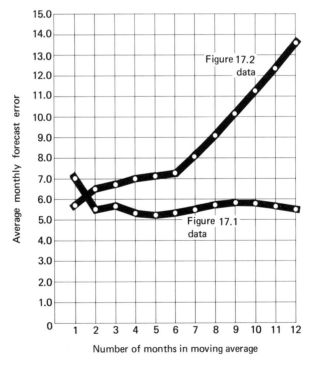

Fig. 17.3 Moving average forecast errors.

Weighted Moving Averages

In deciding what sort of moving average model to use, we found that the basic choice involved a number of periods to be included in a moving average where a greater number of periods tended to do a better job of damping out randomness but at the same time was less responsive to genuine changes in demand. We found the moving average model appealing because it tended to remove obsolete data. We can generalize these remarks to say that the conflicting surrogate criteria of stability and responsiveness lead to choices in the extent to which past data are used.

In the weighted moving average model, in addition to the number of periods to be included in the moving average, we have a choice of the various weights to be put on the data. Thus the first five monthly data in Fig. 17.2 are 45, 50, 45, 55, and 55. If we placed equal weight on all these data (a straight moving average) our forecast for period 6 would be 50 units. If, however, we adopted a weighted scheme where the most recent observation would be given a weight of 30%, the next most recent observation given a weight of 25%, the third most recent observation given a weight of 20%, the fourth observation given a weight of 15%, and the fifth observation given a weight of 10%, our forecast would be determined as follows:

$$
\begin{array}{ll}
30\% \text{ of } 55 = & 16.5 \\
25\% \text{ of } 55 = & 13.75 \\
20\% \text{ of } 45 = & 9.0 \\
15\% \text{ of } 50 = & 7.5 \\
10\% \text{ of } 45 = & \underline{4.5} \\
& 51.25
\end{array}
$$

Since the weighted moving average discounts the value of past information, it tends to be more responsive to the genuine changes in demand. Thus for example, it should be clear that the five-period weighted moving average given above will produce results that are superior to a straight five-period moving average for the demand data given as Fig. 17.2.

In using a weighted moving average, the problems involved in selecting the appropriate number of periods for a moving average become compounded. One now has to search for the combination of periods and weights which leads to a good tradeoff between responsiveness and stability, and a concomitant low level of forecast error.

EXPONENTIAL SMOOTHING

The moving average model and the weighted moving average model both attempt to remain responsive by discarding information after n periods.

We noted, however, that for stable demand situations such as that depicted in Fig. 17.1, forecast error tends to be minimized as the number of periods included in the moving average approaches the long-run or overall average. This is equivalent to saying that for steady demand pattern situations, old demand observations are equally as valuable as new demand observations. Although the same kind of statement cannot be made for trend situations such as that depicted in Fig. 17.2, the moving average model and weighted moving average model both assume that data has *no* value after *n* periods. It would seem that *some* value (although possibly very little) remains in any piece of data, and that a model which utilizes all past demand data with appropriate weightings would be superior to a model which discards data.

An additional problem with moving average models and weighted moving average models is the large amount of record keeping, record "sliding" (after each demand observation the actual demand is put at the top of the list of past demand and each observation is pushed down one position, i.e., the demand for 2 periods ago becomes the demand for 3 periods ago, etc.), and the extended multiplications and/or divisions. Even with fast computers, calculation and storage factors are important entities in judging model worth. We will see that the exponential smoothing model offers substantial economies in both of these factors.

The Model

Exponential smoothing is a very elegant term for what is inherently a highly commonsense-oriented idea. Let us illustrate this by returning to the demand data given in Fig. 17.1: If our interest is in forecasting demand for the month starting January 1970 with a 5-period moving average, the first month's forecast would be $(100 + 105 + 100 + 105 + 110) \div 5 = 104$. The actual demand for January 1970 was 90 units, a forecast error of 14. In estimating February's demand, the moving average procedure would be to discard the oldest period of demand (August $1969 = 100$) and to add in the 90 units for January 1970 demand. As noted above, this procedure involves sliding the records so that we will know which demand period to discard at the end of the next demand period; a computationally easier alternative is: instead of retaining the 5 previous individual period demand data, merely retain the average of those data. Thus the average of these five periods of demand is equal to the forecast (104 units). After the actual demand for January has been observed and when a February estimate is being prepared, rather than discard the actual 100 units associated with August demand, we now discard our best estimate of the August demand (which is 104 units) while adding the 90 units. The same mathematical results can be achieved by adding (or subtracting as the case may be) 20% of the difference between the forecasted demand and actual demand to our next forecast (5-period moving average = 20% weight for each observation).

Let us return to the previous example. Our 5-period moving average estimate for January 1970 was 104 units; having observed 90 units (forecast error equals 14 units) a moving average model would estimate February's demand as equal to $(105 + 100 + 105 + 110 + 90) \div 5 = 102$. Our procedure for the the elimination of record sliding starts with the same 104 unit estimate for January's demand, but has not retained the individual monthly demand data which made up the 104 unit estimate. It assumes that the estimate came about as follows: $(104 + 104 + 104 + 104 + 104) \div 5 = 104$ units. When the actual January demand of 90 units is observed, we replace one of the 104 unit demand estimates by 90 units to calculate our demand estimate for February $(104 + 104 + 104 + 104 + 90) \div 5 = 101.2$; clearly the same result is achieved by taking our prior demand estimate of 104 and reducing it by 20% of the difference between the actual demand of 90 and the estimated demand of 104.

The procedure just described *is* exponential smoothing. If we generalize the 20% figure to a parameter called α, we can prepare exponential smoothed forecasts by the following formula:

(1) New forecast = old forecast + α (actual demand – old forecast)

By rearranging some terms, this formula can be restated in a way that is sometimes more convenient:

(2) New forecast = α (actual demand) + $(1-\alpha)$ old forecast.

The reason this model is called exponential smoothing (remember, smoothing is equivalent to averaging) is that the effect of each demand observation is retained forever in our estimates, but with the weight associated with that demand estimate subject to exponential decay. Thus for the example used above where $\alpha = 0.2$, the actual demand for January 1970 will receive a weight of 0.2 in forecasting February's demand and the prior average or forecast will receive a weight of 0.8. Let us examine what the weight of the January demand is in calculating the forecast for March.

March forecast = 0.2(February actual) + 0.8(February forecast)

but since

February forecast = 0.2(January actual) + 0.8(January forecast)

we can substitute terms in the following way:

March forecast = 0.2(February actual) + 0.8[.2(January actual)
+ 0.8(January forecast)]

Therefore, the role of January actual demand in determining March forecast is equal to 0.8[.2(January actual demand)] = 0.16. Similarly, the

SMOOTHING CONSTANT= 0.05   SMOOTHING CONSTANT= 0.1

PERIOD	WEIGHT	CUMULATIVE	WEIGHT	CUMULATIVE
1	0.05	0.05	0.1	0.1
2	0.0475	0.0975	0.09	0.19
3	0.045125	0.142625	0.081	0.271
4	4.28687 E-2	0.185494	0.0729	0.3439
5	4.07253 E-2	0.226219	0.06561	0.40951
6	0.038689	0.264908	0.059049	0.468559
7	3.67546 E-2	0.301663	5.31441 E-2	0.521703
8	3.49169 E-2	0.33658	4.78297 E-2	0.569533
9	0.033171	0.369751	4.30467 E-2	0.612579
10	3.15125 E-2	0.401263	0.038742	0.651322
11	2.99368 E-2	0.4312	3.48678 E-2	0.686189
12	0.02844	0.45964	3.13811 E-2	0.71757
13	0.027018	0.486658	0.028243	0.745813
14	2.56671 E-2	0.512325	2.54187 E-2	0.771232
15	2.43837 E-2	0.536709	2.28768 E-2	0.794109
16	2.31646 E-2	0.559873	2.05891 E-2	0.814698
17	2.20063 E-2	0.58188	1.85302 E-2	0.833228
18	0.020906	0.602786	1.66772 E-2	0.849905
19	1.98607 E-2	0.622646	1.50095 E-2	0.864915
20	1.88677 E-2	0.641514	1.35085 E-2	0.878423
21	1.79243 E-2	0.659438	1.21577 E-2	0.890581
22	1.70281 E-2	0.676466	1.09419 E-2	0.901523
23	1.61767 E-2	0.692643	9.84771 E-3	0.911371
24	1.53678 E-2	0.708011	8.86294 E-3	0.920233
25	1.45995 E-2	0.72261	7.97664 E-3	0.92821

SMOOTHING CONSTANT= 0.2   SMOOTHING CONSTANT= 0.3

PERIOD	WEIGHT	CUMULATIVE	WEIGHT	CUMULATIVE
1	0.2	0.2	0.3	0.3
2	0.16	0.36	0.21	0.51
3	0.128	0.488	0.147	0.657
4	0.1024	0.5904	0.1029	0.7599
5	0.08192	0.67232	0.07203	0.83193
6	0.065536	0.737856	0.050421	0.882351
7	5.24288 E-2	0.790285	3.52947 E-2	0.917646
8	0.041943	0.832228	2.47063 E-2	0.942352
9	3.35544 E-2	0.865782	1.72944 E-2	0.959646
10	2.68435 E-2	0.892626	1.21061 E-2	0.971752
11	2.14748 E-2	0.914101	8.47426 E-3	0.980227
12	1.71799 E-2	0.93128	5.93198 E-3	0.986159
13	1.37439 E-2	0.945024	4.15239 E-3	0.990311
14	1.09951 E-2	0.956019	2.90667 E-3	0.993218
15	8.79609 E-3	0.964816	2.03467 E-3	0.995252
16	7.03687 E-3	0.971852	1.42427 E-3	0.996677
17	5.6295 E-3	0.977482	9.96988 E-4	0.997674
18	4.5036 E-3	0.981986	6.97892 E-4	0.998372
19	3.60288 E-3	0.985588	4.88524 E-4	0.99886
20	2.8823 E-3	0.988471	3.41967 E-4	0.999202
21	2.30584 E-3	0.990777	2.39377 E-4	0.999441
22	1.84467 E-3	0.992621	1.67564 E-4	0.999609
23	1.47574 E-3	0.994097	1.17295 E-4	0.999726
24	1.18059 E-3	0.995278	8.21062 E-5	0.999808
25	9.44473 E-4	0.996222	5.74744 E-5	0.999866

Table 17.1 Sales data aging.

SMOOTHING CONSTANT= 0.4 | | SMOOTHING CONSTANT= 0.5 | |

PERIOD	WEIGHT	CUMULATIVE	WEIGHT	CUMULATIVE
1	0.4	0.4	0.5	0.5
2	0.24	0.64	0.25	0.75
3	0.144	0.784	0.125	0.875
4	0.0864	0.8704	0.0625	0.9375
5	0.05184	0.92224	0.03125	0.96875
6	0.031104	0.953344	0.015625	0.984375
7	1.86624 E-2	0.972006	7.8125 E-3	0.992187
8	1.11974 E-2	0.983204	3.90625 E-3	0.996094
9	6.71846 E-3	0.989922	1.95313 E-3	0.998047
10	4.03108 E-3	0.993953	9.76563 E-4	0.999023
11	2.41865 E-3	0.996372	4.88281 E-4	0.999512
12	1.45119 E-3	0.997823	2.44141 E-4	0.999756
13	8.70713 E-4	0.998694	1.2207 E-4	0.999878
14	5.22428 E-4	0.999216	6.10352 E-5	0.999939
15	3.13457 E-4	0.99953	3.05176 E-5	0.999969
16	1.88074 E-4	0.999718	1.52588 E-5	0.999985
17	1.12844 E-4	0.999831	7.6294 E-6	0.999992
18	6.77066 E-5	0.999898	3.8147 E-6	0.999996
19	4.0624 E-5	0.999939	1.90735 E-6	0.999998
20	2.43744 E-5	0.999963	9.53674 E-7	0.999999
21	1.46246 E-5	0.999978	4.76837 E-7	1.
22	8.77478 E-6	0.999987	2.38419 E-7	1.
23	5.26487 E-6	0.999992	1.19209 E-7	1.
24	3.15892 E-6	0.999995	5.96047 E-8	1.
25	1.89535 E-6	0.999997	2.98023 E-8	1.

SMOOTHING CONSTANT= 0.7 | | SMOOTHING CONSTANT= 0.9 | |

PERIOD	WEIGHT	CUMULATIVE	WEIGHT	CUMULATIVE
1	0.7	0.7	0.9	0.9
2	0.21	0.91	0.09	0.99
3	0.063	0.973	0.009	0.999
4	0.0189	0.9919	0.0009	0.9999
5	0.00567	0.99757	0.00009	0.99999
6	0.001701	0.999271	0.000009	0.999999
7	5.103 E-4	0.999781	9. E-7	1.
8	1.5309 E-4	0.999934	9. E-8	1.
9	4.5927 E-5	0.99998	9. E-9	1.
10	1.37781 E-5	0.999994	9. E-10	1.
11	4.13343 E-6	0.999998	9. E-11	1.
12	1.24003 E-6	0.999999	9. E-12	1.
13	3.72009 E-7	1.	9. E-13	1.
14	1.11603 E-7	1.	9. E-14	1.
15	3.34808 E-8	1.	9. E-15	1.
16	1.00442 E-8	1.	9. E-16	1.
17	3.01327 E-9	1.	9. E-17	1.
18	9.03981 E-10	1.	9. E-18	1.
19	2.71194 E-10	1.	9. E-19	1.
20	8.13583 E-11	1.	9. E-20	1.
21	2.44075 E-11	1.	9. E-21	1.
22	7.32225 E-12	1.	9. E-22	1.
23	2.19667 E-12	1.	9. E-23	1.
24	6.59002 E-13	1.	9. E-24	1.
25	1.97701 E-13	1.	9. E-25	1.

Table 17.1 (Continued)

role of January actual demand in determining the forecast for April is equal to $0.8(.16) = 0.128$. A general formula for expressing the weight of an actual demand in a future estimate is as follows:

(3) $\text{Weight} = \alpha(1-\alpha)^{n-1}$

where n is the number of periods after the original demand estimate.

It should be clear that, as any actual demand always has an impact on the average or forecasted demand, it will retain *some* influence on estimates of future demand. Depending upon the value of α chosen, the influence of a particular demand observation of future forecasts diminishes more or less quickly; and therefore depending upon the value of α chosen, a forecasting model is more or less stable or responsive to actual changes in demand. Thus when $\alpha = 0.2$, the most recent demand observation accounts for 20% of the demand forecast, the next most recent demand observation accounts for 16% of the demand forecast, the next most recent demand observation accounts for 12.8%, the next for 10.24%, and the next for 8.192%. We can say that the five most recent demand observations account for 67.2% of the forecast and the remaining 32.8% is made up of actual demand data more than 5 periods old. Table 17.1 shows how actual sales data are weighted in the forecast as a function of age.

The Smoothing Constant

In using an exponential smoothing approach to forecasting, one must determine what smoothing constant to use. Values for the smoothing constant are typically expressed as being between 0 and 1.0; as smoothing constants approach 1.0, they become more responsive to current demand data or, conversely, they tend to discount past demand data rapidly (a value of 1.0 is our naive forecast, which is based completely on the most recent demand period). On the other hand, as exponential smoothing constants approach 1.0, the forecasts tend to lose stability.

Some forecasters like to compare exponential smoothing forecasts with various smoothing constant values to moving averages with different numbers of periods. Because of the difference between these models, such comparisons tend to be necessarily somewhat inaccurate. However, it is sometimes said that an exponential smoothing constant of 0.1 is roughly equivalent to about a 19 period moving average, an exponential smoothing constant of 0.2 is about equivalent to a 9 period moving average, an exponential smoothing constant of 0.3 is approximately equal to a 6 period moving average, an exponential smoothing constant of 0.4 is approximately equal to a 4-period moving average, and an exponential smoothing constant of 0.5 is about equal to a 3-period moving average. (As can be seen in Table 17.1, the cumulative weights represented by the first 19 periods with $\alpha = 0.1$, 9 periods with $\alpha = 0.2$, 6 periods with $\alpha = 0.3$, 4 periods with $\alpha = 0.4$, and 3 periods with $\alpha = 0.5$ are all about 87%.)

The actual choice of a smoothing constant is a situation-dependent matter that should be based upon the relevant costs of forecast errors and one's underlying theory or model of behavior which generates the demand. Thus it has been shown that for fairly stable forecasting situations, exponential smoothing constants in the neighborhood of 0.1 tend to yield low forecast errors; however, this "cookbook" approach is incompatible with the systems concept, which would consider what one desires to eat before selecting a recipe.

Trend Consideration

In our consideration of various moving average models for forecasting the demand pattern exhibited as Fig. 17.2, we found that the best possibility was based upon a moving average of one period; that is, our best estimate was the previous period's demand; as the smoothing interval increased, the concomitant forecast error also increased. The reason is that any sort of averaging or smoothing procedure will tend to lag behind a significant trend. We noted, however, that a straight line could be drawn through the points on Fig. 17.2 and that the deviations around that line could be regarded as random or noise. It is clear that what we need for trend forecasting is to include an estimate of the trend component based upon the slope of a line such as might be drawn through the points on Fig. 17.2.

One way to estimate the trend line of Fig. 17.2 would be with a regression model. A not mutually exclusive alternative is to obtain some estimate of linear trend and include it in the exponential smoothing model presented above. Thus equation (2) can be expanded to include trend as follows:

(4) New Forecast = α (actual demand) + $(1-\alpha)$ (old forecast + old trend)

Another estimate of trend that is continually available is the difference between the forecasted sales in one period—as determined by equation (4)—and the forecasted sales in the prior period (assuming there is no seasonal factor). Since this estimate will be subject to noise or randomness, it can usefully be averaged or smoothed. One very appealing way to accomplish the smoothing is to use the exponential smoothing model where perhaps the initial estimate of average trend is determined by a regression model (it might also be determined by guessing). Thus our model for trend is:

(5) New trend = β (present or new forecast − preceding or old forecast) + $(1-\beta)$ old trend.

Let us return to the data in Fig. 17.2. If we place a ruler on the data for January 1969 to December 1970, a rough estimate of the trend component of 2.5 units per month is obtained. Let us initialize our estimate of December 1970 sales at 107.5, use a value of α of 0.2, and use a value for β of 0.4. Our estimate of January 1971 sales:

$$0.2(105) + 0.8(107.5+2.5) = 109$$

Actual sales are 110. The estimate of trend and subsequent estimate for February sales thus become:

Trend: $0.4(109-107.5) + 0.6(2.5) = 2.1$
February: $0.2(110) + 0.8(109+2.1) = 110.9$

Figure 17.4 shows how this forecasting model behaves over the 18 months of January 1971 to June 1972.

Seasonal Considerations

Seasonal or cyclic demand patterns are characterized by a recurring pattern of high and low demand activity. Such a pattern may be caused by external circumstances (selling outboard motors in the summertime) or by internal circumstances (annual introduction of a new model). Also, the timing of the seasonal or cyclical peaks and valleys may be regular or somewhat irregular. Thus early snow might lead to an earlier peak in the sales of skis.

It is being increasingly recognized that companies have the ability to strongly influence the timing and magnitude of seasonal demand patterns. Considerable success has been achieved with selling bathing suits in February or March, and a drug company's heavy promotion of vitamins in the fall led to a substantial seasonal demand pattern. The positive feedback loop aspect of operating within a seasonal demand pattern where "appropriate" actions are taken in the light of seasonal demand forecasts is a very interesting problem. It is somewhat analogous to the situation described in Chapter 13, where work measurement models are considered "valid" because they produce labor time estimates that are close to subsequent actual times observed. Outcomes are not independent of forecasts, and one should regard the forecasting process itself as a decision alternative since subsequent actions will be based upon that forecast. Nevertheless, for our present interest let us disregard the cause-effect relationships involved in forecasting and turn to an exposition of some models available for dealing with seasonal demand situations.

In deciding if a demand pattern should be forecasted on a seasonal basis, three tests are usually considered. First, the peak demand must occur with regularity. For example, if one were forecasting monthly sales it would be expected that the peak would occur in approximately the same

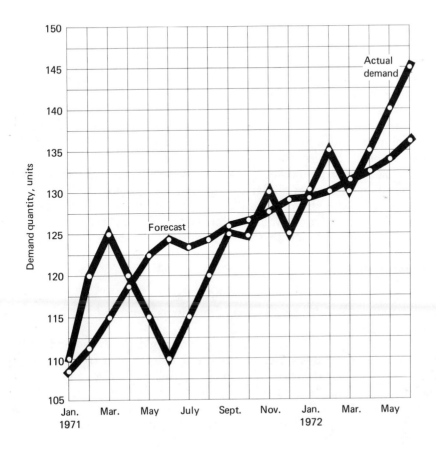

Fig. 17.4 Sales data (growth pattern) and trend model.

month each year. Second, the peak demand should be significantly greater than the randomness or noise and enough higher than the average demand to warrant the additional effort involved in using seasonal forecasting models. Third, one should be able to identify a reason for a seasonal demand pattern. That is, we should not infer that past peaks and valleys due to random causes will be repeated. The terms "regularity," "significantly greater," "enough higher," "warrant," and "reason" obviously infer a set of criteria. Once again we are faced with a highly situation-oriented problem, where one would have to consider the costs and benefits of alternative courses of action (e.g. safety stocks tend to reduce the need for decreased forecast errors).

Exponential smoothing models for either constant or trend conditions can be modified to take account of seasonal variations. The usual procedure is to calculate a set of index numbers or multipliers which represent the expected ratio of demand for individual periods to an average or deseasonalized demand. For example, if the demand rate for December were normally 5% lower than the average yearly demand rate, the index value for December would be 0.95. Actual demand data will differ from forecasted. The forecasted error may be conceived as being made up of noise or randomness, an error in our estimate of base or deseasonalized sales, and an error in our estimate of the appropriate seasonal index. The exponential smoothing process can be used to filter out the noise and to update both the deseasonalized demand and the seasonal indices. The actual demand data are deseasonalized by dividing by index numbers; the resultant deseasonalized or basic demand level (either constant or trend) would be forecasted with an appropriate exponential smoothing model. The index numbers themselves are thereafter updated with an exponential smoothing routine where the index number is equal to the following:

$$(6) \quad \text{New index} = \gamma \left(\frac{\text{actual sales}}{\text{new forecast of deseasonalized sales}} \right) + \frac{(1-\gamma) \text{ old}}{\text{index}}$$

Although we are limiting our attention to additive trend and multiplicative seasonal indices, clearly one could also consider trend as multiplicative, or seasonal factors as additive. In using any seasonal model, there are sometimes situations where the seasonal peaks and valleys vary slightly from year to year due to such causes as weather conditions; base indices are sometimes usefully smoothed with a 3 period moving average.

Since a base index number is updated only once per cycle, relatively high values for γ are typically used (0.3 to 0.5). Thus let us suppose that deseasonalized November sales were forecasted to be 100 units and actual deseasonalized November sales were 120 units. If a single exponential smoothing model with $\alpha = 0.1$ is used for deseasonalized sales (no trend), we would forecast December deseasonalized sales to be 102 units; applying the seasonality factor of 0.95 described above, our forecast for December sales would be 96.9 units. If actual sales were 110 units, we would divide that amount by our seasonal index (0.95) to get an estimate of the present deseasonalized or base level (115.8). Since an exponential smoothing model with $\alpha = 0.1$ is used, our new estimated base or deseasonalized sales level would be:

$$0.1(115.8) + (1-0.1)102 = 103.4$$

In updating our seasonal index for December (smoothing constant = 0.3), we use our new deseasonalized base to obtain the following estimate:

$$0.3(110 \div 103.4) + 0.7(0.95) = 98.4$$

Figure 17.5 shows a strong seasonal pattern of demand (the average demand for Fig. 17.5 is the same as that in Figs. 17.1 and 17.2, i.e., 100 units). We then use the data from the years 1969 and 1970 to determine the initial values for the indices and the base or deseasonalized sales level.

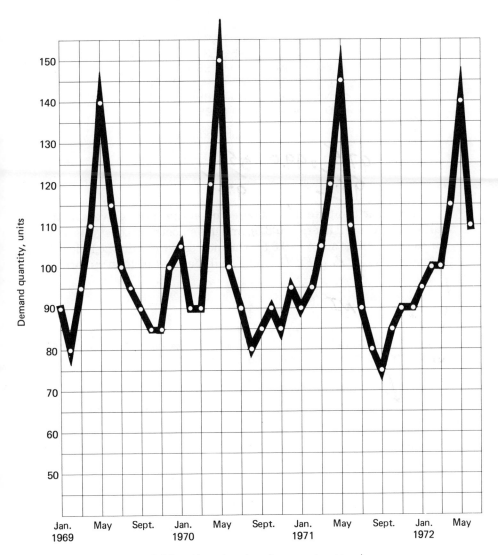

Fig. 17.5 Monthly sales data (seasonal pattern).

Monthly Demand

	1969 1970	Average
January:	$(90 + 105) \div 2 =$	97.5
February:	$(80 + 90) \div 2 =$	85.0
March:	$(95 + 90) \div 2 =$	92.5
April:	$(110 + 120) \div 2 =$	115.0
May:	$(140 + 150) \div 2 =$	145.0
June:	$(115 + 100) \div 2 =$	107.5
July:	$(100 + 90) \div 2 =$	95.0
August:	$(95 + 80) \div 2 =$	87.5
September:	$(90 + 85) \div 2 =$	87.5
October:	$(85 + 90) \div 2 =$	87.5
November:	$(85 + 85) \div 2 =$	85.0
December:	$(100 + 95) \div 2 =$	97.5

Average monthly demand = 98.5

$$\frac{97.5}{98.5} = 99.0 \qquad \frac{85}{98.5}$$

If we now compute indices based upon the ratio of average monthly sales to the overall average (98.5), and use smoothing constants of $\alpha = 0.1$ for the base series and $\gamma = 0.3$ for the indices, we obtain the following (the symbols t, I_{t-12}, $\bar{F}_{t-1}$, F_t, D_t and I_t will be used in later notation):

t 1971 Month	I_{t-12} Initial index	$\bar{F}_{t-1}$ Base	F_t Forecast	D_t Actual demand	D_t-F_t Forecast error	I_t New index
1 (Jan.)	99.0	98.5	97.5	90	− 7.5	96.7
2 (Feb.)	86.3	97.7	84.3	95	+ 10.7	89.6
3 (March)	93.9	98.9	92.9	105	+ 12.1	97.6
4 (April)	116.8	100.2	117.0	120	+ 3.0	117.7
5 (May)	147.2	100.5	147.9	145	− 2.9	146.3
6 (June)	109.1	100.3	109.4	110	+ 0.7	109.3
7 (July)	96.4	100.4	96.8	90	− 6.8	94.4
8 (Aug.)	88.8	99.7	88.5	80	− 8.5	86.2
9 (Sept.)	88.8	98.7	87.6	75	− 12.6	87.5
10 (Oct.)	88.8	97.3	86.4	85	− 1.4	88.4
11 (Nov.)	86.3	97.1	83.8	90	+ 6.2	88.2
12 (Dec.)	99.0	97.8	96.8	90	− 6.8	96.9
		97.1				

An Exponential System

In this major section on exponential smoothing, we started with an exposition of the most basic and simple exponential model, which would be appropriate for a relatively stable system without trend or seasonal influences. We then discussed the necessary model additions for trend and seasonal considerations, but on a somewhat mutually exclusive basis. Let us now consider the three model types; basic, trend, and seasonal, as a system.

We begin by restating equation (2) more tersely:

(7) $\bar{F}_t = \alpha D_t + (1-\alpha)\bar{F}_{t-1}$ $\mathcal{NF}$

where

$\bar{F}_t$ = forecast or estimate of basic sales level at the end of the tth period.

α = exponential smoothing constant for basic demand level.

D_t = actual demand during the tth period.

Let us also add what will initially appear to be a redundant step:

(8) $F_{t+1} = \bar{F}_t$

where

F_{t+1} = forecast of sales in the next or $t+1^{st}$ period.

Equation (8) can be generalized to forecast more than one period into the future:

(9) $F_{t+n} = \bar{F}_t$

where

n = the number of the future period for which a forecast is desired (next period = 1).

To include a trend component, we can restate equation (4) as an expanded version of equation (7):

(10) $\bar{F}_t = \alpha D_t + (1-\alpha)(\bar{F}_{t-1} + T_{t-1})$

equation (5) as:

(11) $T_t = \beta(\bar{F}_t - \bar{F}_{t-1}) + (1-\beta)T_{t-1}$

and equation (9) as:

(12) $F_{t+n} = \bar{F}_t + nT_t$

where

T_t = estimate of trend made at the end of the tth period.

β = exponential smoothing constant for trend.

To include a seasonal influence, we can now expand equation (10) as:

(13) $\bar{F}_t = \alpha \dfrac{D_t}{I_{t-m}} + (1-\alpha)(\bar{F}_{t-1} + T_{t-1})$

equation (6) can be restated as:

(14) $I_t = \gamma \dfrac{D_t}{\bar{F}_t} + (1-\gamma)I_{t-m}$

and equation (12) as:

(15) $F_{t+n} = (\bar{F}_t + nT_t)\, I_{t-m+n}$

where

I_t = seasonality index for the tth period.
γ = exponential smoothing constant for seasonality indices.
m = number of periods in a seasonal pattern ($m=12$ for monthly data with an annual seasonal pattern).

We are now faced with the question of what weights to place on α, β, and γ, as well as how to obtain initial values for $\bar{F}_t$, T_t, and I_t's. Appendix A is devoted to a consideration of these issues.

FORECAST MONITORING

We have discussed several models for forecasting demand under various circumstances. Thus far we have assumed that once the model is selected, we can expect good results. Generally speaking, this is correct only if the conditions for which the model was designed are maintained. In the real world, this is often not true; for example, the demand pattern for a particular item might change from constant to trend, or various factors might cause an increased noise or randomness factor to be exhibited in the demand pattern. To account for these kinds of situations, various tests or monitors are typically included in forecasting schemes to aid in the identification of those demand situations for which the established forecasting models no longer seem valid. Box 17.1 describes one ingenious approach to the problem.

An executive in charge of a large computerized management information system for a pharmaceutical company described their approach to forecast errors: Any forecast error is caused by an epidemic, not by any fault in the forecasting model—sometimes they experience epidemics of good health.

Box 17.1

Naive Comparison

In our discussion of common forecasting models, we started with a naive method based solely upon the prior period sales. We thereafter compared other models to the naive model with varying results. Torfin and Hoffmann use this comparison to evaluate several forecasting methodologies under differing error criteria where percentage error reductions over the naive model are presented.[*] Theil also uses the naive model, and with an assumed interest in squared error minimization calculates a statistic that would take on a value of 0 for perfect forecasts and 1 for no change extrapolation.[†] Although testing against the naive model is most often used to initially compare competing models, there is no reason why some continued assessment could not be made of actual performance relative to expected performance over the naive model. Control limits could be established which when violated would call for a new comparison of alternative forecasting models.

Mean Absolute Deviation

In our discussion of statistical quality control, we observed the need for controlling both the central tendency and the variability in a process. Thus for a process where variables are controlled, it is necessary to have both an $\overline{X}$ or mean chart and an R or range chart. We also noted in our discussion of quality control that several measures of variability exist, and that the range can be used as an approximation to the standard deviation which is the best known and most powerful (in a statistical sense) measure of variability. In forecasting problems, we desire to keep track of the variability between actual and forecasted results.

In our discussions up to this point, we have calculated forecast errors by summing (on an absolute value basis, i.e., without regard to sign) the deviations of actual demand minus forecasted demand. We have also expressed this result as an average error (that is, we have divided by the number of forecasts); that result can now be stated as the mean absolute deviation or MAD:

$$(16)\ \text{Mean absolute deviation of forecast errors} = \frac{\sum_{t=1}^{t=n} \left| F_t - D_t \right|}{n}$$

where F_t = forecasted sales for the tth period, D_t = actual sales for the tth period, n = the number of periods, and $|\ |$ denotes absolute value.

---

[*]G. P. Torfin and T. R. Hoffmann, "Simulation Tests for Some Forecasting Techniques," *Production and Inventory Management*, 2nd Qtr., 1968, pp. 71–78.

[†]Henri Theil, *Applied Economic Forecasting*, Rand McNally & Co., Chicago, 1966, Chapter 2.

Just as the standard deviation could be approximated with the range, so can the standard deviation be approximated with MAD. For a normal distribution, the following relationship between the standard deviation and MAD exists:

(17) Standard deviation $= 1.25$(MAD)

In our prior calculations of mean absolute deviation, we made our computation on the basis of a series of n pieces of data after all n actual forecast deviations had been observed. In practice, we will find the current value of the mean absolute deviation to be quite useful; it too can be estimated with the exponential smoothing model. Thus, to obtain a continually updated estimate of the current MAD, we can proceed as follows:

(18) New MAD $= \delta$|Actual Demand-Forecasted Demand| $+ (1-\delta)$Old MAD

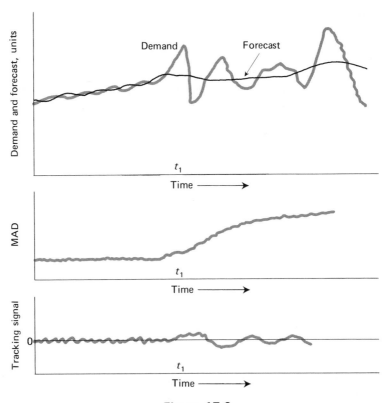

Figure 17.6

With the current estimate of MAD maintained over time, it is possible to develop a control chart-like device (analogous to the R chart) that will indicate whether or not the underlying assumptions of demand variability are still valid. Figure 17.6 shows this phenomenon in a general way.

In this figure, at time t_1 something caused the variability in demand to change drastically from what it was prior to time t_1. We can see that the accompanying forecast error as measured by MAD starts to grow at time t_1 and tends to level off at a much higher rate. Figure 17.6 also shows a tracking signal which we will discuss in the next section; for the present, the tracking signal may be regarded as analogous to a test of means in a quality control process and the conditions depicted in Fig. 17.6 as analogous to those where the mean in a quality control situation has not changed but the variance has increased sharply. Depending upon where we choose to establish an "upper control limit" on MAD, we might or might not decide that the forecasting methodology utilized in Fig. 17.6 is "out of control."

Defining exact control limits on MAD cannot be accomplished without consideration of δ. As can be seen in our smoothing equation (18), higher values of δ will make our estimate of MAD more responsive to current forecast errors. Control limits on MAD are also clearly dependent on the costs of particular errors. It is to be expected that limits would vary for different products in a company; high cost errors call for more detailed manual monitoring.

Tracking Signal

The tracking signal is oriented toward identifying situations where the forecast is lagging behind a genuine change in demand. The tracking signal is based upon the appealing notion that forecast errors should tend to balance out; that is, in the long run, if the forecasting procedure is working correctly there should be just about as many underestimates as overestimates. The tracking signal could be established either on the basis of noting positive and negative forecast errors and judging significance levels with a nonparametric sign test, or by keeping track of the cumulative sum of the forecast errors. The latter procedure is more often used and the tracking signal is expressed as:

$$(19) \quad \text{Tracking signal} = \frac{\text{cumulative sum of forecast deviation}}{\text{MAD}}$$

If demand variations are assumed to be random, control limits of ± 6 MAD will insure that random variations will only account for being outside the tracking signal control limits about 4% of the time. As was true for quality control problems, different control limits can be used with concomitant type I and type II errors. That is, wider limits will lead to fewer out of control signals for random reasons but be more inclined toward permitting nonrandom changes to go undetected. Again, the appropriateness of particular control limits depends on the associated costs. It is also again true that the tracking signal will be affected by the value of smoothing constant δ used in equation (18). Let us now turn to Fig. 17.7, which illustrates a problem that is somewhat different from that depicted in Fig. 17.6.

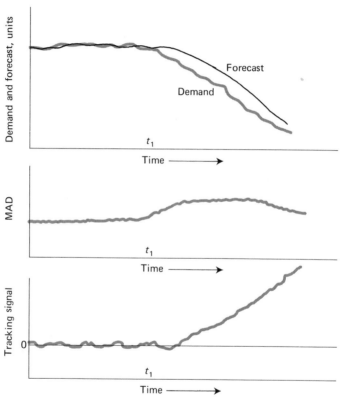

Figure 17.7

As can be seen, at time t_1, a relatively stable demand pattern has become downward trending. Our forecasting procedure lags the actual demand when this occurs which causes a slight increase in MAD; but the significant increase in the tracking signal should go beyond a control limit fairly quickly (this condition is commonly referred to as a tracking signal "trip").

When tracking control signals are tripped, various procedures might be adopted. Some of these procedures call for immediate manual intervention, and others attempt to make machine-oriented corrections such as changing the value of an exponential smoothing constant or switching to an exponential smoothing model with trend. Clearly the procedure to be used is somewhat situation-oriented, and depends upon experiences gained, how to diagnose and treat various kinds of forecast monitoring exceptions, and the relevant costs associated with various kinds of forecast errors.

Demand Filter Test

The demand filter test is an additional procedure for assessing forecast errors. Rather than being based upon a series of error conditions, the demand filter test picks up unusual one-time occurrences such as a clerical error, sudden large change in actual demand, or unforecasted special promotion. A demand filter test is based on testing individual forecast errors against a specified number of MADs. A typical number of MADs is 4, which corresponds to a probability of less than 0.2% of experiencing a demand filter trip for random reasons. When a demand filter trip occurs, manual intervention is usually called for.

Data Editing

Perhaps one of the most overlooked ingredients in a successful forecasting system is a provision for knowledgeable users to be actively involved in forecast monitoring. The monitoring models described above are a useful adjunct to, but not a replacement for, the knowledgeable user. If a chair has been selling at an average rate of 5 per week and one order from a restaurant comes in for 100, what do you do with this datum? Do you allow it to bias the forecast for a long time into the future? Do you discard it from the forecast?

For most companies, disturbances such as this are quite normal. Other examples include hedge buying for anticipated strikes or price changes, "negative" sales because of returns, surges to fill sales quotas, and "pipeline" sales for new dealers. These "dirty" data need to be carefully considered by users who can override purely mechanistic approaches to forecasting, but who are wise enough to make sparing use of the override procedure.

At Baumritter, one person has the authority to override the forecast, the responsibility to do so when needed, and the charge to do so only when necessary. Monitoring models help her to isolate "odd" sales data, but she systematically finds the cause of each abnormality and clearly decides that it is an abnormality before overriding the forecasting system.

SPECIAL CONDITIONS

The forecasting models and monitoring devices described above will tend to work quite well for the large majority of operations management forecasting problems. Now we will identify some additional forecasting problems or situations that will call for modifications to the "standard" forecasting models. To some extent, the construction of mathematically oriented models for unusual forecasting situations is uneconomical. We must return to our distinction between forecasts and predictions where both are aimed at providing a "good" estimate of future demand. For many kinds of estimation problems, better results may be achieved through predictions (based upon intuitive judgment) than by most statistical extrapolations of past data.

Since we have been talking about a forecasting system with an implied use of the computer to make routine forecasts, it is clear that the system must be designed in such a way as to permit, and perhaps to foster, interaction with those who can provide predictive modifications to forecast data. If possible, the system should isolate those situations where predictive data seem to be most necessary.

Changes

It is unrealistic to assume that demand patterns will not change. Products are continually being added or deleted from lines, changed in quality, redesigned to appeal to different market groups, or made obsolete in various degrees by competing products. Some of these changes involve an abrupt shift in the scope or level of operation. Thus an independent wholesale grocery operation added about 30% more stores through a merger. Clearly forecasts based upon past data had to be modified to deal with the new level of operation.

For the wholesale grocery operation, one might initially think that the best procedure would be to multiply forecast data based upon previous demand levels by 1.3. Although this procedure would yield results that might be accurate in aggregate terms, it could easily lead to serious errors and concomitant shortages and overstocking for individual items. The demography and associated buying patterns for the added stores are not necessarily the same as those incorporated in the present mix of stores; if the new stores were in an area where the people have a high concentration of Scandinavian ancestry, our forecasted sales for pickled herring might be woefully inadequate. Baumritter continually faces a similar but less severe problem in the opening of new Showcase Stores in different areas of the country.

In considering how to deal with such a problem, one has to come back to the set of criteria. A desire by the wholesale grocer to meet the demands of all stores with high probability during a short transitionary period led to a decision to increase safety stock levels and to temporarily change the value of α in the exponentially smoothing models from 0.1 to 0.35. This change meant that present data received a much higher weight in forecasts. Baumritter typically handles new store openings on a predictive basis, outside of the regular forecasting effort.

Causality

Many businesses periodically engage in various kinds of sales promotions. Since forecasts are based upon past data assumed to be the result of a series of interacting factors which will continue in the future, forecasts cannot properly estimate future demand when promotional activities are involved. Similarly, as noted in our previous discussion of demand estimation for a restaurant in a college town, the effects of special conditions (big weekends or promotions) should be removed from the data base for forecasting demand under "normal" conditions.

Conceptually, there is considerable appeal in treating promotional activities in a way similar to that used for seasonal forecasting. That is, we can deseasonalize or "depromotionalize" data to obtain a base or normal level, and we can obtain a series of promotional indices. These promotional indices could be initially based upon marketing judgment, and could be updated with exponential smoothing models as done previously for seasonal indices. The indices would, however, be subject to larger amounts of error because of the inherent difficulty in extrapolating promotions of one product to promotions of another and because of the differences in effectiveness of different promotional campaigns. Nevertheless, there is considerable appeal for a company such as Baumritter to make estimates of promotional success on explicit models rather than purely on the basis of optimistic judgments.

The promotional indices should probably be calculated not only for the period of promotional activity, but also for some time periods after the promotional activity has ceased. That is, at least for some items, promotional campaigns seem to cause normal or base level sales in future periods to be realized during the promotional campaign so that sales decrease at the conclusion of the campaign. It would seem that models for promotional campaigns may or may not be useful for particular demand situations, and under most circumstances would act as only one input to the sales estimate; predictive judgments based upon sound knowledge of the market place seem to be a necessity.

Lumpy Demand

Most businesses have items for which the demand per forecast interval is quite likely to be zero or some other low value. Forecasting for these kinds of situations with an exponential smoothing model can sometimes lead to relatively high forecast errors. An alternative procedure for low volume, lumpy-demand items is a technique called probability forecasting. Its basic idea is that for low-volume demand items, the probability of a certain demand in a given period is an independent random event where the pattern of sales should resemble previous history. The methodology is similar to that used in Chapter 12 for simulation based upon an empirical distribution of interarrival or service times.

We simply observe the number of forecast periods for which zero units are sold, one unit was sold, two were sold, etc., and generate sales data based upon random numbers. The major issue involving forecasts of low moving items is concerned with the use of those forecasts. Since a frequent objective is usually tied to customer service, we must be concerned with safety stock levels for these low moving items; we will see in Chapter 18 that most items are manufactured in economic lots and that for items whose sales are low, the effect of lot size or "cycle" inventories is sometimes to create large effective safety stocks.

Forecast data for individual items or SKUs are almost universally subject to greater error than forecasts at a higher level of aggregation. Thus, a machine tool company can forecast total sales for an ensuing year to within ±5%, product divisional sales to within ±25%, major machine group sales to within ±60%, and individual machine sales to within ±100%. For this particular company, individual machine components must be started in production long before actual machine sales are known; needless to say, a large number of production schedule changes are initiated as actual sales uncertainties are eliminated.

For some kinds of situations, forecasts can be based upon sales of a group item with an accompanying error reduction. Thus Baumritter can forecast demand for some grouped items that are identical except for being made with ten different finishes. Since these grouped forecasts are more accurate, the production decisions based upon them will be improved. The actual division of the group item into individual finishes is not necessary before the item is almost completed. By this time, a long lead time (typically 8 to 10 weeks) has elapsed, the actual sales of those items is largely known and acknowledged, and division of the order quantity into individual finishes can be made on actual rather than on forecasted sales data.

Another lumpy demand problem sometimes faced by firms is due to forecasts being based upon internal considerations rather than externally generated demand patterns. One such common problem is to base forecasts on shipment data rather than on orders received. That is, shipments may be limited by many internal considerations such as inventory availabilities, production schedules, or freight rates. A closely related situation has to do with the demand for individual components. Thus an attempt to forecast weekly usage for individual items for a large scale manufacturer uncovered patterns such as: 0, 0, 0, 600, 0, 0; the average demand is 100, but MAD (calculated for the total 6 weeks) is 167! The obvious answer is that the "demand" data were based upon production schedules and an inventory control model based upon requirements planning is superior to one based upon forecasts with assumed random patterns. We will treat this distinction in detail in Chapter 19.

SUMMARY REMARKS

In this chapter we have attempted to describe a forecasting methodology that is easily comprehensible and will yield good forecast results for the majority of demand estimation problems. There are, however, extensions that can be made from the basic exponential smoothing models presented in this chapter. We dealt with only one way to handle trend and seasonality; trend was considered as a linear or additive component and seasonality was considered as a multiplicative or index component. There are obviously trend situations that are better considered as a constant percentage growth, and one can think of seasonality patterns where the peaks and valleys are a straight addition to, or subtraction from, the basic level rather than a function of the level itself. Also, there are extensions that can be added to the exponential smoothing approach itself. Some forecasting models, for example, utilize a series of computer programs which attempt continually to "learn" about a particular demand pattern as new data are incorporated.

Thus we find ourselves again at the end of a chapter saying that the ultimate weapon is not at hand. Nevertheless, the exponential smoothing models presented in this chapter should allow one to have a basic understanding of forecasting methodology. With that understanding should come the ability to identify appropriate models for various kinds of forecasting problems.

REFERENCES

Brown, Robert Goodell, *Smoothing, Forecasting, and Prediction of Discrete Time Series,* Prentice-Hall, 1963.

Geoffrion, Arthur M., "A Survey of Exponential Smoothing." *The Journal of Industrial Engineering,* **13,** no. 4 (Aug. 1962): 223–26.

Gross, D., and J. L. Ray, "A General Purpose Forecast Simulator," *Management Science,* **2** (April 1965): 119–35.

Torfin, Gary P., and T. R. Hoffman, "Simulation Tests of Some Forecasting Techniques," *Production and Inventory Management,* (2nd Qtr., 1968), pp. 71–78.

Winters, Peter R. "Forecasting Sales by Exponentially Weighted Moving Averages," *Management Science,* **6,** no. 3 (April 1960): 324–42.

CHAPTER REVIEW

Chapter 17 is probably the most tersely written chapter in the book. To some of you it may come as a welcome relief from my wordiness; to others, you may feel the desire for the Westfall "security blanket." Some Westfall examples are to be found in the chapter end assignments, but in large measure you will find them somewhat unrealistic. This is so because forecasting is intimately connected with use, and you really will not see this use clearly until Chapter 19.

You need to consider Chapter 17 as a building experience. With a knowledge of how forecasting works at the detailed level, we can add on the basic components of an inventory control system, and see the kinds of real world companies for which such a system will work (we will see that Westfall requires more than basic concepts).

A note of encouragement: Although we have stated that *use* of a forecast is usually more important than accuracy, you will find many companies interested in more accurate forecasts. With a knowledge of the materials presented in Chapter 17 and a limited understanding of their needs, you can deliver those more accurate forecasts. Yes, surprising as it may seem, your education has resulted in your being able to *do* something!

OUTLINE OF THE CHAPTER

Introduction	(goals of the chapter)
The forecasting problem	(estimate of the future)
Forecasts *versus* predictions	(projection of past data)
Criteria	(error, stability, responsiveness, use, speed)
The forecasting interval	(data collection and use)
Extrinsic *versus* intrinsic forecasts	(individual item orientation)
Common forecasting models	(naive forecast)
Smoothing	(averaging)
Moving averages	(average of n most recent periods)
Weighted moving averages	(increased weight on most recent)
Exponential smoothing	(improved forecasts and efficiency)

The model	(related to moving average)
The smoothing constant	(stability-responsiveness)
Trend consideration	(exponential average growth)
Seasonal considerations	(exponential average indices)
An exponential system	(base-trend-seasonal)
Forecast monitoring	(routine validity checks)
Naive comparison	(model *versus* last period)
Mean absolute deviation	(variability measure)
Tracking signal	(sustained error)
Demand filter test	(one time error)
Special conditions	(predictive inputs)
Changes	(incorporating with model)
Causality	(sales stimulation)
Lumpy demand	(low volume items)
Summary remarks	(a basic capability)
Appendix A	(initialization)

CENTRAL ISSUES

The exponential smoothing model is directed toward forecasting of many individual items on a repetitive basis. The model does not take account of predictive data such as expected sales promotions, but *use* of the model can incorporate such data. The model is based on statistical extrapolation of the past. It achieves better forecast results than competing models, and it is superior on economic grounds as well. The model produces results especially important for production planning and inventory control which necessarily is concerned with individual items.

The basic exponential smoothing model is an averaging technique where the new average or forecast is equal to the old average or forecast plus some percentage of the difference between the forecasted and the actual demand. The percentage is a parameter which depicts the rate of exponential decay with which any one piece of actual demand data affects the average or forecast.

The parameter or smoothing constant is set between 0.0 and 1.0 with higher values depicting more rapid decay. Higher values also imply increased responsiveness to recent demand and less reliance on past data. Smaller values of the smoothing constant imply less responsiveness to recent demand and increased stability. Smaller values filter out noise or randomness, but are less able to detect actual shifts in the underlying pattern of demand. Larger smoothing constants will better react to change, but will also react to noise as if it were change.

The basic exponential smoothing model can be expanded to account for trend or steady growth as well as for recurring seasonal patterns of demand. Whether such additions should be made depends upon the relative weight of trend and seasonal components and the use to which the model is to be put. In many cases, the basic model can achieve very good results.

A forecasting system also includes a set of monitors which routinely examine the accuracy of the models. The process is essentially one of statistical hypothesis testing where the validity of a model is being continually assessed. As users become more aware of how they react to various monitor information, parts of the reaction process can be codified into a set of decision rules. The forecasting system tends to evolve over time with more and more aspects becoming routinized, with a concomitant release of creative time which can be devoted to *use* of the forecasts.

ASSIGNMENTS

1. Westfall Furniture Company has provided biweekly sales data for one of the tables made at the Westfall plant and asked you to forecast sales for the periods 6–15 with the following models:

a) 3-period moving average;
b) 5-period moving average;
c) Exponential smoothing, $\alpha = 0.1$;
d) Exponential smoothing, $\alpha = 0.5$;

Use periods 3, 4, and 5 to initialize model (a); 1, 2, 3, 4, and 5 for (b); and the average of periods 1–5 for (c) and (d).

Biweekly sales data, table #15-6023

1.	50
2.	70
3.	90
4.	30
5.	30
6.	40
7.	30
8.	50
9.	60
10.	70
11.	60
12.	40
13.	40
14.	40
15.	50

2. Calculate the average forecast errors for each of the four models in problem 1. What conclusions do you draw?

3. Westfall has also provided biweekly sales data for a newly designed dry sink; forecast sales for this item in the same way as in problem 1.

Biweekly sales data, dry sink #12-6055

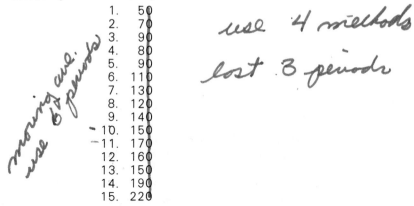

1.	50
2.	70
3.	90
4.	80
5.	90
6.	110
7.	130
8.	120
9.	140
10.	150
11.	170
12.	160
13.	150
14.	190
15.	220

use 4 methods

last 3 periods

moving ave. use 6 periods

4. Calculate the average forecast errors for each of the four models used in problem 3. What conclusions do you draw?

5. Redo problem 3 with the two additional following models:

a) Exponential smoothing, $\alpha = 0.1$, $\beta = 0.2$
b) Exponential smoothing, $\alpha = 0.5$, $\beta = 0.2$

Initialize the trend component as ¼ of the difference between the demand in period 5 and the demand in period 1. Accept the demand in period 1 as the base, and run the models for periods 2, 3, 4, and 5 to achieve an initialization for period 6.

6. Calculate the average forecast errors for the two models used in problem 5. In what way would you revise your conclusions from problem 4?

*7. Using the procedure given in Appendix A of Chapter 12, generate weekly demand from a normal distribution, $\mu = 100$, $\sigma = 10$. Forecast demand and calculate the average error for 1000 weeks (not including the first 40) with the following moving average models:

a) 5 period
b) 10 period
c) 20 period
d) 40 period

Use periods 36–40 to initialize model (a), 31–40 for (b), 21–40 for (c), and 1–40 for (d).

*8. Redo problem 7 with the following exponential smoothing models:

a) $\alpha = 0.4$
b) $\alpha = 0.2$
c) $\alpha = 0.1$
d) $\alpha = 0.05$

Use the average of the first 40 periods for initialization.

*9. Compare the results of problem 7 with problem 8. What conclusions do you draw?

*10. Redo problem 7 with the following exponential smoothing models with trend:

a) $\alpha = 0.2$, $\beta = 0.4$
b) $\alpha = 0.1$, $\beta = 0.4$
c) $\alpha = 0.2$, $\beta = 0.2$
d) $\alpha = 0.1$, $\beta = 0.2$

Initialize the trend component as 1/39 of the difference between the demand in period 40 and the demand in period 1. Accept the demand in period 1 as the base, and run the models for periods 2–40 to achieve an initialization for period 41.

*11. Repeat problems 7, 8, and 10 with the following trend addition to the weekly demand generating procedure: Let demand = demand (as previously generated), + a random integer from 1 to 5 (inclusive), + 3 times the week number. That is, if for week 50 the demand generated was 108 and the random number was 4, the trend adjusted demand would be 108 + 4 + 3(50) = 262.

*12. Redo problem 11 with the trend component reduced to: demand (as previously generated) + a random integer from 1 to 5 inclusive, + 0.5 times the week number.

*13. Redo problem 8, but instead of calculating the average error, estimate the average error with the following exponential smoothing constants for MAD:

a) $\delta = 0.1$
b) $\delta = 0.2$
c) $\delta = 0.4$

Use the average error for the first 40 periods for initialization. What conclusions do you draw when you compare these error measures to those obtained in problem 8?

*14. Redo problem 11 with the error estimated by the procedures of problem 13.

APPENDIX A TO CHAPTER 17

INITIALIZATION

We noted that the exponential system left us with a choice of weights for α, β, and γ, as well as with the choice of initial values for F_t, T_t, and I_t. We also need a weight for δ and an initial value for MAD.

There are three related questions which must be considered in making these choices:

1. The measure of effectiveness for selecting between alternative weights or smoothing constants and initial values

2. Techniques for comparing alternative smoothing constants and initial values

3. The time series over which we wish to make comparisons

The measure of effectiveness is typically assumed to be minimization of the standard deviation or MAD of forecast errors. This criterion does, however, not explicitly take account of a situation dependent loss function. We noted this problem in the chapter; in most instances, minimization of forecast errors is assumed, with forecast use set out as a separate issue.

Techniques for comparing alternative smoothing constants and initial values typically involve some cut and try or simulation. A fairly typical procedure would be to take five years of data, establish $\bar{F}_t$ as the average of either the first or fourth year's data, T_t as one third of the difference between the average of the first year's data and the average of the fourth year's data, the I_t's as the average ratio of each period in the four years to that year's average (normalized so the I_t's sum to 100%), and MAD as the average forecast error for the first year where the forecast is

$$(\bar{F}_t + n\,T_t)\, I_{t-m+n}.$$

Various weights for α, β, γ, and δ can be selected, and combinations can be tried, either by hand or with a computer. One way would be to use the initial values ($\bar{F}_t$ = fourth year) and keep track of forecast errors for the fifth year of demand data (which was not used to calculate initial values). It should be fairly obvious, however, that the initial values will remain very important in the forecasts if the data are monthly (as opposed to shorter time periods), and if the smoothing constants are small (if $\alpha = 0.05$ and data are monthly, the initial value still accounts for 57% of the forecast for year five December sales).

An alternative is to obtain the initial values in approximately the same way ($\bar{F}_t$ = first year), but use the alternative models to forecast over the entire five years of demand with forecast errors only calculated for year five. That is, we can "run in" the model over the first four years to eliminate most of the transient conditions.

Still another alternative is the same as either of the above, but to simply use SWAG (systematic wild guessing) for the initial values for $\bar{F}_t$, T_t, I_t and MAD. In order to decide whether this alternative is good or bad, we need to consider the last of the three opening questions, which is probably the most important.

The process of comparing alternative initial weights and smoothing values described above was done on past data (year five). Whether we should have used three years for constructing our estimate and two for testing is somewhat pedantic. The real issue is whether or not the future will be like the past.

Our interest is in choosing initial values and smoothing constants that will perform well *in the future.* To the extent that one feels the future will be like the past, refinements in methods for selecting initial values and smoothing constants seems appropriate. To the extent that the future is not believed to be like the past, we may be deluding ourselves with sophisticated analyses.

The comparisons of smoothing constants in the literature typically involve a nonchanging demand generator. That is, there is one and only one "stone tablet" that we are trying to estimate with our models. In the real world, the stone tablets can change due to new markets, competitive pressures, etc.

We therefore find ourselves once again returning to the notions of stability and responsiveness. The forecasting problem is to trade off past data and future expectations; choices made in smoothing constants directly indicate how this tradeoff is perceived, and perception is an individual, situation-dependent matter.

The initial values and choice of smoothing constants needs to be related to forecast monitoring. That is, use of the model will generate exception or error reports, and considerable fine tuning can and should be expected. This fine tuning should involve forecast users because one of the expectations is related to the first of our initial related questions. As use occurs, the kinds of errors that are most and least important (in terms of user criteria) will become better understood and the models can evolve accordingly.

Finally, it is worth noting that if a curve were plotted for MAD with various smoothing constants, the bottom of the curve would be fairly flat —some fairly simple experimenting will get one into the general area of the best set of smoothing constants. Whether further analysis is justified comes back again to use.

CHAPTER 18

BASIC INVENTORY
MODELS

This chapter presents some of the most basic concepts or building blocks of a production planning and inventory control system. After an initial categorization of inventories based upon functions served, models for cycle stock and uncertainty stock are presented; thereafter inventory control systems based upon these models are described.

Because of the close interaction between production planning and inventory control, particularly in terms of the proper criteria set for joint consideration of the two subsystems, definitive statements of general applicability are difficult to achieve. For this reason, the approach used in this and the next three chapters will be first to understand basic models and the simplified problems for which they are appropriate; then, we can critically examine the underlying assumptions of the models and develop more encompassing methodologies for more inclusive problem statements.

Some of the previous chapters will be particularly useful to us in this endeavor, especially Chapters 3 and 4 for the underlying process of developing a more inclusive approach to problem solving, Chapters 5 and 7 for assessing the appropriateness of cost data inputs, the flow orientation of Chapter 11 which noted that all flow stoppages or inventories can be usefully regarded in a queuing context, the appropriate measures of required work developed in Chapters 13 and 14, and of course the understanding of forecasting methodology developed in Chapter 17.

INVENTORY CATEGORIZATION

The two basic questions in an inventory control system are timing in terms of acquisition or manufacture and quantity in terms of volume. For most systems of interest, the answers comprise a set of explicit decision rules whose performance can be evaluated over time. In order to make that evaluation, it is useful to divide inventories into the following four categories and to understand the functions that they serve: cycle or lot size stock, uncertainty or fluctuation stock, anticipation or seasonal stock, and transit or movement stock.

Cycle Stock

Cycle or lot size inventories occur when material is purchased or made in infrequent large batches to satisfy more frequent but smaller uses, demands, or needs. The functions fulfilled by cycle stock include the making of material in economic run sizes where expensive one-time setup charges are amortized over many units, and the purchase of large lots to hold down clerical and other costs associated with requisitions, purchase orders, stock receipts, accounts payable, etc. Also, cycle stock helps to permit "job shop" operation where individual work requirements can be economically determined independent of other requirements, helps to take advantage of distribution costs and factors, of favorable purchase prices, and helps to speculate against cost or price changes as well as to hold by-products.

Uncertainty Stock

Uncertainty or fluctuation stocks are held as a cushion against unpredictable variations in both the supply of, and the demand for, various items or materials. The notion of "customer service" plays a significant role in the need for such inventories. If customers are willing to wait, uncertainties associated with the demand rate can be ignored. This situation exists for many products; one would not expect to find aircraft carriers, refineries, steel rolling mills, or jumbo jets being stockpiled to provide instant customer delivery. The furniture industry typically operates in a backlog position where customers have to wait for goods to be produced. Baumritter's franchise policy implies a quite different customer service level. The resulting inventories to support this customer service well might differ from those of other furniture manufacturers.

Other functions fulfilled by uncertainty stocks include the ability to tolerate variability in the output rate of a prior operation or conversion process; the storage of overruns, misruns, or cancelled orders; the ability to tolerate errors in measurement and recording of quantities; protection against fires, hurricanes, acts of God; and protection against unforeseen strikes or work stoppages.

Anticipation Stock

Anticipation or seasonal stocks are built when the production or purchasing rate is higher than the present demand rate, in order that the reverse condition may take place at a later planned time. Thus companies such as Baumritter who face a seasonal demand pattern for their goods often smooth out employment and production rates by building inventories during periods of low demand and subsequently depleting them during periods of high demand. Alternatively, anticipation stocks may be built to meet conditions such as special promotions, plant vacation shutdowns, or potential strikes. Seasonal stocks also derive from anomalies in supply conditions such as those associated with agricultural products which mature at one point in the year but are consumed more uniformly throughout the year. Additional functions fulfilled by anticipation stocks are productive flexibility through building an inventory in expectation of a particular order, a more intensive use of plant capacity, and the ability to postpone the capital expenditures necessary to increase plant capacity. Since the models for building anticipation or seasonal inventories necessarily involve trading off inventories with production plans and productive capacity, discussion of these models will be taken up in Chapters 19 and 20.

Transit Stock

Transit or movement stock exists because of the time required to move material from one location to another; although usually thought of in regard to goods moving between different geographic locations, large amounts of inventory in process are properly regarded as transit or movement stock. The amount of transit stock required is a function of the transit time and the demand rate. Thus, if the average demand for an item is 50 units per week and the goods are sold from a warehouse which takes three weeks to replenish from the factory, the average amount of goods in transit is 150 units. Alternatively, at any time when no goods are in transit, at least 150 units must be in inventory at the warehouse if stockouts are to be avoided. Transit or movement stocks in themselves yield no benefits to an organization; they are a necessary evil, often overlooked, but which can be reduced by changing transportation methods. The determination of proper transit stock levels involves consideration of distribution channels and transportation means as well as other factors; Chapter 21 is devoted to these matters.

In a later section we will see that "a unit in inventory is a unit in inventory;" that is, although a particular unit might reside in inventory because of lot size considerations, it nonetheless acts as uncertainty or fluctuation stock insofar as its existence precludes the possibility of a stock shortage. The same kind of cross functional benefits accrue to transit stocks.

CYCLE STOCK MODELS

As noted above, cycle or lot size inventories come about because goods are purchased or made in batches in order to amortize one-time fixed expenditures, such as setup, transportation, and clerical costs, over many units. Obviously, the more units that are made in one batch, the smaller the amount of fixed charge which each unit has to bear. Offsetting this cost function which encourages ever increasing lot sizes is the cost of holding inventories which increase with lot sizes; if goods are produced only as needed there is no storage, but if produced in batches they must be held until demanded. The problem is to strike a balance between these two offsetting cost functions in such a way that total cost (their sum) is at a minimum.

Trial and Error Solution

Let us consider the following problem:

> The Westfall Furniture Company uses 5000 of a particular knob per day which are purchased from a vendor at $0.005 each. Management feels that it costs about $5 every time an order is processed for such things as filling out the requisition and purchase order, postage, and incoming inspection. In addition, transportation costs $10 per trip; because of the size of the item, transportation cost does not vary significantly with the size of the order. The costs associated with holding knobs in inventory include storage, obsolescence, and an opportunity cost for having capital tied up in inventory. The total of these costs is estimated to be 20% of the purchase price. The company operates 250 days per year.

Concerning ourselves only with the avoidable costs, the cost of the knobs themselves is not incremental to the inventory or buying decision. Therefore, if each day's supply was purchased individually the total avoidable costs would be $15 per day times 250 days or $3750 per year since no storage costs are involved.* At the other extreme, if the company purchased an entire year's supply at once, the $15 fixed charge per order would only be incurred once per year but the average inventory would be ½ of the annual requirement or 625,000 knobs (0.5 X 5000 X 250) and the annual inventory carrying cost would be $625 (0.5 X 5000 X 250 X 0.005 X 20%) or a total annual cost of $640.

Let us examine a less extreme policy. Suppose the knobs were purchased in lots of 100,000. Since the annual usage is 1,250,000 knobs, 12½ orders per year would be placed for a total cost of $187.50; the average inventory would be 50,000 knobs with an annual cost of $50. Total annual cost of this ordering rule is $237.50. Figure 18.1 depicts this policy.

Other trial and error solutions might or might not lead to a reduction in total annual costs. For example, a policy of buying 50,000 knobs (10 day's supply) at a time would double the order cost per year from $187.50 to $375 while halving the carrying cost from $50 to $25 for a total cost of

---

*The assumption of zero storage cost is not entirely correct; since 5000 knobs are purchased once each day, on the average the company would be carrying 2500 knobs in inventory for a yearly increase in cost of $2.50 (2500 X $0.005 X 20%).

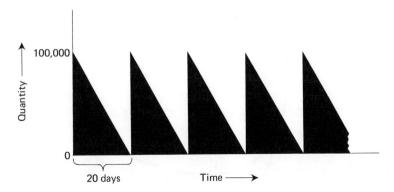

Figure 18.1

$400 per year. On the other hand, if the 100,000 quantity were doubled, the $187.50 for ordering would be reduced to $93.75 while doubling the inventory carrying cost from $50 to $100; the net cost would, therefore, be reduced from $237.50 to $197.75. Let us now turn to an explicit model for trading off these costs.

Economic Order Quantity (Instantaneous Receipt)

Figure 18.2 depicts the annual cost behavior patterns as a function of the order quantity for ordering costs, inventory carrying costs, and the sum or total of these two costs.

Note that the minimum point of the total cost curve is slightly below an order quantity of 200,000 units (we will see presently that it is 193,500). Note also that the minimum point occurs at that order quantity where the ordering costs and inventory carrying costs are equal. This has intuitive appeal and is in keeping with the trial and error solutions calculated above; for a particular order quantity, if the ordering cost was greater than the inventory cost, the total cost would be decreased by increasing the order quantity and vice versa.

The economic lot size formula will yield the minimum cost quantity directly; it can be shown that the following equation will yield the optimum economic order quantity (See Appendix A for a mathematical derivation.)

$$Q = \sqrt{\frac{2RS}{I}}$$

where

Q = order quantity
R = total annual requirements
S = set up or fixed charges
I = annual cost of holding one unit in inventory

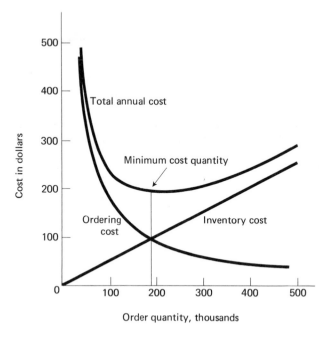

Fig. 18.2 Furniture knob economic order quantity.

Thus, for our furniture knob example, we would find the minimum cost order quantity as follows:

$$Q = \sqrt{\frac{2 \times (5000 \times 250) \times \$15}{\$0.005 \times 20\%}} = \sqrt{37,500,000,000} \approx 193,500$$

A word of caution about the units used in the economic order quantity: Note that R denotes annual requirements rather than daily or monthly requirements, and that I denotes the cost to hold one unit in inventory one year. If monthly or daily requirements are to be used, care must be exercised to maintain consistency of units; if a monthly requirements rate is used, the variable I must then denote the cost to hold one unit in inventory one month rather than one year. I is expressed as a dollar amount per year per unit. If a percentage charge is used for inventory, it must be multiplied by the unit price or cost to make the appropriate conversion.

Calculation of the economic order quantity implies a mode of action or explicated decision rule; for the knob example, the rule is: issue an order for 193,500 knobs when our supply is 0, and receive them instantly.

This supply will last for 38.7 days, at which time a new economic order quantity will be obtained.

Lead Time

With the economic order quantity expressed as the above decision rule, one sees the unrealistic nature of the assumption that orders need not be placed until inventories are entirely depleted. Typically, time is required for requisitions and purchase orders to be processed, for vendors to make the goods and prepare them for shipment, for transportation, and for receipt. The combination of these activities is called *lead time*; i.e., the total time required between the initial signal for inventory replenishment and receipt of the replenishment order. Thus, if the lead time for our knob example were five days, we would restate the inventory decision rule as follows: when the stock of knobs gets down to 25,000, place an order for 193,500; five days later when the inventory has been entirely depleted, the order will arrive. Thus, 25,000 units becomes the level at which we place orders, or the "order point." Figure 18.3 depicts the operation of these decision rules over time in a manner similar to that of Fig. 18.1.

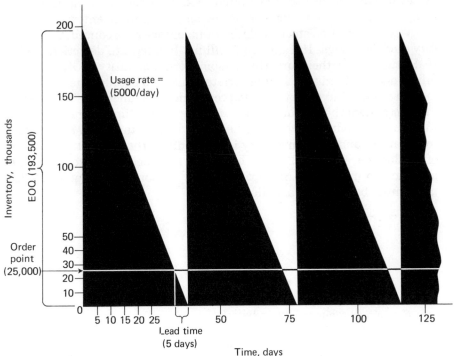

Fig. 18.3 Furniture knob inventory (instantaneous receipt).

Figure 18.3 starts out with an economic order quantity of 193,500 knobs in inventory at day 0. Knobs are used at the rate of 5000 per day for 33.7 days, at which time the inventory stands at 25,000 units. Since 25,000 units is the order point, an order for the economic quantity (193,-500 knobs) is issued at that time. In five days, the order is received and placed in inventory (day 38.7).

There are some obvious faults in the underlying assumptions of this model, and concomitant revisions of the inventory decision rules are necessary. Perhaps the most unrealistic assumption relates to the complete lack of uncertainty in our model; how to cope with uncertainty will be the subject of the next major section in this chapter, but it will behoove us first to examine some additional features of the basic cycle stock model.

Economic Order Quantity (Noninstantaneous Receipt)

In Figs. 18.1 and 18.3, the receipt or delivery of an economic order quantity is depicted as being instantaneous; that is, the entire quantity is received at the same time. For some situations, most notably where stock is produced rather than purchased, the instantaneous delivery assumption is inappropriate. It is not always inappropriate for fabricated items, however, since such items are often held at producing centers until a complete "batch" is finished before being placed in inventory.

When fabricated stock is placed in inventory as produced, the inventory models of Figs. 18.1 and 18.3 will not be accurate depictions of the real situation; furthermore, the economic order quantity (EOQ) as determined above will also be inappropriate. This is so because the basic EOQ model trades off inventory carrying cost which is a function of the average number of items held in inventory, and fixed or one time charges incurred in buying or producing a batch; when stock is simultaneously being added to inventory and used, inventory is built only to the extent that the rate of production exceeds the rate of usage. To reflect this excess or "net accretion to inventory" concept, the basic economic order quantity formula must be modified as follows:

$$Q = \sqrt{\frac{2RS}{I(1 - r/p)}}$$

where

Q = order quantity
R = annual requirements as before
S = fixed or setup cost as before
I = annual inventory holding cost per unit as before
r = requirements or usage rate
p = production rate

The r and p must be established in consistent units such as per day or per week; since the units cancel out through the division, the choice of units is unimportant. However, if p is stated as a rate that could be produced if the item were continuously fabricated all year, then r would be equal to R. As noted above, we are concerned with the net accretion to inventories. The $(1- r/p)$ term reflects this accretion. Thus, if r and p were equal, the division would yield unity, the subtraction would yield zero for the accretion term, and the subsequent arithmetic operations would yield an infinite economic order quantity. Such a result does not mean that the formula is "wrong." The building of cycle stock inventory is due to the economics of production. We produce things at the most speedy and economical rate of production; for that utopian situation where this most efficient production rate just happens to equal the demand rate, we do in fact engage in continuous production without ever building cycle stock inventories.

Conversely, as the ratio of r to p grows smaller (i.e., the economic production rate far outstrips the demand rate) the effect of noninstantaneous delivery or receipt becomes smaller and the resultant economic order quantity approaches that obtained with the formula for purchased stocks.

For the furniture knob example, if Westfall decided to manufacture their own knobs and the knobs were placed into inventory as fabricated, the appropriate order quantity would have to reflect the production rate.

As noted above, if by some chance the production rate for these knobs happened to be 5000 per day, then they would be produced continuously. A much more likely prospect, however, is that some piece of capital equipment would be purchased which would produce the knobs at a rate greater than that of usage (it has to be at least equal to the usage rate unless purchased stocks are also used to satisfy demands). The importance of the incremental cost concepts developed in Chapter 5 are clearly quite pertinent to the decision as to whether to make or buy the knobs and to the appropriate capacity of the capital equipment; the extent to which the production rate exceeds the usage rate is unimportant unless the capital equipment is used for the satisfaction of other needs as well.

Suppose that a knob-making machine was purchased that could fabricate knobs at the rate of 15,000 per day. For comparative purposes, let us also assume that the fixed cost (set up, etc.) remained at $15. The appropriate economic order quantity would now be determined as follows:

$$Q = \sqrt{\frac{2 \times 1{,}250{,}000 \times \$15}{0.005 \times 20\% \, (1-5/15)}} = \sqrt{56{,}247{,}187{,}000} \approx 237{,}000$$

If we continue the assumption of a five-day lead time, the decision rule would now be to issue an order to manufacture 237,500 knobs when the

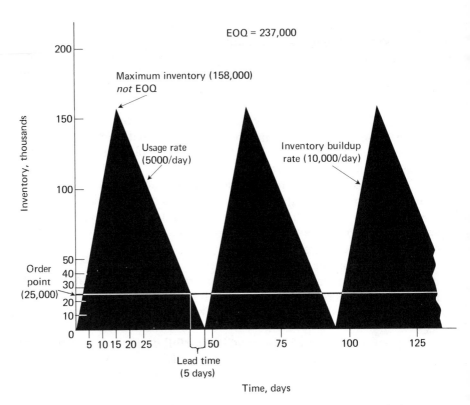

Fig. 18.4 Furniture knob inventory (noninstantaneous receipt).

stock of existing knobs reaches 25,000 units; Fig. 18.4 depicts this situation.

As seen in Fig. 18.4, the inventory again starts to be replenished at time 0 with a portion of the production run. The economic order quantity of 237,000 units takes 15.8 days to produce (15,000 per day). During these 15.8 days, although 15,000 units are produced each day, since the daily usage rate is 5000 units, the net buildup is 10,000 units per day with an inventory peak of 158,000 units reached after 15.8 days. The inventory is then depleted at the rate of 5000 units per day for 26.6 days; at that time an EOQ (237,000) is issued. A 5-day lead time goes by during which the inventory is completely depleted. At the end of that time production from the new run is available for use and inventory buildup.

A comparison of Figs. 18.3 and 18.4 which are drawn on the same scale may be informative since the only cost change in the two inventory models is the addition of the $(1 - r/p)$ term. Since we are still trading off the costs of holding inventory with the fixed or setup costs, it should not be surprising that the areas inclosed by the inventory buildup and depletion triangles in both figures are equal. Thus, although the average inventory in Fig. 18.3 is 96,750 (193,500 ÷ 2), the average applies to a cycle of 38.6 days; in Fig. 18.4 the average inventory is 79,000 (158,000 ÷ 2), but this average is associated with a cycle time of 47.4 days. The total inventory held per cycle is identical in both cases (except for differences in rounding).

Quantity Discounts

The cycle stock models discussed above assume that the price or cost per unit does not vary with the size of the order placed. Clearly this is not true for purchasing situations where quantity discounts are offered; to the extent that we believe in the appropriateness of the learning curve model described in Chapter 14, a fixed cost per unit assumption also becomes untenable for fabricated items. Other economic phenomena which result in the equivalent of quantity discounts include differences in payment terms, freight allowances, and alternative cost shipment methods.

To illustrate the effect of quantity discounts, let us return to our belabored knob example where we will now assume purchase from a vendor with the following discount structure: 0–100,000 = 0% 100,000–300,000 = 3%, 300,000–500,000 = 5%, and over 500,000 = 6%. Since the economic lot size for this problem had previously been calculated to be 193,500, it is clear that at least the 3% discount should be taken. If the 3% discount is reflected in the basic EOQ model, the I (cost to carry one unit in inventory one year) would be decreased by 3%; the resultant economic order quantity would be approximately 196,500 units. Of course the total cost including purchase price for the annual requirements would also be reduced by 3% (a savings of 0.005 X 5000 X 250 X 0.03 = $187.50). The total annual cost of ordering under this policy would be comprised as follows:

Cost of units = 0.005 X 5000 X 250 X 0.97	= $6062.50
Purchasing cost = (1,250,000 ÷ 196,500) X $15	= 95.42
Inventory carrying cost = (196,500 ÷ 2) X ($0.005 X 0.97) X 20%	= 95.30
Total cost	$6253.22

In order to ascertain whether the next price break would be attractive, we need to calculate a comparable annual total cost of operating under that policy:

Cost of units = 0.005 X 5000 X 250 X 0.95	= $5937.50
Purchasing cost = (1,250,000 ÷ 300,000) X $15	= 62.50
Inventory carrying cost = (300,000 ÷ 2) X ($0.005 X 0.95) X 20%	= 142.50
Total cost	$6142.50
Net advantage ($6,253.22 – $6,142.50)	$ 110.72

We therefore conclude that an increase in lot size from 196,500 to 300,000 is economically advantageous; the net disadvantage in the tradeoff of ordering costs and holding costs is more than offset by the decrease in purchase price. If we now increase our lot size from 300,000 to 500,000 in order to gain an additional 1% savings in purchase price, we would find that the total annual costs would be increased to $6,147.50 (note that the small net disadvantage of $5.00 may be regarded as close enough to call the two alternatives equal and to suggest that the decision be made on the basis of other criteria.)

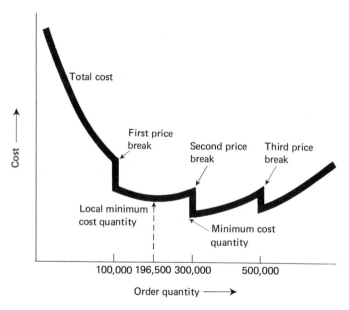

Fig. 18.5 Furniture knob EOQ with price breaks.

In essence we are attempting to find the minimum cost point on the total cost curve depicted in Fig. 18.5. The total cost function in Fig. 18.5 has a general shape like that of the total annual cost depicted in Fig. 18.2, except that it is discontinuous at the price break points. It can be proven that the minimum point for such a function will be either at a point of discontinuity or where the derivatives equal zero as determined by the economic order quantity. Thus in Fig. 18.5 we obtained a local minimum based on a valid economic order quantity of 196,500 units (it is cheaper to make 196,500 unit lots than to make 100,000 or 299,999 lots). The discontinuity occurring at the lot size quantity of 300,000 units yields the absolute minimum for the total cost function, but this would not be true if this cost segment reached a local minimum below the point of discontinuity as was true for the previous cost segment. An alternative way of saying the same thing is that no valid economic order as determined through the EOQ models exists between 300,000 and 500,000 units; a similar statement can be made for the last cost segment.

Magee and Boodman suggest the following method for the direct calculation of the minimum cost order quantity:*

1. Calculate the economic order quantity using the minimum unit price; if this quantity falls within the range for which the vendor offers this price, it is a valid economic order quantity and will result in the minimum cost for the particular item

2. If the EOQ calculated in 1 is not valid, find the total cost for each price break quantity

3. Calculate an EOQ for each unit price

4. Calculate the total cost for each valid EOQ determined in 3

5. The minimum cost order quantity is that associated with the lowest cost found in either 2 or 4

Production Cycling

One of the most unrealistic assumptions associated with the cycle stock models presented above is that they completely ignore the interaction of many items. That is, the decision rule for each item presumes that items can be purchased, fabricated, or stored without regard to the status of other items; furthermore, since the summation of individual item decision rules leads to total production demands, there is an implied assumption of infinite capacity and/or no significant costs being associated with idle capacity. Clearly, ignoring the interrelationships of individual item inventory decision rules is unrealistic; Chapters 19, 20, and 21 are largely devoted to models balancing individual item needs with aggregate needs and more global criteria. There is, however, a cycle stock model for dealing with the more specialized case of several similar products being fabricated by the same productive process or piece of equipment.

Real world examples of this problem include several brands of detergent being manufactured on the same equipment, various grades of paper being made on the same paper machine, different soft drinks being bottled by a bottling plant, different kinds and qualities and sizes of steel in a rolling mill, the scheduling of a general purpose packaging line, or the scheduling of assembly lines such as those at Westfall where several kinds of tables or chairs might be made on one line. In these cases where various products compete for the common production facility, some sort of produc-

---

*John F. Magee and David M. Boodman, *Production Planning and Inventory Control,* 2nd Ed., McGraw-Hill, 1967, pp. 76–77.

tion plan must be developed if stockouts are to be avoided and capacity utilized effectively.

In many of these problems, there are distinct advantages to running the competing jobs in a particular order; thus changeover costs are less for detergents when going from white to colored brands than vice versa, and on the paper-making machine it is advantageous to go from fine to coarser grades. With a planned sequence of products to be run, the question is how much to run of each, or conversely how long a time period should elapse between runs of the same product.

The basic approach used for such problems is to state the demand for each product on a common base, usually hours of production sold per year. Within each cycle, the relative amount of productive hours devoted to each product will be a constant ratio of that product's relative productive requirements; i.e., if products A, B, and C sold at the rates of 100, 200, and 400 hours of production per year respectively then in any production cycle, for every hour devoted to the manufacture of product A, 2 would be spent for B, and 4 for C.

To determine the appropriate order quantity measured in common hours for the total cycle of n products, we can use the noninstantaneous receipt economic order quantity formula given above as follows:

$$Q = \sqrt{\frac{2RS}{I(1-r/p)}}$$

where

Q = total hours devoted to one cycle of n products

R = total annual requirements in hours for all n products

S = total setup or changeover costs for an entire cycle

I = weighted average of the n individual annual holding costs per hour of production (weighted in the ratio of individual annual demand to R)

r/p = average ratio of requirements to production $\left(\sum_{i=1}^{i=n} \frac{r_i}{p_i} \right) \div n$

Once Q has been determined, Q_i (the number of productive hours devoted to each of the n products) is determined by the ratio of annual individual demand requirements to total requirements.

It is worth noting that Q or total hours devoted to a cycle of n products is an attempted optimization for the total cycle which does not necessarily produce results for the n individual products in the cycle that are as good as would be achieved if each were considered independently. This is so because S (fixed or setup costs) in the model is an aggregate which does not reflect significant differences in fixed or setup costs between individual items; similarly, I (annual cost to hold one unit) is a weighted average. Since the cycle sequence is specified and nonvarying, the way in which the total productive hours Q are apportioned between the end jobs is on the basis of their relative annual hourly requirements. If the setup costs for each job were independent of the order in which they were produced, potential savings in total cost would accrue if independent decision rules were calculated for each item which reflected its unique tradeoff of fixed or setup costs with inventory holding costs. The savings are, however, indeed only potential savings since the assumptions of independence imply that no competition for a producing activity exists or that there is sufficient capacity in the producing activity so that scheduling difficulties will not be encountered.

Other kinds of production cycling models can be formulated which relax some of the assumptions in the above model, such as the fixed order for running each job in every cycle. These models would be more appropriate for the Westfall assembly lines. At this time, however, we must appraise the data inputs and assumptions that underlie all of the cycle stock models discussed so far.

Underlying Assumptions and Data Requirements

All of the cycle stock models considered above incorporate some underlying assumptions which are violated in varying extent in the real world. We want to understand clearly what these assumptions are, the kinds of real world situations which lead to violations of differing significance, and the ways in which these models can be adapted or augmented to cope with real world phenomena.

One important assumption pertains to the complete lack of uncertainty in the models considered so far. Thus in Figs. 18.1, 18.3, and 18.4 we assumed that the usage or demand rate was known with certainty and was constant. We made similar assumptions for lead time and for production rates. Clearly these assumptions often will be inappropriate for particular items, companies, and situations. To a large extent, the degree of error in these assumptions depends upon data and the models and procedures used to obtain those data; thus a good forecasting system can decrease errors in requirements, proper attention given to work measurement techniques and the importance of the learning phenomenon can yield more realistic estimates of productive output, and lead time is not an abstract mathematical constant such as π—it is strongly influenced by productive capacity, by work load at a particular moment, and by production scheduling techniques.

Obtaining some of the data inputs required for cycle stock models is not an easy matter; the notions of relevance developed in Chapters 5 and 7 are particularly germane to this data collection. In regard to the basic EOQ model, we have already noted the fallacy in assuming that R, r, and p estimates are constant and error free; a related consideration has to do with needs exhibiting seasonal patterns and with requirements being determined by internal considerations which call for batch withdrawals from inventory. We will consider this kind of withdrawal situation in our discussions of inventory control systems later in this chapter.

Another underlying assumption in the economic order quantity formulae is that S, the fixed or setup cost, can be specified with certainty and that the cost so specified is relevant. Just how does one go about ascertaining what the relevant fixed or setup cost is for an EOQ model? A typical procedure for estimating the cost to place a purchase order involves the division of total annual costs associated with running a purchasing department by the number of purchase orders processed in a year. Clearly, however, the result of this calculation does not yield a reasonable estimate of incremental costs; if one more purchase order were written that amount would not be expended, nor would that amount be saved if one fewer purchase order were written. Figure 18.6 illustrates what is involved in this assumption.

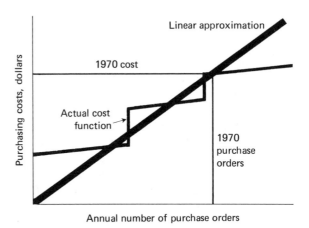

Fig. 18.6 Purchasing costs as a function of orders.

Figure 18.6 plots the number of purchase orders per year on the abscissa and the total purchasing oriented costs on the ordinate. As can be seen, the actual cost function begins with a high initial step (perhaps a purchasing agent's salary) and a small variable cost (perhaps for postage and supplies) which increases linearly until the capacity to place purchase orders must be increased by a discrete step (perhaps by the hiring of an assistant purchasing agent). A similar step increase is necessitated when the new purchasing capacity is exceeded (perhaps the addition of a clerk). Figure 18.6 also shows what happens when a point on the actual cost function is approximated linearly.

A similar kind of problem exists in estimating relevant setup costs for fabricated parts. The problem is not as widely recognized, however, because in many companies highly precise (but not necessarily accurate) estimates of setup time have been determined. If specialized setup men are hired for these tasks, the total cost function would exhibit a pattern of behavior quite similar to that of Fig. 18.6. If those who perform the setups are direct labor workers who are creating salable products when not engaged in setup, then perhaps a linear setup cost assumption is appropriate. Moreover, if setups lead to a reduction in output that could be sold, the appropriate setup cost well might reflect the loss in contributions to overhead and profit.

If Fig. 18.6 does represent a reasonable approximation of fixed or setup cost behavior for a particular company, what should be done? Should the company use the small variable cost per purchase order illustrated by the slope between major steps of Fig. 18.6? Although this might be a fair approximation to incremental cost over certain ranges, the net result of using that approximation would very likely call for an aggregate number of purchase orders large enough to require one or more discrete jumps in total purchasing costs. In our furniture knob example the fixed or setup costs were assumed to be $15; if we now decided that $.50 was a better approximation of the incremental cost we would obtain a purchase order quantity of about 36,500 instead of 173,500; this would mean that approximately 5½ times as many purchase orders per year would be written for this item. Although the magnitude of this change might not be crippling for one item, for Westfall the total change would call for a different scale of operations for the purchasing function.

For a given company or operating department within a company, a practical way out of this dilemma is somehow to choose values for S which result in aggregate setup or purchasing capabilities that are considered "appropriate" or "valid." In the validation process, one should carefully consider the tradeoffs involved in providing various capacities or levels of operation to purchasing or manufacturing operations. That is, one should not casually accept the existing level of operation (number of purchase orders written per year, number of setups per year, etc.) as necessarily being "best." Perhaps an assistant purchasing agent would permit orders to be placed more frequently enough to avoid acquiring additional storage facilities. Perhaps increased working capital would more than offset the relevant costs associated with a different level of aggregate purchasing operation. Perhaps an expected increase in demand for a particular machine center justifies much longer runs so that unproductive downtime due to setups is reduced.

One method for analyzing aggregate cycle stock inventory is called the LIMIT technique which essentially compares aggregate setup hours under an existing operation with anticipated aggregate setup hours based upon EOQ decision rules; thereafter, an implied inventory carrying cost rate is calculated that, when used in the EOQ formulation, would result in anticipated total setup hours equal to the present situation and in individual order quantity decision rules which yield that aggregate.*

The *I* in cycle stock models is also difficult to state with a high degree of reliability. A well-known consultant giving a guest lecture to the author's class once stated that "on every assignment at least one afternoon was devoted to a discussion of the proper inventory carrying cost rate, but that at the end of the discussion the decision was always to use 20% like everybody else." A few years later a different guest speaker was quizzed about the universality of the mystical 20%; he stated that the 20% rule was now outdated and that sophisticated computer installations were now using 24%, because when divided by 12 the result is an even 2% per month!

The value chosen for the cost to carry inventory should depend upon the unique situation that prevails within a company in regard to such considerations as obsolescence, overall financial position, working capital, short-term borrowing capacity, cash forecasts, plans, alternative uses of capital, customer service considerations, employment policies, and economic forecasts. Clearly these considerations are quite different for Baumritter than for other furniture manufacturers or for companies in different industries. Also, these considerations vary over time. Complicating the matter still further is the fact that managers are concerned with aggregate inventories which include uncertainty stocks, anticipation stocks, and transit stocks as well as cycle stocks. Since these inventories satisfy different functions, the desire to change one might or might not be complimentary with other desires. For example, an anticipated change in import laws for Canadian lumber might cause Westfall to stockpile this raw material; a constraint on total inventory value might require a compensating reduction in other raw materials or in work in process or finished goods inventories.

One important segment of the inventory holding costs is storage costs (for example, warehousing). Obtaining storage costs for cycle stock models is not an easy matter. Warehouse men, shelving and other storage devices, material handling equipment, and warehouse space are added in discrete steps; incremental costs are different to segregate, and associations based upon the value of the goods or storage space requirements can be quite tenuous. Even for those items which seem directly based upon valuation such as taxes and insurance, odd results can occur because of

---

*For a description of the LIMIT technique, see G. W. Plossl and O. W. Wight, *Production and Inventory Control,* Prentice-Hall, 1967, Chapter 6.

practices such as drastic inventory reductions just prior to inventory taking for tax purposes.

In many ways an abstract investigation to find proper long-run inventory carrying cost represents an improper view of the inventory function. The decoupling function of inventories allows for mismatches in the outputs of various production stages and the inputs or requirements of succeeding stages (including distribution, sales, and consumption). The mismatch is an expense that is hopefully compensated for by efficiencies and by customer service. With this view in mind, inventories should be viewed as an investment alternative; the choice of interest rate is a decision variable which should be continually updated or revised to reflect current business conditions such as available working capital and forecasted cash requirements.

Responsiveness and Sensitivity

If inventory carrying cost is viewed as a decision variable, a natural question concerns responsiveness or the time required for a change to be reflected in inventory levels; a related consideration is the sensitivity of cycle stock inventory decision rules to changes and errors in input data.

In Fig. 18.2 we plotted the annual ordering costs as monotonically decreasing as a function of the order quantity. The inventory carrying cost was a linear function which intersected the order cost function at the minimum cost order quantity; that is, the total annual cost function was minimized at that point where the annual ordering cost was exactly equal to the annual inventory carrying cost. The inventory carrying cost function used in Fig. 18.2 was based upon an assumed 20% capital or inventory carrying cost. If that rate were changed, a new linear inventory carrying cost function could be drawn which would intersect the same annual ordering cost function at a different point and lead to a new total annual cost function which would be minimized at the order quantity corresponding to the point of intersection. What this means is that by changing the inventory carrying cost percentage, we change the slope of the inventory cost function and the associated minimum cost order quantity; conversely, for any order quantity we can derive an implied inventory carrying cost.

Since a change in the carrying cost yields a change in the economic order quantity, the average inventory held and inventory decision rules would also change. Thus, if for our previous example the inventory carrying cost were reduced from 20% to 10%, the economic order quantity would be increased from 193,500 to 274,000. We can readily analyze the effects of such changes by restating the I term in the cycle stock models as follows:

I = Unit cost X % carrying cost.

Thus:

$$\sqrt{\frac{2RS}{I}} = \sqrt{\frac{2RS}{\text{Unit cost}}} \times \sqrt{\frac{1}{\% \text{ Carrying cost}}}$$

and

$$\sqrt{\frac{2RS}{I(1\text{-}r/p)}} = \sqrt{\frac{2RS}{\text{Unit cost } (1\text{-}r/p)}} \times \sqrt{\frac{1}{\% \text{ Carrying cost.}}}$$

By restating the EOQ formulae in the manner above, we can see how for any one item its economic order quantity would increase or decrease as changes are made in the percentage carrying cost.

A company contemplating a change in the carrying cost would be interested in the effect of the change on its total inventory. For those items that are ordered infrequently, more time would be required before the effect of a change in the carrying cost percentage would influence a particular order. In a later section of this chapter, we will consider inventory control systems for a total set of stock needs; at that time we will discuss a categorization scheme based upon annual dollar volume of each item which allows one to make assessments about aggregate inventories. For now, we will deal briefly with a related cycle stock issue, sensitivity.

Look again at Fig. 18.2. Although the minimum point on the total annual cost curve is reached at an order quantity of 193,500 units, it is worth observing that the curve is relatively flat near this minimum and that the indicated economic lot size could be "violated" somewhat with a small cost penalty. The size of the cost penalty is described by R. G. Brown; he shows that a 100% error in the economic lot size input data (R or S overstated, I understated) would only lead to a 41% increase in the economic lot size ($\sqrt{2} = 1.414$) and a 6% increase in total annual cost.[*]

The moral to the story seems clear: The economic lot size formulae yield "ball park" estimates based upon cost minimization with somewhat tenuous assumptions. Resultant order quantities can easily be rounded to convenient sizes, to fit storage devices, or to match convenient units of production such as a day. In addition, if other criteria call for a fairly substantial shift in the order quantity, the resultant increase in total annual cost may well not be large. However, one should be continually wary of the cost functions depicted in Fig. 18.6 and the danger of decision rule changes which when aggregated call for substantial shifts in operations.

---

[*]Robert G. Brown, *Decision Rules for Inventory Management,* Holt, Rinehart, and Winston, 1967, p. 16–17.

Extensions

The economic lot size formulae and associated decision rules developed above lead to the purchasing or creation of fixed amounts of cycle stock whenever existing stocks reach the reorder points. Many other models and associated decision rules also exist, such as fixed interval systems where orders of varying amounts are issued depending upon the inventory position at specified time intervals. Additional models include placing of constraints on whether orders will be initiated and the size of such orders depending upon inventory status at the fixed interval inspection point. There is a large literature on such models, which are beyond our present scope. The kind of extension that we will find most interesting is to go beyond the basic cycle stock inventory models with their static assumptions and take up the matter of uncertainty. With a basic understanding of uncertainty behind us, we can then turn to inventory control systems with the goal of designing a set of routine inventory control decision rules which cope with the problems of uncertainty as well as with the interactive nature of individual actions.

UNCERTAINTY STOCK MODELS

As noted above in several places, the basic cycle stock models have somewhat untenable assumptions in regard to the constancy of demand, replenishment rates, and lead times. In this section, we now wish to relax those assumptions so that the uncertain nature of the real world can be adequately treated in our models.

Safety Stock

In Figs. 18.3 and 18.4 cycles of nonvarying time lengths and constant usage rates were depicted. In both cases the usage rate was 5000 units per day and the lead time was five days, which meant that the order point was 25,000 units; if the usage rate over the lead time period was indeed 5000 units per day, the replenishment order would arrive without experiencing a stockout. However, both usage rates and lead times are variable. In Fig. 18.7, this variability is illustrated.

The first cycle in Fig. 18.7 is the same as that of Fig. 18.3: an economic order quantity of 193,500 units arrives on day 0 and is depleted at the rate of 5000 units per day for 33.7 days until the stock on hand reaches the 25,000 unit reorder point; thereupon, another economic order quantity is issued which arrives five days later when stocks are down to 0. The second cycle depicted in Fig. 18.7, however, exhibits an increased usage rate of 10,000 units per day. At day 55.55, a 25,000 unit reorder point is reached, whereupon an economic order quantity for 193,500 units is issued. Since the lead time is five days, an order does not arrive until 60.55. However, since stocks are being depleted at the rate of 10,000 units per day, a

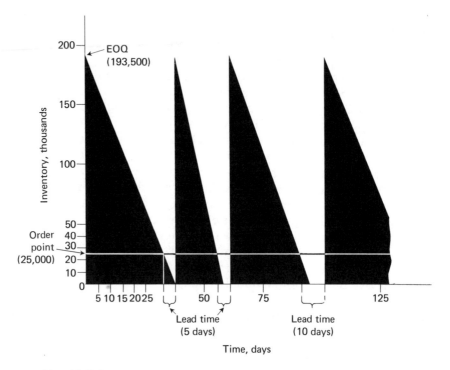

Fig. 18.7 Furniture knob example (varying usage and lead times).

stockout condition commences at day 58.05. In the third cycle depicted in Fig. 18.7, the demand or usage rate remains at 5000 units per day, but the lead time is increased from 5 to 10 days. Thus, although the reorder point is reached on day 91.75 and the usage rate remains at 5000 units per day, the expected delivery date of day 96.75 is missed by 5 days with a resultant stockout condition.

Depending upon how costly or undesirable stockouts are for a particular item in a particular company (a matter of criteria), extra inventories may be carried as a hedge against possible stockouts. Such inventory is typically called "safety stock" or "buffer stock." The amount of safety stock required is a function of two things—the desired safety level and the combined uncertainty in usage rate and lead time. By desired safety level we mean the degree of tolerance for stockout conditions or the long-run percentage of the time that a company wishes to hedge successfully against uncertainty. Clearly, this is a matter of criteria where some out-of-stock conditions are more tolerable than others. A sharply decreasing marginal return in safety from additional stocks makes very low probabilities of stockouts quite expensive. We will see that if a certain level of safety stock allowed us to hedge successfully against uncertainty

84.1% of the time, a doubling of the safety stock would increase our expectation to 97.7% and a tripling would increase it to 99.9%; the first 100% addition to safety stock yielded an incremental percentage increase of 13.6% while the second increment only provided 2.2%.

The extent of variability in the usage or demand rate as well as variability in the lead time determines the amount of safety stock that will be required for a specified level of service. The two factors can be combined and thought of as the variability in demand over a lead time period, but it is perhaps more straightforward to separate them since the usage or demand is normally computed from a forecasting subsystem which operates with a fixed forecasting interval. The forecasting subsystem also provides data on demand variability, typically expressed as MAD (Mean Absolute Deviation). As noted in Chapter 17, for a normal distribution the standard deviation may be approximated by $1.25 \times$ MAD. If we assume that forecast errors are normally distributed, we can compute safety stocks from the required multiples of MAD in Table 18.1.

Table 18.1

Desired % safety	Required multiple of MAD
50	0
55	.157
60	.316
65	.482
70	.655
75	.843
80	1.052
85	1.294
90	1.605
95	2.056
96	2.191
97	2.352
98	2.564
99	2.909
99.1	2.957
99.2	3.012
99.3	3.065
99.4	3.139
99.5	3.217
99.6	3.312
99.7	3.440
99.8	3.600
99.9	3.860

The multiples given in Table 18.1 will yield directly the desired safety stock if the lead time is equal to the forecast interval. This equality rarely holds in practice: the following adjustment takes account of differing lead times:

$$\text{Safety stock} = \text{MAD} \times \text{required multiple of MAD} \times \sqrt{\begin{array}{l}\text{Lead time expressed} \\ \text{as a multiple of} \\ \text{forecast interval}\end{array}}$$

If a weekly forecast for our furniture knob example had an associated MAD of 3000 units, the desired safety stock level were 95%, and the 5-day lead time were considered as one week, then the required safety stock would be 6168 units; if the lead time were 10 days (two weeks) required safety stock would be 8697 units (6168 × $\sqrt{2}$).

In both of these sample calculations, a static approach to lead time has been taken. That is, lead time is considered as a constant known time. If the lead time is considered as a random variable, then the required safety stocks will have to be determined in light of the interaction of both probability distributions.

Although the treatment of lead time as an abstract constant seems inappropriate, in Chapter 19 we will find ourselves equally unhappy with considering lead time as a random variable. The lead time for a particular item will indeed vary, but the variation is strongly influenced by conditions within a fabricating plant, and the reduction of lead time is often present in the criterion system for judging performance. In addition, the actual lead time for a given order is often purposely lengthened or shortened by expediting decisions based upon up to the minute need information. Thus, if parts for 20 different pieces of furniture were in process at Westfall and the demand situation for one indicated an expected stockout while the others were not expected to require the use of safety stock, it would not be unusual for the "hot" item to be pulled ahead with a resultant shortening of its lead time and lengthening of lead time for those items not presently required.

If we accept the 95% safety stock level and 10-day lead time for the knob example, our model for cycle stock and safety stock can be depicted as Fig. 18.8.

Figure 18.8 is an enlarged version of one cycle from Fig. 18.3 with the addition of safety stock. Instead of the reorder point being 25,000 units, a replenishment order is issued when the stock drops to 33,697 units, the safety stock of 8697 units plus 25,000 which is our expected usage over an expected lead time of 10 days. The solid line in Fig. 18.8 shows this expected usage rate; at the end of the solid line, a replenishment order is expected which would increase our stock on hand to 202,197 (193,500 + 8697). The dashed line continuing beyond the solid line at the expected replenishment date with the same slope or usage rate intersects the ab-

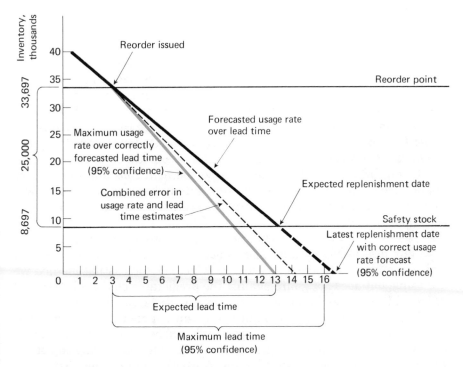

Fig. 18.8 Furniture knob inventory (with safety stock).

scissa at a point representing the maximum lead time we would expect with 95% confidence (assuming a correct usage rate forecast). The lighter line from the reorder point which intersects the abscissa at the expected replenishment date represents our estimate of the maximum usage rate which could occur over a correctly forecasted lead time with 95% confidence. The dashed line between these two lines represents one of the many maximum combinations of error in usage rate and lead time estimates (95% confidence).

Interaction with the Forecasting System

The usage rates depicted in Figs. 18.1, 18.3, 18.4, 18.7, and 18.8 are shown as being constant. Clearly, actual usage rates would vary around these expected or forecasted usage rates. In our calculation of safety stocks above, we in fact made the assumption that the variance around the expected or forecasted usage rate was normally distributed. We also assumed that the forecast was constant throughout an inventory buildup and depletion cycle; clearly both of these assumptions are somewhat inaccurate.

The extent to which the forecasted usage rate over a complete inventory cycle is a constant is obviously dependent upon the forecasting methodology. If a single exponential smoothing model is used, the value of α chosen for the smoothing constant quite clearly will influence the extent to which the forecasted usage rate remains stable over time. Since the major criterion for a forecasting system is minimum forecast error, we certainly cannot assume that only single exponential smoothing models with low smoothing constants are used. If the usage rate situation is one better forecasted with a trend, seasonal, or trend-seasonal model, then the variance from a constant usage rate assumption can be dramatic.

In Fig. 18.8, if the lead time is accepted as a constant 10 days, we might exceed our maximum usage rate simply because of trend or seasonal phenomena. One might initially think that we have allowed for such phenomena in our calculation of safety stock, but in reality we have not. This is so because the calculation of safety stock is based upon MAD from our forecasting system. The safety stock so calculated serves as a hedge against randomness or error in whatever forecasting method we are using, but does not guard against the predictable changes in demand reflected in the trend and seasonal components of our forecast.

If trend and/or seasonal conditions are anticipated, their effect on the expected usage over the lead time period should be included in our model. One way to account for these conditions would be to continually adjust the reorder point to reflect expected usage. Apropos of our earlier discussions on lead time variability, the predictable component of lead time variability might also be reflected in a more dynamic approach to the establishment of reorder points; e.g., lead times and associated reorder points might increase during peak capacity operations. However, in Chapter 19 we will see that one needs to be quite careful in making automatic changes to lead time estimates; the result can amplify the demands issued to peak capacity operations and vice versa.

One kind of variation or deviation from the constant usage rate assumption that can be very pronounced comes about from usage rates or inventory depletions occurring in batches for production planning purposes. For example, although use of the knobs might closely approximate the 5000 units per day, perhaps a two-month supply is used up in one day in the assembly of a particular batch of furniture; if so, the "demand" for knobs is not an even 5000 units per day but in fact is determined by the production schedule. We will refer to this kind of dependent demand situation as "Requirements Planning," and have more to say about such systems in Chapter 19. In our present context, it is important to note that the routine application of a statistical forecasting routine to the "demand" for such an item will result in a high error estimate (MAD), and a concomitant high safety stock. The models assume that the usage rate is a random variable when in fact a large component (or perhaps all) of the usage rate may be based upon internal circumstances which are highly predictable.

Safety Stock—Cycle Stock Interaction

A sage once said that "a banquet is a banquet—anyway you slice it." A paraphrase for our present purposes might be "inventory is inventory, no matter what you call it." One of the important reasons for carrying inventory is to protect against stockouts or unsatisfied demands. Although safety stocks are designed specifically for this purpose, cycle stock nonetheless also provides stockout protection. Furthermore, the amount of protection provided from cycle stock is a function of the economic lot size. This can be seen by again referring to Fig. 18.3. The only time that a stockout seems plausible is when the cycle stock is depleted. If the economic order quantity is increased, the length of the cycle also increases and the number of opportunities per year for a stockout to occur are diminished accordingly. Thus, if an entire year's supply were made in one batch, then a stockout condition would only seem plausible at one time during the year. On the other hand, if one month's supply were manufactured at a time, the vulnerability to stockout would occur 12 times per year.

The process of determining cycle stocks and safety stocks independently is a fairly common practice that does not lead to serious errors in most cases. The kind of situation where joint determination of safety stock requirements and the economic order quantity will lead to important savings is where the ratio of safety stock to cycle stock is significantly higher than that for other items. A high ratio of safety stock to cycle stock can come about for several reasons, including low fixed ordering or setup costs, especially high carrying costs, or a high desired percent safety level; a more fundamental cause of the high ratio, however, is often due to large forecast errors and/or long lead times. For example, we noted that a doubling of the lead time for our knob example caused an increase in required safety stocks of approximately 40%. For many purchased parts, quite long lead times are required and the safety stocks necessarily need to reflect these long lead times. The moral to this story seems clear: a reduction in lead time can permit significantly lower safety stock levels. Lead time reduction should rightly be included in the system of criteria used for evaluating purchasing agents and internal fabricating activities. In addition, the effect of a difference in lead time should not be overlooked in make-buy cost analyses.

INVENTORY CONTROL SYSTEMS

Up to this point, we have largely devoted our attention to the development of inventory control decision rules for individual items. For most inventory situations, there are far too many items for individual attention (perhaps thousands, tens of thousands, or even hundreds of thousands). What is needed is a set of routine policies or decision rules which can monitor individual demand forecasts and the status of stocks, and thereafter issue replenishment orders at "good" times for "good" quantities. Use of the term "good" again connotes a statement of relative desirability that is not "best" or "optimum"; the interaction of many criteria suggests an evolution in inventory decision rules as the environment reacts to the decision rules and as new criteria or opportunities are discovered.

The use of a computer for inventory control encourages the explication of decision rules. Once a set of consistent decision rules has been formulated, the set may be evaluated in some modeling environment (probably digital simulation) or by applying the decision rules to the real world inventory system. Although we would certainly argue that the use of a model is more appealing than experimenting with the real world, for many systems the major benefit is achieved through the formulation and routine application of a consistent set of decision rules.

A set of decision rules for routine inventory monitoring allows us to be concerned with more global criteria such as aggregate inventory balances and the resultant loads placed upon production activities. The routinization of an inventory control system allows for a more encompassing approach, one that continually adapts to permit better control over activities that are closely related to inventory control such as buying, product line choices, and warehousing methods.

For the firm desiring a computerized inventory control system, computer manufacturers offer inventory control application packages for use on their equipment. The best known of these is IBM's IMPACT, but Honeywell's PROFIT and RCA's WISDOM are essentially equivalent systems. Systems like IMPACT are primarily devoted to the inventory problem faced by a wholesaler, although retail IMPACT systems also exist.

The inventory problem faced by a wholesaler or retailer is much less complex than that faced by a manufacturer. This is so because wholesalers and retailers do not have to worry about the effect of their ordering policies on their suppliers; for a manufacturer, decisions to replenish finished goods inventories result in demands for men, materials, and capital equipment that must be kept within certain ranges. Westfall would find it unacceptable to operate the plant for 100 hours one week and close it down the next, so inventory decisions necessarily must be balanced with production planning and scheduling criteria. We will see what these additional criteria mean in Chapter 19. In the balance of this chapter, we will be concerned with the more straightforward problems associated with the development of a computerized inventory control system for wholesaling and distribution activities. When these activities are performed independently of manufacturing, the cycle stock and safety stock models developed above tend to be appropriate.

Distribution by Value

In virtually every inventory control problem for which a computerized system is being contemplated, one will find significant differences in the sales and/or profit contributions made by the various items held. It is not at all unusual for 20% of the items held to account for 60 to 80% of the total annual sales. This phenomenon was described by Dickie in 1951; he suggested dividing inventory items into 3 categories, A, B, and C, where A items are those relatively few whose high dollar volume warrants detailed control procedures, C items are those many relatively unimportant items for which crude rules of thumb will suffice, and B items are intermediate in terms of contribution as well as appropriate control effort.*

The decision to segregate stock into 3 categories is arbitrary; the more general procedure is to prepare an item listing in rank order of item annual sales with the associated cumulative percentage of the items and cumulative percentage of dollar sales. This listing is typically called a distribution by value and can thereafter be plotted in a manner similar to Fig. 18.9.

In Fig. 18.9, the top 20% of the best-selling items account for almost 70% of the annual sales, while the lowest selling 60% of the items constitute only about 15% of the total sales. For other companies in other industries, the extent of the "extremeness" of the distribution by value will vary. A linear function connecting the origin of Fig. 18.9 with 100% on both the abscissa and ordinate would be the least possible degree of imbalance or extremeness in a distribution by value; the most extreme case would be a right angle from the origin to 100% on the ordinate to 100% on the abscissa. R. G. Brown has shown how distribution by value data can be approximated with a lognormal distribution. If the data are plotted on logarithmic normal paper, the cumulative percentage of items will form one straight line and the cumulative percentage of total sales will form another; the lines are parallel and the slope (also called the standard ratio) is a measure of "extremeness." The standard ratio can be calculated directly by dividing item sales for that item which makes up either the 50th percentile in cumulative sales or cumulative units by the corresponding items sales for the 84.1th percentile.† The standard ratio

---

*H. Ford Dickie, "ABC Inventory Analysis Shoots for Dollars Not Pennies," *Factory Management and Maintenance,* July 1951.

†The 84.1% corresponds to one standard deviation in a normal distribution. For a further exposition of the lognormal model, see Brown, *op. cit.* pp. 23–27.

tends to be stable within industries and typically takes on values of 2 to 3 for retail firms, 4 to 7 for wholesale firms, about 10 for industrial firms, and about 25 for firms with a high degree of technological change. Once the standard ratio for a particular company is known, it is possible to make good estimates of the effects of policy changes on the aggregate inventory. Examples include inventory requirements for increased sales, changes in carrying cost, changes in the service level, and the effects of smaller order quantities.

With the advent of high-speed computers utilizing internal decision rules for inventory management, the variable control suggested by Dickie is no longer quite the same issue. With the elimination of manual inventory control, inventory decision rules requiring many calculations can be handled with costs not significantly different from rough rules of thumb. However, distribution by value analysis can still be a useful input to decision making. It can also lead to erroneous conclusions, and it is essential to understand how and under what conditions they might occur.

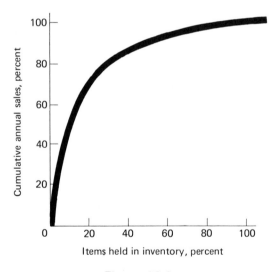

Figure 18.9

One use of the distribution by value report is as an aid in assessing the size of a product line. Thus one particular wholesale grocer forms a distribution by value analysis quarterly with the last 100 items on the list being dropped almost routinely. The modifier "almost" should not be overlooked, however. One of the continually weakest selling items for this wholesale grocery operation is black pepper. A terrible pun might be: "a store without black pepper is not worth its salt." In Chapter 5 and elsewhere we noted the need for a complete product line and the definite constraints one faces in indiscriminately culling out low-selling items.

Another kind of distribution by value formed by the wholesale grocer is on products within categories or groups, such as canned vegetables or dairy case items. Thus, although all oleomargarine item sales are relatively high in the distribution by value for the total store, there are significant differences among oleomargarine brands. Still additional distribution by value reports can be prepared by vendor so that buyer attention is expended in relation to value received, and so that within particular vendors those items which contribute most and least can be identified. Still one more distribution by value analysis is a comparison of item rank within each store to item rank for the wholesaler whose analysis comprises all stores. This wholesaler has managed to keep the number of items carried down to about 5200 while most grocery wholesalers carry 7000 to 8000; this has been achieved by carrying only one brand of baby food, one brand of spices, etc.

Implied in all of these analyses is some kind of action, usually of a marketing variety such as product line changes, promotional efforts, shelf space allocations, allocations of most desirable shelf space, positioning of major categories within a store, and relative stockout desirabilities. Such decisions must not, however, be made indiscriminately. The causal effects of promotions, spacings, etc., can lead to important shifts in sales. Also, perhaps some of the best-selling items such as Campbell's tomato soup should be stocked in relatively poor locations and not given special promotions; perhaps the demand for these items is relatively inelastic and a search for the items might stimulate impulse buying.

An even more fundamental concern has to do with the use of the term "value" in our analyses. We must be eternally wary of casually accepting a criterion of sales maximization as an appropriate surrogate for enterprise well-being. Perhaps the markup on Campbell's tomato soup is such that although it ranks number 1 in dollar sales, it is not nearly the number one annual contributor to profit and overhead. Perhaps a better analysis might be to proceed in the same way as outlined above, but to rank items in terms of their annual usage times gross margin (total annual contribution to profit and overhead).

Another kind of problem with distribution by value analyses can occur after an existing inventory is categorized on the basis of A, B, and C items (or some other classification scheme). If one were asked what inventory mix of A, B, and C items a company should have, a fairly common answer might be to only stock A items since those are the items whose sales we wish to support the most strongly. Conversely, if an analysis of an existing inventory were made and a higher number of C items were found, a not infrequent conclusion would be that the inventory was poorly constituted (this is precisely the situation at Westfall—see Fig. 2.4). However, these conclusions might be entirely erroneous. Slower moving items or items of low value may be ordered or produced in large quantities, such as an entire year's supply so that attention does not need to be devoted to them. On the other hand, fast moving items may be ordered or produced so frequently that very little cycle stock is held. An appropriate action for A items might well be to cut the lead time so that quick reactions and concomitant low safety stock and transit stock levels can be achieved; one way such lead times are achieved in manufacturing firms is to make slow moving items in lots large enough that productive capacity is not bottlenecked.

Still another dangerous application of the distribution by value concept is found in an analysis of component parts. The old saw about "for lack of a nail the war was lost" seems particularly appropriate in this regard; a low value part can cause just as much expense and delay in shipping the finished product as any other component.

Joint Ordering

For most computerized inventory control systems where goods are purchased, it is quite common for more than one item to be purchased from a single vendor. It is also quite common for quantity discounts to be offered by such vendors, and the combining of orders to minimize transportation costs represents the same phenomenon to the purchaser. As a result, wholesalers tend to buy from suppliers in full carload lots. Thus, the wholesale grocer places combined orders for merchandise such as Jello, Maxwell House coffee, and other General Food items. A combined purchase involves the cost tradeoffs already discussed as pertinent to the basic economic lot size problem as well as quantity discounts, safety stocks, combined weights, and bulk. Thus freight advantages might be associated with ordering breakfast cereal, facial tissue, marshmallows, or some other light weight bulk item from the same vendor who supplies high weight-low bulk items such as canned goods.

Conceptually, the joint ordering problem requires no new model. Total annual usage from a vendor can be computed in dollars and the total economic order quantity thereafter determined. As an ongoing system, however, the joint ordering problem necessarily has to cope with safety stock levels and the associated probabilities of stockout. Operationally, the usual procedure is to continually attempt to equalize the inventory position of all joint items in terms of desired safety levels. Thus, if sales of one product are higher than expected, we will tend to run out and require an order from the vendor sooner. The computerized systems sequentially examine all products supplied by a vendor to find the time when an order must be placed to satisfy safety stock requirements. Ideally, the order issued will be for quantities of all items provided by this vendor such that upon arrival we would expect to reach the reorder point level for each item simultaneously and thereby to maximize the time between orders. The desired safety level percentage for each item supplied by a particular vendor need not be equal. Thus, our wholesale grocer uses a service level of 99.5% for Campbell's tomato soup and 85% for Campbell's black bean soup. The size of the actual order issued will be tempered by quantity discount schedules, weight and bulk considerations, and sometimes by internal matters such as warehouse space or capital availabilities.

In many ways, the same sort of dynamic approach could be used for the production cycling problem considered in our discussions of cycle stocks. That is, perhaps each day a soap manufacturer should view existing stocks of each item and forecast the effect of continuing the manufacture of the same brand of soap for one more day (thereby decreasing changeover costs) in terms of anticipated stockout conditions in other brands.

Cost and Benefits

An inventory control system such as that utilized by the wholesale grocer can provide important benefits to a firm. Some of these have been presented above, but a more fundamental review is in order. First, because the system performs much tedious work that formerly was done by buyers and clerks, personnel savings are possible; the wholesale grocery operation employed only two buyers after the computer system became fully operational where five or six would be required under the old method of operation, and the amount of routine clerical work performed by the computer (e.g., printing checks and purchase orders) was substantial.

More importantly, with the computerized systems in operation, the activities performed by personnel such as buyers can be much more in line with the fundamental criteria of the firm. Time formerly devoted to drudgery is now spent on market analysis and improved buying policies. An example can be seen in grocery buying for special sales. A computer report based on stock positions during and after special promotions clearly indicated that a desire not to run out of a sale item was often carried to extremes.

Other advantages have been to reduce back-room inventories held at retail stores to almost zero; to reduce lead times by more frequent review; to reduce lead time variability by placing orders with delayed shipment dates; to increase inventory turnover to the extent that a 400% increase in volume over a six-year period required only a 60% increase in inventory and a 10% increase in the number of items carried; to take advantage of many more discounts in price, advertising, and payment terms; and to readily accommodate transient conditions such as warehouse additions (increasing the carrying cost when space was tight allowed the expansion to be postponed to a convenient time) and significant volume changes, such as addition of a chain of independent retailers. An interesting side benefit was highlighted by detailed reports on stock-picking performance in the warehouse; method changes and an incentive system caused the average number of cases picked per hour to be increased from 120 to 300.

On the cost side, the inventory control system used by the wholesale grocer presently accounts for about 10 to 15 hours of IBM 360/30 computer time per month. Since the hourly rental rate on this machine in the commercial market is in the neighborhood of $50, the monthly computer cost can be estimated at about $500 to $750.

The Other Side of the Coin

An intriguing aspect of computerized inventory control systems is the output from such systems insofar as they establish patterns of buying behavior or demand with which suppliers or manufacturers must cope. The impact of this phenomenon can be quite clearly seen in the field of wholesale grocering. The definite economics of scale associated with large grocery wholesaling have been well exhibited in the United States over the last 20 years. It is simply very costly for companies such as General Foods to fill independently small orders to all the Ma and Pa and even large grocery stores in the United States. It is much more economical to follow the pattern developed by the chain stores. That is, each food manufacturer can send large shipments to regional wholesalers who in turn can combine all the needs of a particular store into one shipment. The advent of computer programs like IMPACT, PROFIT, and WISDOM have made large wholesale grocering even more advantageous.

All of the computer programs for wholesale inventory management embody similar sets of decision rules for the timing and quantities of purchase orders. Since the decision rules are responsive to quantity discounts and freight allowances, the kind of ordering patterns experienced by a producer who distributes through such wholesalers will be quite dependent upon the particular discount structure adopted. The wholesale grocery operation discussed above found that manufacturers' discount structures almost invariably just managed to push them over to the purchase of the next larger lot. This causal ability possessed by the manufacturer should not be overlooked and the criteria set for establishing discount policies should not be limited to marketing goals. In some situations, pronounced "lumpiness" in sales patterns may be directly attributed to the discount structure. The lumpiness may or may not cause problems for the manufacturer in his own internal operation; in any event, the lumpiness will tend to make forecasting more difficult, to create larger forecasting errors, and accordingly to necessitate larger safety stock levels. In Chapter 21 we will consider the design of systems for materials flow; the ability of a firm to "cause" or create its own destiny will be a central theme in that chapter.

Requirements Planning

The causal aspects of inventory replenishment orders are particularly important in the design of requirements planning systems. The explosion of assembly schedules back into component part requirements results in a dependent pattern of component part "demand" that is not only lumpy, but largely predictable. The prediction accuracy, however, does not come about from using a statistical forecasting approach; it derives from deterministically planned assembly schedules. In our discussions of uncertainty stock models, we noted that increased predictability decreases the need for safety stock. This is but one reason for the wisdom of exercising as much control as possible over the factors which create demands on productive capacities. Chapter 19 is devoted to the exercise of this control and the additional criteria which come into play when one moves away from the rather detached view of inventory control and its related decision rules developed in this chapter.

SUMMARY REMARKS

In this chapter we have attempted to provide a basic understanding of inventory models and the costs which these models attempt to minimize. In some situations minimization of these costs represents a criterion or goal that is congruent with fundamental enterprise objectives. In other cases we have noted that strict adherence to this criterion will lead to suboptimal results, most notably when the demands issued by a set of inventory control decision rules must be satisfied by a producing facility within the same enterprise. Such a result should not be terribly surprising; in our earlier discussions of queuing models, we noted that all inventories could be considered as queues or waiting lines, and that such queues can be used to permit individualized increased performance levels for the servicing activities separated or decoupled by the inventories. Thus criteria applied to some "reasonable" approach to the makeup of inventory levels on any basis that does not consider the effect of those inventory levels and decision rules on preceding and succeeding stages in the production-distribution-consumption chain will be shortsighted. The fact that a complete view of this chain often crosses the boundaries of enterprises is widely used as a reason for individual attention being devoted to areas only within their scheme of influence; a more global view often turns up potential advantages of combined production and distribution systems which more than outweigh their costs. In Chapter 19 we will consider the addition of production oriented criteria to an inventory control system. Chapter 20 will expand that treatment into the necessity for coordinating individual item needs with overall needs and capacities, and Chapter 21 will treat more integrated systems of production and distribution.

REFERENCES

Brown, Robert G., *Decision Rules for Inventory Management,* Holt, Rinehart, and Winston, 1967.

Naddor, Eliezer, *Inventory Systems,* Wiley, 1966.

Niland, Powell, *Production Planning, Scheduling, and Inventory Control,* Macmillan, 1970.

Prichard, James W., and R. H. Eagle, *Modern Inventory Management,* Wiley, 1965.

Starr, Martin K., and D.W. Miller, *Inventory Control: Theory and Practice,* Prentice-Hall, 1962.

Wagner, H. N., *Statistical Management of Inventory Systems,* Wiley, 1962.

CHAPTER REVIEW

To some extent, I am setting you up in Chapter 18. You may be a bit chagrined in Chapter 19 to see how much of the logic we developed in Chapter 18 has to be discarded when our materials-flow orientation encompasses manufacturing criteria. Don't get uptight about it; the basic cost tradeoffs reflected in the EOQ are still applicable, but we need to reconsider application of these ideas in terms of an evolving larger criteria set. Now that you have a clear understanding of the basic inventory concepts, we can build upon that base in important ways.

There are many real world systems for which the sets of decision rules described in Chapter 18 are appropriate. When manufacturing is not part of the system being controlled, the basic concepts of this chapter and the forecasting chapter can be combined to yield routine ordering decisions that will be consistently better than those made on an *ad hoc* basis. In Chapter 19 we will try to deliver an expanded set of routine decision rules for more complex problems.

OUTLINE OF THE CHAPTER

Introduction	(basic building blocks)
Inventory categorization	(four categories or functions)
Cycle stock	(economic order quantities)
Uncertainty stock	(hedge for supply and demand variability)

Anticipation stock	(seasonal buildups)
Transit stock	(material in movement)
Cycle stock models	(tradeoff of setup and holding costs)
Trial and error solution	(minimize total cost)
Economic order quantity (Instantaneous Receipt)	$(Q = \sqrt{2RS \div I})$
Lead time	(required replenishment time)
Economic order quantity (Noninstantaneous receipt)	$(Q = \sqrt{2RS \div [I(1-r/p)]})$
Quantity discounts	(incremental cost analysis)
Production cycling	(several products on one machine)
Underlying assumptions and data requirements	(relevant cost issues)
Responsiveness and sensitivity	(total cost curve quite flat near minimum)
Extensions	(other approaches)
Uncertainty stock models	(relaxation of assumptions)
Safety stock	(usage variability over lead time)
Interaction with the forecasting system	(trend or seasonal influences)
Safety stock—cycle stock interaction	(cross functional benefits)
Inventory control systems	(set of decision rules)
Distribution by value	(relative importance)
Joint ordering	(multiple items from single vendor)
Costs and benefits	(managerial time for creative work)
The other side of the coin	(changing the rules)
Requirements planning	(demand dependent upon internal actions)
Summary remarks	(a queuing context)
Appendix A	(derivation of economic lot size)

CENTRAL ISSUES

Any inventory is a queue or stoppage in the flow of material from basic raw material to final consumption. The primary function of an inventory is to decouple successive stages in that total flow of material. Four categories of inventory are described. Cycle stocks occur when the economics of production call for batches larger than current usage rates. Uncertainty or safety stocks are held as a cushion against unpredictable variations in the flows into and out of an inventory which might otherwise cause an out of stock condition. Anticipation stocks are built for seasonal buildups to allow production and consumption to be less rigidly coordinated. Transit stocks exist whenever goods are being moved between successive stages in the total flow of material.

The basic cycle stock models are based upon a tradeoff of fixed costs which can be amortized over the number of units in a batch, and holding costs which increase when the batch size is increased because each unit is held longer. Models are discussed for situations where all of the goods come into inventory at the same time, where the goods come into inventory over time, and for situations where several products are made on the same price of equipment.

Safety stocks are presented as a way of insuring customer service. Determination of proper safety stock levels requires knowledge of demand variability and managerial assessments of appropriate customer service levels.

Models for cycle stock and safety stock can be combined into a formal set of decision rules for routine purchasing decisions. The result is a better, less costly set of ordering decisions, and an ability for managerial personnel to consider more fundamental features of the system. In short, the orientation shifts to the structure of the system rather than the outputs from the system.

ASSIGNMENTS

1. Given the following data:
   order cost = $18 per order
   unit holding cost = $6 per year
   demand = 1350 units per year

   a) Calculate the optimal order quantity, the average number of orders per year, and the total annual inventory cost.
   b) Suppose the firm in question decides arbitrarily to order 5 times per year. What is the total annual inventory cost?
   c) Plot annual inventory cost as a function of the number of orders, N, placed per year for $N = 1$ to 26. If the firm was willing to incur costs as much as 10% above the minimum cost policy, how much flexibility would they have in picking the number of orders placed per year?
   d) Assume that the firm in question incorrectly estimates the order cost to be $25 per order. What order quantity will the firm use? What actual annual inventory costs will be incurred?

2. James Lewis, staff manager for Prominent Eastern Consulting Group, is considering a knotty problem. Jim's group has recently finished a small job for Piddly Midwestern, a small, struggling firm which is a jobber for Washers. Washers are a steady and profitable item for Piddly Midwestern. Sales have

been about 10,000 units per year. Piddly Midwestern buys these units for $100 each and sells them for $250. Piddly has been using an EOQ formula computed for them at great cost by United States Gilfish, since defunct. The Gilfish formula assumes the transaction cost for ordering is $50 and that holding cost is 16% of their purchase cost. Prominent has done a cost analysis and found these figures to be inaccurate. Transaction cost is $30 and holding cost is 20% of purchase cost.

Prominent would like to charge Piddly no more than Piddly's first year increase in profits when Piddly installs the new system.

How much should Prominent charge Piddly?

3. Carl LaFong is deliberating over the purchase policy to use for some particular product. He knows:

order cost = $5
demand = 1000 units per year
annual holding cost = 50 percent

The difficulty is that the supplier for this product offers a choice of three purchase plans:

Plan 1: Cost of Q units = $.32Q$
Plan 2: Cost of Q units = $.32Q$ if $Q < 500$ units
$.16Q$ if $Q \geq 500$ units

To participate in Plan 2 the buyer must pay a flat fee of $100 per year to the supplier.

Plan 3: Cost of Q units = $.32Q$ if $Q < 500$ units
$.16Q$ if $500 \leq Q < 4000$ units
$.08Q$ if $Q \geq 4000$ units

To participate in Plan 3 the buyer must pay a flat fee of $200 per year to the supplier.

What plan should LaFong select and what Q should he use? (Hint: Determine the best Q for each plan, then pick the best plan by comparing total annual costs plus additional fees.)

4. A machine can be used to produce 3 different products with the following data:

	Product 1	Product 2	Product 3
Demand/year	10,000	20,000	5,000
Production rate/year	50,000	50,000	50,000
Holding cost/unit/year	$1.00	$2.00	$4.00

a) Assume that the machine is used for Product 1 only and that it takes a setup man 4 hours to set up each production run every time a run is begun. Assume the setup man earns $10 an hour. What is the production lot size? What is the total annual setup and inventory cost for Product 1?

b) Repeat (a) for Product 2 only. Assume setup man takes 3 hours to set up machine for Product 2.

c) Repeat (a) for Product 3 only. Assume setup man takes 1 hour to set up machine for Product 3.

d) Apply the EOQ's determined in (a), (b), and (c) to the allocation of machine time among the three products. Assume a 50-week year. Simulate hand several cycles using these rules: place an order when inventory reaches zero, order the economic quantity, order the product with the biggest backlog first. Your starting inventories are:

Product 1 = 100
Product 2 = 800
Product 3 = 160

What is the result with respect to backorders? Why?

e) Assume that the production rates of 50,000 units were based on an operating year of 2000 hours. Use the production cycling model to determine the length of the three-product cycle and the quantity of each product to be produced per cycle.

5. a) Assume demand for an item during its lead time is normally distributed with mean 1000 and standard deviation of 20. What reorder point should be used in order to average no more than one stockout every 20 reorder cycles? If safety stock is 30, how often will a stockout occur during a reorder cycle?

b) The forecast interval for an item is three months. Lead time is six months. MAD = 290. Management would like to know the annual costs of service levels (percent safety) of 70, 80, 90, 95, and 99%. Prepare a table for their use. Assume holding cost is $10 per unit per year.

6. Great Eastern is now offering quantity discounts of 4% on orders over 1000 units and 8% on orders over 5000 units. You currently order 800 units five times a year to meet annual demand of 4000. Your purchase cost is now $2.00 and sales price is $3.95 per unit. Orders are placed and filled at an incremental cost of $32 per order. Inventory cost is figured at 20% of purchase cost to hold one unit one year. Under the new discount policy what is the best strategy for you to follow?

7. The Stick M Up Clothespin Company has a machine that is capable of assembling 40,000 clothespins per day. Setup cost for this machine is $50.00, a case of 1000 pins is valued at $8.00, and the cost of capital is 15%. Demand for the clothespins is estimated to be 8000 per day or 2000 cases per 250 day year. Each clothespin is made from 2 wooden "splints" and 1 metal spring. The company produces its own splints on a different machine with a production rate of 160,000 per day or 80 cases of finished pins per day; setup cost for this machine is $60.00, and splints are valued at $4.00 per case of pins. Springs are purchased from an independent supplier in cases of 1000. Lead time is five days, MAD is one day, order cost is $5.00, and cost of springs is $3.00 per case.

a) What is the assembly quantity?
b) What is the lot size for splints?
c) What is the lot size for springs?
d) What is the 95% safety stock required to guard against variability in spring lead time?

8. A knuten valve manufacturer has provided you with the following data and wants you to provide him with a set of inventory control decision rules:

Cost per unit	$3.00
Annual storage cost (per unit)	$0.15
Monthly demand	400

Setup cost	$75.00
Paperwork cost to place an order	$5.00
Cost to write a purchase order	$10.00
Monthly capacity	600
Capital cost	30%
Average lead time	1-1/2 months
MAD of usage over the lead time period	75
Normal return on investment	20%
Interest rate (Next to Last National Bank)	12%
Desired in-stock percentage	95%

Dispatching decision rule: First come-first serve.

9.

Uniproduct (A)

The Situation: Uniproduct, Inc. makes a single standardized product which is in continuous, though fluctuating, demand. The product is manufactured and stocked in the factory warehouse. Demand for the product is received from wholesalers, who stock the product themselves, and from regional sales representatives, who do not stock the product. The demand for the product in a given time period is filled from the finished goods inventory available at the beginning of that period and from production during the period. There are costs associated with stocking the inventory. There are also costs associated with unfulfilled sales orders due to a shortage of inventory. These costs are shown in the cost summary.

Production capacity

The maximum one-shift capacity is 2000 units per period while overtime can increase this amount to a maximum of 3000 units per period. The minimum production rate is 500 units below which the factory is shutdown. The process is most efficient when producing 1000-2000 units per period. Above and below this range, production inefficiencies cause an increase in the variable unit cost.

Production planning

The production schedule for each period is determined at the end of the preceding period. Because the production process is segmented, any changes in the production schedule must be made in 100 unit increments. There are costs associated with making a production change from the previous period's rate and these costs are a function of the magnitude of the change.

Raw materials

Each unit of finished product is fabricated from one unit of raw material. Uniproduct, Inc. has the following contract with its raw materials vendor. At the start of every odd-numbered period, a raw materials order can be placed for delivery two periods later, at the beginning of the next odd-numbered period. A special order can be placed at any time for delivery in the same period; however, under the terms of the contract, Uniproduct, Inc. will pay the vendor a fixed penalty charge for each unit of raw material specially ordered. As with finished goods inventory, there are inventory costs associated with the stocking of raw materials.

The Problem: You will become the production planner of Uniproduct, Inc. In this position, you will be required to make three decisions each period:

a) The rate of production
b) The size of the regular order of raw materials (odd-numbered periods only)
c) The size of the special order of raw materials, if required

Three exhibits follow which will aid you in your decision-making:
    1) a summary of costs;
    2) a production and inventory planning sheet; and
    3) a production and inventory cost sheet.
The planning sheet shows the decisions your predecessor made for periods 1 through 5. In the beginning, let us assume you have perfect foresight and know the future demand for periods 6 through 10.

a) Enter the decisions that you would make in terms of raw materials orders and production rates, as indicated above
b) Calculate your new inventory levels and the number of back orders, if any
c) Compute the costs incurred as a result of your decisions and enter them on the cost sheet
d) When period 10 has been reached, calculate the subtotal of your costs
e) On which factors (raw material inventories, production rates, etc.) do you believe you should focus your attention and why?

Do not attempt to minimize costs by playing an end strategy, such as no inventory at the end of period 10.

Summary of costs

Inventory holding:
    a) Raw materials $2/unit
    b) Finished goods $4/unit

Production changes:
    a) 100-500 units change $750
    b) 600-1000 units change $1500
    c) 1100-1500 units change $2500
    d) Over 1500 units change   Impossible

Increased variable unit cost:
    a) 500-900 units produced $.005 × (1000 − production rate)/unit

    b) 2001-3000 units produced $.0007 × (production rate − 2000)/unit

Shutdown $1000

Special raw materials order $3.50/unit

Back orders $9/unit

Production and inventory planning sheet

Period	Raw materials						Finished goods			
	Regular orders	Beginning inventory*	Receipts	Special orders*	Available	Production	Beginning inventory*	Available	Sales orders	Back orders*
1	1200	700	3000		3700	600*	700	1300	900	
2	—	3100			3100	0*	400	400	1200	800
3	0	3100	1200		4300	800	0	0	1300	1300
4	—	3500			3500	2100*	0	800	1300	500
5	3300	1400	1200	1200	2600	2600*	0	2100	1100	
6	—	0					1000		1300	
7									1300	
8	—								1400	
9									1700	
10	—								1200	
11										
12	—									
13										
14	—									
15										

*Used in cost calculations

Production and inventory cost sheet

Period	Raw materials holding cost	Raw materials special orders	Finished goods holding cost	Production change	Production level	Shutdown	Back orders	Total Avoidable costs
1	1400*		2800†		1200**			5400
2	6200		1600	1500§		1000‡	7200 ‖	17500
3	6200		0	1500	800		11700	20200
4	7000		0	2500	147		4500	14147
5	2800	4200 #	0	750	1092			8842
							Subtotal	66089
6								
7								
8								
9								
10								
							Subtotal	
11								
12								
13								
14								
15								
							Subtotal	

*Beginning raw material inventory x raw material holding cost = 700 x $2 = $1400

†Beginning finished goods inventory x finished goods holding cost = 700 x $4 = $2800

‡Shutdown = $1000

§Production change = 600 − 0 = 600 units/period which is in 600−1000 range at $1500 per change.

‖ Back order quantity x back order charge = 800 x $9 = $7200

#Special raw material order quantity x penalty charge = 1200 x $3.50 = $4200

**Variable cost x production = .005(1000−600)x600 = $1200

10.   **Uniproduct (B): Decision rule formulation**

With the information and experience gained in Uniproduct (A), you are now asked to develop an explicit set of decision rules or policies for operating the Uniproduct production system. That is, after reflecting on how you would make decisions for regular orders, special orders and production, see if you can explicitly state how these decisions would be made.

Explicit rules will thereafter be programmed in BASIC and their efficiency will be tested by the Uniproduct simulator.

It is strongly advised that you jot down the rationale for your initial rules because after the rules have evolved, it will be quite educational to compare changes in the criteria that directed the rule formulation.

Your FORTRAN or BASIC decision rules should be stored as a program named UNIPRO.

Testing of the rules' efficiency is accomplished by merging your program with the Uniproduct simulator.

Decisions to be made

$\emptyset$ = Regular orders placed in odd numbered periods (when $C = 1$) for delivery two periods hence

P = Your scheduled production for this period

S = Special orders for use this period

Information available to help your decision-making

A = Regular ordered materials to arrive this period

B = Back orders to be shipped (if possible) this period

C = Regular order clock ($A = 0$ when $C = 2$)*

D = Demand last period (also subscripted as $D(M{-}1)$)

F = Finished goods inventory at start of period

M = The period in which you are making your decisions now

PO = Actual production last period

R = Raw materials inventory at start of period

Other programming instructions

Your instructor will give you detailed instructions based upon the particular computer system used at your school.

Output description

Column heading

M = Current period

R = Raw materials inventory at start of period in hundreds

A = Regular orders which arrived this period in hundreds

S = Special orders which arrived this period in hundreds

F = Finished goods inventory at start of period in hundreds

(P) = Actual production this period in hundreds

---

*Regular orders placed when $C = 2$ (even numbered periods) are ignored. In odd numbered periods ($C = 1$) regular orders placed two periods previously are in beginning inventory ready for use in that period. Other rule violations will also be monitored by the system, e.g., changes greater than 1500, production over 3000, production between 0 and 500, and negative special ordering.

$D(M)$ = Demand this period in hundreds
B = Back orders this period in hundreds
$COST$ = Total cost this period in dollars

Initialization information

$A = 3000$
$D = 1300$
$F = 700$
$PO = 1300$
$R = 700$

APPENDIX A TO CHAPTER 18

DERIVATION OF THE ECONOMIC LOT SIZE

Recall from Fig. 18.2 that our objective is to find the minimum point on the total annual cost curve. Also recall that that point will yield an order quantity Q, an average inventory of $Q/2$, a resultant annual inventory carrying cost of $QI/2$, an annual number of setups of R/Q, and an annual setup cost of RS/Q. As a result the total annual cost (TC) will be equal to the following:

$$TC = \frac{QI}{2} + \frac{RS}{Q}.$$

Since this function will be minimized at the point where its derivative is zero, we can take the derivative of the total annual costs with respect to quantity as follows:

$$\frac{dTC}{dQ} = \frac{I}{2} - \frac{RS}{Q} = 0.$$

Solving for Q yields: $\quad Q = \frac{2RS}{I}, \quad Q = \sqrt{\frac{2RS}{I}}.$

In making the adjustment for noninstantaneous receipts, recall that the peak inventory achieved in Fig. 18.4 is not Q. Since Q units are produced in a cycle at the rate of p units per time period and $p-r$ units are added to inventory during each time period, the peak of the inventory cycle stock will be: $\quad \frac{Q}{p} \times (p-r)$,

and the average inventory will be: $\quad \dfrac{\frac{Q}{p} \times (p-r)}{2} = \dfrac{Q(1-r/p)}{2}.$

substituting into our basic formula given above we obtain:

$$TC = \frac{Q(1-r/p)I}{2} + \frac{RS}{Q}.$$

differentiating TC with respect to Q yields:

$$\frac{dTC}{dQ} = \frac{I(1-r/p)}{2} - \frac{RS}{Q} = 0, \quad Q = \frac{2RS}{I(1-r/p)}, \quad Q = \sqrt{\frac{2RS}{I(1-r/p)}}.$$

PRODUCTION PLANNING AND INVENTORY CONTROL SYSTEMS

Chapter 17 provided a detailed understanding of forecasting methodologies, and Chapter 18 some basic inventory concepts and inventory control systems which could be built upon these basic concepts. With this material behind us, we can now proceed to manufacturing criteria, models for production planning and inventory control, and the implementation of an integrated system in an ongoing company.

THE PROBLEM—AN OVERVIEW

At the end of the last chapter, we noted that inventory decision rules by themselves can often trigger orders at "inopportune times." A detached set of inventory control decision rules simply cannot yield production orders that are always within the capabilities of men and machines to produce, unless substantial amounts of overcapacity are built into the system. Let us examine where we stand in our evolutionary understanding of production planning and inventory control systems; thereafter we can include additional criteria and see how additional system modules will work toward satisfying these criteria.

Recapitulation

Figure 19.1 depicts an inventory control system based upon the concepts explained in Chapters 17 and 18. The top half of the figure shows the input data and modeling procedures for preparing an adjusted item forecast.

The models and files contained in the lower half of Fig. 19.1 recap the order point-order quantity philosophy of Chapter 18. The output from this inventory control system is a set of orders which would be issued to vendors.

In a wholesaling operation, the character of the order file over time is of no direct concern to the organization. A firm that manufactures its needs, however, will be concerned with the character of the order file. Lumpy demand situations can no longer be casually passed on to an

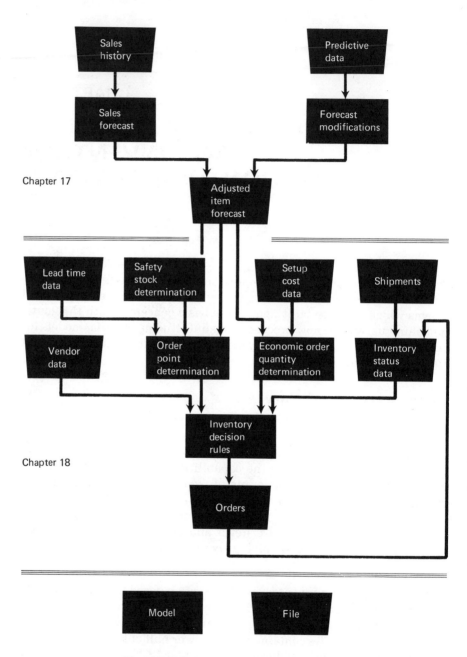

Fig. 19.1 Basic inventory control system.

independent supplier. Moreover, the manufacturer necessarily breaks down or "explodes" an order for an end item into its component parts; we will see that treatment of demand for component parts with the statistical methodologies underlying the order quantity–order point approach is particularly inappropriate.

Additional Criteria

Figure 19.2 depicts the interactions between the production planning and inventory control system and the functions of manufacturing, personnel, finance, marketing, purchasing, and engineering. For each of these functions a set of surrogate criteria concerned with production planning and inventory control is listed; critical inputs from each function are also listed.

Relatively speaking, the functions depicted in the bottom half of Fig. 19.2 (purchasing, marketing, and finance) are not greatly different in criteria and inputs from the roles played by these functions in the less complex inventory control system depicted in Chapter 18. Although the purchasing function may now be more intimately concerned with component parts, a good part of the inherent activity and evaluative criteria remain essentially the same. Similarly, the marketing function retains essentially the same orientation, with perhaps a somewhat more active role in setting priorities for the company-owned manufacturing facilities. The financial role is extended to include investments in the plant, equipment, and inventories necessary to create products, and the capital budgeting necessary to make changes in plant and equipment.

The top half of Fig. 19.2, however, was largely absent in the inventory control systems developed in Chapter 18. The engineering, manufacturing, and personnel functions each have important surrogate criteria and inputs which will influence the design and operation of the production planning and inventory control system.

The engineering function as depicted in Fig. 19.2 includes both activities related to the design of the product and those related to job and method design. The design of the product itself clearly has a strong influence on the way in which the product must be manufactured, kinds of equipment required, skills needed by the work force, capabilities required in vendors, and the extent to which particular pieces of equipment and worker skills are utilized. Thus for example, if Baumritter decided to add wrought iron patio furniture to the Ethan Allan product line, it would be necessary for the engineering function to understand the design requirements and limitations of wrought iron, the kinds of equipment required to make such furniture, the extent to which existing workers might be able to work with this material, and the expected utilization of additional equipment and personnel if the decision was made to manufacture rather than to purchase these items.

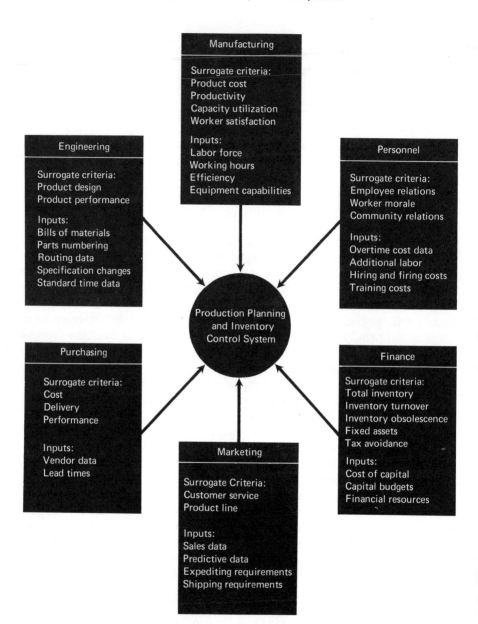

Fig. 19.2 Production planning criteria and inputs.

Critical inputs from the engineering function include specifications for parts and purchased components, the sequence of manufacturing or conversion operations necessary to create each component part and assembly, the times required for each of these conversion operations, a part numbering scheme which facilitates the knowledge of parts required for each item as well as the items each part is used on, and a system for implementing and standardizing specification changes. An important interaction between engineering and purchasing involves continual communication of vendor capabilities, changes in those capabilities, and the resultant influences on product design, manufacturing methods, make-buy decisions, and lead times.

The manufacturing function is concerned with creating component parts, and assembling components as well as purchased parts into salable items. The cost of manufacturing salable items is strongly influenced by labor productivity, utilization of equipment, and the length of time funds must be invested in inventories. Clearly all of these surrogate criteria are related to the flow of material and the way in which that flow is planned and controlled. Material flow is influenced by the size of the labor force, number of working hours, efficiency of the labor force, capabilities of the equipment, and past flow-oriented decisions (we will see how the time to manufacture an item is influenced by the level of work-in-process inventory).

The personnel function is concerned with maintenance of the required labor force. Changes in the size of the labor force, working hours, and employee morale are all influenced by the pattern of material flow-over time.

Although interactions between purchasing, engineering and manufacturing criteria exist, for production planning and inventory control systems the most profound interactions of surrogate criteria are between manufacturing, marketing, and finance (and to a lesser extent personnel). Marketing desires for customer service tend to support larger inventories and shorter manufacturing lead times; an interest in a more extensive product line supports greater diversity of worker skills and larger equipment capabilities. The desires of the manufacturing function to achieve good worker productivity support larger lot sizes and concomitant cycle stocks; a desire to utilize labor and equipment capacity to the fullest supports the building and depleting of seasonal inventories and the existence of high work-in-process inventory levels. A financial interest in maximizing the return on invested capital is manifested in pressures for small inventory levels, constraints on purchases of new equipment, and periodic inventory depletions and additions for tax purposes.

All of the above interactions and surrogate criteria influence the design of a production planning and inventory control system. The system depicted in Fig. 19.1 needs to be expanded to include additional system modules that perform a better job in terms of our expanded criteria set.

Additional System Modules

In Fig. 19.1, the final output is depicted as a file of orders for purchased items. In a gross sense, we may now regard that file as a desire for finished goods that can be fed to additional models which will temper the character of that file to meet the additional criteria enumerated above. To accomplish this tempering, we will want to include the following five major system modules:

1. Long-range capacity planning
2. Major assembly scheduling
3. Major work-center scheduling
4. Shop floor control
5. Purchasing

Long-range capacity planning is the process of determining what productive capabilities the manufacturing function shall have. Although the capability may be expressed in fairly gross terms such as annual output dollars, a more appropriate level of aggregation is to think in terms of major product groups and major productive activities or work centers. Thus for Baumritter an appropriate level of aggregation is to think in terms of assembly lines and major machine groupings (e.g., Westfall's chair or large case line and Westfall's rip saw or molder capability).

Long-range capacity determination represents the major interface between the interfunctional criteria enumerated above. The activity is vital to the business because commitments are made which can lead to proper or improper fixed asset purchases, staffing decisions, financial requirements, and marketing capabilities.

There have been several important models suggested in the literature for doing a better job of long-range capacity planning. Chapter 20 will consider some of these models in an attempt to put their use into proper perspective. It may seem conceptually appealing to examine long-range capacity planning models before considering major assembly scheduling, major work-center scheduling, shop floor control, and purchasing models, since this activity logically precedes the others; we will take the opposite approach in this chapter. That is, in the balance of this chapter we will take long-range capacities as given. It is my belief that a thorough understanding of the rest of the system permits a much improved perspective of long-range capacity planning considerations.

As we examine the remaining four major system modules in this chapter, we will see a shift in manufacturing orientation from a "push" strategy to a "pull" strategy. That is, the manufacturing function within many firms tends to be based upon a logical progression from product creation through engineering design, component part manufacture, assembly, into finished goods, and on to the marketing function; an alternative orientation is to begin with the customer need and then progress backward.

Almost all companies in the furniture industry make a commitment to the final end item at the cutoff saw and proceed to push the committed material through a long lead time which may or may not end in a match between item availability and customer need. A pull strategy focuses on customer needs, assembly schedules to meet those needs, component parts to meet assembly schedules, and purchasing and manufacturing activities necessary to provide those component parts. The pull strategy recognizes the need for faster reaction times, benefits to be obtained from standardized parts, and a principle of not committing component parts or work in process to specific end items any earlier than absolutely necessary. For Baumritter, a pull orientation brings the production function into much better congruence with the marketing function and overall enterprise objectives; the result is a more viable total economic unit.

Other companies can achieve similar benefits. Reductions in throughput time, work-in-process inventories, finished goods inventories, and back orders are common; a somewhat more surprising benefit from a well-organized production planning and inventory-control system seems to be frequently manifested in a 10 to 20% increase in worker productivity: the amount of lost time from poorly coordinated operations and expedited jobs is rarely appreciated.

MAJOR ASSEMBLY SCHEDULING

Major assembly scheduling is the process of deciding which finished goods end items shall be completed in each time period over a planning horizon of several months. The process begins with a specified set of capacities per time period in aggregate terms such as direct labor hours. This set of aggregate capacities comes from the long-range capacity planning model, which specifies the gross level of output from each major assembly operation; major assembly scheduling allocates this capacity to particular products. This allocation represents a primary commitment; all the other system modules act to support this commitment, and the demands made on those modules are known with certainty. Let us now turn to an example of this process. Thereafter we should be able to understand more clearly the basic change in philosophy from push to pull and the ways in which other production-planning and inventory control system modules interact.

PRODUCTION SCHEDULE

WEEK #	1	2	3	4	5	6	7	8	9	10	11	12
10-6003	30	0	30	0	30	0	30	0	0	30	0	30
10-6004	0	0	30	30	30	0	30	0	30	0	30	0
10-6013	0	0	0	35	35	0	35	0	0	35	0	35
10-6023	0	40	0	0	0	0	0	0	0	0	0	0
10-6034	0	0	80	0	40	40	0	40	0	40	0	40
10-6063	0	0	0	0	0	50	0	0	0	50	0	0
10-6073	80	40	40	0	40	0	40	40	0	40	0	40
10-6084	30	30	60	30	0	30	30	30	30	30	30	0
10-6093	0	0	0	45	0	45	0	45	45	0	45	0
10-6114	30	30	0	30	0	30	0	30	30	0	30	0
10-6123P	0	0	0	0	0	0	40	0	0	0	40	0
10-6133	0	0	0	0	0	0	0	30	0	0	30	0
15-6003	0	0	0	30	30	0	30	0	30	30	0	30
15-6004	60	60	0	30	30	30	0	30	30	0	30	30
15-6024	0	30	0	0	0	30	0	0	30	0	0	30
10-6004P	0	0	50	0	0	50	0	0	0	0	0	50
10-6013P	0	0	0	0	0	0	40	0	40	0	40	0
10-6014P	30	160	0	0	0	0	0	0	0	80	0	0
10-6023P	0	0	100	100	0	100	0	50	50	100	0	0
10-6024P	160	160	0	160	0	0	160	0	160	0	320	0
10-6034P	0	0	240	120	0	0	120	120	120	0	120	0
10-6044P	240	240	0	120	0	120	0	120	60	60	0	120
10-6053P	0	0	0	0	0	0	90	0	0	0	0	0
10-6063P	0	0	0	0	0	0	90	0	0	0	0	0
10-6073P	0	0	0	40	40	0	0	0	0	0	80	0
10-6074P	0	0	30	30	30	30	30	30	30	30	30	30
10-6083P	0	0	100	0	100	0	0	100	0	100	0	100
10-6093P	120	0	0	0	120	120	0	0	120	0	0	120
10-6103P	0	0	0	0	80	80	0	80	0	80	0	0
10-6104P	0	0	0	0	120	0	0	0	0	0	0	120
10-6133P	0	0	0	0	0	0	0	0	0	0	0	0
10-6008	0	0	0	50	0	50	0	0	0	0	0	50
10-6009	0	70	0	70	0	0	0	0	70	0	0	0
10-6018	0	0	120	60	0	0	60	60	60	60	60	60
10-6028	0	0	90	0	45	0	0	45	45	45	0	45
10-6039	200	0	0	0	100	0	100	0	100	0	0	0
10-6048	0	70	0	0	0	0	70	0	0	0	70	0
10-6058	0	0	0	0	25	0	25	0	0	0	25	0
10-6459	0	70	0	0	70	0	0	70	0	0	0	70
10-6068	0	50	0	0	50	0	0	0	0	0	50	0
10-6069	50	0	0	0	0	50	50	0	0	0	50	0
10-6125	0	0	0	0	0	0	0	0	0	0	0	0
15-6008	0	50	0	50	0	50	0	50	0	50	0	0
15-6018	25	0	25	25	0	25	0	25	25	25	0	25
15-6028	50	0	0	0	0	50	0	0	0	50	0	0

Figure 19.3

The Westfall Scheduling Process

Figure 19.3 is a portion of the Westfall major assembly schedule. Twelve weeks of scheduling data are provided for three major assembly lines, a table line, a plastic table line, and a hutch-top line.

Turning to the first item or pattern listed for the table line, we see that the schedule calls for completing 30 units in weeks 1, 3, 5, 7, 10, and 12. The second item, 10-6004, is not scheduled to be produced until the third week. Thirty units are produced in periods 3, 4, and 5; thereafter, 30 are produced every other period. The third item has an assembly lot size of 35, the fourth and fifth have an assembly lot size of 40, and the sixth has an assembly lot size of 50. Note that for the fifth item, 10-6034, two lots of 40 are assembled in week 3. A similar situation occurs for other items such as the next to last (15-6004), which has 60 units being assembled in weeks 1 and 2.

The way the model works is quite straightforward. For any given item, if we have an accurate sales forecast, knowledge of the present inventory position, and the assembly lot size, we can determine when we would ideally like to schedule completion of the next assembly lot for that item. For example, if a ladder-back chair is assembled in lots of 200 and the weekly demand rate is 25 and we now have 150 units in inventory, then six weeks from now the inventory will be depleted and we would like to have a batch of 200 units assembled which will last for the following eight weeks. Thereafter an assembly lot of 200 units would be completed every eighth week. A similar "idealized time series" of production output can be constructed for each item. When these individual idealized time series are summed by weekly period for each major assembly line, the result is an idealized major assembly schedule.

The term "idealized," however, is appropriate. The resultant schedule will undoubtedly call for flurries of activity in some weeks and little or no activity in others. It is necessary to assemble some lots before their idealized schedule date and to assemble others after their idealized schedule date. We will want to pull items ahead and push them back so that the weekly capacity of each major assembly line is utilized more fully.

The method used for pushing items back or pulling items forward from their assembly dates as determined by the idealized time series is to schedule each line so that all items assembled on that line will have an equal inventory or backorder position as measured in weekly sales units. That is, if one item sold at the rate of 100 units per week and another sold at the rate of 200 units per week there should be twice as much inventory or backlog for the second as for the first.

The schedule will have to take account of uncertainties. One kind of uncertainty is our demand estimate. Another is productive output; that is, although the schedule calls for 30 units of 10-6003, 80 units of 10-6073,

30 units of 10-6084, 30 units of 10-6114, and 60 units of 15-6004 to be assembled in week 1, the actual output will be somewhat different than the plan. The extent of this variation will influence inventory positions, activities in subsequent weeks, and timing for subsequent assembly batches.

For all Baumritter plants, the scheduling time unit chosen is one week. Initially a month had been proposed. The weekly level of aggregation permits a periodic accounting which is in line with the way Baumritter manufacturing people should control their organizations. Wages are paid weekly, and the incentive calculations for workers are figured accordingly. Before the weekly major assembly schedule was put into full operation, all Baumritter plants were evaluated on the basis of output measured in wholesale price dollars produced per month. This criterion led to flurries of activity near the end of each month with work-in-process being expedited through completion stages. The resultant "dry pipeline" which inaugurated each new month resulted in low dollar output during the first half of the next month, and the resultant need for expediting during the second half of the month to meet dollar output quotas. The weekly accounting has greatly diminished this kind of activity.

Use of the weekly production schedule quickly led to the realization that the criterion of output dollars was a poor surrogate for enterprise well-being. The fact that some items were inherently easier to assemble than others meant that more output dollars could be turned out per time period when these items were produced. The resultant orientation toward easy-to-assemble items had an interesting feedback loop; the short assembly time items would be produced instead of long assembly time items until the resultant backlog on long assembly time items led to pressure from the marketing function; as a result, long assembly time items would be produced but only for a portion of the accounting period—as the end of the period approached they could no longer "afford" to make long assembly time items.

The weekly major assembly scheduling model clearly pointed out the absurdity of the situation. Thereafter the evaluative measure of factory output became the degree to which the assembly schedule was met. An interesting feature of working with the weekly schedule under the criterion of equalizing inventory/backlog position was that after several months of operation, the output as measured in dollar terms became relatively stable. It seems that the former orientation toward dollar output had actually amplified the problem. That is, increases in weekly dollar output came at the expense of dollar output in subsequent weeks which in turn had to disrupt even more subsequent weeks.

The assembly schedule for each item is also monitored in terms of how well assembly dates as determined by the idealized time series are being met. That is, if the idealized time to assemble a batch of a particular item is in week 7, we would expect to see that item scheduled for week 7, 6, or 8, 5 or 9, etc. If items that should have been assembled in week 7 are the only items being assembled in week 15, we have an indication that capacity problems exist for this line and that remedial action may be necessary. On the other hand, if in week 5 items are being assembled that are not needed until week 18, the opposite sort of problem exists.

Additional data inputs required for the major assembly scheduling model were assembly time estimates and assembly lot sizes. The capacities for each line were specified in total weekly labor hours, and it was necessary to know the assembly time for a batch of each item. The initial use of standard times from industrial engineering led to substantial underestimates of weekly output since the efficiency or performance indices of particular workers had not been taken into account (one man who assembled plastic top tables consistently worked at approximately 250%). When adjustments were made for this phenomenon, predictions for weekly output became relatively accurate. Further refinements included changes in the estimated setup times as methods of stock picking and assembly became more oriented toward smaller lot sizes. In fact, companywide output predictions became so accurate that a much improved system of customer order acknowledgment could be built around the major assembly scheduling model.

Consideration of the proper assembly lot sizes led to some important insights. All furniture companies try to manufacture in relatively large lot sizes in order to achieve good equipment utilization and to minimize setup costs. Most firms attempt to never cut less than 50 of a particular item and rarely cut less than 100. A "push strategy" means that minimum assembly lot sizes are also 50 or 100. However, a completely separate lot size problem exists at the assembly stage. There are setup costs and carrying costs which need to be traded off; the high cost of storing bulky finished goods items and the possibility of designing assembly methods so that changeovers are facilitated has led us to much smaller assembly lot sizes for Baumritter. As a result, the constitution of finished goods inventories is considerably enhanced, the ability to react more quickly to actual demand has improved, and the production function has become more congruent with the strong consumer orientation of the marketing function.

Dependent versus Independent Demand

The approach embodied in major assembly scheduling runs counter to much of the order point-order quantity decision rules developed in Chapter 18. Although the basic cost tradeoffs reflected in the economic order quantity models still apply, the statistical nature of safety stocks and order points are discarded. The concern with utilizing capacity effectively forces us into a fixed or deterministic production schedule that results in inventories and/or backlogs; safety stock becomes a residual rather than a method for driving the system.

The fixed or deterministic nature of the major assembly schedule does not, however, mean that the firm is necessarily unresponsive to demand. It is possible to have a fairly rapid updating in the major assembly schedule, and a continuing goal is to reduce the time span over which we are locked into a particular schedule. That is, at the end of one week it is probably too late to change the assembly schedules for the following week or perhaps even the week after that, but careful attention to the production planning and inventory control system and the makeup of work-in-process inventories within that system should allow us to be free of a rigid assembly plan for long time periods. In fact, the pull strategy embodied in the major assembly-dependent demand approach can substantially shorten the reaction time to changes in final demand.

The safety stock-order point philosophy for finished goods or end items is violated by major assembly scheduling. For component parts, the safety stock-order point philosophy needs to be more than violated, it needs to be completely discarded in most companies. The consideration of each component part as if the demand for it were a random process to be estimated with statistics can lead to serious problems. If a product is assembled from 10 components, and the safety stock level for each component is set at 95% (there is a 95% probability that each part will be in stock), the probability of all 10 parts being in stock simultaneously is only approximately 60%; if the number of component parts increases to 20, the probability of all being in stock decreases to approximately 36%, and for 50 component parts the probability is approximately 8%.

The joint probability phenomenon is disturbing enough in its own right, but a more subtle problem arises from the nature of the demand for component parts. Perusal of the stock withdrawal records for a chair leg at Westfall well might yield the following weekly "demand" over a six week period: 0, 0, 0, 0, 0, 600. The average demand is 100 units; the mean absolute deviation from this average, however, is 166.7 and a resultant 95% safety stock level would be 343 units. Moreover, if the same pattern of "demand" continued, 343 units would be unneeded for five weeks out of six and insufficient for the sixth week.

The simple fact is that demand for component parts is usually not a random process. Baumritter sells chairs, not chair legs; the demand for chair legs is completely determined by assembly needs. We do not need a safety stock of chair legs when we are not assembling chairs. If the assembly schedule calls for 100 chairs in week 5, the demand for the components which make up that chair can be ascertained with relative certainty.

Requirements Planning

The pull strategy based upon the demand for component parts being dependent upon assembly schedules results in the need for a requirements planning subsystem. Essentially, the function of this subsystem is to determine the raw materials, purchased parts, fabricated parts, and subassemblies necessary to meet the major assembly schedule (repair parts are sometimes added to these needs).

In order to accomplish requirements planning, it will be necessary to maintain bill of materials type data; i.e., the raw materials, purchased parts, and conversion operations necessary to create end items. The process of converting end item demands into required components is usually referred to as "explosion."

Although it is possible to perform the explosion process manually, the benefits of a computer increase as the number of end items and component parts goes up. The advantages of a computer system are also felt as the number of end items on which a particular component is used increases. A computer system facilitates "where-used" analyses so that a time series of total needs for each component part can be determined.

The time series of component part needs will usually be somewhat lumpy, and poorly approximated by some uniform usage rate assumption. One important ramification of this pattern of lumpy demand is that the economic lot size formulae presented in Chapter 18 lose some validity. If the economic lot size calculation yielded a batch quantity of 90 units for one part, but the assembly lot size was 100 units, then two batches of component parts would be required to make one assembly lot; moreover, 80 units of that unneeded component part inventory would be carried until the next assembly lot was scheduled. This does not mean, however, that the economic lot size concept should be completely discarded. Economic lot sizes can be viewed as starting points for incremental analyses based upon the time series of dependent demand; e.g., the cost tradeoff between making one batch of 100 units to satisfy an assembly schedule versus the cost of making two batches of 90 units with 80 units being stored until the next assembly schedule time.

In determining the time series of component part needs, it is necessary to continually update those needs as actual events materialize. That is, although we might plan to assemble 100 chairs every other week for the next 12 weeks, the actual production in week 3 might turn out to be 95 chairs or 103 chairs. Similarly, although we planned on using 200 chair arms, the amount consumed might have exceeded this due to quality problems. Also, the batch of 200 arms manufactured for this assembly order might have come through as 215 arms. Another possibility is that a salvage operation requires several replacement chair arms to repair damaged merchandise. All of these situations imply a need for some subsystem to determine the net requirements based upon latest inventory and withdrawal information.

An important part of the requirements planning system is to convert the time series of dependent component part demand into a plan for when batches of component parts should be started into production or purchased. This resultant or "offset" time series requires lead time data in addition to lot size decisions. Some components require considerably more lead time than others, both for internal manufacture and for purchased items. If offsetting is properly done, the purchasing function can operate more effectively and the manufacturing process can reduce work-in-process inventories as well as expediting activities.

The costs of not properly offsetting are easily seen in the furniture industry. Demand for an end item is typically converted into a "cutting order" where proper multiples of each part are simultaneously cut and pushed through the production process. Since some parts require much more extensive machining than others, we end up with most of the parts waiting for the parts with long lead times and expediting being used to remedy the situation. Similarly, the lead times for purchased components such as hardware vary substantially; the only way to properly hedge is to carry large inventories of these items.

A somewhat more subtle cost borne by furniture companies because of improper requirements planning procedures is related to the cutting order and the push strategy which it embodies. Because wood is committed to an end item at the cutoff saw, there is little pressure for part standardization. Since parts are unique to an item, once all the component parts for an item are available, manufacturers tend to assemble and finish the entire batch; this leads to large cycle stocks and poorly constituted inventories of finished goods. Because of large assembly lot sizes, the time between assembly batches for a given item tends to be long, and the result is both large inventories and backlogs for the finished items. Furniture manufacturers rarely treat the assembly lot size as a problem separate from that of a lot size for individual components.

The lack of standardized parts tends to prohibit larger lot sizes of component parts and technology improvements based upon those larger lot sizes. In addition, lack of standardized parts limits the length of the product line because each new item calls for an entire set of new parts. A part standardization program coupled with an ABC type analysis well might indicate which final items have sales insufficient to support more than a few nonstandard parts.

The benefits of a pull strategy and standardized parts also exist at levels below that of completed component parts. That is, just as it is advantageous to not commit component parts to a particular end item until the last possible time, it should be possible in many industries to maintain the same noncommitment policy for work-in-process inventories. In Baumritter, it should be possible to standardize lengths of wood or glued up panel sizes of wood so that the need for many component parts can be satisfied from a set of standardized pieces of wood.

Data Requirements

In order for a major assembly scheduling module to operate properly, the following data will be required:

1. Bills of material
2. Parts numbering
3. Efficiency data
4. Manufacturing lead times
5. Vendor lead times

As noted above, bills of material contain lists of all the component parts required to make up subassemblies and final assemblies; they also provide routing data for the conversion steps necessary to fabricate items and vendor information for purchased items. These data are highly dynamic, and in most companies a system for properly maintaining and updating bill-of-material information (a bill-of-material processor) has been specially designed.

The kinds of questions which typically come up include: which parts will be affected by an equipment change? What parts need to be changed for a new item or changed quality standard? Are any of these parts currently being produced? What is the effect of a change in status on these parts? Can we use them up? Are they useful for another item? Should we stop putting any further effort into these parts? What are the tool requirements for a change in method? For what items can we use a new improved purchased part? How will changes in manufacturing methods affect the times required?

A discussion of bill-of-material processor designs is somewhat beyond our present scope. Nevertheless, we need to recognize the necessity of bill-of-material processor data for both major assembly scheduling and for other modules in the production planning and inventory control system. Computerized bill-of-material processor systems are readily available which meet these needs.

Another data input required for efficient production planning and inventory control systems is a part-numbering system. Although at first glance part numbering may seem like a relatively trivial problem as long as each part has one and only one number, in some companies this objective is difficult to achieve.

Parts can be numbered according to some classification system which uses the last digit for expressing whether or not the item is a component part, subassembly, or major assembly. Other techniques include decimal notation for component parts. Still additional schemes attempt to use numbers or letters to indicate type of material, shape of the item, or other attributes which seem to make sense in the particular situation.

Although these sophisticated part-numbering systems provide extra information, they do so usually at the expense of extra digits or redundant numbering. It is not unusual to find a company with 15 digit part numbers. The probability of recording or transmission errors increases with the number of digits. Moreover, these systems never seem quite able to have the "ultimate scheme." This observation should not come as a great surprise; individual users of the system have distinct sets of criteria. The engineering interest in size of the blueprint is probably not important to the expediter for getting all the component parts for some assembly.

The unique nature of user needs calls for an ability to sort part numbers (entities) by particular attributes. Any scheme which attempts to second-guess all of the ways in which users might like to sort seems doomed to failure. Once again we find ourselves interested in some sort of user-oriented modeling environment. Moreover, a system which helps individuals to pick out one component part or job from the many going through a manufacturing operation can have considerable benefits in expediting the flow of materials to meet requirements.

Efficiency data are required to convert industrial engineering-type standard data to predicted actual data. Clearly, if one work center area or man operates at an 80% performance index and another at 120%, the second will achieve 50% more output than the first. These kinds of data need to be estimated and included in the production-planning and inventory control system. At Westfall Furniture Company, there are substantial differences in the efficiencies as measured by engineered standards between the major assembly lines. We noted that one plastic table assembler performs at a rate of about 250%; an occasional table line usually runs at about 125% and can get down as low as 75% when new employees are being trained.

An important data input for production-planning and inventory control systems is manufacturing lead times or the time required between the decision to make an end item and the receipt of that end item into finished goods inventory. Manufacturing lead times are comprised of the times required to manufacture components, times required to purchase components, final assembly times, and times required for inspection and packaging. In Fig. 19.2 we showed a data input from the purchasing function for the lead times for purchased items; no such input is shown for manufacturing lead times.

Manufacturing lead times are not an abstract constant like π. The elapsed time is a function of the work load in the manufacturing activity, the complexity of each component part, and the goodness of our production planning and inventory control system. Manufacturing lead time in fact should be considered as a criterion entity rather than a data input. Marketing criteria of responsiveness to customer demands and financial criteria associated with inventory investment imply a surrogate criterion of reduced manufacturing lead time. Clearly the pull strategy discussed above can provide more responsive production planning and shorter lead times than a push strategy where lead times necessarily are constrained by the longest time to buy or produce any component part plus assembly, inspection, and packaging times.

In actual practice, estimates of manufacturing lead times are often based upon the number of conversion or manufacturing operations required in each component part. The lead time is expressed as some multiple of this number of operations in days, e.g., each operation requires two days. This method of estimating lead times discounts the time required for actual conversion operations as being unimportant relative to the transit and waiting times required to get from operation to operation. Although this estimating procedure tends to give results that are superior to a fixed lead time estimate, we again must conclude that the basis for the calculation is highly dependent upon the ability of the production planning and inventory control system to move material through the manufacturing facility. For this reason, we will want to look at manufacturing lead time again after we understand some of the other major production-planning and inventory control system modules.

Vendor lead times are also a critical data input for production planning and inventory control. Again however, these times are not independent of actions which the purchasing company can initiate. Many times the absence of a major assembly schedule does not allow a purchasing function to adequately predict vendor requirements far enough into the future. The result is frequent scurrying to meet demands, variable lead times because of the scurrying, and larger than necessary inventories to protect against unnecessary uncertainties. With a reliable major assembly schedule, it is often possible to closely coordinate purchasing activities so that vendor production schedules are aligned with those of the purchasing company.

Outputs

The primary output from a major assembly scheduling module is a period by period schedule similar to that presented as Fig. 19.3. In addition, major assembly scheduling also provides the ability to report on performance after each time period has elapsed and to take account of upsets or significant deviations in the schedule such as an entire batch of finished assemblies which do not meet quality requirements or the unavailability of one or more component parts.

This "upsetting" feature can be particularly important for companies that have stringent final inspection and quality requirements as is true in chemical or pharmaceutical firms. A large batch of a particular end product may be judged inadequate, and that knowledge will not be obtained until the entire batch is completed. The resultant impact upon back orders and inventory positions can be dramatic, and it is necessary to have rapid reaction times to rectify those situations.

Similarly the assembly of a particular item may be scheduled, and we subsequently find out that one or more purchased or manufactured components will be unavailable at that time. Obviously, expediting actions are used when feasible, but there will be times when a component simply will not be available at the required time. The sooner that knowledge can be obtained, the more readily the major assembly schedule can be shifted so that assembly capacity is utilized and so that items required for the changed assembly schedule can be expedited where necessary.

The extent to which component part due-dates are missed is largely influenced by other major modules in the production planning and inventory control system. Some systems will be much more reliable than others. The extent of unreliability will determine the need for hedging in the due dates for component parts and the need for a system which can examine the impact of a shortage on all items which use that component. It is also possible to use upset data to inform customers in advance that a delay is anticipated; sometimes sales people can "ration" short supplies of a particular item so that no customer is in serious trouble.

MAJOR WORK CENTER SCHEDULING

In major assembly scheduling, we started with an idealized set of assembly outputs based upon market needs that were subsequently modified to meet capacity criteria and constraints. The same sort of a process can be conceptualized for the scheduling of major manufacturing departments or work centers. If we view the major assembly schedule as an input to work center scheduling, we should be able to derive the implied activities in each major work center in each time period. To the extent that the implied schedule exceeds the capacity for a particular work center, jobs necessarily need to be pulled ahead or pushed back. Also, a feedback can take place between major work-center scheduling and major assembly scheduling; that is, if a particular assembly schedule calls for an unattainable throughput in a major work center, then perhaps the major assembly schedule can be shifted to more appropriately balance required conversion activities over time.

Explosion

In major assembly scheduling, we saw how data from bills of material, efficiency data, and lead times were used to both load or schedule assembly tasks into a particular time period and to know when to initiate the purchase and fabrication of component parts. Using the same basic data, it is possible to estimate when each component part will require the capacity of each particular work center. The resultant demands upon the work centers can be summed by period into an idealized time series of work center activity.

The actual activity performed in each time period may vary from the idealized time series, but by having a plan it is often possible to complete the most critical items during each time period. It is also possible to know when more work is required in a particular area or work center so that transit times for items coming to that area can be reduced and other corrective actions taken.

Additional actions that might be taken include the temporary shift of men between major work centers, possible changes in routing so that conversion activities are performed in different work centers, the use of overtime in a bottleneck department, more intensive use of indirect labor in a particular work center to decrease setup and changeover times between jobs, and temporary reassignment of particularly skilled workers into the bottleneck work center.

Another way to handle the work-center scheduling problem is to ascertain that sufficient capacity exists so that problems do not occur. At first this may seem like a rather odd suggestion, but in fact the process is used in varying degrees in most companies. That is, certain work centers are inherently tighter than others and certain pieces of equipment are far from fully utilized. Many times this comes about from the economics of a particular device. Thus at Westfall there are special machines used for drilling leg holes in the bottoms of chair seats which operate less than one day per week on the average. On the other hand, some of the more expensive equipment like the double-end tenenor and moulders are utilized much more intensely.

Another way to take care of the major work-center scheduling problem is to accept long lead times and high work-in-process inventories. Someone once wisely said "inventories buy management." If our interest is in maintaining high utilization rates on expensive equipment, one way to satisfy that interest is to keep work piled up in front of the equipment. The result of these piles, however, is that each job sits for long periods of time between operations and large investments in work-in-process inventories are required. The lead times in Baumritter factories are generally calculated as two days for each operation; since the average machining operation rarely takes more than a couple of hours for a lot size, the percentage of lead time taken up by actual conversion processes is less than 10%. This is an interesting statistic to calculate for any manufacturing or fabricating operation, because it indicates the kind of potential reduction in work-in-process inventories and increase in responsiveness to final demand that is possible. The objective is not to ignore the surrogate criteria associated with machine and worker utilization; it is to recognize important additional criteria and to find a means whereby all of the criteria can be reasonably satisfied.

Outputs

The outputs from a major work-center scheduling module are somewhat similar to those provided from major assembly scheduling. The principal difference tends to revolve around a typically somewhat shorter time horizon and a greater degree of detail. Both major modules provide a standard of comparison by which actual results can be evaluated. The upset provision of major assembly scheduling will also be desirable for major work-center scheduling. For example, we would like the ability to know what effects will be felt from a run of component parts being scrapped or a machine breakdown. Which component parts need not be further processed till the scrapped part is produced? What products can be assembled from components which do not require capacity on the broken equipment? If all work going through a particular work center is delayed by three days, what will the work loads be on subsequent operations?

SHOP FLOOR CONTROL

The fourth major additional module required for a production-planning and inventory control system is a method for dispatching individual jobs through the production facility so that major assembly schedules are met, work centers are efficiently utilized, work-in-process inventories are kept low, and fast reaction times are attainable. It is not sufficient to merely schedule major work centers in the aggregate and allow individual jobs to meander through conversion stages in any way they might. Clearly some system is required to make sure that assembly runs are not held up for lack of one component part and that decisions made on which jobs to run are not solely based upon worker preference.

The flow of many individual jobs through various operations or fabricating stages is a queuing problem; in the management-science literature, this problem is referred to as the "job shop scheduling problem." Considerable research has focused on different dispatching rules or queue disciplines for the order in which jobs waiting to be processed by a particular conversion activity should be run.

A few of the best-known queue disciplines are first come-first served, the shortest processing time next, earliest assembly or due date next, job with the shortest queue at the next processing stage next, and job with the least amount of slack (defined as time remaining before due in assembly minus processing time) next. The first come-first served rule is one we are all familiar with as customers in supermarkets, gasoline stations, toll booths, etc. However, its "fairness" to customers is not a particularly appealing criterion when the customers are batches of component parts. The shortest-operation-next dispatching rule will result in the shortest queues behind each machine and the lowest in-process inventories; however, since jobs with long processing times are continually passed over for jobs with short processing times, the shortest-operation-next rule can result in certain jobs requiring very long overall fabricating times which can interfere with assembly schedules. The job with the shortest queue at the next-processing-stage-next rule attempts to maximize the utilization of equipment by picking jobs which are needed if subsequent operations are to avoid idle time. The earliest assembly or due-date-next rule focuses on the criterion of meeting assembly schedules by always putting the productive capacity into jobs that are needed earliest in assembly. The job with the least amount of slack next rule attempts to improve the earliest assembly date next rule; it takes account of not only due date, but the amount of necessary work required. Let us now turn to another dispatching rule which goes even further.

Critical Ratio Scheduling

The major criterion in critical ratio scheduling is similar to that used for earliest-assembly-date-next rule and job with the least amount of slack next: we want to work on those jobs which are most likely to be required before they can be finished. The critical ratio technique continaully compares the need for an item with the remaining lead time required to complete the item. The technique is particularly valuable for items with long lead times; as the item is processed, up-to-date actual information can be substituted for the forecasted or expected information which was used to originally put the item into production.

The critical ratio is the demand time divided by the supply time. If a batch of an item is needed in 20 days and it takes 25 days to make it, the critical ratio is $20/25 = 0.8$. This ratio implies that in order to satisfy the need it will be necessary to make the item in 80% of the expected time. This item would take priority in each machine center over all items which have a higher critical ratio. By keeping track of the average critical ratio as well as the number of jobs with critical ratios less than 1.0 for each machine center, important insights on day-to-day operations can be obtained.

There are several ways in which the critical ratio may be computed. One way is to subtract the present date from the assembly or due date and divide the result by the number of days required to complete this particular order, including processing, transit, and waiting times. If the resultant ratio is 1.0 or greater we can say that this job is proceeding on or ahead of schedule. On the other hand, if the critical ratio is less than 1.0 it will be necessary to accomplish the remaining work in less time than the figure indicated in the denominator of our critical ratio calculation; that is, in order to meet the due date, the remaining lead time will have to be reduced by expediting.

The critical ratio technique itself is an expediting procedure since the dispatching rule is always to run that job next with the lowest critical ratio. With a daily report of all jobs that are in a department and those that are expected to arrive in that department shortly, it is possible for a strict schedule of jobs to be maintained and for setup times to be reduced by having all tooling and procedures for the next job waiting in advance. With this "look ahead" provision, it is also possible to overlap start and finish times in consecutive operations; that is, a highly critical job may be started on an operation before all of the batch is completed on the preceding operation.

Another way of calculating the critical ratio applies when stock for an item is continually being randomly depleted instead of being completely dependent upon the assembly schedule. In such a case, this critical ratio compares the rate of depletion with the rate of progress in fabricating the replenishment order. For example, if an order had a total lead time of 30 days and 1/3 of the work on this order has been done, then 2/3 of the lead time is still required. If we initiated this order with a stock of 50 pieces and we still have 40 or 80% on hand, the critical ratio may be calculated as $0.8/0.667 = 1.2$. The critical ratio is greater than 1.0 because although 1/3 of the required activities to complete the replenishment order have been completed, only 1/5 of the reserve stock has been depleted.

Manufacturing Lead Time Revisited

We have discussed the need for lead time data in production planning and inventory control systems and at several points have noted the appropriateness of including reduced lead time in the criteria set by which production planning and inventory control systems should be judged. When one sees a shop floor control system as a queuing problem, it is clear that lead time represents time in the system and that in many manufacturing firms the percentage of time in the system associated with waiting or idle time is quite high.

Few managers fully appreciate the benefits to be obtained from a reduction in lead time. Furthermore, estimates of lead times can involve some rather insidious feedback loops. One of these feedback loops is based upon expectations; that is, if historically the lead time for an item to be manufactured in a furniture factory is 14 weeks, one expects a 14 week lead time and orders are started into process 14 weeks ahead of when they are needed. Moreover, the 14 week actual lead time is borne out because there is no particular reason to decrease it.

It should be clear that the average lead time is directly related to the average work-in-process inventory level; we showed this explicitly in Chapter 11, where we indicated that for the Poisson arrival rate/negative exponential service time models the mean time in the system, including the service time, was equal to the mean number in the system divided by the arrival rate. In our present terms this means that if we put jobs into the manufacturing facility at some given rate, the expected average lead time is directly proportional to the number of other jobs in the system. The fact that the Poisson arrival rate/negative exponential service time assumptions may not apply does not change the phenomenon.

Another interesting feedback has to do with forecasting the expected lead times and changing the order point (or time when orders are initiated) as the expected lead time changes. As the expected lead time goes up, orders will be issued to manufacturing sooner which will result in a higher work-in-process backlog and even longer expected lead times. As is true for so many problems, the "solution" worsens the problem.

By now it should be clear that reducing lead times is intimately involved with reducing work-in-process inventories. It should also be clear that larger backlogs cannot solve problems of inadequate capacity. Essentially, work-in-process inventories are often used as a cushion in place of adequate management; there tends to be little control over work-in-process inventories and actual levels are a result of independent actions.

When lead times and work-in-process inventories are reduced, the ability to react to actual demand patterns is greatly enhanced. Forecasts and commitments over extended lead time periods no longer have to be made and the deviations of actual results from expected results are decreased.

The difference between the push and pull strategies influences the level of work-in-process inventories. The push strategy embodies a specific commitment to an end item at the beginning of the manufacturing process. As a result, jobs will be going through the manufacturing facility which are not required to meet final consumer demand and these jobs will delay those that do meet customer needs. The pull strategy attempts to allocate our various manufacturing capacities to actual items at the latest possible time. It makes sense for Baumritter to forecast demand for end items with several different finishes as a group and to only commit the actual items to particular finishes at the last moment, probably when actual customer demand is known. Similarly, it makes sense to assemble items in small lot sizes so that cycle stocks are reduced and so that assembly capacities are devoted to the items required. It also makes sense to only utilize manufacturing capabilities for those items designated for assembly schedules.

An interesting lead time, work-in-process inventory problem came up at a new facility which manufactured items for Baumritter. An initial order for several items in large quantities was split into two orders. Although setup costs were doubled, the amount of work-in-process and machine time per operation were cut in half. The result was that finished goods were being shipped at the end of five weeks instead of eight weeks and the cash flow pattern was quite different.

Outputs

The outputs from a shop floor control system include a report on all jobs that are in or expected to be in a particular work center this day and the next few days. It is essential that this report be furnished often enough to account for the dynamic nature of a job shop. The frequency will be dependent upon the time that jobs usually require; if jobs stay on the same piece of equipment for a week or two then perhaps daily reporting is not necessary. In most cases, however, a daily run based upon conditions at the end of the previous day will be required.

Other outputs include packets of shop orders and a means for capturing actual information. The latter is often a series of punched cards that are submitted when operations are completed. Cards include data such as quantities, scrappage, and elapsed labor hours. In some systems this information is obtained from data collection systems installed in the factory which are activated as each operation is completed.

PURCHASING

At several points in this chapter we have indicated the need for close coordination with suppliers and how a strategy of production planning and inventory control based upon dependent needs from a master assembly schedule can lead to more reliable data for our suppliers. Purchasing is an area of the business that is too often overlooked; when one calculates the percentage of sales dollars spent on purchased items, the result can be sobering. Poor production planning and inventory control procedures often degrade the purchasing function into little more than an outside expediting operation. As the primary source of communication between company needs and the capabilities of outside firms, the degradation of purchasing into an expediting activity can have significant costs.

Duties

The purchasing function is responsible for the procurement of items from outside vendors within the criteria of cost, performance, availability, and dependability. To the extent that better understanding of company needs is accomplished through a production planning and inventory control system, and with automation of portions of the purchasing activity, more attention can be devoted to the more basic function.

Many times it is possible to go beyond the strict terms of vendor agreements to coordinate vendor activities with those of the purchasing company in such a way that improvements are felt by both parties. The result is a set of more viable dependable vendors and a stronger economic position. Essentially, vendor capacities should be as carefully planned as those of the company.

A case in point again relates to the push versus pull strategy. Proper interaction with a vendor can often lead to the vendor's provision of capacities over time in some gross sense without those capacities being committed to specific items. Thus for example, it might be possible for a company which buys castings from a foundry to reserve capacity in terms of some tons of gray iron castings with the exact items to be cast determined much later. Similarly, it should be possible for Baumritter to order stains and finishes with the exact composition of the colors determined subsequently or lumber of unspecified thickness.

At the risk of overstating the point, the benefits that a well designed production planning and inventory control system can provide to the purchasing activity are very substantial. Closer interactions between the purchasing company and its vendors can be derived from time that is made available for creative thinking. This can easily be seen in Baumritter. The pattern of decentralized operations has led to each plant doing independent purchasing, yet the payoffs from joint purchasing could be substantial (the company's collective purchases of yellow birch lumber represents approximately 1/3 of the demand in the entire northeastern part of the United States). Before these benefits can be achieved, however, it is necessary for the needs as expressed in the major assembly schedule to be accurate. As we shall see in a later section of this chapter, that day is coming.

Outputs

Although the purchasing function obviously produces purchase orders and records on vendors which contain names, addresses, telephone numbers, activities, pricing information, quality history, and delivery history, there are other kinds of analyses that are more interesting. It is possible to do ABC type analyses on individual items as well as on total purchases made from particular vendors. It is also possible to apply the logic developed in critical ratio scheduling to items provided by vendors. With good interaction between the purchasing company and the vendor, it should be possible to inform the vendors as to which items are becoming more critical and which ones are not as important based upon up-to-date information. With the right kind of communication, it should also be possible for vendor upset data to be brought into the production planning and inventory control system so that changes in the major assembly schedule can be made before due dates are missed. Just as the criterion of lead time reduction and work-in-process inventory reduction is important in a manufacturing firm, it is important to the vendors, both for their own well-being and for the well-being of the purchasing company. Essentially, the boundary line between the vendor and purchasing company based upon enterprise ownership should not interfere with the benefits of coordination.

IMPLEMENTATION

Implementation of an integrated production planning and inventory control system requires a change in attitude and orientation on the part of many people. The issuance of work orders to the manufacturing facility and subsequent efforts to get material through the various conversion stages into finished goods is a central problem in almost all manufacturing firms; because of the problem's pervasiveness, most managers "understand" the problem all to well. This "understanding" in many cases is a major source of the problem. That is, some firms have some of the highest paid expediters imaginable; presidents of companies have been observed moving material through the manufacturing stages.

As stated before, expediting is a good barometer of organizational efficiency. The feedback loop associated with pulling hot jobs ahead today which results in today's regular work becoming tomorrow's hot jobs has been discussed also. Similar but less obvious self-perpetuating problems are the result of other "corrective" actions. This kind of problem is particularly prevalent in production planning and inventory controls since this area represents the major interface between the production and marketing functions. Thus for example, the effects of special promotions on manufacturing lead times for regular items is poorly understood in most companies.

Because of the conflicting criteria and the dynamic nature of the problem, production planning and inventory control is often thought of as requiring a high degree of art and an ability to react quickly. The quick reaction time usually means that "fire-fighting" is the rule of the day, and little time is available to codify the art into a science. Moreover, the individuals involved in production planning and inventory control often have neither the abilities or the tools (comprehensible models) to make such a codification.

Many elegant models have been suggested for production planning and inventory control systems, and some of these models indeed might have done a good job. However, the history of management science and operations research is replete with nonimplemented good ideas. Feasibility is a necessary but not sufficient condition; it is my belief that the ultimate test is implementation.

I see the user designer concept as the road to implementation. What is required is a means for sequentially codifying and testing intuitive feelings about the kinds of decisions that should be made in a particular production planning and inventory control environment. The word *means* implies a modeling environment; the modeling environment necessarily has to be designed so that users (who have the criteria) can be a significant part of the investigative activity. Moreover, there is more to the process than investigation to find, discover, or design a good production-planning and inventory-control system; the critical need is for those people who will use the system to become educated and to believe in the validity of the model. Since we know at the outset that many decisions from a good production-planning and inventory-control system will be counterintuitive, it is essential that those whose intuitions are inappropriate understand why.

It is hard to overemphasize the benefits derived from an understanding of the system by people who will work with the system. First, on the negative side it is worth noting that nonbelief can be manifested in very subtle kinds of sabotage; initial predictions about the environment within which the system will operate can be far from accurate. On the positive side, belief reduces perceived threat, and belief is an infectious thing. That is, it is well worth the investment to get even *one* person convinced that the system is right and that it produces results superior to those obtained previously. The investment in convincing additional people that the system is superior quickly drops off. The moral: nothing succeeds like success.

Let us now return to the discussion of production planning and inventory control at Baumritter which was started in Chapter 4.

Major Assembly Scheduling at Westfall

Figure 19.3 presented a portion of the major assembly schedule for Westfall, and we have spent a good part of this chapter explaining the model and how it fits into an overall attack on production planning and inventory control. Let us examine how this model came to be implemented at Westfall.

The author and some colleagues were empirically investigating the process of system design as it was being carried out in a production planning and inventory control/materials management system at Baumritter. One facet of this investigation led to the conclusion that a critical need for aggregate capacity planning (Chapter 20) existed and that Baumritter personnel did not fully comprehend the problem. It was felt that this situation represented a fertile opportunity for the design of a user-oriented model. Our intent was to prepare a seed which could be planted in the Baumritter system and thereafter nurtured on a cooperative basis with our relative role decreasing over time. The model was built and demonstrated to the vice-president of manufacturing, assistant vice-president of manufacturing, plant managers, assistant plant managers, other manufacturing executives, and systems analysts working on the materials flow system.

The reactions of these people was highly positive; an improved recognition of the seriousness of this problem was felt, and we expected that cooperative implementation would take place shortly. However, no amount of prodding on our part caused this to happen.

Each of the manufacturing executives was faced with an extensive schedule of problems and time commitments. Aggregate capacity planning was on no one's list; it was unclear whose list it should go on, whether anyone had the time to do the job, and whether the problem might either go away or be changed significantly in character by the solution of problems already on the "lists."

I believe there is a moral to be learned from this story: the top down approach of selecting the most critical problem first is conceptually elegant, but the bottom up approach of finding a problem of present concern will usually produce implementable results. We backed off from the aggregate capacity planning problem and initiated a search for a pervasive lower level problem which was of present concern. We chose major assembly scheduling at Westfall.

The process of scheduling assembly lines at Westfall was somewhat chaotic. A push strategy involved putting a cutting for a finished item into the rough mill and expecting that it would be ready for assembly eight weeks later. As time elapsed, however, the standard eight-week lead time from cutoff saw to the start of final assembly was often missed. Although the stated goal was to assemble an entire manufacturing lot size upon completion, this goal was rarely met. Short list requirements, poorly constituted inventories, marketing demands, and pool car shipments all led to quite variable quantities being assembled. An interesting feature of assembling smaller lot sizes was that for the first time manufacturing people began to seriously question the validity of assembly lot sizes being identical to cutting lot sizes. An attempt was made to schedule assembly lines on the basis of smaller lot sizes which varied from 1/10 to 1/4 of the cutting lot size. It was felt that in this way cycle stocks of finished goods would be reduced, constitution of finished goods inventory would be improved, and there would be less need for short listing items through final assembly operations.

Three of the key manufacturing executives at Westfall attempted to design an assembly schedule on this basis. They attempted to determine what items to make week-by-week for the next seven or eight weeks on each major assembly line. The effort involved one to two days or about five man-days per week. The procedure was to arrange pieces of paper on a long table where each piece of paper represented a particular assembly lot of an item. Demand forecasts, standard assembly times, part availabilities, pool car requirements, and dollar output objectives were used.

The actual output from the assembly lines was at considerable variance with what the schedule had predicted. As one week's output was off, corrective actions were taken in subsequent weeks which made the validity of estimates for future time periods ever more dubious.

It was at this time that the author and his colleagues proposed that the major assembly scheduling process be attacked with a time-shared computer model. The reaction to this suggestion was overwhelmingly negative. Comments included statements such as the computer is no substitute for manufacturing judgment, go back to your Ivory Tower, and you are wasting your time and I will not permit anyone in my organization to waste his time by cooperating with you. The last comment required the subtle imposition of higher authority; we came to a compromise where no Westfall employee was forbidden to work with us, but no one was encouraged to do so either.

Our approach to the problem was to send a research assistant to the factory to stay until someone could be convinced. We were looking for an entree and that entree had to be an individual—someone who had the problem and who could become convinced that we could help *him* in the solution of problems with which *he* was personally involved. We have since become convinced that finding this kind of individual and getting him on your side is essential (A colleague, Professor Lee Schwarz, suggests that this individual may be the 21st century equivalent of F. W. Taylor's "first class man").

The individual we found at Westfall was one of the three men involved in the major assembly scheduling process. His job in the organization was industrial engineer—time study man—assistant to the assistant plant manager. He had had two years of college and no exposure to computers. He didn't see how he could participate in the development of a computer model, nor did he understand why it was necessary for him to be involved. Convincing him of the necessity for his involvement and our role to provide user-oriented modeling power was a key step in the implementation process. It was accomplished largely by our research assistant playing golf, drinking beer, and generally gaining credibility as both a human being and someone who was trying to help.

When our inside man or user (perhaps shill) became convinced that the effort was worth trying, he received a substantial amount of personal harassment from his fellow workers. Some were friendly such as "I always knew you was a college professor at heart," but others were more substantive; he was essentially told that no company time was to be devoted to this project—he did it largely on his own time.

As the model was being developed, considerable interest was being generated around the plant. Most of the interest was negative, and when the first run produced results that were clearly wrong many individuals had a good time saying "I told you so." We had, however, indoctrinated our user with the user-designer philosophy. He expected the first run to be invalid, but the reason for the lack of validity to be apparent; this proved to be correct. His fellow workers only saw the invalid model, not the glaring inconsistencies that could be remedied. The model's requirement for explicitness quickly pointed out major inconsistencies in data inputs, criteria, and the process of scheduling itself. Within a month these inconsistencies were largely removed and the model was generating valid assembly schedules 18 weeks into the future.

Use and Evolution of the Model

The modeling environment established for major assembly scheduling at Westfall was user-oriented in several important ways. First, all of the computer coding was done in an easy to understand computer language. Second, the model itself was written in small modules with painstaking care to use the simplest possible coding and lavish use of comment statements to explain what each module and even each individual line of code was accomplishing.

Third, and perhaps most important of all, was the use of time-sharing as the experimental vehicle. By having the model programmed for a time-shared computer, we were able to make change after change after change as quickly as inconsistencies were discovered. It just does not seem possible that the number of necessary recyclings could have been accomplished in the turn-around times required in the usual batch-processing computer environment. Interestingly enough, within six months the development efforts on the model had tapered off to zero and it was possible to reprogram the model for the company's in-house batch processing computer; at the time of this writing this system has been running very effectively in batch processing for over four years.

Once the model became operational at Westfall and actual results began to match the schedule, people who had been openly hostile became believers virtually over night. There was no arguing with success, and the amount of managerial talent made available for other activities was significant. News of the success quickly spread through other Baumritter factories, and the author and his colleagues were besieged with requests for the scheduling model.

Our approach to these requests was to promote our original user to the status of expert major assembly-scheduling model builder with the job of transplanting the model to other locations. We helped him in the first 2 or 3 transplantations, with our role gradually diminishing. He was thereafter able to implement the system in several factories by himself. Interestingly enough, the problems experienced by Westfall were largely universal and the model did fit in most other applications. In some of these other applications, new problems were uncovered and at least one of these problems was found to also exist at Westfall. The model went through several stages of generalization, but most of this work was accomplished by Baumritter employees.

The benefits from the major assembly scheduling models are somewhat difficult to tie down explicitly. We noted earlier in the chapter that companies who implement a good system of production planning and inventory control often achieve a 10 to 20% increase in productivity due to the better utilization of equipment, reduced expediting, etc. Productivity has increased at Westfall since the scheduling system was put in, but the major benefits are difficult to measure. Major assembly scheduling became so predictable in all Baumritter plants that order acknowledgement was changed and is now based upon the production schedule. An anticipated problem with filling railway cars did not materialize since improved scheduling allowed for much better planning of railway car needs. Purchasing activities were similarly made easier with a more clear understanding of needs. However, it is my opinion that the most fundamental benefit coming from major assembly scheduling model was the clearly perceived need for rationalizing the rest of the production planning and inventory control-materials flow system.

A Systems Orientation

With a firm major assembly schedule which was reasonable and attainable in terms of the criteria and constraints of major assembly operations, the dependent nature of the demand for component parts to meet those schedules became quickly felt throughout the Baumritter organization. A prior feeling at Westfall toward shop floor control not unlike that toward major assembly scheduling was much easier to change. The tie into other parts of the system such as improved forecasting systems was also more easily attained. As production output became predictable with accuracy, more fundamental attention became devoted to the locations of the finished goods in factory warehouses, regional warehouses, field warehouses, and the transportation system which connects these inventories. Perhaps most interestingly of all, about a year after major assembly scheduling was working, the vice-president of manufacturing became convinced that his most significant problem was aggregate capacity planning; the systems approach had now evolved the problem definition to where the author and his colleagues had seen it a year and a half to two years earlier.

SUMMARY REMARKS

In this chapter we have tried to take some building blocks from prior chapters, add some new ideas, and put them all together with a problem or systems orientation. The production-planning and inventory-control system is a pervasive part of the business enterprise that brings together many separate functional goals. In trying to cope with separate functional goals, disjoint approaches often result in larger than necessary inventories, long manufacturing lead times, poor customer service, and extra cost to the enterprise. A pull versus push philosophy of production planning and inventory control has been presented in this chapter as a way to make important advances along a front of unified and congruent criteria.

Implementation of a pull-oriented production planning and inventory control system requires a systems orientation and a user-oriented approach which builds upon existing strengths, weaknesses, and personnel in an organization. Although the degree of initial antagonism felt by individuals within the Westfall organization may appear to be somewhat extreme, it is a fair bet that equally negative feelings exist in almost any company. If these feelings which are largely based upon fear and lack of understanding are not overcome, the best conceived system in the world has little chance of being implemented.

With the material presented in this chapter as background, let us now go on to Chapter 20 where we will consider the capacity issues which necessarily have been taken as given in Chapter 19. Once again we will find important linkages which broaden our evolving understanding of complex materials-flow systems.

REFERENCES

Greene, James H., *Production Control—Systems and Decisions,* Irwin, 1965.

Magee, John F., and D. M. Boodman, *Production Planning and Inventory Control,* 2nd Ed., McGraw-Hill, 1967.

Plossl, George W., and O. W. Wight, *Production and Inventory Control,* Prentice-Hall, 1967.

Smith, Spencer B., "An Input-Output Model for Production and Inventory Control," *The Journal of Industrial Engineering,* vol. XVI, no. 1, January–February, 1965.

Voris, W., *Production Control,* 3rd Ed., Irwin, 1966.

CHAPTER REVIEW

I think that this chapter may well be the most important and pertinent chapter in the book. The concept of dependent demand and the resultant control provided over production planning and inventories is not well understood in many companies. Implementation of the kind of systems discussed in this chapter can lead to important improvements in several enterprise criteria. It is quite possible for you to advance rapidly in a company by participating in the design and implementation of a dependent demand-based production planning and inventory control system.

I also think this chapter serves as a good vehicle for you to crystalize your understanding of the systems approach. Remember that we stated a working knowledge of the systems approach as a course goal both initially and after Chapter 3. Chapter 19 should pull many things together for you. The limitations of traditional operations management problems were stressed in Chapters 13–16. Chapters 17 and 18 provided some building block concepts, and we saw how systems could be designed from these entities if certain criteria were valid. In Chapter 19 we greatly expanded the criteria set, saw how our prior systems needed to be overhauled, and came up with a broader approach which put it all together. We saw how it all fit for Westfall, and how the user-designer concept was necessary for the actual implementation of the system in the real world.

Support for one further systems approach concept: There is no such thing as the ultimate or total system; Chapter 20 considers the capacities we took as given in Chapter 19, and Chapter 21 goes on to logistics, marketing considerations, and further thoughts on system design to control one's own destiny.

OUTLINE OF THE CHAPTER

Introduction	(builds on chapters 17 & 18)
The problem—an overview	(chapters 17 & 18 as a system)
Recapitulation	(pattern of orders must be manufactured)
Additional criteria	(efficient utilization of capacities)
Additional system modules	(pull *versus* push strategy)

Major assembly scheduling	(the primary commitment)
The Westfall scheduling process	(balance of items made on a line)
Dependent *versus* independent demand	(saftey stock = residual)
Requirements planning	(exact specification of components)
Data requirements	(components and times)
Outputs	(plans and control)
Major work-center scheduling	(planning by department or type of conversion activity)
Explosion	(planned work loads by dept.)
Outputs	(upset features)
Shop floor control	(queue discipline)
Critical ratio scheduling	(select "hotest" job next)
Manufacturing lead time revisited	(benefits from reducing)
Outputs	(job status by department)
Purchasing	(large cost category)
Duties	(plan vendor capacities)
Outputs	(reduced distinction between purchased & owned capacities)
Implementation	(user-designer concept needed)
Major assembly scheduling at Westfall	(establishing credibility)
Use and evolution of the model	(nothing works like success)
A systems orientation	(related problems clarified)
Summary remarks	(building blocks put together)

CENTRAL ISSUES

The forecasting models developed in Chapter 17 and the basic inventory models presented in Chapter 18 can be combined with lead time data to yield an idealized set of production orders. This process, however, ignores limitations on facilities or capacities to produce and criteria associated with intensive utilization of those facilities.

A pull-oriented strategy begins with major assembly scheduling where an idealized time series of assembly orders is adjusted to fully utilize the capacity of each major assembly line. The adjusted time series is a commitment to an exact plan for assembly lot sizes; needs for the component parts which make up the assemblies are known with certainty for as long as the assembly schedule commitment is firm or frozen. Adjustments for forecast errors are reflected in the "unfrozen" portion of the schedule; the benefits of shorter lead times are reflected in length of the frozen period and a corresponding ability to react to change.

Major work-center scheduling employs the same approach as major assembly scheduling. The exploded list of component part needs to meet the assembly schedule results in a period by period expected work load for each major work center or department. In order to more effectively utilize the capacities of these departments, specific orders are pushed ahead or pulled back in time.

Shop floor control is a system to monitor the flow of particular jobs through the required conversion stages. It specifies which job to run next in order to meet the criteria for major assembly scheduling and major work-center scheduling.

The role of purchasing in a manufacturing organization should not be underestimated. The same utilization of capacity problems face the vendors of a company as the company itself, and it is to the company and their vendors collective benefit to effectively plan. A well-designed production-planning and inventory control system should not be restricted to boundaries specified by company ownership.

Implementation of a major assembly scheduling system and some supporting systems was accomplished at Westfall. The process of establishing user credibility was tedious, but once the model started to produce valid results the sales job was over. As the system became used, important linkages with other problem areas became apparent. Evolution toward a broader definition of the problem continues to this day.

ASSIGNMENTS

A captain's chair is made at Westfall out of four legs, two leg stretchers, one stretcher brace, one seat, two arm supports, six spindles, two arms, and a backrest. The standard setup times to make each of these parts are 2.5 hours, 2.5 hours, 2.5 hours, 9.5 hours, 2.5 hours, 2.5 hours, 1.0 hour, and 5.0 hours, respectively. The setup time for all assembly and finishing operations is estimated to be 2.0 hours (total setup=30.0 hours). This chair sells at the rate of approximately 500 per year, the cost of capital is 20% and setup time is valued at $8.00 per hour. The total cost of the chair is estimated at $25.00, with each of the legs $1.00, each stretcher $0.75, the stretcher brace $0.75, the seat $4.50, each arm support $0.50, each spindle $0.25, each arm $1.00, and the back $2.75; the remaining $7.00 is made up of assembly, finishing, and packaging costs.

1. Calculate the economic lot size for the chair.

2. Westfall presently makes this chair in lots of 150. What extra costs are incurred?

3. Calculate the economic lot size for each part.

4. What are the extra costs of making each part in multiples of 220 chairs?

5. Without making detailed calculations, would the extra costs be increased or decreased if each part were made in multiples of 150 chairs? Why?

6. What is the economic assembly quantity (on a value added basis)?

7. Baumritter's vice-president of manufacturing feels that the cost to carry parts is significantly lower than that to carry finished goods inventory for the following three major reasons:

a) The physical volume required for finished items averages 10 to 15 times greater than that for parts.

b) Finish commitments do not have to be made to parts (e.g. red chairs when blue are out of stock).

c) Interchangeable cartons are not tied up in merchandise which is not sold.

What is the implied carrying cost if the assembly quantity for captain's chairs is reduced to 50?

8. If Westfall decides to assemble this chair in lots of 80, in what lot sizes should the parts be made?

9. Suppose Westfall had a backlog of demand for the captains chair and established the following assembly schedule:

Week	Quantity
4	80
7	80
8	80
12	160
13	80
16	80
19	80
20	80

Let us also assume the following data on parts:

Part	Inventory	Lead time (working days: 5 = week)
leg	360	14
stretcher	40	13
stretcher brace	20	13
seat	100	30
arm support	150	13
spindle	2000	15
arm	40	12
back	90	23

Prepare a schedule for part manufacturing.

10. What is the week-by-week load on the cutoff saw in terms of the number of jobs started?

11. An order of seats is needed for week 13 and an order of arms is needed for week 12. Assuming that each job is 50% complete and it is now week 9, what are the critical ratios for these two jobs? If they are both waiting to go on a particular machine, which one should be picked?

12. What savings would result if the legs for this chair were the same for another chair which also sold 500 per year? What if the other chair sold 1000 per year? 50 per year?

13. The answers to problem 7 in Chapter 18 are:

a)≈460 cases
b)≈670 cases
c)≈210 cases
d)≈16 + cases based on sales rate, 82 + cases based on assembly rate.
In what ways is the approach of that problem incorrect?

14. Suppose you are given the following data on a chair line which has a capacity of 45 hours per week.

Style	Inventory	Sales per week	Assembly lot size	Assembly hours per lot size
1	− 25	5	50	15
2	10	20	200	70
3	100	10	100	35
4	30	6	75	25
5	− 40	8	75	30
6	200	40	350	120
7	40	10	100	25
8	15	5	75	35
9	− 20	10	150	55
10	60	30	300	100

a) Prepare a production schedule for the next 10 weeks using the following rules:

let p = priority at beginning of each week = inventory ÷ weekly sales
load items on line with smallest value of p next.

break any ties in p by numerical order of style

do not calculate a p for any item which is carried over in production from one week to the next

b) Calculate the mean value of p for the 10 items at the beginning of each week. What is the significance of this statistic and what conclusions can you draw about this line?

CHAPTER 20

AGGREGATE CAPACITY PLANNING

In Chapter 19 we developed an understanding of production-planning and inventory-control systems. A good part of that chapter was based upon utilizing capital assets and manpower. We also noted the need for understanding the inherent abilities or capacities of a firm's capital assets and manpower, but in Chapter 19 we took the capacities as a given; we now want to examine the ways in which these capacities are established and utilized over differing planning horizons.

The establishment of aggregate capacities is a planning process encompassing medium to long-range planning horizons which are determined for a particular firm by the kinds of actions possible and the necessary lead times to change capacity. The kinds of decisions involved range from research into new technologies to the construction of new physical facilities, additions to existing facilities, adding additional shifts, purchasing additional equipment, changing the level of subcontracting, building inventories in anticipation of seasonal peaks, the making of additions or deletions from the size of the work force, to working overtime or short hours.

In order to understand the ways in which these kinds of decisions interact as well as the interactions between aggregate capacity planning and production planning and inventory control, let us examine capacity decisions for Baumritter; thereafter, we will examine some models of potential aid for these kinds of decisions and then consider the kind of modeling environment which might be most congenial to implementation of aggregate capacity planning model results.

AGGREGATE CAPACITY PLANNING AT BAUMRITTER

I wish it were possible to say that what is presented here has been thoroughly tested in operation; as noted in the last chapter, however, the importance of aggregate capacity planning at Baumritter has only recently become appreciated in a fundamental way. What follows, then, is an exposition of pertinent issues, and some ways in which the problem might have been attacked; thereafter it will behoove us to examine some explicit models proposed in the literature of aggregate capacity planning. With that understanding, we can then return to the Baumritter problem and assess the kind of modeling environment that was necessary and the model currently being implemented.

We will start with a consideration of capacity for the total Baumritter organization. This level of aggregation will permit us to derive a gross understanding of what the manufacturing function needs to produce over the next year, and a "good" way of satisfying this next year's needs. We will also see how the same basic approach can be utilized for planning horizons for more than one year. After considering capacity planning for the total Baumritter operation, we will look at the problem on an individual factory basis and see how our frame of reference ties in with major assembly scheduling and major work-center scheduling.

Total Manufacturing Capacity

Table 20.1 presents a monthly sales forecast for 1972. Let us say that the time is now early November 1971, and we are preparing a total manufacturing plan for the next calendar year. (The numbers used in this section are disguised slightly from actual company data.)

Table 20.1 Baumritter Corporation: Monthly sales forecast (1972)

Months	Forecasted sales (in thousands of $)
January	3,800
February	4,200
March	5,100
April	4,500
May	5,900
June	3,500
July	4,300
August	6,300
September	7,200
October	6,400
November	7,900
December	5,900
Total	65,000

The company keeps a productivity statistic which can be used to convert sales dollars into manpower needs. The statistic is the number of sales dollars produced from one man hour of direct labor; as of November 1, 1971 that statistic is $18.00, and it is expected that the statistic will hold

Table 20.2 Baumritter Corporation: Manufacturing capacity needs (1972)

	A	B	C	D	E	F	G	H
Month	Sales in man hrs. (000)	Regular working days	Saturdays	Sundays and holidays	Vacation	Implied work force	Implied work-week	Implied inventory
January	211	20	5	6	0	1320	28.4	86.2
February	233	21	4	4	0	1390	29.6	167.4
March	283	23	4	4	0	1540	33.1	226.4
April	250	20	5	5	0	1560	33.7	273.2
May	328	22	4	5	0	1860	40.2	271.6
June	195	22	4	4	0	1110	23.9	403.2
July	239	10	5	6	10	2990	64.4	312.5
August	350	23	4	4	0	1900	41.0	304.0
September	400	20	5	5	0	2500	53.8	201.6
October	355	22	4	5	0	2020	43.5	173.0
November	438	20	4	6	0	2740	59.1	31.2
December	328	20	5	6	0	2050	44.2	0
Total	3,610	243	53	60	10	1857	40.0	0

for calendar year 1972. By applying this relationship of sales dollars to direct labor hours, we can restate Table 20.1 as sales measured in direct labor man hours; column A in Table 20.2 makes this conversion. This kind of a statistic, which converts all productive outputs to a common base, is required for aggregate capacity planning. For other companies, measurements such as tons of steel, gallons of paint, tons of paper, or cases of mayonnaise are appropriate.

Columns B, C, D, and E indicate the ways in which the calendar year 1972 is divided into regular working days, Saturdays, Sundays and holidays, and vacations. There are 243 regular working days, 53 Saturdays, 60 Sundays and holidays, and 10 days of vacation.

Column F is the implied work force that would be required to produce the expected sales in each month with an eight hour day, 40-hour workweek. For example, the January sales of 211,000 man hours could be produced by 1320 workers each working 8 hours per day for the 20 working days in January. Similar calculations are made for each month. The 1857 figure at the bottom of column F is obtained by dividing the total sales for the year, 3,610,000 man hours, by 243 eight hour working days; that is, if 1857 labor workers were employed from January 1 to December 31, eight hours per day on only regular working days, the total direct labor man hours during the year would equal the expected sales in direct labor man hours.

Column G, "Implied Workweek," is the number of hours that direct labor workers would be employed each week if the direct labor force were held constant at 1857 employees throughout the year and no inventory were tolerated. That is, if 1857 direct labor employees worked 28.4 hours per week during the 20 working days in January, 211,000 man hours of production would result. As can be seen from column G, the implied workweek varies from a low of 23.9 hours to a high of 64.4 hours; moreover, this variance occurs in one month, primarily because of low expected sales in June and a two-week vacation in July. Ignoring that severe fluctuation (it would seem reasonable to produce some of July requirements in June) still leaves a fluctuation in the implied workweek from 28.4 to 59.1 hours. Column H, "Implied Inventory," is the cumulative thousands of man hours that would be carried in inventory if a work force of 1857 employees worked 8 hours per day for the 243 working days. Thus for example, 86,200 man hours of production would go into inventory in January if the labor force of 1857 employees worked 8 hours per day for the 20 working days. As can be seen from column H, the inventory builds up to a peak of 403,200 man hours at the end of June and thereafter decreases to 0 at the end of December. Any of the implied inventory figures in column H can be converted into an implied finished goods inventory through multiplication by the $18 per direct labor hour statistic; thus the 403,200 hours of inventory accumulated at the end of June converts to $7,257,600.

Columns F, G, and H each depict certain ramifications of an underlying production strategy. The strategy implied for column F is to vary the work force as needed to produce the required production with no inventory; the policy is hire and fire as required. Column G is based upon a constant work force strategy where the number of hours worked per week is varied so that no inventory is accumulated. Column H is based upon a production strategy of constant work force and constant 40-hour workweek with inventory absorbing all mismatches between production output and demand.

Clearly some production plans can be derived which are a mixture of these three strategies. Thus for the column F strategy, we noted that it makes little sense to decrease the labor force from 1860 in May to 1110 in June and thereafter increase it to 2990 in July. To say that it makes little sense, however, implies a criterion; namely, costs of hiring and firing associated with the indicated magnitudes are more than the cost of carrying inventory. Once again we find ourselves concerned with trading off different kinds of costs and with establishment of appropriate surrogate criteria.

The three primary costs associated with the "pure" production strategies implied in Table 20.2 are hiring and firing, overtime and undertime and inventory carrying cost. A related cost might be the possibility of letting inventory go negative, that is to accumulate backlog. Additional criteria include desired and actual starting and end conditions. That is, if the direct labor force is less than 1857 employees in January 1972 it would seem reasonable not to add additional direct labor personnel until a date nearer that when their efforts will be required. Similarly, the beginning inventory and/or backlog position needs to be taken into account, as does the desired ending inventory, backlog, and labor force. Still additional criteria are associated with utilization of the company's fixed assets. If a company works three shifts, the amount of overtime that can be added is limited; moreover, many nondirect labor costs such as supervision or maintenance are not unaffected over all ranges of activity. Our model is based upon direct labor cost, with other costs assumed nonincremental.

Alternative Plans

We indicated that columns F, G, and H in Table 20.2 each implied a production plan. Let us now attempt to evaluate each of these plans as well as some alternatives.

In order for us to evaluate alternative plans it will be necessary to attach costs to the activities which are different from or incremental to the alternatives. However, it is important to emphasize that if we were not "us," but Baumritter management, we could do considerable analysis without attaching costs to alternative actions. A conducive modeling environment might allow for "users" to make choices with unexplicated criteria, and for implied criteria to be deduced from choices.

The production strategy associated with column F in Table 20.2 involved hiring and firing to meet each month's demand exactly. Let us for the sake of argument assume that it costs $200 to hire and train a direct labor employee and $100 to fire him. The production strategy in Column G was based upon a constant labor force which varied the number of hours worked per week to meet the requirements exactly. We will need costs of overtime and undertime. Let us further assume that the average hourly direct labor cost within Baumritter is $2.50; the overtime premium based on time and one half would be $1.25. The costs associated with undertime production are more difficult to assess, but let us assume that $0.50 per hour is appropriate. Column H was based upon a constant work force and a constant 40-hour workweek where all fluctuations were absorbed in inventory. We need an inventory carrying cost; applying a 2% per month rate and the $18 of output direct labor hour yields approximately $0.35 per direct labor hour.

Table 20.3 costs out these three alternative production plans. Column A is the easiest to understand; it is based upon a constant work force of 1857 direct labor employees and a constant 40-hour workweek with differences between productive output and demand absorbed in inventory. The resultant costs are obtained by multiplying figures from column H in Table 20.2 by $0.35. Column B in Table 20.3 is the next simplest plan; it corresponds to column F in Table 20.2, with a constant 40-hour workweek, no inventory, and the work force varied to meet month-to-month demands. The entries in the table are obtained by multiplying the month-to-month positive differences from Table 20.2, column F by $200 and the negative differences by $100. Thus for example, we assume that the beginning work force is 1320 employees so no cost is associated with January; February requires 70 more workers at $200 each for a cost of $14,000. Column C in Table 20.3 is based upon the overtime and undertime costs of varying the hours worked to eliminate inventory while maintaining a constant work force of 1857 employees. The figure for January, $43,200, is obtained by multiplying the difference between 40 hours and 28.4 hours (11.6) by 4 weeks; the result is the number of undertime hours worked in January by each direct labor employee. Since there are 1857 employees and each hour of undertime has an associated cost of $0.50, the total cost for the month of January is $43,200. Similar calculations are made for the months where overtime is required, but the overtime premium rate is $1.25.

Table 20.3 Costs of alternative production plans.

	A	B	C	D
Month	Work force = Constant 1857. Workweek = constant 40 hrs.	Workweek = constant 40 hrs. Inventory = 0	Work force = constant 1857. Inventory = 0	Workweek = constant 40 hrs. Build work force as needed but do not fire until Dec.
January	$ 30.2	$ 0	$ 43.2	$ 0
February	58.6	14.0	40.5	14.0
March	79.3	30.0	29.5	30.0
April	95.6	4.0	23.4	4.0
May	95.0	60.0	2.0	60.0
June	141.2	75.0	65.8	46.2
July	109.3	376.0	106.5	14.6
August	106.4	109.0	10.7	11.9
September	70.5	120.0	128.3	86.0
October	60.6	48.0	35.8	16.8
November	10.9	144.0	177.4	30.0
December	0	69.0	39.0	39.0
Total	$857,600	$1,049,000	$702,100	$352,500

The total cost associated with columns A, B, and C in Table 20.3 might lead one to believe that, based upon our assumed cost structure, column C, overtime-undertime, is the best alternative. However, these three alternatives are "pure" strategies; mixtures can be better. We referred above to just such a mixture in a rather casual way when we noted the possibility of maintaining the May work force level through June so that some of July's requirements would be produced in June. Column D in Table 20.3 expands on this idea. It is based upon a production strategy beginning with 1,320 direct labor employees, building as needed, but not firing any employees until December (so that annual requirements are exactly met).

The costs of column D are the same as those of column B for January through May. In June the work force level of 1,860 men which has been built up through May is maintained; this is 750 more men than required for June production. If each of these 750 men work 8 hours a day for 22 days we will end up with 132,000 man hours in inventory at the end of June. Applying our $0.35 inventory carrying cost per direct labor hour results in a June cost of $46,200. The July needs of 239,000 man hours are partially met by the 132,000 man hours inventoried from June. The 107,-000 man hours remaining are less than will be produced if we maintain the 1,860 direct labor employees. At the end of July's 10 working days we will still have 41,800 man hours in inventory for a cost of $14,600. August needs of 350,000 man hours are partially met by the 41,800 man hours inventoried from July. The 1860 workers can produce 342,200 man hours during the 23 working days of August; we end the month with 34,000 man hours in inventory for a cost of $11,900. The September requirements of 400,000 man hours cannot be met by the 34,000 man hours of inventory plus the 1,860 direct labor employees working for 20 days. In order to meet September needs, it will be necessary to hire an additional 430 employees, bringing the total direct labor force up to 2,290. The October needs of 355,000 man hours are less than can be produced by our 2,290 direct labor employees working for 22 days. We end the month of October with 48,000 man hours in inventory. In November the need for 438,000 man hours results in a net need for 390,000 man hours. Since our labor force of 2,290 men working 8 hours a day for 20 days only results in total production man hours of 366,400, we require 23,600 additional direct labor hours; we need to hire an additional 150 men. In December we will need to cut the labor force to the 2050 level shown in column F, Table 20.2, for a net reduction of 390 employees. As shown in column D, Table 20.3, this production plan results in a total cost of $352,500.

Column D is by no means the last word. If the production plan in column D is modified so that November requirements are not translated into men who will be hired one month and laid off the next, the total cost can be decreased. If the 23,600 additional man hours required above that which can be furnished by the 2,290 direct labor employees is obtained through overtime, the associated cost is $29,500. Although this $29,500 is just slightly less than the $30,000 associated with hiring 150 additional personnel, $15,000 of severance pay is avoided in December for a total savings of $15,500. Additional changes could be made to reduce the cost still further. But at this point it is more useful to return to the assumptions underlying our analysis.

Data Requirements

Our analysis to this point has been somewhat cavalier about data sources, possible imperfections in data, constraints where data estimates no longer maintain linear relationships (can we really increase our direct labor force by 170% in one month as indicated in the June-July increase of column F, Table 20.2?), additional criteria, additional capacity variables, and the ubiquitous problem of surrogate criteria relationships.

Perhaps the most fundamental data assumption made in our analysis (and in aggregate planning models described in the literature) is the existence of an overall capacity measure that is truly meaningful. It may well be academic to view a paint company in terms of gallons of paint—they might have plenty of oil base and no lucite. Similarly, although overall dollars of output sounds good for Baumritter, customers buy items, and most customers are unwilling to take two tables instead of one table and six chairs. If this problem sounds like our old friend, the ubiquitous level of aggregation question, you are quite correct. We will see how this affects the actual model presently being implemented at Baumritter. Let us first, however, turn to some detailed considerations.

Most of the data used in our analysis will not be found in the accounting records of a firm. About the only piece of "hard" data used was the overtime premium rate. Even this datum is deceptive. For one thing, we have assumed that each hour of direct labor time is equally productive. Clearly this is not the case, and some adjustment for efficiency seems appropriate. Figure 20.1 is suggestive of the way in which labor efficiency might be influenced by the length of the workweek.

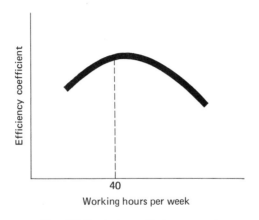

Fig. 20.1 Labor efficiency cost.

The shape of the curve in Fig. 20.1 illustrates that a 40-hour week is a norm where employees can be expected to produce at maximum efficiency. Relatively small increases above 40 hours are achieved with little loss in productivity, but major extensions of the work week incur a high cost in terms of efficiency. Reductions below 40 hours also cause efficiency losses as workers tend to "stretch out" their jobs. Figure 20.1 is a model of labor efficiency as influenced by the length of the workweek and perhaps should be modified to include week-to-week considerations. That is, if the efficiency coefficient of working a 70-hour week in week 1 is $X\%$, the efficiency coefficient for another 70-hour week for week 2 will be less and will continue to decrease as time goes on, both because of worker fatigue and because of a growing disinterest in substituting leisure time for overtime dollars.

Our cost coefficient for working undertime was a WAG (Wild Guess); clearly costs associated with undertime operation must include the influence on employee morale, the ability to hold good workers, and the effects on efficiency. The increasing efficiency loss depicted in Fig. 20.1 seems much more appropriate than a linear relationship.

The number of overtime hours possible in a given day must approach some limit. Similarly, there are only so many Saturdays in a month. Working on Sunday requires even higher overtime premiums (usually double time). One interesting possibility for the Baumritter Corporation example would be to change the date for the annual vacation. July is the time of the year when a major push awaits the company, and it well might be better to build inventory during that month rather than to deplete it, both in aggregate terms and more importantly in terms of inventory constitution.

The problems concerned with identifying inventory carrying costs have already been discussed in Chapter 18. Although the 2% per month calculation is widely enough used to perhaps warrant the title SWAG (Systematic Wild Guess), casual use of any such statistic can be dangerous for a specific firm.

A related cost should probably be included for negative inventories or backlogs. In the plans considered above, we implicitly did not allow backlogs; clearly this is somewhat unrealistic, particularly in industries such as furniture manufacturing. Figure 20.2 suggests the way in which costs might be affected by inventory, both positive and negative.

The cost function in Fig. 20.2 is made up of two segments, a linear cost segment for positive inventories, and a nonlinear cost segment for negative inventories which indicates a certain "flatness" or willingness of customers to tolerate relatively small backlogs but an unwillingness to tolerate large backlogs. Clearly the validity of the model as depicted in

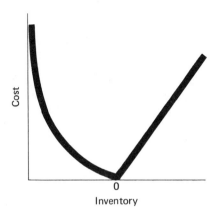

Fig. 20.2 Inventory and backlog cost.

Fig. 20.2 is a situation-dependent matter. Large backlogs are not uncommon in the furniture industry but are intolerable in other situations.

A closely related inventory cost concerns stockouts. In Chapter 18 we noted that safety stock and cycle stock were related (if a year's supply of an item is made in one batch, the item is only subject to potential stockout once per year). Although stockouts as a function of aggregate inventory are necessarily determined by the constitution of the aggregate inventory, there nonetheless is a decreasing tendency to experience stockouts as aggregate inventories grow large. That is, as aggregate inventory is larger the probability of a stockout becomes less. One way to model stockout costs for short-run aggregate capacity planning purposes might be as an exponential decay function where the shortage costs (a) are equal to a parameter (b) times e^{-cx} where c is a parameter of decay and x represents the aggregate inventory (See Fig. 20.3).

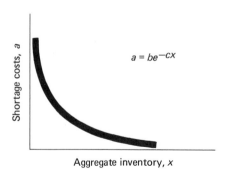

Fig. 20.3 Stockout costs as influenced by aggregate inventory.

Perhaps the most difficult data to estimate are costs associated with hiring and firing. Costs that are associated with the personnel operation may be somewhat nonincremental. On the other hand, the cost associated with interviewing prospective employees by supervisory personnel may be substantial, particularly when such interviewing occurs during peak demand periods, which is usually the case. The firing costs of severance pay and increases in unemployment compensation are relatively easy to estimate, but layoffs can lead to significant enterprise costs in terms of employee morale. Both hiring and firing costs are affected by geographic considerations. The impact of employment decisions on a small company town is quite different than that upon an urban area with a variety of employers.

For many companies learning or training costs are also a significant cost component in terms of varying employment levels. Our studies of the learning phenomenon provide a conceptual base for examining learning and training costs. In those studies learning or improvement was modeled by an exponential decay function described by the parameter "percent progress." Perhaps a suitable model for learning or training cost might be similar to our model of stockout costs as expressed in Fig. 20.3 with the ordinate now labeled either training costs or perhaps efficiency index and the abscissa labeled average employment length of the current work force.

The real costs of changing employment levels are even less visible. The reputation and integrity of a firm and the spirit with which the enterprise is treated in a community are strongly influenced by employment changes. These feelings can be manifested in tangible things such as property tax rates, but the intangibles are perhaps even more important.

One way that employment levels can be changed without firings or layoffs is by controlling the rate at which employees who leave through natural attrition are replaced. There will always be employees leaving for better jobs, to retire, etc. The rate at which such employees are replaced can be varied as a function of anticipated needs. Moreover, not all additions to the direct labor force come in small increments. Indeed, one of the purposes of aggregate capacity planning is to know far enough in advance when capacity needs are such that it is time to initiate purchase or design of a new productive unit. Thus, for Baumritter, at some point it is unrealistic to assume that more direct labor employees can be found for the Westfall Vermont plant, and to conclude that a new factory in a different location is in order.

Another kind of problem associated with our previous analyses involves starting and ending conditions. Thus in one plan we started with a labor force of 1857 direct labor workers, and in another with 1320. Similarly, in one plan we finished with a direct labor force of 1857 direct labor workers and in another with 2050. Although this seems somewhat unreasonable and does in fact affect the cost calculations (the cost of column B in Table 20.3 includes hiring costs for workers who already "existed" in column A), the actual conditions would be known in a particular company. The end condition is a somewhat different problem, yet the practical solution is again prevalent in the real world. In actuality, there never is an "end." The aggregate capacity planning process should be done periodically, perhaps monthly, for some planning horizon such as a year. The goal is to make those decisions within our control in the best way possible in light of a continually extending horizon. Aggregate capacity planning should not be done on a basis where large discrepancies exist before corrective action is taken. Rather, it makes more sense to perform the function routinely, capturing the latest up-to-date information, and making relatively minor adjustments rather than major changes.

Still another practical problem has to do with "offsetting." In Tables 20.1 and 20.2 we produced monthly requirements for the month when they were to be sold. The notions of lead time clearly would make this condition somewhat different for particular firms and particular production processes.

Still another issue has to do with surrogate criteria and the opportunities considered for aggregate planning. A distinct possibility for short-run as well as long-run capacity utilization is a varying amount of subcontractor use. If seasonal peaks can be smoothed through subcontracting, plant investments and many headaches can be eliminated. On the other hand, increasing dependence upon subcontractors can be a potential danger. In 1971 Baumritter was quite concerned about this problem because although many other furniture companies were anxious to do subcontract work for them, they were skeptical about the reliability of this source of capacity when the furniture market turned up.

The influence of subcontracting has an interesting effect upon the statistic we used to convert sales dollars into required labor hours. A company should be extremely careful to not let this statistic in any way become a surrogate criterion. Although it is tempting to think that a plant which turns out $25 per direct labor hour is somehow "better" than a plant which turns out $15 per direct labor man hour, the difference can be entirely due to use of purchased components. The $18 average figure for Baumritter is, in fact, made up of similar statistics for each factory which vary from about $15 to $25. Moreover, we will see that model results can be quite sensitive to this statistic and that the "average" sales dollar or can of paint is never made.

With all of these estimation problems, possible criteria conflicts, and needs for constant updating, the value of some kind of user-oriented explicit model becomes obvious. Production plans need subjection to sensitivity analyses, the implications of various "what if" questions (which usually lead to even more questions) need to be quickly and efficiently evaluated, and the proper surrogate criteria set needs to be evolved.

Planning Individual Factory Capacity

The aggregate capacity-planning approach described above is based upon a level of aggregation which includes the entire Baumritter manufacturing function. Although we described the process on a one-year basis, it should be clear that planning horizons can be extended out to include several years. When this is done for a company experiencing steady growth, it will usually be found that at some point in the future the kinds of alternatives available to meet capacity are felt to be uneconomic. For example, our knowledge of compounding tells us that if sales grow by 10% per year, they will double in less than eight years; a firm must ask whether it is possible for its production function to double its volume in its present configuration, what mode of operation would be required to achieve that volume, and what alternative production capabilities should be considered. The need is for some kind of master plan based upon long term needs and the required lead times to make changes in productive capacity.

Obviously, in a multiplant company such as Baumritter some factories are inherently more capable of expansion than others. We noted the constraints on labor availabilities for a plant located in a town such as Westfall, Vermont. An equally important constraint revolves around managerial capability; expansion of capacity in some factories cannot be achieved without substantial changes in managerial capabilities. Other factors include proximity of raw materials, transportation considerations, and the product line manufactured. Sales growth will probably not be achieved in equal weights among all items currently manufactured. Thus bedroom furniture factories are less able to make dining room furniture than vice versa, and Baumritter is beginning to market a line of cherry furniture which requires manufacturing skills different than those for yellow birch. Capacity decisions involve commitments to specific product lines.

A breakdown of the total company planned production into a factory-by-factory schedule is needed. One way this can be done is to essentially duplicate the capacity-planning process described above on a plant-by-plant basis with the forecast broken down by factory of production. We noted in our discussion of forecasting, however, that forecasts which are segmented like this tend to be less accurate than those at a higher level of aggregation.

By planning capacity on a factory-by-factory basis, inequities in loads can be better anticipated and redivision of products among the factories can be made more rationally. For example, if growth in regular dining room furniture and cherry furniture both lead to an anticipated large demand on the Westfall plant, we have the choice of expanding capacity (in one way or another) or of manufacturing some Westfall items in other Baumritter factories.

At a still lower level of aggregation, if the forecast is broken down into items, we can determine the implied capacities in major assembly stations and in machine centers. The approach utilized in the scheduling models described in Chapter 19 can lead to feedbacks where stated or expected capacities may or may not be sufficient for anticipated volumes.

An important feedback between major assembly scheduling and capacity planning has to do with mismatches between planned and actual capacity. We will always experience some deviations between actual output and planned output, but the cumulative affect of minor deviations should tend to balance out. However, occasionally a "nonrandom" mismatch between planned and actual capacities persists long enough to cause problems. Baumritter experienced this problem in 1971 when the two largest factories took on production of cherry furniture. The conversion problems led to losses in output volume over several months. The cumulative volume loss represented more than an entire month in companywide production capacity.

The significance of a one month loss in production can be staggering. Many of the most important costs (e.g. influence on customer service) are not directly reflected, but the hard data associated with five months of Saturday work is sobering enough by itself. If those overtime hours are already committed to use, it may be even longer before the productive loss can be replaced.

Within each individual factory, the satisfaction of capacity constraints for major item groups involves plant management in whatever shifting of resources is possible (can some small hutches be assembled in the large case lines or can some occasional tables be assembled in the table line?). The same process exists for bottlenecks in the machine centers (which parts can be manufactured with alternative routings, and what parts can be purchased from outside suppliers or other Baumritter factories?). Essentially, the plant capacity planning process attempts to make relatively short-range changes in the stated capacities by these means. The plant is also concerned with longer term changes in assembly capacities and work-center capacities through the purchase of additional or improved equipment and through the addition of manpower, but a clearcut plan for those resources is clearly needed to rationally make such capacity changes.

These plans obviously do not take place in a vacuum. There is little point in expanding occasional table production at Westfall when another Baumritter plant could easily take on production of these items. Similarly, there is little point in buying a new special piece of equipment when capacity exists on a similar piece of equipment in a nearby Baumritter factory. Thus we see that the aggregate capacity planning problem exists at different levels in the company and for both different levels of aggregation and for differing time horizons. Moreover, it is necessary for these activities to be related and congruent to whatever extent possible, and for whatever planning model used to be consistent with realizable ways to change capacity. Let us now turn to the major analytic models proposed for these problems. Thereafter we can see why a somewhat different approach was needed at Baumritter.

THE LINEAR DECISION RULE

Several quantitative models have been proposed for the aggregate capacity planning problem. The output from these models is a set of decisions or decision rules specifying the way in which capacity should be adjusted in the light of current and expected conditions. We have already examined several rather naive decision rules. One was to produce at a constant level throughout the year. A second was to vary production by changing the length of the workweek to exactly meet demand. A third was to vary the size of the labor force to exactly meet demand. We found that these three decision rules led to less than optimal tradeoffs of the costs we assumed appropriate for the planning situation. We also examined two additional schemes which traded off strategies so as to reduce the overall cost. The linear decision rule is the best-known explicit model for trading off production strategies.

The Problem

The linear decision rule for aggregate capacity planning was developed by Holt, Modigliani, Muth, and Simon. The technique was described in the October 1955 and January 1956 issues of *Management Science* and more completely in a book published in 1960.* The work evolved from a series of empirical investigations in industrial decision making where the goal was to apply techniques of management science to the development of improved operational decision rules. One of the major empirical investigations was performed in a paint company with problems not unlike those of Baumritter. Box 20.1 describes the authors' statement of the problem environment faced in the paint company.†

Background: The effort to carry sufficient inventory of each product at warehouses and retail stores had built up total inventories that seemed excessively large. Nevertheless, demand runs on individual products resulted in stockouts, lost sales, and extreme demands on factory production during the peak sales season. One technique for coping with this situation was use of several types of priority orders on the factory in addition to normal replenishment orders. There was some interest in the company in the possibility of ameliorating the situation by centralizing information on stocks and sales at all levels, with the probable exception of information from independent retailers. That such a policy might pay off was indicated by the fact that an informal and partial system of this sort was said to have worked quite well.

The company was also interested in stabilizing production throughout the year. It was felt that employees tended to reduce their efforts in the off season in an attempt to spread out the work. A policy of smooth production would possibly remove fear of seasonal layoffs and improve efficiency. It might also reduce the premium costs associated with overtime payments during the peak season. However, stabilized production would lead to higher inventory costs because of wide seasonal fluctuations in sales.

---

*Charles C. Holt, Franco Modigliani, John F. Muth, and Herbert A. Simon, *Planning Production, Inventories, and Work Force*, Prentice-Hall, 1960.
†*Ibid.* p. 16.

> The factory management wanted to schedule economical production runs of each product without excessively large inventories at the factory warehouse. The factory problem was further complicated by emergency orders from the warehouses, which required prompt filling to keep customers satisfied and to minimize lost sales.

Box 20.1

The linear decision rule does not attempt to solve all of these detailed problems; rather it is a mathematical model to control the planning of aggregate factory operations, with the detailed allocation of capacity to particular products as a subsequent problem. The model takes into account the costs of regular payroll, overtime, finished goods inventory at the factory warehouse, backorders, hiring, and layoffs. The two resultant decision rules specify the changes that must be made in aggregate size of the work force and production so as to provide "optimum" costs for a planning horizon taking into account the present inventory position, number of employees, and forecasted demands on the factory.

The word "optimum" is in quotation marks because of approximations made in fitting cost functions similar to those presented as Figs. 20.1, 20.2, and 20.3. Essentially, the methodology is to approximate cost functions with linear and quadratic equations which can be solved by techniques of differential calculus to yield a set of linear decision rules. Figure 20.4 depicts the four cost components and quadratic approximations for the paint company example. Let us now examine these cost relationships and the resultant capacity rules in more detail.

Cost Data

The regular payroll cost function given in Fig. 20.4 (a) is a linear relationship with a fixed and variable component. Derivation of this function by simple linear regression methods is a straightforward analytical operation. Since the fixed portion is nonincremental to capacity planning decisions, it can be ignored. The resultant regular payroll cost function is a multiple of the work force W in each period (month). For the paint company example, the following relationship was established:

$$\text{Regular Payroll Cost} = 340 \ W_t$$

where \$340 is the average monthly cost of each regular production worker who would be added or deleted from the work force and W_t is the total work force in the month.

The cost component shown in Fig. 20.4 (b), the cost of hiring and firing, is minimized (zero) when no change takes place, and increases more rapidly for workers laid off than for workers hired. The asymmetry in the

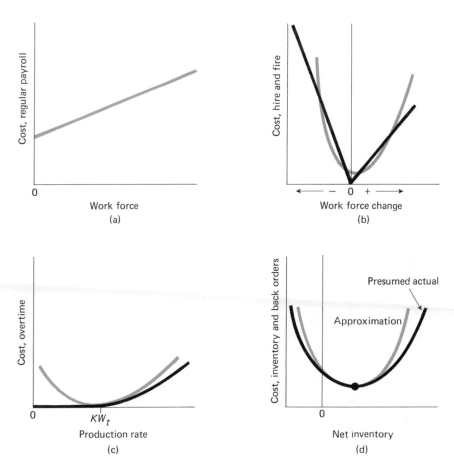

Fig. 20.4 Linear decision rule (monthly costs). Presumed actual costs are shown in black; approximation is shown in gray.

cost function can be handled with the addition of a cost constant which Holt, Muth, Modigliani, and Simon say is irrelevant in obtaining optimal decisions. The black presumed actual cost line is only approximated by the quadratic function; however, in some ways the quadratic approximation has more intuitive appeal. The thought that each additional person added to or deleted from the labor force incurs a higher cost is somewhat more pleasing than a linear relationship. For the paint company example the approximating function was:

$$\text{Hire and fire cost} = 64.3\,(W_t - W_{t-1})^2,$$

where W_t is the work force to be established for t^{th} month, and W_{t-1} is the work force in the prior month. If $W_t - W_{t-1} > 0$, the decision rules have resulted in hiring; if $W_t - W_{t-1} < 0$, we are going to lay off some workers.

The squaring of the difference between work force in one month and work force in the previous month reflects the steadily increasing cost of making changes, and the coefficient of 64.3 indicates the best fit for converting squared differences in work force into out-of-pocket costs.

The third cost function depicted, Fig. 20.4 (c), is the cost of overtime production. The presumed actual cost of overtime is zero until production reaches some point KW_t; thereafter an overtime premium rate (nonlinear) is paid. The nonlinearity is conceptually appealing since initially, only a few bottleneck operations will have to work overtime to increase total output; later, overtime may involve use of Sunday and other double-time pay periods. The approximation that perhaps is most tenuous in Fig. 20.4 (c) is the quadratic cost segment for rates of production less than KW_t. Again, however, we can find possible intuitive appeal; perhaps inefficiency losses are magnified as workers react to laxity in productivity standards.

The treatment of undertime cost involves both the regular payroll cost function and the overtime cost function. Rather than treat undertime and overtime in a combined cost function as we did in Fig. 20.1, Holt, Muth, Modigliani, and Simon account for undertime by having workers on the payroll who are not producing. That is, if the possible regular time productivity from each worker is some constant K, then the monthly production rate P must be less than or equal to KW_t without use of overtime. If $P > KW_t$, then overtime must be used. When $P < KW_t$, unused labor capacity exists which although not shown as a cost in Table 20.4 (c), nonetheless is a cost in Table 20.4 (a).

For the paint company, the following overtime production cost function was established:

$$\text{Overtime cost} = 0.2\,(P_t - 5.67\,W_t)^2 + 51.2\,P_t - 281\,W_t,$$

where W_t is again the work force for the tth month, and P_t is the aggregate monthly production in gallons (a pseudounit used to disguise the actual paint company data). The expression $(P_t - 5.67\,W_t)$ indicates the extent of variations in production away from a norm for the existing labor force; that is, the coefficient 5.67 for W_t is essentially the productivity constant K described above. When the desired production rate $P_t > 5.67\,W_t$ then overtime must be used. When the desired production $P_t < 5.67\,W_t$, then inefficiencies are incurred above and beyond those of unused labor capacity. The symmetry of the quadratic approximation implies that these inefficiency costs are similar in magnitude to these associated with overtime production. Once again, the result of the difference is squared, and the multiplication by 0.2 indicates the cost weighting. The authors state that the final portion of the overtime cost expression, $+51.2$ $P_t - 281\,W_t$ is added to improve the approximation and has no separate intuitive meaning (note, however, that the ratio of the coefficients is similar to the productivity constant).

The cost segment depicted in Fig. 20.4 (d), the cost of inventory and backordering, is based upon the differences in planned inventory at the end of the tth month, I_t, and some "ideal" inventory level, I. For the paint company example, the cost function is:

$$\text{Inventory} + \text{Backorder cost} = 0.0825 \, (I_t - 320)^2,$$

where 320 pseudo gallons represents the ideal inventory in terms of customer service—carrying cost tradeoffs, etc.

The total cost for each month, C_t, is made up of the above four cost components:

$$C_t = 340 W_t + 64.3 \, (W_t - W_{t-1})^2 + 0.2 \, (P_t - 5.67 W_t)^2$$
$$+ 51.2 P_t - 281 W_t + 0.0825 \, (I_t - 320)^2.$$

The Paint Company Rules

The problem is to find the P_t's and W_t's over a planning horizon so that the sum of the C_t's is minimized. We also have an inventory constraint: I_t must be equal to I_{t-1} plus $P_t - O_t$ (the orders or sales in the tth month). Analytic solution for the paint company problem was obtained through calculus. The following two rules were derived for production rate, P_t, and work force level, W_t:*

$$P_t = \left\{ \begin{array}{l} + \; 0.458 \; O_t \\ + \; 0.233 \; O_{t+1} \\ + \; 0.111 \; O_{t+2} \\ + \; 0.046 \; O_{t+3} \\ + \; 0.014 \; O_{t+4} \\ - \; 0.001 \; O_{t+5} \\ -0.007 \; O_{t+6} \\ - \; 0.008 \; O_{t+7} \\ - \; 0.008 \; O_{t+8} \\ - \; 0.007 \; O_{t+9} \\ - \; 0.005 \; O_{t+10} \\ - \; 0.004 \; O_{t+11} \end{array} \right\} + 1.005 \, W_{t-1} \; + \; 153.0 \; - \; 0.464 \, I_{t-1}$$

$$W_t = 0.742 W_{t-1} + 2.00 - 0.010 I_{t-1} + \left\{ \begin{array}{l} + \; 0.0101 \; O_t \\ + \; 0.0088 \; O_{t+1} \\ + \; 0.0071 \; O_{t+2} \\ + \; 0.0053 \; O_{t+3} \\ + \; 0.0042 \; O_{t+4} \\ + \; 0.0031 \; O_{t+5} \\ + \; 0.0022 \; O_{t+6} \\ + \; 0.0016 \; O_{t+7} \\ + \; 0.0011 \; O_{t+8} \\ + \; 0.0008 \; O_{t+9} \\ + \; 0.0005 \; O_{t+10} \\ + \; 0.0004 \; O_{t+11} \end{array} \right.$$

*Coefficients for the decision rules given in the *Management Science* articles are slightly different from those in *Planning Production, Inventories and Work Force*, given here.

The first part of the production equation, P_t is made up of the influences of demand forecasts over the entire planning horizon. Note that the intention is to produce 45.8% of the expected demand for the current period, plus 23.3% of the expected demand for the next period, etc. The most interesting aspect of the demand treatment in setting production rates is the rate at which future period demand influences decrease. Thus, although the current period demand is weighted by 45.8%, the weight given expected demand for the next period falls off by about 1/2, and that rate of decline is approximately the same for two additional periods; after that point, we find the coefficients becoming quite small, although any intuitive appeal of negative values for months $t + 5$ to $t + 11$ is difficult to derive. Essentially, the rule tells us that present production levels are not sensitive to demand estimates more than three or four months ahead. The reason for this insensitivity is undoubtedly related to the tradeoff between costs for varying production and inventory carrying cost; this tradeoff defines the extent to which it is economical to carry present production forward to meet expected demands of subsequent periods.

The next term in the production equation ($1.005\ W_{t-1}$) is a weight given to work force size in the previous period. The coefficient is essentially unity. Since the final result of the production equation is expressed in gallons and W_t is in workers, it is helpful to recall the productivity constant of 5.67 for converting workers into gallons. This statistic means that the magnitude of the W_t's will be about 17.6% of the magnitude of the P_t's ($1.005 \div 5.67 = 0.176$). The sum of coefficients derived for future orders is 0.821; the addition of 0.176 yields 99.7% which is intuitively appealing (weighting 0.176 by 1.005 instead of 1.0 yields 99.8%).

The last two terms in the production equation are best considered together, since they describe the inventory adjustment process. If inventory at the end of the prior month is low, then the influence of subtracting 46.4% of this inventory from 153 units will cause an upward inventory adjustment. The same reasoning will decrease production when inventory levels exceed 330 (46.4% of 330 $\not\approx$ 153). The 46.4% rate at which inventories in excess of 330 pseudo gallons will decrease production rates has particular significance in showing how forecast errors will be reflected in setting production levels, since these errors are directly reflected in the closing inventory for the prior month, I_{t-1}.

The work force decision rule, W_t, starts with a strong indication of stability. The first term ($0.742\ W_{t-1}$) indicates that as a starting condition we want to stay about 75% the same as last period. The next two terms are the inventory adjustment as it influences work force determination. The pivotal point for upward or downward adjustments is 2.00 men (or equivalently 10.34 gallons), but it is interesting to note that the adjustment rate of 0.010 implies that only 5.67% of inventory imbalance will be used to influence the work force level instead of the 46.4% rate used for production.

The influence of forecasted future monthly demands is also considerably smaller for work force determination than for production rate setting. Note that the largest single coefficient is just over 1%. The sum of coefficients is only 0.0452. After converting the gallons into workers, we see that the role of future sales is only 25.6% as opposed to 82.1% for production. The rate of decrease in weights, however, is not nearly as sharp as that for production. It would seem that long-term needs are more relevant in work force level setting or conversely that short-term needs are more readily satisfied through adjustments in production (overtime-undertime).

It should be clear that the two rules interact. Both rules make inventory adjustments, and treat forecasted sales in different ways. Moreover, the output of the W_t equation becomes a direct input to the P_t equation.

The general reaction of the rules will be for W_t to be much less responsive to change than P_t. In order for substantial changes in work force levels to occur, there will have to be a long-term movement in capacity needs. Short-term needs and demand fluctuations are much more likely to be satisfied through overtime-undertime adjustments in P_t. That is, each month as the rule is applied to the following 12-month planning horizon, deviation from optimal conditions brought about by forecast errors and revised short-term forecasts will be largely compensated for by changes in the effective workweek.

Results

Holt, Modigliani, Muth, and Simon were anxious to test their set of linear decision rules against company performance. Since the rules work on a 12-month planning horizon; it was necessary to have monthly forecast data for the test. As prior company forecasts did not exist, the researchers worked with two alternative schemes, a simple moving average and a perfect forecast based on the actual data. The thought was that these two methods would give a range within which most forecasting schemes would perform.

The linear decision rules, based upon moving average forecasting, performed about 8% better than actual company performance over a three-year period. The same linear decision rules with perfect forecasts were an additional 5% better than moving average forecasting. One conclusion the authors drew was that expenditures for a sophisticated forecasting scheme might be a good investment.

Another cost comparison for the paint company involved use of the linear decision rules for a five-year period, but this time span included the Korean War and a recession. The authors concluded that the anomalies associated with these extreme conditions (e.g., appropriate backorder costs for war material) make cost comparisons for the more normal business operation more significant. The cost savings for the entire five-year period were approximately 29% with moving average forecasting and an additional 10% with perfect forecasts. Analysis of these cost savings, however, leads to the conclusion that the savings were entirely due to backorder costs.

The three-year cost comparison is presented as Table 20.4.* Note that in this case the cost savings are spread between categories. The major savings seem to be in regular payroll and backorders, with these savings being partially achieved through modest overtime and inventory costs.

Table 20.4 Paint company cost comparisons ($000) 1952–1954

Cost category	Company performance	Linear decision rules (moving average forecasts)
Regular payroll	$1256	$1149
Overtime	82	95
Inventory	273	298
Backorders	326	246
Hiring and firing	16	12
Total	$1953	$1800
%	100.0	92.2

It is important to note that the cost calculations were not based upon the quadratic approximations; rather, to whatever extent possible they were based upon the "exact" cost structure. In our evolving understanding of operations management problems, we have attempted to instill a healthy skepticism of cost measurements. It is tempting to believe that the 8% improvement shown for the paint company might be entirely due to poor cost estimations, but the authors present a convincing rebuttal which is presented as Box 20.2†

The authors conclude that the 8% saving based upon a simple forecasting scheme and the additional 5% potential from improved forecasting are reasonable estimates. They correctly point out that although the percentages may appear to be small, the bases are large, including such major expenses as total factory payroll. Perhaps even more importantly,

---

*Charles C. Holt, Franco Modigliani, and Herbert A. Simon, "A Linear Decision Rule for Production and Employment Scheduling," *Management Science,* **2,** no. 1 (October 1955): 28.

†Charles C. Holt, Franco Modigliani, John F. Muth, and Herbert A. Simon, *Planning Production, Inventories and Word Force, op. cit.,* pp. 24–25.

It may be objected that our estimates of the factory cost structure might be in error, so that the factory performance is being judged by an erroneous criterion. Such errors are possible, but it should be remembered that the decision rule is designed to minimize a given cost function. If the cost estimates were changed, the costing of factory performance would be different, but also a new decision rule would be calculated—the decision behavior of which would be different. Consequently, if in the cost structure changes were made that would reduce the estimated cost of the factory performance, the estimate would then have to be compared with the cost performance of a decision rule changed to be optimal under the new cost function.

Box 20.2

the authors conclude that the routine application of a set of carefully derived rules will perform significantly better than judgmental methods used by operating managers—explicit models are better than "black cigar models."

The conclusions tend to be bolstered by similar studies in other applications. In particular, three MIT masters' theses apply the methodology to an ice cream company, a chocolate company, and a candy company. In these three applications the moving average forecasting technique improved performance by 0.5%, 3.3%, and 8.0% respectively; using a perfect forecast increased the expected savings to 5.4%, 5.3%, and 11.5% respectively.

Of special interest in evaluating any model is the extent to which robust decisions are produced; that is, decisions that tend to be insensitive to minor changes in the environment and to minor changes in input parameters. Holt, Modigliani, Muth, and Simon perform sensitivity analyses on the cost relationships used in the linear decision rule and conclude that large errors lead to relatively small differences in the decisions. In some later research, however, it is concluded that changes in the statistic depicting worker productivity can lead to important changes in expected results.*

Implementation

The amount of effort required to calculate work force and production levels with the linear decision rule model is quite modest, well within the capabilities of clerical workers with desk calculating equipment. The use of a computer potentially allows for extensions, for more detailed analyses, and for better interaction between users and the models. The real

---

*C. Van De Panne and P. Josje, "Sensitivity Analysis of Cost Coefficient Estimates: The Case of Linear Decision Rules for Employment and Production," *Management Science,* **9,** no. 1 (October 1962): 82–107.

issue, however, is whether the users can understand the model enough to believe in it, and whether the decisions addressed by the model are those made by the users.

Results of the investigation and linear decision rules were presented to the paint company managers. The policies were supposedly adopted, and the linear decision rule took its place among models that have led to implementable changes in actual company operations.

A few years later, however, a different research team returned to the paint company to make an assessment. Buffa presents the following revealing quotation from Gordon's Ph.D. dissertation:*

After considerable study and investigation it became apparent that although top management thought the rules were being used to determine aggregate production and work force, a more intuitive and long-standing system was in fact being used. The production control clerk whose responsibility it was to calculate the production and work force sizes, as well as convert these into item orders, was doing just that and posting the results in the form of job tickets on the production control board. When the foremen came into the production control office for a job ticket, they surveyed the available tickets for one that agreed with their intuitive feeling or judgment. If they found one they took it but if they did not they simply wrote out a ticket which corresponded with their feeling. Over the history of the use of the rules it turned out that about 50 percent of the tickets were used and the others ignored. Management, however, had the feeling that the rules were being used except in the odd case when judgment indicated that they should be overruled. At a later date the calculations associated with the rules were centralized with the installation of a data processing center. The personnel in the center became concerned when their reports indicated that many of the production orders that they had issued were ignored. Consequently, and with the compliance of higher management, they instituted a reporting system which fed back to the plant management, and the foremen, a cumulative listing of outstanding production orders. After a short delay the length of this cumulative list began to diminish until it all but vanished. But in the meantime the inventory of finished goods associated with this plant rose steadily to alarming proportions, especially in some obsolete items. Further investigation revealed that although the rules were indicating the size of the work force, no action was ever taken to reduce the work force because it was against the policy of the company. This meant that the work force rule was indicating a reduction in the work force; the production rule, attempting to minimize costs given the present work force level but anticipating layoff, called for some production for the excess work force. The rules are interactive, but in this case the interaction had been eliminated.

Box 20.3

---

*Gordon, J.R.M. "A Multi-Model Analysis of an Aggregate Scheduling Decision," Unpublished Ph.D. dissertation, Sloan School of Management, M.I.T., 1966; published in Elwood S. Buffa, *Production-Inventory Systems: Planning and Control*, Richard D. Irwin, 1968, pp. 168–69.

Once again, we see the pervasiveness of the user-designer concept where it is essential for those who use the model results to understand the methodology and for the methodology to adequately reflect the proper criteria set; evolution in both user needs and modeling mechanisms is quite natural but if not closely coordinated the inevitable result seems to be a credibility gap. We will pay particular attention to this when we return to the design of a model for aggregate planning for Baumritter.

Other Models

Additional explicit models exist for the aggregate capacity planning problem but a detailed exposition is beyond our present scope. The problem has been formulated in both distribution and simplex forms of linear programming, with the simplex methodology inherently more adaptable to the complexity of aggregate planning problems. The linear programming formulation also provides an optimal solution (assuming linear costs), and is based upon the same underlying cost phenomena and decision alternatives as the linear decision rule model. The major difference between the two approaches is in the quadratic versus linear cost approximations. It would seem that there are some situations where one model will more closely reflect the actual situation than the other, but my frank opinion is that all of the models are of far more interest to professors than to businessmen.

In both the linear decision rule and the linear-programming approaches to aggregate capacity planning, one of the most important features is a consistent set of decision rules which will be followed, period-by-period, rather than an approach where recent perturbations cause overreactions. An interesting approach to the development of a consistent set of decision rules, suggested by Bowman, capitalizes on the benefits of consistency.* Essentially, Bowman uses regression analysis based upon actual management decisions to estimate the implied "optimal" coefficients that should be used in the weighting of expected sales over the planning horizon, changes in production levels, and desired inventories. The underlying basis for this approach is that managers may be quite aware of both appropriate criteria and system variables which affect those criteria, that the decisions made by managers reflect this awareness, that the imperfections in the decisions will be more erratic than biased, and that decision rules based upon the average or mean coefficients of managerial past decision making will be better than the actual decisions made. When this approach (Management Coefficients Theory) is applied to the paint, ice cream, chocolate, and candy companies, results are achieved that are generally supportive. Two additional strengths of this approach are that noncost criteria can be accommodated

---

*E. H. Bowman, "Consistency and Optimality in Managerial Decision Making," *Management Science*, **4**, no. 1 (January 1963): 310–21.

and that its inherent flattery of managerial behavior may permit easier implementation. On the other hand, the assumptions may be invalid, poor performance perpetuated, and intuitive appeal for the derived coefficients hard to justify.

Still another approach to the aggregate capacity planning problem is the use of computer search techniques. A model developed by Jones is called Parametric Production Planning and another by Taubert and Buffa used a similar approach to find "good," not optimal, solutions to the aggregate capacity planning problem. One major advantage of computer search methodologies is that no constraining assumptions need be placed upon the form of the cost functions. Another is that the underlying analysis seems inherently easier for operating managers to understand. The search models seem to achieve good results, with results superior to those obtained through linear decision rule or linear programming becoming more likely as linear and/or quadratic approximations lose validity.

Extensions

A number of model extensions for the aggregate capacity planning problem have appeared in the literature. Two recent extensions are for multi-item planning* and for the inclusion of shipments as a decision alternative.† The Bergstrom and Smith paper considers the case of capacity planning for major item groups instead of in terms of one aggregate measure of productive output. One of the most interesting features of the analysis is an extension into marketing as well as production-oriented criteria. The combined criteria set no longer takes orders as a given, but recognizes the interdependencies of sales and productive capacities. We will find this broadening of horizons and disaggregation particularly useful in considering the proper modeling environment for Baumritter.

Similarly the Rein paper essentially relaxes the assumption that the ordering pattern received by a manufacturer must be taken as a given. Instead, the model allows for shipping decisions to be different from order or sales patterns. Although somewhat academic, the paper attempts to isolate cost savings that could be generated from smoothing production, and a system of pricing that would pass a portion of the savings along to customers as a partial incentive to tolerate deviations between shipments and orders. The two comments on the paper are critical of the ability to derive a pricing system and the possibility of the smoothing mechanism

---

*Gary L. Bergstrom and Barnard E. Smith, "Multi-Item Production Planning—An Extension of the HMMS Rules," *Management Science,* **16,** no. 10 (June 1970): B614–B629.

†Rein Peterson, "Optimal Smoothing of Shipments in Response to Orders," *Management Science,* **17,** no. 9 (May 1971): 597–607. Also, see Comments on this paper in the same issue by Samuel Eilon and by Charles C. Holt.

leading to a gaming environment between the manufacturer and his customers (e.g., a distributer who needs 100 units orders 150 in the peak period to get 100 at a lower price).

The most appealing aspect of this paper is the notion of considering shipments as a decision alternative. In his comment Holt points out that many firms tend to absorb sales fluctuations more by backorders than by inventories. We also know that some manufacturers (e.g., auto makers) "load" their dealers; that is, they ship more than ordered. We will see how the consideration of shipping as a decision alternative is important to Baumritter. We will also see in Chapter 21 how a manufacturer who controls the distribution system can achieve important economies in his overall operation.

THE MODELING ENVIRONMENT

In most of the chapters of this book, we have concerned ourselves with the application of modeling power and the kind of modeling environment which facilitates and fosters both use and evolution in the models. All of those general ideas apply to the establishment of model building for aggregate capacity planning. However, the aggregate capacity-planning problem exists at different levels of aggregation, and for differing time horizons; as a result, we will find individuals with different orientations addressing various aspects of what we have generally called aggregate capacity planning. It will be necessary to have a congruent set of models which attack problems in ways that the individuals involved find compatible with their own understanding and approaches to the problems.

Use

In order to understand the modeling environment that would be appropriate for any particular company or situation, it is necessary to identify the users. Specifically, which individuals are concerned with aggregate capacity planning? How do they see the aggregate capacity planning problems? What is their planning horizon? level of aggregation? What decisions do they make? Who else in the organization is concerned with this problem? Who is presently not concerned with this problem but needs to be? What are the relationships among the approaches used by these individuals? What should they be? Where should we start?

The answer to the last question is probably going to be provided as it was in the Westfall example described in Chapter 19. That is, the place to start will be based upon the location of an individual who perceives that he personally has a problem and that a model-building approach might be useful—we need our shill or "twenty-first century first class man." This individual could come from almost anywhere in the organization, but it is the author's belief that he is more likely to be found at a higher level in the organization than the major assembly scheduling user. The aggregate capacity planning man must of necessity have a horizon longer than that typically possessed by factory managers. He is an individual concerned with design of the overall production function, who can see the interactions among components of the production function. He is the man whose thinking and criteria are not as oriented to day-to-day operations as they are to medium-to-long range problems, to the design of solutions to recurring problems rather than reaction to current problems, and to issues that transcend departmental and functional boundaries.

In one sense, aggregate capacity planning is a process properly carried out by the board of directors. They can and do consider decisions for major additions or deletions from productive capacity. They also approve major expenditures for research and development which can strongly influence the nature of the production conversion process, both in terms of the items which the production function will be asked to produce and in terms of the methods of production or conversion themselves. Although research and development decisions involve substantial uncertainties, they nevertheless involve decisions that frequently have important capacity ramifications. Thus for example, the decision by American Telephone and Telegraph to invest in automatic dialing equipment well might have noted that the growth in the United States telephone usage would soon require that the entire female work force in the United States be employed as telephone operators.

As the decisions become less esoteric, the need for some kind of explicit model building for board-of-director-type questions becomes more apparent. The lead times and capital investments involved in making major changes in productive capacity will require that needs be carefully anticipated and that investments generate returns as soon as possible. The availability of additional capacity implies marketing and promotional efforts so that it can be utilized.

Many changes in productive capacity require major new sources of capital. It is necessary to coordinate these plans with stock and bond market conditions, and for a company to go after new capital at a time when its financial picture permits favorable terms on capital acquisitions. Thus we can see that some kinds of aggregate planning necessarily involve top executives and boards of directors; these decisions tend to be at a gross level of aggregation, for long planning horizons, and interfunctional.

At a more detailed level of aggregation and a shorter planning horizon, we find the vice-president of manufacturing with an interest in design of additional capacity, the vice-president of marketing with an interest in matching market and productive potentials, and perhaps the vice-president of finance who is necessarily concerned with intermediate range sources and uses of funds and the company's capital budgeting process. The vice-president of manufacturing would also coordinate activities among factories, making decisions as to which products should be manufactured in which factories and the overall extent to which each factory should be utilized (e.g., which factories should be more aggressively attempting to increase their work force or which factories should be not replacing workers who leave through natural attrition).

The Baumritter Environment

We started this chapter with a rather general description of the Baumritter capacity-planning problem. We then took a more detailed look at the best-known explicit model for aggregate capacity planning, at some extensions of the linear decision rule, at some alternative problem formulations, at the all too familiar kinds of implementation problems we have seen in other problem areas, and at the kinds of users who might be interested in capacity planning. Let us now attempt to pull some of these ideas together into a cohesive understanding of issues pertinent to a Baumritter aggregate capacity-planning model.

The initial Baumritter user of an aggregate capacity planning model will be the vice-president in charge of manufacturing. There is little doubt, however, that when feasible results start coming from the model some other key managers within the Baumritter organization will become involved. One of these key managerial personnel is the executive vice-president; this individual has had long experience in the manufacturing function, and has great intuitive (not explicit) understanding of the criteria set. There are at least two individuals from the marketing function who well might become actively involved in certain key issues of capacity planning, particularly in assessing the applied costs of backlogs, extensions in lead times, and influences of special promotional sales.

Another key managerial input will of necessity be financial. The linear decision rule and alternative aggregate capacity planning models discussed earlier in this chapter tend to have an orientation toward the production function in the face of a recurring seasonal demand pattern. Although Baumritter confronts this problem, there is also a strong trend in demand which is superimposed upon the seasonal pattern. The net result is that the solution to last year's problem well may not be appropriate to this year's problem; major periodic additions to capacity will be required and those changes will involve financial commitments that will be the concern of the company president.

The aggregate capacity plan will also be of interest to individual plant managers, since it will be necessary to breakdown the rather nebulous concept of aggregate capacity into capacity at each plant and further into capacities for major product groups. The prior work done in major assembly scheduling will foster a level of aggregation that seems quite natural; it should also permit a feedback on actual results so that the paint company experience is less likely to be duplicated at Baumritter.

The Baumritter aggregate capacity-planning problem, therefore, will eventually involve several individuals, each with a somewhat different orientation or criteria set. The initial user, and perhaps the man who will remain the central user, appears to be the vice-president of manufacturing. It is necessary that the initial model facilitate *his* approach to the problem and be in tune with capacity decisions he makes, yet at the same time be potentially expandable to include other important inputs.

Baumritter's vice-president of manufacturing has an undergraduate engineering degree, is acquainted with computers (but is by no means a computer "expert"), has studied the production planning and inventory control literature, is overseeing the design of Baumritter's total operating system, and is well aware of his own personal need for some means of planning capacity. In going through the aggregate capacity planning literature, however, he has always had the feeling that the models were academic and not particularly pertinent to his problems. Further probing of this uneasiness led to the identification of three related problem areas. First, he feels distinctly at sea about the cost relationships; not only does he not know the cost to hire and fire and employee, he doesn't really know how one might go about trying to properly identify such a cost. A related issue pertains to the reliability of such cost estimates. That is, how sensitive are the final capacity plans to variability and estimates of nebulous concepts such as the economic value of retaining employees not needed for current productive needs?

The second major "hangup" with the aggregate capacity planning models described in the literature turns out to be a lack of appreciation for capacity analyses based solely upon the criterion of manufacturing cost minimization. There is the uneasy feeling that even within the manufacturing function there are other important criteria above and beyond those identified in the linear decision rule. When one goes beyond the manufacturing function, noncost criteria become even more evident. Two examples of important criteria for Baumritter were presented in our earlier discussion of extensions to the linear decision rules. One was the notion of considering shipments as a decision variable. The vice-president in charge of manufacturing at Baumritter has never found the idea of backlog as negative inventory to be netted against positive inventory a comforting one. Baumritter can and does deviate shipments from orders for a myriad of reasons. Moreover, the orders coming in one time period represent shipments in a later time period, and the delay is more than a simple offset; at a minimum the offset time varies as a function of total backlog position.

The third problem comes back again to the level of aggregation. The concept of a global capacity measure simply does not lead to decisions that are like those presently made. Capacity changes are decided for individual factories, with differing cost structures, in fairly large "chunks," for particular categories of product. The decisions are at the level of major assembly scheduling, and use information from that system as an important input.

The Baumritter Model

The author and some students built a prototype capacity planning model for Baumritter which is currently being installed by the company. The model is relatively straightforward, is in agreement with the kinds of decisions presently made by users, and builds upon the successful major assembly scheduling model.

Basically, the model is major assembly scheduling (with the same criteria for loading items onto lines), on a monthly basis, for three years into the future. The outputs are a month-by-month report of "priority," inventory, backlog, and net inventory for each line and for each factory. The priority is the month of sales being produced during the month of production. For example, on line 6, in Factory 3, in month 14, we are producing merchandise that was sold in month 9; we are 5 months behind on capacity for that line. Lines are summed by factory, but only for inventory, back-log, and net inventory since factory priorities seem to involve "apples and bananas." The summation by factory provides important upstream and downstream capacity requirement information, e.g., parts machining, dry kilns, finishing room warehouse space.

The two major decisions made by users of the model are changes in capacity of particular lines at particular times, and reassignments of items to major assembly lines at particular times. For example, a run of the model might indicate that the capacity for building occasional tables at Westfall will be insufficient for the products being made on that line in month 24. The productive hours of capacity might be changed by overtime, second shift, redesign of the method, additional line, etc. Or, some of these tables might be shifted to another plant with an occasional table line that is not as heavily loaded. Other decisions involve marketing, e.g., what items to put on market special in Year 3.

Capacity is defined in productive hours per week, which is the same measure used for major assembly scheduling. Changes in capacity come in chunks, and are decided by *Users* who know the ways in which outputs on the major assembly line can indeed be changed. In fact, one of the important questions is how to make such changes. If the vice-president of manufacturing anticipates a need for more occasional table capacity in two years, interesting issues include how and where to best achieve that added capacity, whether to overbuild, and strategic implications for factory specialization.

The data for the model include a three year marketing forecast by major product group, the present percentage of sales for each item within its major product group, monthly seasonal indices, hours of weekly capacity for each item, the times to assemble lot sizes of each item, and the sales price of each item.

The model breaks the annual group forecast down into a monthly item forecast with the seasonal indices and item percentages. Assembly lines are loaded to capacity for each month (weekly capacities are converted to monthly which reflect working days per month). As in major assembly scheduling the next lot of an item to be produced is that in the shortest inventory or largest backlog position. Mismatches between production capacity and sales result in inventories, backlogs, and priorities.

The process of generating monthly item forecasts for three years into the future by extrapolating present percentages will undoubtably lead to errors. These errors might be reduced by using exponential smoothing forecasting, but the summation of item exponential smoothing forecasts by product groups would very likely be more in error than marketing forecasts. Since our interest is in planning total capacity, we are more interested in product groups than in items. As the actual production times occur, exponential smoothing forecasts over shorter time horizons can be used to load the lines.

The benefits that Baumritter will derive from a well-designed capacity planning model can be substantial. In addition to the savings in production cost due to better tradeoffs of capacity alternatives, there are many important intangible benefits which accrue to proper consideration of aggregate planning issues. We have discussed some of these benefits above; however, perhaps the most fundamental benefit to the organization is an appreciation that managers gain for the importance of planning horizons, when decisions need to be made, the lead times that are required for different kinds of productive capacity changes, and the differences in the environment of a firm that plans for change rather than reacting to it.

In Chapter 19 we noted some fundamental benefits which accrued to the Baumritter organization from a more rational method of production planning and inventory control. The company experienced an evolution in the surrogate criteria used as well as in the drive toward further rationalization of the production function into a set of consistent integrated decision rules. We have every reason to expect that similar and even more fundamental methods will come from improved design of an aggregate capacity-planning system. The system presently being installed is not the last word, but by now you realize that nothing is the last word. As this system comes into use, we can and should expect attention to shift to longer run planning and even more fundamental issues affecting the company.

SUMMARY REMARKS

In this chapter we have once again expanded our evolving understanding of materials-flow systems. A properly designed aggregate capacity-planning system will provide key input data into a pull-oriented production planning and inventory control strategy. We have also seen how data provided from the pull-oriented production planning and inventory control strategy feeds back to capacity planning in important ways.

It is now appropriate to carry our understanding of materials-flow processes even further. Chapter 21 is devoted to the flow of materials beyond the stage of finished goods in factories. This consideration brings us to field and regional warehousing and the entire area of the business commonly referred to as physical distribution or logistics. It is in this area that the production and marketing functions come even more clearly together. We will also see that the logistics notion is once again related to a pull-oriented strategy; in Chapter 21 we will generalize the pull-orientation even further into the notion of control over one's destiny. We will see why manufacturing firms who control the physical distribution system can achieve important advantages. We will also see in Chapter 21 that our evolving definition of materials flow becomes even more difficult to understand without a well-constructed modeling environment. We will see that determination of physical distribution policies often runs counter to what might be suggested intuitively and that the ubiquitous aspects of feedback are particularly relevant in our models.

REFERENCES

Bowman, E. H., "Consistency and Optimality in Managerial Decision-Making," *Management Science* 4, no. 1 (Jan. 1963), pp. 310-21.

Buffa, Elwood S., and W. H. Taubert, *Production-Inventory Systems: Planning and Control,* Irwin, 1972.

Galbraith, Jay R., "Solving Production Smoothing Problems," *Management Science,* 15, no. 12 (Aug. 1969): 665-74.

Holt, Charles C., Franco Modigliani, John F. Muth, Herbert A. Simon, *Planning Production, Inventory, and Workforce,* Prentice-Hall, 1960.

Vollmann, Thomas E., "Capacity Planning: The Missing Link," *Production and Inventory Management* (in preparation).

CHAPTER REVIEW

Chapter 20 is somewhat difficult for many students to understand. The analytical derivation of the linear decision rule is really beyond our present scope, and deeper knowledge of alternative models such as computer search or management coefficients also involves more study than usually available in a survey course in operations management. For some of you the lack of more depth is more than welcome; however, the "accept the number on faith" approach is always upsetting.

In my opinion, it really isn't all that necessary for you to understand the linear decision rule and alternative models at the detailed level. What is necessary is to know that such models exist, to understand the basic problems to which they are devoted, to appreciate the general approaches utilized, to recognize some of their weaknesses, and to consider real world implementation issues.

OUTLINE OF THE CHAPTER

Introduction   (establishing capacities)

Aggregate capacity planning at   (frame of reference)
Baumritter

Total manufacturing capacity   (basic alternatives)

Alternative plans   (cost considerations)

Data requirements   (cost functions)

Planning individual factory capacity   (relation to major assembly scheduling)

The linear decision rule   (classic model)

The problem   (two decision rules)

Cost data   (payroll, hire & fire, overtime & inventory)

The paint company rules   (production rate and workforce)

Results   (5–8% cost savings)

Implementation   (model subverted)

Other models   (best approximation of underlying cost functions)

Extensions   (additional criteria)

The modeling environment   (user orientation)

Use   (level of aggregation)

The Baumritter environment   (pertinent criteria)

The Baumritter model   (production lines and items)

Summary remarks   (expanded analysis)

CENTRAL ISSUES

Capacity planning is a medium to long-range planning process. The results are typically used to plan capital expenditure programs for the addition of product or service creation capabilities. For Baumritter the process involves planning for additional factories, additions to factories, larger major assembly or machine center capabilities, building and depletion of seasonal inventories, and use of outside subcontractors.

The primary focus of the chapter is on the building and depletion of seasonal inventories. Production output levels must be established in light of expected needs over at least a one-year planning horizon. When the company is experiencing growth, it is often necessary to add capacity before it seems needed.

The linear decision rule is the best-known explicit model for aggregate capacity planning. The model utilizes actual data to estimate four cost functions: payroll or basic labor cost, additions or deletions to the labor force, use of overtime, and inventory and backorder costs. These four costs are approximated with quadratic functions, and minimization of the total cost function is derived through calculus. The result is a set of two decision rules which determine how much to produce and how many people to hire or fire based on present workforce levels, inventory levels, and forecasted orders.

The linear decision rule was developed from empirical research in a paint company. A subsequent observer, however, found that the decisions dictated by the model were being subverted in actual practice. The need for a user-oriented modeling environment had not been met.

A user-oriented model is proposed for Baumritter. The basic approach is similar to the existing major assembly scheduling model. The level of aggregation and implied decisions are in accord with the ways in which capacity changes are currently made.

It is worth noting that the model builds upon prior success in major assembly scheduling. This success is critical for three main reasons. First, realistic data have been produced (e.g. time estimates for assembly). Second, users believe in the data and the approach. Third, the systems approach has permitted a problem delineation which matches perceived user needs.

ASSIGNMENTS

1. Referring to the overall Baumritter example in the text of this chapter, several pure production strategies and one combination of strategies were costed out. See if you can improve upon these strategies in terms of minimizing cost.

2. Baumritter management has been considering its responsibility, as the major employer in several communities, for the economic well-being of the communities. They are attempting to not hire anyone who is not retained for at least three months. (Layoffs always start with the last hired.)

   In addition they have notified the planning staff that backorders up to one month may be tolerated but that a cost of $0.15 per direct labor hour will be assigned. Revise the production strategy in assignment 1.

3. The Ogallala Goggle Company, well-known manufacturer of skin diving equipment, is branching into ski goggles to smooth the peak in production requirements. Estimated monthly sales in units for the two products follow:

	Underwater (000)	Ski (000)	Work days
January	3	35	20
February	4	31	21
March	7	15	23
April	8	7	20
May	11	5	22
June	29	3	22
July	41	4	10
August	36	3	23
September	10	4	20
October	4	6	22
November	2	10	20
December	6	43	20

   The underwater goggles require 1.6 direct labor hours, the ski goggles require 0.9 direct labor hours. Develop a production plan for Ogallala.

4. Suppose that you are personnel director for the paint company and that you are carefully following the linear decision rule for work force determination.

   Imagine that it is the end of December and you are deliberating the size of the January work force. You know W_0, I_0, and have been given a forecast of demand by month. The problem is that the forecast of April orders, O_{t+3}, has been so poor in the past that no one has much faith in it anymore.

   By how many gallons may the April forecast vary without affecting work force by more than one man-month?

   How might you use this kind of information in evaluating your forecasting technique?

5. Mr. Silver, operations researcher, used the linear decision rule for Maxwell's Hammer Company. Mr. Silver's most difficult problem was in approximating hiring and layoff costs. These costs are shown in Fig. 20.5 (gray line) along with Mr. Silver's approximation (black line). What is the influence of this approximation on the work force rule and the cost of resulting policy?

Dollars

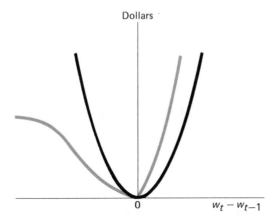

$$0 \qquad\qquad w_t - w_{t-1}$$

Fig. 20.5 Maxwell's Hammer Co., hiring and layoff cost.

6. Consider the problem of scheduling regular and overtime production for each of four future time periods so as to minimize the sum of employee regular time production cost, employee overtime production cost, and holding cost. All demands must be met (no backlogging).

Let:

D_t = number of units demanded in period t.
X_t = number of units produced during regular time in period t.
C_x = employee cost per unit for all goods produced during regular time.
U_t = maximum number of units which can be produced on regular time during period t.
O_t = number of units produced during overtime in period t.
C_o = cost per unit for all goods produced on overtime.
V_t = maximum number of units which can be produced on overtime in period t.
I_t = inventory on hand at the end of period t. $I_o = 0$.
h = holding cost per unit on all goods on hand at the end of any period.

State this problem as a linear programming problem.

7. Returning to assignment 14 in Chapter 19, suppose we add items 11 and 12 at the beginning of week 7 with inventories of –75 and –100, weekly sales of 40 and 50, lot sizes of 300 and 400, and assembly times per lot size of 110 and 150 hours.

a) Evaluate the capacity of the line for weeks 1–20.
b) Evaluate a change in line capacity to 60 hours at the beginning of week 15.
c) Evaluate the same change at week 10.

CHAPTER 21

LOGISTICS SYSTEMS

We conclude our major section on materials management systems by carrying our evolving understanding into the area of logistics. Logistics is the study of materials flow within the manufacturing function, reaching backward toward vendors to encompass activities within purchasing, and reaching forward to encompass physical distribution within the marketing function. However, logistics is more than the physical movement of goods, it is more importantly the study of the interrelationships among flow-oriented subsystems.

The design of logistics systems recognizes the interdependencies of materials-flow subsystems and the kinds of cost/benefit tradeoffs which can result from cooperative efforts. The result of a properly designed logistics system is a marked increase in a firm's control over its own destiny.

Study of logistics systems involves an interest in flows of information as well as in flows of material. We will be interested in models which incorporate information flows, and we will see how interactions between information and materials flows require a feedback orientation to the models. We will also see that solutions obtained from these models tend to run counter to intuition.

The implementation of counterintuitive model results necessitates a modeling environment where those affected by the results have actively participated. Substantial benefits from improved logistics systems seem possible, but they will not be achieved without a step by step evolutionary process involving the people who control existing materials flow subsystems.

THE TOTAL COST CONCEPT

The total cost concept is a valuable way of thinking about logistics problems. Essentially, the notion is that there are costs which accrue to various movement and conversion processes as materials flow from raw materials to final consumption, or perhaps in Baumritter's case from trees in the woods to babies chewing the legs off chairs. The goal is to minimize suboptimization costs associated with considering each conversion or movement stage independently. There clearly are cost tradeoffs between dependent stages which offer potential savings.

If the lumber vendor stacks wood carefully, better lumber utilization can result in manufacturing. If a finish mill operator handles parts carelessly to make greater incentive wages, he may do so at the cost of extra sanding. The establishment of field warehouses allows retailers to carry less inventory. Chemical treatment of upholstery fabrics permits increased product lives for consumers. Just as we have seen that inventory control cannot be considered independently of production planning, we will see that warehousing and transportation means are interrelated and that both of these activities interact with manufacturing criteria.

The obvious goal of the total cost concept is to achieve cooperative efforts among various stages in the production-distribution system; to establish surrogate criteria that are congruent with highest order goals of the firm. Total cost is the highest order cost criterion, to which all surrogate criteria must be evaluated. Further, there is no reason why the total cost concept cannot exist for material flows which cross enterprise boundaries.

Although the total cost concept is easy to state, it is less easy to see in particular instances. Moreover, what represents a good solution to one problem may not be appropriate for another. There is no one answer to all problems, nor indeed, a final answer to one particular problem. Improvement is always possible, it is dependent upon who "you" are and upon the functions or needs that are satisfied by the particular good or service used by the final consumer.

Logistics System Entities

The primary entities in a logistics system are the manufacturing firm, its vendors, vendors of the vendors, storage for purchased materials and components, storage associated with work in process, storage or warehousing of finished goods, various activities associated with movement of the product to the final consumer, and promotional-selling activities to encourage consumption of the product. The major surrogate criteria which lead to profitability are to perform conversion activities so that the final product satisfies consumer needs, to provide place utility by getting the product to the consumer, and to fulfill or satisfy the time requirements attendant to the particular product.

For almost all products, some of the logistic system entities are provided by different organizations. Most manufacturing firms are not large enough to economically produce all of their raw materials and component parts. Furthermore, some companies who might be economically able to justify backward integration into materials and components choose instead to concentrate on subsequent stages in the manufacturing-distribution process. Forward integration is equally difficult. If for no other reason, the location of manufacturing firms is often not in close proximity to their markets. Location and many other reasons usually cause a manufacturer to utilize the services of independent warehousing, wholesaling, and retailing firms.

Warehousing may or may not be within the domain of the manufacturing company or organization; the issue is often decided on the basis of volume requirements and/or physical proximity. The independent warehouse may be used solely for physical storage features or encompass customer and supplier linkages associated with wholesaling. The wholesaler fulfills two major functions, the mixing activity so evident in wholesale grocery operations and/or an economical means of exposing several products to many retailers. Retailing represents a similar mixing and exposure link with final consumers.

When the logistics system entities and their basic functions are identified, the interdependencies become obvious; moreover, the manufacturer's clear interest in the degree of expertise and economic well-being of the other system entities becomes apparent. Although perhaps not so obvious, each logistic system entity has a similar interest in the well-being of other system entities. Whether it be providing raw materials for the producer, converting components into finished products, transporting finished products into wholesale warehouses, or selling the product to the final consumer, any entity which performs the function of getting the proper product to the location where it is wanted at the time that it is wanted must be concerned with the other entities in the same system.

Criteria

The total cost concept implies a criterion: minimize the total cost or maximize the total benefit of the overall production-distribution system. The cost interrelationships and cost tradeoffs among different organizational units in the logistics system need to be coordinated to achieve the overall benefit. For example, if a trucking firm that delivers finished products to the wholesaler is unreliable, the wholesaler may be forced to react in one of two ways; carry a larger safety stock or tolerate a higher probability of stockouts. If the wholesaler increases safety stock, inventory carrying costs also increase. If he allows stockouts, retailer and consumer loyalties are affected. Moreover, retailer and consumer buying patterns result in problems for the manufacturer. He may be forced to deal with more wholesalers and retailers, increase his advertising expenditures, or have more goods in transit.

Independent actions on the part of any one stage in the logistics system have ramifications in other stages; these ramifications in turn lead to new reactions on the part of those stages which later lead to still further ramifications for other stages, corresponding reactions, ad infinitum. Because of the interdependencies and the feedbacks between various actions, it is often quite difficult to fully appreciate what system ramifications result from "corrective" actions.

To a great extent, the criteria associated with the total cost concept are well described by an old children's song which states "watch the doughnut, not the hole." We need to begin with an examination of the function or service that our product provides to the ultimate consumer. The logistics system includes both manufacturing and marketing, in as many separate firms as necessary. Although the total cost concept is the only major goal, the establishment of surrogate criteria for the evaluation of separate organizational activities can often detract from the common purpose, and coordination of efforts can be difficult to achieve.

Our functional analysis model can be usefully applied to logistics systems. Insightful answers are often obtained from asking questions such as, what is the inherent function provided by retailers to my product? What activities do these retailers perform that are directly in line with superior achievement of that function? What activities do they perform that are at cross-purposes to the basic objective? How can I as a manufacturer help them to do a better job? What activities can I more economically undertake? What activities are impossible for me to undertake? What policies do I now have which encourage retailers to act in accordance with their inherent function? What policies or actions am I now engaged in which inhibit retailers from achieving their function? If I owned the retail firms, what retail policies would I change? What manufacturing policies would I change?

Similar questions can be asked for any stage in the logistics system, and definitive or ultimate answers are difficult if not impossible to achieve. Even though ultimate answers are hard to come by, large improvements are still possible. This is clearly shown by the difference between retailing of Ethan Allen furniture and furniture retailing in general. Baumritter regards the retailer as the final link to the ultimate consumer, and the mission of the company to mass market interior decorating to the consumer rather than to sell furniture. A belief in individual entrepreneurship has led to a system of franchises rather than company ownership of retail outlets. A key feature of the franchise concept is an important division of labor between Baumritter and the franchisees. Baumritter regards its role as franchiser to invest in finding the best way to perform any marketing activity that can be transplanted from store to store. This is easily seen in the architectural design of showcase stores and in the use of highly skilled interior decorators for room plans, but the proper division of labor is even more important in some more subtle areas. Baumritter naturally feels that it can do a much better job of designing advertising copy and special promotions, but they also run a school for sales training. Each salesman is continually attempting to gain decorating expertise in order to help the consumer design her home properly. Baumritter provides franchisees with detailed step-by-step plans for how to open and run a business including market surveys, location studies, blueprints for the store itself, construction cost control, financial assistance, and performance-oriented accounting systems. In this way the franchisee is not required to devote significant time to nonfunctional activities. Rather, the franchisee can devote himself almost exclusively to his mission, consumer contact and the identification and satisfaction of basic customer needs.

It is worth noting that because many aspects of the retailing process have been designed by Baumritter as the franchiser, the attributes which make for a successful franchisee tend to be different from those possessed by the average furniture retailer. The cornerstone of the showcase store is the spirit of individual entrepreneurship. It is not unusual for showcase stores to produce sales dollars per square foot ratios triple those of other furniture stores and furniture sections in department stores. It is also not unusual for franchisees to earn $30,000 to $50,000 per year in their second year of operation.

In sharp contrast to the cooperative nature of Baumritter's franchised dealership are the typical furniture industry retail practices. The typical furniture retailer is very cost conscious and makes his major purchasing decisions at periodic furniture markets held throughout the country. The basis for a retailer's decision, once he has decided upon a general style, is made almost entirely upon price. By mixing items from different manufacturers he can get "almost" the same set of furniture that a particular manufacturer is showing that seems to have customer appeal. There are very few strong manufacturing brands within the industry, and retailers often remove manufacturers brands from the items. Their approach to selling is a move-it-out-the-door strategy based primarily on price. As a result, furniture retailing remains one of the few areas where significant "horse trading" exists. Physical distribution represents an appreciable cost component of the delivered price to the retailer. Most retailers request the lowest cost transportation means which tends to result in long lead times for furniture and poor customer service. Furniture retailers spend large portions of their time in negotiations with various manufacturers, they know little about sophisticated furniture displays, have little understanding of the ultimate consumer problems, and as a result don't do nearly as good a job of fulfilling their inherent function as do the Ethan Allen Showcase Store franchisees.

It is easy to look upon the Baumritter system of retailing in an after the fact way and agree with the choices made. However, some of those choices required considerable intestinal fortitude. In 1970 Baumritter decided to no longer sell Ethan Allen furniture through one of the largest department stores in New York City. This was Baumritter's largest single account, yet it was not possible for the sales personnel within the department store to understand the Baumritter consumer orientation to the degree deemed adequate by Baumritter management. Many executives talk a good story about the mission of their company, but the test always comes with the hard decisions.

Even though fundamental benefits require the kind of devotion to company mission illustrated above, there are still improvements that can be made in any logistics system through a better understanding of the ultimate mission and resultant changes in surrogate criteria. Tradeoffs between higher cost transportation methods and reduced damage or packaging costs are relatively easy to understand. Similarly, faster transportation methods can often decrease the number of warehouses required, and mixed modes of shipping (slow and cheap for the majority with fast and expensive for infrequently needed items) can result in inventory reductions at a specified level of customer service. More difficult and potentially more rewarding tradeoffs involve production and marketing criteria. Thus for example, cost pressures felt by retailers often lead to minimal inventories and rush delivery requests. In some cases sales on consignment can significantly reduce manufacturing rush orders as well as stimulate sales; if the retailer is loaded up with inventory he well may sell it.

The kinds of cost tradeoffs we have been discussing are not likely to be represented by hard data in the accounting system of a firm. However, soft as they are, the data are pertinent and should be estimated even while recognizing full well their lack of precision. As Forrester states, "there is no reason, except lack of courage on the part of the investigator, for omitting these concepts from our system representation."*

The importance of time in the design of logistics systems must be recognized. Time requirements of particular systems vary a great deal and the variation has a direct impact on the choice of system entities. If time were not important, firms could delay deliveries until the lowest cost means of transportation could be utilized. Although some furniture manufacturers tend to act like time is no problem, there is clearly a feedback influence upon repeat business and the general level of consumer interest in home furnishings. As noted in Chapter 15, for products such as life-

---

*Jay W. Forrester, "The Structure Underlying Management Processes," paper presented at the Academy of Management Meeting, Chicago, December 30, 1964, p. 10.

saving drugs or repair parts for expensive computers, the time between
need recognition and product delivery must be quite small; waiting costs
are high. For others, such as books in a bookstore the transit times associated with ordinary mail are usually sufficient and the provision for
telephone requests and air mail special delivery bring the times within
those required by the vast majority. This is not to say, however, that a
company shipping books should always use air mail special delivery; the
fact that most customer orders are known with much longer inherent lead
times makes a mixed mode of transportation very appealing, and even
faster transportation means may be appropriate for some needs.

Evolution

Throughout this book, we have talked about evolution in problem delineation and solution. The evolutionary context is terribly important for materials management or logistics systems, both because of the complex and
encompassing nature of the problem, and because of the complex and
encompassing criteria system which necessarily must be used to evaluate
these problems.

The concept of evolution is particularly important for logistics problems since there is virtually no such thing as the ultimate weapon; improvements are always possible and can usually only be seen or
understood sequentially. That is, each change in the logistics system
permits new ideas to be generated.

Because evolution is always possible and future improvements are
more easily identified after present improvements are implemented,
changes in logistics methods should be expected. It is important for a
company to not become wed to a particular logistics or physical distribution system; it is difficult to avoid, however, because individual prestige
is often at stake. Since implementation of a change often requires crusad-
ing on a very personal basis, proposed changes are often viewed quite
personally with a resultant impedance of the evolutionary process.

The kind of evolution possible in logistics systems is well illustrated
by Baumritter's experience. We have already noted how a view of the
distribution system which was not constrained to company owned facilities led to establishment of the New York metropolitan area warehouse
and additional regional warehouses in other parts of the country. Subsequent actions involved decisions as to which goods to hold in each warehouse, based largely upon customer service criteria. When decision rules
for this system began to cause orders for warehouse replenishments to be
given preference over orders for sold merchandise, a broader definition of
the problem began to emerge. The field warehousing system was conceived and implemented largely on the basis of marketing criteria. Maintaining field warehouse inventories had important implications for

manufacturing which fed back to marketing in several ways, but most immediately through the order acknowledgment system. The marketing function has no desire for regional warehouses per se; the interest is in customer service measured in terms of delivery time and reliability of delivery promises. Improvements in these measures of effectiveness intimately involve the manufacturing function. When the interdependencies of marketing and production criteria are better recognized, system design efforts should aim at developing a reliable and responsive production function that is congruent with more clearly understood marketing policies and fundamental objectives of the firm.

Although changes such as closing certain field warehouses have been implemented, much remains to be done. Physical distribution cost represents more than 20% of the final cost to the consumer. It is a potential source of saving which has been relatively unexploited in comparison with manufacturing activities. Some pertinent questions for Baumritter are whether all field warehouses should be condensed into two or three large field warehouses, whether a mixed mode transportation scheme and one large factory type warehouse could eliminate all regional warehousing, how much of the actual physical distribution should be accomplished by Baumritter owned facilities, and whether Baumritter should undertake responsibility for distribution to the final consumer. The latter possibility, although quite complex, opens up some new avenues for investigation; one of the more interesting being returnable packaging which could substantially reduce damage while simultaneously reducing unit packaging cost.

Other questions concern allocation of finished goods to regional warehouses, the amounts that should be held back for replenishment, the possibility of trans-shipments between warehouses, and the influence on appropriate solutions to all of these problems if reductions in manufacturing lead time can be achieved.

Transportation Technology

With two primary objectives of any physical distribution system being to provide time and place utility, it is essential to consider the various transportation methods for providing place utility and their associated times. The importance of transportation technology to proper design of a logistics system is hard to overemphasize.

In a societal sense, national wealth is strongly affected by transportation means and many less developed countries find that transportation systems represent one of the key investments for economic growth. The effects of transportation cost reductions can be profound since in some countries the transportation cost can be at least as much as the cost of production. Historically, the United States government has subsidized transportation means including the building of canals, railroads, highways, and airports; to this day, shipbuilding, railroads, trucks, and aircraft firms receive direct or indirect government subsidies. Governmental encouragement of transportation has often resulted in more effective transportation means; when the Erie Canal was opened, the cost of moving grain was reduced by 90%, and the C5A promises to cut the air cost per ton-mile by 25 to 50%.

Almost every firm needs to concern itself with transportation technology. The conclusion that air freight is only for extremely high value low weight items is often not true when a total cost and/or mixed mode transportation scheme are considered. Thus a Chicago meat packer shipped beef to California via air freight; high altitudes eliminated any need for refrigeration, in transit inventory was minimized, California safety stocks were eliminated, and a reduction in accounts receivable was experienced. In terms of mixed mode transportation, there are many companies that achieve customer service levels comparable to those obtained with field warehousing by using fast transportation methods instead of safety stocks.

Changes in transportation technology are affecting relative costs. In the 1960s the costs of truck transportation were in the range of five to ten cents per ton mile, but all indications are for these costs to increase. Air freight rates, on the other hand, were about ten to twenty cents per ton mile but should be decreasing as improved aircraft and ground handling systems are developed.

Although air freight is an exciting transportation mode, there are many other interesting developments in transportation technology and in ways to more effectively utilize transportation means. Water transportation remains one of the cheapest possible ways of moving material; even before the days of supertankers, the cost of transporting crude oil by ship was less than half that by pipelines, which in turn was only a fraction of the cost by railroad tank car. A specially designed ship which can transport fully loaded barges across the ocean serves to connect any town on the United States inland water system with most of the inland European cities.

Creative uses of existing transportation technology also can lead to substantial savings. A firm which mines a raw material in southern California and refines it in Iowa ships all of its ore cars via Seattle since the transportation cost is the same; the railroad ends up carrying the inventory (in more ways than one). Other firms cut cost through long term leases of ships and railroad cars and by figuring out very compatible backhaul deals (e.g., California rice to Puerto Rico and Puerto Rico phosphates to California).

A more imaginative use of transportation modes is something that almost every firm should consider; however, the viewpoint should not be limited to changes in the flow of materials from the factory warehouse out. Just as changes in production methods call for or permit changes in methods of physical distribution, changes in physical distribution can call for or permit changes in production. Moreover, all of these changes can have strong influences upon marketing and the competitive advantage of the firm. Let us now consider some of these issues.

Management Technology

Although changes in physical distribution methods sometimes lead to spectacular cost savings, many times the more important changes are in understanding of the basic material flows. It is necessary to be highly creative in defining the proper roles to be played by successive stages in the production-distribution chain and in generating important improvements in those roles. For example, some appliance manufacturers have found, as did Baumritter, that by increasing their own warehousing costs they can increase sales to more than offset the additional costs. Dealer inventories are reduced and effective customer service is increased to the point of providing a competitive advantage. Similarly, many companies who distribute through jobbers have found that these firms often make choices on inventory levels which inhibit sales and necessitate rush orders. Sales on consignment and other means for pushing inventory closer to the final consumer often yield substantial sales increases and decrease the need for highly reactive distribution systems.

One of the intriguing aspects of logistic systems study is that there is very little that can be generalized about problem solutions. Some involve more warehouses while others involve fewer warehouses. Some involve increased use of fast transportation methods while others decrease their use of fast transportation methods. Some facilitate larger inventories while others permit inventories to be reduced.

There are two basic reasons for disparity in logistic system problem solutions. First, if we apply our functional analysis model, we see that the inherent function fulfilled by a warehouse or other entity in the distribution system is quite different for differing firms and products. Second, we noted that evolution was always possible and that adding warehouses today well may create a situation where warehouses can be eliminated at a future date.

The role of the computer in logistic systems improvements is very large. The computer has allowed us to routinize segments of the logistics function and to examine the interactions between logistics subsystems, both actual and proposed. The central thrust of Chapters 17, 18, 19, and

20 has been to develop a set of computerized decision rules which when applied will yield production decisions superior to those made in isolation and by intuitive means. When the additional criteria connected with the logistics—total cost point of view are added, the set of decision rules becomes larger, and the intuitive appeal of individual rules becomes increasingly difficult to determine without a well-designed modeling environment.

Control

In Chapters 19 and 20 we described a pull-orientation to manufacturing based upon a strategy of effectively utilizing capital and manpower capacities. A logical extension of the pull strategy is the belief in control over one's destiny. The logistics system of a firm does not exist merely to satisfy some externally generated demand function. The entire logistics system including manufacturing capability exists to meet and to influence the demand for the firm's products. Sales are as strongly influenced by the way in which products are created as by the time and place utility of those products. It makes sense to influence sales in ways that are consistent with the most fundamental criteria of the firm.

When one views the kinds of advantages that can accrue from a well thought out logistics system or conversely the suboptimal behavior patterns caused by many existing systems, it is clear that large potential benefits are often possible. The primary cause of suboptization is due to the behavior patterns established by firms or portions of firms acting in what they think is their own individual interest. This is well illustrated by the furniture industry, and we have noted in several places how furniture retailers and manufacturers typically fail to recognize their mutual dependence. We have also pointed out how Baumritter's franchise concept goes a long way towards ameliorating those problems.

Baumritter, however, has not found the ultimate weapon; improvement possibilities will always exist. For example, at the time of this writing dealers are still able to specify transportation means. This policy can interfere with overall goals in several ways. Dealers may choose lower cost factory shipment when the desired item is in a nearby factory warehouse; the result can be a long wait in delivery to the final consumer and unnecessary expediated manufacture.

Distribution issues faced by Baumritter are quite similar to those facing firms in other industries. A critical variable in one's ability to deal with any of these problems is the extent of control exercised over the distribution system. A manufacturer who has his demand determined by a distribution system but has no control over inventory levels within that system is simply not in the same economic position as the firm which uses all inventories to decouple in ways suitable to the whole system. The notion of logistics carries with it the total cost concept including profit maximization for the production or conversion process as well as for the distribution system which provides the time and place utility. A manufacturer's control over his own destiny is directly related to his control over the distribution system.

Control does not necessarily imply ownership. Many firms do indeed achieve control over the distribution system through vertical integration. However, Baumritter's franchise system achieves the same objective without actual ownership. Even for firms that have looser ties to their subsequent distribution channels, there is considerable power or control over the actions of these firms that manufacturers can exercise.

A very appropriate form of analysis is to assume that complete control exists; this assumption allows the manufacturer to ask what policies on the part of subsequent stages in the distribution chain would he like to see. When such policies have been identified, the next question is what actions can the manufacturer take which will cause those policies to be implemented? Many times fairly straightforward answers come out of these questions. When the answer is that there is virtually no way to influence independent wholesalers or retailers to act in the manufacturer's interest, the benefits of vertical integration may justify the expenditure.

It is worth stating emphatically that control does not imply some Machiavellian game played by the manufacturer at the expense of wholesalers and retailers. Mutual benefit is the goal. The manufacturer potentially can better understand the interdependencies of the total system than can the wholesaler or retailer; moreover, many of the fundamental cost savings occur in the form of better utilization of manufacturing capacities. Part of the total cost concept is to recognize benefits, but another part is to divide them equitably.

Now let us consider a class of models which is particularly well suited to improved understanding of the firm's ability to control its destiny.

INDUSTRIAL DYNAMICS MODELS

The industrial dynamics view of the world is flow oriented; the models are made up of levels and rates where the levels are reservoirs, inventories, or queues of men, material, money, or information. Rates are essentially the sets of decision rules which indicate how flows go from level to level.

Industrial dynamics connotes much more than a form of model building. It is a philosophy or way of looking at real life situations that approaches being a religion. The most essential aspect of this philosophy is the feedback orientation which causes one to view all problems not as being caused by outside forces but, indeed, to continually ask what is it that insiders are doing to cause the problems. Jay Forrester describes the objective of industrial dynamics as "enterprise design." The fundamental idea is that a firm has control over its own destiny, that the problems it experiences are influenced by its own internal actions through complex feedback mechanisms, and that it is possible to redesign the set of decision rules within the control of the firm so as to achieve desired conditions.

To illustrate, if finished goods inventory were to increase, pressure might be placed on sales people which would increase sales and decrease finished goods inventories. This is a rather simple negative or self-correcting feedback loop; the condition (excess inventory) caused an action (extra sales efforts) which corrected the condition (inventories returned to normal) and the action is stopped (sales effort returns to normal). Even this simple feedback loop is somewhat more complex in the real world since a delay will occur between the point at which the undesirable condition is noticed and when the condition is corrected. Moreover, the nature of our industrial systems often causes the corrective action to take place in ways that are out of proportion to the problem; i.e., amplification takes place.

Another kind of feedback loop is of the positive or explosive variety. For example, if advertising expenditures are established as a fixed percentage of sales, and advertising has the usual effect (more advertising results in more sales), then if sales increase, advertising expenditures increase, causing sales to increase, causing advertising expenditures to increase, ad infinitum. Of course this positive feedback mechanism would work in the other direction as well; if sales go down, advertising expenditures are reduced, which causes sales to go down, which causes advertising expenditures to be reduced, etc. The features of amplification and delay are equally applicable to positive feedback loops. Thus one can see that advertising expenditures do not produce immediate results, and reactions to advertising expenditure changes may be in different proportion to the changes.

Four Foundations

Forrester lists the following four foundations as necessary to the construction of industrial dynamics models:*

1. The theory of information-feedback systems
2. A knowledge of decision making
3. The experimental model approach to complex systems
4. The digital computer as a means to simulate realistic mathematical models

---

*Jay W. Forrester, *Industrial Dynamics,* MIT Press, Cambridge, Massachusetts, 1961, p. 14.

Information-feedback control systems pervade operations management problems since so many situations lead to actions which in turn change the situations. The way in which changes occur in the behavior of information-feedback systems is determined by the structure of the system, by delays, and by amplification. System structure refers to the ways in which attributes of system entities are related; recalling our framework for the system design process from Chapter 3, we can see that enterprise design is concerned with changes in system structure and with the inclusion of additional system entities.

We noted the existence of delays in the inventory and advertising examples presented above. The importance of delays in the behavior of information-feedback control systems largely derives from both the average length of the delay and the pattern or transient response of the delay. Both of these delay characteristics tend to be poorly understood in the business world. An example of delay length and transient response is the time required for large shipments of merchandise from Baumritter to its showcase stores. We are not only interested in the average length of time for the goods to arrive, but the pattern of arrival. Do they all arrive at once? How are the arrivals spread over time? How do the dealers react to the arrivals insofar as additional orders are concerned? How would a different arrival pattern influence subsequent orders?

Amplification takes place when we examine problem situations or system states and take actions which do not properly consider the relationships between timing of the examination process and the timing as well as the pattern of system state changes resulting from actions. Amplification occurs when actions lead to larger than desired changes in system states. Amplification is closely related to delay, since many systems overreact in an attempt to compensate for delays, with the transient response of the delay often leading to further overreactions.

The second foundation of industrial dynamics, a knowledge of decision making, is what we have called explicit decision rule formulation in this book. It is necessary to replace informal or "black cigar" models with rigorous statements of how subsystems are structured if the communication necessary for the systems approach is to be achieved. The substitution of an explicit set of decision rules for rules of thumb will generally lead to improved system performance, but the substitution becomes absolutely essential when counterintuitive changes are made in system design. Information-feedback control systems almost always involve counterintuitive improvements.

The third foundation, the experimental approach to complex systems, is digital simulation. All of the arguments presented in Chapter 12 as to the elegance of this general purpose technique are applicable. Basically, industrial feedback-control systems are far too complex to be studied with formal mathematical analysis. Digital simulation gives us the rigor of mathematical models without the constraints. Digital simulation provides the modeling environment where the information-feedback relationships of explicit sets of decision rules can be studied.

The last foundation of industrial dynamics is digital computation power. The elegance of the experimental or simulation methodology is offset by its computational cost. Without the advent of modern electronic digital computers, simulation models would be far too expensive. Forrester notes that the cost per calculation has been reduced by a factor of 100,000 in twenty years, and that this technological improvement is greater than that experienced in the change from chemical to atomic explosives.*

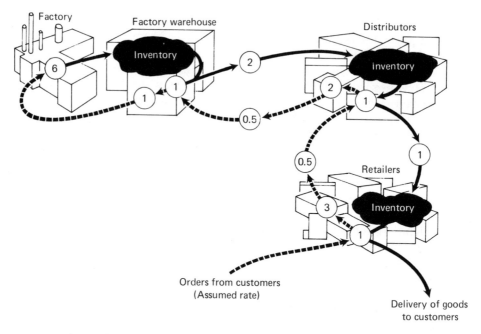

Fig. 21.1 Organization of production-distribution system.

Simulation of a Logistics System

Although the industrial dynamics approach is applicable to a wide range of problem situations, it is particularly germane to our understanding of important interactions between production, distribution, and marketing.

*Forrester, *op. cit.,* p. 19.

To illustrate these interactions, let us examine the example proposed by Forrester in Fig. 21.1.*

Figure 21.1 shows that the factory is a source of supply for goods held in inventory in the factory warehouse, by distributors, and by retailers. The solid lines represent flows of goods from the factory through the distribution system to the final consumer and the dashed lines depict information flow shown as orders placed on preceding stages in the distribution chain. The circled numbers represent the time delays in weeks for movement of both physical goods and information.

Starting at the factory level, we see that factory output is based upon order input with a six-week lead time or delay. Output from the factory is stored in the factory warehouse, and there is a two-week transit time for shipments between the factory warehouse and the distributors. Orders coming from the distributors to the warehouse arrive in 0.5 weeks, but are batched for a week before acted upon; it takes an additional week to convert the orders received by the factory warehouse into replenishment orders to the factory. The distributors ship to retailers with a one-week time delay and an additional week passes between the receiving of the customer order at retail and delivery of the merchandise to the final customer. The retailer has a three-week delay due to accounting and purchasing requirements before a retail sale is reflected in a replacement order to his distributor. The order requires a 0.5 week mail time before received by the distributor who takes a week to process the order and an additional two weeks to convert the retail order into his replenishment order to the factory warehouse.

Inventories will obviously be affected by these delays and will be adjusted as volume changes. The model calls for gradual upward or downward adjustments based upon smoothing out sales fluctuations with an eight-week averaging period. Both orders and goods in transit are proportional to the level of business activity and delay times so that either an increased sales volume or an increased lead time will result in increases in the supply pipeline.

An industrial dynamics model constructed for this logistics system yielded the output presented as Fig. 21.2 when a 10% increase in final customer demand was input to the model. What we see in Fig. 21.2 as a set of curves is the underlying anatomy, character, or structural interaction of this system. By examining how the model responds to various stimuli and how changes in the model produce responses which we judge

---

*This example and the exhibits are described in Jay W. Forrester, "Industrial Dynamics: A Major Breakthrough for Decision Makers," *Harvard Business Review*, July-August 1958; and more completely in his *Industrial Dynamics*.

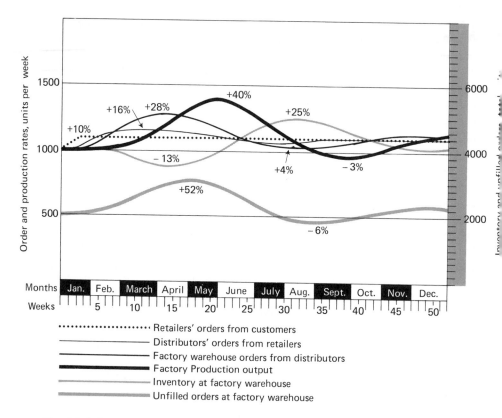

Fig. 21.2 Response of production-distribution system to a sudden 10% increase in retail sales

to be superior, we can make inferences and changes in real world systems described by such models; that is, we can engage in enterprise design.

An examination of Fig. 21.2 yields a somewhat surprising result. When the rate of retail sales goes up 10%, the orders placed by retailers on their distributors lags behind and does not reach the additional 10% level for several weeks. Note, however, that the rate of orders placed on the distributors does not approach and thereafter stop at 10%; it overshoots and reaches a peak of 16% in March, thereafter decreases to less than 10% in July, and finally stabilizes at 10% in about September. The cause for this amplification is primarily to make adjustments in both inventories held and inventories in transit.

Unfortunately, the accentuation of retailers' orders from customers in the distributors' orders from retailers is further accentuated in the factory warehouse orders placed by distributors. The distributors, looking at several months of steadily increasing orders, find their inventories being depleted at the same time their expectations of future sales are increasing (the model does not use trend forecasting, which would only accentuate the amplifications). As shown in Fig. 21.2, the response of distributors to the order pattern received from retailers is to increase their orders to a peak in April which is 28% higher than December.

The effect on factory production is even more dramatic. The peak in factory warehouse orders received from distributors naturally leads to a low point in the inventory held at the factory warehouse. The delays involved in adjusting factory production and the natural processes for adjusting inventories lead to a peak production output in June that is 40% higher than December.

Thus we have seen that a 10% increase in retail sales results in an increase in factory production four times as great. Since the factory has overproduced, new inventories throughout the system will thereafter be in excess of needs. The result will be cuts in orders placed by all levels which will be amplified back to the factory. Consequently, factory production output in September is 3% lower than the preceding December. We also can see that more than an entire year is required to bring factory production into line with actual retail sales. Moreover, the initial stimulus of a 10% increase in sales was small relative to the kinds of fluctuations faced by most companies.

Forrester expands the basic model to analyze the effects of randomness in retail sales, the effects of a gradual swing up to 10% additional customer orders which thereafter swings down to 10% below normal, and the effect of limitations on production capacity. Somewhat different kinds of instability result from these additions, but the net result is similar: the underlying anatomy or character of this logistics system is unstable and we are interested in changes which reduce the instability.

Counterintuitive System Design

Even for this relatively simple logistics system model, enterprise design is not easy. Many changes which are believed to be especially beneficial for an enterprise often turn out to have limited value; changes which result in fundamental improvements are sometimes quite surprising. As an example of an intuitively pleasing change, Forrester reduces the delay times associated with clerical and data-processing activities (1, 2, and 3 weeks for factory warehouse, distributors, and retailers, respectively) by two-thirds. The result is only slight improvement; Forrester concludes that clerical delays are a small factor and that resources used to reduce clerical delay will yield little return in this logistics system.

Two policy changes which do have a fundamental effect on system operations are to base factory production on smoothed retail sales information instead of the information as amplified by the distribution chain, and to eliminate the distributor level with retail orders placed directly on the factory. In both cases the degree of fluctuation in factory production is decreased (in the first by about one-half, in the second by about one-third). Basing factory production on retail sales does, however, lead to larger savings in factory warehouse inventories and backlogs. Stability achieved through elimination of the distributor level leads Forrester to question whether instability might not be endemic to industries with more than three distribution levels such as textiles.

Basing production levels on retail sales would take a considerable degree of intestinal fortitude. There are times when production does not vary significantly even though inventories are rising and backlogs falling substantially. Similarly, elimination of one or more stages in the production-distribution channel runs counter to industry traditions.

A closely related idea is critical to implementation of results from industrial dynamic models. Enterprise redesign almost invariably calls for changes in organizations and methods of operation, which in turn result in changes in the authority structure of a company. It is unwise to casually assume that such changes can be made easily. We will return to this issue in our appraisal of industrial dynamics models.

An interesting aspect of counterintuitive enterprise design relates to the pull-orientation developed in Chapter 19. The policy change of establishing factory production levels as a function of final retail sales is somewhat akin to the notion of basing production on the utilization of manpower and capital equipment capacities. In both cases, inventories are relegated to a subservient position rather than one that drives operation of the entire system. The placement of inventory in a subservient role is consistent with Forrester's conclusion that fluctuating behavior of logistic systems is more affected by the practices used to adjust inventories and orders in process than by any other single characteristic. Amplification is largely due to decision rules which do not properly recognize that the patterns of information received are distorted by the basic structure of delays in the system as well as by how other equally unknowledgeable individuals react in what they believe to be their self-interest.

A further reinforcement of the role of inventory policies is shown in Fig. 21.3. This figure is essentially the same as Fig. 21.2 with only retailers' orders from customers and factory production output shown. Four different factory production output curves are given; the one labeled ¼ per week is the same as that presented in Fig. 21.2.

The four different factory production output curves are based upon the same general policies used previously except that the time intervals for making inventory adjustments vary. That is, when inventories at the factory warehouse are different from the desired levels, all of that differ-

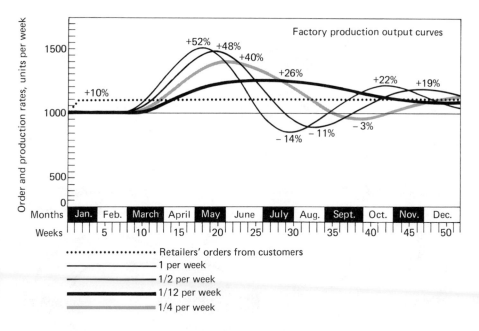

Fig. 21.3 Changing the time to make inventory and in-process order corrections

ence or some portion of it can be reflected as an adjustment to the production order issued to the factory in the next week. The four factory production output curves indicate the implied variability when imbalances are smoothed over different periods. Thus the curve that peaks at 52% above normal is based upon transmitting the entire imbalance as an inventory adjustment in the next week, the curve that peaks at 40% only passes along one-half of the imbalance, etc.

Marketing Influence

Up to this point, marketing aspects of the logistic system have not been included. Figure 21.4 exhibits one possible kind of marketing component that could be added to the model. It is worth emphasizing that it is indeed only a "possible" marketing sector. Criticisms of the industrial dynamics approach based upon a perceived lack of general applicability of this marketing function seem to miss the point; the intent is illustrative and a different marketing policy or customer reaction to the policy can be designed for a different perception of the real world as applied to a particular company, product, or situation.

Forrester's marketing component involves advertising expenditures based upon sales, as reflected in the factory production schedule, and excess inventories held in the factory warehouse. A six-week delay is used

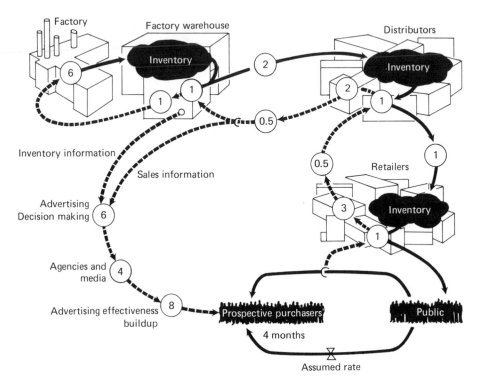

Fig. 21.4 The addition of a marketing function

to smooth out fluctuations before changes are made in the advertising expenditure rate, a four-week delay is required for advertising agencies and media to get advertising before prospective purchasers and eight weeks are required before the full impact of advertising buildups are felt in the market place. The model essentially assumes a replacement market with advertising rates lengthening or shortening the time between when a prospective purchaser becomes an actual purchaser.

The addition of this marketing component to the logistics system is to create recurring cycles of boom and bust. Forrester concludes that advertising is a possible cause of long-term cyclic patterns in companies, and that by changing advertising policies in ways that are not intuitively obvious, one might be able to exert strong countercyclical influences.

An Appraisal

Industrial dynamics models represent a good culmination of both our study of materials flow and the operations management course. The approach recognizes the complex and individual nature of logistics systems and how proper treatment of these complexities requires a policy orientation. The approach also illustrates the counterintuitive nature of solutions to complex problems, and why explicit models are needed to investigate such problems.

A study of industrial dynamics models sufficient to truly understand the methodology and philosophy requires far more time than we can devote in an introductory operations management course. Interesting as these concepts are, we must leave them for another pedagogical experience.

The author would be remiss, however, if he did not temper his enthusiasm by noting that real world applications of industrial dynamics are few and far between. The best known real world example of the application of industrial dynamics was at the Sprague Electric Company. The study extended over several years and uncovered some fundamental improvements which would result in stabilizing production and employment levels. Implementation of the changes in enterprise design required some fundamental changes in operations of the company which were difficult for company personnel to appreciate. After a period of time, the company reverted back to prior methods of operation in a manner similar to that described for the paint company in Chapter 20.

It is my strong opinion that there is nothing conceptually wrong with the industrial dynamics approach. Operationally, however, implementation attempts seem to have always followed the top-down approach with emphasis on the most fundamental or encompassing aspects of the company. Unfortunately, few people in the company have that orientation as a day-to-day concern; moreover those executive officers who might have that viewpoint tend to not understand complex models and therefore cannot take on the proper role of the user in an evolutionary sense.

In my opinion, the answer to this problem is to teach students of business administration about industrial dynamics, to simplify the methodology as much as possible, and to initially apply the methodology to less encompassing problems that are less apt to call for fundamental changes in the authority structure of an organization. The user-designer concept should permit evolution to higher level problems as user understanding grows.

AN APPROACH TO LOGISTICS SYSTEM DESIGN

In Chapter 17 we considered a fairly straightforward kind of problem. Each succeeding chapter has treated material and problems that are less easy to define. There simply are no magic formulae which can be applied to the design of all logistic systems. Each situation is somewhat unique both in terms of the inherent needs and the criteria systems to be satisfied. Nevertheless, some general guidelines can be formulated from our previous discussions.

The Logistics Czar Fallacy

Both the total cost concept and the broad definition of logistics imply an attempt to reduce suboptimization which largely derives from functional divisions of authority. Physical distribution represents the interface between marketing and production, and the logistics connotation encompasses the entire production conversion process including flows of materials from vendors and even their vendors. Functional authority divisions have always been somewhat artificial but necessary devices to effectively divide the tasks associated with managing this complex job of buying, converting, distributing, and selling.

There are those who suggest that a new "function" defined as physical distribution or logistics will allow for significant improvements to be generated in the organization. This temptation toward simple answers to complex problems should be avoided. The flow of materials through production into distribution channels to the final consumer involves some of the most basic production and marketing activities. Included are questions of when and which products are to be made; this in turn implies questions of staffing, capital equipment capacities and all of the issues considered in Chapters 17 through 20. Similarly, on the marketing side, flows of materials involve basic questions of market stimulation.

There simply is not a set of distinct criteria that applies to logistics or even to the narrower term distribution. Distribution objectives involve many more things than minimization of freight bills. Essentially, the determination of distribution policies involves integrative efforts between functional areas of the firm; it represents a task orientation to the systems approach. That is, determination of distribution policies potentially permits improved understanding between functional divisions of a company with a resultant improvement in basic company criteria.

Skepticism of the distribution czar approach does not mean in any way, however, that attempts to improve physical distribution cannot yield very important benefits. I believe that the attack on physical distribution is most properly mounted by a team of individuals with knowledge of production, marketing, traffic, and (perhaps) purchasing activities and criteria. It would seem wise to have additional team members with some degree of model-building expertise, and for the team to be further supported with staff model building and data-gathering capabilities.

The final result of a logistics system analysis well might be a new "function" called logistics, but if properly done, it will be very closely related to both production and marketing. The overall control and integration implied in a logistics function is indeed desirable, but that control must be creditable in terms of broadly defined production and marketing criteria. Dogmatic control or control exercised by formal delegation of authority that impedes existing function objectives can only lead to circumvention. Moreover, all of the notions of the user-designer concept are terribly applicable to implementation of an integrative logistics concept. At the outset it will not be possible to operationally define the concept, the problems, or the solutions. Evolution can and should be expected, and implementation will necessitate intimate involvement of those most likely to be affected by the resultant problem solution.

The Modeling Environment

There are three major implications for a modeling environment which can be derived from our previous discussions. First, logistics systems are basically interfunctional activities that will affect many different people in the organization who probably have quite different analytical or problem-solving styles. It will be necessary for any model to foster communications between people of diverse interests; since belief in model results is a necessary but not sufficient condition for implementation, substantial investments in developing communication and understanding seem warranted.

The second major implication for modeling environments makes the recommendations based on the first more paramount; improvements in logistics systems will often be based upon changes that are not intuitively pleasing. Coordination of activities that are now handled in diverse ways within a company can be difficult to implement. Some of these coordinated activities well may call for redelegations of authority that cross functional lines, e.g. authority over something currently in the domain of marketing may be transferred to production. Since many of these changes cannot be readily understood by one's intuitive understanding of company operations, communication and belief in the model becomes even more critical.

A related implication that follows from a belief in counterintuitive design improvements is the need for a quantitative model which can evaluate such improvements. "Black cigar" models rely upon intuitive validation procedures and are largely inappropriate.

The third major implication for a logistics system model derives from the presumption of significant evolutionary changes in the model and in user understanding of the problem. The model necessarily has to be open-ended enough to accommodate and foster evolution based upon intimate user involvement.

It should come as no surprise that digital simulation is the only model that I think can satisfy all of these conditions. It should also come as no surprise that my approach to the model would be to start with a fairly inelegant model that is consistent with at least one user's present perception of the problem and that an immediate goal would be to involve the key users on the team formed to investigate logistics.

A choice of initial problem area is not crucial if the team concept is viable. A likely starting point is the kind of analysis we examined in Chapter 15 for the location of warehouses. Such an investigation is a natural jumping off point for considering additional criteria and a broader point of view. At the same time, the methodology utilized is potentially expandable to a more inclusive logistics study.

A fully fledged logistics study should attempt to include the feedback aspects of industrial dynamics. Our interest will be in the long-run implications of sets of decision rules or policies. The interactions of those policies should be reflected in the model.

Another feature of the industrial dynamics simulation approach that is particularly useful is graphical output. Our ability to clearly specify criteria for such systems and investigate the "anatomy" of a set of policies will be enhanced. Looking at a state history of the simulation will tend to be much more valuable than at results based merely on summary statistics.

SUMMARY REMARKS

Our investigation of logistics systems completes the series of chapters devoted to materials flow and its pervasive nature within the operations of the firm. Except for one last attempt at implementation, this investigation also completes the text and your course in operations management.

It is appropriate that we consider logistics as the capstone to the course, because logistics involves both an integration of concepts developed in the course and an outreach toward new materials to be added in the spirit of the system approach.

REFERENCES

Ammer, Dean S., *Materials Management,* Irwin, 1968.

Forrester, Jay W., *Industrial Dynamics,* M.I.T. Press, 1961.

Heskett, J. L., Robert M. Ivie, and Nicholas A. Glaskowsky, Jr., *Business Logistics, Management of Physical Supply and Distribution,* Ronald Press, 1964.

Magee, John F., *Physical Distribution Systems,* McGraw-Hill, 1967.

McGarrah, Robert E., *Production and Logistics Management,* Wiley, 1963.

Mossman, Frank H., and Newton Morton, *Logistics of Distribution Systems,* Allyn and Bacon, 1965.

CHAPTER REVIEW

I see this chapter providing a good wrap-up to your course in operations management for three major reasons. First, since the general area of logistics represents the interface between production and marketing, a bridge is built toward another important area in your business administration curriculum. Second, many important ideas we have considered in isolation, such as decision rule formulation and digital simulation models, are unified in the industrial dynamics approach. Third, and perhaps most important, the systems approach we have been building spirally throughout your operations management course is reinforced; industrial dynamics represents a specific modeling approach for implementing the systems concept.

OUTLINE OF THE CHAPTER

Introduction — (relationships among flow-oriented subsystems)

The total cost concept — (minimize suboptimization)

Logistic system entities — (different organizations)

Criteria — (treat entire flow system as a whole)

Evolution — (continuing improvement)

Transportation technology — (mixed modes)

Management technology — (emphasis on function)

Control — (manufacturer assessed tradeoffs)

Industrial dynamics models — (enterprise design)

Four foundations — (relate to systems approach)

Simulation of a logistics system — (decision rule amplification)

Counterintuitive system design — (stabilization difficult)

Marketing influence — (counter to common perceptions)

An appraisal — (need for user orientation)

An approach to logistics system design — (uniqueness of logistics problems)

The logistics czar fallacy — (not a separate function)

The modeling environment — (critical model attributes)

Summary remarks — (capstone to the text)

CENTRAL ISSUES

Logistics represents a logical step in our interest in flow-oriented systems. The interest necessarily involves more than the production function; indeed, a proper focus often includes other business firms or entities not under the direct control of the manufacturer.

The total cost concept is represented as a way to view logistics systems. The primary goal is for each entity to be designed to best harmonize with total flow criteria. If total cost can be reduced through an increase in one sector, it is imperative for the distribution of costs and benefits to not impede such savings. Creative ways to allocate costs and benefits can reduce suboptimization.

The design of total materials-flow or logistics systems is not an easy task. Many individual actions or decision rules seem intuitively correct, but when coupled with other such rules, feedback properties often result in poor system performance levels. Counterintuitive sets of decision rules are often required.

Decision rules that run counter to individual validity procedures imply a need for a user-oriented modeling environment. Results of logistics studies often imply changes in authority relationships. It is necessary for those who will be affected by the authority changes to believe in their value. Since a continuous evolution can be expected, a different view toward the tenure of authority will go a long way toward achieving the results indicated by the models.

ASSIGNMENTS

1. Chapter 5 included a discussion of an industrial supplier who arranged to buy a three-year supply of merchandise with a noninterest bearing note payable one year from the date of purchase. The industrial supplier sold the entire order within six months.

   a) How does the total cost concept apply to this situation?
   b) What are the implications to manufacturers?

2. What kinds of distribution systems might be used for the following:

   a) A textbook company (e.g., Addison-Wesley)
   b) A food company (e.g., General Mills)
   c) A drug company (e.g., Upjohn)
   d) A drug wholesaler (e.g., McKesson-Robbins)
   e) A franchised food company (e.g., McDonalds)
   f) A farm equipment manufacturer (e.g., John Deere)

3. In what important ways are the marketing and operations functions of these firms related to the distribution systems?

4. Describe how a decrease in the delivery time for Ethan Allen Furniture might be part of a negative feedback loop which results in the delivery time returning to its prior value.

5. Describe how an increase in plant capacity might cause an increase in sales.

6. Suppose a retailer uses the rule of ordering at the rate of sales for the prior month, plus any inventory adjustment to keep one month of sales (current)

in inventory. Determine the pattern of orders that would result from the following sales data (beginning inventory = 50).

Month	Sales
1	60
2	70
3	40
4	50
5	30
6	60
7	50
8	40
9	70
10	30
11	50
12	60

7. How would the pattern of orders calculated in problem 6 change if the estimated sales and desired inventory levels were based on an exponential smoothing, model = 0.1, initial value = 50?

8. Describe how the conditions given in assignments 4 and 5 might interact.

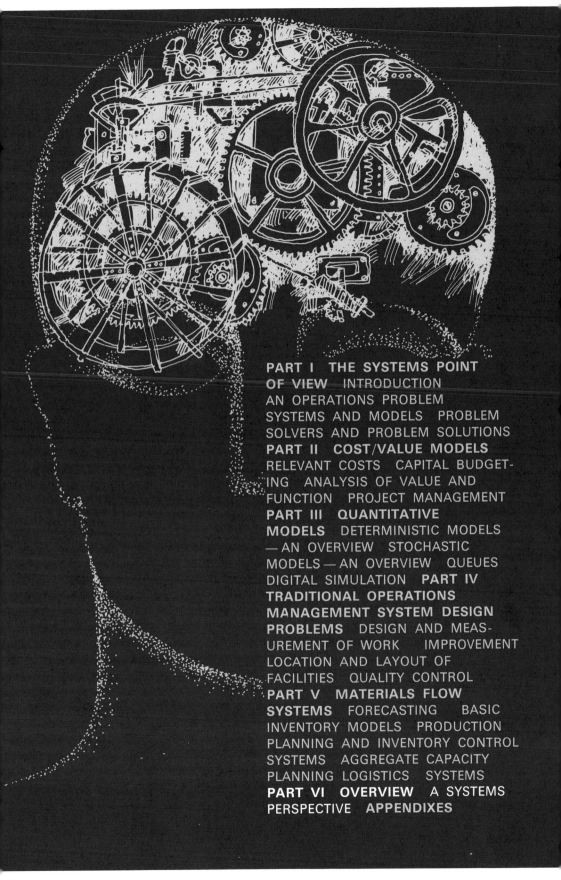

INTRODUCTION
TO PART VI

How do you go about writing an introduction to the end of something? The textual material is completed, and you well may be getting tired of these chatty introductions. However, if you have survived this far, you have been through an experience that is worth trying to pull together, even if only for your final examination.

A review of each of the five previous introductions to major parts is a good place to start and you are well advised to go over the chapter reviews. You should also find it interesting to go back to the question posed in Chapter 2 and see how you would answer it now. If you still have your written report, you might benefit by now attempting a critical appraisal. Part of your appraisal should be in terms of specific ideas or entities considered, and part should be in terms of the organization or structure of those ideas.

Our orientation has been on applications, and the structure for viewing these applications is the systems approach. By now each of you should have an internally viable understanding of what this approach is all about and the kinds of payoffs that can be derived from viewing specific problems in a systems context.

Chapter 22 foregoes my inclinations to make puffy statements about what you have learned or what you can expect to see happen in the field within the next decade. We finish the book in the way it was started, with another open-ended case study. In this way you are provided with an opportunity once again to apply what you have learned which, in the last analysis, is what really counts.

BIRO FEED AND
COAL COMPANY*

In June 1970 Mr. Joseph Biro received his baccalaureate degree from a Midwestern state university and went into the family business located in Thetford, Pennsylvania, about 150 miles northwest of Philadelphia. The business had been started by Mr. Biro's grandfather, Ezekiel Biro, who had immigrated from Hungary in 1898. From a humble beginning as a tenant farmer, Ezekiel Biro managed to accumulate 7,500 acres of farm land before he died in 1935. His two sons, James and Amos, carried on the business and became involved in cattle and hog fattening operations in the late 1930s. Their success in this venture prompted them to go into the feed business on a commercial scale at the end of World War II.

Although the Biro lands were adjacent to considerable anthracite coal-mining activity, it was not until 1951 that commercially exploitable deposits of coal were found on the property. In that year a contract was drawn with a small independent coal company to develop a "slope" or mine shaft; by 1960, 21 such independent contractors were mining coal on Biro land. In addition, a 22nd independent contractor was involved in river dredging activities on a small river which flowed through the property.

In 1967 the Biro brothers were approached by Mr. Bernard Aquilano, who owned a nearby preparation plant, with a proposal to buy him out. The primary function of a preparation plant or "breaker" is to break up large pieces of coal, remove undesirable impurities, and separate the coal into standard sizes. Mr. Aquilano claimed that he was having a hard time maintaining an adequate profit margin because of an insufficient source of coal and that the Biro production could be profitably integrated with his preparation plant.

---

*Some important ideas for this case were derived from a case written by Professor R. W. Merry of the Harvard Business School, Safford Breaker, Inc. (EA-P 171). Professor Merry has given his permission to use materials from that case.

After considerable negotiation, the Biro brothers bought out the Aquilano Preparation Plant in August, 1968, for $400,000 on the understanding that Mr. Aquilano's crew would become Biro employees.

The initial months of the new integrated operation were unsatisfactory, and poor service discouraged independent coal operators from delivering their coal to the preparation plant. Neither James nor Amos Biro knew much about coal mining and preparation, and neither was particularly interested in learning; both were fully concerned with the feed business. They were both delighted when Amos' son Joseph indicated an interest in taking over this aspect of the family business upon completion of his education.

ANTHRACITE COAL—A BACKGROUND NOTE

Coal has been formed from the remains of trees and plants that grew in swampy jungles hundreds of millions of years ago. The sinking of these jungle remains and their subsequent burial under layers of mud and sand caused them to be slowly squeezed into coal of various qualities or properties. Coal quality or properties are determined by the extent of pressure from the rock strata overlaying the coal. Thus peat is a soft, high water content, coal-like material which is relatively new and near the surface of the earth; lignite is a peat-like material which is more solid with most of the water having been squeezed out by layers of sand and soil; soft or bituminous coal is covered by additional layers of sand and rock, contains still less moisture, burns easily, gives off more heat than lignite, does not crumble in shipment, and is the most abundant and widely used type of coal; anthracite is coal that has been subjected to even more extensive pressure from overlaying soil and rock. Anthracite is a slow, even burning fuel that is found in small quantities relative to bituminous. The United States anthracite industry produces approximately 12,000,000 tons per year compared with an annual U.S. bituminous production of approximately 440,000,000 tons.

Production

In the United States virtually all anthracite coal is found in the state of Pennsylvania. Table 22.1 presents production figures for the ten largest anthracite-producing countries which collectively account for about 95% of the world production.

United States production of anthracite coal is from four major sources: underground mines, strip pits, culm banks, and streams. Underground mining involves tunneling beneath the surface of the earth to follow seams of coal. Coal seams vary in quality and thickness and in degree of pitch and slant. Different methods of mining or tunneling are

Table 22.1 1967 world production of anthracite

Ten largest countries	Thousands of short tons
U.S.S.R.	91,500
China (mainland)	19,840
North Korea	18,700
South Korea	13,708
France	12,840
U.S.A.	12,256
West Germany	12,103
Belgium	5,503
United Kingdom	4,630
Netherlands	4,275

Source: Adapted from 1967 Bureau of Mines Materials Yearbook, *Coal— Pennsylvania Anthracite,* United States Department of the Interior, U.S. Government Printing Office, Washington, D.C.

used for different seams; generally chambers are carved out, leaving supporting columns or pillars of coal in place; the coal is removed from the chambers by blasting and hauled to the surface by material handling equipment. In strip mining large-scale earth moving equipment completely exposes coal seams relatively near the surface. Stripping depth is limited by the ratio of overburden to seam thickness; present anthracite strip mines rarely go below about 700 feet. However, economies effected by new larger earth moving equipment continually increase the feasibility of deeper strip pits. Culm banks and streams both represent secondary recovery sources of anthracite coal. Small pieces of anthracite coal, discarded as waste product from early preparation plants, can now be scooped up and reprocessed for use in modern coal burning equipment, particularly by public utilities. Since much of this waste was discharged directly into streams or later eroded into them, large deposits of presently salable coal are found in the rivers draining the Pennsylvania anthracite production areas. These deposits are now being dredged from the rivers.

A preparation plant or breaker accepts raw coal with various kinds of impurities and in various sizes; the percentage of impurities and the sizes received depend upon the vagaries of particular coal sources and the mining methods used. Preparation plants break larger pieces of coal into usable sizes, remove the impurities, and separate the coal into standard sizes. The breaking operation typically utilizes toothed crusher rolls and screens to select coal of the proper size for the appropriate crusher rolls.

After crushing coal is separated into standard sizes by a set of vibrating screens with increasingly smaller holes. The two major categories of coal sizes are domestic, or large sizes, and industrial, or small sizes. Do-

Table 22.2 Anthracite quality standards

Size	Round test (inches)	Percentage				Maximum impurities*		
		Maximum oversize	Maximum undersize	Minimum undersize	Slate	Bone	Ash
Broken	Over 3-1/4 through 4-3/8	—	15	7-1/2	1-1/2	2	11
Egg	Over 2-7/16 through 3-1/4	5	15	7-1/2	1-1/2	2	11
Stove	Over 1-5/8 through 2-7/16	7-1/2	15	7-1/2	2	3	11
Chestnut	Over 13/16 through 1-5/8	7-1/2	15	7-1/2	3	4	11
Pea	Over 9/16 through 13/16	10	15	7-1/2	4	5	12
Buckwheat no. 1	Over 5/16 through 9/16	10	15	7-1/2	—	—	13
Buckwheat no. 2	Over 3/16 through 5/16	10	17	7-1/2	—	—	13
Buckwheat no. 3	Over 3/32 through 3/16	10	20	10	—	—	15
Buckwheat no. 4	Over 3/64 through 3/32	20	30	10	—	—	15
Buckwheat no. 5	<3/64	30	No limit				16

Source: Adapted from Vaughn, J.A., *Anthracite, a chapter from Mineral Facts and Problems, 1965 Edition*, United States Department of the Interior, U.S. Government Printing Office, Washington, D.C.

*Impurities defined as "slate" are any material with less than 40% fixed carbon. Impurities defined as "bone" are any material with more than 40% but less than 75% fixed carbon. Ash is the residual after burning and is determined on a dry basis.

mestic sizes are further divided into four subgroups: egg (3 1/4 in. to 2 7/16 in.), stove (2 7/16 in. to 1 5/8 in.), chestnut (1 5/8 in. to 13/16 in.), and pea (13/16 in. to 9/16 in). Industrial sizes are divided into five subgroups: buckwheat no. 1 (9/16 in. to 5/16 in.), buckwheat no. 2 or rice (5/16 in. to 3/16 in.), buckwheat no. 3 or barley (3/16 in. to 3/32 in.), buckwheat no. 4 (3/32 in. to 3/64 in.), and buckwheat no. 5 (smaller than 3/64 in.).

After sizing, impurities are removed by machines which take advantage of the differences in specific gravity of coal and its impurities. Various devices or machines are used for different sizes of coal and typically involve movement or flotation of the coal over the impurities in conjunction with water or some other type of slurry. Table 22.2 sets out the quality standards for anthracite coal adopted by the industry in 1947.

Marketing

The United States usage of anthracite coal falls into two major classifications: as a fuel for energy and as a source of industrial carbon. Anthracite coal was once an important source of fuel for United States domestic heating, but this market has diminished as alternative, more convenient sources of energy such as natural gas have become more readily available. However, worldwide use of anthracite for domestic heating continues and represents an important market for U.S. production of larger sizes. The classification of anthracite coal into the two major categories of domestic and industrial sizes is based on the historical use of pea and larger sizes for domestic heating. The use of pea and buckwheats no. 1 and 2 for domestic heating is possible with automatic or stoker fired furnaces. Many commercial establishments still use anthracite coal as a source of heat and rely largely on buckwheat no. 3 for this purpose. Buckwheats no. 4 and 5 are generally used solely for industrial use with public utilities being a primary customer. Although most electricity is presently generated from bituminous coal, anthracite's lower sulfur content may increase its use near population centers. The steel industry uses a considerable amount of anthracite for the manufacturing of coke and for other purposes. As a source of industrial carbon, anthracite is used in telephones, filters and purifiers, battery cases, carbides, and in electrodes and other electrical equipment.

The prices for anthracite coal are quite variable depending upon size and to a lesser extent upon location and quality. Table 22.3 gives a list of average prices at the preparation plants for 1967.

Retail or delivered prices to the consumer are more variable than wholesale prices because in addition to profit margins they often include varying transportation costs, storage costs, and local sales taxes. In December 1963, stove and chestnut coal sold at an average retail price of

Table 22.3 1967 average prices for Pennsylvania anthracite at preparation plants

	Per short ton
Egg	$12.65
Stove	12.25
Chestnut	12.03
Pea	9.75
Buckwheat no. 1	9.19
Buckwheat no. 2	9.16
Buckwheat no. 3	7.51
Buckwheat no. 4	5.51
Buckwheat no. 5	4.95

Source: Adapted from 1967 Bureau of Mines Minerals Yearbook, *Coal—Pennsylvania Anthracite*, United States Department of the Interior, U.S. Government Printing Office, Washington, D.C.

$33.50 per ton in Boston, $30.09 in New York City, $29.00 in Washington, D.C., $26.20 in Philadelphia, and $24.37 in Baltimore. Buckwheat no. 1 retailed at $27.56 in Boston, $24.21 in New York City, $22.95 in Philadelphia, $21.84 in Washington, D.C., and $21.26 in Baltimore.*

Since rail rates on anthracite are seldom based on mileage, the cost per ton mile tends to decrease as the length of the haul increases. On the other hand, operating costs of trucks remain relatively constant on a per ton mile basis; a rule of thumb is that rail transportation is generally used for hauls greater than 200 miles.

Distribution of anthracite coal is largely from preparation plants via railroad cars or trucks to wholesalers, dock operators and exporters who in turn sell to consumers. A few of the large producing companies do, however, maintain their own sales forces. Some truck shipments of coal occur as sales to consumers in the immediate vicinity of the preparation plants, and to some extent to retailers who dispatch their trucks to the preparation plants. Table 22.4 gives a breakdown of coal sizes shipped by rail and truck.

The anthracite industry operates with a seasonal demand for its products. Although some industrial customers and wholesalers carry in-

---

*J. A. Vaughn, *Anthracite, a chapter from Mineral Facts and Problems, 1965 edition,* United States Department of the Interior, U.S. Government Printing Office, Washington, D.C., p. 14.

Table 22.4 1967 sales of coal by sizes and methods of shipment

	Percentage		
	Shipped by rail	Shipped by truck	Total
Egg	5.9	.1	2.6
Stone	14.8	7.2	10.5
Chestnut	10.0	14.3	12.4
Pea	4.9	12.6	9.3
Buckwheat no. 1	9.0	13.4	11.5
Buckwheat no. 2	4.0	13.0	9.2
Buckwheat no. 3	9.1	11.5	10.4
Buckwheat no. 4	7.1	4.2	5.4
Buckwheat no. 5	21.3	4.7	11.9
Other (mixtures of low value)	13.9	19.0	16.8

Source: Adapted from 1967 Bureau of Mines Minerals Yearbook, *Coal— Pennsylvania Anthracite*, United States Department of the Interior, U.S. Government Printing Office, Washington, D.C.

ventories of coal, the inventories are fairly small relative to demand so that in an unusually cold winter it is not unusual for shortages to occur and for appreciable price increases to be made. Data on monthly shipments, retail stocks, retail deliveries, and prices are given in Table 22.5.

Technology
Research in the anthracite coal industry has been largely directed towards reducing the costs of mining and preparation plant operation as well as towards finding new uses and expanding old ones for anthracite coal. Many of these efforts involve governmental agencies rather than individual firms because the research is necessarily general and will benefit the entire industry as well as other industries and society as a whole. A good example is the attempt to control surface water so that mine seepages are minimized and water returned to the surface does not pollute rivers and lakes. Other research efforts are continually being directed towards improved mining methods and equipment, improved material-handling equipment, market studies, the use of anthracite in making metallurgical coke, and increased safety for mine workers. An additional research effort conducted by Bituminous Coal Research Incorporated is concerned with making gasoline and natural gas substitutes from coal.

Table 22.5 1967 monthly shipment, inventory, delivery, and price data for Pennsylvania anthracite

(Thousands of short tons except for indices)

	Jan.	Feb.	Mar.	April	May	June	July	Aug.	Sept.	Oct.	Nov.	Dec.
Preparation plant shipments												
Rail	384	303	377	466	550	600	450	602	569	498	421	401
Truck	578	574	500	375	410	344	283	354	391	445	523	535
Total	962	877	877	841	960	944	733	956	960	943	944	936
Retail dealer stocks												
Chestnut and larger	217	163	135	149	178	229	245	279	265	252	240	219
Pea	28	24	20	21	24	28	31	30	29	38	28	31
Buckwheat nos. 1 & 2	113	93	66	65	87	116	109	135	120	115	103	106
Total	358	280	221	235	289	373	385	444	414	405	371	356
Retail dealer deliveries												
Chestnut and larger	201	213	160	77	80	55	64	109	150	192	218	222
Pea	33	36	30	17	17	66	58	93	87	38	27	26
Buckwheat nos. 1 & 2	59	60	56	31	44	57	68	54	71	65	50	61
Total	293	309	246	125	141	178	190	256	308	295	295	309
Wholesale price indices (1957-59 = 100)												
Chestnut	93.4	93.4	93.4	83.2	83.2	83.2	86.6	86.6	90.0	90.0	93.4	95.8
Buckwheat no. 1	93.7	93.7	93.7	86.2	86.2	86.2	88.1	88.1	91.4	91.4	93.7	96.4

Source: Adapted from 1967 Bureau of Mines Minerals Yearbook, *Coal — Pennsylvania Anthracite*, United States Department of the Interior, U.S. Government Printing Office, Washington, D.C.

BIRO COAL OPERATION

Joseph Biro spent the summer of 1970 studying the Biro coal operation. Although his attention was primarily directed to the operation of the preparation plant, he also spent time at several of the mines and talked with some of the customers for processed coal.

Mining

The contractual arrangements between the Biro Feed and Coal Company and the 21 independent mine shaft operators plus the one dredge operator were fairly simple. Biro Feed and Coal Company was paid a straight royalty per ton for all processed (clean) coal recovered. The royalty payments were computed monthly based upon each operator's proportion of the total raw coal processed and the overall recovery percentage. The per ton royalty was, however, less for the dredge operator than for the mine shaft operators because the dredge operation was limited to the smaller coal sizes with an attendant smaller per ton revenue. When the Aquilano preparation plant was bought out by the Biro brothers, the contractual terms with the miners were modified so that all coal mined would be delivered to the Biro preparation plant. The miners were initially quite willing to add this additional contractual constraint, since the Biro preparation plant was relatively close to the mining operations. The additional contractual constraint did not affect the dredge operation because that contractor cleaned and sized his coal as it was recovered from the river.

The prices paid for the raw coal by the Biro preparation plant were identical to those paid by other preparation plants in the vicinity; the prices were on a per ton basis for "run of the mine" quality coal that was to have no more than 35% impurities. The prices varied seasonally in line with the wholesale and retail seasonal discount structure of the industry.

The quality of coal brought to the preparation plant varied considerably. Some mine operators always seemed to have a higher rock content in their coal than others; whether this was deliberate or a matter of local mine conditions was difficult to ascertain. In addition, the amount of impurities from any given mine operation varied over time as different conditions in the mine were met.

An additional kind of quality variation had to do with the size of the incoming coal. Larger sizes or chunks of coal could be processed into the larger or domestic sizes which had a higher revenue per ton than smaller or industrial sizes. One factor affecting the size of coal received was the particular blasting or dynamiting technique used. In mining the face of a coal seam, an operator had to decide how many blasting holes to drill. A small number of blasting holes led to the dislodgment of fairly large chunks of coal, whereas a large number of blasting holes led to pulverization of the coal. Although fewer dynamiting holes decreased blasting expense, pulverized coal was much easier to load and remove from the mine by mechanized material-handling equipment.

The amount of coal received varied considerably from hour to hour, day to day, week to week, and month to month. Weather conditions affected mining and trucking operations and there were considerable variations in the work patterns of particular mining contractors. Some worked longer hours and more days per week than others. In addition, almost all of the operators would step up their output just prior to the spring price reductions.

Joseph Biro found that present relationships with the mine operators left much to be desired. The initial enthusiasm for the additional contractual constraint of delivering all coal to the Biro preparation plant was quickly dissipated. Trucks often had to wait one-half hour before they could be unloaded, and waiting times of 1½ hours had been experienced on occasion. In addition to the miners' unhappiness with this situation, some of the truckers (who were employed by the miners) were paid on a per truck basis and found their earnings cut because of waiting times at the preparation plant.

Because of miner and trucker pressures, the acting superintendent, Mr. Nicholas Hamilton, had started to allow trucks to go to competitive preparation plants when expected waiting times became excessive. Unfortunately, Mr. Biro feared that what had started as a reasonable solution to an immediate problem was becoming a widespread practice. He also feared that some mine operators were not reporting all such shipments and were thereby evading royalty payments.

Preparation Plant

Figure 22.1 is a diagram depicting the flow of material through the preparation plant. As depicted in the lefthand side of Fig. 22.1, the plant had an area for truck weighing, inspection, and unloading. This area was on the top of a small hill so that gravity could be employed to move the raw coal into the crusher. Trucks were weighed with their loads of raw coal, and loads were visually inspected for percentage of impurities. Trucks then backed up to the chute area, dumped coal, and were reweighed empty. The chute between the truck unloading area and the breaker also acted as a storage device and held up to 15 tons of raw coal.

The crusher utilized two large slightly inclined screens, one several feet above the other, which were agitated to facilitate the flow of coal over them. The top screen had 5" diameter holes and the lower screen 3" diameter holes. Coal passing through both screens was ready for further sizing; coal passing through the first screen but not the second went to a set of crusher rolls which broke the coal into smaller standard sized pieces. Coal not passing through either screen went to a different set of

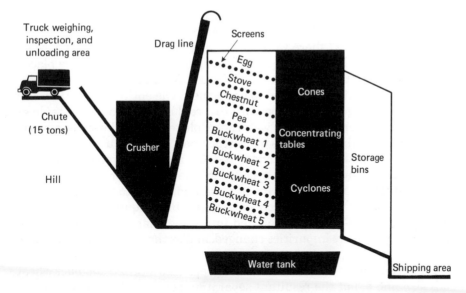

Figure 22.1

crusher rolls which accomplished the same purpose; these large pieces of coal were examined before crushing by a man who removed large pieces of rock so that they did not damage the crusher rolls. The coal coming from the crusher (both crushed and that which did not require crushing) was then elevated to a set of sizing screens by a chain link conveyor belt called a drag line.

The coal then passed through or failed to pass through a series of eight inclined screens that separated the coal into the nine standard coal sizes. Streams of water and vibration were used to move the coal across the screens. The angle of incline, extent of vibration, and intensity of the water streams were varied depending on the amount of coal passing through the screens. Most effective sizing was achieved when the screens were completely covered with a single layer of coal.

The various sizes of raw coal coming from the sizing screens were then fed to devices for removing impurities. Egg, stove, and chestnut sizes were cleaned in cones, which were so named because of their overall shape. A sand and water mixture which had a specific gravity slightly higher than the coal was agitated by a revolving paddle in the center of the cone, allowing the coal to float off and the impurities to sink. Efficient operation of the cones required a fairly even or steady feed of coal. Variations in feed rates tended to cause inadequate separation so that coal was discarded and impurities remained mixed with the coal.

The pea and buckwheats no. 1 and 2 were cleaned in concentrating tables which looked like wooden boxes 16' long by 8' wide by 6" deep. Inside these "boxes" there were ¼" wide grooves running lengthwise on about 3" centers. In these ¼" grooves, strips of ¼" wide wood were placed that protruded above the bottom of the box from about ¼" to about ¾" depending upon the size of coal to be cleaned. The entire table or box was inclined in a diagonal direction with raw coal being fed onto the table at the highest corner. Streams of water were played across the strips of wood (downhill) and the table was vibrated. Coal, being of a lower specific gravity than the impurities, tended to cross the wooden strips and accumulate for removal through a chute in the lowest corner. Impurities tended to travel along the strips of wood and feed into a disposal chute at the end of the table. The concentrating tables required continual adjustments as the volume of coal fed into them changed, as the relative proportion of coal to impurities changed, and as the wooden strips became worn.

Concentrating tables at one time were also utilized for buckwheat nos. 3, 4 and 5, but the resultant separation achieved was not very good. One of Mr. Hamilton's first requests as a Biro employee was to buy three cyclones for cleaning the three smaller sized coals. The cyclones also operated on the difference in specific gravities of coal and impurities but utilized centrifugal force and water to achieve the separation.

The cleaned coal coming from the cones, concentrating tables, and cyclones was gravity fed into nine coal storage bins or "pockets" of 75 ton capacity.

One man was employed at the truck unloading area to weigh the empty and full trucks and visually inspect the coal for quality. Two men were necessary for the crushing operation, one for removing large pieces of rock so they would not damage the larger crusher rolls and the other for controlling the gate or feed rate into the crusher. The drag line required no personnel except when it was broken. Two men were concerned with making the proper adjustments to the sizing screens. Each of the cones and concentrating tables required a full-time employee, but the three cyclones were operated by two men. One man handled the shipping area. In addition to this contingent of workers, the preparation plant employed one general maintenance man, a foreman, an office girl and a general superintendent. The foreman, Nicholas Hamilton, was covering his job and acting as general superintendent while waiting for Joseph Biro to take over. The total payroll amounted to approximately $9,500 per month, including $700 per month for the foreman and $900 a month for the general superintendent. The direct laborers were unionized, and although there were minor labor disputes from time to time, in general the workers were cooperative and interested in seeing improvements made.

The Biro brothers were disappointed in the productivity of the preparation plant. Mr. Aquilano had assured them that he thought it possible to achieve an output rate of 900 tons per day. Appendix A, a production report for May 1970, is typical of the kind of performance the preparation plant was achieving.

The preparation plant was usually standing idle for one-half to one-and-a-half hours each morning. Union rules called for all preparation plants in Pennsylvania to start operations at the same time as the miners. It took some time for the first truck load of coal to arrive and usually several truck loads would arrive at about the same time. Since truck loads averaged about 6 tons, if several trucks arrived at the same time some would necessarily have to wait.

When trucks were waiting to unload, the man at the bottom of the chute tended to increase the feed of coal through the crusher in order to cut down the waiting time and the consequent temptation for the truck drivers to deliver their coal to competitive preparation plants. Unfortunately, an increased rate of flow through the crushing operation meant an increased rate of flow to the sizing screens and thereafter to the cleaning equipment. Variations in flow rates to sizing screens tended to cause improper sizing. Improper sizing led to customer complaints and also to more difficult cleaning operations and excessive equipment adjustments. Variations in the rate of flow to the cleaning operations produced equally, if not more, adverse effects.

Although the preparation plant often operated under extremely hectic conditions, it was not at all unusual to experience a two-hour lull between truck arrivals; one day in February, 5½ hours elapsed between the arrival of two trucks.

Equipment failures were another source of constant problems. Even under proper operating conditions, teeth on the crusher rolls were subject to breakage. The drag line consisted of a series of chain links; if one gave way a working conveyor belt became a tangled mass of chain links and coal. When this occurred, one-half to one hour usually elapsed before the drag line became operational again. Sizing screens were bolted to frames; constant vibration caused the bolts to break or work themselves loose. With the screens not properly bolted down, coal worked its way under the screens and they would tear. Screens also became torn from the constant abrasive action of the moving coal. The equipment manufacturer claimed that his screens should last for about 6 weeks at the Biro preparation plant; for the 5 months ending May 30, 1970, the average screen life was 3.2 weeks. The cleaning equipment also required replacement due to gradual wear and tear, but usually not urgently enough to stop the flow of coal. Thus the wooden strips in the concentrating tables and the paddles in the cones gradually wore out. The cyclones were relatively new and as yet had not required any significant overhauls.

A considerable amount of water was used in the preparation plant, most notably for sizing and cleaning (one estimate was 10 tons of water for 1 ton of coal). The water was reprocessed by settling out the coal dust in a large tank located beneath the screens and cleaning equipment. New water was continually added, as were chemicals to make the water less corrosive. Nevertheless, the water tank and pumping equipment were subject to breakdowns and the sludge needed to be removed from the bottom of the water tank every 3 or 4 days, a job which required 1 to 2 hours work depending upon conditions.

Sales

Biro coal was sold almost exclusively to coal wholesalers in Philadelphia and New York City. Joseph Biro talked to several of these wholesalers; he also attempted to review past dealings both with these men and with prior customers. He was disappointed by what he found. The preparation plant's past quality performance seemed poor relative to established industry standards, and the existing set of wholesale customers seemed to be oriented toward coal of a slightly inferior quality at cut rate prices.

Much haggling complicated the present relationships with customers. Biro maintained no testing equipment for analyzing shipments and customers seemed always to find some deficiency that required a price reduction. There also had been some experience with poor payment practices; several customers were months in arrears and one customer went bankrupt with a settlement of ten cents to the dollar.

Specific customer complaints covered a wide range: impurity overages—most particularly for the pea and buckwheat sizes, although such complaints for buckwheats no. 3, 4, and 5 had diminished since the purchase of the cyclones; improper sizing—particularly for the larger sizes, with the major complaint concerning oversize egg; and unkept delivery promises—the two long-term contracts for supplying coal had been terminated because of unmet delivery schedules, although delivery promises were also linked to quality since some loads were returned for quality deficiencies.

ASSIGNMENT

1. You have been hired as Mr. Joseph Biro's assistant. In a four page (maximum length) written memorandum, tell him what you think he should do.

APPENDIX A TO CHAPTER 22

BIRO FEED AND COAL CO.—PREPARATION PLANT MAY 1970 PRODUCTION STATISTICS

Date	Coal input (tons)	Coal output (tons)	Recovery percentage	Egg	Stove	Chestnut	Pea	Buckwheat #1	Buckwheat #2	Buckwheat #3	Buckwheat #4	Buckwheat #5
1	547	323	59	4	14	9	5	11	9	11	8	29
2	493	311	63	5	16	8	4	12	11	14	9	21
3	Sunday											
4	621	342	55	6	15	9	5	13	10	13	7	22
5	423	241	57	4	16	11	6	11	10	12	8	22
6	1071	557	52	4	17	14	4	11	10	9	10	21
7	1089	587	54	3	16	12	6	10	11	10	9	23
8	306	196	64	5	14	7	6	12	12	11	8	25
9	934	532	57	3	12	11	5	12	11	13	9	24
10	Sunday											
11	842	463	55	8	14	12	5	11	10	14	9	17
12	1280	652	51	4	17	10	5	12	9	13	8	22
13	1119	593	53	4	21	11	4	13	8	12	6	21
14	429	266	62	6	16	10	8	11	11	13	5	20
15	319	210	66	8	13	9	7	12	11	11	9	20
16	489	288	59	6	15	9	6	11	10	14	8	21
17	Sunday											
18	490	309	63	5	19	10	5	12	12	10	9	18
19	0											
20	310	205	66	6	14	11	4	12	13	12	7	21
21	473	314	64	6	14	10	6	11	10	11	5	27
22	418	259	62	5	19	9	5	13	8	10	5	26
23	915	522	57	4	18	8	5	16	7	9	8	25
24	Sunday											
25	215	133	62	8	16	13	4	14	9	14	9	13
26	175	112	64	8	15	12	7	11	10	10	10	17
27	0											
28	980	549	56	4	13	9	6	12	11	14	9	22
29	1175	635	54	4	15	10	5	13	10	13	8	22
30	Holiday											
31	Sunday											

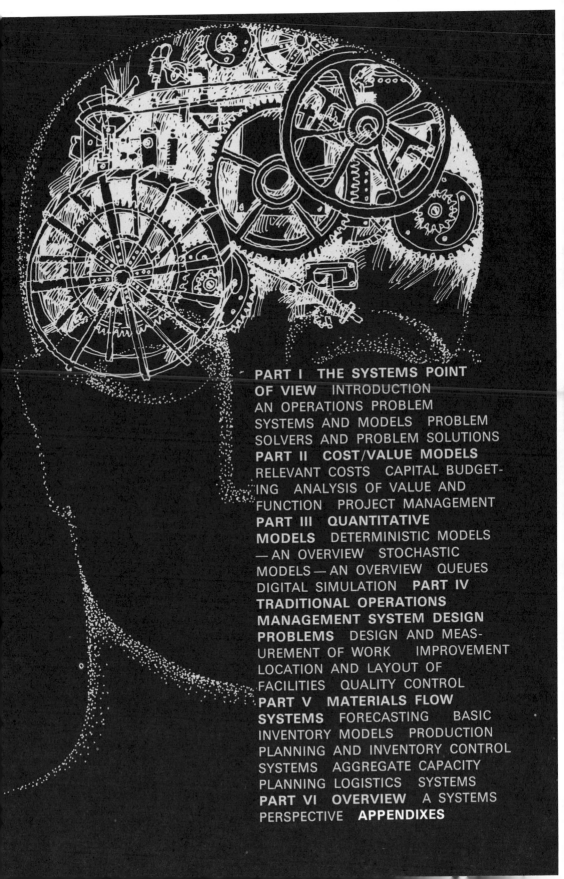

APPENDIX A

APPENDIX A

PRESENT VALUE FACTORS FOR FUTURE SINGLE PAYMENTS

PRESENT VALUE FACTORS FOR FUTURE SINGLE PAYMENTS

	0.5%	1.0%	1.5%	2.0%	2.5%	3.0%	3.5%	4.0%	4.5%	5.0%	
1	0.9950	0.9901	0.9852	0.9804	0.9756	0.9709	0.9662	0.9615	0.9569	0.9524	1
2	0.9901	0.9803	0.9707	0.9612	0.9518	0.9426	0.9335	0.9246	0.9157	0.9070	2
3	0.9851	0.9706	0.9563	0.9423	0.9286	0.9151	0.9019	0.8890	0.8763	0.8638	3
4	0.9802	0.9610	0.9422	0.9238	0.9060	0.8885	0.8714	0.8548	0.8386	0.8227	4
5	0.9754	0.9515	0.9283	0.9057	0.8839	0.8626	0.8420	0.8219	0.8025	0.7835	5
6	0.9705	0.9420	0.9145	0.8880	0.8623	0.8375	0.8135	0.7903	0.7679	0.7462	6
7	0.9657	0.9327	0.9010	0.8706	0.8413	0.8131	0.7860	0.7599	0.7348	0.7107	7
8	0.9609	0.9235	0.8877	0.8535	0.8207	0.7894	0.7594	0.7307	0.7032	0.6768	8
9	0.9561	0.9143	0.8746	0.8368	0.8007	0.7664	0.7337	0.7026	0.6729	0.6446	9
10	0.9513	0.9053	0.8617	0.8203	0.7812	0.7441	0.7089	0.6756	0.6439	0.6139	10
11	0.9466	0.8963	0.8489	0.8043	0.7621	0.7224	0.6849	0.6496	0.6162	0.5847	11
12	0.9419	0.8874	0.8364	0.7885	0.7436	0.7014	0.6618	0.6246	0.5897	0.5568	12
13	0.9372	0.8787	0.8240	0.7730	0.7254	0.6810	0.6394	0.6006	0.5643	0.5303	13
14	0.9326	0.8700	0.8118	0.7579	0.7077	0.6611	0.6178	0.5775	0.5400	0.5051	14
15	0.9279	0.8613	0.7999	0.7430	0.6905	0.6419	0.5969	0.5553	0.5167	0.4810	15
16	0.9233	0.8528	0.7880	0.7284	0.6736	0.6232	0.5767	0.5339	0.4945	0.4581	16
17	0.9187	0.8444	0.7764	0.7142	0.6572	0.6050	0.5572	0.5134	0.4732	0.4363	17
18	0.9141	0.8360	0.7649	0.7002	0.6412	0.5874	0.5384	0.4936	0.4528	0.4155	18
19	0.9096	0.8277	0.7536	0.6864	0.6255	0.5703	0.5202	0.4746	0.4333	0.3957	19
20	0.9051	0.8195	0.7425	0.6730	0.6103	0.5537	0.5026	0.4564	0.4146	0.3769	20
21	0.9006	0.8114	0.7315	0.6598	0.5954	0.5375	0.4856	0.4388	0.3968	0.3589	21
22	0.8961	0.8034	0.7207	0.6468	0.5809	0.5219	0.4692	0.4220	0.3797	0.3418	22
23	0.8916	0.7954	0.7100	0.6342	0.5667	0.5067	0.4533	0.4057	0.3634	0.3256	23
24	0.8872	0.7876	0.6995	0.6217	0.5529	0.4919	0.4380	0.3901	0.3477	0.3101	24
25	0.8828	0.7798	0.6892	0.6095	0.5394	0.4776	0.4231	0.3751	0.3327	0.2953	25
26	0.8784	0.7720	0.6790	0.5976	0.5262	0.4637	0.4088	0.3607	0.3184	0.2812	26
27	0.8740	0.7644	0.6690	0.5859	0.5134	0.4502	0.3950	0.3468	0.3047	0.2678	27
28	0.8697	0.7568	0.6591	0.5744	0.5009	0.4371	0.3817	0.3335	0.2916	0.2551	28
29	0.8653	0.7493	0.6494	0.5631	0.4887	0.4243	0.3687	0.3207	0.2790	0.2429	29
30	0.8610	0.7419	0.6398	0.5521	0.4767	0.4120	0.3563	0.3083	0.2670	0.2314	30
31	0.8567	0.7346	0.6303	0.5412	0.4651	0.4000	0.3442	0.2965	0.2555	0.2204	31
32	0.8525	0.7273	0.6210	0.5306	0.4538	0.3883	0.3326	0.2851	0.2445	0.2099	32
33	0.8482	0.7201	0.6118	0.5202	0.4427	0.3770	0.3213	0.2741	0.2340	0.1999	33
34	0.8440	0.7130	0.6028	0.5100	0.4319	0.3660	0.3105	0.2636	0.2239	0.1904	34
35	0.8398	0.7059	0.5939	0.5000	0.4214	0.3554	0.3000	0.2534	0.2143	0.1813	35
36	0.8356	0.6989	0.5851	0.4902	0.4111	0.3450	0.2898	0.2437	0.2050	0.1727	36
37	0.8315	0.6920	0.5764	0.4806	0.4011	0.3350	0.2800	0.2343	0.1962	0.1644	37
38	0.8274	0.6852	0.5679	0.4712	0.3913	0.3252	0.2706	0.2253	0.1878	0.1566	38
39	0.8232	0.6784	0.5595	0.4619	0.3817	0.3158	0.2614	0.2166	0.1797	0.1491	39
40	0.8191	0.6717	0.5513	0.4529	0.3724	0.3066	0.2526	0.2083	0.1719	0.1420	40
41	0.8151	0.6650	0.5431	0.4440	0.3633	0.2976	0.2440	0.2003	0.1645	0.1353	41
42	0.8110	0.6584	0.5351	0.4353	0.3545	0.2890	0.2358	0.1926	0.1574	0.1288	42
43	0.8070	0.6519	0.5272	0.4268	0.3458	0.2805	0.2278	0.1852	0.1507	0.1227	43
44	0.8030	0.6454	0.5194	0.4184	0.3374	0.2724	0.2201	0.1780	0.1442	0.1169	44
45	0.7990	0.6391	0.5117	0.4102	0.3292	0.2644	0.2127	0.1712	0.1380	0.1113	45
46	0.7950	0.6327	0.5042	0.4022	0.3211	0.2567	0.2055	0.1646	0.1320	0.1060	46
47	0.7910	0.6265	0.4967	0.3943	0.3133	0.2493	0.1985	0.1583	0.1263	0.1009	47
48	0.7871	0.6203	0.4894	0.3865	0.3057	0.2420	0.1918	0.1522	0.1209	0.0961	48
49	0.7832	0.6141	0.4821	0.3790	0.2982	0.2350	0.1853	0.1463	0.1157	0.0916	49
50	0.7793	0.6080	0.4750	0.3715	0.2909	0.2281	0.1791	0.1407	0.1107	0.0872	50

PRESENT VALUE FACTORS FOR FUTURE SINGLE PAYMENTS

	6.0%	7.0%	8.0%	9.0%	10.0%	11.0%	12.0%	13.0%	14.0%	15.0%	
1	0.9434	0.9346	0.9259	0.9174	0.9091	0.9009	0.8929	0.8850	0.8772	0.8696	1
2	0.8900	0.8734	0.8573	0.8417	0.8264	0.8116	0.7972	0.7831	0.7695	0.7561	2
3	0.8396	0.8163	0.7938	0.7722	0.7513	0.7312	0.7118	0.6931	0.6750	0.6575	3
4	0.7921	0.7629	0.7350	0.7084	0.6830	0.6587	0.6355	0.6133	0.5921	0.5718	4
5	0.7473	0.7130	0.6806	0.6499	0.6209	0.5935	0.5674	0.5428	0.5194	0.4972	5
6	0.7050	0.6663	0.6302	0.5963	0.5645	0.5346	0.5066	0.4803	0.4556	0.4323	6
7	0.6651	0.6227	0.5835	0.5470	0.5132	0.4817	0.4523	0.4251	0.3996	0.3759	7
8	0.6274	0.5820	0.5403	0.5019	0.4665	0.4339	0.4039	0.3762	0.3506	0.3269	8
9	0.5919	0.5439	0.5002	0.4604	0.4241	0.3909	0.3606	0.3329	0.3075	0.2843	9
10	0.5584	0.5083	0.4632	0.4224	0.3855	0.3522	0.3220	0.2946	0.2697	0.2472	10
11	0.5268	0.4751	0.4289	0.3875	0.3505	0.3173	0.2875	0.2607	0.2366	0.2149	11
12	0.4970	0.4440	0.3971	0.3555	0.3186	0.2858	0.2567	0.2307	0.2076	0.1869	12
13	0.4688	0.4150	0.3677	0.3262	0.2897	0.2575	0.2292	0.2042	0.1821	0.1625	13
14	0.4423	0.3878	0.3405	0.2992	0.2633	0.2320	0.2046	0.1807	0.1597	0.1413	14
15	0.4173	0.3624	0.3152	0.2745	0.2394	0.2090	0.1827	0.1599	0.1401	0.1229	15
16	0.3936	0.3387	0.2919	0.2519	0.2176	0.1883	0.1631	0.1415	0.1229	0.1069	16
17	0.3714	0.3166	0.2703	0.2311	0.1978	0.1696	0.1456	0.1252	0.1078	0.0929	17
18	0.3503	0.2959	0.2502	0.2120	0.1799	0.1528	0.1300	0.1108	0.0946	0.0808	18
19	0.3305	0.2765	0.2317	0.1945	0.1635	0.1377	0.1161	0.0981	0.0829	0.0703	19
20	0.3118	0.2584	0.2145	0.1784	0.1486	0.1240	0.1037	0.0868	0.0728	0.0611	20
21	0.2942	0.2415	0.1987	0.1637	0.1351	0.1117	0.0926	0.0768	0.0638	0.0531	21
22	0.2775	0.2257	0.1839	0.1502	0.1228	0.1007	0.0826	0.0680	0.0560	0.0462	22
23	0.2618	0.2109	0.1703	0.1378	0.1117	0.0907	0.0738	0.0601	0.0491	0.0402	23
24	0.2470	0.1971	0.1577	0.1264	0.1015	0.0817	0.0659	0.0532	0.0431	0.0349	24
25	0.2330	0.1842	0.1460	0.1160	0.0923	0.0736	0.0588	0.0471	0.0378	0.0304	25
26	0.2198	0.1722	0.1352	0.1064	0.0839	0.0663	0.0525	0.0417	0.0331	0.0264	26
27	0.2074	0.1609	0.1252	0.0976	0.0763	0.0597	0.0469	0.0369	0.0291	0.0230	27
28	0.1956	0.1504	0.1159	0.0985	0.0693	0.0538	0.0419	0.0326	0.0255	0.0200	28
29	0.1846	0.1406	0.1073	0.0822	0.0630	0.0485	0.0374	0.0289	0.0224	0.0174	29
30	0.1741	0.1314	0.0994	0.0754	0.0573	0.0437	0.0334	0.0256	0.0196	0.0151	30
31	0.1644	0.1228	0.0920	0.0691	0.0521	0.0394	0.0298	0.0226	0.0172	0.0131	31
32	0.1550	0.1147	0.0852	0.0634	0.0474	0.0355	0.0266	0.0200	0.0151	0.0114	32
33	0.1462	0.1072	0.0789	0.0582	0.0431	0.0319	0.0238	0.0177	0.0132	0.0099	33
34	0.1379	0.1002	0.0730	0.0534	0.0391	0.0288	0.0212	0.0157	0.0116	0.0086	34
35	0.1301	0.0937	0.0676	0.0490	0.0356	0.0259	0.0189	0.0139	0.0102	0.0075	35
36	0.1227	0.0875	0.0626	0.0449	0.0323	0.0234	0.0169	0.0123	0.0089	0.0065	36
37	0.1158	0.0818	0.0580	0.0412	0.0294	0.0210	0.0151	0.0109	0.0078	0.0057	37
38	0.1092	0.0765	0.0537	0.0378	0.0267	0.0190	0.0135	0.0096	0.0069	0.0049	38
39	0.1031	0.0715	0.0497	0.0347	0.0243	0.0171	0.0120	0.0085	0.0060	0.0043	39
40	0.0972	0.0668	0.0460	0.0318	0.0221	0.0154	0.0107	0.0075	0.0053	0.0037	40
41	0.0917	0.0624	0.0426	0.0292	0.0201	0.0139	0.0096	0.0067	0.0046	0.0032	41
42	0.0865	0.0583	0.0395	0.0268	0.0183	0.0125	0.0086	0.0059	0.0041	0.0028	42
43	0.0816	0.0545	0.0365	0.0246	0.0166	0.0112	0.0076	0.0052	0.0036	0.0025	43
44	0.0770	0.0509	0.0338	0.0226	0.0151	0.0101	0.0068	0.0046	0.0031	0.0021	44
45	0.0727	0.0476	0.0313	0.0207	0.0137	0.0091	0.0061	0.0041	0.0027	0.0019	45
46	0.0685	0.0445	0.0290	0.0190	0.0125	0.0082	0.0054	0.0036	0.0024	0.0016	46
47	0.0647	0.0416	0.0269	0.0174	0.0113	0.0074	0.0049	0.0032	0.0021	0.0014	47
48	0.0610	0.0389	0.0249	0.0160	0.0103	0.0067	0.0043	0.0028	0.0019	0.0012	48
49	0.0575	0.0363	0.0230	0.0147	0.0094	0.0060	0.0039	0.0025	0.0016	0.0011	49
50	0.0543	0.0339	0.0213	0.0134	0.0085	0.0054	0.0035	0.0022	0.0014	0.0009	50

PRESENT VALUE FACTORS FOR FUTURE SINGLE PAYMENTS

	16.0%	17.0%	18.0%	19.0%	20.0%	22.0%	24.0%	26.0%	28.0%	30.0%	
1	0.8621	0.8547	0.8475	0.8403	0.8333	0.8197	0.8065	0.7937	0.7812	0.7692	1
2	0.7432	0.7305	0.7182	0.7062	0.6944	0.6719	0.6504	0.6299	0.6104	0.5917	2
3	0.6407	0.6244	0.6086	0.5934	0.5787	0.5507	0.5245	0.4999	0.4768	0.4552	3
4	0.5523	0.5337	0.5158	0.4987	0.4823	0.4514	0.4230	0.3968	0.3725	0.3501	4
5	0.4761	0.4561	0.4371	0.4190	0.4019	0.3700	0.3411	0.3149	0.2910	0.2693	5
6	0.4104	0.3898	0.3704	0.3521	0.3349	0.3033	0.2751	0.2499	0.2274	0.2072	6
7	0.3538	0.3332	0.3139	0.2959	0.2791	0.2486	0.2218	0.1983	0.1776	0.1594	7
8	0.3050	0.2848	0.2660	0.2487	0.2326	0.2038	0.1789	0.1574	0.1388	0.1226	8
9	0.2630	0.2434	0.2255	0.2090	0.1938	0.1670	0.1443	0.1249	0.1084	0.0943	9
10	0.2267	0.2080	0.1911	0.1756	0.1615	0.1369	0.1164	0.0992	0.0847	0.0725	10
11	0.1954	0.1778	0.1619	0.1476	0.1346	0.1122	0.0938	0.0787	0.0662	0.0558	11
12	0.1685	0.1520	0.1372	0.1240	0.1122	0.0920	0.0757	0.0625	0.0517	0.0429	12
13	0.1452	0.1299	0.1163	0.1042	0.0935	0.0754	0.0610	0.0496	0.0404	0.0330	13
14	0.1252	0.1110	0.0985	0.0876	0.0779	0.0618	0.0492	0.0393	0.0316	0.0254	14
15	0.1079	0.0949	0.0835	0.0736	0.0649	0.0507	0.0397	0.0312	0.0247	0.0195	15
16	0.0930	0.0811	0.0708	0.0618	0.0541	0.0415	0.0320	0.0248	0.0193	0.0150	16
17	0.0802	0.0693	0.0600	0.0520	0.0451	0.0340	0.0258	0.0197	0.0150	0.0116	17
18	0.0691	0.0592	0.0508	0.0437	0.0376	0.0279	0.0208	0.0156	0.0118	0.0089	18
19	0.0596	0.0506	0.0431	0.0367	0.0313	0.0229	0.0168	0.0124	0.0092	0.0068	19
20	0.0514	0.0433	0.0365	0.0308	0.0261	0.0187	0.0135	0.0098	0.0072	0.0053	20
21	0.0443	0.0370	0.0309	0.0259	0.0217	0.0154	0.0109	0.0078	0.0056	0.0040	21
22	0.0382	0.0316	0.0262	0.0218	0.0181	0.0126	0.0088	0.0062	0.0044	0.0031	22
23	0.0329	0.0270	0.0222	0.0183	0.0151	0.0103	0.0071	0.0049	0.0034	0.0024	23
24	0.0284	0.0231	0.0188	0.0154	0.0126	0.0085	0.0057	0.0039	0.0027	0.0018	24
25	0.0245	0.0197	0.0160	0.0129	0.0105	0.0069	0.0046	0.0031	0.0021	0.0014	25
26	0.0211	0.0169	0.0135	0.0109	0.0087	0.0057	0.0037	0.0025	0.0016	0.0011	26
27	0.0182	0.0144	0.0115	0.0091	0.0073	0.0047	0.0030	0.0019	0.0013	0.0008	27
28	0.0157	0.0123	0.0097	0.0077	0.0061	0.0038	0.0024	0.0015	0.0010	0.0006	28
29	0.0135	0.0105	0.0082	0.0064	0.0051	0.0031	0.0020	0.0012	0.0008	0.0005	29
30	0.0116	0.0090	0.0070	0.0054	0.0042	0.0026	0.0016	0.0010	0.0006	0.0004	30
31	0.0100	0.0077	0.0059	0.0046	0.0035	0.0021	0.0013	0.0008	0.0005	0.0003	31
32	0.0087	0.0066	0.0050	0.0038	0.0029	0.0017	0.0010	0.0006	0.0004	0.0002	32
33	0.0075	0.0056	0.0042	0.0032	0.0024	0.0014	0.0008	0.0005	0.0003	0.0002	33
34	0.0064	0.0048	0.0036	0.0027	0.0020	0.0012	0.0007	0.0004	0.0002	0.0001	34
35	0.0055	0.0041	0.0030	0.0023	0.0017	0.0009	0.0005	0.0003	0.0002	0.0001	35
36	0.0048	0.0035	0.0026	0.0019	0.0014	0.0008	0.0004	0.0002	0.0001	0.0001	36
37	0.0041	0.0030	0.0022	0.0016	0.0012	0.0006	0.0003	0.0002	0.0001	0.0001	37
38	0.0036	0.0026	0.0019	0.0013	0.0010	0.0005	0.0003	0.0002	0.0001	---	38
39	0.0031	0.0022	0.0016	0.0011	0.0008	0.0004	0.0002	0.0001	0.0001	---	39
40	0.0026	0.0019	0.0013	0.0010	0.0007	0.0004	0.0002	0.0001	0.0001	---	40
41	0.0023	0.0016	0.0011	0.0008	0.0006	0.0003	0.0001	0.0001	---	---	41
42	0.0020	0.0014	0.0010	0.0007	0.0005	0.0002	0.0001	0.0001	---	---	42
43	0.0017	0.0012	0.0008	0.0006	0.0004	0.0002	0.0001	---	---	---	43
44	0.0015	0.0010	0.0007	0.0005	0.0003	0.0002	0.0001	---	---	---	44
45	0.0013	0.0009	0.0006	0.0004	0.0003	0.0001	0.0001	---	---	---	45
46	0.0011	0.0007	0.0005	0.0003	0.0002	0.0001	0.0001	---	---	---	46
47	0.0009	0.0006	0.0004	0.0003	0.0002	0.0001	---	---	---	---	47
48	0.0008	0.0005	0.0004	0.0002	0.0002	0.0001	---	---	---	---	48
49	0.0007	0.0005	0.0003	0.0002	0.0001	0.0001	---	---	---	---	49
50	0.0006	0.0004	0.0003	0.0002	0.0001	---	---	---	---	---	50

PRESENT VALUE FACTORS FOR FUTURE SINGLE PAYMENTS

	32.0%	34.0%	36.0%	38.0%	40.0%	42.0%	44.0%	46.0%	48.0%	50.0%	
1	0.7576	0.7463	0.7353	0.7246	0.7143	0.7042	0.6944	0.6849	0.6757	0.6667	1
2	0.5739	0.5569	0.5407	0.5251	0.5102	0.4959	0.4823	0.4691	0.4565	0.4444	2
3	0.4348	0.4156	0.3975	0.3805	0.3644	0.3492	0.3349	0.3213	0.3085	0.2963	3
4	0.3294	0.3102	0.2923	0.2757	0.2603	0.2459	0.2326	0.2201	0.2084	0.1975	4
5	0.2495	0.2315	0.2149	0.1998	0.1859	0.1732	0.1615	0.1507	0.1408	0.1317	5
6	0.1890	0.1727	0.1580	0.1448	0.1328	0.1220	0.1122	0.1032	0.0952	0.0878	6
7	0.1432	0.1289	0.1162	0.1049	0.0949	0.0859	0.0779	0.0707	0.0643	0.0585	7
8	0.1085	0.0962	0.0854	0.0760	0.0678	0.0605	0.0541	0.0484	0.0434	0.0390	8
9	0.0822	0.0718	0.0628	0.0551	0.0484	0.0426	0.0376	0.0332	0.0294	0.0260	9
10	0.0623	0.0536	0.0462	0.0399	0.0346	0.0300	0.0261	0.0227	0.0198	0.0173	10
11	0.0472	0.0400	0.0340	0.0289	0.0247	0.0211	0.0181	0.0156	0.0134	0.0116	11
12	0.0357	0.0298	0.0250	0.0210	0.0176	0.0149	0.0126	0.0107	0.0091	0.0077	12
13	0.0271	0.0223	0.0184	0.0152	0.0126	0.0105	0.0087	0.0073	0.0061	0.0051	13
14	0.0205	0.0166	0.0135	0.0110	0.0090	0.0074	0.0061	0.0050	0.0041	0.0034	14
15	0.0155	0.0124	0.0099	0.0080	0.0064	0.0052	0.0042	0.0034	0.0028	0.0023	15
16	0.0118	0.0093	0.0073	0.0058	0.0046	0.0037	0.0029	0.0023	0.0019	0.0015	16
17	0.0089	0.0069	0.0054	0.0042	0.0033	0.0026	0.0020	0.0016	0.0013	0.0010	17
18	0.0068	0.0052	0.0039	0.0030	0.0023	0.0018	0.0014	0.0011	0.0009	0.0007	18
19	0.0051	0.0038	0.0029	0.0022	0.0017	0.0013	0.0010	0.0008	0.0006	0.0005	19
20	0.0039	0.0029	0.0021	0.0016	0.0012	0.0009	0.0007	0.0005	0.0004	0.0003	20
21	0.0029	0.0021	0.0016	0.0012	0.0009	0.0006	0.0005	0.0004	0.0003	0.0002	21
22	0.0022	0.0016	0.0012	0.0008	0.0006	0.0004	0.0003	0.0002	0.0002	0.0001	22
23	0.0017	0.0012	0.0008	0.0006	0.0004	0.0003	0.0002	0.0002	0.0001	0.0001	23
24	0.0013	0.0009	0.0006	0.0004	0.0003	0.0002	0.0002	0.0001	0.0001	0.0001	24
25	0.0010	0.0007	0.0005	0.0003	0.0002	0.0002	0.0001	0.0001	0.0001	---	25
26	0.0007	0.0005	0.0003	0.0002	0.0002	0.0001	0.0001	0.0001	---	---	26
27	0.0006	0.0004	0.0002	0.0002	0.0001	0.0001	0.0001	---	---	---	27
28	0.0004	0.0003	0.0002	0.0001	0.0001	0.0001	---	---	---	---	28
29	0.0003	0.0002	0.0001	0.0001	0.0001	---	---	---	---	---	29
30	0.0002	0.0002	0.0001	0.0001	---	---	---	---	---	---	30
31	0.0002	0.0001	0.0001	---	---	---	---	---	---	---	31
32	0.0001	0.0001	0.0001	---	---	---	---	---	---	---	32
33	0.0001	0.0001	---	---	---	---	---	---	---	---	33
34	0.0001	---	---	---	---	---	---	---	---	---	34
35	0.0001	---	---	---	---	---	---	---	---	---	35
36	---	---	---	---	---	---	---	---	---	---	36
37	---	---	---	---	---	---	---	---	---	---	37
38	---	---	---	---	---	---	---	---	---	---	38
39	---	---	---	---	---	---	---	---	---	---	39
40	---	---	---	---	---	---	---	---	---	---	40
41	---	---	---	---	---	---	---	---	---	---	41
42	---	---	---	---	---	---	---	---	---	---	42
43	---	---	---	---	---	---	---	---	---	---	43
44	---	---	---	---	---	---	---	---	---	---	44
45	---	---	---	---	---	---	---	---	---	---	45
46	---	---	---	---	---	---	---	---	---	---	46
47	---	---	---	---	---	---	---	---	---	---	47
48	---	---	---	---	---	---	---	---	---	---	48
49	---	---	---	---	---	---	---	---	---	---	49
50	---	---	---	---	---	---	---	---	---	---	50

APPENDIX B

APPENDIX B

PRESENT VALUE FACTORS FOR ANNUITIES

PRESENT VALUE FACTORS FOR ANNUITIES

	0.5%	1.0%	1.5%	2.0%	2.5%	3.0%	3.5%	4.0%	4.5%	5.0%	
1	0.9950	0.9901	0.9852	0.9804	0.9756	0.9709	0.9662	0.9615	0.9569	0.9524	1
2	1.9851	1.9704	1.9559	1.9416	1.9274	1.9135	1.8997	1.8861	1.8727	1.8594	2
3	2.9702	2.9410	2.9122	2.8839	2.8560	2.8286	2.8016	2.7751	2.7490	2.7232	3
4	3.9505	3.9020	3.8544	3.8077	3.7620	3.7171	3.6731	3.6299	3.5875	3.5460	4
5	4.9259	4.8534	4.7826	4.7135	4.6458	4.5797	4.5151	4.4518	4.3900	4.3295	5
6	5.8964	5.7955	5.6972	5.6014	5.5081	5.4172	5.3286	4.2421	5.1579	50.757	6
7	6.8621	6.7282	6.5982	6.4720	6.3494	6.2303	6.1145	6.0021	5.8927	5.7864	7
8	7.8230	7.6517	7.4859	7.3255	7.1701	7.0197	6.8740	6.7327	6.5959	6.4632	8
9	8.7791	8.5660	8.3605	8.1622	7.9709	7.7861	7.6077	7.4353	7.2688	7.1078	9
10	9.7304	9.4713	9.2222	8.9826	8.7521	8.5302	8.3166	8.1109	7.9127	7.7217	10
11	10.6770	10.3676	10.0711	9.7868	9.5142	9.2526	9.0016	8.7605	8.5289	8.3064	11
12	11.6189	11.2551	10.9075	10.5753	10.2578	9.9540	9.6633	9.3851	9.1186	8.8633	12
13	12.5562	12.1337	11.7315	11.3484	10.9832	10.6350	10.3027	9.9856	9.6829	9.3936	13
14	13.4887	13.0037	12.5434	12.1062	11.6909	11.2961	10.9205	10.5631	10.2228	9.8986	14
15	14.4166	13.8651	13.3432	12.8493	12.3814	11.9379	11.5174	11.1184	10.7395	10.3797	15
16	15.3399	14.7179	14.1313	13.5777	13.0550	12.5611	12.0941	11.6523	11.2340	10.8378	16
17	16.2586	15.5623	14.9076	14.2919	13.7122	13.1661	12.6513	12.1657	11.7072	11.2741	17
18	17.1728	16.3983	15.6726	14.9920	14.3534	13.7535	13.1897	12.6593	12.1600	11.6896	18
19	18.0824	17.2260	16.4262	15.6785	14.9789	14.3238	13.7098	13.1339	12.5933	12.0853	19
20	18.9874	18.0456	17.1686	16.3514	15.5892	14.8775	14.2124	13.5903	13.0079	12.4622	20
21	1 .8880	18.8570	17.9001	17.0112	16.1845	15.4150	14.6980	14.0292	13.4047	12.8212	21
22	20.7841	19.6604	18.6208	17.6580	16.7654	15.9369	15.1671	14.4511	13.7844	13.1630	22
23	21.6757	20.4558	19.3309	18.2922	17.3321	16.4436	15.6204	14.8568	14.1478	13.4886	23
24	22.5629	21.2434	20.0304	18.9139	17.8850	16.9355	16.0584	15.2470	14.4955	13.7986	24
25	23.4456	22.0232	20.7196	19.5235	18.4244	17.4131	16.4815	15.6221	14.8282	14.0939	25
26	24.3240	22.7952	21.3986	20.1210	18.9506	17.8768	16.8904	15.9828	15.1466	14.3752	26
27	25.1980	23.5596	22.0676	20.7069	19.4640	18.3270	17.2854	16.3296	15.4513	14.6430	27
28	26.0677	24.3164	22.7267	21.2813	19.9649	18.7641	17.6670	16.6631	15.7429	14.8981	28
29	26.9330	25.0658	23.3761	21.8444	20.4535	19.1885	18.0358	16.9837	16.0219	15.1411	29
30	27.7941	25.8077	24.0158	22.3965	20.9303	19.6004	18.3920	17.2920	16.2889	15.3725	30
31	28.6508	26.5423	24.6461	22.9377	21.3954	20.0004	18.7363	17.5885	16.5444	15.5928	31
32	29.5033	27.2696	25.2671	23.4683	21.8492	20.3888	19.0689	17.8736	16.7889	15.8027	32
33	30.3515	27.9897	25.8790	23.9886	22.2919	20.7658	19.3902	18.1476	17.0229	16.0025	33
34	31.1955	28.7027	26.4817	24.4986	22.7238	21.1318	19.7007	18.4112	17.2468	16.1929	34
35	32.0354	29.4086	27.0756	24.9986	23.1452	21.4872	20.0007	18.6646	17.4610	16.3742	35
36	32.8710	30.1075	27.6607	25.4888	23.5563	21.8323	20.2905	18.9083	17.6660	16.5469	36
37	33.7025	30.7995	28.2371	25.9695	23.9573	22.1672	20.5705	19.1426	17.8622	16.7113	37
38	34.5299	31.4847	28.8051	26.4406	24.3486	22.4925	20.8411	19.3679	18.0500	16.8679	38
39	35.3531	32.1630	29.3646	26.9026	24.7303	22.8082	21.1025	19.5845	18.2297	17.0170	39
40	36.1722	32.8347	29.9158	27.3555	25.1028	23.1148	21.3551	19.7928	18.4016	17.1591	40
41	36.9873	33.4997	30.4590	27.7995	25.4661	23.4124	21.5991	19.9931	18.5661	17.2944	41
42	37.7983	34.1581	30.9941	28.2348	25.8206	23.7014	21.8349	20.1856	18.7235	17.4232	42
43	38.6053	34.8100	31.5212	28.6616	26.1664	23.9819	22.0627	20.3708	18.8742	17.5459	43
44	39.4082	35.4555	32.0406	29.0800	26.5038	24.2543	22.2828	20.5488	19.0184	17.6628	44
45	40.2072	36.0945	32.5523	29.4902	26.8330	24.5187	22.4955	20.7200	19.1563	17.7741	45
46	41.0022	36.7272	33.0565	29.8923	27.1542	24.7754	22.7009	20.8847	19.2884	17.8801	46
47	41.7932	37.3537	33.5532	30.2866	27.4675	25.0247	22.8994	21.0429	19.4147	17.9810	47
48	42.5803	37.9740	34.0426	30.6731	27.7732	25.2667	23.0912	21.1951	19.5356	18.0772	48
49	43.3635	38.5881	34.5247	31.0521	28.0714	25.5017	23.2766	21.3415	19.6513	18.1687	49
50	44.1428	39.1961	34.9997	31.4236	28.3623	25.7298	23.4556	21.4822	19.7620	18.2559	50

PRESENT VALUE FACTORS FOR ANNUITIES

	6.0%	7.0%	8.0%	9.0%	10.0%	11.0%	12.0%	13.0%	14.0%	15.0%	
1	0.9434	0.9346	0.9259	0.9174	0.9091	0.9009	0.8929	0.8850	0.8772	0.8696	1
2	1.8334	1.8080	1.7833	1.7591	1.7355	1.7125	1.6901	1.6681	1.6467	1.6257	2
3	2.6730	2.6243	2.5771	2.5313	2.4869	2.4437	2.4018	2.3612	2.3216	2.2832	3
4	3.4651	3.3872	3.3121	3.2397	3.1699	3.1024	3.0373	2.9745	2.9137	2.8550	4
5	4.2124	4.1002	3.9927	3.8897	3.7908	3.6959	3.6048	3.5172	3.4331	3.3522	5
6	4.9173	4.7665	4.6229	4.4859	4.3553	4.2305	4.1114	3.9975	3.8887	3.7845	6
7	5.5824	5.3893	5.2064	5.0330	4.8684	4.7122	4.5638	4.4226	4.2883	4.1604	7
8	6.2098	5.9713	5.7466	5.5348	5.3349	5.1461	4.9676	4.7988	4.6389	4.4873	8
9	6.8017	6.5152	6.2469	5.9952	5.7590	5.5370	5.3282	5.1317	4.9464	4.7716	9
10	7.3601	7.0236	6.7101	6.4177	6.1446	5.8892	5.6502	5.4262	5.2161	5.0188	10
11	7.8869	7.4987	7.1390	6.8052	6.4951	6.2065	5.9377	5.6869	5.4527	5.2337	11
12	8.3838	7.9427	7.5361	7.1607	6.8137	6.4924	6.1944	5.9176	5.6603	5.4206	12
13	8.8527	8.3577	7.9038	7.4869	7.1034	6.7499	6.4235	6.1218	5.8424	5.5831	13
14	9.2950	8.7455	8.2442	7.7862	7.3667	6.9819	6.6282	6.3025	6.0021	5.7245	14
15	9.7122	9.1079	8.5595	8.0607	7.6061	7.1909	6.8109	6.4624	6.1422	5.8474	15
16	10.1059	9.4466	8.8514	8.3126	7.8237	7.3792	6.9740	6.6039	6.2651	5.9542	16
17	10.4773	9.7632	9.1216	8.5436	8.0216	7.5488	7.1196	6.7291	6.3729	6.0472	17
18	10.8276	10.0591	9.3719	8.7556	8.2014	7.7016	7.2497	6.8399	6.4674	6.1280	18
19	11.1581	10.3356	9.6036	8.9501	8.3649	7.8393	7.3658	6.9380	6.5504	6.1982	19
20	11.4699	10.5940	9.8181	9.1285	8.5136	7.9633	7.4694	7.0248	6.6231	6.2593	20
21	11.7641	10.8355	10.0168	9.2922	8.6487	8.0751	7.5620	7.1016	6.6870	6.3125	21
22	12.0416	11.0612	10.2007	9.4424	8.7715	8.1757	7.6446	7.1695	6.7429	6.3587	22
23	12.3034	11.2722	10.3711	9.5802	8.8832	8.2664	7.7184	7.2297	6.7921	6.3988	23
24	12.5504	11.4693	10.5288	9.7066	8.9847	8.3481	7.7843	7.2829	6.8351	6.4338	24
25	12.7834	11.6536	10.6748	9.8226	9.0770	8.4217	7.8431	7.3300	6.8729	6.4641	25
26	13.0032	11.8258	10.8100	9.9290	9.1609	8.4881	7.8957	7.3717	6.9061	6.4906	26
27	13.2105	11.9867	10.9352	10.0266	9.2372	8.5478	7.9426	7.4086	6.9352	6.5135	27
28	13.4062	12.1371	11.0511	10.1161	9.3066	8.6016	7.9844	7.4412	6.9607	6.5335	28
29	13.5907	12.2777	11.1584	10.1983	9.3696	8.6501	8.0218	7.4701	6.9830	6.5509	29
30	13.7648	12.4090	11.2578	10.2737	9.4269	8.6938	8.0552	7.4957	7.0027	6.5660	30
31	13.9291	12.5318	11.3498	10.3428	9.4790	8.7331	8.0850	7.5183	7.0199	6.5791	31
32	14.0840	12.6466	11.4350	10.4062	9.5264	8.7686	8.1116	7.5383	7.0350	6.5905	32
33	14.2302	12.7538	11.5139	10.4644	9.5694	8.8005	8.1354	7.5560	7.0482	6.6005	33
34	14.3681	12.8540	11.5869	10.5178	9.6086	8.8293	8.1566	7.5717	7.0599	6.6091	34
35	14.4982	12.9477	11.6546	10.5668	9.6442	8.8552	8.1755	7.5856	7.0700	6.6166	35
36	14.6210	13.0352	11.7172	10.6118	9.6765	8.8786	8.1924	7.5979	7.0790	6.6231	36
37	14.7368	13.1170	11.7752	10.6530	9.7059	8.8996	8.2075	7.6087	7.0868	6.6288	37
38	14.8460	13.1935	11.8289	10.6908	9.7327	8.9186	8.2210	7.6183	7.0937	6.6338	38
39	14.9491	13.2649	11.8786	10.7255	9.7570	8.9357	8.2330	7.6268	7.0997	6.6380	39
40	15.0463	13.3317	11.9246	10.7574	9.7791	8.9511	8.2438	7.6344	7.1050	6.6418	40
41	15.1380	13.3941	11.9672	10.7866	9.7991	8.9649	8.2534	7.6410	7.1097	6.6450	41
42	15.2245	13.4524	12.0067	10.8134	9.8174	8.9774	8.2619	7.6469	7.1138	6.6478	42
43	15.3062	13.5070	12.0432	10.8380	9.8340	8.9886	8.2696	7.6522	7.1173	6.6503	43
44	15.3832	13.5579	12.0771	10.8605	9.8491	8.9988	8.2764	7.6568	7.1205	6.6524	44
45	15.4558	13.6055	12.1084	10.8812	9.8628	9.0079	8.2825	7.6609	7.1232	6.6543	45
46	15.5244	13.6500	12.1374	10.9002	9.8753	9.0161	8.2880	7.6645	7.1256	6.6559	46
47	15.5890	13.6916	12.1643	10.9176	9.8866	9.0235	8.2928	7.6677	7.1277	6.6573	47
48	15.6500	13.7305	12.1891	10.9336	9.8969	9.0302	8.2972	7.6705	7.1296	6.6585	48
49	15.7076	13.7668	12.2122	10.9482	9.9063	9.0362	8.3010	7.6730	7.1312	6.6596	49
50	15.7619	13.8007	12.2335	10.9617	9.9148	9.0417	8.3045	7.6752	7.1327	6.6605	50

PRESENT VALUE FACTORS FOR ANNUITIES

	16.0%	17.0%	18.0%	19.0%	20.0%	22.0%	24.0%	26.0%	28.0%	30.0%	
1	0.8621	0.8547	0.8475	0.8403	0.8333	0.8197	0.8065	0.7937	0.7813	0.7692	1
2	1.6052	1.5852	1.5656	1.5465	1.5278	1.4915	1.4568	1.4235	1.3916	1.3609	2
3	2.2459	2.2096	2.1743	2.1399	2.1065	2.0422	1.9813	1.9234	1.8684	1.8161	3
4	2.7982	2.7432	2.6901	2.6386	2.5887	2.4936	2.4043	2.3202	2.2410	2.1662	4
5	3.2743	3.1993	3.1272	3.0576	2.9906	2.8636	2.7454	2.6351	2.5320	2.4356	5
6	3.6847	3.5892	3.4976	3.4098	3.3255	3.1669	3.0205	2.8850	2.7594	2.6427	6
7	4.0386	3.9224	3.8115	3.7057	3.6046	3.4155	3.2423	3.0833	2.9370	2.8021	7
8	4.3436	4.2072	4.0776	3.9544	3.8372	3.6193	3.4212	3.2407	3.0758	2.9247	8
9	4.6065	4.4506	4.3030	4.1633	4.0310	3.7863	3.5655	3.3657	3.1842	3.0190	9
10	4.8332	4.6586	4.4941	4.3389	4.1925	3.9232	3.6819	3.4648	3.2689	3.0915	10
11	5.0286	4.8364	4.6560	4.4865	4.3271	4.0354	3.7757	3.5435	3.3351	3.1473	11
12	5.1971	4.9884	4.7932	4.6105	4.4392	4.1274	3.8514	3.6059	3.3868	3.1903	12
13	5.3423	5.1183	4.9095	4.7147	4.5327	4.2028	3.9124	3.6555	3.4272	3.2233	13
14	5.4675	5.2293	5.0081	4.8023	4.6106	4.2646	3.9616	3.6949	3.4587	3.2487	14
15	5.5755	5.3242	5.0916	4.8759	4.6755	4.3152	4.0013	3.7261	3.4834	3.2682	15
16	5.6685	5.4053	5.1624	4.9377	4.7296	4.3567	4.0333	3.7509	3.5026	3.2832	16
17	5.7487	5.4746	5.2223	4.9897	4.7746	4.3908	4.0591	3.7705	3.5177	3.2948	17
18	5.8178	5.5339	5.2732	5.0333	4.8122	4.4187	4.0799	3.7861	3.5294	3.3037	18
19	5.8775	5.5845	5.3162	5.0700	4.8435	4.4415	4.0967	3.7985	3.5386	3.3105	19
20	5.9288	5.6278	5.3527	5.1009	4.8696	4.4603	4.1103	3.8083	3.5458	3.3158	20
21	5.9731	5.6648	5.3837	5.1268	4.8913	4.4756	4.1212	3.8161	3.5514	3.3198	21
22	6.0113	5.6964	5.4099	5.1486	4.9094	4.4882	4.1300	3.8223	3.5558	3.3230	22
23	6.0442	5.7234	5.4321	5.1668	4.9245	4.4985	4.1371	3.8273	3.5592	3.3254	23
24	6.0726	5.7465	5.4509	5.1822	4.9371	4.5070	4.1428	3.8312	3.5619	3.3272	24
25	6.0971	5.7662	5.4669	5.1951	4.9476	4.5139	4.1474	3.8342	3.5640	3.3286	25
26	6.1182	5.7831	5.4804	5.2060	4.9563	4.5196	4.1511	3.8367	3.5656	3.3297	26
27	6.1364	5.7975	5.4919	5.2151	4.9636	4.5243	4.1542	3.8387	3.5669	3.3305	27
28	6.1520	5.8099	5.5016	5.2228	4.9697	4.5281	4.1566	3.8402	3.5679	3.3312	28
29	6.1656	5.8204	5.5098	5.2292	4.9747	4.5312	4.1585	3.8414	3.5687	3.3317	29
30	6.1772	5.8294	5.5168	5.2347	4.9789	4.5338	4.1601	3.8424	3.5693	3.3321	30
31	6.1872	5.8371	5.5227	5.2392	4.9824	4.5359	4.1614	3.8432	3.5697	3.3324	31
32	6.1959	5.8437	5.5277	5.2430	4.9854	4.5376	4.1624	3.8438	3.5701	3.3326	32
33	6.2034	5.8493	5.5320	5.2462	4.9878	4.5390	4.1632	3.8443	3.5704	3.3328	33
34	6.2098	5.8541	5.5356	5.2489	4.9898	4.5402	4.1639	3.8447	3.5706	3.3329	34
35	6.2153	4.8582	5.5386	5.2512	4.9915	4.5411	4.1644	3.8450	3.5708	3.3330	35
36	6.2201	5.8617	5.5412	5.2531	4.9929	4.5419	4.1649	3.8452	3.5709	3.3331	36
37	6.2242	5.8647	5.5434	5.2547	4.9941	4.5426	4.1652	3.8454	3.5710	3.3331	37
38	6.2278	5.8673	5.5452	5.2561	4.9951	4.5431	4.1655	3.8456	3.5711	3.3332	38
39	6.2309	5.8695	5.5468	5.2572	4.9959	4.5435	4.1657	3.8457	3.5712	3.3332	39
40	6.2335	5.8713	5.5482	5.2582	4.9966	4.5439	4.1659	3.8458	3.5712	3.3332	40
41	6.2358	5.8729	5.5493	5.2590	4.9972	4.5441	4.1661	3.8459	3.5713	3.3333	41
42	6.2377	5.8743	5.5502	5.2596	4.9976	4.5444	4.1662	3.8459	3.5713	3.3333	42
43	6.2394	5.8755	5.5510	5.2602	4.9980	4.5446	4.1663	3.8460	3.5713	3.3333	43
44	6.2409	5.8765	5.5517	5.2607	4.9984	4.5447	4.1663	3.8460	3.5714	3.3333	44
45	6.2421	5.8773	5.5523	5.2611	4.9986	4.5449	4.1664	3.8460	3.5714	3.3333	45
46	6.2432	5.8781	5.5528	5.2614	4.9989	4.5450	4.1665	3.8461	3.5714	3.3333	46
47	6.2442	5.8787	5.5532	5.2617	4.9991	4.5451	4.1665	3.8461	3.5714	3.3333	47
48	6.2450	5.8792	5.5536	5.2619	4.9992	4.5451	4.1665	3.8461	3.5714	3.3333	48
49	6.2457	5.8797	5.5539	5.2621	4.9993	4.5452	4.1666	3.8461	3.5714	3.3333	49
50	6.2463	5.8801	5.5541	5.2623	4.9995	4.5452	4.1666	3.8461	3.5714	3.3333	50

PRESENT VALUE FACTORS FOR ANNUITIES

	32.0%	34.0%	36.0%	38.0%	40.0%	42.0%	44.0%	46.0%	48.0%	50.0%	
1	0.7576	0.7463	0.7353	0.7246	0.7143	0.7042	0.6944	0.6849	0.6757	0.6667	1
2	1.3315	1.3032	1.2760	1.2497	1.2245	1.2002	1.1767	1.1541	1.1322	1.1111	2
3	1.7663	1.7188	1.6735	1.6302	1.5889	1.5494	1.5116	1.4754	1.4407	1.4074	3
4	2.0957	2.0290	1.9658	1.9060	1.8492	1.7954	1.7442	1.6955	1.6491	1.6049	4
5	2.3452	2.2604	2.1807	2.1058	2.0352	1.9686	1.9057	1.8462	1.7899	1.7366	5
6	2.5342	2.4331	2.3388	2.2506	2.1680	2.0905	2.0178	1.9495	1.8851	1.8244	6
7	2.6775	2.5620	2.4550	2.3555	2.2628	2.1764	2.0957	2.0202	1.9494	1.8829	7
8	2.7860	2.6582	2.5404	2.4315	2.3306	2.2369	2.1498	2.0686	1.9928	1.9220	8
9	2.8681	2.7300	2.6033	2.4866	2.3790	2.2795	2.1874	2.1018	2.0222	1.9480	9
10	2.9304	2.7836	2.6495	2.5265	2.4136	2.3095	2.2134	2.1245	2.0420	1.9653	10
11	2.9776	2.8236	2.6834	2.5555	2.4383	2.3307	2.2316	2.1401	2.0554	1.9769	11
12	3.0133	2.8534	2.7084	2.5764	2.4559	2.3455	2.2441	2.1507	2.0645	1.9846	12
13	3.0404	2.8757	2.7268	2.5916	2.4685	2.3560	2.2529	2.1580	2.0706	1.9897	13
14	3.0609	2.8923	2.7403	2.6026	2.4775	2.3634	2.2589	2.1630	2.0747	1.9931	14
15	3.0764	2.9047	2.7502	2.6106	2.4839	2.3686	2.2632	2.1665	2.0775	1.9954	15
16	3.0882	2.9140	2.7575	2.6164	2.4885	2.3722	2.2661	2.1688	2.0794	1.9970	16
17	3.0971	2.9209	2.7629	2.6206	2.4918	2.3748	2.2681	2.1704	2.0807	1.9980	17
18	3.1039	2.9260	2.7668	2.6236	2.4941	2.3766	2.2695	2.1715	2.0815	1.9986	18
19	3.1090	2.9299	2.7697	2.6258	2.4958	2.3779	2.2705	2.1723	2.0821	1.9991	19
20	3.1129	2.9327	2.7718	2.6274	2.4970	2.3788	2.2712	2.1728	2.0825	1.9994	20
21	3.1158	2.9349	2.7734	2.6285	2.4979	2.3794	2.2717	2.1731	2.0828	1.9996	21
22	3.1180	2.9365	2.7746	2.6294	2.4985	2.3799	2.2720	2.1734	2.0830	1.9997	22
23	3.1197	2.9377	2.7754	2.6300	2.4989	2.3802	2.2722	2.1736	2.0831	1.9989	23
24	3.1210	2.9386	2.7760	2.6304	2.4992	2.3804	2.2724	2.1737	2.0832	1.9999	24
25	3.1220	2.9392	2.7765	2.6307	2.4994	2.3806	2.2725	2.1737	2.0832	1.9999	25
26	3.1227	2.9397	2.7768	2.6310	2.4996	2.3807	2.2726	2.1738	2.0833	1.9999	26
27	3.1233	2.9401	2.7771	2.6311	2.4997	2.3808	2.2726	2.1738	2.0833	2.0000	27
28	3.1237	2.9404	2.7773	2.6313	2.4998	2.3808	2.2726	2.1739	2.0833	2.0000	28
29	3.1240	2.9406	2.7774	2.6313	2.4999	2.3809	2.2727	2.1739	2.0833	2.0000	29
30	3.1242	2.9407	2.7775	2.6314	2.4999	2.3809	2.2727	2.1739	2.0833	2.0000	30
31	3.1244	2.9408	2.7776	2.6315	2.4999	2.3809	2.2727	2.1739	2.0833	2.0000	31
32	3.1246	2.9409	2.7776	2.6315	2.4999	2.3809	2.2727	2.1739	2.0833	2.0000	32
33	3.1247	2.9410	2.7777	2.6315	2.5000	2.3809	2.2727	2.1739	2.0833	2.0000	33
34	3.1248	2.9410	2.7777	2.6315	2.5000	2.3809	2.2727	2.1739	2.0833	2.0000	34
35	3.1248	2.9411	2.7777	2.6315	2.5000	2.3809	2.2727	2.1739	2.0833	2.0000	35
36	3.1249	2.9411	2.7777	2.6316	2.5000	2.3809	2.2727	2.1739	2.0833	2.0000	36
37	3.1249	2.9411	2.7777	2.6316	2.5000	2.3809	2.2727	2.1739	2.0833	2.0000	37
38	3.1249	2.9411	2.7778	2.6316	2.5000	2.3809	2.2727	2.1739	2.0833	2.0000	38
39	3.1249	2.9411	2.7778	2.6316	2.5000	2.3809	2.2727	2.1739	2.0833	2.0000	39
40	3.1250	2.9412	2.7778	2.6316	2.5000	2.3810	2.2727	2.1739	2.0833	2.0000	40
41	3.1250	2.9412	2.7778	2.6316	2.5000	2.3810	2.2727	2.1739	2.0833	2.0000	41
42	3.1250	2.9412	2.7778	2.6316	2.5000	2.3810	2.2727	2.1739	2.0833	2.0000	42
43	3.1250	2.9412	2.7778	2.6316	2.5000	2.3810	2.2727	2.1739	2.0833	2.0000	43
44	3.1250	2.9412	2.7778	2.6316	2.5000	2.3810	2.2727	2.1739	2.0833	2.0000	44
45	3.1250	2.9412	2.7778	2.6316	2.5000	2.3810	2.2727	2.1739	2.0833	2.0000	45
46	3.1250	2.9412	2.7778	2.6316	2.5000	2.3810	2.2727	2.1739	2.0833	2.0000	46
47	3.1250	2.9412	2.7778	2.6316	2.5000	2.3810	2.2727	2.1739	2.0833	2.0000	47
48	3.1250	2.9412	2.7778	2.6316	2.5000	2.3810	2.2727	2.1739	2.0833	2.0000	48
49	3.1250	2.9412	2.7778	2.6316	2.5000	2.3810	2.2727	2.1739	2.0833	2.0000	49
50	3.1250	2.9412	2.7778	2.6316	2.5000	2.3810	2.2727	2.1739	2.0833	2.0000	50

APPENDIX C

TABLE OF RANDOM NUMBERS

406533	927599	264283	789368	976272	948228	165784	328597
552183	615669	912571	512762	535560	825354	777282	907836
884522	99916	883958	109132	742572	362751	216531	858972
133681	420067	786135	310895	374835	130711	161053	149596
455110	988753	965144	395932	415651	13749	647235	312497
365608	690798	179551	716747	342285	761621	87534	889553
487791	617989	924166	340217	678262	125227	450979	512554
349432	503265	816043	375439	362177	18332	360685	457066
340203	904575	485404	736051	655591	498840	832552	304206
673600	6558	208355	205230	539676	230845	972338	335989
525734	874795	173782	632809	390053	843679	763392	272311
27565	581199	815064	110662	393175	972133	464463	890967
902303	745199	658967	76173	710670	820559	302584	80474
553505	816875	430388	637756	859343	781761	922056	791852
643362	616683	712190	127116	59648	851745	863633	77098
11461	766426	980803	918449	978759	2915	666185	115543
152664	695494	658696	448831	978393	49989	796205	209142
293390	898615	267523	426316	862888	519471	921617	199396
952742	890301	624157	357340	19619	115233	446267	937730
243020	775945	608904	97362	9721	734924	946461	644882
842496	625537	231186	760581	790064	246324	903963	266505
106419	230236	233168	513105	515494	719096	262499	27603
594356	339184	264799	421845	809505	453014	241712	412861
244635	568093	941125	232195	927028	421390	240085	152657
703512	627313	116252	989318	929515	374541	572773	342229
435045	975293	663905	291574	903316	495838	346565	738377
503938	23174	993537	13705	872763	825859	17899	713105
988312	94870	418276	999403	837628	609930	667547	632120
121103	820248	588750	573742	397484	783034	825486	119874
723762	862086	377444	46716	768644	707626	867623	35779
181466	804419	780871	299181	923492	968942	259002	613208
245235	120170	518473	171554	590725	406415	460685	701957
859744	352063	342265	148005	10480	178650	624760	458105
548309	816245	855601	337927	496875	219214	539174	457414
915189	630713	689221	466948	638792	612922	813624	353647
983964	161531	828658	865469	737788	312176	254183	960474
255219	782878	377848	4528	48342	835455	807616	866507
791865	366133	532815	963776	117475	263379	279703	893408
847180	583208	55438	959386	679840	892439	846917	115703
95330	740356	948207	431883	536245	583067	624014	720128

APPENDIX D

APPENDIX D

AREAS UNDER THE NORMAL CURVE

Area under the standard normal curve from 0 to z, shown shaded, is $A(z)$.

Examples. If Z is the standard normal random variable and $z = 1.54$, then

$$A(z) = P(0 < Z < z) = .4382,$$
$$P(Z > z) = .0618,$$
$$P(Z < z) = .9382,$$
$$P(|Z| < z) = .8764.$$

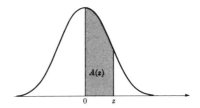

z	.00	.01	.02	.03	.04	.05	.06	.07	.08	.09
0.0	.0000	.0040	.0080	.0120	.0160	.0199	.0239	.0279	.0319	.0359
0.1	.0398	.0438	.0478	.0517	.0557	.0596	.0636	.0675	.0714	.0753
0.2	.0793	.0832	.0871	.0910	.0948	.0987	.1026	.1064	.1103	.1141
0.3	.1179	.1217	.1255	.1293	.1331	.1368	.1406	.1443	.1480	.1517
0.4	.1554	.1591	.1628	.1664	.1700	.1736	.1772	.1808	.1844	.1879
0.5	.1915	.1950	.1985	.2019	.2054	.2088	.2123	.2157	.2190	.2224
0.6	.2257	.2291	.2324	.2357	.2389	.2422	.2454	.2486	.2517	.2549
0.7	.2580	.2611	.2642	.2673	.2704	.2734	.2764	.2794	.2823	.2852
0.8	.2881	.2910	.2939	.2967	.2995	.3023	.3051	.3078	.3106	.3133
0.9	.3159	.3186	.3212	.3238	.3264	.3289	.3315	.3340	.3365	.3389
1.0	.3413	.3438	.3461	.3485	.3508	.3531	.3554	.3577	.3599	.3621
1.1	.3643	.3665	.3686	.3708	.3729	.3749	.3770	.3790	.3810	.3830
1.2	.3849	.3869	.3888	.3907	.3925	.3944	.3962	.3980	.3997	.4015
1.3	.4032	.4049	.4066	.4082	.4099	.4115	.4131	.4147	.4162	.4177
1.4	.4192	.4207	.4222	.4236	.4251	.4265	.4279	.4292	.4306	.4319
1.5	.4332	.4345	.4357	.4370	.4382	.4394	.4406	.4418	.4429	.4441
1.6	.4452	.4463	.4474	.4484	.4495	.4505	.4515	.4525	.4535	.4545
1.7	.4554	.4564	.4573	.4582	.4591	.4599	.4608	.4616	.4625	.4633
1.8	.4641	.4649	.4656	.4664	.4671	.4678	.4686	.4693	.4699	.4706
1.9	.4713	.4719	.4726	.4732	.4738	.4744	.4750	.4756	.4761	.4767
2.0	.4772	.4778	.4783	.4788	.4793	.4798	.4803	.4808	.4812	.4817
2.1	.4821	.4826	.4830	.4834	.4838	.4842	.4846	.4850	.4854	.4857
2.2	.4861	.4864	.4868	.4871	.4875	.4878	.4881	.4884	.4887	.4890
2.3	.4893	.4896	.4898	.4901	.4904	.4906	.4909	.4911	.4913	.4916
2.4	.4918	.4920	.4922	.4925	.4927	.4929	.4931	.4932	.4934	.4936
2.5	.4938	.4940	.4941	.4943	.4945	.4946	.4948	.4949	.4951	.4952
2.6	.4953	.4955	.4956	.4957	.4959	.4960	.4961	.4962	.4963	.4964
2.7	.4965	.4966	.4967	.4968	.4969	.4970	.4971	.4972	.4973	.4974
2.8	.4974	.4975	.4976	.4977	.4977	.4978	.4979	.4979	.4980	.4981
2.9	.4981	.4982	.4982	.4983	.4984	.4984	.4985	.4985	.4986	.4986
3.0	.4987	.4987	.4987	.4988	.4988	.4989	.4989	.4989	.4990	.4990

INDEX

INDEX